SNMP

Versions 1 & 2

Simple Network Management Protocol Theory and Practice

SNMP

Versions 1 & 2
Simple Network Management Protocol
Theory and Practice

Mathias Hein
David Griffiths

INTERNATIONAL THOMSON COMPUTER PRESS

I(T)P An International Thomson Publishing Company

London • New York • Bonn • Boston • Madrid • Melbourne • Mexico City • Paris • Singapore
Tokyo • Toronto • Albany, NY • Belmont, CA • Cincinnati, OH • Detroit, MI

SNMP Versions 1 & 2
Simple Network Management Protocol
Theory and Practice

I(T)P A division of International Thomson Publishing Inc.
The ITP logo is a trademark under licence

British Library Cataloguing-in-Publication Data
A catalogue record for this book is available from the British Library

---

First printed 1995

Made in Logotechnics C.P.C. Ltd., Sheffield

Project Management:	Sandra Potestà
Production:	Marco V. Potestà + team
Artistic Direction:	Stefano E. Potestà

Printed in the U.K. by Clays Ltd, St Ives plc

ISBN 1-850-32139-6

International Thomson Computer Press
Berkshire House
High Holborn
London WC1V 7AA
UK

International Thomson Computer Press
20 Park Plaza
14th Floor
Boston
USA

You can shake a milk bottle
as much as you like,
but the cream
always goes to the top.

F.P., December 1990

To Frank Patterson
Graham Williams
Jeremy Major

Contents

Foreword

Network users today face an unstoppable expansion of ever more complex networks with features such as biennial doubling of the number of connected terminals and the consequential increase in demand for additional applications, protocols and operational tasks for the network. Administration, maintenance, development and efficient network operation have thus become of vital importance. The various approaches and attempts at organizing these factors are generally called network management.

The importance given to network management has been on the increase for about five years now, with a marked acceleration since 1992. Interest is no longer focused on the use of certain tools for fault tracing or protocol analysis, but instead extends to providing integrated and largely automated operational support for medium sized and large multi-vendor networks. Management solutions must therefore take into account all – or perhaps more realistically, as many as possible – of the network components used.

From 1991 to mid-1992, available products (even those running with SNMP) were at best rudimentary in their functions, despite the promises made in their documentation. Since then, however, products have matured to provide a satisfactory basis of operational functionality. This development was reflected in 1993 in an increased investment expenditure on network management solutions.

As usual in the field of data communications, 'rival' approaches co-exist in the network management market. Established yet proprietary network management solutions in a host environment (NetView, TransView *et al.*) may be considered the precursors and inspiration for more general network management approaches. The all-encompassing management approach provided by the OSI standardization movement with CMIP/CMIS (as supported by the Network Management Forum in its Omnipoint specifications and Implementation Agreements) attempts to integrate all the various system worlds and management functions. Unfortunately, not all the specifications are yet complete, so certain implementations and compatibility tests are not available. CCITT-class manufacturers in particular maintain that appropriate solutions will be developed. This book will provide a short discussion on the subject.

SNMP is the third and currently the leading player in the network management arena. No manufacturer, whether of LAN components, client-server network systems, mini, midi or maxi systems, can afford not to fly the flag for SNMP (even though some of the flags tend to resemble mere fig leaves). Even manufacturers of WAN components are moving ever closer to the SNMP standard rejected by the CCITT when it comes to integrating LAN interfaces in their components (as most of them will in future). SNMP's immensely practical and sometimes all too literally implemented network philosophy is based on Marshall T. Rose's axiom:

> 'Equipping managed network components with network management functionality must be done with the minimum effort; it must represent the greatest common factor.'

With frequent expansions, SNMP is well on the way towards a step-by-step implementation of the crucial OSI ideas. SNMP underwent the development from 'Gateway Monitoring Protocol' (gateway = router) through 'Internetwork Management Protocol' to 'LAN/WAN System Management Protocol' at a breathtaking pace.

Both the protocol and the management philosophy behind it have long since overcome their teething problems, especially since the specification of SNMPv2 in 1993, which eliminates a number of the weaknesses apparent in Version 1. (One network specialist comments: 'Now SNMP has finally become just as complicated as OSI.')

This book is intended for all readers who require more detailed information about the management approach that will be the most prevalent in the medium term. We hope you will join us in tracing the development, potential and limitations of SNMP.

Stolberg, December 1993

Petra Borowka

1

Introduction to network management

This book aims to provide the reader with a basic understanding of network management and deals with the following questions:

- What does network management achieve?
- What effect does it have on the network components?
- What are the tools available today?
- How will network management develop in future?

Our extensive hands-on experience in network management has equipped us to guide the reader through the terminology labyrinth surrounding this lively technology and to introduce the components that are its building blocks. We intend to explode the myth that network management must be left to boffins in white laboratory coats. These days, network management should be a fundamental and necessary part of any well-structured computer system. This book is aimed especially at readers who have gained some experience in network management and those who intend to implement network management within their organization and networks. Others with less technical knowledge will find this book a useful source of information providing them with a basic understanding of the role of network management.

It is fair to say that many computer networks exist with no form of management. The number of connected users can range from fewer than five to as many as 30 to 50. No information is available to those responsible for the upkeep and management of the network to indicate if the installation is efficient and cost-effective. Reliability and availability cannot be measured. Faults are frequently difficult to pin down, especially those which are intermittent or transient in nature. Many network owners are unaware of the benefits that even the simplest network administration can provide. Consideration may be given to the selection of computers and peripherals, but little to the infrastructure to connect them. The market is awash with network components for 'plug 'n play' installation by the adventurous DIY networker. Computer systems are becoming faster and less expensive. It is now possible for a PC to boast the same performance as a minicomputer of ten years ago. Disk read/write speeds coupled with high-speed interfaces such as FibreChannel have brought power to the desktop at a fraction of the cost of the mini of the mid-1980s. The network is now the bottleneck and frequently the least considered and misunderstood element in the equation. In reality, the network is 'the tail that wags the dog'.

Network management can be compared with domestic contents insurance policies. In areas where crime is high, and particularly where burglaries and housebreaking are common, it is to be expected that more insurance policies are sold, even if the premiums are high. In a rural area where such things are rare, the insurance company has to work harder to sell its policies, since the client may never have been affected by crime. It only takes one or two neighbors to be affected before the price of the policy doesn't seem so expensive after all. The same can be said for the network and the management system to control and support it. Society has become dependent on computer systems. It is only when they or the connections between them fail that we realize how much we have entrusted to them. Few organizations maintain a manual fallback procedure which can be adopted until service is restored.

1.1 The whys and wherefores of network management

Imagine a company run with no management. These days we have come to accept the necessity in principle for some form of management. All organizations, no matter what their size, require some management structure. Even the human body has been equipped with a management system by Mother Nature. Without management, for example, limbs would execute uncoordinated motions. A very small company may achieve and maintain a certain amount of order with limited management. But once staff and workload increase, the organization needs a structure to hold it together and provide the foundation for growth.

Without a structure, problems and difficulties will increase to the point where only 'serious talking' will keep the organization from falling apart. The word 'management' may mean many things to different people. Some people regard management as a necessary evil. Others regard it as a career objective. Basically, management encompasses the administration, organization and regulation of a unit. In a company, management is key to the smooth functioning of all departments.

It is fair to compare the management of networks with their organic counterparts. As organizations become more dependent on high technology, the associated networks grow increasingly larger and more complex. Network components are added to provide users with an increasing range of services. Comparatively recently, every computer needed a dedicated printer. Today printers, disk drives, fax servers and modems can be shared by a number of users. Users at remote sites can access the resources in headquarters' networks (for example, databases). The number of users connected to LANs is rising steadily and there are many networks with several hundred simultaneous users. In almost all cases, network faults can create disruption and generate high costs for the operators.

Network system downtime is very expensive. A high proportion of faults originate in the most costly part of the network, the cabling infrastructure. Frequently, cables and transceivers are installed in ceiling voids, in conduits or under floors. This looks neat and tidy and serves the interests of safety. But in case of a fault, it may cause problems. It will not only affect those whose computers and terminals have been put out of action. Those around them may be disturbed as engineers are forced to run tests, and disconnect and reconnect network segments until the problem has been diagnosed and service restored. Large networks often employ alternative pathways in the event of localized faults, but small to medium network operators cannot justify the investment.

Without a network management system fault tracing and diagnosis almost always starts with a telephone call from a user to the network administrator. Common complaints range from poor network response time to intermittent or complete network access failures. It may take hours for the problem to be located, diagnosed, repaired and the network returned to service. The costs arising from lost working hours alone can be enormous. With the support of a network management system on the other hand, the network administrator may be aware of faults before the user notices them. But this is not the only strength of network management systems. A good system may locate the fault, advise the network administrator to reconfigure the system to minimize disruption (if possible), and refer to databases containing cabling and network component data to establish the nature of the fault. Such a database should contain equipment descriptions, serial numbers, software and hardware revision levels, installation dates, and so on. Last but not least it should contain the telephone number of the person responsible for the relevant section of the building or organization.

Retrieving such information should take only moments. Should the user now call the network administrator, all the relevant information will be available and fault diagnosis can be under way immediately. Localizing the source should ensure that valuable time is not wasted on a widespread search for the fault.

Network management systems have proved their investment value. Designing a LAN with performance goals based on theoretical throughput is something of a black art. Few organizations are willing to invest in the planning of a network infrastructure to establish their current and future network demands. Frequently, LAN capacity is underestimated from the beginning, or over-engineered to allow for significant corporate growth (which may or may not happen).

High network loads may not appear to be a problem for some time. In the absence of network management tools, throughput limitation will be noticed by users who eventually will complain about low network performance or limited services. A network management system would have already displayed the information to the administrator by identifying bottlenecks, and generated statistical information and reports. The resulting data could be used to modify or extend the network to ensure greater availability and resilience.

By 1985, intelligent LAN management systems had been developed to supervise functions proprietary to vendor-specific products. This provided limited functionality, and no provision was made for the exchange of information between LAN products from different vendors. This meant that clients who wanted to build a network management framework were forced to commit to one LAN vendor for the major network components. Ideal for the LAN vendor with a complete solution, but a strain for the client faced with difficult decisions to make. Whose products and network management best suited their needs? Would the LAN vendor be in business five years from the decision date? Would the LAN vendor maintain an upward product technology path?. In the days of proprietary LANs, purchasing decisions were far more difficult to make than they are today. Thanks to open standards, clients have more freedom to choose equipment from an ever-increasing supplier base with the confidence that the LAN or WAN components will be compatible with their network.

The twentieth century has been the most dynamic in the history of the world. Change has become both the driving force and philosophy of our age and the rate of change has accelerated dynamically since the turn of the century. The moment a new technology has been implemented and launched on the market, the next generation is announced. The fall in prices of electronic components and the growing mass market have contributed to the fact that even apparently simple products embody a high degree of complexity. This trend towards constantly accelerating and progressive development has taken the high technology market by storm. Not that long ago for example, one could buy a camera with some basic and easily used functions. Learning to use it took little time. These days, the proud owner of most new compact cameras will need to spend hours studying the manual before he or she can shoot the first picture. Of course, the improved technology should result in better pictures – provided the instructions are correctly followed. Even with the most advanced technology, the results can be disappointing. The technology isn't at fault; the problem is the lack of appreciation of the benefits built into the system. Network management is also subject to these fundamentals.

Well-designed network management should consist of a simple to operate human to machine interface (usually termed MMI for Man–Machine Interface), a clear and unambiguous portrayal of the system (usually graphically represented) and the ability to control the network infrastructure with some security safeguards. A happy medium must be maintained between the amount of detailed information available and too selective a view of the system. Let us turn to some of the points relevant to selection and operation of realistic network management, its position in the global framework and its future.

The most widely used network is the telephone system which is global and homogeneous. Consider for a moment the size of this worldwide network, a complex web of interconnected services where voice, data, video and other services are carried on a variety of physical media. Copper and glass-fibre cables, ground to satellite links, ground to ground microwave connections, radio and laser combine to tie the system together. Complex network management systems are employed by the various telecommunications carriers to meet subscriber needs.

The forerunner of today's telephone networks was the simplest possible network. The first call took place between two instruments linked by a single cable. Few considered that this experiment would lead to the creation of the largest network in the world. Once the telephone left the experimental stage, lines were laid to permit calls to be exchanged between users or subscribers. In the early days, all calls were connected manually by human operators who checked the validity of the connection by asking the remote party for their name or number. This form of partial network management was progressively improved until the operator was no longer required. The connection was effected by automatic systems based on electrical and electronic exchanges with little or no human intervention.

The early telephone networks provided little to help the operators in their management task. Exchanges were simple in construction and primarily electro-mechanical in design. Simple indicators alerted the operator that one subscriber wished to connect to another. Lamps, solenoid-operated semaphores and frequently 'listening in' were the only means to ensure that the operator had identified the called party prior to completing the connection between subscribers. As telephone networks increased in size, their management became more labour intensive. In the thirties and forties, city telephone exchanges were vast, with hundreds of operators at work.

A similar network management structure operated for years in railway networks. Simple signalling and control systems enabled operators to guide trains safely through complex rail networks. Communication between two signalling and control centers was effected by semaphore devices. The semaphore was essentially an enclosure containing a needle, or pointer, normally at rest in a vertical position. Electrical charges initiated by an operator device at the next station deflected the pointer one way or the other at both the transmitting and receiving stations. The combination of movements and positions of the pointer followed a simple code to inform the adjacent operators what was happening on their part of the network. A bell was connected to provide an audible warning of a change of semaphore state, and to provide a greater number of signalling permutations. A form of management protocol was based on the combination of these optical signals with acoustic sequences. Until some years ago, this simple but effective system was the only management function, assisted later by the installation of telephone systems.

No matter which network we use as an example, four basic components are necessary for any network management system:

- Display
  The indication of changes of state
- Control
  The ability to control or change the network status
- Diagnosis
  To understand the condition of the network
- Database
  To record and store information relevant to the network

We have become used to working with computer systems capable of displaying data in graphical form. Icons, plans, maps and graphics including on-line help functions can all be shown on a high-resolution color monitor. Early proprietary management systems sometimes used several displays, each depicting a part of the network. It was not uncommon to find several proprietary systems standing side by side in an administration center, each responsible for a single vendor system. This meant that the network administrator had to learn how to operate a number of different systems, each with its own method of control and display.

In today's more open environment, one management station is often all that is required for even the most complex system. The ability to point and click, zoom, have several open windows and still receive alarm information is basic to most NCC (Network Control Center) platforms. The operator can create and print relevant reports which can be used by management teams to determine the performance, condition, availability and growth requirement of the system while maintaining network control.

Let us turn to the four basic elements of a network management station.

Display

Most of the early proprietary network management systems were text-based; some could only display crude wire-frame figures, others were more sophisticated. Today's monitor or computer screen can depict managed objects in the context of the complete network, their position relative to other network components and their current status. If possible, the icons representing network elements should characterize their function. Software vendors offer object libraries, enabling the network management designer to chose from pre-designed icons. These vendors have increased their efforts to establish a standard for object libraries. For example, the NM Forum's Omnipoint program has been instrumental in focusing on standardizing objects and object management.

Most *de facto* standards management systems indicate the state of the managed objects using established color conventions: green to indicate a steady, normal condition; red to indicate a problem or potential danger; amber to signal impending change, with audible alarms to warn of status change. The basic alarm is a 'beep'. Most PCs and workstations can reproduce this signal, usually used to alert the operator to an alarm condition. Additionally, speech synthesis software can be employed to enhance the flow of information.

Even the most modestly priced GUI-based packages provide the tools to help the administrator create diagrams of the network. Usually, a LAN is too large to be comfortably displayed in one screenful of information. The picture would be too busy and detail would be lost. In all but the smallest systems, the network may need to be broken down by sections or layers. The top layer is usually the global view, indicating the major network components such as servers, subnetworks, hubs, routers, and so on. Packages like OpenView™ enable the designer or administrator to build hierarchic network layers on screen via windowing techniques. In this way, the administrator can build a 'top down' graphic representation of the network from the global view to the smallest part of the system. By pointing and clicking with the aid of a mouse or trackball, the user can display, examine and review information occurring in real time on the network. In fact, few packages operate in a real-time manner. They depend on a polling technique which is described later in the book. The polling time is usually user-configurable within certain parameters and adequate for most installations.

Network management packages designed to run on various hardware platforms, such as PCs running DOS/Windows and OS/2, workstations running UNIX, VAXen and IBM 6000, are popular. The least expensive and most commonly used platforms in small to medium networks are based on DOS/Windows. The management of devices may be shared as shown in Figure 1.1, but consideration must be given the fact that conflicts may arise if the two management stations initiate different commands to each agent process.

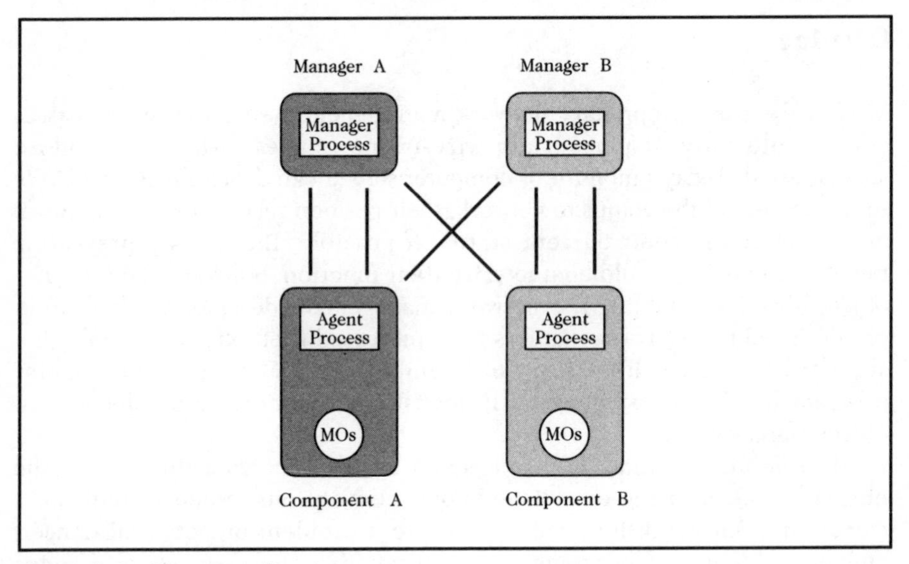

Figure 1.1 Shared applications

DOS-only network management platforms have limitations. The operating system is single tasking in nature and can only handle tasks in a sequential manner. For example, alarms generated by more than one network component need to be queued by a process independent of DOS to be able to be serviced by the management application. Windows NT does not suffer from this limitation, nor of course do multitasking applications which can, as the term implies, handle more than one task or process independently.

The friendliness of the user interface is critical to its adoption by network administrators. Early proprietary systems did not allow the user much flexibility, due to the fact that the application software was primarily text-based. The user was limited to a number of menu options and few developer packages existed for greater customization at the client site. The majority of application packages available today enable the network administrator to customize the system easily. Even so, the user interface must be as intuitive as possible. On-line contextual help, auto discovery and 'drag and drop' object manipulation are common to most packages. The network administrator should know the network under control intimately; a well-thought-out user interface makes life far easier for the administrator to build and modify the management equivalent of the 'real' network.

Network control

Network management systems should allow for manual and automatic responses to events. The type of response depends on the quantity and quality of information available and the critical or non-critical nature of the event. The network administrator requires precise information in order to change or modify system parameters. In addition, all alarm conditions should be logged with a time stamp, description of the fault and a record of the response by the management system, whether manually or automatically initiated. All critical decision paths initiated via keyboard or mouse for example, should be challenged by the management software. It is possible to allow some limited automated control for some alarm conditions; however, the administrator should consider the effect of each automatic or computer-controlled response to an event. If too many events are handled in this way without careful consideration, unexpected permutations can lead to complete network failures. It is good practice to automate some functions and monitor the effect on the system before putting more decision making under the control of the software application.

Diagnosis

Diagnosis is directly related to the information available. Networks that incorporate embedded controllers in the system elements can be interrogated to provide administration with timely and accurate information on the condition of the system being managed. Devices can be attached temporarily or permanently to subnetworks to assist in the diagnostic task. For example, hand-held protocol analyzers and traffic monitors enable the technician or network administrator to obtain a clear picture of the performance of a system at close range. The ability to download this information for later retrieval and analysis makes report generation easier to handle. Diagnostic tools not only help at times of network failure, but can also be used for predictive monitoring. In Ethernet and Token Ring networks, RMON (Remote MONitoring) is an invaluable technology for gathering information on traffic statistics for planning purposes and for detecting bottlenecks in a system. Many networks have neither management systems nor diagnostic tools. When problems arise, an external contractor is often called in. Depending on the nature of the fault, some or all of the network may be 'down' and unavailable to the users. In many cases, as noted earlier, no manual fallback procedures can be initiated and the workforce (and the eventual customer) is denied service. If we take, for example, the failure of a single transceiver in an Ethernet coaxial segment, it is possible that the whole segment with many connected users may be out of service. Several hours can elapse before a technician arrives (if available at short notice), locates the faulty unit with a TDR (Time Domain Reflectometer) or similar device and replaces the faulty transceiver. The cost of the technician and the component is minor compared with the loss of service revenues. Internal diagnostics, common in most 'intelligent' network components, RMON probes and network management packages, become invaluable diagnostic aids.

One Ethernet vendor exploited the market potential of transceivers with integrated diagnostic functionality. Color-coded LEDs were fitted on the front of the transceiver. Rumour has it that the sales staff followed a simple strategy. They encouraged the customer to place the transceiver in a strategic position in the building, for example in the reception area. In the event of a problem on the segment, the condition of the LEDs would be seen by all and fault finding could begin. This simple use of LEDs brought huge success to the supplier, Cabletron Systems, one of the world's largest network system vendors. Simple diagnostic equipment can minimize expensive network failures. It is important to choose diagnostic equipment appropriate to the network.

Many networks grow without a clear plan or strategy. Not all organizations can afford to employ a network consultant to advise them. However, network management should be a basic part of an organizational model as shown in Figure 1.2. Experienced network designers should always be consulted before a network is installed. They will be able to provide valuable advice before the system is purchased. Few organizations have the resources or know-how required to design a network, and frequently networks are over- or under-dimensioned from the start. In consequence, the time required from system design to commissioning a stable network cannot be accurately predicted.

The many networks in operation vary in efficiency. Most users do not collect information about the performance achieved by their network. The network market offers a wide range of diagnostic components for LANs and WANs. In addition, it is advisable to have the network evaluated from time to time by a reputable network consultant.

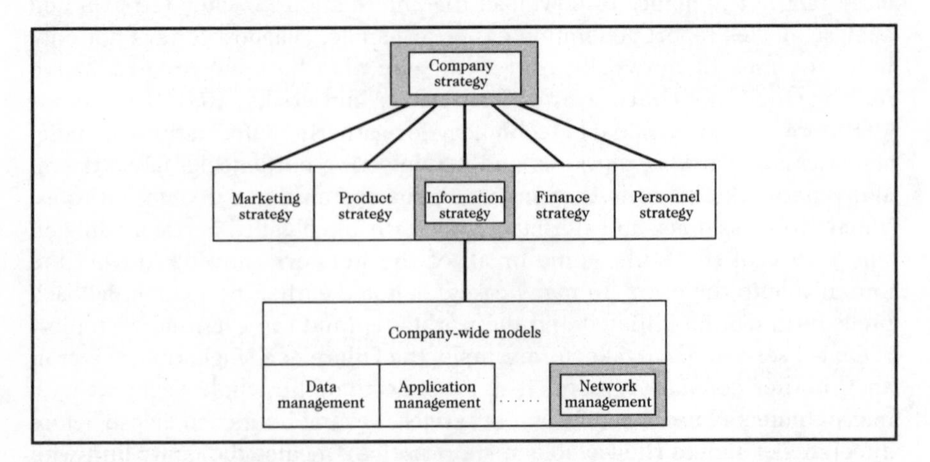

Figure 1.2 Network management as company strategy

Periodic expert network diagnoses are adequate for small static networks. Larger and continually expanding networks however, correspondingly increase the need for permanently installed diagnostic equipment and continuous surveillance. Dedicated terminals or PCs running diagnostic software can trace all network activity.

Few networks are static. Their tendency is to grow, which should be taken into account at the design stage. Another consideration is the extent to which the network can adjust to a new environment. This applies for example, to organizations with the same number of users but frequent changes of equipment location.

Database

What is a database? Bus, train or plane timetables for example, are databases, as are hotel registers. Even the much used phone book is a well-organized database. The word database is so closely associated with computers that we do not think of it in the context of hard-copy notebooks, diaries, address books, price or telephone lists anymore, although all of these are in fact databases.

Databases are an elementary part of every network management system. They contain the information relevant to network management as well as management of the database itself. Examples of database entries are as follows:

Personnel data
: Job title, place of work and telephone number may be listed alongside each individual.

Inventory
: Most hardware components have an inventory number referring to the owner, plus a serial number specific to the device. Inventories should contain additional information such as purchase date, type name and number, manufacturer's serial number, and so on. Normally the inventory will provide information on the location of the device.

Maps
: Maps may contain security information, fire equipment locations, emergency exits, power points, telephones, furniture, office equipment, windows and doors.

Service lists
: These lists contain information about status and availability of the hardware. Records showing the date of the most recent maintenance of each system element may be kept.

Emergency records
: This list should show who is responsible for the installation during normal hours, at night or at the weekend.

The list is by no means complete. In most cases, lists and inventories will be updated and changed at regular intervals and should be circulated or made available to relevant personnel. When a problem occurs, the relevant database should be readily available to the individuals responsible.

Selection of an object on screen could generate the following information:

- device serial number;
- date of purchase;
- version number of hardware;
- version number of software;
- various data, for example, load capacity;
- cable links, origin and termination of cables, cross-connections within the cabling plan;
- persons responsible, their place of work and availability (telephone number, and so on);
- printout of map on which all devices can be identified, along with their location.

Some vendors provide additional information such as the total number of packets received or sent, the number of bad packets transmitted and the total number of faults that occurred during a fixed time period.

1.2 User demands on network management

User demands have increased in line with the growth in network complexity. In the early days of network management, a fault indication was often displayed on a KSR printer (Keyboard Send-Receive) and consisted of a time stamp and a short fault report. As a result the fault report was limited in content. Once vendors began to integrate microcomputers, programmable controllers and minis into their networks, they increased the amount of information that could be displayed and provided the option to save the information on magnetic tape. In general, information was displayed on a terminal. When fault reports were generated, the management station was often unable to test the status of a device or to examine the network in detail.

Network systems now provide the network administrator with more functions than generally required. The administrator could be flooded with network information too voluminous to process. Fortunately, selection processes permit the filtering, display and storage of relevant data.

Some network administrators configure their system in such a manner that any fault automatically activates a recovery process. There are no fixed rules for handling network management fault conditions. Individual approaches will always be determined by the specific network conditions. Some administrators are opposed to permitting software to make decisions, others are equally in favor.

We have already mentioned the possibility of being flooded by information. Administrators can turn this to their advantage by compiling statistics on their networks. This information can be used to identify bottlenecks and weak points within a network. Once problems have been identified, the network administrator can take appropriate measures to ensure network operations function smoothly.

1.3 Basic functions in a mixed hardware environment

The late 1970s saw the development of specialized management systems for integration into computer and communication systems. Network management was mainly restricted to telecommunication systems and some large computer vendors. These systems were designed to increase availability and reliability of resources. As they were based on proprietary specifications and applications, the management systems were customized to suit their environments. This meant that management technology was not openly available.

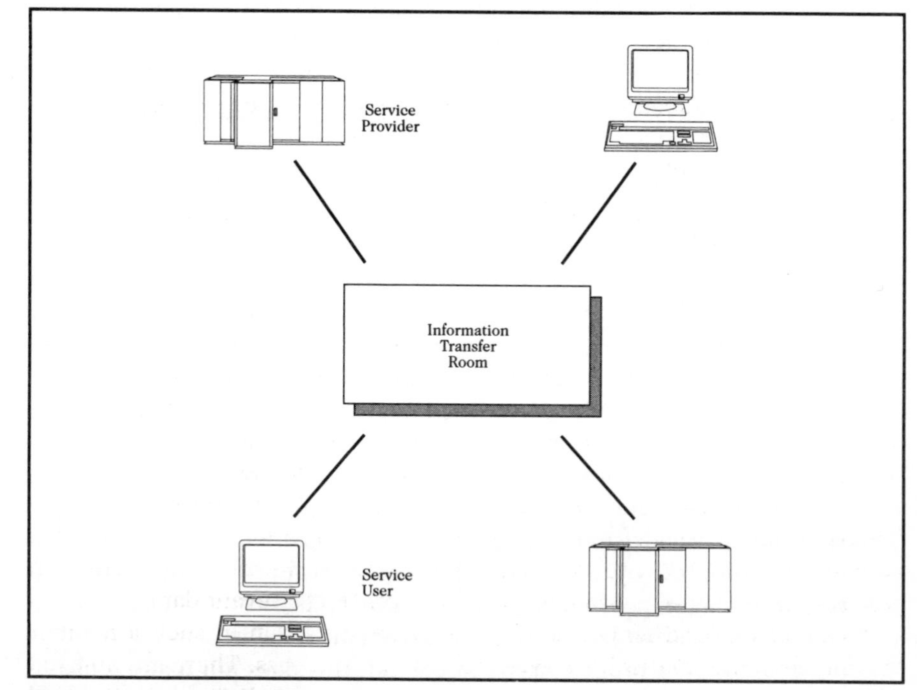

Figure 1.3 Open systems

Network management objectives had not been fully identified. Applications took up computer resources without providing maximum benefit to the user. The introduction of standards forced harmonization of the various network management concepts. Today, vendors ignore the term 'standards-based' at their peril. Harmonization and integration of systems took many years.

Before we review functions and standardization mechanisms, their contents and the products resulting from them, the requirements for operating a network management system should be explained.

The following components must be available in a mixed hardware environment:

- network interface;
- common protocols;
- sufficient CPU and memory resources.

Network interface

The network interface allows the network management station to communicate with the network in some form or another. In Ethernet for example, the choice is in-band or out-of-band management. In the case of in-band management, the management information, carried by a suitable transport-layer protocol, is transported around the network along with the network traffic. The network management platform may be sited anywhere within the network and connects to the network via a suitable interface such as a transceiver and an appropriate adapter card. In an out-of-band management system, the network management device will be connected directly to the device to be managed. This is less practical since the management platform is local to the device and may not be able to manage devices other than the one it is directly connected to. Physical interfaces vary: some use an AUI port, some a 25-way connector, some a 9-pin connector, and so on.

Common protocols

All components participating in the network management process need a common protocol to communicate with each other. The network management protocol described in this book is SNMP, although any reliable protocol may be used. It is important though to realize that in a mixed hardware environment, different management protocols would require translation or gateway processes in order for them to interact. This is not efficient, can be expensive to implement and is pointless since standards exist. The management protocol itself must be carried or transported by a transport-layer protocol. Again, standard transport-layer protocols such as UDP/IP, TCP/IP, OSI, and so on should be used to convey the management data in a network. It is possible to use a proprietary protocol, but this does not make sense in a mixed hardware environment.

Sufficient CPU and memory resources
Network management applications are CPU-intensive. It is important to recognize this fact when choosing a hardware platform for the network management station. As hardware devices in the network have themselves become more sophisticated, the amount of information they can deliver to the management station has increased. Bridges, routers, hubs and even adapter cards generate data which will be carried across the network to and from the management station. Reports and calculations will be generated within the management platform, and this takes up processor and memory resources. It is important to ensure that the RAM and disk space is more than sufficient to meet the current and future needs of the management platform.

Some computer management applications have been seen to generate high loading on a system and require the user to increase the amount of memory, disk space and even processing resources to provide the functionality demanded by the application. Fortunately, the majority of SNMP-based management applications do not produce this undesirable effect.

1.4 National add-ons

In recent years, the employment of staff and resources has undergone a remarkable change. For example, it is becoming common practice for individuals or small groups to be located at sites other than the organization headquarters. The term 'homeworker' has become common, where staff work from home and communicate with the main computer system via dial-up or leased lines with the aid of remote bridges and routers. These devices can be controlled by the network management system, assuming they incorporate some degree of intelligence and the relevant management and transport-layer protocols.

Likewise, the increasing number of multimedia video and voice applications available have enabled remote users to transfer visual information to and from central sites and to conduct virtual meetings across the network. For efficient operation of such networks, the management system should be extended to provide cover for remote users and services. Many organizations have decentralized their operations: for example, moved out from a city center to the suburbs, opened regional offices and provided the infrastructure for homeworkers to communicate with the central and regional centers.

With such a system, decentralized network management can be utilized. Regional centers can have their own management station which in turn may communicate with a master station at the central office. Network management may be distributed, providing local support for the regional offices and outworkers or homeworkers, with a link between the regional offices and the central site. In this way, the complete network may be managed from different locations.

It is important to consider the security aspects of distributed management across a national or regional network. With SNMP version 1 there is a need for strict control over the SET function (described later in the book), to prevent more than one network administrator making changes to the network from other locations. SNMP version 2 provides a security mechanism to deal with this situation, allowing secure management from remote sites.

The management station can display the complete network as a set of sites, presented with a map overlay to provide some sense of scale. Selecting the various subnetworks by pointing and clicking should reveal the network as seen at the remote sites. Statistics, reports and alarms generated at the remote locations can be delivered to a central management station as well as being held locally at the regional sites (if required).

Taking this strategy further, it is feasible to put a management system together on a global scale. For example, a bank with its headquarters in Tokyo has regional centers in New York, London and Geneva. The regional centers each have branch offices across the USA, the UK and Europe. At each regional center, the network management system is responsible for the regional office and the branch offices in its territory. During normal (local to the regional center) working hours, each regional office controls its own network. In the event of network problems at a regional office or a branch office supported by a regional office, the fault can be dealt with locally and within the time zone. If no action is taken locally, for example if the regional network center is unmanned, alarms could be sent to another regional network center for the appropriate action to be taken. The head office in Tokyo may wish to exercise the right to override all regional office network management systems and take control of the whole network at any time.

The aforementioned scenario provides for flexibility across time zones, a global view from each regional center and master control by agreement at one site. As organizations become more decentralized and global, network management will develop likewise.

All these features and functions require an integrated management framework. The next chapter reviews the OSI standards which were developed to provide a structured and cohesive mechanism for network management on a local, regional and global basis.

2

OSI Network Management

The OSI network management specification was produced by the International Standards Organization (ISO) in the mid-1980s and made public in 1988. The OSI standards for network management were and remain of considerable importance as they offered the first non-proprietary basis for the exchange of management information. Without such standards, multi-manufacturer management and the transparent exchange of management data would be impossible. In general terms, Open Systems Management describes all the mechanisms required to observe, control and coordinate the resources to be managed within an open system.

2.1 OSI Management Framework

The OSI Management Framework establishes the model and guidelines for all management standards. All later management standards refer to these standards, analogous to the OSI reference model. The total standards package comprises the following functions:

- definition of terminology and OSI management concepts;
- specification of an abstract model and the structure of all management objects;
- specification of a management protocol including all management activities.

The global OSI Management Framework contains three components: system management, layer management and protocol management.

System management
System management manages all controlled objects within the OSI management environment.

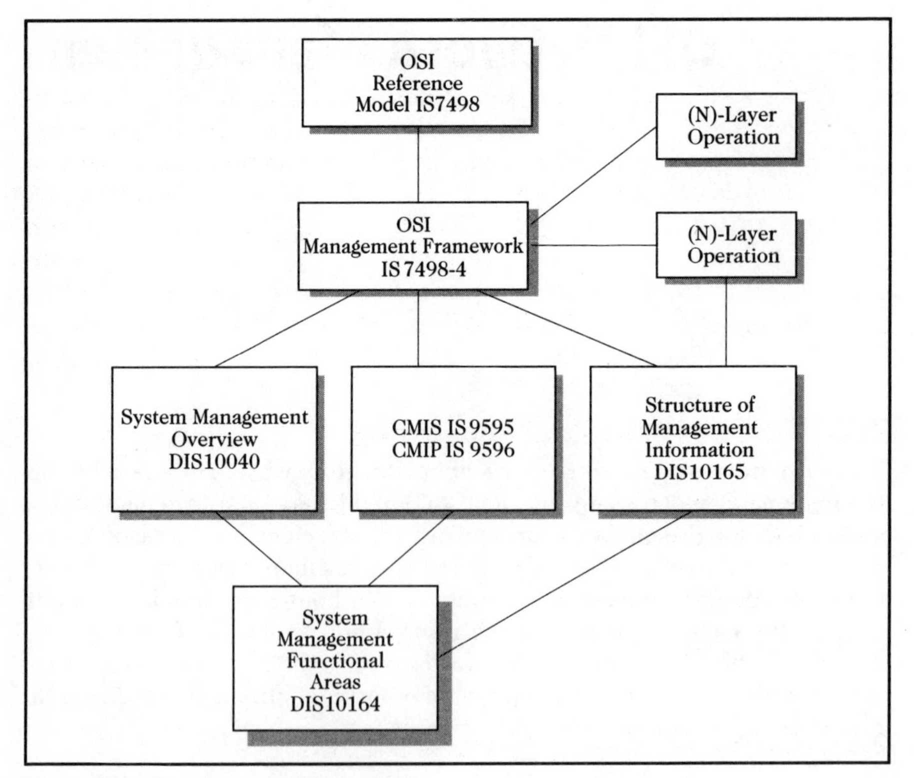

Figure 2.1 Development of standards

Layer management
Layer management provides management mechanisms for the seven layers of the OSI reference model and their coordination. It ensures the integrity of the individual layers, so management parameters may be exchanged and modified on a peer-to-peer basis without any impact

on the other layers. The management process for one level may be a separate process, or it may be part of an integrated management of all seven levels. With an N-layer management protocol, the ability to communicate is restricted to services offered by the lower level (N–1). Consequently, an N-layer management environment is less secure than an integrated system management environment. Layer management functions comprise the following:

- reading layer parameters;
- modifying layer parameters;
- active testing of layers;
- activating layer services.

Protocol management

Protocol management realizes all control functions for individual communication transactions on the respective protocol layers. Associated management functions must have agreed a certain set of parameters for a particular communication or its management. N-protocol actions are local, that is, only effective for a particular communication; once this has finished, the system returns to its original status. Management options of this nature are implied requests to the management entity operating in parallel with current communication protocol activities.

2.2 OSI System Management

The Open Systems Interconnect (OSI) System Management is separated into two overlapping concepts:

- system management models;
- system management standards.

2.2.1 OSI System Management Models

The OSI 'System Management Models' standard describes three models:

- functional model;
- organizational model;
- information model.

2.2.2 Functional model

The functional model defines the concept of Specific Management Functional Areas (SMFAs). SMFAs comprise the functions of configuration management, fault management, performance management, security management and accounting management. Each SMFA forms a separate standard, which specifies a function quantity implementing the SMFA functions and associated function procedures, CMIS services used, and object categories within the SMFA as well as subfunctions in accordance with certain conformity categories.

2.2.3 Organizational model

The organizational model illustrates the following concepts: domains, managed open system and manager and agent processes.

A domain may cover an organizational unit within a company, a company site or a certain manufacturer's devices within a company. Domains may include a number of sub-domains. Managed open systems are end systems that use OSI protocols to communicate and are administered via OSI management. The organizational model illustrates how OSI management administration may be spread across management domains and management systems within a domain. This involves linking abstract objects to abstract ports which communicate in synchronous or asynchronous mode and may be visible or hidden from the outside (internal ports). Abstract objects may be subdivided into object components. A management domain as an abstract object serves to shield management environment aspects from those of the application environment within the domain. It may be subdivided into sub-domains and/or object components. In principle, this is where the connection with real management centers is made; that is, a method to create structured management activity domains is extended; complex nets are established. The OSI organizational model arose from the fact that all management activities require the existence of a large information base, along with a number of associated data manipulation tools. The ISO describes management details as objects and attributes. 'Object' is an abstract term for resources that make up a specific segment of the net, which may in turn have many options (parameters/attributes). If an object can be integrated into a management concept, it is called a manageable object. A management function then, is nothing but a consequence of operations on an object carried out according to the parameters supplied. The total managed object is known as a Management Information Base (MIB). Objects and attributes are entries in the MIB; they appear in hierarchical form in the Management Information Tree. Objects may be combined in groups. The characteristics of 'super-groups' will extend to their sub-categories. Communication from network management stations to managed objects is never direct, but takes place via agents: see Figure 2.2. The agents must respond to service demands made by the network management station and forward alarm signals and event reports to this station. Communication between management station and agent is governed by the communication protocol.

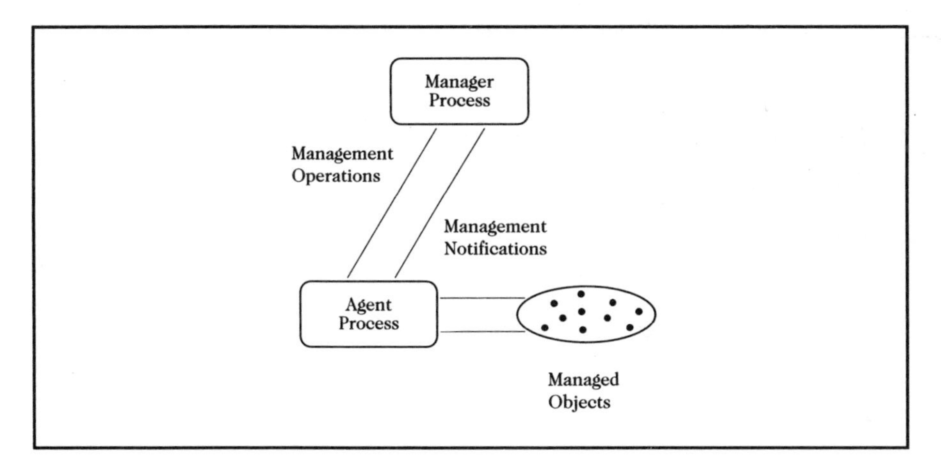

Figure 2.2 Manager – Agent

The three models listed above provide a conceptual and terminological framework for the following system management standard elements:

- Common Management Information Services Elements (CMISE).
- Specific Management Functional Areas (SMFA).
- Structure of Management Information (SMI).
- Generic Definition of Management Information (GDMI).

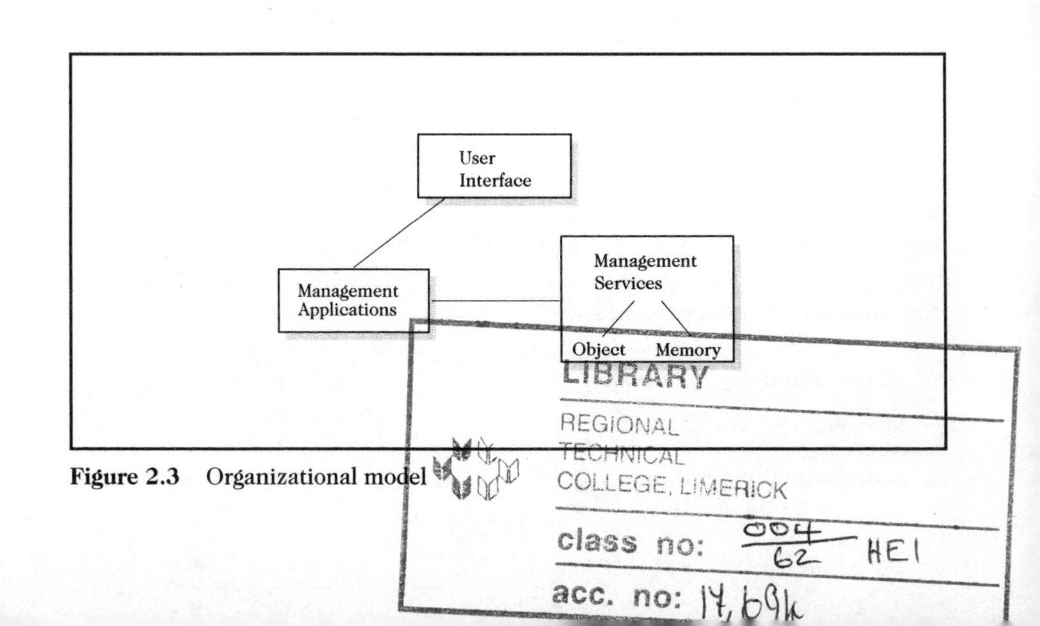

Figure 2.3 Organizational model

2.3 OSI System Management Standards

The OSI System Management Standards comprise a number of individual standards:

- CMIS/CMIP protocol specification.
- Configuration SMFA.
- Fault SMFA.
- Performance SMFA.
- Security SMFA.
- Accounting SMFA.
- Structure of Management Information (SMI).

2.3.1 Common Management Services and Protocols (CMIS/CMIP)

Common Management Services and Protocols support the peer-to-peer exchange of information on the application level. They include the CMIS (Common Management Information Services), CMIP (Common Management Information Protocols), ACSE (Association Control Service Elements) and ROSE (Remote Operations Service Element) standards.

2.3.1.1 Common Management Information Services

Common Management Information Services (CMIS) are an Application Service Element (ASE) as established in ISO Standard 9595. CMIS defines the service and the functions each network component must support to effect network management. The services described in CMIS are of a very general nature. Implementation of these services as real functions requires actual implementation. A CMIS application supporting the system management is known as a CMIS Service User. CMIS defines three communication service classes:

- Management Association.
- Management Notification.
- Management Operation.

2.3.1.2 Management Association Services

Management Association Services supervise communication between CMIS systems and serve to establish and disconnect links. The following Management Association Services have been defined:

M–Initialize
This service regulates the cooperation of CMIS service users within the system management.

M–Terminate
The M–Terminate service is concerned with disconnecting a link between CMIS users.

M–Abort
The M–Abort service is only used in case of severed links between CMIS service users.

2.3.1.3 Management Notification Services

Management Notification Services enable a CMIS agent to transmit autonomously any extraordinary conditions or information. The agreed Management Notification Service is the M–Event Report Service.

2.3.1.4 Management Operation Services

The following services are intended to transfer communication between a CMIS manager and CMIS agent:

M–Get
The M–Get service permits management information to be collected on a CMIS agent.

M–Set
The CMIS M–Set service allows variables to be set and modified on a CMIS agent.

M–Action
The M–Action service allows a command to be sent to the CMIS agent, causing it to perform a specific action.

M–Create
The M–Create service enables the network administrator to establish a new management object on a CMIS agent.

M–Delete
The M–Delete service allows management objects on a CMIS agent to be deleted.

2.3.1.5 Management Associations

Communication between two CMIS systems is always effected via virtual connection. The following connection functions are supported:

Event

Event links are used to send M–Event report messages between two CMIS applications.

Event/Monitor

Event/Monitor links are used to send M–Event report messages and M–Get messages between two CMIS applications.

Monitor/Control

A Monitor/Control link between two CMIS applications permits communication using M–Get, M–Set, M–Create, M–Delete and M–Action requests. These types of link do not support event reporting.

Full Manager/Agent

A Full Manager/Agent supports all CMIS Services (M–Get, M–Set, M–Create, M–Delete, M–Action and M–Event).

CMIS services are implemented via the Common Management Information Protocol (CMIP). OSI/OSI network management protocols are intended to offer a network architecture of general validity for all devices and all layers of the ISO reference model.

2.3.2 Specific Management Functional Areas

Each of the Specific Management Functional Areas is defined in its own OSI management standard, which describes the number of possibilities to support the SMFA functions. There are five groups of Specific Management Functional Areas (SMFAs):

- Configuration SMFA.
- Fault SMFA.
- Performance SMFA.
- Security SMFA.
- Accounting SMFA.

Specific Management Functional Areas (SMFAs) describe how CMIS and CMIP are used for SMFA functions. A range of procedures and associated information (the facilities) are set out for each SMFA. Management information is exchanged via Management Application Protocol Data Units

(MAPDU). MAPDUs contain management commands, responses, messages or other management information and are exchanged between a management process and an agent process. MAPDUs are standard vehicles for the exchange of information between tools of equal priority within the management protocol framework of an application layer.

2.3.2.1 Configuration Management SMFA

The Configuration Management SMFA defines the configuration data. This permits operations such as initializing or modifying configuration parameters. The following functions form part of the Configuration Management SMFA:

- Presence, name and relation of network components.
- Addressing.
- Hardware parameters.
- Activity/inactivity of network components.

Managed objects are controlled via their presence, attributes, conditions and relation to other objects. Normal network operation is controlled and supervised on the basis of collected, supervised and controlled configuration data, which contains both statistical and dynamic information about:

- Inventory management.
- Network design.
- Current configuration/reconfiguration.
- System generation.
- Operator support.

2.3.2.2 Fault Management SMFA

The Fault Management SMFA permits detection and identification of faults in an OSI environment. These faults may be of a temporary or permanent nature. Relevant management stations maintain error logs and fault traces and initiate diagnostic tests at regular intervals. The SMFA standard defines function modules for the support of fault recognition and diagnosis, associated procedures and CMIS services, managed objects and subsets of the conformity classes. Fault management comprises three primary activities:

- fault recognition (during normal operation, on exceeding specific threshold values or through confidence tests);
- fault diagnosis (event/fault reports, diagnostic tests);

- fault removal (automatically via configuration management or by operator intervention).

2.3.2.3 Performance Management SMFA

The Performance Management SMFA provides analysis and long-term evaluation, and thus effectively measurements for all communication processes. Relevant events, monitor intervals and threshold values can be defined, and performance reports generated. When a loss in performance is detected, the appropriate changes to the performance parameters are the responsibility of configuration management. Performance reports may be real-time reports or historical reports (long-term analysis/summary) and refer to individual systems or the whole net. Accumulated reports covering performance behavior over days, weeks or years regarding efficient load, work load, overhead, peaks and response times should be available. The functions of performance management SMFAs are divided into two categories:

- Monitor functions.
- Control of monitor functions (adjusting threshold values, events, operational modes, measurement characteristics, log functions).

2.3.2.4 Security Management SMFA

The functions of the Security Management SMFA refer only to the security of services and protocol mechanisms of the OSI levels. The Security Management SMF standard defines the relevant function modules, associated procedures and CMIS services, managed objects and subsets for conformity classes. This includes a (security) strategy for protection against unauthorized receipt of data and falsification of data during transfer, access authorization and identification of entities wishing to communicate on a peer-to-peer basis. This strategy is defined analogously to all other OSI services (service offer, service call-up, PDUs). The function modules are:

- Security-oriented object management
- Security-oriented event/fault trail management
- Security management.

2.3.2.5 Accounting Management SMFA

The Accounting Management SMFA defines all services necessary to use and restrict the available services with regard to individual end users. Costs arising from the use of certain services can be measured in cost units. This applies only to communication services, not to any system services outside the communication infrastructure. Two areas must be distinguished:

- Accounting for the medium itself.
- Accounting for the use of resources in the network end systems.

These areas may fall into different management domains which must, of course, be able to maintain a mutual exchange of information. The SMFA standard defines the exchange of information for accounting management data, associated procedures and CMIS services, managed objects and subsets for conformity classes. Security management comprises the following areas:

- Accounting system administrator.
- Accounting information.
- Accounting limit.
- Accounting unit.
- Charging unit.
- Accounting report.
- Network subscriber.
- Application subscriber.

If accounting management is operated in a distributed manner, that is, on several systems, a central control system is recommended. All systems involved in accounting must exchange information with each other. This may lead to information chains. The standard places no length restriction on these chains. A system collecting accounting data is called an Accounting Management Agent. A system requesting (and processing) this data is an Accounting Manager. A single system may be both agent and manager in the information chain.

2.4 Common Management Information Protocol (CMIP)

The Common Management Information Protocol is defined in OSI Standard 9596. It offers a transport mechanism in the shape of a request/response service for OSI peers. The relevant protocol specification defines precisely how this protocol executes individual CMIS services. The CMIP protocol is based on the CMIP Machine. The CMIP Machine is also known as CMIPM and offers the following functions:

- The CMIS Service User hands over certain operations to the CMIP Machine via a CMIS Service. These operations provide the necessary sequence of net operations.

- The CMIP Machine then sends the messages as received CMIS Service Requests to the CMIS Service User via the network.

One part of the CMIP specification is the definition of the abstract syntax (ASN.1) for coding and decoding CMIP Protocol Data Units (PDUs). The CMIP Protocol offers no further guidelines for the processing of the information contained in the PDUs by the CMIP Service User. The CMIP specification relies completely on the efficient functioning of the management system. The management system can receive any information from a manageable object and interpret it freely.

2.5 Additional protocols and functions

Alongside CMIS and CMIP, the functional standards also use ACSE and ROSE from the application layer. Neither ACSE nor ROSE form part of the OSI–NM specification, but they do provide the basis for the essential functionality of information exchange.

2.5.1 Association Control Service Element (ACSE)

The Association Control Service Element is defined in OSI Standards 8649 and 8650. It describes the service elements required to establish links, a precondition for the use of CMIS primitives.

2.5.2 Remote Operation Service Element (ROSE)

OSI Standard 9072 gives the specification for the Remote Operation Service Element. It supports CMIS with options for remote services, for example, invoke, result, error or reject operations. ROSE in turn utilizes the service options of the OSI Presentation Layer.

2.5.3 Problems with CMIS/CMIP

The definition of CMIS/CMIP permits a range of executable functions. The comprehensive nature of CMIS/CMIP standard definitions creates some difficulties with the actual implementation of these standards. The following problems arise:

- CMIS/CMIP require a great deal of memory and CPU capacity.
- Vast amounts of protocol overheads are generated.

- Programmers find the specifications difficult to realize and consequently tedious to implement.

2.6 Structure of Management Information (SMI)

The OSI Structure of Management Information contains a very abstract definition of all elements of other OSI standards. These elements are used by the OSI management and define the logical structure of any information able to form part of OSI management communications. The following structuring elements have been established:

- Managed objects.
- Attributes.
- Operations on objects.
- Information regarding these objects.

In addition, the SMI handles the naming of almost all managed objects, attributes, object sub-groups and attribute types. These definitions apply to all object classes. They encompass the general semantics and relations between different types. Management information categories are:

- Managed objects and their relations.
- Object characteristics.
- Attribute characteristics.
- Management operations.
- Naming.
- Object selection.

2.7 Common Management Information Services and Protocol over TCP/IP (CMOT)

Use of the Common Management Information Services and Protocol on a TCP/IP protocol stack is generally referred to as CMOT. This standard was published in October 1990 in Request for Comments (RFC) 1189 under the title 'Common Management Information Services and Protocols for Internet (CMOT and CMIP)'. Like other ISO/OSI specifications, it is rarely available in real products. When considering the CMOT specification, the working parties aimed for a gentle migration towards OSI management. CMOT is an attempt to add the ISO/OSI management protocol to existing and available

IP transport methods in such a manner that it would behave like CMIP at the application level. This adaptation of CMIS to the popular TCP/IP protocols was seen as a temporary measure until a complete OSI solution became available on the market. CMOT relies on the presence of the CMISE, ACSE and ROSE protocols as a basis on the application levels. Due to the fact that there is still no complete version of the OSI presentation layer protocols, CMOT builds on the Lightweight Presentation Protocol (LPP) as defined in RFC 1185. This protocol permits a direct take-up of the UDP and TCP service. Systems supporting the CMOT specification must support one or all of the service definitions. This means that CMOT can execute event, event/monitor, monitor/control or full manager/agent functions, depending on the hardware. CMOT's biggest problem is the reluctance displayed by manufacturers to invest time and money in what is after all, only intended to be an interim solution. For this reason, most manufacturers have decided to support the SNMP protocol.

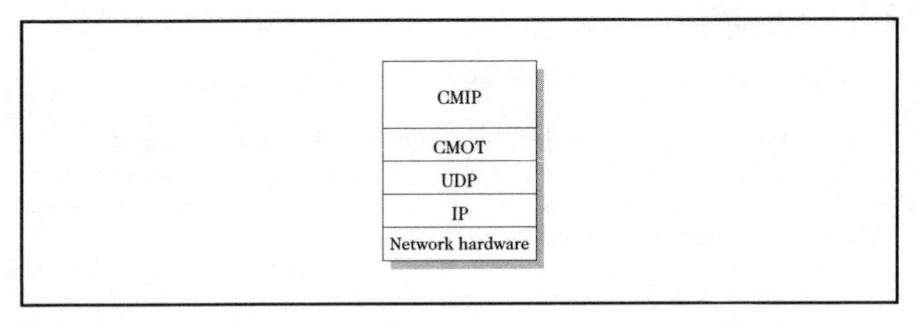

Figure 2.4 The CMOT protocol stack

2.8 The reality of OSI Specific Management Functional Areas

Investigation of local data networks has shown that a LAN is not available to the user (network downtime) for approximately 6% of the total running time. The reason for this frequently lies with cable faults, insufficient regard for relevant specifications, component failures, and so on. The order of magnitude of this failure rate is best illustrated by comparison with other communication resources within a company. The failure rate for telephones, for example, is less than 0.1%. It is therefore essential to equip the network with management tools that permit safe and reliable fault tracing within the LAN. This means that a faulty data network develops into a controllable factor, thus significantly reducing running costs.

In order to implement a refined network management system that fulfils all demands made on it, certain preconditions must be met, for example, standards.

In its System Management Overview (ISO10040), the International Standards Organization described mechanisms to observe, control and coordinate all manageable objects in an open system environment. This includes the conceptual framework for management in the Specific Management Functional Areas (SMFAs). Currently, five independent functional areas are available:

- Fault Specific Management Functional Area.
- Configuration Specific Management Functional Area.
- Performance Specific Management Functional Area.
- Accounting Specific Management Functional Area.
- Security Specific Management Functional Area.

2.8.1 Specific Management Functional Areas (SMFA)

The Specific Management Functional Areas are defined by ISO in individual OSI Management Standards. These definitions are expected to be generally available from 1994 as International Standards (IS). The following is an overview of the ISO definitions for the individual SMFAs.

Fault Specific Management Functional Area
Fault management serves to recognize fault conditions. This should enable the system to trace a fault automatically, analyze it via integrated diagnostic programs, find its cause and remove or isolate the fault.

Configuration Specific Management Functional Area
Configuration management deals with identification, supervision and control of manageable objects. It defines functions to initialize manageable objects, supervise their operation, reconfigure them as necessary and possibly take them out of operation. Furthermore, all manageable parameters are continually supervised during operation, so that any changes in a variable are recorded.

Performance Specific Management Functional Area
As its name implies, performance management defines statistical functions to generate certain data based on integrated analysis options for evaluating object performance.

Accounting Specific Management Functional Area
Accounting management defines functions that permit accounting by user of certain services or resources provided by the data net.

Security Specific Management Functional Area
Security management provides protection from unauthorized access to a data net or any connected resources.

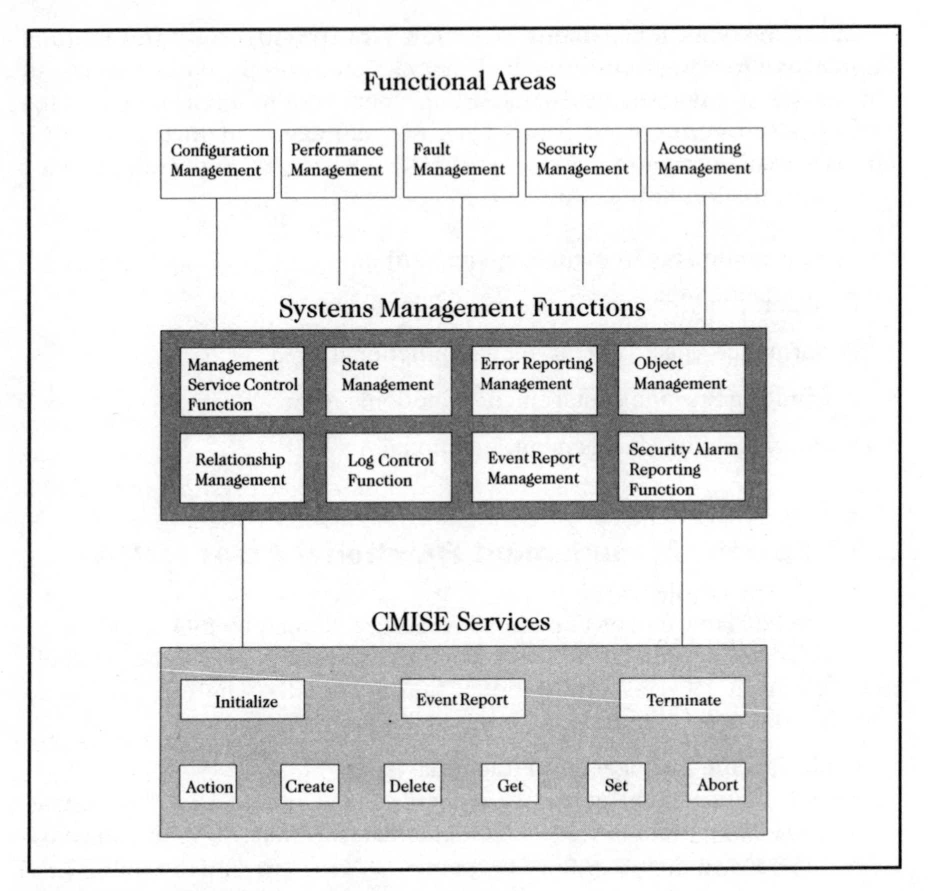

Figure 2.5 OSI Management Functional Areas

The following chapter describes OSI Management Functional Areas in greater detail. The technology and hardware available today illustrates not only the functions already available, but also the areas in which realization lags a long way behind theoretical definitions.

2.8.2 Fault management

Faults go hand in hand with the invention of technical hardware. The speed of fault tracing is largely determined by the qualifications and experience of the person conducting the search. No matter what the hardware, fault tracing will always require the classic three-step procedure:

- Tracing the fault
- Isolating the fault
- Eliminating the fault

Local network users notice a problem when data transfer fails (Network unreachable). Users will then pick up the phone and try to describe the symptoms to the responsible network administrator or technician. Once the user's fault report has been recorded, the technician will saddle up his or her troubleshooting horse and patrol the whole length of the network to trace the fault. After several hours, the fault (a disconnected bridge) is isolated in another segment, and regular LAN operation can be resumed.

If the technician or network administrator had been equipped with a troubleshooting tool, that is, network management, the same fault could have been located within a couple of minutes through analysis of all the information available. A simple component reset would have eliminated the problem.

A sensible mechanism for locating and eliminating faults is one of the most important troubleshooting tools available to the network administrator. In order to analyze and solve a problem, certain data about the network and its components (for example, data throughput and error rates) must first be gathered. This is done via the threshold and polling mechanisms.

2.8.2.1 Threshold mechanism

All data traffic throughout the network is analyzed automatically. Once certain threshold values established by the network administrator (for example, error rate, data throughput exceeding 80% of bandwidth, the device was restated 20 times in the past hour) are exceeded, alarm messages are generated on the network management station and may be highlighted by color coding. In order to ensure the greatest possible clarity, network managers should be able to set their own color coding. Table 2.1 illustrates a possible alarm differentiation on the basis of the currently required bandwidths (per second) on the LAN.

Priority	Color	Bandwidth required
Highly critical	Flashing red	>80%
Critical	Red	>60%
Warning	Blue	>50%
Information	Yellow	>35%
OK	Green	<35%

Table 2.1

A major disadvantage of the threshold mechanism lies in the fact that it can only supervise active or functional components. If a device or a whole net has ceased to operate and persistently refuses to resume communication, no data on this system can be gathered.

2.8.2.2 Polling mechanism

In addition to the threshold mechanism, continuous supervision (polling) of all existing transfer routes and all available components is used. The best known polling tool is based on ICMP echo packets, the PING. This tool is implemented in almost all IP terminals and relies on ICMP ECHO requests sent by the processor that require an ICMP ECHO response. Depending on the implementation, a success or failure message is generated (HOST ALIVE/ NO RESPONSE FROM HOST), perhaps including the response time. Some processors send several ICMP packets numbered in sequence and provide detailed information on the number of packets sent and received, along with the minimum, maximum and mean response times. This is one way to establish whether a processor or a relevant transit system is available.

The SPRAY function on certain UNIX devices fulfils an equivalent function at a higher level. SPRAY works on level 5 with Remote Procedure Calls (RCP) to send a precisely specified data stream to a target computer which then returns a response packet with the number of data packets received and the data throughput.

Different tests exist on the physical level for Ethernet and IEE 802.x networks, but these may not run via routers. In Ethernet, we use Ethernet Loop Packets which are received by the target computer's controller and, assuming the relevant driver is installed, return the data packet to the network after switching network addresses (source for destination). 802.x networks have the 802.2–TEST and 802.2–XID packets. 802.2–TEST is similar to the Ethernet Loop test, while the response to an XID request includes additional information about the system.

Unfortunately, polling routines have an unpleasant side effect in that they tie up part of the transfer bandwidth to transmit the polls. This presents the network administrator with a tough choice. All currently gathered data can be displayed in the on-line mode, which causes a high polling rhythm and uses a vast part of the available transfer bandwidth. Alternatively, the polling frequency can be reduced. Although data gathered in this manner is less precise and up to date, it still permits a reasonable information display within a certain bandwidth. Management systems supporting fault management functions should therefore permit the adjustment of the polling frequency individually for specific components and network segments. Polling frequencies between the network management station and a device on a local net may be much higher than those between the station and a device or LAN that is linked via a remote bridge with an open line of 64 kbit/s. For devices or LANs communicating via a router and ISDN-type links, it is advisable to reduce the polling frequency quite drastically (perhaps to only one poll every 30 minutes), as each poll means that a short-term link is established.

Because of the disadvantages of threshold and polling mechanisms alike, it is now common practice to use both mechanisms simultaneously in fault management. In local nets, the polling procedure is supplemented with the occasional threshold value, while data gathering in remote networks relies more heavily on the threshold mechanism.

Resource	Polling rate	Bandwidth required
In a local net	High	Low
In a remote net (linked via a bridge and 64 kbit/s line)	Low	Medium
In a remote net (linked via a bridge and 2 Mbit/s line)	Medium low	Low
In a remote net (linked via router with several 64 kbit/s (X.25) lines)	Low	High
In a remote net (linked via router with a choice of several 64 kbit/s lines)	Very low	Medium

Table 2.2 Polling (example)

The priority rating for faults and alarms is of course, determined to some extent by the size of the network. In smaller networks with some LAN components, the network administrator can respond to, trace and probably eliminate any fault or threshold value transgression. In larger data networks, lack of time and staff make this a very unrealistic approach. Fault display in such networks should be in order of priority as outlined above. The information may be displayed in a variety of ways. The simplest form of display uses a database which contains all faults and threshold values as ASCII text. When a fault occurs or a threshold value is exceeded, the stored text is displayed on screen, and the network administrator can deal with the causes. The display of events as ASCII text is cost-efficient, fast and easy to implement.

Example

Connection interrupted in router Stockach–Netz Airach; Beaconsfield, Marlborough and Tel Aviv can no longer be contacted.

If a fault generates a number of messages (sometimes from each of the connected stations), this system may drown the network administrator in a flood of messages. The administrator may find it impossible to maintain an overview, draw the right conclusions from the mass of incoming information and take steps to remedy the fault.

Far greater clarity is achieved by a graphical display of the network and its components. The standard tools readily available in the market today are an obvious basis for this, for example Windows in a DOS environment or X.11–Motif for UNIX. These standard tools have the advantage that many applications build on these interfaces, and many programmers will already be familiar with them. Specific messages can be integrated in the terminals, so that an alarm is automatically set off and transmitted to the network management station when the device is switched on (initialized). When this alarm is received by the management processor, it activates a display of the device which is stored in a database (bitmap). The bitmap is a graphical representation of the device and may be a circle, a specific symbol (PC, processor, router, bridge, and so on) or even a picture of the device (with all specific details). Symbols thus generated may be co-related, and with a display of the links this gives us the net map (*see* Figure 2.6).

If a threshold value is exceeded or no poll response is made, the color of the device on the graphic display changes. Individual priorities should be color coded to ensure greater clarity. Each network manager should be free to choose his or her preferred color coding. Table 2.3 illustrates how color coding could look when based on the polling rate (polls responses) on a LAN.

Priority	Color	Poll responses
Very critical	Flashing red	<20%
Critical	Red	<50%
Warning	Blue	<70%
Information	Yellow	70%–80%
OK	Green	80%–100%
Not active	Gray	None

Table 2.3

The advantage of a color graphics display lies in the ease with which the network administrator can see the condition of the network and take fast action. A flat network display showing all net resources can however, become very cluttered in medium sized and larger networks when faults generate a variety of messages.

The network administrator must draw the right conclusions from the many elements displayed on the bitmap before he or she can take the correct action to remedy the fault.

In medium sized and larger networks, the display of the individual nets or network segments as network clouds is preferable to maintain clarity. This requires a display mode that can separate all information into individual layers. Table 2.4 illustrates such a Layer View.

Layer	Network cloud
5	Complete network
4	Subnetwork
3	Components
2	Parts of component
1	Port

Table 2.4

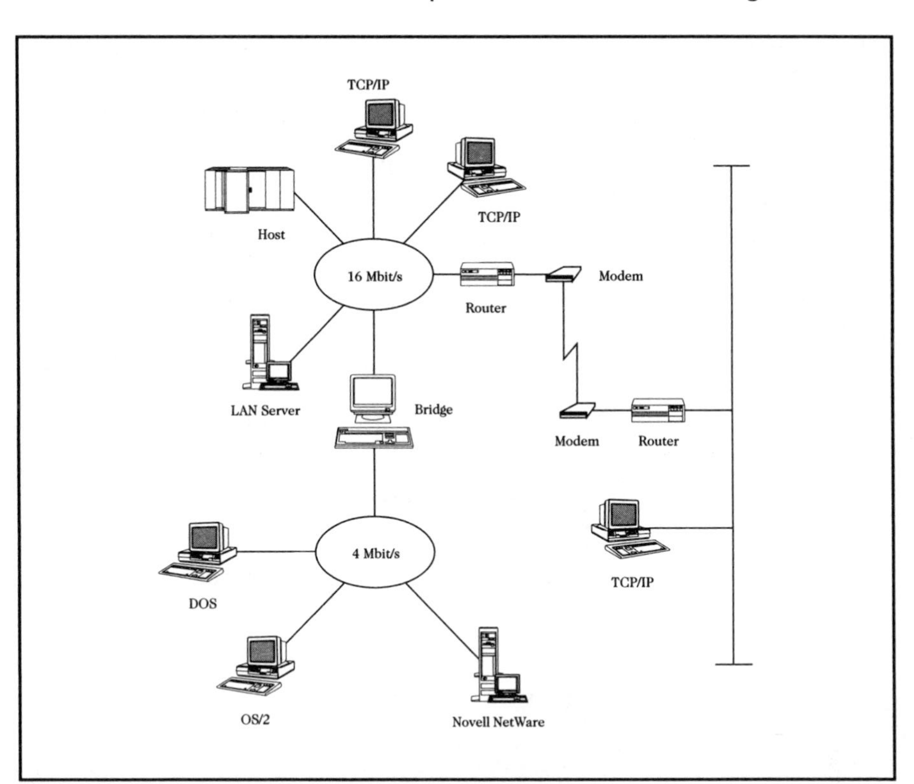

Figure 2.6 Graphical display of the components

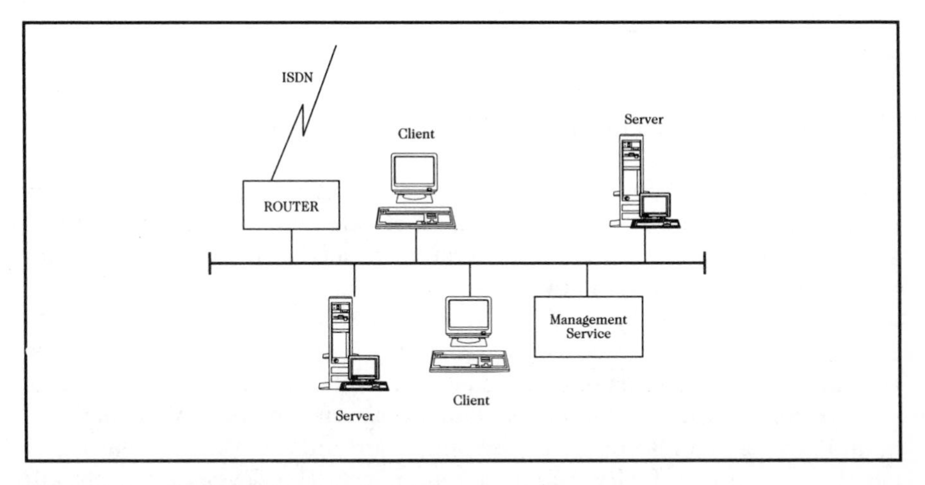

Figure 2.7 Graphical display of a LAN

The top display layer shows all the data nets in the shape of circles or network clouds. Each cloud indicates by color the condition of all nets and components it contains. In case of an alarm (that is, a flashing red cloud), the network administrator zooms to the next lowest display level and takes a close look at the relevant subnets. If one or more components indicate a fault, the net administrator moves to the next lowest level and looks at the components in detail. The information displayed (LEDs, switch positions) may already give a clue to the nature of the fault. In the next level, the relevant part of the component (for example, Net interface board, CPU board, memory) can be displayed and checked. If analysis at this level gives rise to the assumption that the fault may be located at a physical port on the interface board, the network administrator moves to the lowest level and investigates the appropriate port.

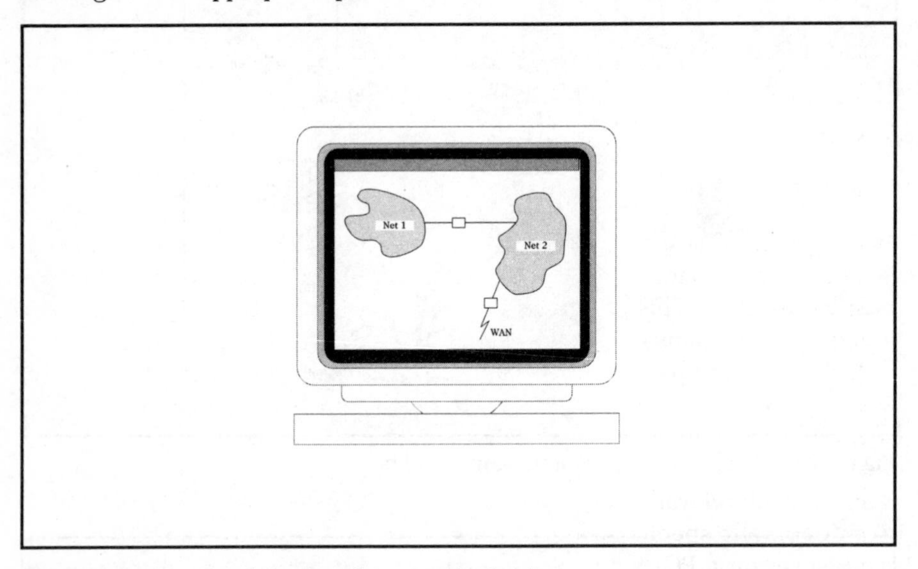

Figure 2.8 Graphical display of a network cloud

All alarms collected by fault management, and all associated data should be stored in a database. This enables the network manager to reconstruct any problems arising during his or her absence and to take precautions against future incidents. It is also possible to link certain alarm categories or alarm sequences with an automatic call system to advise the appropriate net administrator of his or her network's condition.

The integrated database offers further possibilities of linking alarms with specific reports. These reports may consist of simple lines of text and give certain fault-tracing hints or contain certain methods for solving a fault. It is also possible for these reports to contain a program compiled by the network administrator which could, for example, automatically establish other circuits to bypass a faulty router or router line. The development of fault management tools towards systems that no longer require highly specialized and highly paid experts, but merely far less specialized operators, will increase the marketability of such a system (particularly to companies operating a three-shift system).

2.8.3 Configuration management

All computers and the software installed on them, must be configured. Without this specific adaptation, the device would remain a mere lump of electronics. Basic configuration is followed by constant supervision, and possibly modification of the parameters entered during set-up, for example threshold values, filters, routing tables, and so on. By the same token, the software (and its versions) must be supervised and documented. In network management, these functions are carried out by configuration management which comprises the following functions:

- Supervision of the current configuration of all devices.
- Modification of individual configurations to suit demand.
- Storage of current configurations.
- Inventory of all devices used.

During the first configuration, the set-up, of a device connected to the network, certain parameters (for example, addresses, services, name tables) must be installed. This basic configuration procedure is usually carried out manually by the network administrator or the technician responsible.

If the device is portable (depending on size and weight), the set-up may be carried out in the administrator's or technician's office before the device is connected at its proper location. If the computer is not portable, configuration must take place on site. Once configuration has been completed, all relevant information about this computer is noted and stored in a document specific to it. This document is usually generated as a spreadsheet on a PC. When a fault occurs, all information required can be drawn manually from the configuration file and compared with the computer's current settings. Table 2.5 shows an example.

Computer etc. /hosts	IP address (Ethernet address)	Operating system	TCP/IP version	Function (location)	Serial number
Alex	192.5.6.3 (080002001234)	DOS 5.0	FTP 6.4	Fileserver (Accounting)	677883
Alison	192.5.6.4 (095670200123)	DOS 4.1	FTP 6.0	Workstation (Admin.)	2345878
Andrew	192.5.6.5 (0800124576D0)	BSD 386	BSD 0.3	Workstation (Boss)	8647840
Brian	192.5.6.6 (082345673434)	SCOUnix	SCO3.5	Workstation (Marketing)	7783542
Stockach	192.5.6.9 (080002001235) 192.5.6.10 (080002001236)	Griff 1.1	TRY 1.1	Router (Net Airach) (Net Beaconsfield)	9863

Computer etc. /hosts	IP address (Ethernet address)	Operating system	TCP/IP version	Function (location)	Serial number
	192.5.6.11 (080002001239)		(Net Marlborough)		
	192.5.6.11 (080002001239)		(Net Tel Aviv)		
Virginia	192.5.6.7 (0AA234567234)	Solar 2.1	SUN 2.0 (Development)	Gateway SNA	67459
Marlon	192.5.6.8 (080002845634)	MAC 7	MAC 6.8 (Accounting)	Workstation	87456

Table 2.5

In a small data net with only a few LAN components, the network administrator may of course, keep a manual inventory and register of the components and enter each change in the appropriate document. In medium sized and large networks, there is rarely sufficient staff and time to do this. These networks therefore require configuration management to enable the network administrator to gather automatically certain information (data) about his or her system (net) and the devices connected to it. In a large data net, a vast amount of configuration data is generated and should be stored in a relational system database. The database permits fast location and co-relation of the data stored in search or co-relation categories. In cases of system failure or even if the management computers crash, modern databases will automatically restore the data, so a computer failure no longer automatically entails loss of data. Defined interfaces can import existing ASCII data into a database system. Traditional configuration reports generated manually in spreadsheet format can thus be included in a modern configuration management tool.

As soon as a computer has been set up manually and initialized, it will generally send an initialization alarm to the management station connected to the network:

```
Computer > NM Station: I, '192.5.6.20', am now active.
```

The management station responds to the initialization alarm by initializing all relevant operational data and reads this information from the device to be managed. In our example, the following data will be read in sequence via a secure transfer mechanism: computer name, IP address, Ethernet address, operating system, TCP/IP version, serial number, function, location, and so on. This complete procedure is known as the automatic recognition of all managed devices in the net. Once the basic configuration has been transferred to the management station, the network administrator can confirm to have it frozen, so that it can only be changed through renewed access (description and confirmation) to the same set of data. By means of a poll routine, this file is continually compared to the data currently set in the supervised device.

Each change to the basic configuration automatically causes an alarm on the network management station. The network administrator can either identify the change in configuration as a fault, or signal his or her approval with an authorized confirmation.

System failure and repeated start-up on a device administered by the network management station leads to a renewed initialization alarm. Because the basic configuration data for the device is already present on the management station, it will immediately check whether the current data matches the basic configuration data. If the values in both files correspond, normal operation continues. Should they differ, an alarm will be given, enabling the network administrator to take corrective action. All changes made externally or by the network administrator, and all alarms, should be recorded automatically in a log file in order to facilitate future checks.

Computer	Event	Date	Time
Virginia	Cold Startup	31.12.92	08:00
Marlon	Cold Startup	31.12.92	08:30
080002001234	10BaseT Link down	31.12.92	12:00
080002008976	Config Change New IP Version	02.01.93	09:00
080002008976	Download	02.01.93	09:01
080002008976	Reset	02.01.93	09:02
080002008976	Startup	02.01.93	09:03
Virginia	Cold Startup	02.01.93	10:00
034561234567	Config Change New IP Address (192.1.1.76)	02.01.93	09:06
034561234567	Reset	02.01.93	09:06
034561234567	Restart new IP Address	02.01.93	09:06
Brian	10BaseT Link down	03.01.93	10:23
Stockach	Link Tel Aviv up	03.01.93	10:23
034561234567	Spanning Tree config change	03.01.93	10:24
Alex	Root Password change	03.01.93	10:25
Alex	New Root Password active after restart	03.01.93	10:25
Alex	Restart	03.01.93	10:30
Brian	10BaseT Link up	03.01.93	11:48

Table 2.6 Example: Log file

2.8.3.1 Inventory

Keeping an inventory of the hardware used in large organizations is by far the most thankless task.

An investigation of heterogeneous data nets showed that approximately 8% of all PCs change location within an organization in the space of 30 days. The network manager may find it difficult to locate these PCs. Frequently, PCs disappear for so long that they are considered lost, and then suddenly resurface.

The database integrated in the management application should therefore be able to document the real inventory. A simple program (Select) assists in reading the required data from the database and printing it as a report (*see* Table 2.7).

Computer	Brian	Alison	Andrew
Function	Workstation	Workstation	Workstation
Location of installation	Marketing Building 5 3rd floor, room 25	Administration Building 3 8th floor, room 5	Office Manager Building 3 8th floor, room 3
IP address	192.5.6.6	192.5.6.4	192.5.6.5
Ethernet address	082345673434	095670200123	800124576D0
Software version	SCO 3.5	FTP 6.0	BSD 0.3
Operating system	SCO UNIX 3.5	DOS 4.1	BSD386
Serial number	7783542	2345878	8647840

Table 2.7 Example: Inventory

2.8.4 Performance management

A network can be compared to a wide bridge (like the Golden Gate Bridge or Bay Bridge in San Francisco) used by all car traffic between two parts of a city. During the rush hour, the traffic volume on the bridge may peak at the absolute maximum possible. Even in off-peak times, minor interruptions (like a car that has broken down or an accident) may cause a severe performance reduction on the bridge.

For this reason, an efficient traffic control system was installed in the San Francisco area. Traffic is thus diverted partly or in total well ahead of accident or road maintenance sites. By camera and helicopter, the traffic control system gathers all the data at critical junctions and transmits the data to a traffic control center. The center analyzes the incoming data and controls traffic flow via radio or traffic signals.

Traffic flow in a data network (LAN and WAN) behaves in a manner not unlike the cars crossing the bridge. If too much data is sent on a data network, long waiting times may result. These waiting times may cause repeat data transmissions, which in turn increase the load on the line and may ultimately lead to the collapse or at least a severe reduction in the data throughput of the line. Accidents, for example a repeater defect or a faulty cable, may take whole branches of the network out of action. Network management should target its information-gathering measurements in such a manner that a system failure, whether in whole or in part, is anticipated and prevented. This is a function of performance management. Performance management gathers current performance and error rates in the individual network segments. This data can be displayed as statistics. Performance and fault management interlink, so certain threshold values can be set for all parameters. If a value is not reached or exceeded, an error message is sent automatically. Possible bottlenecks and excessive loads can be spotted in time, and remedial action taken before they lead to a network failure. Efficient network management requires certain tools to track events on devices and in the transfer links.

The three most important functions of performance management should be carried out at regular intervals, ideally constantly:

- Gathering and analysis of data, and its presentation as statistics.
- Monitoring, a procedure to analyze certain communication processes.
- Simulation, the deliberate provocation of certain events.

2.8.4.1 Gathering data

The main purpose of gathering data and statistics is the evaluation of current network conditions. Among the numerous options for the collection of statistical data, information on network load and error rates takes priority. Network administrators will find a statistical overview of all current network activity particularly helpful.

Popular presentations include bar diagrams and constantly updated tables in which all important information (for example, network load in % (or in frames/s and byte/s), all collisions, CS and alignment errors in %, CPU load required by certain resources, response times) is displayed. It is particularly helpful to network administrators if peak values are shown alongside the current and average values. Network management systems should have a statistic generator implemented, which should permit free configuration of the values to be monitored and their relationship. Great importance should be given to the length of the intervals between measurements. If faults occur, short measurement intervals (for example, one second) may be the only way to capture short load or error peaks.

In order to run a background history of network events, it may be advisable to use an integration interval of an hour or more for the display of average values. Long-term observations, maybe for network planning purposes, require in addition the capacity to display the above data related to time, that is, as a curve (X/T diagram). Again, it is of vital importance that measurements and interval lengths can be set individually. This will provide information on low load times (apart from the lunch break) as well as load peaks (for example, at night, due to backup procedures).

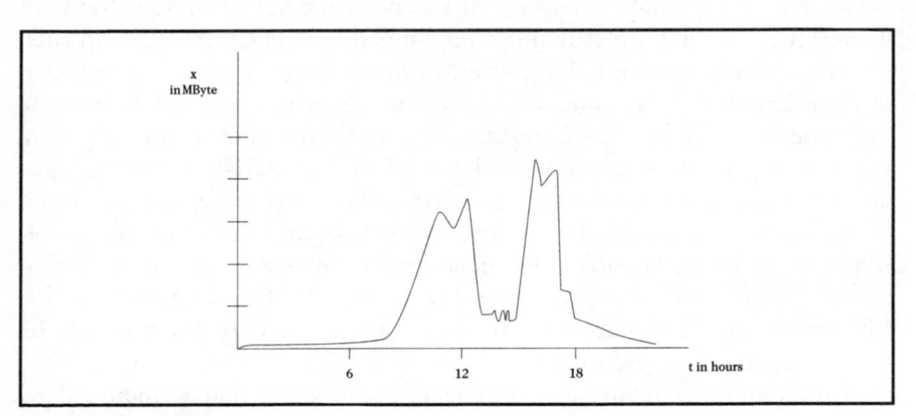

Figure 2.9 X/T diagram

From		To	Percentage	Packet/s
Computer A	⟷	Computer B	10 %	153
Computer B	⟷	Computer C	35%	478
Computer A	⟷	Computer C	8%	122
Computer A	⟷	Computer X	2%	15
Computer B	⟷	Computer Y	0,1%	20

Figure 2.10 Performance data

Performance management should be able to conduct all the measurements mentioned above simultaneously, in order to establish the correlation between for example, load, packet sizes and collisions. In addition, a cursor that can be started at any given point during a measurement might turn out to be very useful to serve as a further point of reference, along with the start and end of the measurement, for the comparison of various X/T diagrams. See Figure 2.9. When carrying out long-term observations, the system administrator should be given the option to store reference values or reference curves he or she has specified in separate files. Only by comparison with these reference values will the administrator be able to discover certain long-term, creeping trends. Reference curves may for example, assist in the recognition of defective or ageing transceivers or LAN cards that display faulty behavior such as increased error rates, response times, excessive signal processing times, jitters, and so on. A further aid in the supervision of networks are the node statistics. These show the data transfers from and to one computer or between two computers.

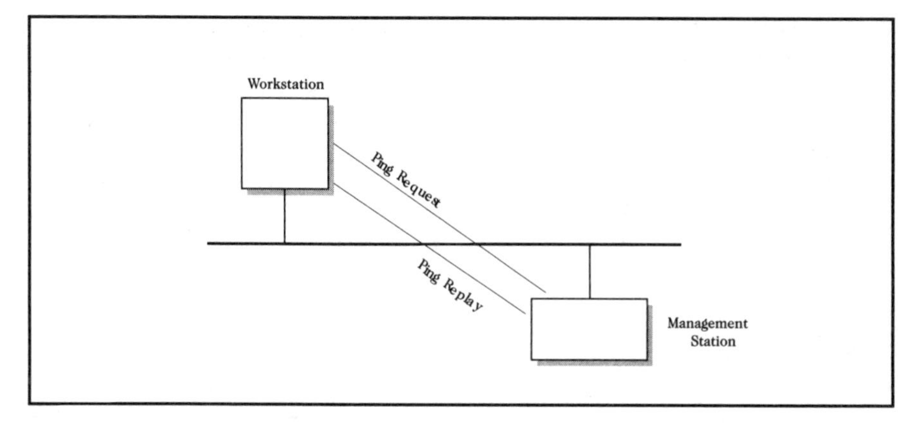

Figure 2.11 Node statistics

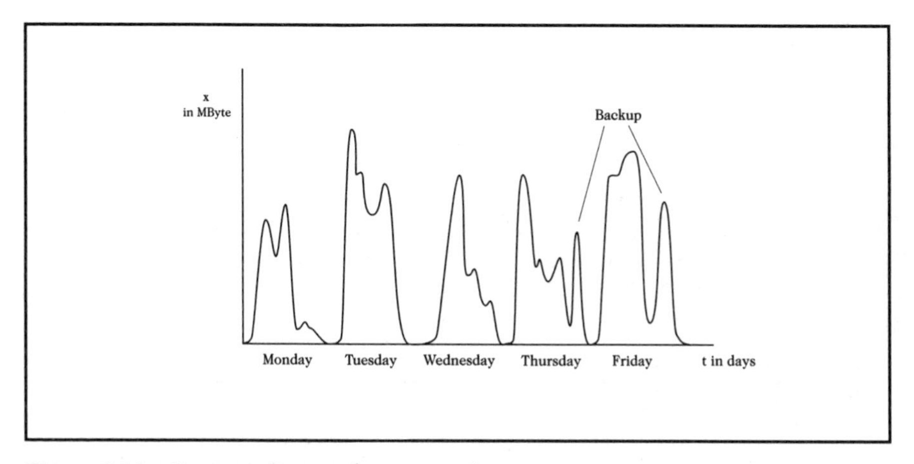

Figure 2.12 Progress diagram for one week

Analysis of node statistics goes a long way towards avoiding, or at least minimizing, misplanned data networks. Looking at Figure 2.14, we can see that the intensive load between computers A and E would make the installation of a bridge – or even a router – completely pointless. Each data packet between these two computers would be transmitted via the bridge or router, thus putting unnecessary strain on the resource. If the node statistics are combined with a data packet size display, nodes increasing the net load with numerous small packets or generating an excessively high rate of faulty packets could be traced. This makes for easy display, whether as graphics or tables, of packets that match certain conditions. The distribution of the network protocols on the activities of certain addresses (computers) or address areas (for example, IP-Subnet) are possible examples of this.

Computer link	Load %			Error rate %		
	Average value	Low mark	High mark	Average value	Low mark	High mark
Alex	27	3	67	2	0	3
Alison	37	4	75	0	0	0
Stockach	20	8	45	1	0	1.5
Link Airach	35	20	47	20	18	25
Link Beaconsfield	56	45	59	1	1	1.5
Link Tel Aviv	70	56	90	2	1	5

Table 2.8 Performance report

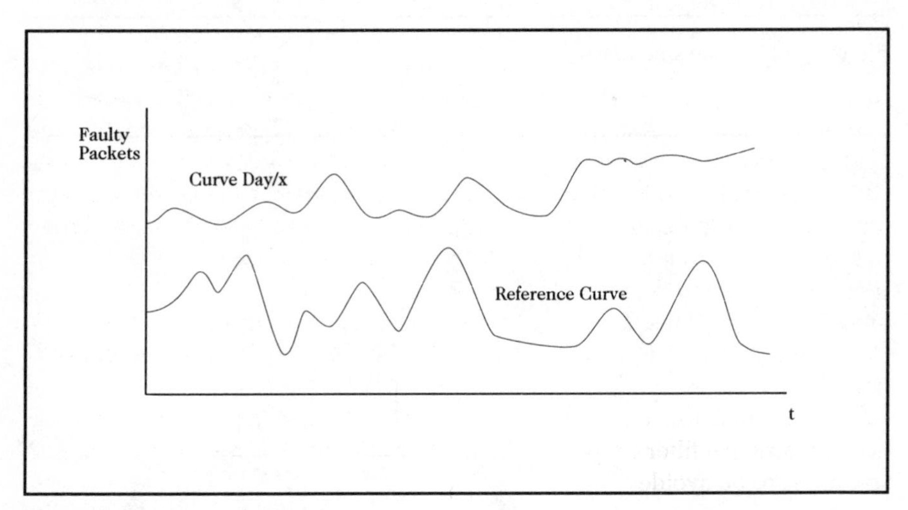

Figure 2.13 Example Ping

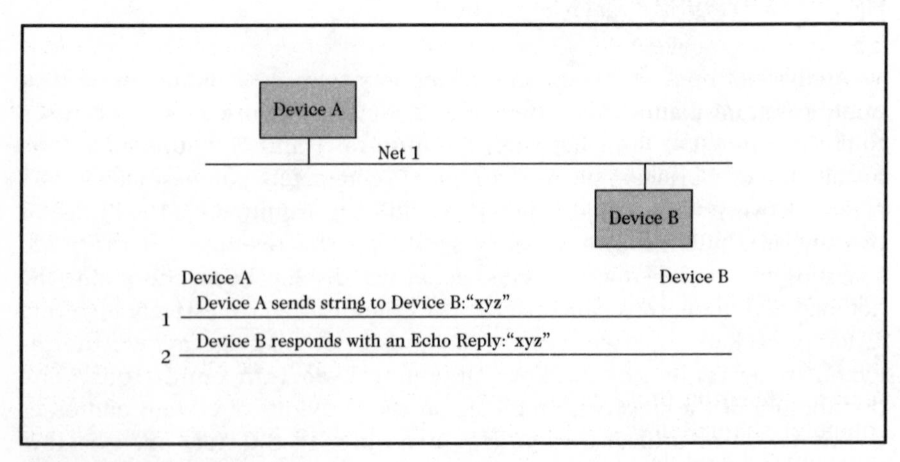

Figure 2.14 Example Ping

2.8.4.2 Monitoring

Monitoring data traffic is an important tool in fault tracing and elimination. Although most of these functions are executed by fault management, some of them also form part of performance management. There is no clear differentiation between the individual management functions. Effective monitoring offers the chance to trace the cause of problems such as 'computer not communicating' or 'connection is failing'. Monitor function users should be aware of the fact that 75–80% of all faults will be traced to the lower three layers. It is therefore of great importance that the software and hardware used are able to recognize certain events and forward them to the appropriate function modules. The Analyzer function implemented in performance management (and fault management), for example the Remote Management Information Base, RMON, can record certain selected data packets. Access to a range of filter options is important. In an Ethernet for example, it should be possible to filter out Ethernet addresses and the type field. If routers are used in a data net, the facility to filter Layer 3 addresses (IP addresses) is needed. Equally sensible is the option to 'match' each byte (or even bit) in a packet. Additional support may be provided by a function to use packets taken from the net in part or in total as filters.

All unprocessed data gathered during active monitoring should be stored in a separate file. This facilitates later processing of this data (postprocessing), for example by using new or different filters. This applies especially if network traffic is recorded without precise ideas about which events are being searched for, and the risk of losing relevant information through overly restrictive filter definitions, that is, the recording of an incomplete data stream, is to be avoided.

2.8.4.3 Simulation

It is difficult to make a clear statement about certain performance data in a network. Questions about network performance are usually answered in a vague manner: I think...I believe...last week (month)... .The network administrator simply does not have precise data and values that would permit a clear statement. Taking the example of a bridge, it is possible to simulate all bridge capacities on a computer. This requires the input of all relevant values (parameters), for example weather, minimum and maximum traffic flow, traffic volume to a simulation program. By changing certain parameters, an accident or a breakdown can be simulated, and the reduction in performance for the bridge can be shown. Thanks to advanced computer technology and the comparatively clear area of a bridge and its environment (access roads), such a simulation program is easily created in a cost-effective way. Before computer simulation was available, bridge operators had to analyze certain statically gathered data manually, or they had to close a lane (to simulate an accident) to get a result. This result was never quite reliable, as certain extreme conditions (such as pile-ups in snow or ice) could not be provoked for obvious safety reasons.

Computer and network technology today provides a range of very simple simulation tools. The best known tool is the PING command which is implemented in almost all terminals that support the Internet Protocol (IP). Ping is based on an ICMP ECHO request sent by a computer which will then wait for the ICMP ECHO response. Depending on the implementation, the result will be given as a simple success/failure message (HOST ALIVE / NO RESPONSE FROM HOST), or it may include details such as the waiting time for the response.

Some computers will send numbered ICMP packets in sequence and provide detailed information about the number of packets sent and received (percentage lost), and minimum, maximum and mean response times. This provides details about the availability of a computer (or even a relevant transit system), and with constant supervision it offers an indirect network supervision.

```
PING 126.1.1.6

64 bytes from 126.1.1.6: icmp_seq=1. time=10. ms
64 bytes from 126.1.1.6: icmp_seq=2. time=5. ms
64 bytes from 126.1.1.6: icmp_seq=3. time=5. ms
64 bytes from 126.1.1.6: icmp_seq=4. time=5. ms
64 bytes from 126.1.1.6: icmp_seq=5. time=11. ms
64 bytes from 126.1.1.6: icmp_seq=6. time=8. ms
64 bytes from 126.1.1.6: icmp_seq=7. time=5. ms
64 bytes from 126.1.1.6: icmp_seq=8. time=5. ms
64 bytes from 126.1.1.6: icmp_seq=9. time=5. ms
64 bytes from 126.1.1.6: icmp_seq=10. time=5. ms
64 bytes from 126.1.1.6: icmp_seq=11. time=5. ms
64 bytes from 126.1.1.6: icmp_seq=12. time=5. ms
64 bytes from 126.1.1.6: icmp_seq=13. time=5. ms
64 bytes from 126.1.1.6: icmp_seq=14. time=5. ms
64 bytes from 126.1.1.6: icmp_seq=15. time=8. ms
64 bytes from 126.1.1.6: icmp_seq=16. time=6. ms
64 bytes from 126.1.1.6: icmp_seq=17. time=19. ms
64 bytes from 126.1.1.6: icmp_seq=18. time=6. ms

      126.1.1.6 PING Statistics
18 packets transmitted, 18 packets received, 0% packet loss
round trip (ms) min/avg/max = 5/6/19
```

Table 2.9 Screen input/results of a PING in a local net

A load generator with ability to specify the packets to be sent in greater detail (addresses, packet types, higher protocols, and so on) provides the option to send a highly specific load on the net and check the net's behavior via performance management. The following example behavior tests can be executed:

- Reaction to Layer 2 broadcast load.
- Reaction to Layer 2 Unicast/Multicast load.
- Reaction to Layer 3 broadcast load.
- Reaction to Layer 3 Unicast/Multicast load.
- Reaction to faults in Layer 1.

Because these load tests (stress tests) have to be run during normal network operation, they will provide realistic load data for the network. A possible disadvantage of the tests may be an interruption of normal data traffic. The results will give the network administrator the option to react to certain network loads by diverting data traffic to network segments that are not used or hardly ever used, or by dynamic operation of additional lines (for example, with modems with multi-line fallback). A possible scenario would be to equip routers/bridges and computers with filters that will only accept data up to a certain load and then reject all additional traffic.

Unfortunately, it is not possible to simulate heterogeneous computer networks with a computer supported tool. The sheer number of different devices would make it practically impossible to create a realistic and cost-effective simulation program that would take account of all the values (parameters) of the individual devices. Perhaps there will be some activity in this direction in future years.

2.8.5 Accounting management

All Heads of Department dream of charging for the network resources made available to users. The requirement can be compared to the operation of a motorway toll. The access road to the motorway is free of charge. The user must identify himself on entry, that is, he inserts his ID card into the appropriate ID box, which in turn gives access by raising the barrier. Once the driver has crossed this border, he can use the resource motorway for as long as he likes (unlimited time and mileage). On leaving the motorway, time and place of exit are recorded at a further barrier. This information (motorway entry, ID, motorway exit and time taken) is sufficient for simple accounting of the resource used.

If this motorway mechanism is transferred to a network, it comes very close to meeting the requirements of the Heads of Department. Each network user identifies himself at a barrier (log-in) when he starts to use the net. Once the barrier is crossed, he is free to use the network. An accounting system could be based on the services used (motorway exit) and the amount of data transmitted on the network.

That is the theory. In reality, an open network does not provide for many of the mechanisms mentioned above. Any terminal may be connected to a LAN and start to communicate with the net resources through widely available communication software, especially in a DOS environment. Identification usually only takes place at the target computer (if a user account has been established). This means that, in principle, the network is open to almost any user.

This dilemma gives rise to the following approaches:

- Introduction of a fixed connection fee.
- Accounting by Layer 2, Layer 3 or addresses.

2.8.5.1 Fixed fee

The easiest way to implement an accounting procedure is to introduce a one-off connection fee for each terminal. This connection fee could be based on the real cost (cable, wages, components), to which a multiplication factor for certain protocols may be added. This protocol-determined multiplication factor enables the network operator to regulate user demands. Protocols acceptable in the network (for example, DECnet, TCP/IP and IPX) could be charged at Factor 1, while undesirable protocols (for example, LAT, XNS, LANManager) would attract Factor 10. This would still enable the user to employ the protocol of his or her choice. The real monthly or annual costs are invoiced on the basis of the costs incurred for personnel, material, measuring devices, and so on. The easiest calculation would be to divide all costs by the number of stations (terminals) on the network. This model may create some hardship, as a DOS station (single user) would attract the same monthly/annual cost as a multi-user station.

2.8.5.2 Accounting by addresses

The problems arising from a monthly/annual accounting procedure on the basis of terminals could be reduced by accounting on the basis of hardware (Layer 2) or net (Layer 3) addresses. This requires an appropriate procedure on Layer 2 or Layer 3.

2.8.5.3 International Layer 2 addresses

The LAN Controller hardware has a unique address (burnt into the chip). Administration and allocation of the hardware address by manufacturer used to be carried out by Xerox, but the IEEE took over this task some years ago. The first three octets of a LAN hardware address represent the manufacturer's code and clearly identify the make of a LAN card. The standard supports the use of group (broadcast, multicast) and individual addresses. Address types are distinguished by the coding of the lowest bit (1 – group address, 0 – individual address). The broadcast address belongs to the multicast addresses (FF–FF–FF–FF–FF–FF).

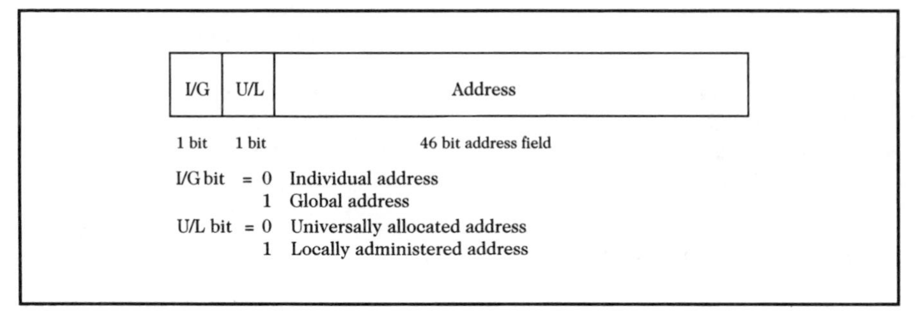

Figure 2.15 LAN address

00000C	Cisco
00000F	NeXT
00001D	Cabletron
00005A	S & Koch
000093	Proteon
0000A2	Wellfleet
0000AA	Xerox
00802D	Xylogics
00DD00	Ungermann-Bass
00DD01	Ungermann-Bass
02608C	3Com
080002	3Com
080003	ACC
080009	Hewlett-Packard
080020	Sun
080039	Spider Systems
08005A	IBM
080090	Retix
AA0003	DEC
AA0004	DEC

Table 2.10 Known hardware manufacturer codes

01-00-5E-00-00-00-bis 01-00-5E-7F-FF-FF	Internet Multicast
01-80-C2-00-00-00	Spanning Tree
09-00-09-00-00-01	HP Probe
09-00-1E-00-00-00	Apollo DOMAIN
09-00-2B-00-00-03	DEC Lanbridge
09-00-2B-00-00-0F	DEC LAT
09-00-2B-01-00-00	DEC Lanbridge
09-00-2B-02-00-00	DEC DNA Level 2
09-00-2B-02-01-01	DEC DNA Naming
09-00-4E-00-00-02	Novell IPX
09-00-77-00-00-01	Retix Spanning Tree
0D-1E-15-BA-DD-06	HP
AB-00-00-01-00-00	DEC MOP
AB-00-03-00-00-00	DEC LAT
AB-00-04-01-xx-yy	Local Area VAX Cluster
CF-00-00-00-00-00	Ethernet Loopback
FF-FF-FF-FF-FF-FF	Broadcast

Table 2.11 Ethernet addresses

2.8.5.4 Local Layer 2 addresses

The LAN Controller universal hardware address may be overwritten in the local area. These addresses are then referred to as 'locally administered addresses'. The practical consequence of this is that a user can compose an address to suit his or her requirements from each hardware address while maintaining his or her ability to communicate with every other device in the LAN.

Layer 2 addresses are frequently overwritten in Token Ring applications and in the DECnet Protocol. After initializing the computer, the universal hardware address is overwritten with a DECnet specific address.

If accounting is based on Layer 2 addresses, unknown addresses must be excluded from the exchange of data. If a communication controller in a terminal (for example, a PC) is changed, the hardware address will, of course, change with it. This means that the network administrator must know all controller addresses at all times to ensure fair accounting.

A further problem for Layer 2 accounting lies in the treatment of data traffic via routers. On Layer 2, the controller address stands for all computers connected to the linked data nets. As shown in Figure 2.16, router 1 re-packages all responses from computer 2 and computer 3 as data packets with its own Ethernet address as the source address. Layer 2 accounting will therefore only capture part of the data traffic in a network containing routers.

2.8.5.5 Layer 3 addresses

Because computers in a LAN tend to be from more than one manufacturer, chances are that there will be several communication protocols present. The major protocols are the SNA/SDLC or IBM Netbios in IBM environments, TCP/IP in UNIX environments, DECnet and LAT in the DEC world and the XNS derivative Network Operating System in PC nets (for example, Novell's SPX/IPX).

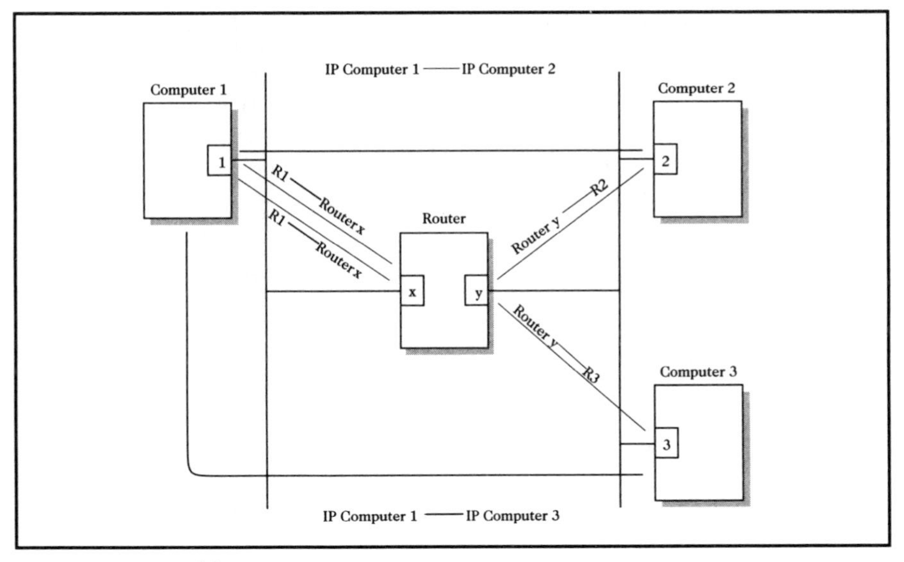

Figure 2.16 Problem area in router communication

Gateways can form a bridge between the individual transmission protocols and ensure that the different computer worlds are not operated in isolation. Each of the above protocols supports an addressing scheme best suited to its own purposes. The consequence of Layer 3 accounting is that each protocol used must have a definitive capture mode for the specific address mechanism.

2.8.5.6 TC/IP address: length 32 bits

Of this, 8 to 24 bits are the net address, and 24 to 8 bits are the address area for the individual computer address.

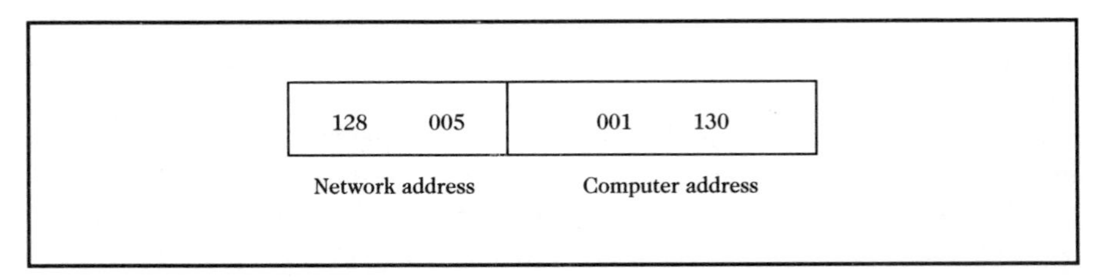

Figure 2.17 Different Layer 3 address formats

Example:	128.5.1.130 (decimal)
XNS address:	Length 80 bits of which 32 bits are the network address, and 48 bits are the address area for the individual computer address.

001565	080002003456
Network address	Computer address

Figure 2.18 Different Layer 3 address formats

Example: 001565.080002003456 (hexadecimal)
DECnet address: Length 16 bits
of which 16 bits are the area address, and 10 bits are the address area for the individual computer address.

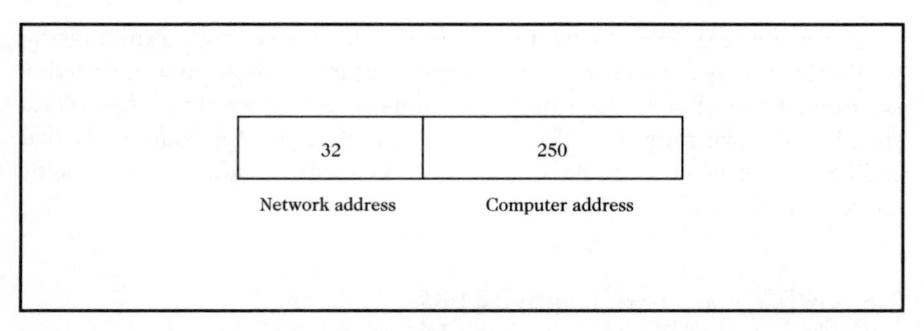

Figure 2.19 Different Layer 3 address formats

Example: 32.250 (decimal)

Even in data nets with only one protocol family present, for example TCP/IP, accounting on the basis of the TCP/IP address is not easy. The router problem outlined above would be solved on this layer, because each datagram contains the complete IP source and IP destination addresses. Routers do however, create additional problems: ICMP packets and routing packets.

2.8.5.7 ICMP packets

The Internet Control Message Protocol (ICMP) is located on Layer 3 as an assistant program. It facilitates the exchange of fault and information messages between the devices in the net. The ICMP protocol builds on the IP protocol; that is, IP treats it like a higher-level protocol.

2.8.5.8 RIP

The Routing Information Protocol (RIP) is based on a version of the XNS protocol. RIP builds directly on the User Datagram Protocol (UDP). The RIP protocol is one of the Interior Gateway Protocols which enable routers to exchange information within an Autonomous System Routing. A poll mechanism permits constant mutual updating of the routers, enabling them to know at all times how each resource can be reached.

The RIP protocol guarantees instant availability of routing information to new routers, and fast availability of information on network topology changes (interrupted lines, failed routers) to other network participants. The drawback of the routing protocol lies in the unprompted broadcast of the routing tables to all network participants by each router, every 30 seconds.

The ICMP and RIP packets illustrate the dilemma of Layer 3 accounting. The ICMP protocol enables the network operator to trace the originator of ICMP replies on the basis of the information contained in the data packet. The RIP protocol sends this information automatically. Costs for RIP packets would have to be shared between all network participants.

Accounting management should equip the network operator with tools to record user-relevant data in order to establish a tariff for network use. The ideal of accounting demands true measurements of all the network resources used. In effect, this would entail collecting statistics on net load for each user. Measurement of network resources used could be based on the following criteria:

- number of packets;
- number of bytes;
- number of transactions.

2.8.5.9 Number of packets/bytes

If measurement is to be based on bytes or packets, this should include either the amount of information sent onto the network, or the amount of information taken from the network.

2.8.5.10 Number of transactions

If accounting is based on the number of transactions per user, various information about user behavior may be gathered. It is very easy for example, to establish the number of logins on a certain computer, the amount of e-mail sent, and so on. These functions are simple and cost- effective to implement, but they have their disadvantages: each transaction would be charged at a flat rate, irrespective of which resource was used for what time. This means that a user who has sent several gigabytes of data via the network is charged the same amount as the user who only transferred a short e-mail message. Because this strategy flies in the face of fairness, it must be discounted as a solution.

The number of packets transferred via the network gives a truer reflection of the network resources currently used. Each data packet sent or received by the user increases his or her bill. If only the number of packets received or sent is counted, the differences in size are disregarded. Users of the virtual terminal protocol Telnet for example, will send a great number of short packets onto the net. Frequently, these packets contain only one or two ASCII characters. Short packets may in certain circumstances, place a considerable strain on the network. For this reason, the File Transfer Protocol ensures that data is sent in reasonably large packets, which create a far lower network load than short packets. In order to ensure fair network accounting, service and type of data packet transfer must be taken into consideration.

The disadvantages inherent in accounting on the basis of transactions and the number of data packets transferred may easily be bypassed by counting the number of data bytes transferred. In this case, the user is charged for each data byte transferred. This method does of course, have its own set of disadvantages, although the apparently irrefutable logic of charging by the number of bytes sent tempts one to consider it the fairest of accounting methods.

In today's computing environment, particularly in the client–server architecture, this approach is hardly feasible. The client–server model means that the user sends short packets to the server and receives in response long information segments. Does this mean that the sender of this information (that is, the server) should be held responsible for the costs incurred? For reasons of fairness, the server costs would again need to be split among all users. How then should we treat computers that act as both client and server? In a fair accounting system, all data resources made available on a computer (server) should lead to a 'voucher' in the charging system each time they are used. Each computer in the net (provided it is equipped with a sensible operating system) can make its resources and services available to the community of network users, as long as they are of some economic benefit (not games, for example), and thus reduce individual network operating costs.

At the same time, the load on all network resources would need to be supervised as part of the network management accounting system. High loads on a computer or a WAN line should lead to higher costs for data transfer or required services than on a computer or line with the same services operating at a lower load.

All accounting information from the individual network areas would need to be collected in a central database. Accounting applications should run on diverse systems. The charging computer, that is the computer on which the amount of network resources used is calculated, must have access to this information. This seems to be the only way to create valid accounts for individual users or user groups.

Some network operators have already implemented (or tried to implement) various accounting models, but the results of these field studies have usually been far from satisfactory. The biggest hurdle in the implementation of accounting is the requirement for a fair charging system for all network resources. Accounting applications do not come ready-made for nets with diverse computers and hardware and software components. An individual software application needs to be written for each individual device. Implementation and operation of these services requires qualified personnel, which makes it very expensive. In addition, software updating is of great importance. Maintaining proper operation of a network with a heterogeneous hardware structure and securing the investments made in the long term demands updating the devices at regular intervals with the latest software releases and associated functions and features. This constant change in the software and hardware versions in turn requires constant adaptation of the accounting application. This is why consequential costs should be considered when accounting is introduced. The accounting project must also be thoroughly documented.

This documentation must contain the following: a plan of the complete network, and details of devices (for example, configuration and specific values (physical/logical parameters)) of individual network users. This last point is of particular importance to ensure that slow, creeping errors can be traced by means of readily available reference values. The documentation can turn out to be an invaluable resource in fault tracing, so special emphasis should be placed on this point. In general, it can be said that the more attention has been paid to this point, the easier the search for certain accounting and configuration faults will be. Data network operators should be aware of the fact that nothing is more obsolete than yesterday's documentation. For this reason, the documentation should always be available on an electronic medium, for example AutoCad or similar. Extensions or modifications that will no doubt occur in the net should of course, always be entered in the documentation.

2.8.6 Security management

One of the tasks of network management is the supervision of access to the data net and its resources and services. This requires certain supervision mechanisms and rules, for example passwords, access codes, and so on. Security management enables the network operator to protect his or her network resources:

- Access to computers and other terminals at user level.
- Notification to network management of any attempted unauthorized access to protected resources.

As these functions need to be integrated on all network resources, the following functions should be implemented:

- A mechanism to clearly identify net resources relevant to security.
- Clearly defined access points to protected resources.
- Security mechanisms for these functions.
- A management protocol for the administration of network resources to be protected.

Network management security functions are often confused with operating system security functions or physical access protection for the network. Security mechanisms on the network are created through special configuration of all resources connected to the network and supervision of all network activities. Supervision of resources also entails the inclusion of special access points to software services (applications), hardware components or the network medium. Security functions may be realized through different approaches:

- Protecting the operating system.
- Physical protection.
- Protecting protocols.

2.8.6.1 Protecting the operating system

Each operating system contains a number of minimum security functions, for example access for certain users to certain files, directories or programs. These rights are stored along with the relevant passwords in the user accounts. This enables the user to access a fixed range of files, directories and programs. Resources not cleared for this user cannot normally be accessed.

2.8.6.2 Physical protection

Physical protection encompasses many areas, for example protecting of computer rooms or electric cabinets with special keys or through an electronic staff recognition system.

A physical protection system naturally includes protection of the individual computers. This can be achieved by lockable keyboards or disk drives. In addition, access by unauthorized users to important components, for example the fileserver, must be prevented. One important point frequently neglected in physical security concepts is the barring of access to the network medium. With Ethernet, a new user can just plug his or her device, for example a network analyzer, into the cable and read all information (user ID and associated passwords) without being noticed. This information equips any hacker to break into the relevant computer and copy the desired data. Cable in certain areas (easily accessible cable shafts in workshop areas) should therefore be laid in steel pipes or be replaced with glass-fibre lines.

2.8.6.3 Protecting protocols

In any network, the highest priority must be given to security concerns specific to protocols. Protocol specific security functions include coding mechanisms, network access protocols that clear access to certain network resources for the individual user, and administration tools used to manage security aspects relating to the running of the net.

Many of the points listed, for example physical security, protecting the operating system and some elements of protocol protection, are not included in security management. It would far exceed the tasks of a network system if these special services were expected from an open protocol and system. In general, computer specific security and physical access protection are a precondition for security management. Without them, we do not have the technology to give complete protection against unauthorized access to net and terminals.

We used the example of a motorway to illustrate the basic functions of security management. Access to the motorway is controlled by an access mechanism. The user has to identify himself on entering the motorway; that is, he must insert an ID card into the appropriate ID box. At the same time, the user states his destination, that is, the motorway exit. The user administration computer will check whether the user has access clearance for his destination. If the check result is negative, the barrier to the motorway will not rise. If the result is positive, the user may access the motorway and continue his journey to his destination. The security mechanism can be tightened by giving each motorway user an electronic key (code). This electronic key is transmitted on the User ID card magnetic strip. On leaving the motorway, this card must be inserted in an exit clearance box to be checked. If the values (electronic key) match the information entered at the entrance barrier, the barrier will rise. Even better security is achieved if the electronic key is negotiated dynamically between entrance and exit through a set algorithm. Only cars reaching the destination within a certain time and with this dynamic key will be let out. All other traffic will be denied exit. As an additional function, the motorway security system needs a management tool. Alarms must be generated if faults occur in the procedure, that is, if the car attempts to leave the motorway at the wrong exit. Electronic keys are also administered by the management system (*see* Figure 2.20).

If the control system for motorway entry and exit is applied to a network, it will become obvious that many of these mechanisms are already in place today, but use of the security management options is not generally established. A top-down approach is advisable when introducing and implementing security management. This approach derives demands on network security from demands made on applications. Only in this manner can the aims relevant to security be implemented efficiently, and problems in later operation be kept to a minimum. The security demands made on applications and services will almost automatically define the quantity and quality of the net resources and network services worthy of protection. The top-down approach requires slow and steady planning and an attempt to anticipate future problems and take them into account in the total concept. Unlike the technical bottom-up approach, it demands a much more global strategy.

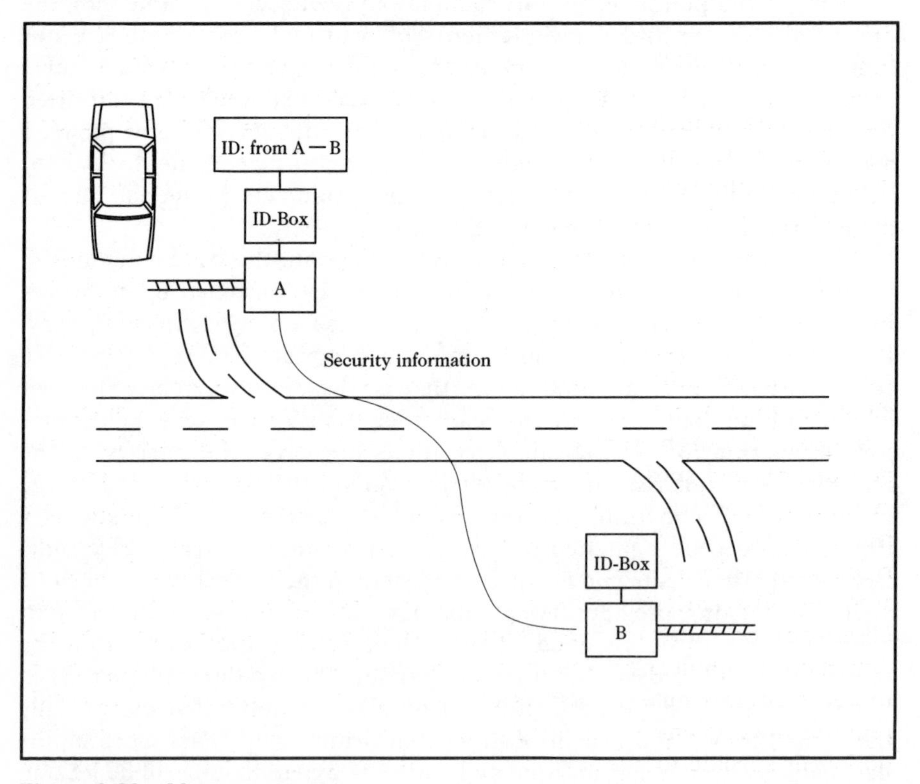

Figure 2.20 Motorway security

By analyzing demand in detail prior to implementing a global security system, the effort required to realize the total concept is increased. A security system defined in all details will, however, pay off in the long run, as far fewer problems occur during implementation. Faults arising during operation of the complete system will be resolved more quickly and easily.

Security management must therefore be understood as a comprehensive entrepreneurial, organizational and technical measure. For this reason, the top-down approach requires the cooperation of all areas of the company. Company management must establish the demands of the lower company levels, and on this basis, individual company levels must define the services they require for their day-to-day operation. The IT department must plan the resources required to fulfill the demands made on the network and the associated network management. This analysis of all components of a global security strategy must not stop at obsolete applications or computers merely because they are still running, or because people have become fond of them. Global thinking also means the introduction of new and more effective mechanisms.

A global security concept encompasses all seven layers of the ISO/OSI reference model, from the physical up to the application layer. The application layer however, only defines services provided by the net during actual applications. These applications, which enable the user to do his or her work, in turn use the application layer of the network system. For this reason, it is crucial to extend the total system and thus security management, to include this eighth layer. Application security management administers the specific demands of each application and provides dynamically the resources and configurations required by the applications, depending on the security level. Unfortunately, the network management products currently available do not permit the integration of applications into a unified system on this level. A global security concept and the general network management concept resulting from it would provide the framework for integrating all services in the network into one security system. The security concept must allow for growth and dynamic expansion, because demands on communication philosophies are constantly changing through new strategies; for example multimedia, video networking, and so on, and companies will need to redefine their goals to remain competitive. Static computer worlds and old organizational hierarchies are things of the past. Keywords such as downsizing or rightsizing dominate the debate in modern computer culture. Central IT services are split into smaller units or replaced by decentralized client–server solutions with diverse applications. Restricted and one-dimensional applications are replaced with open applications capable of integration and network operation. On the lower network layers, this requires the implementation of standards and open interfaces and protocols no longer specific to one manufacturer. The resulting flexibility places new competence and wider responsibilities on the individual company units. Classic terminal networks must be replaced with the modular structure of LANs and WANs. New communication structures constitute new challenges to system security in each specific area. In order to adapt a data net to constantly changing demands, and to implement these changes without delay, management functions for the simulation of all relevant parameters are required. Only by checking all relevant data of a plan can potential security problems on a technical level be spotted in the early stages. Operational bottlenecks (net, application and maintenance) or security gaps in the total system can be found and dealt with at the planning stage, thus avoiding any negative impact on future users of these services. A complete simulation enables the network operator to take preventive action in order to minimize potential flashpoints and the costs resulting from them. The more pronounced the change in demands on a network, the more important early simulation of the target aspired to becomes.

Introducing a security management system in a company requires a strategic approach. The system must be considered to be a management tool that goes beyond the technical administration of bits, bytes and parameters. A security system is a management tool and must therefore derive from the demands of company strategy. It must support the operational framework and operate as a combination tool for both software and hardware platforms. In addition, it should be capable of expansion, so that it can be adjusted to suit new organizational conditions at any time. But even the best network management system will only produce its maximum benefits if the aims for and demands on the total system have been clearly defined.

In order to introduce a security system in a company, the following parameters must be established:

- Net resources worthy of protection must be clearly identified.
- Access mechanisms for the network resources to be protected must be developed.
- The access mechanisms for the net resources to be protected must be administered and maintained in a management system.

2.8.6.4 Identifying net resources worthy of protection

In order to protect certain resources on the net and in the computer systems, they must first be identified. From the variety of data, applications and resources that network users can access, individual security levels must be established with the aid of a matrix. Not every resource available is necessarily a security relevant resource/application. Table 2.12 shows a simple net security matrix.

The security matrix shown, and the applications, resources and security classifications it contains, illustrate clearly that no security demands are made on certain services in the net. These services are therefore generally available, without restrictions. Access privileges for all other services must be defined with a further matrix.

Application/resource	Security classification				
	None	Low	Medium	High	Very high
Printers, general	X				
Laser printer		X			
Network fax				X	
e-mail			X		
Word processing program on File Server	X				
User-relevant text files				X	
Computer, Personnel					X
Computer, Directors					X
Computer, departmental			X		
Internet access				X	
Multi Line modems					X
Common database	X				
Games	X				
Customer database				X	

Table 2.12 Security matrix

Application/resource	Users
Laser printer	Personnel department
	Directors
	Research team A
	Research team B
	Research team D
	Support team D
	Hans Karl Steffan
	Brian Frederik
	Virginia Grace
Network fax	Personnel department
	Directors
	Research team D
	Support team A
	Lothar Aberle
	Uwe Bold
	Virginia Grace
e-mail	Personnel department
	Directors
	Research team A
	Research team B
	Research team C
	Research team D
	Support team A

Application/resource	Users
	Support team B
	Support team C
	User group 1
	User group 2
	User group 3
	User group 4
	User group 5
User-relevant text files	Support team A
	Respective user
Computer, Personnel	Personnel department
	Directors
	Support team A
Computer, Directors	Directors
	Support team C
	Carla Spätzle
Computer, departmental	Support team A
	Respective departmental user
Internet access	Directors
	Research team A
	Research team B
	Research team C
	Research team D
	Support team A
	Support team B
	Support team C
	User group 1
Multi-line modems	Research team A
	Support team A
	Support team B
	Support team C
	User group 1
Customer data base	Directors
	Support team C
	User group 2

Table 2.13

This matrix illustrates at a glance which user groups or individual users should be allowed access to certain net services. Once the important resources are known, the next step is the implementation of a security strategy to search for or develop suitable access mechanisms for these protected network resources.

2.8.6.5 Establishing access mechanisms

Normally, a user wishing to access the network via a computer must identify himself to the target computer with a password. The effort of user identification in a remote computer is justifiable if a user logs in to a remote system and works on it for some time. When a single command is executed on the remote computer (for example, an RSH command), this additional effort is more often a hindrance. Also, the option to demand a password is not available with some commands, for example RCP. In order to facilitate access to a remote computer without password queries, UNIX computers with TCP/IP protocols have an integrated two-step equivalence system. Access entitlement to a remote computer is governed by two files: /etc/hosts.equiv. and .rhost in the user's remote Home directory. It is up to the system administrator to make access to the files and the computer as simple as possible, and to create system security in accordance with his or her ideas.

The lowest security level in a UNIX computer uses the etc/hosts.equiv file. All computer names are entered in this file, with each name on a separate line. In the case of the Network fax computer, this file would look as follows:

```
Personnel
Directors
ResearchD1
ResearchD2
ResearchD3
SupportA
Aberle
Bold
Virginia
```

If a user attempts to reach a remote computer from a different computer via the network (for example with rlogin, RSH or RCP), the target computer will consult the /etc/hosts.equiv file. If the computer is entered in the /etc/ hosts.equiv file, the etc/passwd file will be checked next. This ensures that the user does indeed have a user account for the system. If the user is present on the system, system access is granted without any further password queries. An important point to consider is that only the /etc/hosts.equiv file on the target system is relevant for access entitlement; the /etc/host.equiv file on the user's system is of no importance in this.

If a user tries to access a remote system under a different user name (by adding the –L option on RSH or rlogin), the /etc/hosts.equiv file will not be used. The /etc/hosts.equiv file does not facilitate supervisor access under root to a remote system. This makes sense, because system administrators in a network generally use different system passwords.

The minimum security mechanism provided by entries in the /etc/hosts.equiv file can be extended with a security mechanism on the account level. Security mechanisms on the account level are realized via the rhosts file in the Home directory of the target account. Each line of the rhosts file consists of a computer name and an optional user name. Adding this line means that the user (username) may access this account on computer (hostname). If no user name is stated, only the user with the same name as the owner of the rhosts file may access the remote computer (hostname). The following example shows the rhosts file in the Home directory of user FAX:

Personnel	Aspach Donald Otto
Directors	DDuck Lemmon
ResearchD1	GGlaser AGlaser Juppy WAberle
ResearchD2	MMueller KMueller
ResearchD3	Chaos Disaster WAberle
SupportA	Rainer Ludwig WAberle
Aberle	WAberle
Bold	UBold
Virginia	Grace

The rhosts file permits user WAberle to access the resource Network fax via computers SupportA, ResearchD3, Aberle and ResearchD1. The personnel computer permits users Aspach, Donald and Otto to establish a link. If, during login on a remote computer, access is denied by the security mechanism at computer level, the target computer will check the rhosts file in the Home directory of the relevant account. If the computer name and username of the accessing computer or user are found, access will be granted without any further password queries.

2.8.6.6 Physical protection

Another security mechanism that is easily implemented is the incorporation of an access box in front of each network access. This access box consists of a simple MAC-level bridge that contains all (network specific) addresses of computers entitled to access the system. All unauthorized network addresses will have the appropriate data packet filtered out. In comparison with computer specific security mechanisms, the advantage of this system lies in the fact that all information in a data packet may be used as criteria for filtering, giving a highly effective method of determining access criteria. The disadvantage lies in the high administration load.

2.8.6.7 Encoding

Encoding of some highly sensitive data is an important criterion for network security. Only data already coded before it is transferred onto the network is protected against unauthorized listening or copying. All (!) transfer protocols can be used by a practised hacker to read all information (including all passwords) with a data analyzer without much effort, and to store this data in memory for future processing. Data encoding is currently handled in two ways: net specific encoding and computer specific encoding.

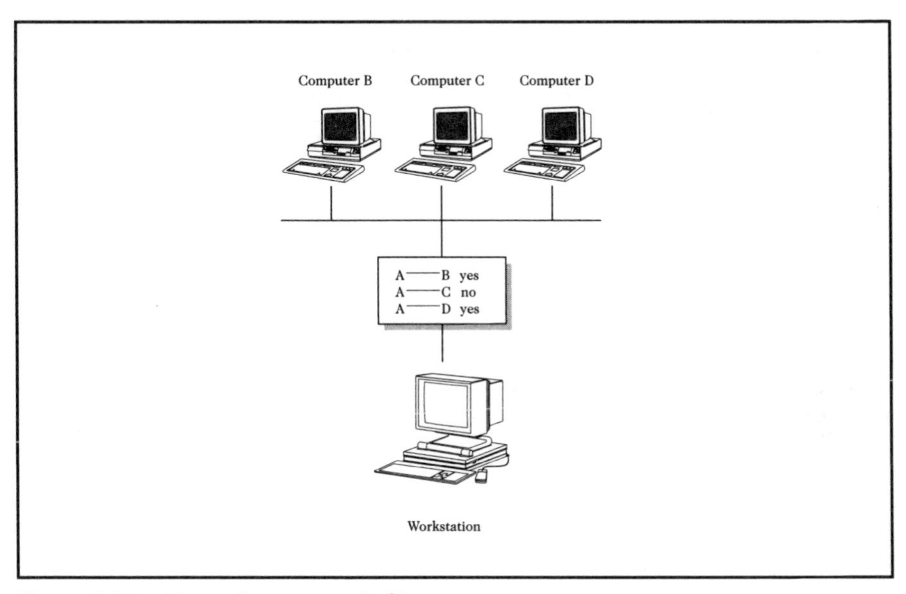

Figure 2.21 Network access with filters

2.8.6.8 Net specific encoding

Net specific encoding means that all data transmitted via the network is encoded by a coding mechanism provided by a chip on the network controller. Computers equipped with a coder chip conduct a dynamic exchange of the codes and apply them to the data in accordance with set rules. The major advantage of this approach lies in the fact that all data transmitted is encoded (including the header information). It is a disadvantage, however, that only computers with an additional integrated coder chip can communicate.

2.8.6.9 Computer specific encoding

In computer specific encoding, all data relating to applications relevant to security is encoded with a special program in the computer. This means that the computer only contains coded information, which may be sent on the net at any time without further coding mechanisms. The network applications only need to exchange decoding mechanisms for the data to be transferred. The advantage of computer specific encoding lies in the fact that coding may be restricted to certain data and applications. It is a disadvantage, however, that not many of the applications on the market today support such an encoding mechanism.

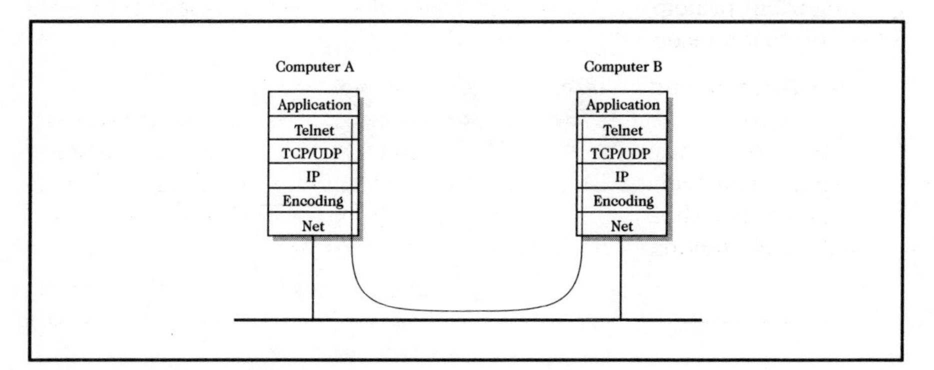

Figure 2.22 Net specific encoding

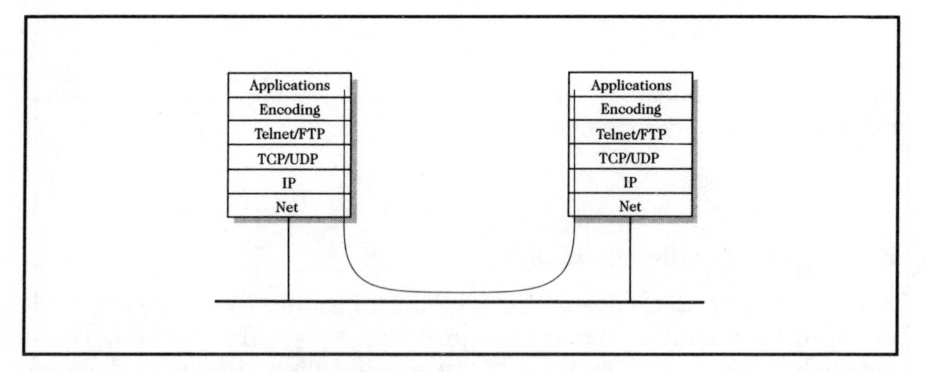

Figure 2.23 Computer specific encoding

Dynamic access key

A further mechanism that contributes to the security of information to be protected relies on the dynamic distribution of access keys. A network contains one or more access key servers. After logging into a local computer, a user attempts to establish a connection with a network resource. The connection request is forwarded to the access key server. This device checks whether the user in question is entitled to access the resource under the account stated. If the result of this check is negative, the request for connection is refused. A positive result will mean that the access key generator will issue a code (1231). The user must multiply this code by, for example, his date of birth (040760), result = 50175560. The access key computer will also carry out the multiplication and relay the result to the actual target computer. The user may now log in at the target computer by using the access key represented by the result within a certain time and work on that computer for this session.

The above access key server model may be refined considerably by the use of complex mathematical algorithms or additional queries. The important principle is the dynamic administration of access entitlement to protect a resource against unauthorized access.

Administration and maintenance of access mechanisms

In a modern data network, net resources to be protected must of course be administered and maintained on a central management system. This requires all net resources to be equipped with mechanisms that permit their integration into a global security system. The following function modules are necessary for this:

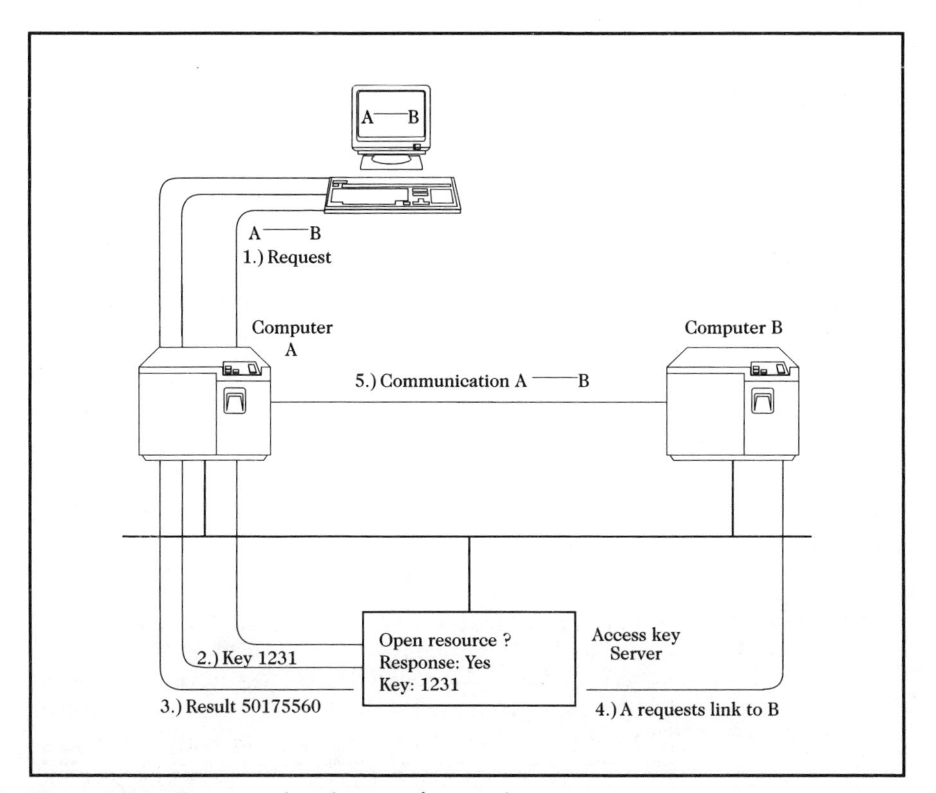

Figure 2.24 Dynamic distribution of access keys

- Parameters for the definition of security structures.
- Secure management protocol.
- Database for the administration and maintenance of security criteria.
- Application for the visual display of all network events.
- Protection mechanisms for the central management system.

Security parameters

Data net security management requires all parameters set in resources relevant to security (objects) to have access mechanisms (filter, key, user ID/password) that are administered by a central resource. This collection of parameters is known as a Management Information Base (MIB). By setting individual parameters specific to the user, access may be granted or barred. Table 2.14 illustrates how such a set of parameters might look for user Brian Frederik, using a fictional security system as an example.

```
User ID: Brian Frederik
Source computer HW Address: 08002001234
Source computer IP address: 192.1.1.23
Password: Chicken&Egg
Dynamic key: 50176660
Entitled to access the following services: Telnet, FTP
Password: Onthefly
Entitled to access the following directories: Reports
                                               Service
                                               Online
Password: Flora
Entitled to access the following files in the Reports directory:
                                               Planning.txt
                                               Editorial.txt
                                               Bookreviews.txt
                                               Muesli.txt
                                               News.txt
                                               Bridges.txt
Password: Ottocar
Entitled to access the following files in the Services
directory:
                 ..................
                 ..................
                 ..................
Password: Huber
Entitled to access the following files in the Online directory:
                 ..................
                 ..................
                 ..................
Password: LANnal
```

Table 2.14

An additional function is the collection of statistics for the individual parameters, for example the number of logins that succeeded/failed, changes of password, changes in access entitlements, and so on. Only by gathering this incidental information can security in the total system be maintained in the long term. In addition, fault management must report each failed login to the operator console immediately in order to prevent any unauthorized access straight away.

Secure management protocol

A further characteristic of a LAN security concept is the importance of the management protocol. This protocol transfers the individual parameters (password, filter, user ID, and so on) between network management and the computer (terminal). Encoding mechanisms must be used to prevent unauthorized reading of data on the network.

Database

Security parameters can soon mushroom into an avalanche on the network and resist any efforts at maintenance and administration the network administrator may make. For this reason, security parameters must be administered in a database. In order to maintain security, it is advisable to establish a separate database that contains only security data.

Application

An important component of all network management systems is the graphical user interface which permits easy handling of the data and information to be administered. This application should be mask based to facilitate easy entry of users, access entitlements and passwords. In addition, alarms (login errors) should be shown automatically. Alarm messages should contain a range of additional information (time, user ID, cause of alarm, and so on). This information is essential to trace any hackers in the network.

Protection mechanisms

One point frequently overlooked in security management systems is the protection of the management system itself. The computer running the management system must be protected against unauthorized access, for example with lockable keyboards and disk drives. Only this protection ensures that data and resources in a net can be administered and protected safely.

2.8.7 The future

Many of the functions described in this chapter are already implemented on various devices and systems today. Standardization of certain cornerstones, for example accounting and security management, is now a top priority with the relevant bodies. More and more companies and new product areas discover network management and base their long-term strategies on it. The philosophy of global network management is now undisputed in the world of computer networks, but it will be some time before all functions are available in all products.

2.9 Executing the management functions

All data required by the management application for the administration of each managed object in the net is exchanged on a firmly defined path between the management station and the agent module. The way in which this data and the commands, information and functions contained in it are transferred on the physical link permits a more detailed distinction of the communication paths. In general, these communication paths are associated with the somewhat confusing terms 'in-band management' and 'out-of-band management'.

2.9.1 In-band management

In-band management describes the communication between network management and terminal via direct access (net interface) on the respective data net. With this in-band data path, all SNMP agents can be accessed and configured (setting threshold values, switching connected links and ports) directly. SNMP agents send trap (alarm) and other messages directly to the management station on this data path. In general, SNMP data is packaged as UDP/IP frames for in-band communication and sent directly on the respective medium (Ethernet, Token Ring, FDDI). Many devices have the option to switch off any available ports to the data nets connected with an SNMP command.

This function, although very useful for fault tracing, carries with it the danger of switching off a desired management function. If the network manager accidentally switches off the port (the interface) currently used for communication, he or she can no longer contact this device. Some manufacturers recommend configuration of the main communication paths in such a manner that they cannot be switched off in error. The practical implication of this may be that this port (interface) can no longer be managed, because the manufacturer has not provided for a selective block on commands.

In order to exclude errors, procedures to ensure that the system manager can always read or modify the data are necessary. Especially with such a difficult matter as data modification, a secure communication link between management station and agent must be maintained. For this reason, a further communication strand, the out-of-band management, is usually laid in parallel with the in-band management.

2.9.2 Out-of-band management

An out-of-band management method is present when the managed device can be contacted by the network management station via a V.24 port directly on a serial data link or with a connected multi-line modem. The out-of-band management path offers the same functions as the in-band management, albeit, due to the capacity of the available links, at much lower data speeds.

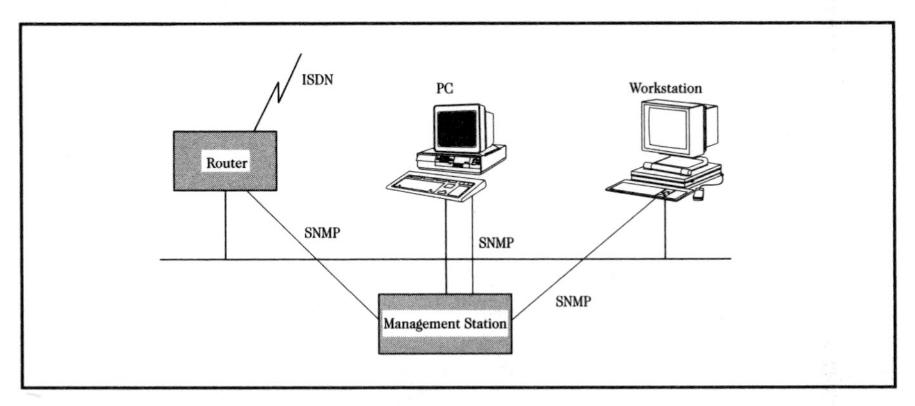

Figure 2.25 In-band communication

Out-of-band cabling should always be included in the planning of a managed data network as retrospective installation of lines costs both time and money. Special communication protocols are used in out-of-band communication, the most common being the Serial Line Interface Protocol (SLIP) and the more modern Point-to-Point Protocol (PPP).

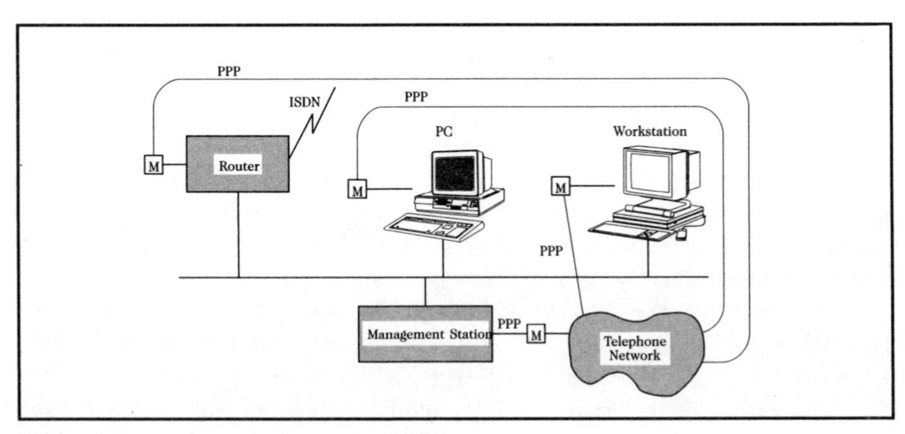

Figure 2.26 Out-of-band communication

2.9.3 The SLIP protocol

Data nets were created in response to the requirement to link various resources (computers) from different manufacturers. Data nets may thus be based on a variety of media and access mechanisms. As a rule, these data nets are clearly defined by international standards, for example X.25, FDDI, token ring and Ethernet, which are available as RFC publications.

The bodies concerned with standardizing TCP/IP protocols have, since the TCP definition was produced, operated from the premise that the network layer (Layer 3) must provide its services while remaining wholly independent of the lower physical layers. The best known representative of Layer 3 protocols is the Internet Protocol (IP). Data blocks transferred by the IP protocol on the network layer are known as datagrams. IP transfers these datagrams via a connection-free communication mechanism between the communicating partners.

The Internetwork Protocol offers some additional functions during data transfer, for example an addressing mechanism, fragmentation and reassembly of data packets and the transfer of data packets between separate networks (routing). For this, IP adapts the higher layers to the net specific protocols and conditions. This Layer 2 service is known as the Network Service.

A simple and cost-effective alternative method of linking two IP networks is a simple point-to-point connection. This only requires an asynchronous RS-232 interface for the physical connection. Data is transported on this link using a pseudoprotocol, the Serial Line Interface Protocol (SLIP). SLIP originated in 3Com's UNET TCP/IP implementation which was first published in early 1980. It found a wider market when it was implemented in 4.2 Berkeley UNIX (Rick Adams' version) in 1984. Today, we meet SLIP in almost any device, for example routers, terminal servers, cable concentrators (hubs) and almost all UNIX implementations. The SLIP protocol was published in mid-1988 as 'RFC 1055 A non-standard for Transmission of IP datagrams over several lines'.

SLIP permits data transfer between two computers via a serial link. This serial link may be implemented as a single line or multi-line. For multi-line, an alternate line modem is required ahead of the actual IP link – change to the serial IP protocol takes place only after a connection has been established. The SLIP mechanism is based on the fact that IP datagrams are enclosed between certain characters and transferred via the link. The characters marking the beginning and end of a SLIP packet are known as framing characters. Two framing characters are defined as the END and ESC symbols. The END symbol is represented by the decimal value 192 (hexadecimal C0), the ESC symbol by the decimal value 219 (hexadecimal DB). Each SLIP packet starts with the ESC symbol, followed by the IP data. Each SLIP packet is terminated with the END symbol.

If the values of the ESC and END symbols occur in the actual IP data, they are replaced by special symbols. The value corresponding to the END symbol is shown as END DD – decimal value 192 221 (hexadecimal C0 DD), ESC appears as ESC DC – decimal value 219 220 (hexadecimal DB DC). These symbols are converted back into their original values by the receiver.

Symbol	Decimal value	Hexadecimal value
End	192	C0
ESC	219	DB
END DD	192 221	C0 DD
ESC DC	219 220	DB DC

Table 2.15 SLIP characters

As no real standard has been published for the SLIP protocol, maximum SLIP packet lengths may vary between manufacturers. A general guideline for this value is the maximum packet length of 1006 bytes as defined in the Berkeley UNIX SLIP driver. These 1006 bytes refer to all higher protocol headers included in the packet, but do not include the SLIP framing characters.

SLIP is a very simple transfer mechanism and does not support the following mechanisms:

Addressing

Because SLIP does not support any address mechanisms, no address information can be combined with the serial link.

Type field

Because SLIP is not equipped with any function similar to the TYPE field in Ethernet (EtherType in the IEEE/SNAP format), only one set protocol can be transferred on this link.

Fault recognition and rectification

SLIP permits the transfer of data via serial links (modem links) between two computers. As a rule, these modem links offer only low transmission speeds (1200 bit/s–9.6 kbit/s), and the telephone lines used are frequently susceptible to faults (overtalking, noise). SLIP does not carry out any fault recognition or rectification services. It leaves these tasks to the lower protocols. Each IP, TCP or UDP datagram has a checksum calculation field in its header. By analyzing the checksum field, a higher protocol can trace faults on the transfer link and, if necessary, request that a defective data packet be resent.

2.9.4 The Point-to-Point Protocol

Applications and protocols must be capable of flexible use on LANs. In modern communication architecture, this means that a wide range of different media and access mechanisms must be supported. These access mechanisms are defined by international bodies, for example CCITT (X.25), ANSI (FDDI), IEEE 802.x (Token Ring, token bus and Ethernet). These standards are published worldwide and available to anyone interested in them. Some manufacturer specific solutions still exist, most widely represented by the ARCNET and Hyperchannel networks. In order to transmit the LAN protocol via alternate WAN connections, the transfer protocol must be defined in the lower layers. SLIP, the Serial Line Interface Protocol, now a decade old, operates in WAN line data transfer between TCP/IP computers. Because no common standards are available for other protocols (DECnet, AppleTalk, IPX and so on), this information must be transferred through individual mechanisms on Layer 2. One solution to this dilemma appears to be the availability of the Point-to-Point Protocol (PPP).

Layer 3 (the network layer) of the ISO reference model is completely independent of the lower physical layers. For this reason, lower protocols such as Ethernet, Token Ring, FDDI, and so on are at least in theory, interchangeable. These functions have been implemented in theory for a long time, but the idea could not be realized as long as no reasonable Modem/Point-to-Point protocol was available. Earlier solutions, such as SLIP in the IP area, were too imperfect to be accepted as a general standard. Today, the PPP protocol is widely used and tipped by experts to replace all other solutions in the near future. In both its structure and the protocol mechanisms it supports, the specification of PPP is far more elaborate than that of SLIP. The Point-to-Point Protocol specification has been defined by the Internet Engineering Taskforce (IETF) in RFC 1331 (The Point-to-Point Protocol (PPP) for the Transmission of Multiprotocol datagrams over Point-to-Point links), RFC 1332 (The PPP Internet Protocol Control Protocol) and RFC 1333 (PPP Link Quality Monitoring). Because PPP was developed to suit the multiprotocol character of the Internet community rather than specifically for the IP world, it has found an additional use in the definition of the integration of further protocols (RFC 1376 – The PPP DECnet Phase IV Control Protocol, RFC 1377 – PPP OSI Network Layer Control Protocol, RFC 1378 – PPP AppleTalk Control Protocol). The end user can find the PPP protocol as public domain software for SUN workstations, or as a manufacturer specific implementation for certain LAN devices (routers, hubs, bridges, terminal servers, and so on).

The PPP protocol permits the transfer of data via synchronous (bit serial) or synchronous (start–stop operation) single line WAN link. PPP operates independently of the respective physical interface. Its only requirement is a totally transparent data link with full duplex capacity. The data format established for PPP is 8 Bit, No Parity. In addition, a flow control mechanism is supported on the link. The PPP protocol consists of three main components:

- Data encapsulation.
- Link Control Protocol (LCP)
- A family of Network Control Protocols (NCPs).

Data encapsulation

The familiar HDLC (High-Level Data Link) protocol is the basis specified for the PPP protocol transfer of data packets on Layer 2. The HDLC protocol has been standardized worldwide since the mid-1970s and was published in the ISO standards ISO 3309–1979 and ISO 3309:1984/PDAD1.

2.9.4.1 The PPP data format

For the Point-to-Point Protocol, the data format, significance and values of the individual fields are specified exactly. Figure 2.27 shows the data format structure.

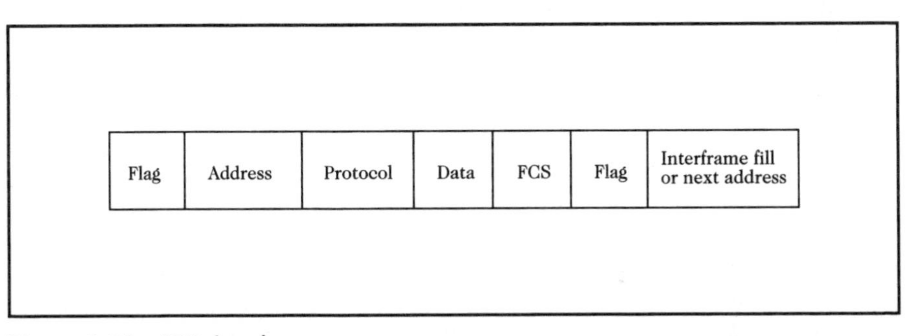

Figure 2.27 PPP data format

Flag sequence

Each PPP data packet opens with an 8-bit value, the flag sequence. This flag sequence is always given the binary value 01111110 (hexadecimal 0x7e).

Address field

The address field always defines the all station address and is set to the binary value 11111111 (hexadecimal 0xff). In its current versions, PPP does not support an addressing mechanism to address individual stations.

Control field

The control field always defines the Unnumbered Information (U) command, for which the P/F bit is set to 0. The binary sequence for the control field is 00000011 (hexadecimal 0x03). Data packets with different values are invalid and will be rejected.

Protocol field

The protocol field has a length of two octets and defines the way in which the following data is to be treated. Protocol field values are published in the RFC Assigned Numbers. Table 2.16 shows the set groups.

0– to 3–	Set Network Layer Protocols
8– to b–	Network Control Protocols (NCPs)
4– to 7–	Freely available for data traffic with low transfer volume
c– to f–	Link Control Protocols (LCPs)

Table 2.16

The values currently defined for these fields are shown in Table 2.17.

Value (in hexadecimal)	Protocol
0001 to 001f	Reserved
0021	Internet Protocol
0023	OSI Network Layer
0025	Xerox NS IDP
0027	DECnet Phase IV
0029	AppleTalk
002b	Novell IPX
002d	Van Jacobsen Compressed TCP/IP
002f	Van Jacobsen Uncompressed TCP/IP
0031	Bridging PDU
0033	Stream Protocol
0035	Banyan Vines
0037	Reserved
00ff	Reserved
0201	802.1d Hello Packets
0231	Luxcom
0233	Sigma Network Systems
8021	Internet Protocol Control Protocol
8023	OSI Network Layer Control Protocol
8025	Xerox NS IDP Control Protocol
8027	DECnet Phase IV Control Protocol
8029	AppleTalk Control Protocol
802b	Novell IPX Control Protocol
802d	Reserved
802f	Reserved
8031	Bridging NCP
8033	Stream Protocol Control Protocol
8035	Banyan Vines Control Protocol
c021	Link Control Protocol
c023	Password Authentication Protocol
c025	Link Quality Report
c223	Challenge Handshake Authentication Protocol

Table 2.17

Companies may reserve their own protocol field for the development of individual PPP sub-protocols by contacting the Internet Assigned Numbers Authority (IANA) at the following e-mail address:

```
IANA@isi.edu.
```

Information field
The information field contains protocol specific information (header and data) for the Network Layer Protocol defined in the protocol field. The information field default length can range from 0 to a maximum of 1500 bytes (default value). Communicating partners are always free to negotiate a larger value as the Maximum Frame Size.

Frame Check Sequence field
The Frame Check Sequence (FCS) field is 16 bits long and permits fault checks on transferred data frames.

2.9.4.2 Link Control Protocol

The Link Control Protocol is responsible for establishing, configuring, testing and quitting a PPP data link. Before the datagrams themselves are transferred via a PPP link, each participating PPP interface sends a number of LCP packets onto the link. The LCP goes through five phases:

Phase 1: Link Dead
At this phase, there is no connection to the modem, or the link was interrupted. Each PPP connection begins and ends with this phase.

Phase 2: Link Establishment
Before higher-layer data (for example, IP) transferred via the link, it is prepared through the exchange of configuration packets.

Phase 3: Authentication
Optional mode, during which both PPP peers are identified with an authentication protocol.

Phase 4: Network Layer Protocol Configuration
Configuration of the Network Layer Protocol used for the link by the respective Network Control Protocol (NCP). Several Network Control Protocols may be used in parallel on one link.

Phase 5: Link Termination
The LCP protocol may terminate the link at any time. Termination is caused by a user-initiated event, an expired timer or a missing hardware interface signal.

Link Quality Testing

An optional step between phases 3 and 4 is a Link Quality Test (in accordance with RFC 1333) to investigate the transmission quality offered by the data link. This may provide the basis for a decision on whether the quality meets the requirements of the higher-layer protocol (usually the Network Layer Protocol).

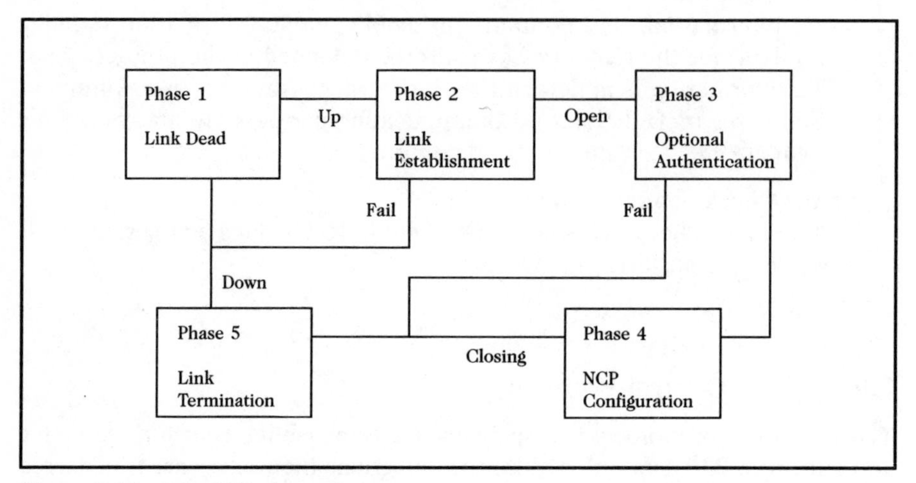

Figure 2.28 The PPP phase diagram

2.9.4.3 The LCP data format

Link Control Protocol information is sent as PPP datagrams. If the protocol field has the value c021 (hexadecimal), this signals that LCP information is present in the data field. Only one LCP information can be sent per datagram. There are three defined packet types:

- **Link Configure packets**

  These packets are used to establish and configure a link (Configure Request, Configure Ack, Configure NAK and Configure Reject).

- **Link Termination packets**

  Link Termination packets signal controlled termination of a link between two PPP peers (Termination Request, Termination Ack).

- **Link Maintenance packets**

  To ensure that a link is established properly, Link Maintenance packets are sent between PPP peers (Code Reject, Protocol Reject, Echo Request, Echo Reply and Discard Request).

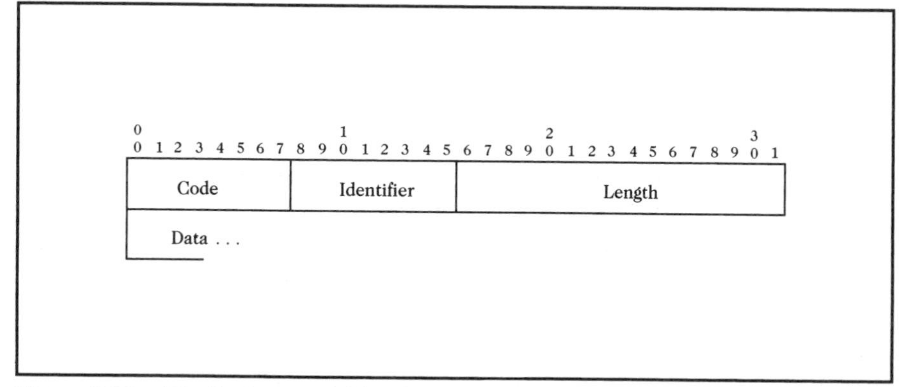

Figure 2.29 The Link Protocol header

Code

The code field is one byte long and defines the type of LCP information. The following values are currently defined:

1	Configure–Request
2	Configure–Ack
3	Configure–Nak
4	Configure–Reject
5	Terminate–Request
6	Terminate–Ack
7	Code–Reject
8	Protocol–Reject
9	Echo–Request
10	Echo–Reply
11	Discard–Request
12	Reserved

Identifier
The identifier field is one byte long and permits requests and replies to be matched.

Length
The length field, two bytes long, sets the total LCP packet length, including the code, identifier, length and data fields.

Data
The data field contains the actual LCP information and always ends with a code field.

2.9.4.4 LCP Configuration Options

The Link Control Protocol permits dynamic negotiations about configurations between PPP peers. The data format shown in Figure 2.30 has been defined for configuration options negotiations.

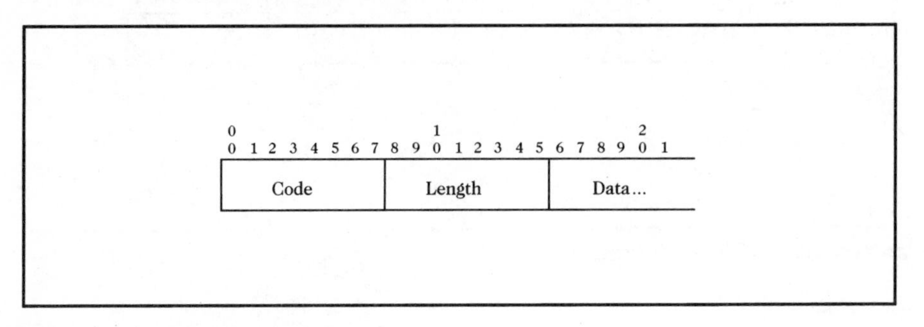

Figure 2.30 LCP data format

Code
The code field, one byte long, defines the type of LCP configuration. The following values are currently defined:

1	Maximum–Receive–Unit
2	Async–Control–Character–Map
3	Authentication–Protocol
4	Quality–Protocol
5	Magic–Number
6	RESERVED
7	Protocol Field Compression
8	Address and Control Field Compression

Length
The length field, one byte long, sets the total length of the LCP configuration packet, including the code, length and data fields.

Data
The data field contains the expanded LCP configuration information.

2.9.4.5 Network Control Protocols

A family of Network Control Protocols (NCP) permits the preparation and configuration of various protocols on the network layers. PPP is designed to support the simultaneous use of different network protocols.

Network Control Protocol for IP

The Internet Protocol Control Protocol (IPCP) enables activation, deactivation and configuration of IP protocol modules on both sides of a point-to-point link. As with the Link Control Protocol, these functions are achieved through the exchange of special data packets. The exchange of IPCP packets takes place after the conclusion of phase 4 (NCP configuration) of the LCP protocol.

The IPCP Data Format

IP Control Protocol information is sent as PPP datagrams. The protocol field with the value 8021 (hexadecimal) signals that IP Control Protocol information is contained in the data field. Only one IPCP information can be sent per datagram. Figure 2.31 shows the IP Control Protocol header.

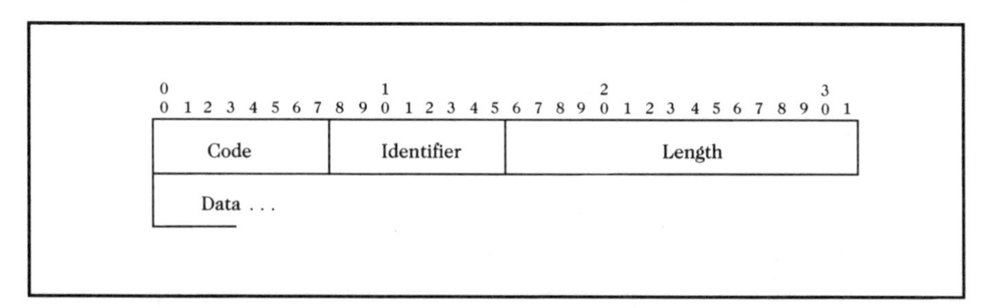

Figure 2.31 IP Control Protocol header

The code field, one byte long, defines the type of IPCP information. The following values have been defined:

1	Configure–Request
2	Configure–Ack
3	Configure–Nak
4	Configure–Reject
5	Terminate–Request
6	Terminate–Ack
7	Code–Reject

Identifier

The identifier field, one byte long, permits requests and responses to be matched.

Data

The data field contains the actual ICPC information. It always closes with a code field.

Prior to the transfer of IP datagrams, the IPCP protocol can exchange configuration options with the IP communication partner. The following IPCP options have been defined:

1	IP Addresses
2	IP Compression Protocol
3	IP Address

IP Addresses
An option supported for early PPP versions, of no relevance with later versions.

IP Compression Protocol

Permits the exchange of data between IP peers in a compressed format. The only compression mechanism integrated so far is the Van Jacobsen mechanism (value 002d).

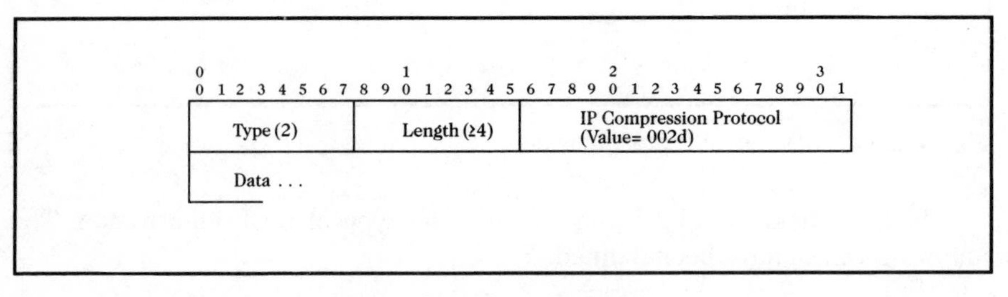

Figure 2.32 IPCP header with compression option

IP Address
Permits the dynamic use of IP addresses between two communicating partners.

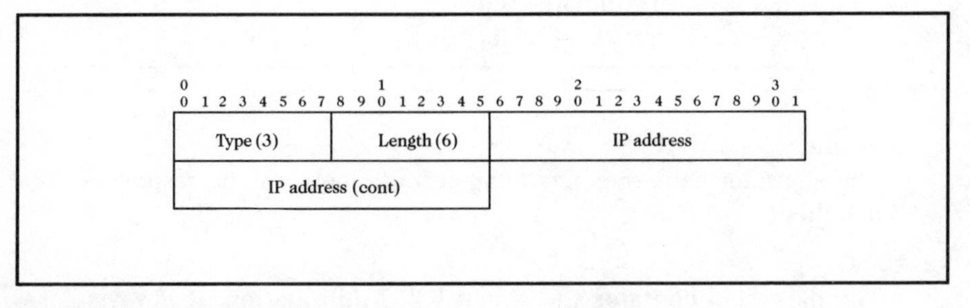

Figure 2.33 IP Address format

2.9.4.6 Marketing potential

Many companies already offer commercial products on the basis of the PPP protocol. RFC standardization will have a significant impact on the importance of this comparatively new protocol. Manufacturers who habitually include the SLIP protocol in their products will need to rethink their policy very quickly. PPP will finally put an end to the squabbles over the 'right' data Link Layer Protocol for Point-to-Point and Multipoint.

3

Introduction to SNMP Management

The SNMP protocol serves as a mechanism to provide and transport management information between network components. It permits interactive network administration via parameter checks, or supervision of certain network conditions. In general, the SNMP protocol makes it possible to manage all SNMP devices in the network. Based on the SNMP protocol, all data required for management applications (status, performance, faults, alarms, reports, and so on) is transferred between managed devices. The acronym 'SNMP' leaves wide scope for the interpretation of its actual meaning and function. The term 'simple' is the source of most misunderstandings. SNMP is simple neither in its specification nor in its aims. It was not designed to be 'simple'. But concepts integrated in the SNMP protocol are of a simplicity ranging from the beautiful to the trivial. This made SNMP version 1 deceptively easy to implement. Many manufacturers of communication products embarked on the development of their own SNMP version 1 implementation to cash in on this apparent simplicity and triviality. Frequently however, they underestimated the work required to turn the simple specification into a marketable product, an expensive error of judgement. Following the failure of planned implementations, they usually fell back on various SNMP source codes available in the Public Domain or the open market. SNMP version 2 is far more complex than the old version 1. Calling version 2 'simple' is a mere nod towards its historical origins. Strictly speaking, SNMP should now stand for 'Standard Network Management Protocol' to express suitably both its significance and its complexity.

In the current form of SNMP management, a Network Management system consists of five components:

- Hardware platform.
- SNMP protocol stack.
- Transport layer protocol.
- Network management applications.
- Physical link.

Hardware platform

This is where the actual SNMP 'Client' software runs. This enables the network administrator to survey the network and provides the information basis for his or her decisions. Network management stations can be based on a multitude of hardware platforms, for example a PC with Windows or a workstation with a multitasking operating system such as OS/2, VAX/VMS or UNIX.

SNMP protocol stack

The SNMP protocol stack, along with the collection of managed parameters and variables (for example, counters, timers, text strings, physical and logical addresses, object identifiers, and so on) permit administration and targeted management of network resources. This information is made available to the transport layer protocol.

Transport layer protocol

It is the task of the transport layer protocol to transport the information provided by the SNMP protocol across the net. Among the transport protocols used in the SNMP world are: UDP/IP, TCP/IP, Novell IPX, XNS and DECnet.

Network management applications

Network management applications run on the network management station and convert the information provided by the transport layer protocol into management functions. The best known examples of management applications, among others are SunNet Manager from Sun Microsystems, HP Open View from Hewlett Packard, NMC from Network Managers, IBM's NetView/6000, Multinet's Lance+, Overlord System from NetLabs, Multiman from the RAD Group, and SNMPC from Castle Rock.

Physical link

A secure physical link to the managed components is an essential precondition for a functional network management system. The physical connection is either effected via the network (Ethernet, Token Ring, FDDI) or it is established indirectly via a modem link.

Background

The concept of the SNMP standard is derived from the Management Framework specified by the International Standards Organization (ISO). Included in the OSI specification are defined tools that enable a user to access all information about the complete net and to exercise targeted control over individual components. From its early versions in 1989, SNMP has followed the OSI guidelines. It rapidly became established in the LAN Market. OSI opponents have spread the heresy that SNMP was the only actually available management protocol for heterogeneous systems. In the Internet community, SNMP had a predecessor in SGMP, the Simple Gateway Monitoring Protocol. The SGMP protocol was victorious in the race towards standardizing network management. Other runners were HEMS, the High-Level Entity Management System, and the OSI-based CMOT protocol (Common Management Information Protocol over Transmission Control Protocol). Many debates and Internet tests later, the HEMS group decided to abandon their approach, thus withdrawing from the field. Although the SGMP protocol was intended only for IP environments, it was soon deployed in many other areas and products. This process was no doubt aided by the integration of certain OSI characteristics in the protocol (for example, the Management Information Base and the Structure of Management Information). Although the OSI management specification never gained complete dominance, technical and political reasons led to the integration of the SGMP concept into the OSI management parameters. SGMP's developers intended to provide for a later migration towards OSI.

In the end, the Ad-hoc Network Management Review Group under the IETF, influenced by politics and time scales, decided to continue experiments with both approaches. The next months saw the introduction of new and expanded protocol specifications. With their SNMP standard, the SGMP group presented the IETF with a far more comprehensive and easy to implement solution than their CMOT competitors. Because of these advantages, SNMP was promoted to *defacto* standard, and all further experiments by the CMOT group ceased. In May 1988, the SNMP protocol was finally defined and duly published as an Internet Proposed Standard (August 1988). In April 1989, it received Draft Standard status. In the end, it took until May 1990 before the IAB finally accepted it as an Internet Standard. The specification was first published as RFC 1067. Some specification changes necessitated renewed publication (RFC 1098). The definitive standard was finally published in May 1990 under the title *Simple Network Management Protocol (SNMP)* (J.D. Case, M. Fedor, M.L. Schoffstall and C. Davin (RFC1157)).

The first MIB was defined in May 1988 and published in August 1988. In May 1990, this specification became the Internet Standard MIB I. It contained 100 objects. Development continued, and in 1991, MIB I's successor was published in RFC 1213. The new MIB II contained approximately 180 objects. MIB I was completely integrated into MIB II. With the standardization of MIB II, massive progress was made in the Internet world, especially with the development of SNMP. In order to avoid the need for frequent publications of new MIB standards, the Internet community decided to use newly published MIB sub-specifications as MIB II appendices. These MIBs are now available for a multitude of media and technologies. They are expanded almost on a weekly basis. Specific documentation regarding individual MIBs and their current status is available on Internet Electronic Mail and can be accessed free of charge on any of the many Internet Mail Servers.

The Structure of Management Information (SMI) underwent a similar development. It was agreed in May 1988 and published in August 1988. Again, it took until May 1990 before Recommended Internet Standard status was achieved.

When development of the SNMP protocol commenced in 1987, none of the people and companies involved could have foreseen the stormy events to follow. At that time, only a few organizations and companies took any interest in the SNMP protocol. As early as 1988, the first commercial implementation of the SNMP protocol was implemented. It was envisaged that the SNMP development would shortly be superseded by a migration towards the OSI standard. When the exact opposite occurred, it caused some astonishment. Due to the simplicity and fast availability of a generally accepted standard, the communication market decided in favour of the SNMP protocol. Today, more than 600 manufacturers and organizations support the protocol, and the number of installations implemented worldwide is beyond count. The critical mass required to establish a standard was reached by the SNMP protocol some time ago. OSI network management solutions form a minority today, and it seems unlikely that they will ever catch up with the SNMP protocol. The clear head start SNMP has on its competitors has led to implementation of SNMP technology in all communication industry markets. SNMP also builds bridges towards technologies that have little or nothing to do with the classical concept of the communication industry, leading to the implementation of security systems, measuring stations, alarm systems, printers, plotters, even electric railways (as introduced by the American company TGV), simple toasters (as introduced by Epilogue Technology) and fully automated toilets (as introduced by SNMP Research). The resulting publications of a Railway MIB and a Toaster MIB indicate that some implementations should not be taken too seriously.

Although SNMP is supported by almost all manufacturers, leading to wide distribution, some resistance and prejudice is encountered in security, preventing use of the protocol in certain areas (for example, WAN). The protocol mechanisms defined in the original SNMP specification and the security issues were the major impetus towards changing the SNMP. A short-term SNMP security variation, the Secure SNMP Proposal, was published as an RFC. This paper defined an independent authentication and coding mechanism. The Secure SNMP Proposal was heavily criticized for its lack of compatibility with the existing SNMP version 1. All installed SNMP products would have had to be replaced or upgraded. SNMP version 2 provides the foundations for all requirements made on a modern management protocol. The MD5 algorithm for authentication and a coding mechanism are integrated in SNMPv2. The MD5 authentication mechanism contained in the SNMPv2 protocol was a joint development by Ronald L. Rivest (MIT Labs for Computer Science, Cambridge MA, USA) and RSA Data Security Limited. The specification of this algorithm and the complete source code were published as *The MD5 Message-Digest Algorithm* (RFC 1321) in April 1992. The MD5 algorithm takes a type of checksum and a time stamp to form an individual 16-byte fingerprint for each SNMPv2 packet. This fingerprint permits the receiver to check the origin and transfer quality of any messages received. The MD5 algorithm is a Public Domain product, but is subject to the import and export restrictions of certain European countries. The import of the source code to Great Britain, for example, was until recently governed by an agreement between the governments of Britain and the USA and thus required a separate licence. This has some implications for the SNMPv2 code, because MD5 is part of the SNMPv2 specification. As with so many politically motivated decisions, the reasoning behind this import and export restriction is impossible to follow. Anyone with access to the Internet can download and decode the MD5 algorithm without any problems or customs paperwork.

SNMP also provides for data coding. This prevents unauthorized network participants from understanding a transferred message. As a further security aspect, a time stamp for the life span of an SNMP message was integrated to prevent the repetition of a valid message at a later time. The intended encoding mechanism is the National Institute of Standards' DES (Date Encryption Standard). Any software containing DES is subject to US government export restrictions, even though the algorithms are available as Public Domain software. Users of licences outside the USA need to make do without this addition to their SNMPv2.

When the SNMP protocol came into being in 1988, it was designed solely as a management protocol for Ethernet-based products. During SNMP's evolution, other LAN media such as Token Ring, Fiber Distributed Data Interface, AppleTalk and SNA came to be supported. In addition, expansions to support Wide Area Networks (WAN) technologies were created, e.g. T1/E1, X.25, ISDN, Frame Relay, ATM and SMDS. Far from being an insider protocol, SNMP has become the accepted market standard and is used in many areas of the communication industry.

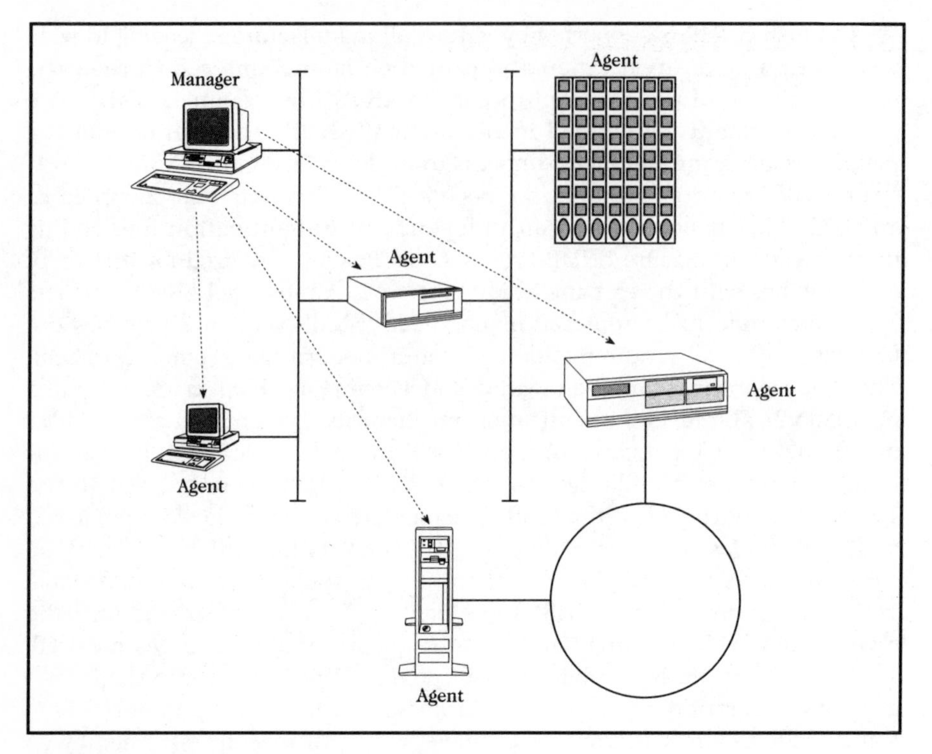

Figure 3.1 Manager – Agent relations

How to access SNMP information

All MIBs and SNMP protocol specifications are available via the Internet on individual Internet Servers as RFCs (Requests for Comment). The Internet Architecture Board (IAB) serves as the highest authority for matters concerning the standardization of the TCP/IP standards. Every three months, an RFC with the title *IAB Official Protocol Standard* is published. It details the status of current standardization processes and lists all valid standards. Readers without E-mail access to the Internet can obtain hard copies of the RFCs from the following address (for a small administration charge):

Government Systems, Inc. Attn:
Network Information Center
14200 Park Meadow Drive
Suite 200 Chantilly, VA 22-21
Tel.: +1-800-365-3642
+1-703-802-4535
Fax: +1-703-802-8376
Network address: 192.112.36.5 (NIC.DDN.MIL)
Root Domain Server: 192.112.36.4 (NS.NIC.DDN.MIL)

3.1 The Structure of Management Information

The last decade has seen the evolution of computer networks from unknown, hardly developed niche products to essential systems. Users demand ever higher reliability from the communication medium. This level of demand results in increasingly complex networks. The rise in complexity is reflected in the transparent integration of many different network services and networks. Experts assume that the trend towards increasingly complex networks will snowball. Network administrators face problems, not only the constant progress of complex network services, but also the trend towards ever more different hardware and software within a small environment.

Network administration and network management in the original sense were underdeveloped for many years. Manufacturers of hardware and software spared no effort to prove that their administration tool was the best for their products. Integration of components produced by competitors or any reference to the condition of OSI network management was scrupulously avoided. Some manufacturers were led into rash promises about a golden future when OSI and all its protocols would be available, leading them to abandon their current strategy towards supporting a generally valid network management. This ignorant attitude meant that some areas of network development were quite simply missed, although it was obvious after the early 1980s that the administration of complex networks in the near future would no longer be possible without adequate tools.

Development of an open standard for network management started roughly simultaneously for both OSI and TCP/IP. A first, very early and consequently incomplete example of practical network management was the Simple Gateway Monitoring Protocol (SGMP), published in November 1987 as a Standard (RFC 1028). The results of the OSI developments – or rather definitions – were defined in the OSI network management framework and the CMIP protocol.

Certain fundamental factors are necessary to establish a standard that is not dependent on any manufacturer(s). Standards must be made available to all users (manufacturers) as cheaply as possible. At the same time, specifications of a standard must be checked in practice before they are set. Resulting experimental implementations should be made available to all interested persons and companies (Public Domain software) in order to ensure speedy implementation of these standards in current products.

In early 1988, the Internet Architecture Board (IAB), acting as coordinating committee for the planning, structure and administration of the complete Internet, passed a two-tier network management strategy:

1. As a solution for the short to medium term, the Simple Gateway Monitoring Protocol was to be improved and developed according to OSI guidelines.
2. The long-term solution was full integration of all OSI solutions and protocols.

The SGMP protocol was reworked fundamentally and published in May 1990 as RFC 1157, *Simple Network Management Protocol (SNMP)*. This pragmatic network management protocol soon became the *de facto* standard for TCP/IP network management.

As the name implies, the SNMP protocol designers aimed to keep the protocol simple. SNMP architecture is based on a model comprising one or more network management stations and several network elements. It is the task of network management stations to supervise and control the network elements. All devices connected to the net with one or more network management agents implemented are known as network elements. The agent acts as an intelligent front-end processor for all network management functions. This means that certain network management tasks are passed to the agent and processed on site in the network elements. Communication between the agents and the network management station is governed by the SNMP protocol.

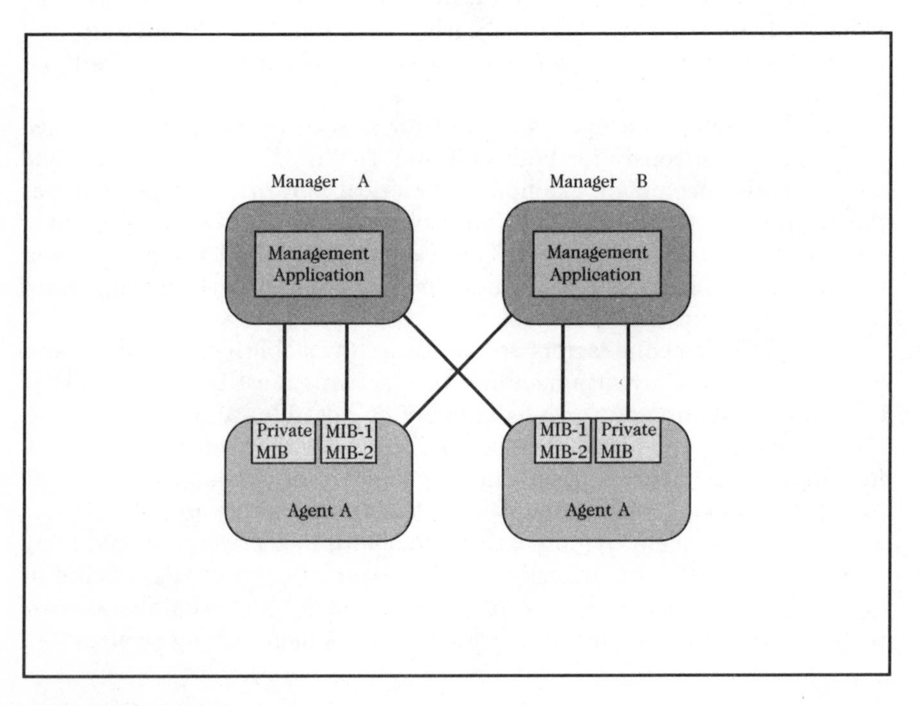

Figure 3.2 SNMP architecture

In order to keep agent complexity to a minimum, the following considerations were allowed for in the SNMP specification:

Cost
It must be possible to keep development costs low for management agent software.

Openness
Network management options and functions within one agent are not limited.

Functionality
Its open design permits the implementation of SNMP in a multitude of devices. The resulting spread of SNMP devices ensures maximum penetration of all worlds.

Availability
Thanks to its simple functions and specification structure, SNMP can be implemented quickly and at low cost.

Independence
Definitions are so general in nature that the SNMP concept can be implemented independently of hardware and software conditions in the individual device, thus making it a realistic general basis for network management in heterogeneous environments.

The SNMP architecture establishes the following parameters:

- The extent of management information transferred via the protocol.
- The way data transferred via the SNMP protocol is displayed.
- The management operations the SNMP protocol can execute.
- The way data is exchanged between management entities.
- The establishment of relations between all administrative entities.

3.1.1 Management information

All management information transferred via the SNMP protocol is shown as non-aggregate object types. These object types are gathered in one or more Management Information Bases (MIBs) and defined by the Structure and Identification of Management Information (SMI). The SMI for the Simple Network Management Protocol (Version 1) was defined in May 1990 in the Request for Comment (RFC) entitled *Structure and Identification of Management Information for TCP/IP based Internets*. This RFC stated that all Management Information Base data and information must be coded according to ISO Standard 8824, *Specification of Abstract Syntax Notation One (ASN.1)*. Showing all information and objects according to ASN.1 was intended to facilitate a later migration towards an OSI-based network management protocol without the need for a renewed definition of all objects and MIBs to date.

Objects, names and syntax

The SMI defines the following components for each object type:

- name.
- syntax.
- coding instruction.

Object name

The name of an object type clearly represents an object and is also known as the 'object identifier'. The identifier 0 must never be allocated to an object type as part of the name. For easier reading, the standard documentation also contains a written object description next to the object identifier. Object identifiers are structured according to a strict hierarchy established in the OSI MIB tree. Object identifiers are always a unique integral sequence that describes the MIB tree starting from the root. The combination of object identifier and descriptive text is known as a label.

Example

The object identifier for the Internet is structured as follows: `iso (1), org (3), dod (6), internet (1) or 1.3.6.1.`

3.1.2 The management tree

The SMI states clearly that all managed information and data are identified by the management tree. This management tree comes from the OSI definition. It is strictly hierarchically structured from the root (/). Branches and leaves of the management tree are shown both numerically and alphabetically. The numerical code is machine readable; the alphabetical display is better suited to the human eye and assists the user in finding his or her way through the labyrinth of branches. The way through the tree up to a node or leaf is shown by the object identifier.

Individual branches of the tree are represented by numbers, making the object identifier a sequence of integers. The root of the management tree has three direct successors: branches for the CCITT (Comité Consultatif International Télégraphique et Téléphonique), ISO (International Standards

Organization) and Joint-ISO-CCITT (a combination of the above). The branch labels are defined and listed in Table 3.1.

Description	Label
Root	–
CCITT	ccitt(0)
ISO	iso(1)
Joint-ISO-CCITT	joint-iso-ccitt(2)

Table 3.1 The root of the management tree

Under the ISO branch (iso(1)), a further subtree was established for other national and international organizations with the label org(3). The US National Institute of Standards and Technology (NIST) was given free availability of this tree. The NIST subtree has its own set of branches.

One of the NIST subtrees was made available to the US Department of Defense (DoD). The DoD has not yet defined the future appearance of this subtree, so the Internet community have opened another branch with the label 'internet(1)'. The Internet subtree (1.3.6.1.) opens on all management objects relevant to the Internet.

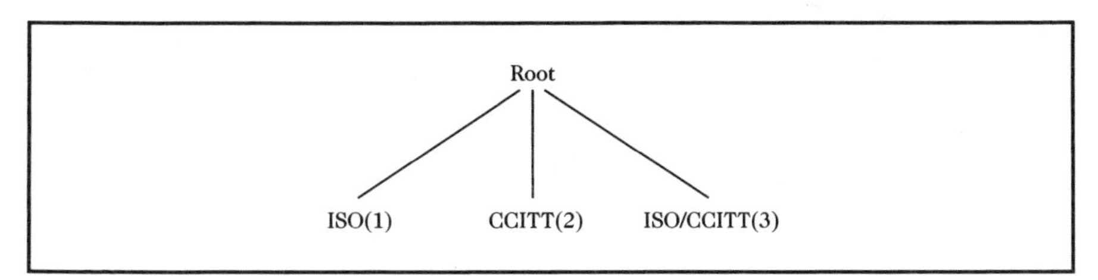

Figure 3.3 Root of the management tree

Description	Label
Root	–
CCITT	ccitt(0)
Joint-ISO-CCITT	joint-iso-ccitt(2)
ISO	iso(1)
ISO Standard	standard(0)
ISO registration-authority	registration-authority
ISO member-body	member-body(2)
ISO org	org(3)
DoD	dod(6)
Internet	internet(1)

Table 3.2 Structure of the management tree up to the 'Internet' branch

Below the Internet label, the tree divides again into four subtrees: Directory, Management, Experimental and Private.

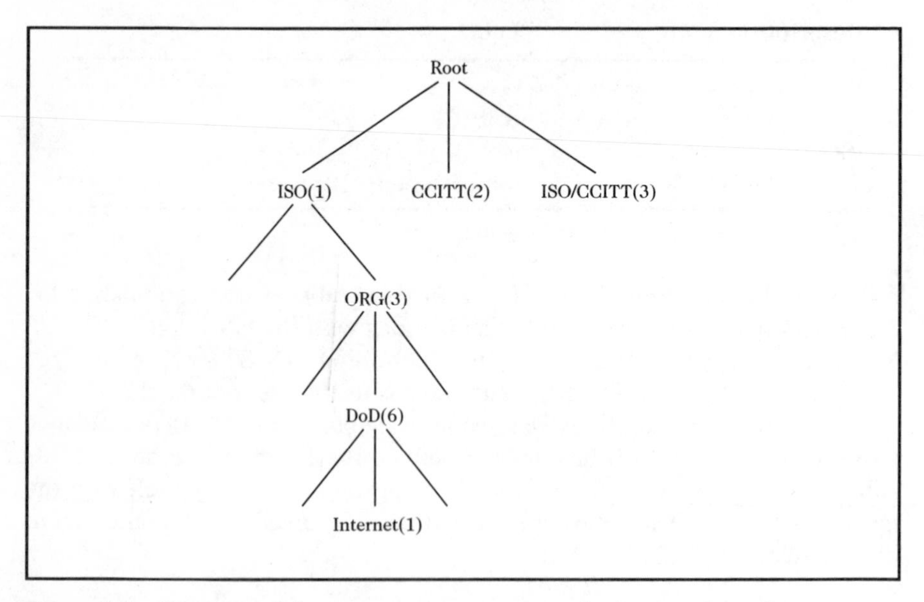

Figure 3.4 Structure of the management tree up to the Internet branch

Directory
The Directory branch label is 'directory (1)'. Currently, it contains no directory objects and remains reserved for future applications.

Experimental
The experimental subtree is labelled 'experimental(3)' and is used exclusively for experiments within the Internet (testing of new objects). The Internet Assigned Numbers Authority (IANA) within the IAB has been given the task of allocating object identifiers in the experimental subtree.

Value	Label	Description
0	Reserved	
1	CLNS	ISO CLNS-Object
9	LANMGR-1	LAN Manager V1-Object
10	LANMGR-TRAP	LAN Manager Trap-Object
11	Views	SNMP View-Object
12	SNMP-AUTH	SNMP Authentication-Object
18	PPP	PPP-Object
22	atsign-proxy	Proxy via Community
24	Alert-Man	Alert-Man

25	FDDI-Synoptics	FDDI-Synoptics
28	IDPR	IDPR MIB
29	HUBMIB	IEEE 802.3 Hub MIB
30	IPFWDTBLMIB	IP Forwarding Table MIB
31	LATM MIB	
32	SONET MIB	
33	IDENT	
34	MIME-MHS	FDDI-Synoptics

Table 3.3 Some defined experimental MIBs

Management

The management branch bears the label 'mgmt(2)'. Implementation of this branch is obligatory in each SNMP implementation. Allocation of object identifiers within the management subtree is the task of the Internet Assigned Numbers Authority.

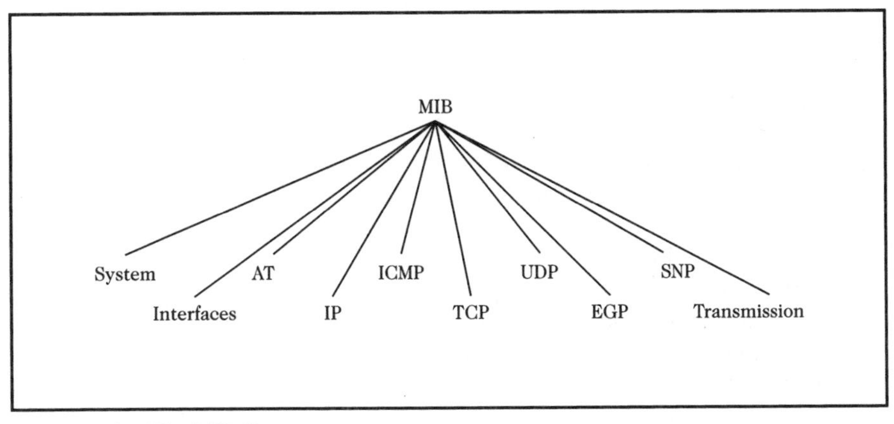

Figure 3.5 The MIB II tree

Because object groups underneath these branches may change in line with technical development, the Internet Assigned Numbers Authority publishes relevant versions of the Standard Management Information Base (MIB) and the associated object identifiers in the RFCs. New MIB standards become effective from the moment of publication and replace all documents published earlier. The version number, therefore, is an important part of any new object identifier.

Example

```
{ mgmt version-number }
```

The now obsolete MIB I defined the following object identifier (with the prefix 1.3.6.1.2.1.):

```
mib   OBJECT IDENTIFIER :: = { mgmt 1 }
```

Then MIB II was published as RFC 1213 and replaced the old MIB I; the following object identifier applies:

```
MIB II OBJECT IDENTIFIER :: = { mgmt 1 }
```

All objects defined under the label MIB II(1) are currently deployed in the management area.

Private

The private branch of the management tree (label 'private(4)') so far only has one further division: the Enterprises branch (label 'enterprises (1)'). Manufacturers may register their own manufacturer code with the IAB and define their own objects under this code. The Private MIB thus provides a tool for the integration of objects specific to one manufacturer that exceed the objects defined as standard for MIB I and MIB II. Application for registration and allocation of a Private Enterprise Number should be made to the following address:

Joyce K. Reynolds
Internet Assigned Number Authority
USC/Information Sciences Institute
4676 Admiralty Way
Marina del Rey
CA 90292-6695, USA

Prefix: 1.3.6.1.4.1.

Value	Description
0	Reserved
1	Proteon
2	IBM
3	CMU
5	ACC
9	Cisco
11	HP
12	Epilogue

15	Xylogics, Inc.
18	Wellfleet
36	DEC
42	Sun Mycrosystems
43	3Com
45	SynOptics
49	Chipcom
52	Cabletron Systems
81	Lannet Company
89	RND
99	SNMP Research
121	FTP Software Inc.
130	Banyan Systems Inc.
164	Rad Data Communications Ltd
179	Schneider & Koch & Co. Datensysteme Gmbh
191	NCR
192	Dr. Materna Gmbh
202	SMC
207	Allied Telesis, Inc.
224	LANOPTICS LTD. Israel
231	Siemens Nixdorf Informationssysteme AG
232	Compaq
247	AEG Electrocom
248	Richard Hirschmann GmbH & Co.
279	Olivetti
306	Gambit Computer Communications
311	Microsoft
328	NeXT Computer, Inc.
249	Compu-Shack
353	ATM Forum
442	PEER Networks
453	ISODE Consortium

Table 3.4 Important Private Enterprise Numbers

directory	OBJECT IDENTIFIER : := { internet 1 }
mgmt	OBJECT IDENTIFIER ::= { internet 2 }
experimental	OBJECT IDENTIFIER ::= { internet 3 }
private	OBJECT IDENTIFIER ::= { internet 4 }

Table 3.5 Object identifiers of sub-branches below the 'Internet' label

3.1.3 Names and syntax

The syntax defines the data type of an object. A subgroup of ASN.1 is used to describe this formally. ASN.1 permits the description of data independent of system and manufacturer. This unified data display means that all SNMP terminals connected to the network can clearly interpret information transferred. ASN.1 coding uses only the Basic Encoding Rules (BER). The SMI defines three data types: Primitive Types, Constructor Types and Defined Types.

Primitive types

Primitive ASN.1 types (Primitive types) are the types Integer, Octet, String, Object Identifier and Null. No other primitive types are used. The primitive type Integer Type was defined for the display of numbers. This type permits the description of all numbers consisting of the digits 0, 1, 2, 3, 4, 5, 6, 7, 8 and 9. The only exception is 0. This is only allowed when combined with another digit and must not stand alone.

Constructor types

The Constructor type is a composite type used for the compilation of lists and tables. For this purpose, SNMP uses Sequence and Sequence of. The constructor type Sequence permits the listing of simple types. The SNMP protocol does not provide for the use of default or optional values within a sequence definition. With type denoting a valid ASN.1. type, the syntax of a sequence is structured as follows:

```
SEQUENCE    { <type1>, ..., <typeN> }
```

Tables are the display of an abstract data structure consisting of a number of components. The syntax of Sequence of is structured as follows, with entry denoting the name of the list:

```
SEQUENCE OF <entry>
```

Defined types

By means of lists and construction, further types can be derived from the basic types (defined types) (Integer, Null, Object Identifier and Octet String). For this reason, the SMI defines six composite types: NetworkAddress, IP Address, Counter, Gauge, TimeTicks and Opaque.

NetworkAddress

The NetworkAddress permits the use of various network address formats. Currently, SMI only supports the Internet protocol family.

IPAddress
Defines the format of the 32-bit IP address.

Counter
Contains a 32-bit counter of which must not be a negative value. This counter counts from Zero to 2^{32}-1 (4294967295 decimal). Once the maximum value is exceeded, the counter starts again from Zero.

Gauge
Contains a 32-bit counter which must not be a negative value. This counter can count down as well as up. The gauge cannot exceed the maximum value (2^{32}-1, 4294967295 decimal) and will start again from Zero.

TimeTicks
Contains a non-negative 32-bit Integer that counts time in 1/100 seconds.

Opaque
This pseudo-datatype was introduced to bypass any restrictions inherent in the restrictive SMI definition. It permits free ASN.1 constructions. It is necessary of course, to reach an agreement between the management station and the agent process on the interpretation of Opaque data.

Managed objects
The Structure and Identification of Management Information does not define individual managed objects, but their formal structure and contents. Each object type consists of five fields: object name, syntax, definition, access and status.

Object
Under 'Object', the numerical object identifier is paired with a text describing the object.

Example

```
atIndex {atEntry 1}
```

Syntax
Syntax uses the ASN.1 syntax types described above.

Example

```
Syntax: INTEGER
```

Definition
The text describing the managed object is stored in this field.

Example

```
Definition: 'The interface number for the physical address.'
```

Access
The access field defines an object as read only, write only, read-write or non-accessible.

Example

```
Access: read-write
```

Status
The object status field contains information regarding its importance. The status field may have the following values:

- Mandatory, must be available in each implementation.
- Optional, integration of this object is at the choice of each implementation.
- Obsolete, this object is no longer used.

Example

```
Status: mandatory.
```

The Concise MIB Definitions published as RFC 1212 contain a substantial revision of the structure of managed objects, that is, their formal structure and their contents. This RFC aimed to simplify the fields contained in each object type in order to explain their contents clearly. Additional explanations of objects were to be reduced to a minimum. MIB definitions always comprise two parts:

- A text summarizing object groups.
- A MIB module, the objects contained in the MIB module being described by means of the ASN.1 macro OBJECT-TYPE.

The following example illustrates such a formal definition:

```
OBJECT: sysLocation { system 6 }
Syntax: DisplayString (SIZE (0)...255))
Definition: 'The physical location of a computer (e.g. cable
shaft. Top Floor Right).'
Access: read-only
Status: mandatory.
```

In a pure ASN.1 display, this definition appears as follows:

```
sysLocation OBJECT-TYPE
   SYNTAX DisplayString (SIZE (0..255))
   ACCESS read-only
   STATUS mandatory
   :: = {system 6}
```

For the sake of simplicity, and in order to avoid errors, these definitions can be summarized in an Object Type Macro:

Definitions

```
RFC1155-SMI DEFINITIONS ::= BEGIN

EXPORTS -- EVERYTHING
    internet, directory, mgmt,
    experimental, private, enterprises,
    OBJECT-TYPE, ObjectName, ObjectSyntax, SimpleSyntax,
    ApplicationSyntax, NetworkAddress, IpAddress,
    Counter, Gauge, TimeTicks, Opaque;


internet      OBJECT IDENTIFIER ::= { iso org(3) dod(6) 1 }
directory     OBJECT IDENTIFIER ::= { internet 1 }
mgmt          OBJECT IDENTIFIER ::= { internet 2 }
experimental  OBJECT IDENTIFIER ::= { internet 3 }
private       OBJECT IDENTIFIER ::= { internet 4 }
enterprises     OBJECT IDENTIFIER ::= { private 1 }

IMPORTS
  ObjectName
    FROM RFC1155-SMI
  DisplayString
    FROM RFC1158-MIB;

OBJECT-TYPE MACRO ::=
BEGIN
  TYPE NOTATION ::=
               -- must conform to
               -- RFC1155's ObjectSyntax
           "SYNTAX" type(ObjectSyntax)
           "ACCESS" Access
           "STATUS" Status
           DescrPart
           ReferPart
           IndexPart
           DefValPart
  VALUE NOTATION ::= value (VALUE ObjectName)
```

```
  Access ::= "read-only"
          | "read-write"
          | "write-only"
          | "not-accessible"
  Status ::= "mandatory"
          | "optional"
          | "obsolete"
          | "depreciated"

  DescrPart ::=
        "DESCRIPTION" value (description DisplayString)
          | empty

  ReferPart ::=
        "REFERENCE" value (reference DisplayString)
          | empty

  IndexPart ::=
        "INDEX" "{" IndexTypes "}"
          | empty
  IndexTypes ::=
        IndexType | IndexTypes "," IndexType
  IndexType ::=
            -- if indexobject, use the SYNTAX
            -- value of the correspondent
            -- OBJECT-TYPE invocation
        value (indexobject ObjectName)
            -- in all others otherwise use named SMI type
            -- must conform to IndexSyntax below
          | type (indextype)

  DefValPart ::=
        "DEFVAL" "{" value (defvalue ObjectSyntax) "}"
          | empty

END

IndexSyntax ::=
  CHOICE {
    number
      INTEGER (0..MAX),
    string
      OCTET STRING,
    object
      OBJECT IDENTIFIER,
    address
      NetworkAddress,
    ipAddress
      IpAddress
  }
```

This does not cause any changes in the syntax and access fields. These fields retain the same significance as in RFC 1157. The new value 'depreciated' was integrated into the status field. The new value permits the depreciation of certain obsolete parts of a MIB. This variable known as 'depreciated' will be eliminated, along with 'obsolete' in a future MIB version. All descriptive text now appears in the description field, rather than under definitions. The length of the definition field is unlimited. Each definition, though, must appear in quotation marks ('xyz'). The optional reference field permits cross-referencing to objects in other MIB modules. The index was introduced for the clear definition of any objects not contained in a table. If no index is given for a MIB module, and we are not dealing with an object that is part of a table, the name of the object is automatically extended by the sub-identifier 0.

Up to now, several object types that use the same object instance could be contained in a MIB.

Example 1

The object: atIfIndex { atEntry 1 } defines the interface number for the respective physical address within a computer.

```
Object: atIFIndex { atEntry 1 }
Syntax: INTEGER
Definition: 'The interface number for the respective physical
address.'
Access: read-write
Status: mandatory
```

Example 2

The object atPhysAddress { atEntry2 } defines the physical address of the respective network controller.

```
Object: atPhysAddress { atEntry 2 }
Syntax: OCTET STRING
Definition: 'The physical address of the respective controller.'
Access: read-write
Status: mandatory
```

Example 3

The object atNetAdress { atEntry 3 } defines the respective network address (IP address) allocated to the physical address.

```
Object: atNetAddress { atEntry 3 }
Syntax: NetworkAddress
```

```
Definition: 'The network address allocated to the respective
physical address.'
Access: read-write
Status: mandatory
```

Lists or lines

In the fourth example, the values of examples 1–3 are used in a line in the address translation table. This line comprises all values of the object type atEntry { atTable 1 } of the information already displayed through other object types (object 1: atIndex, Object 2: atPhysAddress, Object 3: atNetAddress). Such an object construct is also known as a list. Several such lists may form a table.

```
Object: atEntry { atTable 1 }
Syntax: AtEntry :: = SEQUENCE {
   atIndex
   INTEGER
   atPhysAddress
   OCTET STRING
   atNetAddress
   NetworkAddress
   }
Definition: 'An entry in the address translation table.'
Access: read-write
Status: mandatory
```

Tables

As shown in the fourth example, each object distance within the Object atTable represents the values of a number of object lists that have been compiled in an address translation table. The list shown in Table 3.6 may be derived from this.

atIfIndex (Integer)	atPhysAddress	atNetAddress (Octet String)	(Network Address)
1	080002001234	192.1.1.1	
2	040002345678	192.1.1.4	
3	080000287564	192.1.1.240	
4	080908964532	192.1.1.68	

Table 3.6 Structure of the Address Translation Table

In order to access specific values from such a list, the user or the application needs to know the individual objects in the object list and their structure. The following object identifier was defined for the Address Translation Table group (at): MIB II 3 (prefix = 1.3.6.1.2.1.3.1.2). When proceeding down the MIB tree from the Address Translation Table group, one encounters the object identifier atTable (1) which shows the Address Translation Table (prefix = 1.3.6.1.2.1.3.1). Each line of the atTable in turn consists of a number of object identifiers, the atEntry(1) (prefix = 1.3.6.1.2.1.3.1.1), atEntry(2) (prefix = 1.3.6.1.2.1.3.1.2), atEntry(3) (prefix = 1.3.6.1.2.1.3.1.3), and so on. If, for example, the stored hardware address and the relevant IP address of atEntry(3) are to be accessed, the contents of field 2 (atPhysAddress) with the prefix = 1.3.6.1.2.1.3.1.3.2 and the contents of field 2 (atNetAddress) with the prefix = 1.3.6.1.2.1.3.1.3.3 must be read out.

The Option Index introduced by the Concise MIB Definition increases the clear unambiguous identification of associated table groups significantly. The index is also defined by an individual object variable, thus defining the Instance Identifier syntax. The index definitions for the SMI shown in Table 3.7 were defined in RFC 1212.

DEFVAL

The DEFVAL value permits the allocation of certain default values to the object variables. These values remain valid until they are actively overwritten by a network management station. RFC 1213 contains some examples which are listed in Table 3.8.

Object	INDEX
ifEntry	
atEntry	
ipAddrEntry	{ ipAdEntAddr }
ipRouteEntry	{ ipRouteDest }
ipNetToMediaEntry	{ipNetToMediaIfIndex, ipNetToMediaNetAddress }
tcpConnEntry	{tcpConnLocalAddress, tcpConnLocalPort, tcpConnRemoteAddress, tcpConnRemotePort }
udpEntry	{ udpLocalAddress, udpLocalPort }
egpNeighEntry	{ egpNeighAddr }

Table 3.7 Index definitions

Objects	INDEX
INTEGER	1
COUNTER	1
GAUGE	1
TimeTicks	1

Objects	INDEX
OCTET STRING	'ffffffffffff'h
DisplayString	'each NVT ASCII string'
OBJECT IDENTIFIER	sysDescr
OBJECT IDENTIFIER	{ system 2 }
NULL	NULL
NetworkAddress	{ internet 'c0210561'h }
IpAddress	'c0210516'h - 192.33.4.21

Table 3.8 RFC 1213 (examples)

3.1.4 Abstract Syntax Notation 1 (ASN.1)

The document entitled *Structure and Identification of Management Information (SMI)* defines the ISO Abstract Syntax Notation 1 (ASN.1) as the notation for all Management Information Base variables. ASN.1 was developed and published by the ISO during the 1980s:

- *ISO IS 8824 Specification of Abstract Syntax Notation One (ASN.1)*, International Organization for Standardization.
- *ISO IS 8825 Specification of Basic Encoding Rules for Abstract Notation One (ASN.1)*, International Organization for Standardization.

ASN.1 is generally associated with the ISO communication protocols. However, the ISO intended it to be applied far more widely. ASN.1 is a description tool ('language') for the construction of complex data structures and information constructs. ASN.1 is a tool of general validity for the description of data, irrespective of manufacturer, hardware and operation. Data under administration is known as objects (object type). These data objects are characterized by name and attributes. As already described, the structure defined by the SMI is a hierarchical tree shape.

ASN.1 rules

ASN.1 defines some rules that are crucial for understanding the SNMP.

- The standard describes a multitude of defined ASN.1 types.
- ASN.1 type names always start with a capital letter.
- Certain reserved keywords are shown in capital letters throughout. These keywords are of special significance within the standard.
- Certain names start with lower case keywords. These names are only included for easier comprehension of the ASN.1 notation.

Templates

SMI defines all attributes of a managed object as sets of data (templates). These templates comprise five components: Object Description, Syntax, Definition, Access and Status of the object in question. The object template syntax defines the object's ASN.1 coding (Integer, Object String, Null, NetworkAddress, IP Address, Counter, Gauge, TimeTicks, Opaque).

Example: Interface type template

```
Object: ifType OBJECT-TYPE
Syntax: INTEGER {
         other(1),
         regular1822(2),
         hdh1822(3),
         ddn-x25(4),
         rfc877-x25(5),
         ethernet-csmacd(6),
         iso88023-csmacd(7),
         iso88024-tokenBus(8),
         iso88025-tokenRing(9),
         iso88026-man(10),
         starLan(11),
         proteon-10Mbit(12),
         proteon-80Mbit(13),
         hyperchannel(14),
         fddi(15),
         lapb(16),
         sdlc(17),
         ds1(18),
         e1(19),
         basicISDN(20),
         primaryISDN(21),
         propPointToPointSerial(22),
         ppp(23),
         softwareLoopback(24),
         eon(25),
         ethernet-3Mbit(26),
         nsip(27),
         slip(28),
         ultra(29)
         ds3(30),
         sip(31),
         frame-relay(32)
        }
Definition: 'The Interface Type distinguishes between individual
physical protocols at the Data Link Layer.'
ACCESS: read-only
STATUS: mandatory
::= { ifEntry 3 }
```

Primitive types

The object type syntax defines the abstract data structure of the individual object type. Only a subset of the multitude of object types possible with the ASN.1 specification are used as primitive application – wide types for the definition of the SNMP MIB. The primitive application – wide types are also known as non-aggregate types. The following primitive types have been defined: Integer, Null, Object Identifier and Octet String.

Integer type

The basic type for the display of numbers in ASN.1 is the Integer type. An Integer permits the display of any number consisting of the digits 0, 1, 2, 3, 4, 5, 6, 7, 8 and 9. The only exception is the digit 0, which is only valid in combination with other digits and must not stand alone.

Example: INTEGER type

```
OBJECT: tcpConnState { tcpConnEntry 1 }
Syntax: INTEGER {
          closed(1),
          listen(2),
          synSent(3)
          synReceived(4),
          established(5),
          finWait1(6),
          finWait2(7),
          closeWait(8),
          lastAck(9),
          closing(10),
          timeWait(11)
         }
Definition: 'TCP link status.'
Access: read-only.
Status: mandatory
```

The object type TcpConnState defines the state of a TCP connection and has the following defined values: Closed (1), Listen (2), SynSent (3), SynReceived (4), Established (5), FinWait1 (6), FinWait2 (7), CloseWait (8), LastAck (9), Closing (10), TimeWait (11) and DeleteTCB (12). The state of a TCP link can be monitored by demanding the Integer value of the TcpConnState object type.

Null type

The Null type within ASN.1 serves as a marker for information that may be of interest even though the value it contains is not.

Object Identifier type

In ASN.1, the object identifier type describes abstract information objects. Each label in the management MIB tree (object identifier) is marked with an object identifier. Because the individual branches of the tree are represented by numbers, an object identifier is in effect a sequence of Integer numbers.

Example: OBJECT IDENTIFIER type

```
MIB II                             OBJECT IDENIFIER ::= { mgmt 1 }
        system                     OBJECT IDENIFIER ::= { MIB II 1 }
        interfaces                 OBJECT IDENIFIER ::= { MIB II 2 }
        at                         OBJECT IDENIFIER ::= { MIB II 3 }
        ip                         OBJECT IDENIFIER ::= { MIB II 4 }
        icmp                       OBJECT IDENIFIER ::= { MIB II 5 }
        tcp                        OBJECT IDENIFIER ::= { MIB II 6 }
        udp                        OBJECT IDENIFIER ::= { MIB II 7 }
        egp                        OBJECT IDENIFIER ::= { MIB II 8 }
        cmot                       OBJECT IDENIFIER ::= { MIB II 9 }
        transmission               OBJECT IDENIFIER ::= { MIB II 10 }
        snmp                       OBJECT IDENIFIER ::= { MIB II 11 }
```

The object identifier for MIB II is located in the object identifier tree as follows: ISO (1) – Organization (3) – Department of Defense (6) – Internet (1) – Management (2) – MIB II (1), branching out into the individual MIB II sub-groups (System (1), Interfaces (2), AT (3), IP (4), ICMP (5), TCP (6), UDP (7), EGP (8), CMOT (9), Transmission (10), SNMP (11)). The numbers (sequences) for the branches in the tree give an SNMP Object Identifier value of 1.3.6.1.2.11.

Octet String type

The ASN.1 type for the display of text is the Octet String. One Octet is always an 8-Bit sequence and contains all NVT ASCII characters (0–255 decimal). The Octet String types used in the SNMP protocol are DisplayString and PhysAddress.

```
Display String :: =
   OCTET STRING
PhysAddress :: =
   OCTET STRING
```

Example: DisplayString

In the following example, the System Descriptor shows the hardware and software of a device as an Octet String.

```
sysDescr OBJECT-TYPE
   SYNTAX DisplayString (SIZE (0..255))
   ACCESS read-only
   STATUS mandatory
   DESCRIPTION
        'Contains a text describing the
        complete name and version of hardware, operating system
        and network software used.'
   ::= { system 1 }
```

Example: PhysAddress

The following example shows the physical address of the network component used.

```
ifPhysAddress OBJECT-TYPE
  SYNTAX PhysAddress
  ACCESS read-only
  STATUS mandatory
  DESCRIPTION
      "The Interface Address represents the
      address of the protocol layers used
      directly below the network layers."
  ::= { ifEntry 6 }
```

Composite types

In order to compile lists and tables, ASN.1 uses composite types (constructor types). For this purpose, the SNMP protocol has Sequence and Sequence of.

Sequence

The constructor type Sequence permits the construction of a sequence of simple types. The SNMP protocol does not provide for the use of default or optional values within a sequence definition. The syntax of Sequence is constructed as follows, with type denoting a valid ASN.1 type:

```
sequence : { <type>, , <typeN> }
```

Example

```
ifEntry OBJECT: { ifTable 1 }
Syntax: IfEntry ::= SEQUENCE {
          ifIndex
            INTEGER,
          ifDescr
            OCTET STRING,
          ifType
            INTEGER,
          ifMtu
            INTEGER,
          ifSpeed
            Gauge,
          ifPhysAddress
            OCTET STRING,
          ifAdminStatus
            INTEGER,
          ifOperStatus
            INTEGER,
          ifLastChange
            TimeTicks,
          ifInOctets
            Counter,
          ifInUcastPkts
            Counter,
          ifInNUcastPkts
            Counter,
          ifInDiscards
            Counter,
          ifInErrors
            Counter,
          ifInUnknownProtos
            Counter,
          ifOutOctets
            Counter,
          ifOutUcastPkts
            Counter,
          ifOutNUcastPkts
            Counter,
          ifOutDiscards
            Counter,
          ifOutErrors
            Counter,
          ifOutQLen
            Gauge
        }
Access: read-write.
Status: mandatory.
```

Sequence of

The tables are constructed with constructor types. They represent an abstract data structure that contains sequences of components. The syntax of Sequence of is constructed as follows, where every entry is a placeholder or descriptor of the list:

```
SEQUENCE OF <entry>
```

Example: atTable

In the Address Translation Table (atTable), all IP addresses are shown alongside the respective hardware addresses.

```
atTable OBJECT-TYPE
  SYNTAX SEQUENCE OF AtEntry
  ACCESS not-accessible
  STATUS depreciated
  DESCRIPTION
      "The Address Translation table contains
      all network addresses for which a physical
      address has been mapped."
  ::= { at 1 }

atEntry OBJECT-TYPE
  SYNTAX AtEntry
  ACCESS not-accessible
  STATUS depreciated
  DESCRIPTION
      "Each Sequence contains the physical
      address associated with the respective
      network address."
  INDEX  { atIfIndex,
       atNetAddress }
  ::= { atTable 1 }

AtEntry ::=
  SEQUENCE {
    atIfIndex
      INTEGER,
    atPhysAddress
      PhysAddress,
    atNetAddress
      NetworkAddress
  }
```

By means of lists and constructions (tables, lists), additional types can be created from the basic types (Integer, Null, Object Identifier and Octet String). The following constructions are familiar examples of composite types: NetworkAddress, IP Address, Counter, Gauge, TimeTicks and Opaque.

NetworkAddress
The NetworkAddress type permits selection from the available network address formats. Currently, only the Internet protocol family (TCP/IP) is supported.

Example

```
atNetAddress OBJECT-TYPE
   SYNTAX NetworkAddress
   ACCESS read-write
   STATUS depreciated
   DESCRIPTION
   "Contains the network address allocated
   to a physical address."
::= { atEntry 3 }
```

IP Address
The 32-bit Internet protocol (IP) address is shown as an octet string of length four.

Example

```
ipAdEntAddr OBJECT-TYPE
  SYNTAX IpAddress
  ACCESS read-only
  STATUS mandatory
  DESCRIPTION
      "Contains the IP Address of the
      entry in the ipAddrEntry object table."
  ::= { ipAddrEntry 1 }
```

Counter
The Counter type represents a non-negative counter which only counts up. Its value range is defined as 0 to 4294967295 (2^{32}-1). Once the maximum value is reached, a wrap-around occurs, that is the counter starts again at the beginning.

Example

```
icmpInMsgs OBJECT-TYPE
  SYNTAX Counter
  ACCESS read-only
  STATUS mandatory
  DESCRIPTION
      "This counter shows the number
      of all ICMP packets received to date."
  ::= { icmp 1 }
```

Gauge

The Gauge type represents a non-negative counter that counts down as well as up. Its value range is defined as 0 to 4294967295 ($2^{32}-1$). The gauge counter has no wrap-around; once the maximum value is reached, the counter stops automatically.

Example

```
tcpCurrEstab OBJECT-TYPE
   SYNTAX Gauge
   ACCESS read-only
   STATUS mandatory
   DESCRIPTION
      "Number of TCP Connections in the
      following states: ESTABLISHED or CLOSE-WAIT."
   ::= { tcp 9 }
```

TimeTicks

The TimeTicks type represents a non-negative counter which counts the time in 1/100 seconds since the start of an event.

Example

```
sysUpTime OBJECT-TYPE
 SYNTAX TimeTicks
 ACCESS read-only
 STATUS mandatory
 DESCRIPTION
     "Defines the time (in 1/100 seconds) since
     the last time the network management software
     was re-initialized."
 ::= { system 3}
```

Opaque

The Opaque type was introduced as a pseudo-data type to bypass any possible restrictions imposed by the SNMP definition. An Opaque type permits the definition of ASN.1 constructions at will.

3.1.4.1 Encoding

All object types of the SNMP protocol are encoded according to ISO Standard 8824, *Specification of Basic Encoding Rules for Abstract Notation One (ASN.1)*. As defined in the Basic Encoding Rules (BER), ASN.1 data is always transferred onto the data net with the most significant bit, that is, the highest-order bit, as the first value. As shown in Figure 3.6, Bits 8–1 are always transferred in sequence from left to right to the next lowest protocol layer. Bit 8 is the highest-order bit, Bit 1 the lowest-order bit. Accordingly, the recipient of this protocol message will transfer Bits 8–1 as a serial data stream. All other forms of bit ordering, for example, with the highest-order bit on the right-hand side of the Octet (Bit 1), are not valid.

Unlike most TCP/IP protocols, SNMP messages do not consist of a fixed header format. In accordance with the Basic Encoding Rules (BER) of ASN.1, SNMP structures each data type into three fields: Tag field, Length field and Data field.

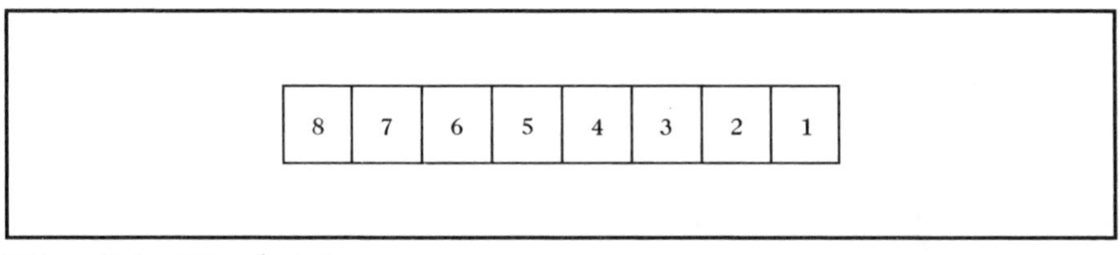

Figure 3.6 Bit ordering

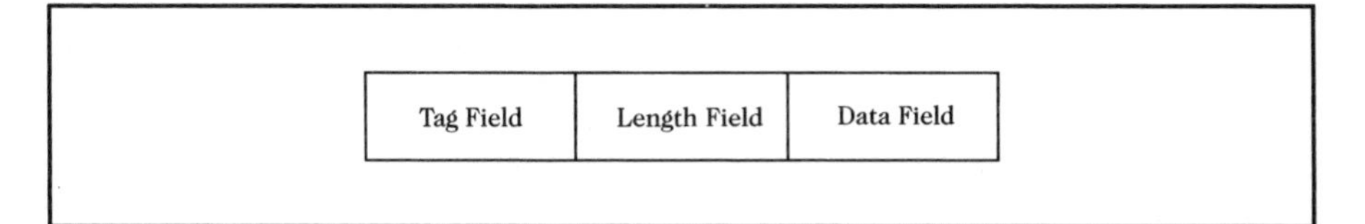

Figure 3.7 The three ASN.1 value fields

The Tag field
The Tag field defines the ASN.1 type. For all SNMP protocol types, the tag field is divided into the components Class field, Format bit and Tag Number field.

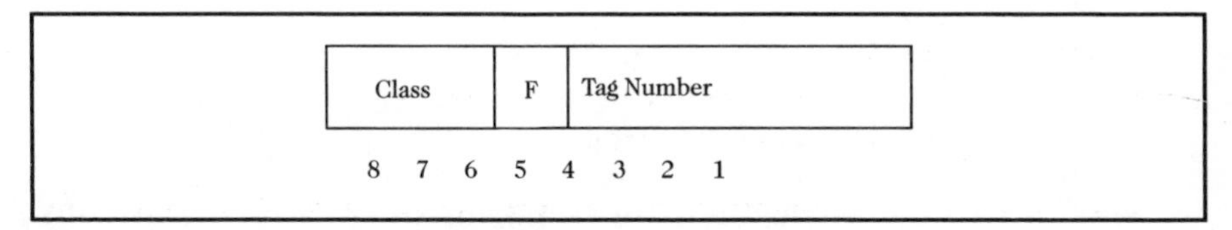

Figure 3.8 The Tag field

Class

The first two highest-order bits (Bits 8 and 7) in the Tag field describe the class of the tag value. The following Tag classes have been defined: Universal, Application Specific, Context Specific and Private.

Bit 8	Bit 7	Class
0	0	Universal
0	1	Application
1	0	Context Specific
1	1	Private

Table 3.9 Distribution of the Tag classes

Universal

The Universal Tag field defines all universally valid and ASN.1 defined (well-known) data types. Table 3.10 shows the Universal tags defined to date.

Value	Description
1	Boolean
2	Integer
3	Bit String
4	Octet String
5	Null
6	Object Identifier
7	Object Description
8	External
9	Real
10	Enumerated
12	Reserved
13	Reserved
14	Reserved
15	Reserved
16	Sequence and Sequence of
17	Set and Set of
18	Numeric String
19	Printable String
20	Teletext String
21	Videotext String
22	IA5 String
23	UTC Time
24	Generalized Type
25	Graphics String
26	Visible String
27	General String
28	Character String
29	Reserved for Character String

Table 3.10 Universal tags

Application Specific
The Application Specific tags permit the expansion of Universal tags for one particular application or one particular standard. An Application Specific tag must be defined clearly in this standard, for example in the application, and must be allocated to one type only.

Context Specific
Context Specific tags permit the introduction of specific tags that can only be interpreted in the context in which they were defined.

Private
Private tags permit the introduction of individual user specific tags. The SNMP protocol only provides for the use of the Universal tags and Application Specific tags.

The Format bit
Bit 6 in the Tag field is known as the Format bit (F-Bit). The F-Bit distinguishes between primitive and composite coding of the following Tag Number. With primitive codes, the F-Bit is set to 0. If the following Tag Number has a composite code, the F-Bit has the value 1.

Tag Number field
The Tag Number field (bits 5–1) shows the Tag Numbers as binary numbers. The Number field is always encoded from left to right, starting with the most significant bit (5) and down to the least significant bit (bit 1). Because only values from 0–31 can be shown by these five bits, the binary value 1111 remains reserved for larger Tag value numbers. For this reason, the five bits can in fact only show the values from 0–30. All larger Tag Numbers are shown instead in the following data octets. In these cases, the most significant bit (bit 8) is always given the value 0.

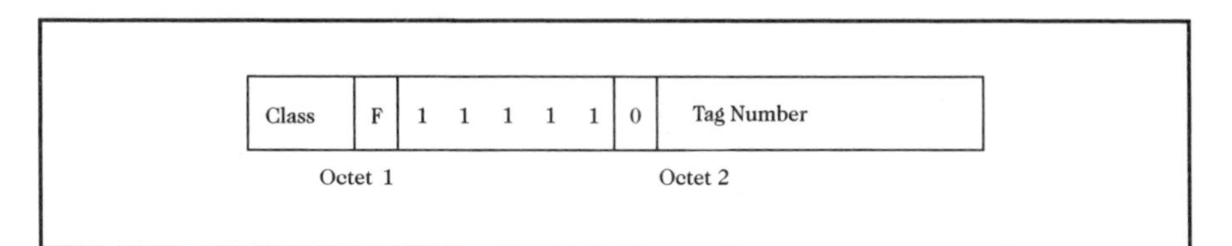

Figure 3.9 The extended Tag field

The Length field
In ASN.1, information is transferred in two different types of length field. These are known as the 'definite form' and the 'undefinite form'. The Simple Network Management Protocol only provides for use of the 'definite form', in which one or more octets define the number of data octets in the following information field. The high-order bit in the first octet of a length field serves to distinguish between a one-octet and multi-octet length field.

The 1-Octet Length field

The number of data octets in the following information field can be defined in a 1-octet length field if the information in the information field (Bits 1–7) is of a length between 0 and 127 octets. The high-order bit in the first octet of the length field is set to 0 to indicate a short form.

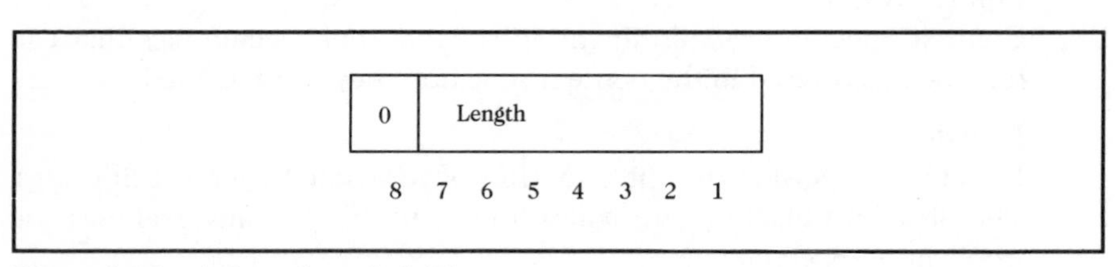

Figure 3.10 1-Octet Length field

Multi-Octet Length field

If the number of data octets in the information field following the length field exceeds 127, several octets are required to show the length. Multi-octet data fields are also known as Long Form. The high-order bit of the first octet of the length field is always set to 1 to indicate the long form. All further bits in the first octet (Bits 1–7) define the number of following length octets (in binary form). SNMP protocol multi-octet length fields are restricted to a maximum length of three octets, because the IP protocol can only process datagrams up to a length of 65,535 data octets.

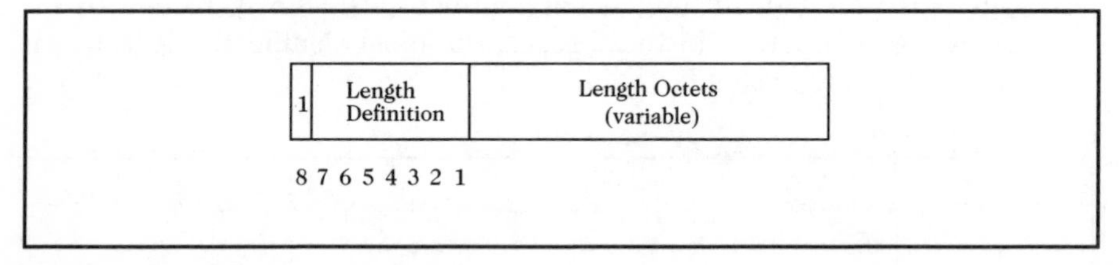

Figure 3.11 Multi-Octet Length field

The Data field

Individual functions of ASN.1 are encoded in the Data field. The SNMP protocol only provides for the use of primitive types: Integer, Null, Object Identifier, Octet String, Sequence and Sequence of.

Integer

ASN.1 has defined Integer as the basic type for the display of numbers. An Integer permits the description of all numbers consisting of the digits 0, 1, 2, 3, 4, 5, 6, 7, 8 and 9. For SNMP, an exception applies to the digit 0. It is only valid in combination with other digits and must not stand alone.

Encoding of Integer values

Example: Value 221 (DD hexadecimal), see also Figure 3.12

Integer	**Length**	**Value**
<02>	<01>	<DD>

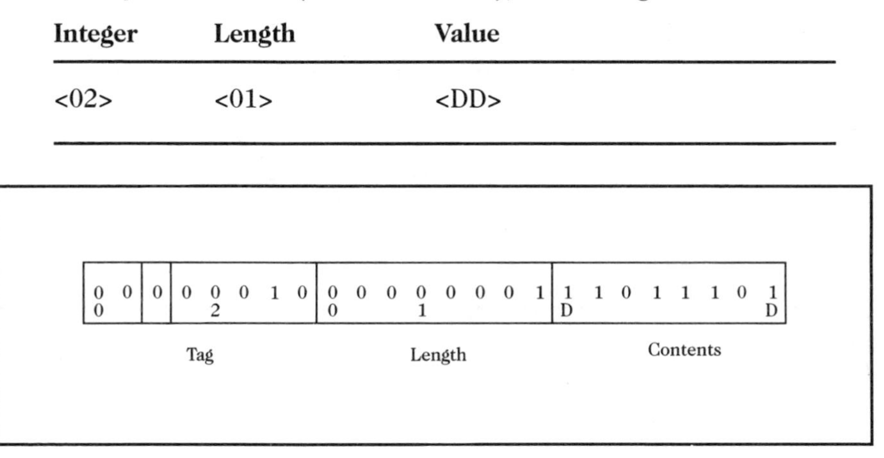

Figure 3.12 Encoding of Integer values

Null
The Null type in ASN.1 serves to mark information that is of interest even though the value contained in it is not.

Encoding of Zero values

Example: Hexadecimal 05 00

Zero	**Length**
<05>	<00>

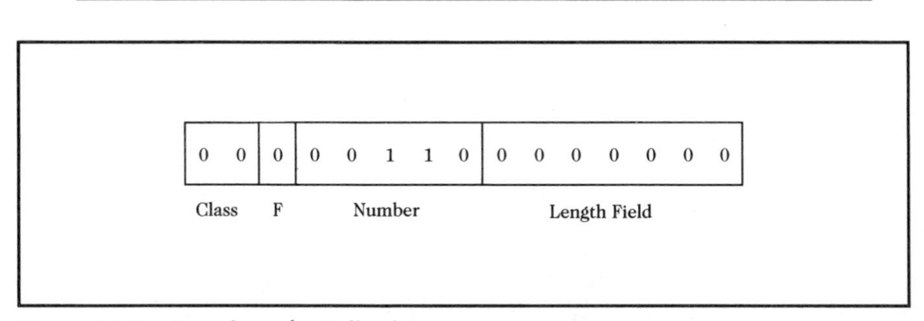

Figure 3.13 Encoding of a Null value

Octet String type
ASN.1 defines the Octet String as the type for the display of data contents (for example, text). One octet is always a sequence of 8 bits.

Encoding of Octet Strings

Example: Chaos & Disaster

Octet String	Length	Value
<04>	<10>	<43> <68> <61> <6F> <73> <00> <26> <00> <44> <69> <73> <61> <73> <74> <65> <72>

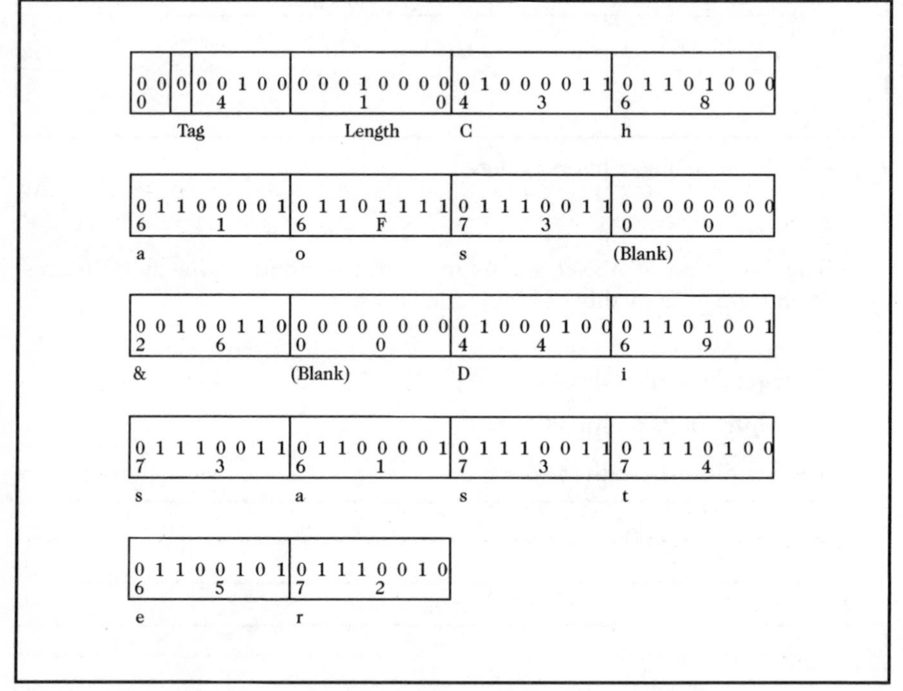

Figure 3.14 Encoding of an Octet String

Object Identifier type

In ASN.1, the object identifier serves to describe abstract information objects. Each label in the Management MIB tree is marked with an object identifier. Because the individual branches on the tree are represented by numbers, the object identifier is in effect a sequence of Integers. Object identifiers are always shown in primitive form and contain one or more data octets. Consequently, encoding of object identifiers always results in a primitive value, with the contents value comprising an ordered list of encodings. Because the values refer to the object identifier tree, their sequence must be preserved at all times.

Object identifiers following the root are also known as sub-identifiers. Each sub-identifier is represented by a sequence of one or more octets. Bit 8 in each octet determines whether the current octet is the last in a sequence. If Octet 8 has the value 0, it signals that this is the concluding octet. Otherwise, further octets encoding the object identifier value follow. The complete sequence of Bits 7 to 1 of all octets are the encoding of the sub-identifier values. These bits are interpreted as a binary number, with Bit 7 of the first octet bearing the highest and Bit 1 of the last octet the lowest value. Sub-identifiers must be encoded in the shortest sequence of octets possible, that is, the leading octet of a sub-identifier must not be the value <8>. The numerical value of the first sub-identifier is derived from the first two object identifier components. The following formula is used for this purpose:

```
(x * 40) + y
```

Value X is the current value of the first object identifier component, that is, 0 for ccitt, 1 for iso and 2 for joint-iso-ccitt. The value of the second object identifier component must be substituted for y. The practical upshot of this is that the number of sub-identifiers is one less than the number of object identifier components.
Using the above formula, we arrive at the following value for the standard value of the first object identifier component (iso-org) of the SNMP protocol:

```
(1 * 40) + 3 = 43 (decimal) or 2B (hexadecimal).
```

Example: OBJECT IDENTIFIER type

```
MIB II    OBJECT IDENTIFIER ::= { mgmt 1 }
        system   OBJECT IDENTIFIER ::= { MIB II 1 }
                sysDescr   OBJECT IDENTIFIER ::= { system 1 }
```

The object identifier for the system descriptor in the object identifier tree is located as follows: ISO (1) – Organization (3) – Department of Defense (6) – Internet (1) – Management (2) – MIB II (1). One subgroup located under MIB II is the System Group (1). The first object in the System Group is sysDescr (1). The numbers (sequences) for the individual branches in the tree result in an SNMP object identifier value of 1.3.6.1.2.1.1.1.

For the sysDescr Object Identifier (1.3.6.1.2.1.1.1), the object identifier components shown in Table 3.11 result.

Component	Decimal	Hexadecimal	Binary
1	43	2B	00101011
2	06	06	00000110
3	01	01	00000001
4	02	02	00000010
5	01	01	00000001
6	01	01	00000001
7	01	01	00000001

Table 3.11 Object Identifier components

OBJECT IDENTIFIER TAG	Length	Value
<06>	<07>	<43> <06> <01> <02> <01> <01> <01>

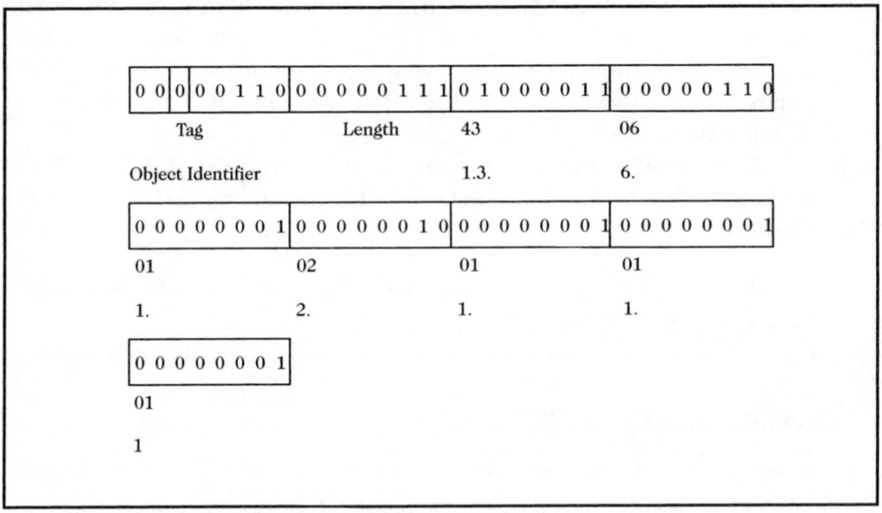

0 0 | 0 | 0 0 1 1 0 | 0 0 0 0 0 1 1 1 | 0 1 0 0 0 0 1 1 | 0 0 0 0 0 1 1 0
Tag Length 43 06
Object Identifier 1.3. 6.

0 0 0 0 0 0 0 1 | 0 0 0 0 0 0 1 0 | 0 0 0 0 0 0 0 1 | 0 0 0 0 0 0 0 1
01 02 01 01
1. 2. 1. 1.

0 0 0 0 0 0 0 1
01
1

Figure 3.15 Encoding of Object Identifiers

Sequence type

The coding of a value of the data type that was defined via a sequence construct is a constructor type and results from a complete coding of the values for the individual component types. Encoding sequences for the individual Sequence components must be in the same sequence as the definition of these types or their relevant value notations. The Constructor type Sequence permits the sequencing of primitive types.

The SNMP protocol does not provide for the use of default and optional values within a sequence definition.

The syntax of a Sequence is constructed as follows, with type denoting a valid ASN.1 type:

```
Sequence { <type1>,..., <typeN> }
```

An example illustrates the encoding of a Sequence data type by means of part of the If Table:

```
ifEntry OBJECT: { ifTable 1 }
Syntax: IfEntry ::= SEQUENCE {
          ifIndex
            INTEGER.
          ifDescr
            OCTET STRING,
        }
```

The name ifIndex is represented by an object name tag. The contents of ifIndex are represented as an Integer. This results in the encoding shown in Table 3.12.

SEQUENCE	TAG	Length	Value
	<30>		<07>
Object names	<06>	<07>	<69> <66> <49>
			<6E> <64> <65> <78>
INTEGER	<02>	<01>	<ww>

Table 3.12 Encoding

The following name, ifDescriptor, is shown as an object name tag. The contents of ifDescr are represented by an Octet String. The resulting encoding is shown in Table 3.13.

SEQUENCE	TAG	Length	Value
Object Name	<06>	<07>	<69> <66> <44>
			<65> <73> <63> <72>
Octet String	<04>		<xy> <ww> <ww>

Table 3.13 Encoding

From these values, the ASN.1 definition shown in Table 3.14 is derived.

SEQUENCE	<30> <07>
ifIndex	<06> <07> <69> <66> <49> <6E> <64> <65> <78>
Integer	<02> <01> <ww>
ifDescr	<06> <07> <69> <66> <44> <65> <73> <63> <72>
Octet String	<04> <xy> <ww> <ww>

Table 3.14 ASN.1 definition

Sequence of type

The data type Sequence of is subject to composite encoding consisting of a sequence of (possibly empty) data values, with the sequence of the data values during encoding determined by the value sequence in the ASN.1 value definition. All elements of the type list are the same in a Sequence of type.

The following example illustrates the encoding of a Sequence of type, using the atTable:

```
atTable OBJECT TYPE
SYNTAX SEQUENCE OF AtEntry
ACCESS non-accessible
STATUS depreciated
DESCRIPTION
   'The Address Translation Table contains all network addresses
   for which a physical address has been mapped.'
:: = { at 1 }
```

The entries under AtEntry are unambiguously represented by a Sequence (`:: = { atTable 1 }`), they represent the contents of the Sequence of fields.

Tagged type

The Tagged type enables you to define newly created types clearly, therefore there are two completely different strategies available.

The Tagged type is a composite, and its contents comprise the complete encoding of the basic types it consists of. The Tagged type was defined as implicit including the keywords. That means, by definition, that this will use the form and the coding of the Basic types.

Example: Composite Tagged type

```
TelNo:: [part]
Octet String
```

The fictional telephone number 0044-71-56783456 has been defined as the value of the Octet String. Combination of both tags and encoding according to the rules for Octet Strings result in the construct shown in Table 3.15.

TAG	Length	TAG	Length	Value
<61>	<12>	<04>	<10>	<00> <00> <04> <04> <2D> <07> <01> <2D> <05> <06> <07> <08> <03> <04> <05> <06>

Table 3.15

In this case, encoding comprises the first two composite tags. It is defined by the first tag (binary value = 0 1 1 0 0 0 0 1) and a length of 12 (hexadecimal) (binary value = 0 0 0 1 0 0 1 0). The actual octet string starts with TAG 04.

In practice, encoding of the basic type tag is not necessary, as the receiver of the encoded value should be aware of the structure of the newly created type. In this case, the Tagged type may look as follows:

```
TelNo: : [part] IMPLICIT OCTET STRING
```

Thanks to the keyword 'Implicit', encoding of the first tag and length is not required. The tag field has the value 10000001 and signals that we are dealing with a content specific, noncomposite tag. This construct is shown in Table 3.16.

TAG	Length	Value
<41>	<10>	<00> <00> <04> <04> <2D> <07> <01> <2D> <05> <06> <07> <08> <03> <04> <05> <06>

Table 3.16

Choice types

Choice types require special treatment. No universal tags have been defined for them so far. For this reason, both the tag and the value of the Choice component must be encoded. Irrespective of the relevant component, the actual encoding may be primitive or composite. In the SNMP protocol specifications, RFC 1157 defines the Protocol Data Units (PDUs) with a Choice type.

```
PDUs ::=
    CHOICE {
          get-request
            GetRequest-PDU,

          get-next-request
            GetNextRequest-PDU,

          get-response
            GetResponse-PDU,

          set-request
            StRequest-PDU,

          trap
            Trap-PDU
        }
```

Individual PDUs are defined via Context Specific tags:

```
GetRequest-PDU ::=
  [0]
    IMPLICIT PDU

GetNextRequest-PDU ::=
  [1]
    IMPLICIT PDU

GetResponse-PDU ::=
  [2]
    IMPLICIT PDU

SetRequest-PDU ::=
  [3]
    IMPLICIT PDU
```

The structure of individual PDUs is defined via Sequence tags:

```
PDU ::=
    SEQUENCE {
      request-id
   INTEGER,

      error-status
        INTEGER {
```

```
            noError(0),
            tooBig(1),
            noSuchName(2),
            badValue(3),
            readOnly(4),
            genErr(5)
          },

        error-index
          INTEGER,

        variable-bindings
          VarBindList
    }
```

The structure of Trap PDUs is defined via a Tagged value:

```
Trap-PDU ::=
  [4]
    IMPLICIT SEQUENCE {
      enterprise
        OBJECT IDENTIFIER,

      agent-addr
        NetworkAddress,

      generic-trap
        INTEGER {
          coldStart(0),
          warmStart(1),
          linkDown(2),
          linkUp(3),
          authenticationFailure(4),
          egpNeighborLoss(5),
          enterpriseSpecific(6)
        },

      specific-trap
        INTEGER,

      time-stamp
        TimeTicks,

       Variable-bindings
        VarBindList
    }
```

VarBindings are defined via a Sequence tag:

```
VarBind ::=
    SEQUENCE {
      name
        ObjectName,

      value
        ObjectSyntax
    }

VarBindList ::=
    SEQUENCE OF
      VarBind

END
```

The GetRequest-PDU gives access to more detailed information on the structure of ASN.1 constructs. The GetRequest-PDU is defined as follows:

```
GetRequest-PDU ::=
  [0]
    IMPLICIT SEQUENCE {
      request-id
                INTEGER,

      error-status
        INTEGER    - always 0

      error-index  - always 0
        INTEGER,

      variable-bindings
        VarBindList
    }

VarBind ::=
    SEQUENCE {
      name
        ObjectName,
      value
        ObjectSyntax
    }

VarBindList ::=
    SEQUENCE OF
      VarBind
```

In the VarBind Sequence, 'ObjectName' represents the Object Identifier and 'ObjectSyntax' its value. In our example, we used the sysDescr OBJECT TYPE (1.3.6.1.2.1.1.1) we explained earlier. Its Syntax is defined as an octet string (SIZE (0..255)).

Table 3.17 illustrates the encoding of the complete GetRequest-PDU.

[0]	IMPLICIT SEQUENCE	A2 19
	error-index INTEGER	02 01 00
	VarBindList SEQUENCE	30 0D
	VarBind SEQUENCE	30 0D
	sysDescr OBJECT-TYPE	06 07 43 06 01 02 01 01 01
	Octet String	04 01 01

Table 3.17 Encoding of the GetRequest-PDU

3.2 The Management Information Base

The ISO describes parameters to be managed as objects and attributes. As mentioned above, 'object' is an abstract term for a resource that constitutes a certain segment of the net. This resource may offer a multitude of options (parameter/attributes). If the object can be integrated into a management concept, it is referred to as a managed object. In principle, management functions are a sequence of parameter-determined operations on an object. The sum total of managed objects is called a Management Information Base (MIB).

3.2.1 Evolution of SNMP MIBs

When SNMP was defined several years ago, the authors of this protocol aimed for maximum simplicity and portability. This concept is responsible for the advance of the SNMP protocol to the market standard for network management. Since the early stages of the SNMP protocol, the Management Information Base (MIB) has been an essential component. In RFC 1066 (published in August 1988), the first group of managed objects was published under the title *Management Information Base for Network Management of TCP/IP-based Internets*. This Management Information Base is known as MIB I. MIB I contained eight object groups with approximately 100 objects.

System Object Group
Interface Object Group
Address Translation Object Group

Internet Protocol Object Group
Internet Control Message Protocol Object Group
Transmission Control Protocol Object Group
UserDatagram Protocol Object Group
Exterior Gateway Protocol Object Group

Table 3.18 MIB I Object Groups

Manufacturers soon perceived MIB I as the foundation for cost-effective implementation of SNMP protocols in their management stations and agent implementations. However, before long it became obvious that a mere hundred variables for a network management system only permits display of a small part of the complete net.

In May 1990, MIB I was replaced by MIB II (RFC 1158). MIB II introduced three new object groups and expanded the groups known from MIB I by many new objects (Table 3.19).

System Object Group
Interface Object Group
Address Translation Object Group
Internet Protocol Object Group
Internet Control Message Protocol Object Group
Transmission Control Protocol Object Group
User Datagram Protocol Object Group
Exterior Gateway Protocol Object Group
Transmission Object Group
CMOT Object Group
Simple Network Management Protocol Object Group

Table 3.19 MIB II Object Groups

From the start, MIBs had three dynamic expansion options implemented:

1. Publication of a new MIB specification;
2. Use of an experimental group;
3. Use of a private object group in the Management subtree.

Experimental Group

All MIBs available as Internet Drafts are anchored in the Experimental Group. This branch permits the use of experimental MIBs as an interim solution, until these objects and object groups are one day accepted as part of the standard MIB. In case of official standardization of an experimental MIB, manufacturers had to carry out software updates on all their products and integrate these objects into the Standard MIB tree.

Private Group

The Private Group in the Enterprise subtree permits the introduction of vendor specific objects. Each vendor has the option to expand the generally accepted MIBs with private MIB information. In many products, a wide range of vendor specific information and functions in addition to the standard are implemented as options. This means that users need to know exactly which management station supports which private MIBs fully, in order to implement the whole range of functions of the products.

MIB II was completely revised in RFC 1213 and adapted to the Concise MIB definitions in RFC 1212. This document invalidates RFC 1158. RFC 1213 amends RFC 1156 in the following respects:

- Text changes for unambiguous display of MIBs. The data type Display String is introduced. A Display String may only contain characters defined in NVT ASCII. The following objects were defined as Display String: sysDescr and ifDescr. In addition, attention should be given to the fact that an octet string may contain binary data (0..255).
- Greater downward compatibility with the SMI/MIB and SNMP is given, for example, by the introduction of Depreciated Objects. Thus, a MIB can be told that certain objects were removed from the standard in later versions. In MIB II, the object is marked as Depreciated in the atTable. In this case, the complete Address Translation Group is removed from the MIB.
- Improved support for multi-protocol environments. The MIB in a multi-protocol network must be able to support more than one Address Mapping Table. Further tables will be implemented in future.
- Creation of additional options for adapting the MIB to the respective implementation. For example, implementation specific positive Integers for identifying IP addresses and routing tables are possible.

The old Object Identifier is still used for the new MIB II:

```
MIB II OBJECT IDENTIFIER : : = { mgmt 1 }
```

Under the Title *Reassignment of Experimental MIBs to Standard MIBs (June 1991)*, RFC 1239 sounded the death knell for any ideas involving a successor to MIB II. Manufacturers of SNMP devices were unable to wait until the draft was declared to be a valid standard before it could be implemented. At the same time, a possible case scenario foresaw constant changes to the standard definition in the final stages of ratification, obliging developers to wait even longer for the final standard before they could write even the first piece of code. The preferred alternative was the option to provide for dynamic expansion of the standard MIB. New object groups, even new objects, could be integrated into the standard MIB simply by adding further branches to the MIB groups (see Table 3.20).

System Object Group
Interface Object Group
Address Translation Object Group
Internet Protocol Object Group
Internet Control Message Protocol Object Group
Transmission Control Protocol Object Group
User Datagram Protocol Object Group
Exterior Gateway Protocol Object Group
Transmission Object Group
Token Bus-like Object Group
Token Ring-like Object Group
T1 Carrier Object Group
DS3 Interface Type Object Group
CMOT Object Group
Simple Network Management Protocol Object Group
Generic Interface Extension Object Group

Table 3.20 RFC 1239 MIB Object Groups

Branching of MIBs and the resulting easy expansion option caused an avalanche of new MIBs. Manufacturers of managed products suddenly found themselves with a far wider choice of objects than could be implemented on the respective devices. In an Ethernet to Token Ring Bridge, only the following MIBs could be implemented: Standard MIB (without EGP Objects), Ethernet MIB, Token Ring MIB and Private Enterprise MIB. The Enterprise MIB is used to define vendor specific objects, for example filters defined by the user, that are not covered by the relevant standard MIB. The sum total of all available MIBs leads inevitably towards a far greater range of options for effective and systematic network management. This variety requires a certain amount of knowledge on the part of the network administrator, who needs to know about the MIBs (parameters) supported by a device he or she is using in order to ensure adequate configuration. At the same time, all information (for example, performance and fault management) offered by a device must be converted into appropriate action in order to exploit all functions offered by a network management system.

3.2.2 New MIBs

It is hardly possible to choose the right component from the mass of comparable devices without an in-depth understanding of MIBs. Network administrators and network planners consequently need to undergo a process of continuous education in order to process the vast amount of new information. The best way to keep up to date is provided by the Internet Architecture Board (IAB) (formerly the Internet Activities Board) or the Internet Engineering Task Forces (IETFs) via E-mail. It is very easy to waste a lot of time chasing information. Not many companies can employ staff solely for the purpose of providing and processing information. In practice, network administrators have no choice but to get hold of the relevant standards (RFCs) and compile the information required to make the 'right' choice in the purchase of a new device. As usual, special attention should be paid to the small print. In practice, not all the MIBs listed on the data sheet necessarily turn out to be fully implemented.

Dynamic development of standards means that vendors face a further problem with certain MIBs that are already obsolete at the time a document goes into print or have been replaced with another version of the same MIB. The implication for the user is the necessity to be aware in detail of the functions and MIBs the device should support. Only detailed examination of all the devices on offer prevents a 'wrong' purchase.

Currently, the MIBs listed in Table 3.21 are available to users.

RFC	Title
1525	Source Routing Bridges MIB
1516	IEEE 802.3 Repeater MIB
1515	IEEE 802.3 Medium Attachment Unit (MAU) MIB
1514	Host Resources MIB
1513	Remote Network Monitoring (RMON) MIB
1512	FDDI MIB
1493	Bridge MIB
1474	Bridge Network Control Protocol MIB for PPP
1473	IP Network Control Protocol MIB for PPP
1472	Security Protocol MIB for PPP
1471	Link Control Protocol MIB for PPP
1461	SNMP MIB for Multiprotocol Interconnect over X.25
1451	Manager-to-Manager MIB
1450	Management Information Base for SNMPv2
1447	Party MIB for SNMPv2
1414	Identification MIB
1407	DS3 and E3 Interface MIB
1406	DS1 and E1 Interface MIB
1398	Ethernet Interface MIB
1389	RIP Version 2 MIB
1382	X.25 Packet Layer MIB
1381	X.25 LABP MIB
1354	SNMP IP Forwarding Table MIB
1353	SNMP Party MIB

1318	Parallel Interface Type MIB
1317	RS-232 Interface Type MIB
1316	Character Device MIB
1315	Frame Relay DTE Interface Type MIB
1304	SMDS Interface Protocol (SIP) Interface Type MIB
1289	DECnet Phase IV MIB Extensions
1269	Border Gateway Protocol (version 3) MIB
1253	OSPF version 2 MIB
1243	AppleTalk MIB
1238	CLNS MIB
1231	IEEE 802.5 Token Ring MIB
1230	IEEE 802.4 Token Bus MIB
1229	Extensions to the Generic Interface MIB
1227	SNMP MUX Protocol and MIB
1214	OSI Management Information Base
1213	MIB II

Table 3.21 MIBs currently available

3.2.2.1 DS1 Interface Type MIB

The DS1 and E1 MIBs were defined in RFC 1406 by the Transmission MIB Working Group of the Internet Engineering Task Force (IETF) and establish the variables and objects required to manage DS1 (T1) and similar interfaces. The DS1 MIB distinguishes between two interfaces (ifType variables): DS1 (18) and E1 (19). The DS1 MIB is based on the AT&T T1 specification and the Extended Superframe (ESF) Format. The DS1 specific interface value was given the following object identifier:

```
DS1 OBJECT IDENTIFIER ::= { transmission 18 }
```

3.2.2.2 IEEE 802.5 Token Ring MIB

The IEEE 802.5 Token Ring MIB published in RFC 1231 (May 1991) is based on the variables for the administration of Token Ring devices and nets developed by the Internet Engineering Task Force (IETF). The specification describes three Token Ring specific tables: the 802.5 Interface Table, the 802.5 Statistics Table and the 802.5 Timer Table.

802.5 Interface Table
Contains all Token Ring specific variables/parameters.

802.5 Statistics Table
Permits records to be kept of statistics and values.

802.5 Timer Table
The optional IEEE 802.5 Timer Table provides for management of the interface specific timer.

The IEEE 802.5 specific interface value in MIB II was given the following object identifier:

```
OBJECT IDENTIFIER ::= { transmission 9 }
```

3.2.2.3 IEEE 802.4 Token Bus MIB

The IEEE 802.4 Token Bus MIB published in RFC 1230 (May 1990) is based on the variables for the administration of Token Bus devices and nets developed by the Transmission Working Group. The specification describes the following three Token Bus specific tables: the Operational Table, the Initialization Table and the Statistics Table.

IEEE 802.4 Operational Table
The Operational Table contains all IEEE 802.4 interface specific variables/parameters.

IEEE 802.4 Initialization Table
The IEEE 802.4 Initialization Table contains information that is activated as parameters during initialization of an 802.4 Interface.

IEEE 802.4 Statistics Table
The Statistics Table provides for Token Bus specific recording of statistics and values.

The IEEE 802.4 specific interface value in the MIB II was given the following object identifier:

```
IEEE 802.4 Object Identifier ::= { transmission 8 }
```

3.2.2.4 Extensions to the Generic Interface MIB

In RFC 1229 (May 1991), the SNMP Working Group of the Internet Engineering Task Force (IETF) expanded MIB II with the definition of the Generic Interface MIB. The Internet Standard MIB contains a number of management objects that may be regarded as standard variables, irrespective of the physical and logical interface used. The Generic Interface MIB contains three tables: Generic Interface Extension Table, Generic Interface Test Table and Generic Receive Address Table.

Generic Interface Extension Table
The Generic Interface Extension Table contains all new objects valid for all interface types.

Generic Interface Test Table
The Generic Interface Test Table contains objects that enable a network manager to run tests defined by an agent on the interface.

Generic Receive Address Table
The Generic Receive Address Table contains objects that are only used with interfaces capable of receiving packets/frames at several physical interface addresses.

The Generic MIB variable in MIB II was given the following object identifier:

```
Generic IF Object Identifier ::= { standard-MIB 12 }
```

3.2.2.5 DS3 and E3 Interface Type MIB

The DS3 and E3 MIB published by the Transmission MIB Working Group in RFC 1407 defines variables and objects required to manage a DS3 interface. The DS3 MIB defines the following ifType variable: DS3 (30). DS3 MIB definitions are based on the ANSI T1.102-1987, ANSI T1.107.1988 and ANSI T1.404-1989 specifications. The DS3 specific interface values of MIB II was given the following object identifier:

```
DS3 Object Identifier ::= { transmission 30 }
```

3.2.2.6 AppleTalk Management Information Base

The AppleTalk MIB published in RFC 1243 (July 1991) permits management of a number of devices supporting various AppleTalk Protocols. The AppleTalk MIB supports the following object groups: LLAP, AARP, ATPort, DDP, RTMP, KIP, ZIP, NBP and ATEcho.

LocalTalk Link Access Protocol Group
The LocalTalk Link Access Protocol (LLAP) defines the Link Layer Protocol for Apple's LocalTalk network. The LLAP group permits management and administration of all devices supporting this protocol.

AppleTalk Address Resolution Protocol Group

The AppleTalk Address Resolution Protocol (AARP) permits the mapping of AppleTalk node addresses (Datagram Delivery Protocol) for the Data Link Layer addresses. The AARP table permits administration of the Address Mapping Table.

The AppleTalk Port Group

All packets of a logical link are transported via an AppleTalk port. This group permits management and configuration of the AppleTalk ports.

Datagram Delivery Protocol Group

The Datagram Delivery Protocol (DDP) (Network Layer Protocol) permits datagram transport (socket to socket) via the AppleTalk net. The DDP group manages the DDP layer of a device integrated into management.

Routing Table Maintenance Protocol Group

The Routing Table Maintenance Protocol (RTMP) used by AppleTalk routers establishes the routing tables. The RTMP group manages both the RTMP protocol and the routing tables.

Kinetics Internet Protocol Group

The Kinetics Internet Protocol (KIP)is used for the routing of AppleTalk Datagrams (Encapsulation) via an IP net. The KIP group manages both the KIP protocol and the routing tables.

Zone Information Protocol Group

The Zone Information Protocol (ZIP) is used for the mapping between network and zone names (Name Binding Protocols). The ZIP group permits both management of this protocol and mapping.

Name Binding Protocol Group

The Name Binding Protocol (NBP) serves as a Transport Level Protocol. Its task is the conversion of Service names into numerical AppleTalk network addresses. The NBP group provides for management of these protocols and of the NBP services.

AppleTalk Echo Protocol Group

The AppleTalk Echo Protocol is used as a Transport Level Protocol. The ATEcho group permits tests and status requests in an AppleTalk network.

The AppleTalk specific interface value in MIB II was given the following object identifier:

```
appletalk Object Identifier ::= { MIB II 13 }.
```

3.2.2.7 OSPF Version 2 Management Information Base

The OSPF Version 2 MIB published in RFC 1253 (August 1991) permits the integration of the Open Shortest Path First Protocol (OSPF) into a management system. The following data types were defined for the OSPF Version 2 MIB: AreaID, RouterID, TOSType, Metric, BigMetric, TruthValue, Status, Validation, PositiveInteger, HelloRange, UpToMaxAge, InterfaceIndex and DesignatedRouterPriority. The OSPF Version II MIB contains the following object groups:

- General variables;
- Area Data Structure;
- Area Stub Metric Table;
- Link State Database;
- Address Range Table;
- Host Table;
- Interface Table;
- Interface Metric Table;
- Virtual Interface Table;
- Neighbor Table;
- Virtual Neighbor Table.

General variables
The General variables define OSPF specific global variables.

Area Structure and Area Stub Metric Table
The Area Structure defines the OSPF areas to which the router belongs. The Area Stub Metric Table describes the metrics offered by the default router in a stub area.

Link State Database
The Link State Database contains information needed mainly for debugging.

Address Table and Host Table
The Address Range Table and the Host Table contain a survey of all configured networks and all Host Route information.

Interface and Interface Metric Tables
The Interface Table and the Interface Metric Table describe the various IP Interfaces within OSPF. The Metric Count values are stored in a separate table.

Virtual Interface Table
The Virtual Interface Table describes the virtual connections with the OSPF process.

Neighbor and Virtual Neighbor Tables
The Neighbor Table and Virtual Neighbor Table describe the OSPF neighbors.

The OSPF Version 2 specific value in MIB II was given the following Object Identifier:

```
ospf Object Identifier ::= { MIB II 14 }.
```

3.2.2.8 Border Gateway Protocol [Version 3] MIB

The Border Gateway Protocol (Version 3) was published in October 1991 as RFC 1269. These variables permit management of devices supporting the Border Gateway Protocol (BGP) as an InterAutonomous System Routing Protocol. The BGP (Version 3) MIB was divided into two tables: the BGP Peer Table and the BGP Received Path Attribute Table.

BGP Peer Table
The Peer Table contains all the information (connection state and current activities) of all BGP Peer connections.

BGP Received Path Attribute Table
The Received Path Attribute Table contains all the routing attributes that were received from the neighbor peers.

The BGP (Version 3) specific value in the MIB II was given the following object identifier:

```
bgp Object Identifier ::= { MIB II 15 }.
```

In addition, the RMON can store current values when freely configured threshold values are exceeded and advise the network manager accordingly, if required.

3.2.2.9 Remote Network Monitoring Management Information Base

The Remote Network Monitoring (RMON) MIB was published in November 1991. It permits management and monitoring of remote networks via a probe. The implementation of the RMON MIB provides for the recording of certain network events even in cases where the network management station is not actively linked to the device (probe) to be monitored. Thus, the probe may be configured to monitor the net continuously and collect statistical data. If certain threshold values are exceeded or certain events occur, the probe will attempt to inform the network management station of these events. Network performance data and fault history may also be recorded by the RMON MIB. The fault history may be accessed at any time in order to conduct targeted fault diagnoses.

Because the probe is directly linked to the monitored device, it is predestined to process network specific data (for example, to check which computers are communicating via the network, which computers cause most network faults and even to record certain data packets). The RMON MIB is divided into the following object groups: statistics, history, alarm, host, hostTopN, matrix, filter, packet capture and event.

Statistics Group

The Statistics Group contains statistics gathered by each probe for each monitored interface. Currently, the Statistics Group contains only the etherStats Table.

History Group

The History Group periodically records statistical net values and stores them for processing at a later date. Currently, the History Group comprises only the historyControl and etherHistory tables.

Alarm Group

The Alarm Group periodically checks the statistical values of a check variable and compares them to set threshold values. If the test variable values exceed the threshold values, an event (alarm) is generated. The Alarm Group contains the alarm table and relies on the implementation of the Event Group.

Host Group

The Host Group records statistics for each computer detected in the network on the basis of Source and Destination MAC addresses of all computers on the network. This group records all valid received packets. The Host Group comprises the hostControl table, the host table and the hostTime table.

HostTopN Group

The HostTopN Group enables the user to filter out computers (hosts) that lead or precede a statistic. The hostTopN Group contains the hostTopNControl and hostTopN tables. This group relies on the implementation of the Host Group.

Matrix Group

The Matrix Group records traffic statistics for two addresses. When communication between the two addresses is first established, a new entry is made in the table. The Matrix Group comprises three tables: the matrix Control table, the matrixSD table and the matrixDS table.

Filter group
The Filter Group provides for the 'diversion' of data packets on a certain channel if these packets match a certain set filter value. The Filter Group contains the filter table and the channel table.

Packet Capture Group
The Packet Capture Group permits the recording of data packets after they were sent to a certain channel. The Packet Capture Group contains the bufferControl and captureBuffer tables. The implementation of the Filter Group is necessary as the basic function for the Packet Capture Group.

Event Group
The Event Group monitors the sending of events and consists of the event table and the log table.

The RMON specific value in MIB II was given the following object identifier:

```
rmon Object Identifier ::= { MIB II 16 }.
```

3.2.2.10 Token Ring RMON

In RFC 1513, the RMON MIB was expanded to include the Token Ring specification; some new groups were introduced and existing groups expanded:

- Token Ring MAC Layer Statistics Group;
- Token Ring Promiscuous Statistics Group;
- Token Ring MAC Layer History Group;
- Token Ring Promiscuous History Group;
- Token Ring Station Group;
- Token Ring Station Order Group;
- Token Ring Station Config Group;
- Token Ring Source Routing Group.

Token Ring MAC Layer Statistics Group
The Token Ring MAC Layer Statistics Group contains the MAC layer statistics (general statistics, fault statistics and ring load) compiled by each RMON agent/probe per monitored Token Ring interface.

Currently, the group contains only the tokenRingMLStats table. Support of the group is optional.

Token Ring Promiscuous Statistics Group
The Token Ring Promiscuous Statistics Group contains statistics on all non-MAC specific data packets (for example, data source, broadcasts/ multicasts, packet sizes, and so on) compiled by each RMON agent/ probe per monitored Token Ring Interface. The group consists of the tokenRingPStats table. Support of the group is optional.

Token Ring MAC Layer History Group
The Token Ring MAC Layer History Group periodically records general statistics for non-MAC layer specific information. These values are stored and processed at a later date. Currently, the group contains only the tokenRingMLHistory table. Support of the group is optional and requires implementation of the historyControl table.

Token Ring Promiscuous History Group
The Token Ring Promiscuous History Group periodically records general statistics for non-MAC layer specific information. These values are stored and processed at a later date. Currently, the group only contains the tokenRingPHistory table. Implementation of the group is optional and requires implentation of the historyControl table.

Token Ring Station Group
All statistics (active stations, ring status, active monitor, sender of Beacon Frames, and so on) for all stations linked to the local ring are stored in the Token Ring Station Group. The group contains only the ringStationControl table. Support of the group is optional.

Token Ring Station Order Group
The physical and logical order of the Token Ring devices in the ring is recorded and stored in the Token Ring Station Order Group. The group contains only the ringStationOrder table. Support of the group is optional.

Token Ring Station Config Group
The Token Ring Station Config Group permits adding and removing of Token Ring terminals, as well as reconfiguring, for example downloading of software. The group contains the ringStationConfigControl and ringStationConfig tables. Support of the group is optional.

Token Ring Source Routing Group
The Token Ring Source Routing Group compiles statistics for all source routing information sent via the ring. The group contains the sourceRoutingStats table. Implementation of this group is optional.

The Token Ring specific value was given the following object identifier in the RMON MIB:

```
tokenRing Object Identifier ::= { rmon 10 }.
```

3.2.2.11 Ethernet MIB

In December 1991, the Ethernet-like Interface Type MIB was published as RFC 1398. The Ethernet MIB permits management and administration of devices supporting the Ethernet (IEEE 802.3) CSMA/CD transfer mechanism. The Ethernet MIB is based on the IEEE 802.3 Layer Management specifications. The following values were defined in the Ethernet Standard MIB (ifType variable) for the different Ethernet specifications: ethernet-csmacd(6), iso88023csmacd(7) and starLan(11). The Ethernet specific interface value (ifSpecific variable) in MIB II was given the following object identifier:

```
dot3 OBJECT IDENTIFIER ::= { transmission 7).
```

3.2.2.12 FDDI MIB

In January 1992, the first version of the FDDI MIB was published. It was thoroughly revised in RFC 1512. This MIB permits monitoring of all FDDI devices by means of the SNMP protocol. FDDI variables and parameters were defined in accordance with the recommendations made by the ANSI X3T9.5 Committee and the SMT Committee. The value defined in the Internet Standard MIB (ifType variable) is fddi(15). The FDDI specific interface value (ifSpecific variable) in MIB II was given the following object identifier:

```
fddi Object Identifier ::= { transmission 15 }.
```

3.2.2.13 Bridge MIB

The Bridge MIB establishes the Management Information Base (MIB) required to monitor and configure an Ethernet bridge via SNMP. The Bridge MIB is based on the IEEE 802.1d draft standard. In addition, options for the support of both Source Routing Bridging and Transparent Bridging in the local and remote areas are implemented. The Bridge MIB is divided into the following object groups: dot1dBase, dot1dStp, dot1dSr, dot1dTp and dot1dStatic.

Dot1dBase Group
All objects required by all bridge types are defined in the Dot1dBase Group.

Dot1dStp Group
The Dot1dStp Group is only implemented for bridges supporting the Spanning Tree Protocol. These objects permit monitoring of all Bridge Spanning Tree states.

Dot1dSR Group
The D ot1dSr Group is only implemented for bridges supporting the Source Routing process. These objects permit monitoring of all Source Routing Bridging states.

Dot1dTp Group
The Dot1dTp Group is only implemented for bridges supporting the Transparent Bridging process. These objects permit monitoring of all Transparent Bridging states.

Dot1dStatic Group
The Dot1dStatic Group is only implemented for bridges supporting Destination Address Filtering. These objects permit monitoring of values relevant to the Destination Address Filtering mechanism.

3.2.2.14 Source Routing Bridge MIB

A revised version of RFC 1286 was published in RFC 1525 under the title *Definitions of Managed Objects for Source Routing Bridges*. This standard expands the Bridge MIB to include all managed objects used for Source Routing Bridges (IEEE 802.5M as a fixed component of IEEE 802.1D). The following new groups are integrated into the Source Routing Bridge MIB: dot1SR and dot1dPortPair.

The bridge specific values in MIB II were given the following object identifier:

```
dot1dBridge Object Identifier ::= { MIB II 17 }.
```

3.2.2.15 IEEE 802.3 Repeater Devices MIB

The Repeater MIB was published as a standard in RFC 1516 (October 1991). This specification enables the user to monitor and manage IEEE 802.3 10 Mbit/s baseband repeaters. The IEEE 802.3 Baseband repeater is also known as a hub or concentrator. The Repeater MIB is based on the IEEE draft standard P802.3K (Layer Management for Baseband

Repeaters), in accordance with Chapter 9, 'Repeater Units for 10 Mb/s Baseband Networks', defined in the IEEE 802.3/ISO 8802-3 CSMA/CD standard. The Repeater MIB is divided into the object groups Basic, Monitor and Address Tracking.

Basic Group
Basic Group objects are basic information and must be implemented in all repeaters. This group contains Status, Parameters and Control Objects referring to the complete repeater, port groups and individual ports.

Monitor Group
The optional Monitor Group contains objects permitting the compliation of statistics on the complete repeater, port groups and individual ports.

Address Tracking Group
The optional Address Tracking Group contains objects permitting the recording of MAC addresses for terminals connected to the repeater ports.

Repeater specific values in MIB II were given the following object indetifier:

```
snmpDot3RptrMgt Object Identifier ::= { MIB II 22 }.
```

3.2.2.16 DECNet Phase IV MIB Extensions

The DECnet Phase IV MIB published in RFC 1289 is based on the variables for the administration of DECnet networks operating jointly in a TCP/IP environment developed by the DECnet Phase IV MIB Working Group. RFC 1289 relies on the Digital Network Architecture Network Management Functional Specification Version 4.0.0 developed by Digital Equipment Corporation (DEC). The DECnet Phase IV MIB contains the following object groups: System Group, Network Management Group, Session Group, End Group, Routing Group, Circuit Group, DDCMP Group, DDCMP Multipoint Control Group, Ethernet Group, Counters Group, Adjacency Group, Line Group, Non Broadcast Line Group and Area Group.

The DECnet specific values in MIB II were given the following object identifier:

```
phiv  Object Identifier ::= { MIB II 18 }.
```

3.2.2.17 Definitions of managed objects for the SIP interface type

The SMDS Interface Protocol MIB published in February 1992 permits management and administration of SMDS devices with the SNMP protocol. Currently, only the value for the ifType variable in the Internet Standard MIB is defined: ip (31). The SIP specific interface values in MIB II were given the following object identifier:

```
sip   Object Identifier ::= { transmission 31 }.
```

3.2.2.18 Management Information Base for Frame Relay DTEs

The Frame Relay MIB was published in April 1992 and permits management of Frame Relay terminals. The basic Frame Relay model assumes the following precondition: the DTE has only one interface with the data net (physical link). This link gives access to a range of destinations via several virtual links. The Frame Relay MIB contains the following object groups: the Data Link Connection Management Interface (DLCMI), Circuit and Errors. The Frame Relay specific interface values in MIB II were given the following object identifier:

```
frame-relay   Object Identifier ::= { transmission 32 }.
```

3.2.2.19 Character Stream Devices MIB

The Character MIB was introduced in April 1992. The Character MIB is to be deployed for each interface (port) that transfers character streams, irrespective of whether it is a virtual or a physical interface/port (serial or parallel) with synchronous or asynchronous data streams. An RS-232 (V.24) interface in a PC or a parallel Centronics interface in a printer are the most common examples. The Character MIB is always used in combination with other MIBs: the PPP MIB, the RS-232-like MIB, and the Parallel printer-like MIB contain the variables for the physical layer, while the Character MIB or the PPP MIB is used as a service above one of these interfaces. The Character MIB should be implemented, for example, in terminal servers.

Character MIB specific values in MIB II were given the following object identifier:

```
char  Object Identifier ::= { MIB II 19 }.
```

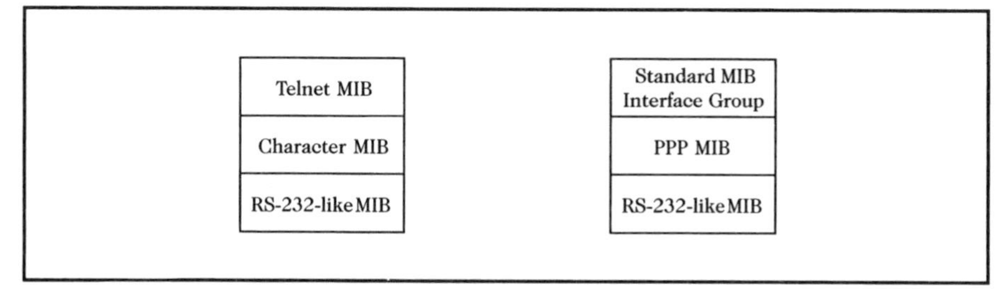

Figure 3.16 Areas of deployment for some MIBs (example)

3.2.2.20 RS-232-like Hardware Devices MIB

The RS-232 MIB was published at the same time as the Character MIB. This MIB decribes objects that enable the network manager to monitor the status of RS-232, RS-422, RS-423, V.35 (asynchronous or synchronous) interfaces and to trace possible faults. The RS-232 MIB is always used in combination with other MIBs: the PPP MIB or the Character MIB. The RS-232 MIB consists of an object group containing the following four tables: all ports, asynchronous ports, input signals and output signals. RS-232 specific values in MIB II were given the following object identifier:

```
rs232  Object Identifier ::= { transmission 33 }.
```

3.2.2.21 Parallel-printer-like Hardware Devices MIB

In April 1992, simultaneously with the Character MIB and the RS-232 MIB, the Parallel Printer MIB was published. This MIB describes objects allowing the network manager to monitor the status of a Centronics or other parallel printer port and to trace possible faults. The Parallel Printer MIB is always used in combination with other MIBs: the PPP MIB and the Character MIB. The Parallel Printer MIB comprises one object group containing three tables: all ports, input signals and output signals. Parallel Printer MIB specific values in MIB II were given the following object identifier:

```
para  Object Identifier ::= { transmission 34 }.
```

3.2.2.22 SNMP Party MIB

In July 1992, the Party MIB created the option to show special parameters of managed objects in their own MIB. The Party MIB contains the following object groups: Party Table, Acl Table, View Table and Context Table.

Party Table
The Party Table defines for each party its name, the appropriate encoding procedure and associated parameters (for example, public and private keys), respective authentication procedures and the transport address for the respective parties.

Acl Table
Access rights for the individual parties are defined in the Acl Table.

View Table
The View Table defines segments of the MIB that individual parties may access.

Context Table
The Context Table contains a list of MIB Views bearing a code which states whether or not the MIB View should be accessible.

Party MIB specific values in MIB II were given the following object identifier:

```
snmpParties   Object Identifier ::= { MIB II 20 }.
```

3.2.2.23 IP Forwarding Table MIB

In July 1992, the IP Forwarding Table MIB specification replaced the ipRouteTable defined in RFC 1213. The IP Forwarding Table MIB defines objects required to manage routes in an IP data net. IP Forwarding Table specific data in MIB II was given the following object identifier:

```
ipForward ::= { ip 24 }.
```

3.2.2.24 SNMP MIB Extensions for X.25 LAPB

The two parts of the X.25 MIB were published as RFC 1381 and RFC 1382 in November 1992. The X.25 LAPB MIB defines the objects required to manage the X.25 Data Link Layer (LAPB). The X.25 LAPB MIB is always used in combination with other MIBs: SNMP MIB Extension for the Packet Layer of X.25 and the Definitions of Managed Objects for RS-232-like Hardware Devices, in order to ensure comprehensive management of the complete X.25 protocol. The X.25 LAPB MIB definition is based on the following documents: *Information processing systems – Data communication – High-level data link control procedure – Description of the X.25 LAPB compatible data link procedures*, International Organization for Standardization, International Standard 7776, December 1986, and *Information technology – Telecommunications and information exchange between systems – High-level data link control (HDLC) procedures – General Purpose XID frame information field contents and format*, International Organization for Standardization, International Standard 8885. The X.25 LAPB MIB defined new data types, the PositiveInteger and the ifIndex types. An LAPB interface is identified in the Internet Standard MIB by the following ifType variable value:

```
lapb(16).
```

The X.25 LAPB MIB contains four tables: the LapbAdmin Table, the LapbOper Table, the LapbFlow Table and the LapbXid Table.

LapbAdmin Table
The LapbAdmin Table contains objects representing Standard LAPB parameters (for example, the T1 Retransmission Timer or the N2 Retransmission Counter).

LapbOper Table
The LapbOper Table contains objects representing the current parameter values of the LAPB interface.

LapbFlow Table
The LapbFlow Table contains objects that permit checks on the LAPB interface performance.

LapbXid Table
The LapbXid table should only be implemented in systems that can send XID frames.

LAPB MIB specific values in MIB II were given the following object identifier:

```
lapb  Object Identifier ::= { transmission 16 }.
```

3.2.2.25 SNMP MIB Extension for the X.25 Packet Layer

In November 1992, the X.25 MIB was published in two RFCs: RFC 1381 and RFC 1382. The X.25 Packet Layer MIB defines the objects required to manage the X.25 network layer. The X.25 MIB is always used in combination with other MIBs, SNMP MIB Extension for X.25 LAPB and the Definitions of Managed Objects for RS-232-like Hardware Devices, in order to ensure comprehensive management of the complete X.25 protocol. The X.25 Packet Layer MIB defines a new data type: the X121Address. A packet layer interface is recognized by the following ifType variable values in the Internet Standard MIB: ddn-x25(4) and rfc887-x25(5). The X.25 Packet Layer MIB contains the following tables: the x25Admn Table, the x25Oper Table, the x25Stat Table, the x25Channel Table, the x25Circuit Table, the x25ClearedCircuit Table and the x25CallParm Table.

x25Admn Table
The x25Admn table defines objects for X.25 interface parameters that can be set or selected by the administrator. These objects are initialized when the interface is initialized.

x25Oper Table
The x25Oper Table defines objects that permit the display of the interface parameters.

x25Stat Table
The x25Stat Table defines objects that may be used to compile statistics for the X.25 interface.

x25 Channel Table
The x25Channel Table defines objects that enable an administrator to manage the channel numbers.

x25Circuit Table
The x25Circuit Table defines objects giving information about certain (PVCs) X.25 links.

x25ClearedCircuit Table
The x25ClearedCircuit Table contains objects that indicate X.25 links aborted due to a fault.

x25CallParm Table
The x25CallParm Table defines the call parameters required to establish connections with certain systems.

The X.25 Packet Layer MIB specific values in MIB II have been given the following object identifier:

```
x25 Object Identifier ::= { transmission 5 }
```

3.2.2.26 RIP Version 2 MIB

RFC 1389 defines the RIP Version 2 MIB for the management of interface specific values when using RIP Version 2. The RIP 2 MIB contains global counters and statistics which will also support RIP Version 1 Protocol functions. The following groups are components of the RIP 2 MIB: the Global Group, the Interface Group, the Interface Status Table, the Interface Configuration Table, the Peer Table and the Peer Group.

Global Group
The Global Group must be implemented in all RIP 2 devices. Counters in this group serve to compile statistics.

Interfaces Group
The Interfaces Group must be implemented in all RIP 2 devices. Because RIP Versions 1 and 2 do not support links without address mapping, RIP interfaces are treated as subnets within a routing domain.

Peer Group
The Peer Group contains all information about active peers communicating via the RIP routing protocol. Implementation of this group is optional.

RIP 2 MIB specific values within MIB II were given the following object identifier:

```
rip2  Object Identifier ::= { MIB II 23}.
```

3.2.2.27 PPP MIB

The PPP Protocol mechanisms are divided into a range of sub-specifications: the Control Protocol, the Network Protocols and the Network Control Protocol.

Control Protocol
The Control Protocol delivers the Link Layer standards which are implemented as follows: Link Control Protocol (LCP), Password Authentication Protocol (PAP), Link Quality Report (LQR) and the Challenge Handshake Authentication Protocol (CHAP).

Network Protocols
The various network protocols serve to transfer protocol specific data via the PPP interface.

Network Control Protocols
Network Control Protocols (NCPs) govern protocol specific data traffic on a point-to-point link.

For this reason, the PPP MIB comprises four MIB sub-standards: Link Control Protocol MIB, Bridge Network Control MIB, IP Network Control MIB and the Security Protocol MIB for PPP. The following groups are introduced in the PPP MIB: PPP Link Group, PPP LQR Group, PPP LQR Extensions Group, PPP IP Group, PPP Bridge Group and the PPP Security Group. PPP MIB specific values in MIB II were given the following object identifier:

```
ppp   Object Identifier ::= { transmission 23 }.
```

3.2.2.28 Link Control Protocol MIB

The Link Control Protocol MIB for the Point-to-Point Protocol (PPP) was specified in RFC 1471. This specification includes the Link Control Protocol and the Link Quality Monitoring Protocol. The following groups are components of the Link Control Protocol MIB: PPP Link Group, PPP LQR Group and the PPP LQR Extensions Group.

PPP Link Group
The PPP Link Group must be supported by all PPP implementations. This group contains two tables, containing statistics and configuration data.

PPP LQR Group
All variables required to manage the PPP LQR protocol are gathered in the PPP LQR Group. This group contains two tables, both containing information about status and configuration. It must be supported by all PPP LQR implementations.

PPP LQR Extensions Group
The PPP LQR Extensions Group stores the last received LQR data packet so it may be analyzed in case of faults. This group is optional and need not be supported by all implementations.

Link Control Protocol MIB specific values within MIB II were inserted below the PPP MIB and given the following object identifier:

```
pppLcp Object identifier ::= { ppp1 }.
```

3.2.2.29 Security Protocol MIB

The Security Protocol MIB was published as RFC 1472. This document contains all PPP Authentication Protocol objects, and it defines the PPP Security Group. Implementation of the Security Group is compulsory for the SNMPv2 protocol, although these objects were not integrated into the

SNMPv1 protocol. The Security Group contains all managed variables required for configuration and monitoring of network security for the PPP protocol. Security protocol MIB specific values were inserted below the PPP MIB and given the following object identifier:

```
pppSecurity  Object Identifier ::= { ppp 2 }.
```

3.2.2.30 IP Network Control Protocol MIB

RFC 1473 defines the IP Network Control Protocol MIB which contains all managed objects for the IP Network Control Protocol. The PPP IP Group is an essential component of the IP Network Control Protocol MIB. It contains all variables regarding configuration, status and checks required for the efficient operation of the Internet Protocol (IP) on Point-to-Point links. This group is mandatory for all PPP implementations supporting the IP protocol. The IP Network Control Protocol MIB was inserted below the PPP MIB and given the following object identifier:

```
pppIp  Object Identifier ::= { ppp 3 }.
```

3.2.2.31 Bridge Network Control Protocol MIB

Request for Comments 1474 defines the Bridge Network Control Protocol MIB which contains all managed objects for the Bridge Network Control Protocol. The PPP Bridge Group is an essential component of the Bridge Network Control Protocol MIB. It contains all variables regarding configuration, status and checks required for correct bridging of transparent information on Point-to-Point links. This group is mandatory for all PPP implementations supporting bridging via PPP. Bridge Network Control Protocol MIB specific values were inserted below the PPP MIB and given the following object identifier:

```
pppBridge    Object Identifier ::= { ppp 4}.
```

3.2.2.32 OSI MIB

RFC 1214 created the option for integration of the variables and objects defined in the OSI into MIB II. Objects in this group may be accessed either via a pure OSI protocol stack or, with the CMIP variation, via TCP/IP. The OSI MIB is derived from the following standards: Open Systems Interconnection – Structure of Management Information: parts 1–4 (ISO/IEC DIS 10165), OSI Common Management Information Service (CMIS) and the Common Management Information Protocol (CMIP). OSI MIB specific values were given the following object identifier:

```
cmot  Object Identifier ::= { mib 9 }.
```

3.2.2.33 CLNS MIB

An experimental MIB was introduced in RFC 1238 under the title *CLNS MIB for use with Connectionless Network Protocol* (ISO 8473) and *End System to Intermediate System* (ISO 9542). All variables and objects required for management with use of the ISO Connectionless-mode Network Protocols and the End System to Intermediate System are defined in the CLNS MIB. CLNS MIB specific values were given the following experimental object identifier:

```
clns  Object Identifier ::= { experimental 1 }.
```

3.2.2.34 SNMP MIB for Multiprotocol Interconnect over X.25

RFC 1461 defines all objects and variables for multiprotocol operation via an X.25 net. The MIB defined in this RFC must be understood as an expansion of the SNMP MIB Extension for the X.25 packet layer, the SNMP MIB Extension for LAPB and the MIB for RS232-like Hardware Devices. The SNMP MIB for Multiprotocol Interconnect over X.25 was given the following object identifier:

```
miox  Object Identifier ::= { transmission 38 }.
```

3.2.2.35 IEEE 802.3 Medium Attachment Unit (MAU) MIB

The Request for Comments 1515 defines the IEEE 802.3 Medium Attachment Unit (MAU) MIB. The MIB definitions are based on draft 5 of the IEEE 802.3p specification entitled *Layer management for 10 Mb/s Medium*

Attachment Units. The MAU MIB contains new groups: the Repeater MAU Basic Group, the Interface MAU Basic Group and the Broadband MAU Basic Group.

Repeater MAU Basic Group
This group comprises all variables regarding configuration, status and checks required for efficient management of IEEE MAUs and capable of connection to a repeater. Implementation of the Repeater MAU Basic Group is mandatory.

Interface MAU Basic Group
The Interface MAU Basic Group comprises all variables regarding configuration, status and checks required for efficient management of IEEE MAU Interfaces. Implementation of this group is mandatory.

Broadband MAU Basic Group
All broadband specific variables needed during configuration are gathered in the Broadband MAU Basic Group. Implementation of the Broadband MAU Basic Group is mandatory for all 10 BROAD 36 MAUs.

The IEEE 802.3 Medium Attachment Unit MIB was given the following object identifier:

```
snmpDot3MauMgt Object Identifier ::= { MIB II 26 }.
```

3.2.2.36 Host Resources MIB

The Host Resources MIB (RFC 1514) defines global variables for use with all computers, workstations and PCs, irrespective of operating system, network services and application software. The Host Resources MIB relies on implementation of the Systems and Interface Groups of MIB II. The following new groups were integrated into the Host Resources MIB: Host Resources System Group, Host Resources Storage Group, Host Resources Running Software Group, Host Resources Running Software Performance Group and the Host Resources Installed Software Group.

Host Resources System Group
The Host Resources System Group must be implemented on all systems supporting this MIB. The group contains global information such as time, date, load device, path name, load parameter, number of active processes, and so on.

Host Resources Storage Group
The Host Resources Storage Group must be implemented on all devices supporting the Host Resources MIB. Information on memory used and

available, platform partitions, file system, swap space, RAM, and so on, is stored in tables in this group.

Host Resources Running Software Group
The Host Resources Running Software Group is optional. It contains information relevant to the software loaded in the physical or virtual memory. Among the information gathered in this group are device driver used, operating system and the applications.

Host Resources Running Software Performance Group
The Host Resources Running Software Performance Group is an optional implementation. It permits certain performance evaluations of currently loaded software products.

Host Resources Installed Software Group
This optional group permits the recording of software products as entries in a table and is used for inventories and diagnosis of incompatible products.

The Host Resources MIB was given the following object identifier:

```
host  Object Identifier ::= { MIB II 25 }.
```

3.2.2.37 Identification MIB

The Identification MIB was published as Request for Comments 1414. This MIB defines objects identifying the user of a TCP connection. The Ident Information System Group is a component of the Identification MIB and is mandatory for each implementation of the Identification MIB. The group contains tables with certain user information about a TCP link.

The Identification MIB was allocated the following object identifier:

```
ident  Object identifier ::= { MIB II 24 }.
```

The SNMP protocol may be expanded at any time by the simple measure of defining new MIBs. The multitude of available MIBs and objects, however, makes it increasingly difficult for the lay person to comprehend the subject with all its variables and functions. The only thing that can help in this situation is a good user interface that relieves the user of the necessity to grapple with individual variables and values.

- System Object Group
- Interface Object Group
- Address Translation Object Group
- Internet Protocol Object Group
    - IP Forward Object Group
- Internet Control Message Protocol Object Group
- Transmission Control Protocol Object Group
- User Datagram Protocol Object Group
- Exterior Gateway Protocol Object Group
- Transmission Object Group
    - Token Bus Object Group
    - Token Ring Object Group
    - T1 Carrier Object Group
    - DS3 Interface Type Object Group
    - DS1 Interface Type MIB
    - Ethernet Object Group
    - FDDI Object Group
    - SIP (SMDS) Object Group
    - Frame Relay Object Group
    - RS-232 Object Group
    - Parallel Printer Object Group
    - X.25 LAPB Object Group
    - X.25 Packet Layer Object Group
    - PPP MIB
        - Link Control Protocol MIB
        - Security Protocol MIB
        - IP Network Control Protocol MIB
        - Bridge Network Control Protocol MIB
- SNMP MIB for Multiprotocol Interconnect over X.25
- IEEE 802.3 Medium Attachment Unit (MAU) MIB
- RIP 2 MIB
- CMOT Object Group
- Simple Network Management Protocol Object Group
- Generic Interface Extension Object Group
- AppleTalk Object Group
- OSPF Version 2 Object Group
- BGP Version 3 Object Group
- RMON Object Group
    - Token Ring RMON MIB
- Bridge Object Group
- Repeater Object Group
- DECNet Phase IV Object Group
- Character Object Group
- SNMP Party Object Group
- Identification MIB
- Host Resources MIB
- Party MIB

Table 3.22 The MIB Object Groups

3.2.3 The SNMPv2 MIBs

At the same time as the SNMPv2 protocol specifications, a number of new SNMPv2 specific MIBs were published (Manager-to-Manager MIB, Management Information Base for SNMPv2 and Party MIB for SNMPv2).

3.2.3.1 Manager-to-Manager MIB

RFC 1451 defines the managed objects for the Manager-to-Manager MIB. This MIB eliminates a weakness of SNMP Version 1. Strict division into Agent (server process) and Network manager (agent process) was overthrown in favour of a flexible approach permitting the network manager in SNMPv2 to act in both an agent process and a server process. This function permits communication from manager to manager. The concepts of alarms, events and notifications was integrated into this MIB. On the basis of set alarm criteria, the consequential actions (events) are defined in the notifications. The Manager-to-Manager MIB contains three individual tables (alarm, event and notification tables) and their associated groups.

Alarm Group

The Alarm Group permits individual definition of alarm parameters. Thus, threshold values that are constantly compared with current values can be set. If a threshold value is exceeded, an event is initialized.

Event Group

An event table may be defined in this group to determine the actions of agent/manager if a certain threshold value is exceeded.

The following object identifier was given to the Manager-to-Manager MIB:

```
snmp2M2MObjects  Object identifier ::= { snmp2M2M 1 }.
```

3.2.3.2 Management Information Base for SNMPv2

RFC 1450 defines a Management Information Base (MIB) specifically for the SNMP Version 2 protocol. The following groups are contained in the SNMPv2 MIB: SNMPv2 Statistics Group, SNMPv1 Statistics Group, Object Resource Group, Traps Group and the Set Group.

The SNMPv2 Statistics Group

SNMPv2 specific statistics may be gathered with these objects.

The SNMPv1 Statistics Group
These objects may be used to gather SNMPv1 specific statistics.

The Object Resource Group
The Object Resource Group comprises all objects defined for an agent that are available for dynamic configuration.

The Traps Group
The Traps Group contains all objects defined for an agent that may be configured to transmit SNMPv2 Trap PDUs.

The Set Group
The Set Group contains all objects defined for a manager that are free to execute the Set function.

The following object identifier was allocated to the SNMPv2 MIB:

```
snmpMIBObjects Object Identifier ::= { snmpMIB I }.
```

3.2.3.3 Party MIB for SNMPv2

The Party MIB published as RFC 1447 enables the administrator to allocate MIB objects individually defined via the Parties to individual users. This means that several network management stations may access one agent. A certain segment of the MIB tree (MIB View) is configured for each of the parties, so each station can only read, or respectively write to, the objects provided for it. The following groups are integrated into the Party MIB: SNMPv2 Party Database Group, SNMPv2 Contexts Database Group, SNMPv2 Access Privileges Database Group and the MIB View Database Group.

SNMPv2 Party Database Group
All locally stored MIB View values for an agent are contained in the Party Database Group.
A number of corresponding values are defined for each defined MIB View, for example Transport Service, message lengths, authentication protocol used, authentication clock, time delay of transport link, encoding mechanism (for example, DES), global variables and variables exclusive to certain parties.

SNMPv2 Context Database Group
Information of purely local significance may be stored in tables in the Context Database Group. This also enables the developer to create SNMPv2 proxy management functions.

SNMPv2 Access Privileges Database Group
This database contains tables that define all party access mechanisms for this device.

MIB View Database Group
This database contains a table of all MIB Views for this device.

The SNMPv2 Party MIB was allocated the following object identifier:

```
partyAdmin   Object Identifier ::= { partyMIB I }.
```

3.2.4 The Management Information Base II

The Management Information Base II (MIB II) was described in Request for Comment 1213. MIB II defines all globally available management objects that can be administered in a TCP/IP data network. MIB II was given the following object identifier:

```
MIB II Object Identifier ::= { mgmt 1 }.
```

The Management Information Base II is divided into the following subgroups:

System (sys), Interfaces (if), Address Translation (AT), Internet Protocol (IP), Internet Control Message Protocol (ICMP), Transmission Control Protocol (TCP), User Datagram Protocol (UDP), Exterior Gateway Protocol (EGP), Common Management Information Protocol on Top of TCP/IP (CMOT), Transmission (Trans) and Simple Network Management Protocol (SNMP). The following object identifiers were given to the individual groups within MIB II:

```
system          OBJECT IDENTIFIER ::= { MIB II 1}
interfaces      OBJECT IDENTIFIER ::= { MIB II 2}
at              OBJECT IDENTIFIER ::= { MIB II 3}
ip              OBJECT IDENTIFIER ::= { MIB II 4}
icmp            OBJECT IDENTIFIER ::= { MIB II 5}
tcp             OBJECT IDENTIFIER ::= { MIB II 6}
udp             OBJECT IDENTIFIER ::= { MIB II 7}
egp             OBJECT IDENTIFIER ::= { MIB II 8}
cmot            OBJECT IDENTIFIER ::= { MIB II 9}
transmission    OBJECT IDENTIFIER ::= { MIB II 10}
snmp            OBJECT IDENTIFIER ::= { MIB II 11}
```

3.2.4.1 The System Group

The System Group variables must be supported by all SNMP implementations.

sysDescr Object Type

The System descriptor defines the device name, the software version and the hardware type exclusively in ASCII characters.

```
Syntax: DisplayString (SIZE (0..255))
Access: read only
Status: mandatory
::= { system 1 }
```

sysObjectID Object Type

The System Object ID defines the position of the managed device in the SMI Enterprise subtree.

```
Syntax: Object Identifier
Access: read only
Status: mandatory
::= { system 2 }
```

sysUpTime Object Type

The Object Type SysUpTime defines the time (in 1/100 seconds) since the last re-initializing of the network management software.

```
Syntax: TimeTicks
Access: read only
Status: mandatory
::= { system 3 }
```

sysContact Object Type

The System Contact contains a text string giving the name and address of the person responsible for this managed node.

```
Syntax: DisplayString (SIZE (0..255))
Access: read-write
Status: mandatory
::= { system 4 }
```

sysName Object Type

The System Name Object Type is a name defined by the system administrator for the node being managed, conventionally used as the fully qualified domain name.

```
Syntax: DisplayString (SIZE (0..255))
Access: read-write
Status: mandatory
::= { system 5 }
```

sysLocation Object Type

The System Location Object Type describes the physical location of the node under management.

```
Syntax: DisplayString (SIZE (0..255))
Access: read-write
Status: mandatory
::= { system 6 }
```

sysServices Object Type

The System Services Object Type is a value indicating the set of services (ISO) layers) provided by the node, where the Services Object corresponds to a sum starting with the basic value zero, then 1 through to 7 for each layer in the range. This applies to Internet and OSI protocols.

```
Syntax: INTEGER (0..127)
Access: read-only
Status: mandatory
::= { system 7 }
```

Interface-Group

The Interface Group implementation is mandatory for all systems.

ifNumber Object Type

The ifNumber Object Type describes the number of network interfaces on the system irrespective of their current status.

```
Syntax: INTEGER
Access: read-only
Status: mandatory
::= { interfaces 1 }
```

ifTable Object Type

The Interface Table Object Type defines a list of interface entries where the number of entries corresponds to the value of ifNumber.

```
Syntax: SEQUENCE OF IfEntry
Access: not-accessible
Status: mandatory
::= { interfaces 2 }
```

ifEntry Object Type

The Interface Entry Object Type contains an entry in a list containing the following information: the interface number, the interface description, definition of interface types, the size of the MTU and the transfer rate of the media specific interface address, the status of the interface, the time point of the latest status change, the total number of octets received, the total number of unicast packets, multicast packets and broadcast packets, the total number of all discarded packets, the total number of faulty packets, the total number of octets sent, the length of the output queue and an interface specific entry.

```
Syntax: IfEntry
Access: not-accessible
Status: mandatory
Index:  { ifIndex }
::= { ifTable 1 }
IfEntry ::=
  SEQUENCE {
    ifIndex
      INTEGER,
    ifDescr
      DisplayString,
    ifType
      INTEGER,
    ifMtu
      INTEGER,
    ifSpeed
      Gauge,
    ifPhysAddress
      PhysAddress,
    ifAdmin     Status
      INTEGER,
    ifOper     Status
      INTEGER,
    ifLastChange
      TimeTicks,
    ifInOctets
      Counter,
```

```
      ifInUcastPkts
        Counter,
      ifInNUcastPkts
        Counter,
      ifInDiscards
        Counter,
      ifInErrors
        Counter,
      ifInUnknownProtos
        Counter,
      ifOutOctets
        Counter,
      ifOutUcastPkts
        Counter,
      ifOutNUcastPkts
        Counter,
      ifOutDiscards
        Counter,
      ifOutErrors
        Counter,
      ifOutQLen
        Gauge,
      ifSpecific
        OBJECT IDENTIFIER
    }
```

ifIndex Object Type

BODY 3PT = The Interface Index Object Type defines the interface number (a unique value for each).

```
Syntax: INTEGER
Access: read-only
Status: mandatory
::= { ifEntry 1 }
```

ifDescr Object Type

The Interface Description Object Type is a text string which contains information about the interface. It should contain the vendor name, product name and hardware interface version number.

```
Syntax: DisplayString (SIZE (0..255))
Access: read-only
Status: mandatory
::= { ifEntry 2 }
```

ifType Object Type

The Interface Type Object Type defines the type of interface (Physical and Data Link Layer). The following interface types are distinguished: other(1), regular 1822(2), DDN 1822(3), ddn-x25(4), rfc 877-x25(5), Ethernet-CSMACD(6), ISO 88023-CSMACD(7), ISO 88024-Token Bus(8), ISO 88025-Token Ring(9), ISO 88026-MAN(10), StarLan(11), Proteon-10Mbit(12), Proteon-80Mbit(13), Hyperchannel(14), FDDI(15), LAPB(16), SDLC(17), DS1(18), E1(19), BasicISDN(20), PrimaryISDN(21), Proprietary serial prop Point-To-Point Serial(22), PPP(23), Software-Loopback(24), EON(25), CLNP over IP, Ethernet-3Mbit(26), NSIP(27), XNS over IP, SLIP(28), Generic SLIP ultra(29), ULTRA Technologies DS3(30), SIP(31), Frame-Relay(32).

```
Syntax: INTEGER
Access: read-only
Status: mandatory
::= { ifEntry 3 }
```

ifMtu Object Type

The Interface Maximum Transmission Unit defines the size of the largest datagram that can be sent and received on the interface (specified as octets).

```
Syntax: INTEGER
Access: read-only
Status: mandatory
::= { ifEntry 4 }
```

ifSpeed Object Type

The ifSpeed Object Type is defined as an estimate (in bits per second) of the interface's current bandwidth.

```
Syntax: Gauge
Access: read-only
Status: mandatory
::= { ifEntry 5 }
```

ifPhysAddress Object Type

Describes the physical hardware address of the interface. For interfaces with no address (for example, a serial line), the object should contain a zero length octet string.

```
Syntax: PhysAddress
Access: read-only
Status: mandatory
::= { ifEntry 6 }
```

ifAdminStatus Object Type

Defines the desired state of the interface as follows: Up(1), Down(2) and Testing(3).

```
Syntax: INTEGER
Access: read-write
Status: mandatory
::= { ifEntry 7 }
```

ifOperStatus Object Type

Describes the current operational condition or state of the interface as follows: Up(1), Down(2) and Testing(3).

```
Syntax: INTEGER
Access: read-only
Status: mandatory
::= { ifEntry 8 }
```

ifLastChange Object Type

Defines the value of sysUpTime when the interface became operational.

```
Syntax: TimeTicks
Access: read-only
Status: mandatory
::= { ifEntry 9 }
```

ifInOctets Object Type

Defines the total number of octets received on the interface (including framing characters).

```
Syntax: Counter
Access: read-only
Status: mandatory
::= { ifEntry 10 }
```

ifInUcastPkts Object Type

Defines the number of subnetwork unicast packets which are delivered to a higher-level protocol.

```
Syntax: Counter
Access: read-only
Status: mandatory
::= { ifEntry 11 }
```

ifInNUcastPkts Object Type

Defines the number of subnetwork multicast or broadcast (not unicast) packets delivered to a higher-level protocol.

```
Syntax: Counter
Access: read-only
Status: mandatory
::= { ifEntry 12 }
```

ifInDiscards Object Type

Defines the nuber of inbound packets discarded even though no errors were detected (often used to free up buffer space).

```
Syntax: Counter
Access: read-only
Status: mandatory
::= { ifEntry 13 }
```

ifInErrors Object Type

Defines the number of inbound packets containing errors which prevents them from being delivered to a higher-level protocol.

```
Syntax: Counter
Access: read-only
Status: mandatory
::= { ifEntry 14 }
```

ifInUnknownProtos Object Type

Defines the number of discarded packets that were received by the interface due to an unsupported or unrecognized protocol.

```
Syntax: Counter
Access: read-only
Status: mandatory
::= { ifEntry 15 }
```

ifOutOctets Object Type

Defines the total number of octets transmitted from the interface, including framing characters.

```
Syntax: Counter
Access: read-only
Status: mandatory
::= { ifEntry 16 }
```

ifOutUcastPkts Object Type

Defines the number of packets requested by a higher-level protocol to a subnetwork unicast address, including those packets not sent or discarded.

```
Syntax: Counter
Access: read-only
Status: mandatory
::= { ifEntry 17 }
```

ifOutNUcastPkts Object Type

The total number of multicast or broadcast packets requested by a higher-level protocol, including those packets not sent or discarded.

```
Syntax: Counter
Access: read-only
Status: mandatory
::= { ifEntry 18 }
```

ifOutDiscards Object Type

The number of outbound packets chosen to be discarded even though no errors were detected (often used to free up buffer space).

```
Syntax: Counter
Access: read-only
```

```
Status: mandatory
::= { ifEntry 19 }
```

ifOutErrors Object Type

The total number of outbound packets that were not transmitted due to errors.

```
Syntax: Counter
Access: read-only
Status: mandatory
::= { ifEntry 20 }
```

ifOutQLen Object Type

Defines the length of the output packet queue (measured in packets).

```
Syntax: Gauge
Access: read-only
Status: mandatory
::= { ifEntry 21 }
```

ifSpecific Object Type

Defines a reference to the MIB definition. For example, in the case of Ethernet, the object value refers to a document defining objects which are Ethernet specific.

```
Syntax: Object Identifier
Access: read-only
Status: mandatory
::= { ifEntry 22 }
```

3.2.4.2 The Address Translation Group

Implementation of the Address Translation Group is mandatory for all systems. This group is included only to provide compatibility with MIB I nodes and will not normally be included in MIB II nodes. From MIB II onwards, every network protocol group incorporates its own address translation tables.

```
atTable Object Type
   Description: 'These tables contain the network address to
   physical address equivalences.' Not all interfaces use
   translation tables to determine the address equivalences.
   Syntax: SEQUENCE OF AtEntry
   Access: not-accessible
   Status: deprecated
   ::= { at 1 }

atEntry Object Type
   Description: 'A table which equates one network address to a
   physical address'. For example, a mapping between a physical
   and an IP address.
   Syntax: AtEntry
   Access: not-accessible
   Status: depreciated
   Index:  { atIfIndex,
           atNetAddress }
      ::= { atTable 1 }

AtEntry ::=  SEQUENCE {
     atIfIndex
       INTEGER,
     atPhysAddress
       PhysAddress,
     atNetAddress
       NetworkAddress  }

atIfIndex Object Type
   Description: 'Contains the interface number.'
   Syntax: INTEGER
   Access: read-write
   Status: depreciated
   ::= { atEntry 1 }

atPhysAddress Object Type
   Description: 'Contains the physical hardware address.'
   Syntax: PhysAddress
   Access: read-write
   Status: depreciated
   ::= { atEntry 2 }

atNetAddress Object Type
   Description: 'The network address that corresponds to the
   media dependent physical address (for example the IP
   address).'
   Syntax: NetworkAddress
   Access: read-write
   Status: depreciated
   ::= { atEntry 3 }
```

3.2.4.3 The Internet Protocol (IP) Group

Implementation of the Internet Protocol (IP) Group is mandatory for all SNMP-based systems that implement the IP.

```
ipForwarding Object Type
   Description: 'Defines if the entity is acting as an IP
   gateway with respect to datagrams forwarded to it, but not
   addressed to it. Values are as follows: Forwarding(1) acting
   as a Router not forwarding. Also Not Forwarding(2) - Not
   acting as a Router.'
   Syntax: INTEGER
   Access: read-write
   Status: mandatory
   ::= { ip 1 }

ipDefaultTTL Object Type
   Description: 'Defines the default value inserted into the
   time-to-live field of the IP header of this entity-originated
   datagram.'
   Syntax: INTEGER
   Access: read-write
   Status: mandatory
   ::= { ip 2 }

ipInReceives Object Type
   Description: 'The total interface-received input datagrams,
   including those received in error.'
   Syntax: Counter
   Access: read-only
   Status: mandatory
   ::= { ip 3 }

ipInHdrErrors Object Type
   Description: 'The total number of input datagams discarded
   due to IP protocol header errors.'
   Syntax: Counter
   Access: read-only
   Status: mandatory
   ::= { ip 4 }

ipInAddrErrors Object Type
   Description: 'The total number of input datagrams discarded
   because the IP address in their IP header destination field
   was not valid for this entity.'
   Syntax: Counter
   Access: read-only
   Status: mandatory
   ::= { ip 5 }
```

```
ipForwDatagrams Object Type
   Description: 'Defines the number of datagrams that were not
   destined for this entity.'
   Syntax: Counter
   Access: read-only
   Status: mandatory
   ::= { ip 6 }

ipInUnknownProtos Object Type
   Description: 'Contains the number of successfully received
   datagrams discarded because of unsupported or unrecognized
   protocols.'
   Syntax: Counter
   Access: read-only
   Status: mandatory
   ::= { ip 7 }

ipInDiscards Object Type
   Description: 'Defines the number of input IP datagrams that
   were discarded even though no problems were encountered.'
   Syntax: Counter
   Access: read-only
   Status: mandatory
   ::= { ip 8 }

ipInDelivers Object Type
   Description: 'Defines the total number of input datagrams
   successfully delivered to IP user protocols (including
   ICMP datagrams).'
   Syntax: Counter
   Access: read-only
   Status: mandatory
   ::= { ip 9 }

ipOutRequests Object Type
   Description: 'The number of IP datagrams that local IP user
   protocols supplied to IP in requests for transmission
   (including ICMP datagrams)'
   Syntax: Counter
   Access: read-only
   Status: mandatory
   ::= { ip 10 }

ipOutDiscards Object Type
   Description: 'The number of output IP datagrams with no
   problems encountered their transmission to their final
   destination but discarded (usually because of limited
   buffer space).'
   Syntax: Counter
   Access: read-only
   Status: mandatory
   ::= { ip 11 }
```

```
ipOutNoRoutes Object Type
   Description: 'Defines the number of IP datagrams discarded
   because no route could be found to deliver them to their
   final destination.'
   Syntax: Counter
   Access: read-only
   Status: mandatory
   ::= { ip 12 }

ipReasmTimeout Object Type
   Description: 'Defines the maximum time in seconds while
   received fragments are held pending reassembly at this
   entity.'
   Syntax: INTEGER
   Access: read-only
   Status: mandatory
   ::= { ip 13 }

ipReasmReqds Object Type
   Description: 'Defines the number of IP fragments received by
   this entity that need to be reassembled by this entity.'
   Syntax: Counter
   Access: read-only
   Status: mandatory
   ::= { ip 14 }

ipReasmOKs Object Type
   Description: 'The number of successfully reassembled IP
   datagrams.'
   Syntax: Counter
   Access: read-only
   Status: mandatory
   ::= { ip 15 }

ipReasmFails Object Type
   Description: 'Defines the number of failures detected by the
   IP reassembly algorithm for whatever reason.'
   Syntax: Counter
   Access: read-only
   Status: mandatory
   ::= { ip 16 }

ipFragOKs Object Type
   Description: 'The number of successfully fragmented IP
   datagrams at this entity.'
   Syntax: Counter
   Access: read-only
   Status: mandatory
   ::= { ip 17 }
```

```
ipFragFails Object Type
   Description: 'The number of discarded IP datagrams that
   should have been fragmented at this entity but could not be,
   for example because their Don't fragment flag was set.'
   Syntax: Counter
   Access: read-only
   Status: mandatory
   ::= { ip 18 }

ipFragCreates Object Type
   Description: 'The number of IP fragments generated as a
   result of fragmentation at this entity.'
   Syntax: Counter
   Access: read-only
   Status: mandatory
   ::= { ip 19 }

ipAddrTable Object Type
   Description: 'The address table information relevant to the
   device's IP addresses.'
   Syntax: SEQUENCE OF IpAddrEntry
   Access: not-accessible
   Status: mandatory
   ::= { ip 20 }

ipAddrEntry Object Type
   Description: 'The address information for one of this
   device's IP addresses.'
   Syntax: IpAddrEntry
   Access: not-accessible
   Status: mandatory
   ::= { ipAddrTable 1 }

IpAddrEntry ::=  SEQUENCE {
      ipAdEntAddr
        IpAddress,
      ipAdEntIfIndex
        INTEGER,
      ipAdEntNetMask
        IpAddress,
      ipAdEntBcastAddr
        INTEGER,
      ipAdEntReasmMaxSize
        INTEGER (0..65535)
   }

ipAdEntAddr Object Type
   Description: 'The device specific IP address information
   (relevant to this device).'
   Syntax: IpAddress
   Access: read-only
   Status: mandatory
   ::= { ipAddrEntry 1 }
```

```
ipAdEntIfIndex Object Type
   Description: 'Contains the interface number of the respective
   entries in the ipAddrEntry Object table.'
   Syntax: INTEGER
   Access: read-only
   Status: mandatory
   ::= { ipAddrEntry 2 }

ipAdEntNetMask Object Type
   Description: 'Contains the IP subnet mask entry in the
   ipAddrEntry Object table.'
   Syntax: IpAddress
   Access: read-only
   Status: mandatory
   ::= { ipAddrEntry 3 }

ipAdEntBcastAddr Object Type
   Description: 'Defines the broadcast address entries in the
   ipAddrEntry Object table.'
   Syntax: INTEGER
   Access: read-only
   Status: mandatory
   ::= { ipAddrEntry 4 }

ipAdEntReasmMaxSize Object Type
   Description: 'Defines for this interface the size of the
   largest IP datagram that the device can reassemble from
   incoming fragmented IP datagrams received on this interface.'
   Syntax: INTEGER (0..65535)
   Access: read-only
   Status: mandatory
   ::= { ipAddrEntry 5 }

ipRouteTable Object Type
   Description: 'This device's own IP Routing table.'
   Syntax: SEQUENCE OF IpRouteEntry
   Access: not-accessible
   Status: mandatory
   ::= { ip 21 }

ipRouteEntry Object Type
   Description: 'Describes the route to a specific destination.'
   Syntax: IpRouteEntry
   Access: not-accessible
   Status: mandatory
   Index: { ipRouteDest }
    ::= { ipRouteTable 1 }

IpRouteEntry ::=  SEQUENCE {
     ipRouteDest
       IpAddress,
     ipRouteIfIndex
       INTEGER,
```

```
    ipRouteMetric1
      INTEGER,
    ipRouteMetric2
      INTEGER,
    ipRouteMetric3
      INTEGER,
    ipRouteMetric4
      INTEGER,
    ipRouteNextHop
      IpAddress,
    ipRouteType
      INTEGER,
    ipRouteProto
      INTEGER,
    ipRouteAge
      INTEGER,
    ipRouteMask
      IpAddress,
    ipRouteMetric5
      INTEGER,
    ipRouteInfo
      OBJECT IDENTIFIER
  }

ipRouteDest Object Type
   Description: 'Defines the destination IP address of this
   route. A device with the value of 0.0.0.0 is considered as a
   default route.'
   Syntax: IpAddress
   Access: read-write
   Status: mandatory
   ::= { ipRouteEntry 1 }

ipRouteIfIndex Object Type
   Description: 'Defines the index value that uniquely
   identifies the local interface relevant to the next hop.'
   Syntax: INTEGER
   Access: read-write
   Status: mandatory
   ::= { ipRouteEntry 2 }

ipRouteMetric1 Object Type
   Description: 'Describes the routing metric for this route.'
   Syntax: INTEGER
   Access: read-write
   Status: mandatory
   ::= { ipRouteEntry 3 }

ipRouteMetric2 Object Type
   Description: 'Describes the alternate routing metric for this
   route. This is determined by the ipRouteProto value.'
   Syntax: INTEGER
```

```
   Access: read-write
   Status: mandatory
   ::= { ipRouteEntry 4 }

ipRouteMetric3 Object Type
   Description: 'Describes the alternate routing metric for this
   Route. This is determined by the ipRouteProto value.'
   Syntax: INTEGER
   Access: read-write
   Status: mandatory
   ::= { ipRouteEntry 5 }

ipRouteMetric4 Object Type
   Description: 'Describes the alternate routing metric for this
   route. This value is determined by the routing protocol
   specified in the route ipRouteProto value.'
   Syntax: INTEGER
   Access: read-write
   Status: mandatory
   ::= { ipRouteEntry 6 }

ipRouteNextHop Object Type
   Description: 'Describes the IP address of the next hop on the
   route.'
   Syntax: IpAddress
   Access: read-write
   Status: mandatory
   ::= { ipRouteEntry 7 }

ipRouteType Object Type
   Description: Describes the type of route. The following
   values are examples: other(1), invalid(2), route to directly
   direct(3) and route to a non-local indirect(4).'
   Syntax: INTEGER
   Access: read-write
   Status: mandatory
   ::= { ipRouteEntry 8 }

ipRouteProto Object Type
   Description: 'Describes the routing mechanism by which this
   route was learned. The following values are examples:
   Other(1), Local(2), set via a network netmgmt(3), obtained
   via ICMP, icmp(4), EGP(5), GGP(6), hello(7), RIP(8), is-
   is(9), es-is(10), ciscoIgrp(11), BBNSpfIgp(12), OSPF(13) and
   BGP(14).
   Syntax: INTEGER
   Access: read-only
   Status: mandatory
   ::= { ipRouteEntry 9 }

ipRouteAge Object Type
   Description: 'Defines the time (in seconds) since this route
   was last updated.'
```

```
   Syntax: INTEGER
   Access: read-write
   Status: mandatory
   ::= { ipRouteEntry 10 }

ipRouteMask Object Type
   Description: 'Defines the subnet mask for this route.'
   Syntax: IpAddress
   Access: read-write
   Status: mandatory
   ::= { ipRouteEntry 11 }

ipRouteMetric5 Object Type
   Description: 'Defines an alternate route metric for this
   route.'
   Syntax: INTEGER
   Access: read-write
   Status: mandatory
   ::= { ipRouteEntry 12 }

ipRouteInfo Object Type
   Description: 'Defines an identifier, or reference to MIB
   definitions specific to the routing protocol used which is
   responsible for this route.'
   Syntax: Object IDENTIFIER
   Access: read-only
   Status: mandatory
   ::= { ipRouteEntry 13 }

ipNetToMediaTable Object Type
   Description: 'The IP address translation table used to map
   betwen physical and IP addresses.'
   Syntax: SEQUENCE OF IpNetToMediaEntry
   Access: not-accessible
   Status: mandatory
   ::= { ip 22 }

ipNetToMediaEntry Object Type
   Description: 'Contains an entry in the ipNetToMedia table,
   containing the following information: the interface number,
   the physical address, the IP address and the address
   equivalence.'
   Syntax: IpNetToMediaEntry
   Access: not-accessible
   Status: mandatory
   Index:  { ipNetToMediaIfIndex,
             ipNetToMediaNetAddress }
      ::= { ipNetToMediaTable 1 }

IpNetToMediaEntry ::=
   SEQUENCE {
     ipNetToMediaIfIndex
       INTEGER,
```

```
    ipNetToMediaPhysAddress
      PhysAddress,
    ipNetToMediaNetAddress
      IpAddress,
    ipNetToMediaType
      INTEGER
  }

ipNetToMediaIfIndex Object Type
   Description: 'Defines the interface number in the
   ipNetToMedia table.'
   Syntax: INTEGER
   Access: read-write
   Status: mandatory
   ::= { ipNetToMediaEntry 1 }

ipNetToMediaPhysAddress Object Type
   Description: 'Defines the physical hardware address in the
   ipNetToMedia table.'
   Syntax: PhysAddress
   Access: read-write
   Status: mandatory
   ::= { ipNetToMediaEntry 2 }

ipNetToMediaNetAddress Object Type
   Description: 'Defines the IP address corresponding to the
   physical address in the ipNetToMedia.table.'
   Syntax: IpAddress
   Access: read-write
   Status: mandatory
   ::= { ipNetToMediaEntry 3 }

ipNetToMediaType Object Type
   Description: 'Defines the procedure, how the IP address and
   the physical address in the ipNetToMedia table map to each
   other according to the following values: Other(1),
   Invalid(2), Dynamic(3) and Static(4).'
   Syntax: INTEGER
   Access: read-write
   Status: mandatory
   ::= { ipNetToMediaEntry 4 }

ipRoutingDiscards Object Type
   Description: 'The number of all the routing entries that were
   chosen to be discarded even if they were valid (for example,
   to free up buffer space).'
   Syntax: Counter
   Access: read-only
   Status: mandatory
   ::= { ip 23 }
```

3.2.4.4 The ICMP Group

The implementation of the Internet Control Message Protocol (ICMP) Group is mandatory for all SNMP protocol implementations that implement the ICMP.

```
icmpInMsgs Object Type
   Description: 'The total number of ICMP messages received by
   the device.'
   Syntax: Counter
   Access: read-only
   Status: mandatory
   ::= { icmp 1 }

icmpInErrors Object Type
   Description: 'The total number of ICMP messages received by
   the device but determined to have specific ICMP errors.'
   Syntax: Counter
   Access: read-only
   Status: mandatory
   ::= { icmp 2 }

icmpInDestUnreachs Object Type
   Description: 'The total number of unreachable ICMP
   destination messages.'
   Syntax: Counter
   Access: read-only
   Status: mandatory
   ::= { icmp 3 }

icmpInTimeExcds Object Type
   Description: 'The total number of ICMP Time Exceeded Messages
   received.'
   Syntax: Counter
   Access: read-only
   Status: mandatory
   ::= { icmp 4 }

icmpInParmProbs Object Type
   Description: 'The total number of ICMP Parameter Problem
   Messages received.'
   Syntax: Counter
   Access: read-only
   Status: mandatory
   ::= { icmp 5 }

icmpInSrcQuenchs Object Type
   Description: 'The total number of ICMP source quench messages
   received.'
   Syntax: Counter
   Access: read-only
   Status: mandatory
   ::= { icmp 6 }
```

```
icmpInRedirects Object Type
   Description: 'The total number of ICMP redirect messages
   received.'
   Syntax: Counter
   Access: read-only
   Status: mandatory
   ::= { icmp 7 }

icmpInEchos Object Type
   Description: 'The total number of ICMP Echo (request)
   messages received.'
   Syntax: Counter
   Access: read-only
   Status: mandatory
   ::= { icmp 8 }

icmpInEchoReps Object Type
   Description: 'The total number of ICMP Echo Reply messages
   received.'
   Syntax: Counter
   Access: read-only
   Status: mandatory
   ::= { icmp 9 }

icmpInTimestamps Object Type
   Description: 'The total number of ICMP Timestamp (request)
   messages received.'
   Syntax: Counter
   Access: read-only
   Status: mandatory
   ::= { icmp 10 }

icmpInTimestampReps Object Type
   Description: 'The total number of ICMP Timestamp Reply
   messages received.'
   Syntax: Counter
   Access: read-only
   Status: mandatory
   ::= { icmp 11 }

icmpInAddrMasks Object Type
   Description: 'The total number of ICMP Address Mask Request
   messages received.'
   Syntax: Counter
   Access: read-only
   Status: mandatory
   ::= { icmp 12 }

icmpInAddrMaskReps Object Type
Description: 'The total number of ICMP Address Mask Reply
messages received.'
   Syntax: Counter
   Access: read-only
```

```
   Status: mandatory
   ::= { icmp 13 }

icmpOutMsgs Object Type
   Description: 'The total number of ICMP Messages that the
   device attempted to send.'
   Syntax: Counter
   Access: read-only
   Status: mandatory
   ::= { icmp 14 }

icmpOutErrors Object Type
   Description: 'The total number of ICMP messages the device
   did not send due to problems discovered within the ICMP
   protocol; in some implementations the value may not directly
   relate to a type of error.'
   Syntax: Counter
   Access: read-only
   Status: mandatory
   ::= { icmp 15 }

icmpOutDestUnreachs Object Type
   Description: 'The number of ICMP Destination Unreachable
   messages sent.'
   Syntax: Counter
   Access: read-only
   Status: mandatory
   ::= { icmp 16 }

icmpOutTimeExcds Object Type
   Description: 'The number of ICMP Time Exceeded messages
   sent.'
   Syntax: Counter
   Access: read-only
   Status: mandatory
   ::= { icmp 17 }

icmpOutParmProbs Object Type
   Description: 'The number of ICMP Parameter Problem messages
   sent.'
   Syntax: Counter
   Access: read-only
   Status: mandatory
   ::= { icmp 18 }

icmpOutSrcQuenchs Object Type
   Description: 'The number of ICMP Source Quench messages
   sent.'
Sxntax: Counter
   Access: read-only
   Status: mandatory
   ::= { icmp 19 }
```

```
icmpOutRedirects Object Type
   Description: 'The number of ICMP Redirect messages sent.'
   Syntax: Counter
   Access: read-only
   Status: mandatory
   ::= { icmp 20 }

icmpOutEchos Object Type
   Description: 'The number of ICMP Echo (request) messages
   sent.'
   Syntax: Counter
   Access: read-only
   Status: mandatory
   ::= { icmp 21 }

icmpOutEchoReps Object Type
   Description: 'The number of ICMP Echo Reply messages sent.'
   Syntax: Counter
   Access: read-only
   Status: mandatory
   ::= { icmp 22 }

icmpOutTimestamps Object Type
   Description: 'The number of ICMP Timestamp (request) messages
   sent.'
   Syntax: Counter
   Access: read-only
   Status: mandatory
   ::= { icmp 23 }

icmpOutTimestampReps Object Type
   Description: 'The number of ICMP Timestamp Reply messages
   sent.'
   Syntax: Counter
   Access: read-only
   Status: mandatory
   ::= { icmp 24 }

icmpOutAddrMasks Object Type
   Description: 'The number of ICMP Address Mask Request
   messages sent.'
   Syntax: Counter
   Access: read-only
   Status: mandatory
   ::= { icmp 25 }

icmpOutAddrMaskReps Object Type
   Description: 'The number of ICMP Address Mask Reply messages
   sent.'
   Syntax: Counter
   Access: read-only
   Status: mandatory
   ::= { icmp 26 }
```

3.2.4.5 The Transmission Control Protocol (TCP) Group

Implementation of the TCP Group is mandatory for all SNMP-based systems that implement the Transmission Control Protocol. Instances of object types that represent information pertinent to a specific TCP connection are transient in nature; they exist only as long as the connection is made.

```
tcpRtoAlgorithm Object Type
   Description: 'Defines the algorithms used to determine the
   value of the timeout timers which are used to retransmit
   unacknowledged octets as in the following examples :
   Other(1), Constant(2), RSRE(3) and VANJ(4).'
   Syntax: INTEGER
   Access: read-only
   Status: mandatory
   ::= { tcp 1 }

tcpRtoMin Object Type
   Description: 'Defines the minimum retransmission timeout
   timer in a TCP session (in milliseconds).'
   Syntax: INTEGER
   Access: read-only
   Status: mandatory
   ::= { tcp 2 }

tcpRtoMax Object Type
   Description: 'Defines the maximum retransmission timeout
   timer in a TCP session (in milliseconds).'
   Syntax: INTEGER
   Access: read-only
   Status: mandatory
   ::= { tcp 3 }

tcpMaxConn Object Type
   Description: 'Defines the maximum number of all TCP sessions
   that can be supported by the device.'
   Syntax: INTEGER
   Access: read-only
   Status: mandatory
   ::= { tcp 4 }

tcpActiveOpens Object Type
   Description: 'The number of times TCP Connections have
   transitioned to the SYN-SENT state from the CLOSED state.'
   Syntax: Counter
   Access: read-only
   Status: mandatory
   ::= { tcp 5 }
```

```
tcpPassiveOpens Object Type
   Description: 'The number of times TCP Connections have
   transitioned from the SYN-RCVD state to the LISTEN state.'
   Syntax: Counter
   Access: read-only
   Status: mandatory
   ::= { tcp 6 }

tcpAttemptFails Object Type
   Description: 'The number of times TCP connections directly
   transitioned to the CLOSED state from either the SYN-SENT or
   SYN-RCVD state, plus the number of times TCP connections have
   directly transitioned to the LISTEN state from the SYN-RCVD
   state.'
   Syntax: Counter
   Access: read-only
   Status: mandatory
   ::= { tcp 7 }

tcpEstabResets Object Type
   Description: 'The number of times TCP connections directly
   transitioned to the CLOSED state from either the ESTABLISHED
   or CLOSE-WAIT state'
   Syntax: Counter
   Access: read-only
   Status: mandatory
   ::= { tcp 8 }

tcpCurrEstab Object Type
   Description: 'The number of TCP connections where the current
   state is either an ESTABLISHED or CLOSE WAIT state.'
   Syntax: Gauge
   Access: read-only
   Status: mandatory
   ::= { tcp 9 }

tcpInSegs Object Type
   Description: 'The total number of TCP segments received
   including those received in error.'
   Syntax: Counter
   Access: read-only
   Status: mandatory
   ::= { tcp 10 }

tcpOutSegs Object Type
   Description: 'The total number of TCP segments sent.'
   Syntax: Counter
   Access: read-only
   Status: mandatory
   ::= { tcp 11 }
```

```
tcpRetransSegs Object Type
   Description: 'The total number of TCP segments transmitted
   which contained one or more previously transmitted octets.'
   Syntax: Counter
   Access: read-only
   Status: mandatory
   ::= { tcp 12 }

tcpConnTable Object Type
   Description: 'This table contains TCP connection-specific
   information.'
   Syntax: SEQUENCE OF TcpConnEntry
   Access: not-accessible
   Status: mandatory
   ::= { tcp 13 }

tcpConnEntry Object Type
   Description: 'Contains information about a particular TCP
   current connection. This is a transient object; it ceases to
   exist at the time (or soon after) the connection transitions
   to the CLOSED state.'
   Syntax: TcpConnEntry
   Access: not-accessible
   Status: mandatory
   Index: { tcpConnLocalAddress,
            tcpConnLocalPort,
            tcpConnRemAddress,
            tcpConnRemPort }
   ::= { tcpConnTable 1 }

TcpConnEntry ::=
    SEQUENCE {
      tcpConnState
        INTEGER,
      tcpConnLocalAddress
        IpAddress,
      tcpConnLocalPort
        INTEGER (0..65535),
      tcpConnRemAddress
        IpAddress,
      tcpConnRemPort
        INTEGER (0..65535)
    }

tcpConnState Object Type
   Description: 'Defines the condition of a TCP connection. The
   following example values are relevant to this TCP Connection
   State Object: Closed(1), Listen(2), SynSent(3),
   SynReceived(4), Established(5), FinWait1(6), FinWait2(7),
   CloseWait(8), LastAck(9), Closing(10), TimeWait(11) and
   DeleteTCB(12).'
```

```
   Syntax: INTEGER
   Access: read-write
   Status: mandatory
   ::= { tcpConnEntry 1 }

tcpConnLocalAddress Object Type
   Description: 'The local address for this TCP connection.'
   Syntax: IpAddress
   Access: read-only
   Status: mandatory
   ::= { tcpConnEntry 2 }

tcpConnLocalPort Object Type
Description: 'The local port number for this TCP connection.'
   Syntax: INTEGER (0..65535)
   Access: read-only
   Status: mandatory
   ::= { tcpConnEntry 3 }

tcpConnRemAddress Object Type
   Description: 'The remote IP address for this TCP connection.'
   Syntax: IpAddress
   Access: read-only
   Status: mandatory
   ::= { tcpConnEntry 4 }

tcpConnRemPort Object Type
   Description: 'The remote port number for this TCP
   connection.'
   Syntax: INTEGER (0..65535)
   Access: read-only
   Status: mandatory
   ::= { tcpConnEntry 5 }

tcpInErrs Object Type
   Description: 'The total number of TCP segments received in
   error.'
   Syntax: Counter
   Access: read-only
   Status: mandatory
   ::= { tcp 14 }

tcpOutRsts Object Type
   Description: 'The total number of TCP segments that were sent
   containing the RST flag.'
   Syntax: Counter
   Access: read-only
   Status: mandatory
   ::= { tcp 15 }
```

3.2.4.6 The User Datagram Protocol (UDP) Group

The implementation of the UDP Group is mandatory for all SNMP-based systems that use the User Datagram Protocol.

```
udpInDatagrams Object Type
   Description: 'The total number of UDP datagrams delivered to
   UDP users.'
   Syntax: Counter
   Access: read-only
   Status: mandatory
   ::= { udp 1 }

udpNoPorts Object Type
   Description: 'The total number of UDP datagrams received for
   which there was no application at the destination.'
   Syntax: Counter
   Access: read-only
   Status: mandatory
   ::= { udp 2 }

udpInErrors Object Type
   Description: 'The number of UDP datagrams received that were
   unable to be delivered for reasons other than the lack of an
   application at the destination port.'
   Syntax: Counter
   Access: read-only
   Status: mandatory
   ::= { udp 3 }

udpOutDatagrams Object Type
   Description: 'The total number of UDP datagrams sent from
   this device or entity.'
   Syntax: Counter
   Access: read-only
   Status: mandatory
   ::= { udp 4 }

udpTable Object Type
   Description: 'A table that contains UDP listener
   information.'
   Syntax: SEQUENCE OF UdpEntry
   Access: not-accessible
   Status: mandatory
   ::= { udp 5 }

udpEntry Object Type
   Description: 'Contains information on a specific current UDP
   listener.'
   Syntax: UdpEntry
   Access: not-accessible
```

```
   Status: mandatory
   Index: { udpLocalAddress, udpLocalPort }
   ::= { udpTable 1 }

UdpEntry ::=  SEQUENCE {
     udpLocalAddress
       IpAddress,
     udpLocalPort
       INTEGER (0..65535)
   }

udpLocalAddress Object Type
   Description: 'Defines the local IP address for this UDP
   listener.'
   Syntax: IpAddress
   Access: read-only
   Status: mandatory
   ::= { udpEntry 1 }

udpLocalPort Object Type
   Description: 'Defines the local port number for this UDP
   listener.'
   Syntax: INTEGER (0..65535)
   Access: read-only
   Status: mandatory
   ::= { udpEntry 2 }
```

3.2.4.7 The Exterior Gateway Protocol (EGP) Group

The implementation of the EGP Group is mandatory for all SNMP-based systems that incorporate the EGP.

```
egpInMsgs Object Type
   Description: 'The number of error-free received EGP
   messages.'
   Syntax: Counter
   Access: read-only
   Status: mandatory
   ::= { egp 1 }

egpInErrors Object Type
   Description: 'The number of EGP messages which were proved to
   have been received in error.'
   Syntax: Counter
   Access: read-only
   Status: mandatory
   ::= { egp 2 }
```

```
egpOutMsgs Object Type
   Description: 'The total number of locally generated EGP
   messages.'
   Syntax: Counter
   Access: read-only
   Status: mandatory
   ::= { egp 3 }

egpOutErrors Object Type
   Description: 'Defines the number of locally EGP messages
   generated that were not sent because of resource limitations
   within an EGP device.'
   Syntax: Counter
   Access: read-only
   Status: mandatory
   ::= { egp 4 }

egpNeighTable Object Type
   Description: 'Contains the EGP Neighbor Table.'
   Syntax: SEQUENCE OF EgpNeighEntry
   Access: not-accessible
   Status: mandatory
   ::= { egp 5 }

egpNeighEntry Object Type
   Description: 'Defines the connection and the status of a
   specific EGP Neighbor relative to this device as defined in
   the EGP Neighbor Table.'
   Syntax: EgpNeighEntry
   Access: not-accessible
   Status: mandatory
   Index: { egpNeighAddr }
   ::= { egpNeighTable 1 }

EgpNeighEntry ::=
   SEQUENCE {
     egpNeighState
       INTEGER,
     egpNeighAddr
       IpAddress,
     egpNeighAs
       INTEGER,
     egpNeighInMsgs
       Counter,
     egpNeighInErrs
       Counter,
     egpNeighOutMsgs
       Counter,
     egpNeighOutErrs
       Counter,
```

```
    egpNeighInErrMsgs
      Counter,
    egpNeighOutErrMsgs
      Counter,
    egpNeighStateUps
      Counter,
    egpNeighStateDowns
      Counter,
    egpNeighIntervalHello
      INTEGER,
    egpNeighIntervalPoll
      INTEGER,
    egpNeighMode
      INTEGER,
    egpNeighEventTrigger
      INTEGER
  }

egpNeighState Object Type
   Description: 'Defines the condition of the local EGP systems
   in relation to this device's EGP Neighbor. The following
   values are applicable: Idle(1), Acquisition(2), Down(3),
   Up(4) und Cease(5).'
   Syntax: INTEGER
   Access: read-only
   Status: mandatory
   ::= { egpNeighEntry 1 }

egpNeighAddr Object Type
   Description: 'Defines the IP address of this entity's EGP
   Neighbors.'
   Syntax: IpAddress
   Access: read-only
   Status: mandatory
   ::= { egpNeighEntry 2 }

egpNeighAs Object Type
   Description: 'Defines the autonomous system number of this
   EGP peer.'
   Syntax: INTEGER
   Access: read-only
   Status: mandatory
   ::= { egpNeighEntry 3 }

egpNeighInMsgs Object Type
   Description: 'The number of all error-free EGP Messages
   received from this EGP peer.'
   Syntax: Counter
   Access: read-only
   Status: mandatory
   ::= { egpNeighEntry 4 }
```

```
egpNeighInErrs Object Type
   Description: 'The total number of EGP messages from this EGP
   peer which were proved to be in error.'
   Syntax: Counter
   Access: read-only
   Status: mandatory
   ::= { egpNeighEntry 5 }

egpNeighOutMsgs Object Type
   Description: 'The total number of locally generated EGP
   messages to this EGP peer.'
   Syntax: Counter
   Access: read-only
   Status: mandatory
   ::= { egpNeighEntry 6 }

egpNeighOutErrs Object Type
   Description: 'The total number of locally generated EGP
   Messages that were not sent to this EGP peer due to resource
   limitations within an EGP entity.'
   Syntax: Counter
   Access: read-only
   Status: mandatory
   ::= { egpNeighEntry 7 }

egpNeighInErrMsgs Object Type
   Description: 'The total n umber of EGP defined error messages
   that were received by this EGP peer.'
   Syntax: Counter
   Access: read-only
   Status: mandatory
   ::= { egpNeighEntry 8 }

egpNeighOutErrMsgs Object Type
   Description: 'The total number of all EGP defined error
   messages that were sent to this EGP peer.'
   Syntax: Counter
   Access: read-only
   Status: mandatory
   ::= { egpNeighEntry 9 }

egpNeighStateUps Object Type
   Description: 'The total number of EGP state transitions to
   the UP state relevant to this EGP peer.'
   Syntax: Counter
   Access: read-only
   Status: mandatory
   ::= { egpNeighEntry 10 }
```

```
egpNeighStateDowns Object Type
   Description: 'The total number of EGP state transitions from
   the UP state to any other state with this EGP peer.'
   Syntax: Counter
   Access: read-only
   Status: mandatory
   ::= { egpNeighEntry 11 }

egpNeighIntervalHello Object Type
   Description: 'Defines the interval (in 1/100 seconds) between
   EGP Hello commands. This value corresponds to the EGP t1
   timer.'
   Syntax: INTEGER
   Access: read-only
   Status: mandatory
   ::= { egpNeighEntry 12 }

egpNeighIntervalPoll Object Type
   Description: 'Defines the interval (in 1/100 seconds) between
   EGP polls. This value corresponds to the EGP t3 timer.'
   Syntax: INTEGER
   Access: read-only
   Status: mandatory
   ::= { egpNeighEntry 13 }

   egpNeighMode Object Type
   Description: 'Defines the polling mode of the EGP device. It
   can be: Active(1) or Passive(2).'
   Syntax: INTEGER
   Access: read-only
   Status: mandatory
   ::= { egpNeighEntry 14 }

egpNeighEventTrigger Object Type
   Description: 'This control variable is used to start and stop
   operator-initiated events. The following variables are valid:
   Start(1) or Stop(2).'
   Syntax: INTEGER
   Access: read-write
   Status: mandatory
   ::= { egpNeighEntry 15 }

egpAs Object Type
   Description: 'Defines the autonomous system number of the EGP
   device or entity.'
   Syntax: INTEGER
   Access: read-only
   Status: mandatory
   ::= { egp 6 }
```

3.2.4.8 The Transmission Group

Based on the underlying transmission media (Ethernet MIB, Token Ring MIB, FDDI MIB, Bridge MIB, and so on), each interface on a system must incorporate the corresponding portion of the Transmission group. When managing the above transmission media using Internet standard definitions, the transmission group is used to provide a prefix for these named objects. Generally these definitions reside in the experimental part of the MIB until they are proven. When standardized they are elevated and defined under a new object identifier.

3.2.4.9 The CMOT Group

The elements of the CMOT Group are for a future OSI management based on the TCP/IP protocol stack. The definition of this MIB is not yet fixed, but this group is under review.

3.2.4.10 The SNMP Group

The implementation of the SNMP Group is mandatory for all systems that support an SNMP protocol device.

```
snmpInPkts Object Type
   Description: 'The total number of messages delivered from the
   transport service to the SNMP device.'
   Syntax: Counter
   Access: read-only
   Status: mandatory
   ::= { snmp 1 }
snmpOutPkts Object Type
   Description: 'The total number of SNMP messages passed to the
   transport service from the SNMP protocol device.'
   Syntax: Counter
   Access: read-only
   Status: mandatory
   ::= { snmp 2 }
snmpInBadVersions Object Type
   Description: 'The total number of SNMP messages delivered to
   the SNMP protocol device that were for an unsupported version
   of SNMP.'
   Syntax: Counter
   Access: read-only
   Status: mandatory
   ::= { snmp 3 }
```

```
snmpInBadCommunityNames Object Type
   Description: 'The total number of SNMP messages delivered to
   the SNMP protocol device that used an SNMP community name not
   recognized by the device.'
   Syntax: Counter
   Access: read-only
   Status: mandatory
   ::= { snmp 4 }

snmpInBadCommunityUses Object Type
   Description: 'The total number of SNMP messages delivered to
   the SNMP protocol device that represented an SNMP operation
   not allowed by the SNMP community named in the,message.'
   Syntax: Counter
   Access: read-only
   Status: mandatory
   ::= { snmp 5 }

snmpInASNParseErrs Object Type
   Description: 'The total number of ASN.1 or BER errors
   encountered by the SNMP protocol device when decoding
   received SNMP messages.'
   Syntax: Counter
   Access: read-only
   Status: mandatory
   ::= { snmp 6 }

snmpInTooBigs Object Type
   Description: 'The total number of SNMP Protocol Data Units
   (PDUs) delivered to the SNMP protocol device where the value
   of the staus field is 'tooBig'.'
   Syntax: Counter
   Access: read-only
   Status: mandatory
   ::= { snmp 8 }

snmpInNoSuchNames Object Type
   Description: 'The total number of SNMP Protocol Data Units
   (PDUs) where the value of the error status field is
   'noSuchName'.'
   Syntax: Counter
   Access: read-only
   Status: mandatory
   ::= { snmp 9 }

snmpInBadValues Object Type
   Description: 'The total number of SNMP Protocol Data Units
   (PDUs) where the value of the error status field is
   'badValue'.'
   Syntax: Counter
   Access: read-only
   Status: mandatory
   ::= { snmp 10 }
```

```
snmpInReadOnlys Object Type
   Description: 'The total number of SNMP Protocol Data Units
   (PDUs) where the value of the error status field is
   'readOnly'.'
   Syntax: Counter
   Access: read-only
   Status: mandatory
   ::= { snmp 11 }

snmpInGenErrs Object Type
   Description: 'The total number of SNMP Protocol Data Units
   (PDUs) where the value of the error status field is
   'genErr'.'
   Syntax: Counter
   Access: read-only
   Status: mandatory
   ::= { snmp 12 }

snmpInTotalReqVars Object Type
   Description: 'The total number of successfully retrieved MIB
   objects (by the SNMP protocol device), and the result of
   valid received SNMP Get-Request and Get-Next PDUs.'
   Syntax: Counter
   Access: read-only
   Status: mandatory
   ::= { snmp 13 }

snmpInTotalSetVars Object Type
   Description: 'The total number of successfully altered MIB
   objects (altered by the SNMP protocol device) resulting from
   valid received SNMP Set-Request PDUs.'
   Syntax: Counter
   Access: read-only
   Status: mandatory
   ::= { snmp 14 }

snmpInGetRequests Object Type
   Description: 'The total number of SNMP Get Request PDUs that
   were received and processed (by the SNMP protocol device).'
   Syntax: Counter
   Access: read-only
   Status: mandatory
   ::= { snmp 15 }

snmpOutGenErrs Object Type
   Description: 'The total number of SNMP Protocol Data Units
   (PDUs) where the error status field was 'genErr'.'
   Syntax: Counter
   Access: read-only
   Status: mandatory
   ::= { snmp 16 }
```

```
snmpInSetRequests Object Type
   Description: 'The total number of SNMP Set Request PDUs
   received and processed.'
   Syntax: Counter
   Access: read-only
   Status: mandatory
   ::= { snmp 17 }

snmpInGet Responses Object Type
   Description: 'The total number of SNMP Get Response PDUs
   received and processed.'
   Syntax: Counter
   Access: read-only
   Status: mandatory
   ::= { snmp 18 }

snmpInTraps Object Type
   Description: 'The total number of SNMP Trap PDUs received and
   processed.'
   Syntax: Counter
   Access: read-only
   Status: mandatory
   ::= { snmp 19 }

snmpOutTooBigs Object Type
   Description: 'The total number of  SNMP protocol Data Units
   (PDUs) sent with an Error Status Field marked 'tooBig'.'
   Syntax: Counter
   Access: read-only
   Status: mandatory
   ::= { snmp 20 }

snmpOutNoSuchNames Object Type
Description: 'The total number of SNMP protocol Data Units
(PDUs) sent with an Error Status Field marked 'noSuchName'.'
   Syntax: Counter
   Access: read-only
   Status: mandatory
   ::= { snmp 21 }

snmpBadValues Object Type
Description: 'The total number of SNMP protocol Data Units
(PDUs) sent with an Error Status Field marked 'BadValue'.'
   Syntax: Counter
   Access: read-only
   Status: mandatory
   ::= { snmp 22 }

snmpOutGenErrs Object Type
   Description: 'The total number of SNMP protocol Data Units
   (PDUs) sent with an Error Status Field marked 'genErr'.'
```

```
   Syntax: Counter
   Access: read-only
   Status: mandatory
   ::= { snmp 24 }

snmpOutGetRequests Object Type
   Description: 'The total number of SNMP Get Request PDUs
   sent.'
   Syntax: Counter
   Access: read-only
   Status: mandatory
   ::= { snmp 25 }

snmpOutGetNexts Object Type
   Description: 'The total number of SNMP Get Next PDUs sent.'
   Syntax: Counter
   Access: read-only
   Status: mandatory
   ::= { snmp 26 }

snmpOutSetRequests Object Type
   Description: 'The total number of SNMP Sent Request PDUs
   sent.'
   Syntax: Counter
   Access: read-only
   Status: mandatory
   ::= { snmp 27 }

snmpOutSetResponses Object Type
   Description: 'The total number of SNMP Set Response PDUs
   sent.'
   Syntax: Counter
   Access: read-only
   Status: mandatory
   ::= { snmp 28 }

snmpOutTraps Object Type
   Description: 'The total number of all SNMP Trap PDUs sent.'
   Syntax: Counter
   Access: read-only
   Status: mandatory
   ::= { snmp 29 }

snmpEnableAuthenTraps Object Type
   Description: 'Enables an SNMP agent to send the
   Authentication Failure Traps. The following values are
   defined: Enabled(1) and Disabled(2).'
   Syntax: Counter
   Access: read-only
   Status: mandatory
   ::= { snmp 30 }
```

3.2.5 RMON – Physical Layer Management

Modern data networks need to be managed. One crucial factor in achieving productivity is the unhindered flow of information within a company. Data must be available at any place at any time. The flip side of the coin is an increasing dependence on the data net and the transmission links. Bottlenecks and system failures can incur high costs. For this reason, companies are introducing suitable network management systems. The generally accepted basis for such network management systems is the Simple Network Management Protocol (SNMP). The functionality of the SNMP protocol far exceeds that of pure TCP/IP protocols. In the course of the development of SNMP, a number of LAN transmission mechanisms and protocols have come to be supported besides Ethernet, such as Token Ring, Fiber Distributed Data Interface (FDDI), AppleTalk, DECNet and SNA. In addition, expansions to support Wide Area Network (WAN) technologies were created, for example V.24, T1/E1, ISDN, Frame Relay and SMDS. SNMP advanced from an insider protocol to become the market standard and is now used in many areas of communication technology. The expansion of SNMP to include the Remote Network Management Information Base (RMON MIB) now provides for the integration of measuring and diagnostic functions on the physical layer via SNMP.

SNMP wholly dominates the management market. In principle, SNMP is not tied to one particular protocol and can thus be used with a number of protocol stacks (ISO, Novell IPX, DECNet, and so on). This makes it exceptionally suited to heterogeneous LANs and Internetworks. The Internet Engineering Task Force (IETF) published the RMON MIB as Request for Comments (RFC) 1271 under the title *Remote Network Monitoring Management Information Base*. In September 1993, RFC 1513 (*Token Ring Extensions to the Remote Network Monitoring MIB*) expanded the RMON MIB to include Token Ring applications. This SNMP subset permits management of the lowest layer of the OSI Reference Model. For the first time it is possible to deploy a management tool literally on the physical and data level of the network.

RMON MIB

The IETF played a leading role in the development of the Remote Network Monitoring Management MIB. Many well-known manufacturers of network management equipment contributed to the work. Since the availability of the SNMP protocol with all its functions and product groups (MIB II, IP Forward, Token Bus, Token Ring, T1, DS3, Ethernet, FDDI, SMDS, Frame Relay, RS-232, X.25, AppleTalk, OSPF, BGP, Bridge, Repeater, DECNet, Phase IV, PPP, SNMP Parties, and so on), there have been increasing demands for a tool for the management of data networks via a network monitor, irrespective of manufacturer and product. In practice, this means that network data is monitored, analyzed, gathered and stored. Then the information is forwarded to one or more SNMP management stations. The management systems include applications to analyze and process these data. The RMON MIB first allowed a unified Remote Management in a heterogeneous environment. The concept is vendor independent. RMON creates full compatibility between individual devices and thus provides the basis for decentralized management in LANs and WANs.

Preventive management

The RMON standard permits preventive management of data nets. The network operator can trace faults occurring in a net, segment or device much quicker and can thus take preventive action against failure of network resources. Communication via RMON information is always conducted between one or more network management stations and the agent, by means of an RMON probe. A probe may consist of a separate, completely independent device, or it may be an expanded function of the SNMP agent. RMON defines a number of functions not available in this form in similar products. Implementation of the RMON MIB permits recording of certain network events, even in cases where the network management station is not actively linked (off-line) with the monitored device (agent, probe). This means that a probe may be configured to diagnose the net and collect statistical data continuously for later analysis by the network administrator.

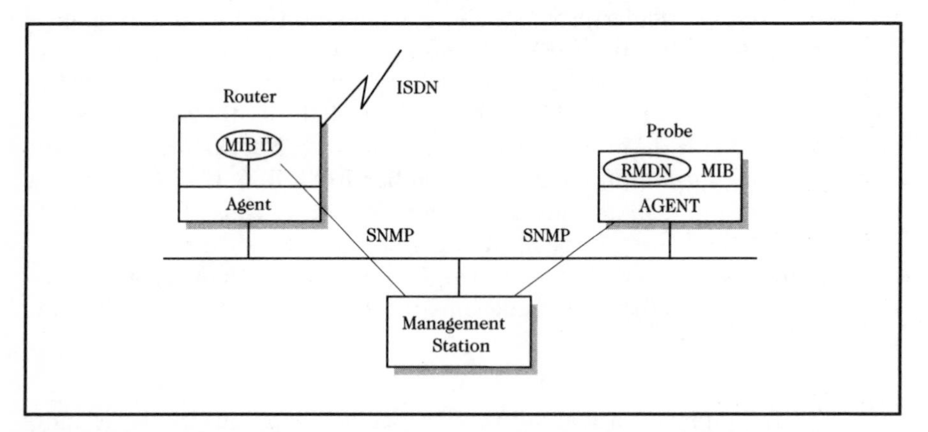

Figure 3.17 Communication between network management station and probe/agent

If certain threshold values are exceeded or certain events occur, the probe attempts to advise the network management station of these events. The RMON MIB may also be used to record network performance data and a fault history. The fault history data may be accessed at any time to assist efficient fault diagnosis.

Because the probe is connected directly to the monitored device, the device is almost predestined to process network specific data (for example, which computers are communicating via the network, which computer produces the most network faults, and so on). The RMON MIB according to RFC 1271 defines only Ethernet objects and is divided into nine object groups:

- Statistics Group;
- History Group;
- Alarm Group;
- Host Group;
- HostTopN Group;
- Matrix Group;
- Filter Group;
- Packet capture Group;
- Event Group.

Expansion of the RMON specification to include Token Ring led to the introduction of some new groups and expansion of some existing ones:

- Token Ring MAC Layer Statistics Group;
- Token Ring Promiscuous Statistics Group;
- Token Ring MAC Layer History Group;
- Token Ring Promiscuous History Group;
- Token Ring Station Group;
- Token Ring Station Order Group;
- Token Ring Station Config Group;
- Token Ring Source Routing Group.

Statistics Group
The Statistics Group contains statistics compiled by each RMON agent/probe for each monitored interface. Currently, the Statistics Group contains only the etherStats table. In future, this group will be expanded to include further interface specific tables (for example, for FDDI).

History Group
The History Group collects periodic recordings of statistical network values and stores them for processing at a later date. Currently, the group contains only the historyControl and etherHistory tables. In future, this group will expand to include further interface specific tables (for example, for FDDI).

Alarm Group

The Alarm Group measures the statistical value of a probe variable at regular intervals and compares it to a set threshold value. If the value of the agent/probe variable exceeds the set threshold value, an event (alarm) is generated. The Alarm Group contains the alarm table. Implementation of the Event Group is required to support the Alarm Group.

Host Group

The Host Group records statistics for each computer detected on the network. This group collects the Source and Destination MAC addresses for all computers on the net by means of valid received packets. The Host Group comprises the hostControl table, the host table and the hostTime table.

HostTopN Group

The HostTopN Group permits the filtering of computers (hosts) that head or lead a statistic. The HostTopN Group contains the following tables: hostTopNControl and hostTopN. This group relies on implementation of the Host Group.

Matrix Group

The Matrix Group records traffic statistics for two addresses. When communication is first established between two addresses, a new entry is made in the table. The Matrix Group consists of three tables: matrixControl, matrixSD and matrixDS.

Filter Group

The Filter Group permits 'diversion' of data packets to a certain channel if these packets match a specific set filter value. The Filter Group comprises the filter and channel tables.

Packet Capture Group

The Packet Capture Group can record data packets after they were sent onto a certain channel. The Packet Capture Group contains the bufferControl table and the captureBuffer table. Implementation of the Filter Group is required for the Packet Capture Group since it is a basic function.

Event Group

The Event Group monitors sending of events and consists of the event and log tables.

Token Ring MAC Layer Statistics Group

The Token Ring MAC Layer Statistics Group contains MAC Layer statistics (general statistics, fault statistics and ring load) compiled by each agent/probe per monitored Token Ring interface. Currently, the group contains only the tokenRingMLStats table. Support for the group is optional.

Token Ring Promiscuous Statistics Group

The Token Ring Promiscuous Statistics Group contains statistics on all non-MAC specific data packets (for example data source, broadcasts/multicasts, packet sizes, and so on) compiled by each RMON agent/probe per monitored Token Ring interface. The Token Ring Promiscuous Statistics group consists of the tokenRingPStats table. Support of the group is optional.

Token Ring MAC Layer History Group

The Token Ring MAC Layer History Group records MAC Layer statistics (general statistics, fault statistics and ring load) about the net at regular intervals and stores them for processing at a later date. Currently, the group contains only the tokenRingMLHistory table. Support of the group is optional and requires implementation of the historyControl table.

Token Ring Promiscuous History Group

The Token Ring Promiscuous History Group records general statistics regarding non-MAC specific information at regular intervals. These values are stored and may be processed at a later date. Currently, the group contains only the tokenRingPHistory table. Support of the group is optional but requires implementation of the historyControl table.

Token Ring Station Group

Statistics about all stations connected to the local ring (active stations, ring status, active monitor, sender of beacon frames, and so on) are stored in the Token Ring Station Group. The group contains only the ringStationControl table. Support of the group is optional.

Token Ring Station Order Group

The physical and logical sequence of Token Ring devices in the ring is detected and stored in the Token Ring Station Order Group. The group contains only the ringStationOrder table. Support of the group is optional.

Token Ring Station Config Group

The Token Ring Station Config Group permits the addition and removal of Token Ring terminals as well as reconfiguration, for example downloading of software. The Token Ring Station Config Group consists of the ringStationConfigControl and ringStationConfig tables. Support of the group is optional.

Token Ring Source Routing Group

The Token Ring Source Routing Group gathers statistics about all Source Routing information sent via the ring. The group contains the sourceRoutingStats table. Implementation of this group is optional.

RMON functionality

In order to handle the complex functions and function groups of the RMON MIB correctly, the user needs to have a good understanding of the respective functions. RMON standardizes the format of the data it

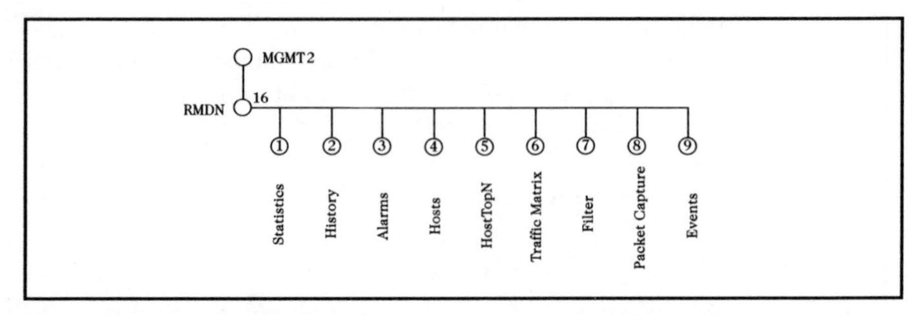

Figure 3.18 The RMON MIB

collects. This enables the management station to display the data via an appropriate user interface. Because support of all RMON groups is not mandatory, its individual components may be implemented in an RMON agent to suit both taste and requirements. For this reason, a multitude of RMON monitors are now available, each of them optimized for one particular task. These devices differ in performance, processing speed and memory capacity. The RMON MIB is supported by all of them, but this does not mean that certain parts of the RMON MIB were implemented. It is up to the user/procurer to examine the device in detail. A test installation under realistic conditions is strongly recommended. This test and the effort it takes will soon pay off because certain problems and incompatibilities can be eliminated from the start.
In principle, RMON enables cooperation of different management stations in the network. Thus, management tasks may be distributed and shared. For example, all statistical data may be sent to an ordinary workstation, while alarms and panic messages are forwarded to disaster management.

In addition to the straightforward gathering of data on the net, an RMON agent may also filter out specific data and compare it to pre-set values. This helps, for example, to find the LAN device with the highest traffic load. An RMON agent may also be configured in such a way that it will monitor potential network problems and fault conditions and spot them automatically.

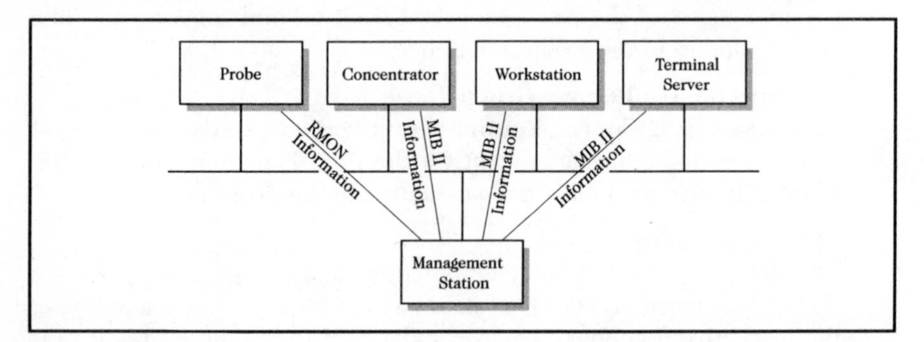

Figure 3.19 Cooperation of RMON with shared management functions

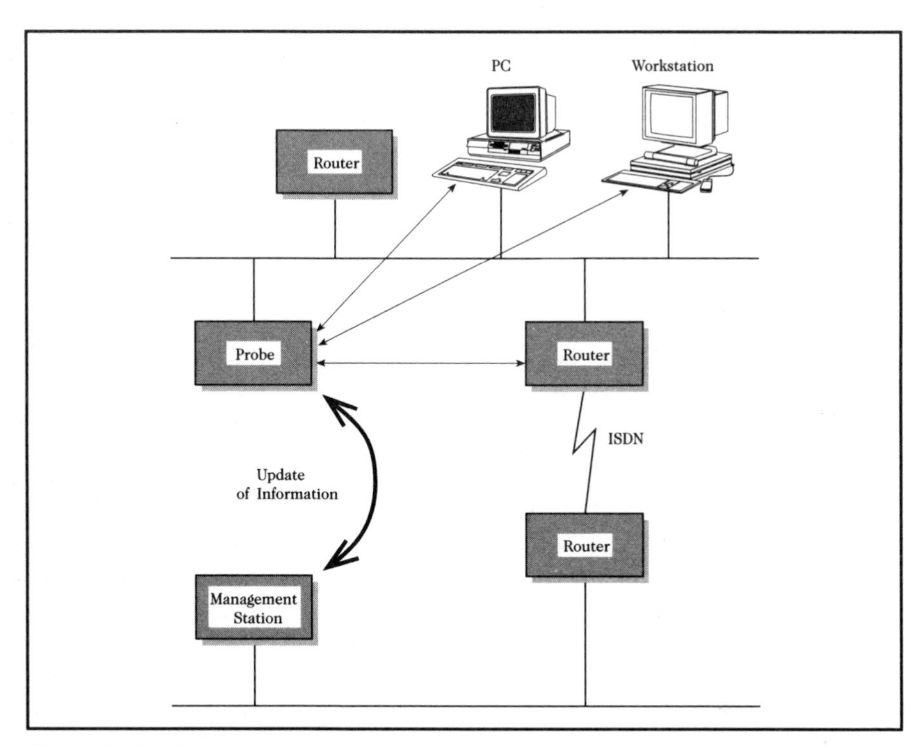

Figure 3.20 Proxy management

If such a fault condition occurs, the agent registers the event and notifies the SNMP management station. In daily operation, diagnostic functions permit continuous recording of network or segment performance data, so that long-term statistics can be compiled.

Proxy management

As a rule, each SNMP station follows the Query Response model and sends regular requests to the managed terminals. In large networks, these data packets may amount to a major part of the data traffic. This will necessarily impair performance and available bandwidths on the data network.

The RMON MIB proxy management capacity reduces current data traffic, particularly in Wide Area Networks (WANs). In these applications, the RMON MIB acts as a network management station and only forwards management information to central management at defined intervals. RMON devices operate on the following settings: Off Line, On Line and On Demand (*see* also Figure 3.20).

Off Line operation

The RMON agent collects and stores the data. The network management stations establish a connection with the RMON agents in the net at defined intervals to read the stored information. Off Line operation is particularly suitable for RMON agents installed in a remote net (via a WAN link).

On Line operation

In On Line operation, all data collected by the RMON agent is automatically forwarded to the network management station. Due to the amount of data likely to accumulate in a network, this function requires a certain amount of bandwidth.

On Demand operation

Two working methods are possible in On Demand operation:

- The network management station cooperates permanently with the RMON agent. If a fault occurs in the link between the RMON agent and the management station, the monitor can be programmed to store the data until the link is re-established.
- As with Off Line operation, the RMON agent does not need a link to a management station. Communication takes place once a value (threshold value, alarm situation) has been exceeded.

Flexibility

The flexible nature of the RMON standard means that data can be gathered at the lowest level and transferred to the management station. The functions available are determined by the respective implementation. Threshold values for many events can be set on almost all devices (probes). An alarm is generated when such a value is exceeded. This alerts the network operator to a problem in time to take corrective action. Grading the alarm according to freely allocated priorities spares the operator from exposure to an uncontrollable flood of information. Continuous collection of statistics and threshold value definitions permits individual characterization of 'normal' network behaviour. Certain data (Number of Packets/Octets, Broadcasts/Multicasts, and so on) will be written to a LOG file, while genuine faults, for example, short packets, packet fragments, CRC/alignment errors, jabber, big packets, beacons, token errors and collisions will change the color of the respective icon on the network management console. The alarm may be combined with an acoustic signal or a PA system so the network management system can alert the operator to a critical situation.

Performance analysis

The RMON is structured for optional delivery of performance data during communications between SNMP management stations and SNMP agents. In practice, this means that data is transported much faster over the network, generating far less overhead. Each line in a table of MIB variables is given an index. This value is used to identify the line. Tables administered by the RMON MIB always start with Index 1 and increase continuously. When accessing the RMON MIB, the management station may access a number of index types. The data contained in them is transferred to the management station as a single data packet. The following example illustrates the functions of statistics and alarms. The basic characteristics of a network are defined during configuration. Normal network load per minute averages 15%. An alarm is to be generated if the mean (per minute) exceeds a load of 40%. Normal statistics are collected by the RMON probe and transferred to the network management stations at the intervals defined. If an alarm occurs, the network manager is informed immediately via a trap (alarm). The manager may now use the TopNTalker function to establish which computer is generating the data traffic. If appropriate, data traffic may be diverted partly or totally with a filter function. Decoding software at the management station enables the administrator to analyze all data transferred on all layers of the OSI/ISO reference model. These tools help to find and eliminate the cause of the problem rapidly.

Management of older devices

Many older LAN devices do not have an integrated management. This excludes them from a global management concept. In practice, this means that they cannot be managed. An RMON agent expands the functionality of data nets and will support such devices indirectly. The network administrator can set special filters and statistics for these devices and collect information about the devices for transfer to the network management station. The availability of RMON can turn an unmanageable device into a managed terminal (see Figure 3.21).

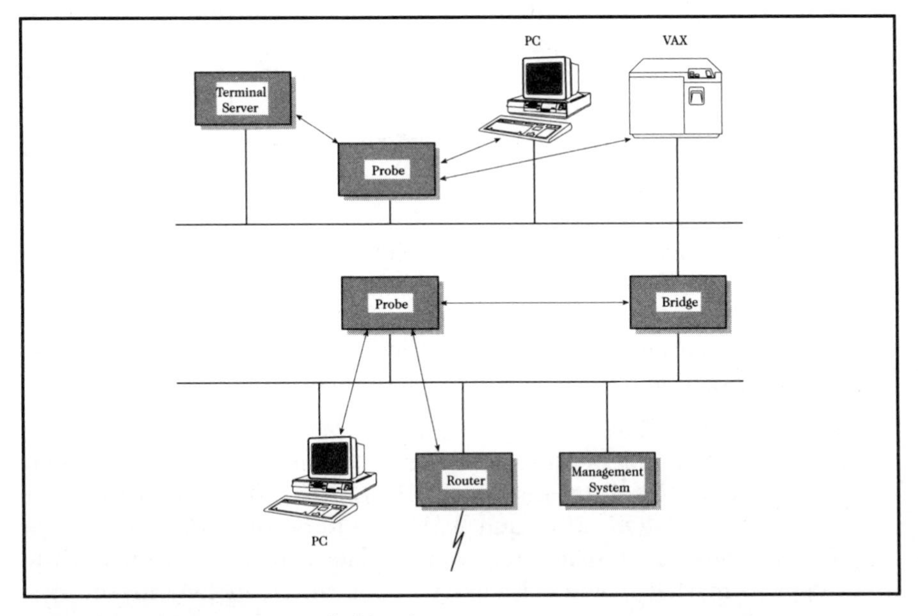

Figure 3.21 Management of older devices

RMON architecture

In loose terms, an RMON application is a low-cost instrument for measurement. Measurements always require one RMON application and one or more RMON probes. The RMON application is always installed on a computer (client), while the server software resides on the individual probes in the net.

RMON applications

RMON applications may be used as stand-alone tools or implemented as an addition to a familiar network management application (for example, HPOpenView, SunNet Manager). The main tasks of RMON applications are as follows:

- Collecting RMON SNMP information;
- Processing collected information;
- Graphical conversion of data (statistics).

RMON probe

RMON implementations on RMON servers may be realized as both hardware and software solutions.

Hardware probe

Due to its high functionality, the RMON MIB necessarily requires a high-performance hardware platform to collect and process the data. Under no circumstances must the hardware or software of the RMON probe lose information transferred on the connected nets. For this reason, most probe hardware platforms use a RISC architecture. This probe must have sufficient memory (2–16 Mbytes) to process and store the data. The number of available LAN interfaces determines memory size. Hardware probes may consist of either an independent device (stand-alone probe) or an add-on module in concentrators (hubs), routers or bridges.

Software probe

Some manufacturers implement the Server Version RMON MIB on the workstations (for example, Sun) by distribution on the network via a download. In this case, the workstation acts as a temporary probe. Unlike the hardware probe, this application restricts functionality and the maximum number of available data packets.

Expandability

Originally, the RMON MIB was designed for use in Ethernets. Thanks to the Token Ring expansion, all IEEE 802.5 devices can now be managed via RMON. FDDI and WANs are to be supported in the near future. RMON is designed to accommodate expansion of this MIB to adapt to market realities. Envisaged applications include inventories, automatic protocol and address recognition, network security, and so on. Development continues at breakneck speed, and there is no end in sight.

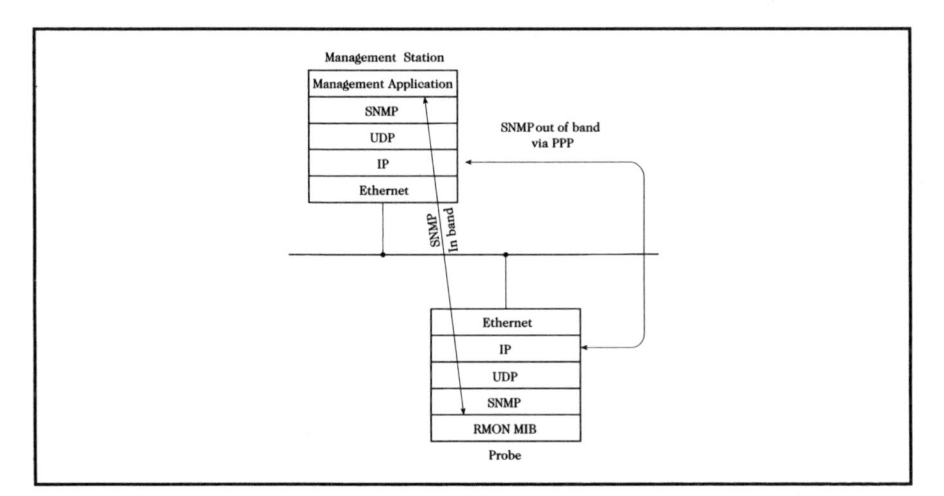

Figure 3.22 RMON architecture

Conclusion

The availability of the RMON MIB means that, for the first time, network management extends to the physical layer. This permits collection of data independently of devices. The built-in tools provide for qualified analysis of the entire traffic without taking up valuable resources (bandwidth). RMON products are already available, and their number will increase steadily in the coming months.

Parameter Group	MIB II	RMON MIB	Hub MIB	Bridge MIB	Host MIB
Interface Statistic	X				
IP Statistic	X				
TCP Statistic	X				
UDP Statistic	X				
SNMP Statistic	X				
Host Job Counts					X
Host File System Information					X
Link Tests			X	X	X
Data Traffic Statistic		X	X	X	
Host Statistic		X	X		
History Statistic		X			
Spanning Tree Performance			X		
WAN Link Performance			X		
Thresholds for each area			X		
Configuration Statistic			X		
Traffic Matrix			X		
Top Talkers			X		
Packet Analysis			X		
Distributed Logging			X		

Table 3.23 Comparison of MIBs

4

Simple Network Management Protocol Version 1

The increasing use of data networks (Local Area Networks/LANs) in many organizations, restructuring and the redefinition of corporate goals over the past decade have led to the important insight that availability of information cannot be underestimated as a factor influencing productivity. In advanced organizations, all forms of data and information can be called up from any workstation at any time. While data transfer has become a vital element of internal procedures within an organization, there is also a corresponding increase in the organization's dependence on the availability of the data network and connected terminals. Any breakdown of these components inevitably leads to considerable costs. Access to a suitable network management system has become an indispensable organizational requirement. In general, data networks are managed from a central office. This helps to minimize network downtime or, using various means, to minimize the risk of power failure. As well as facilitating control over individual network components, the tools contained in management systems enable specific network information and events to be called up via the network. Communication from the network management station to the manageable objects is always carried out via a protocol which converts commands from a network management station into actions. For practical reasons, SNMP has become established as a standard management protocol for use in heterogeneous system environments. The communicative basis is provided by the TCP/IP protocols. SNMP is placed directly on the transport level where it employs the User Datagram Protocol (UDP). The protocol standards for SNMP were drawn up by the Internet Architecture Board (IAB) (formerly the Internet Activity Board) and published as a standard in the Request for Comments (RFCs). The following RFCs contain information on the SNMP standard:

RFC 1213
Management Information Base for network management of TCP/IP-based internets: MIB II

RFC 1157
Simple Network Management Protocol (SNMP)

RFC 1156
Management Information Base for network management of TCP/IP-based internets

RFC 1155
Structure and identification of management information for TCP/IP-based internets

The development of the SNMP protocol began in 1987. As a practical initiative, the TCP community embarked on a completely new direction in network management. The initial basis was the Simple Gateway Monitoring Protocol (SGMP). The actual tasks performed by the SGMP protocol consisted of purely monitoring functions which were implemented on WAN IP Gateways (Routers). The Internet Team, responsible for the implementation of the SGMP protocol, was commissioned by the Internet community to develop a successor protocol offering a wider range of functions. This development led to SNMP. Since the Internet community has always taken account of international standards where available, it was quite natural for the work of the ISO/OSI organization to be used as the framework for the development of the SNMP standard. The specifications of the SNMP protocol were therefore based on Abstract Syntax Notation 1 (ASN.1).

The Management Information Base (MIB) and the Structure of Management Information (SMI) were also integrated into the management standard. Two years of development time, during which the protocol was tested in practice, elapsed before the first official SNMP standard was authorized by the IAB. In 1990, the SNMP protocol was raised to the status of a Recommended TCP/IP Protocol. It has since brought about significant and positive changes in network management.

SNMP architecture

The SNMP architecture is based on the very simple concept of the Query/Response model. The Client, which sends out Queries, is generally described as the 'manager'. The SNMP Server (the device that answers the queries) is referred to as the 'agent'. The SNMP protocol enables a network management station to read and to change (or to write) an agent's parameters according to the rules of SNMP. SNMP also allows the agents to send an unrequested message to the management station under certain circumstances (alarm).

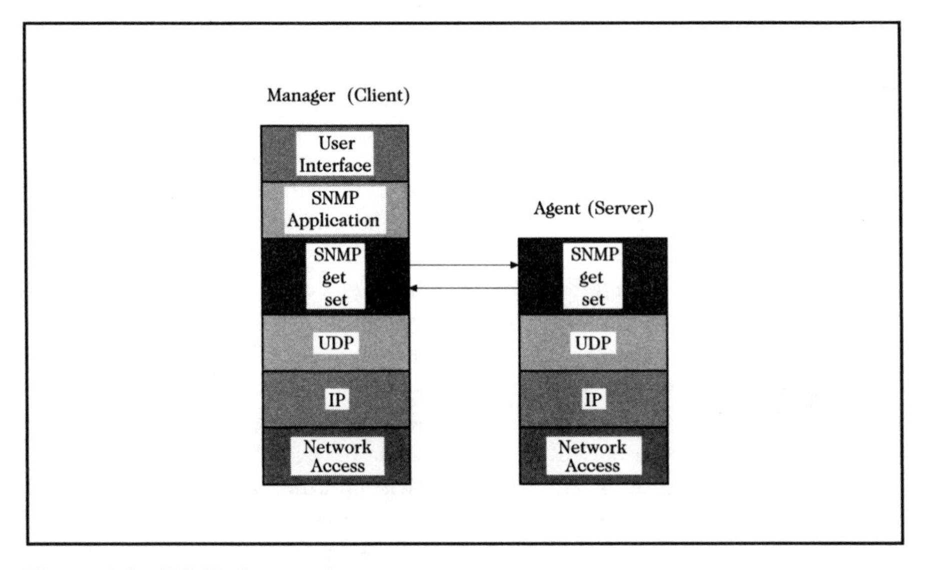

Figure 4.1 SNMP client and server

The simplicity of the SNMP system reduces the complexity of the overall range of functions and contributes significantly to the fulfilment of the following goals:

- Development costs for the implementation of the overall system are reduced.
- The range of functions can be reached from every device via a simple structure, thereby reducing acceptance of network management applications.
- The simple protocol structure makes network management very easy to understand. This means that it is cost efficient to run the network.
- The entire architectural model was defined as simply as possible and is completely independent of hardware and software structures (operating systems). The protocols and mechanisms can be supported by any device.

The SNMP architecture establishes the following fixed points:

- The protocol and its range of functions.
- The information and data that can be transferred via the protocol.
- The protocol mechanisms necessary for the transportation of management functions.
- The functions and tasks of the individual devices participating in the transfer of management data.

The management information transferred by the SNMP protocol complies with the rules set out in the *Structure and Identification of Management Information (SMI) for TCP/IP-based Internets* (RFC 1155) in terms of structure and coding. A subset of the OSI ASN.1 description language and the Basic Encoding Rules (BER) is used for coding. The manageable objects (parameters/attributes), described according to these rules, represent a section of the network. A management function is a sequence of parameterized operations on an object. The complete set of managed objects is referred to as a Management Information Base (MIB). Communication from the network management station to the managed objects is never direct; it always passes through agents. The agents have the task of responding to the services requested by the network management station and passing on alarm and event messages to this station. Communication between the management station and the agent takes place via the communication protocol. In practice, this means that a management station communicates with the agent only by reading (Get) and writing (Set). This relative functional restriction does have two positive consequences:

- The complexity of an agent is dramatically reduced by the minimal functions.
- The command and protocol syntax is considerably simplified and support for imperative management commands is excluded from the outset.

All management requests are reduced to a polling mechanism. Queries are sent to the network components to be managed at regular intervals. The event mechanism offers a way out of this limitation by means of the trap. If an agent recognizes a certain predefined situation, this agent can inform the management station. The decision to use the polling mechanism instead of an event mechanism can be problematic in practice – especially when using SNMP with larger networks. The network can be overburdened by the number of agents involved in communication and the mass of polling requests and replies. The available bandwidth for transmission on the network can also be considerably reduced as a result.

At worst, this can lead to a network error. It is therefore possible to vary the polls sent through the network management by means of a timer.

Application protocols	Simple Network Management Protocol (SNMP)
Transport protocols	User Datagram Protocol (UDP)
Internet work protocols	IP
Network access protocols	Ethernet FDDI Token Ring

Figure 4.2 The IP/UDP/SNMP protocol stack

The SNMP protocol is located on the application layer. It is completely independent of the underlying transport mechanisms. With the SNMP protocol, each message is treated as a unique event and is therefore interpreted individually. The SNMP protocol uses the connection-free datagram service UDP (User Datagram Protocol) for the transport of information. The UDP is defined in RFC 768. The multiplex mechanism in the UDP creates the conditions required for the coexistence of a great many higher protocols and processing routines in a single computer. The use of the UDP is also enabled by a large number of processing routines from a single higher-level protocol. To identify the various data streams, UDP issues port numbers to each computer. The entire data exchange between application processes and UDP takes place through these port numbers. Fixed port numbers are issued for certain frequently used application processes. These port numbers are regularly published in the RFC as Assigned Numbers. The UDP port number 161 is always used for communication between a network management station and an agent, while port number 162 is used for transferring traps.

Direction	Function	UDP port
Network management station —> agent	SNMP messages	161
Agent —> network management station	SNMP trap1	62

Table 4.1 UDP ports

The UDP transport mechanism is not rigidly prescribed. Other transport protocols such as the OSI Transport Layer (TP0–TP4) or Media Access Control (*see* Figure 4.2) can also be used.

Relationship between management levels

The key fixed component of the SNMP architecture is the precise definition of the administrative relationship between the management protocol levels. These management levels, which are implemented both in the management station and in the network element (agent), in conjunction with the SNMP protocol, are referred to as SNMP Application Entities.

All peer processes on which the SNMP has been implemented and which consequently support SNMP application entities are described as Protocol Entities. Network management can be used for the transport of information relevant to safety (for example, in accounting or configuration management) via the data network. For this reason, the SNMP protocol has to implement a mechanism to prevent the abuse of this type of information. SNMP must therefore provide the means of ensuring that data can only be read or altered by selected management stations.

SNMPv1 is capable of subdividing communicative relationships between management stations and agents into groups. SNMP groups communicating with each other are described as an SNMP Community. The SNMP Community has an unambiguous Community Name in the form of an octet string. If SNMP messages are created by one network management station and received by an agent within the same SNMP Community, they are referred to as 'authentic SNMP messages'.

The system of rules which must be observed to check whether an SNMP message belongs to an SNMP Community is called an 'Authentication Scheme'. A subset of objects within the MIB is allocated to every network element. This subset of objects is also known as a MIB View. The names and object types presented within a MIB View need not necessarily belong to a single subtree. Each element of the set (Read Only, Read/Write) is described as an SNMP Access Mode. The agreement between an SNMP Access Mode and an SNMP MIB View is described as an SNMP Community Profile. An SNMP Community Profile represents all specific access privileges in terms of variables within a specific MIB View. For each variable within the MIB View of a Community Profile, access rights are issued according to the following rules:

None

If a variable is marked with access right 'None', then this variable is protected against any access.

Read/Write, Read only

If a variable is marked with the access rights 'Read/Write, Read only' and if the access mode of the relevant profile is marked as 'Read/Write', this variable is available for Set, Get and Trap functions. In the case of the access mode of a 'Read only' profile, the variables are available only for Get and Trap functions. In cases in which a 'Write only' variable is used as the operand for Get or Trap operations, the value of this variable depends on the relevant implementation.

The comparison between an SNMP Community and an SNMP Community Profile is described as an Access Policy. The Access Policy defines the Community Profile required to gain access to an agent. If there is a device in the network that does not support SNMP functions or supports them only to a limited extent, this can still be managed. In this case, the management functions are executed through a Proxy Agent.

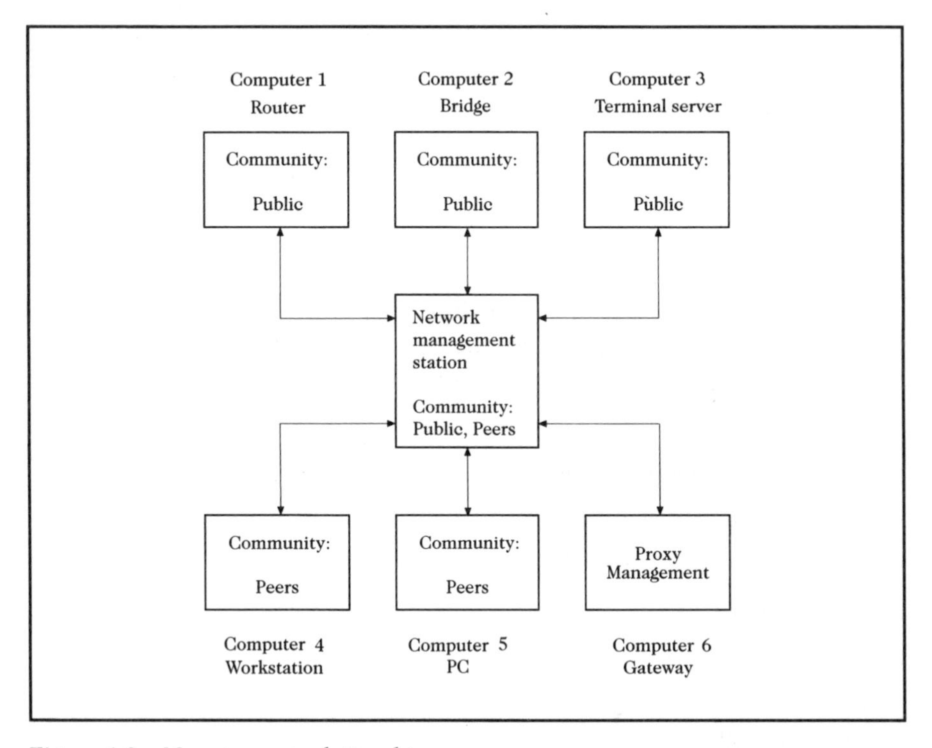

Figure 4.3 Management relationships

Figure 4.3 shows the various communicative relationships between Management Stations, Proxy Agents and Management Agents.

4.1 Client and server

4.1.1 The client

With SNMP Management the client sends all SNMP messages to the server (the agent) and requests specific information which has been collected by the agent. The management protocol is used for the ordered exchange of data between the client and the server components which are to be managed. SNMP supports five types of message. From these five message types, the following functions are available to the client: Get, Get Next and Set.

Get Request

The Get Request command enables a management system to request a given variable in an agent's MIB.

Get Next

The Get Next command enables the client to request several consecutive variables from a MIB.

Set Request

The Set Request command enables a variable within a MIB to be changed. This command is also acknowledged by the agent with a Get Response command.

On the basis of these minimal functions, all forms of information can be transferred between the server and the agent. One of the tasks of the client is to collect and prepare all information received. This involves the following functions:

- Configuration management;
- Performance management;
- Error management;
- Accounting management;
- Security management.

Configuration management

A network management station must be capable of monitoring the configurations of devices connected to the network and storing the relevant data in a system database. As a result, the network administrator can control all devices and register all changes in the network. Configuration management may, for example, comprise the following functions:

- Automatic recognition of all agents in the network;
- Graphically displayed network topology including status information;
- Graphic representation of individual devices in the network;
- Requests for port-user information;
- Requests for link-status information;
- Sending configuration commands to agents.

Configuration management therefore includes the structure and maintenance of a configuration and user database. Configuration management is the basis for all other functional areas.

Performance management

The network management software must respond automatically to given performance parameters. Performance management includes registering, processing, evaluating and preparing performance parameters such as transfer rate, availability, workload, response times, and so on. This process should be carried out automatically or in a form predetermined by the user. It may, for example, involve producing statistics on CPU workload, current memory load, network loading, the ratio of error-free to faulty data packets, and so on. Performance management enables the following parameters to be queried:

- Error-free packets;
- Transfer rate (number of bits per second);
- Packets too short;
- Faulty packets (too long, CRC and alignment errors, and so on);
- Address changes.

It should be possible to define threshold values for these parameters, so that an event will be released automatically if they are exceeded. In this way, potential bottlenecks and overloads can be promptly recognized and counter measures can be taken before the network crashes.

Error management

Error management enables the automatic analysis of the entire flow of data (data transfer rate and error rate) and writes the values registered into the system database. Alarm messages may need to be generated in the network management station. For example, alarm messages or errors can be indicated by means of color coding. It should be possible to store alarm messages in a database together with all the relevant data. This integrated database enables further possibilities for error handling based on user specific reports. These are produced by the administrator for given errors and may indicate the cause of the error or certain procedures for removing the error.

The SNMP server announces errors and operational faults by means of alarms. The identification of faults is dependent on the options provided by the management system in use.

Accounting management

Accounting management is intended to place certain tools at the disposal of the network administrator by registering user-related data and scaling this for use with the network. It is also used for resource allocation according to user needs. The accounting system contains information on the type and scale of resources and/or network services used. User specific cost calculations are based on this information. It is possible to divide up the costs arising in many different ways. For example, costs can be calculated for individual users, groups of users or for a cost point. In terms of resource allocation, accounting management should enable access to individual resources (Server Access) to be

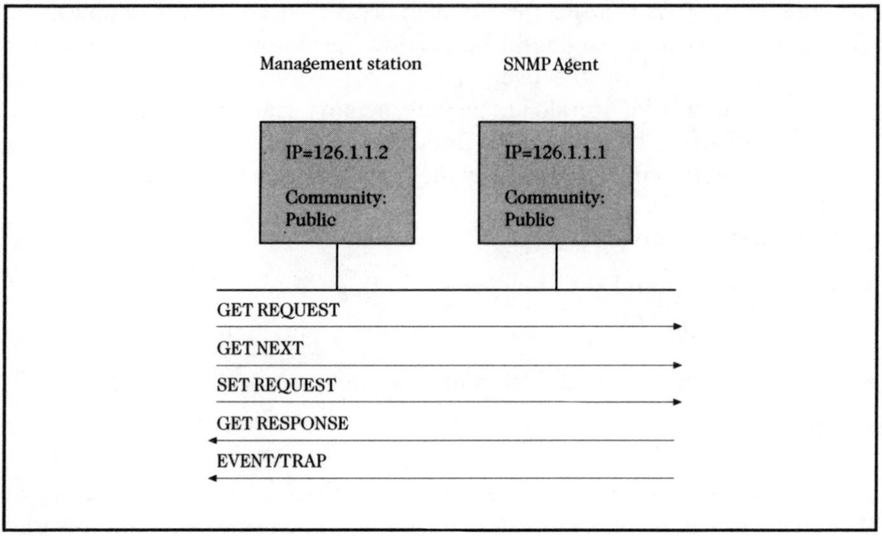

Figure 4.4 Communication Relationships

authorized or restricted according to time or user controls. Accounting management should also enable the definition of upper limits for resource utilization, thereby allowing utilization restrictions to be imposed via accounting management.

Network management should monitor access to the data network, to resources and services. This requires certain monitoring mechanisms and rules, such as passwords, access authorizations, and so on. Security Management provides for the protection of resources required for communication.

Security management

A network must be protected from various risks:

- Passive eavesdropping on messages;
- Active changing of messages;
- Active interruption of a connection;
- Unauthorized access to data.

4.1.2 The server

A server function, in the form of an SNMP agent, is integrated with the relevant components of the SNMP protocol in order to monitor and control the terminals to be managed. This agent acts as an intelligent front-end processor for all network management functions. SNMP supports five types of message. From these five message types, the following functions are available to the agent: Get Response and Event/Trap.

Get Response
The Get Response command represents an agent's answer to a Get Request, Set Request or Get Next query.

Event/Trap
While all communication originates from the management station, the event command enables an agent to send an unrequested message (alarm) to the management station under certain circumstances.

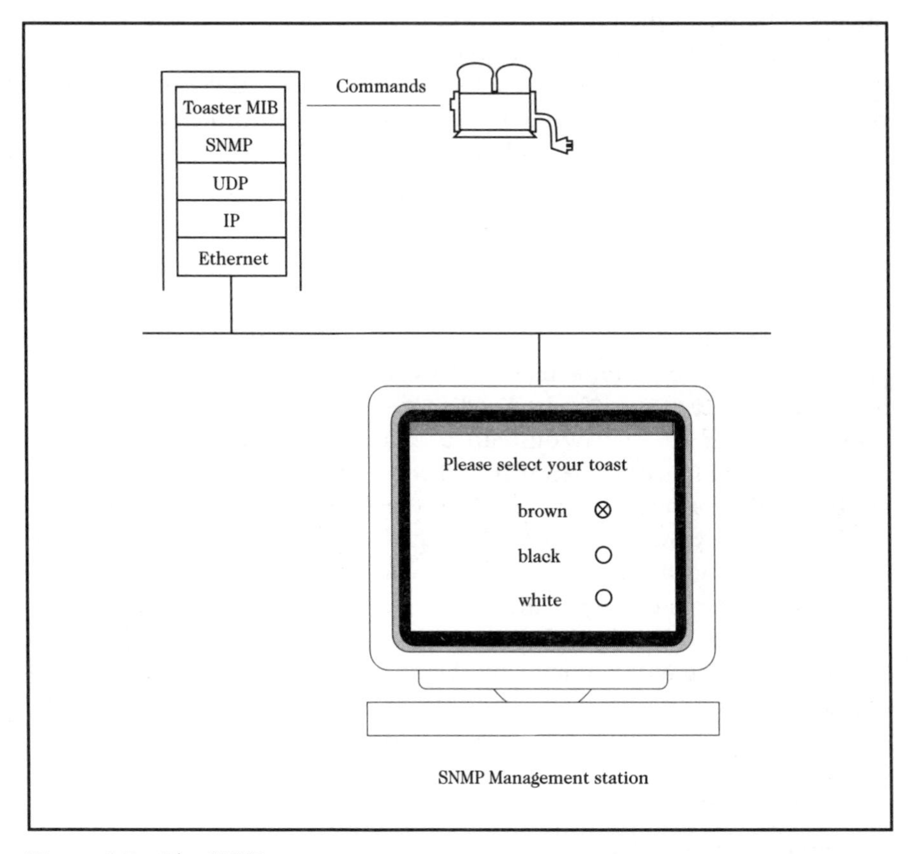

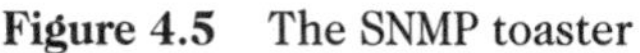
Figure 4.5 The SNMP toaster

In practice, the network management tasks of the SNMP protocol are devolved onto the agent. Information processing is therefore carried out directly on the relevant device. The network management agent communicates directly with all relevant functional and structural groups in the terminal, thereby ensuring that given network management tasks can be preprocessed (collected, grouped and possibly even analyzed) at their place of origin and effect. The agent's task is to access the relevant module data, to bundle it and possibly also to issue control messages. Future developments in networking, especially in the context of SNMP, should enable the network management server (agent) to support all future applications and requirements. It should therefore be possible to download the relevant SNMP software of the network management agent via the network. As a result, it is no longer necessary to change chip sets when software release changes take place (PALs, PROMS, and so on). The currently available SNMP source codes are generally based on modular subroutines. The code is independent of the operating system and of the actual computer environment. This flexibility of the SNMP protocol means that it is already possible to produce agent implementations, which require between 13 and 64 kbytes of memory. As a result, the SNMP is capable of supporting an extensive range of terminal devices (bridges, routers, modems, PABXs, and so on). At various INTEROP trade fairs, SNMP implementations have already been produced for coffee machines, toasters and model railways.

4.2 SNMP PDUs

By contrast with most TCP/IP protocols, the data format of the SNMP protocol is based on one or more defined header formats. Instead of fixed headers, SNMP uses the standard coding specifications for data description. This makes it particularly difficult to read and understand SNMP data formats. Communication between individual protocol levels is guaranteed via the exchange of messages. Each of these messages is dispatched in a single completely independent UDP datagram. The information in the datagram is coded according to ASN.1 rules. A message consists of a version code, an SNMP Community Name and a Protocol Data Unit (PDU). All SNMP messages are received through the UDP port 161. Only traps use UDP port 162. Every implementation must be able to receive messages of at least 484 octets in length.

Each SNMP message always consists of three different components:

- Protocol version identifier;
- Community identifier;
- Data field.

Protocol version identifier

The version field indicates the version of SNMP used. SNMP version 1 always uses the version code 0. Inserting the version number in every SNMP message enables new protocols to be developed and tested during network operation, without disturbing the work of other network participants.

Community identifier

Every communicating SNMP group has an unambiguous Community Name in the form of an octet string. This community name is also transferred with every SNMP message. In SNMP v1, the communicative relationships between management stations and agents are defined in terms of their membership of the respective communities. An agent only executes all management operations of a management station if it belongs to the same community. The management operations act on all object levels implemented in the agent, and are filtered only by a Community Profile which is allocated to every community.

Data field

The SNMP commands are coded in the data field. SNMP supports only five types of message, which are limited to pure utilization data. This data orientation does not permit imperative commands to be issued to the network components managed. Direct instructions such as Reboot System or Performance Self Test are not possible. In practice, however, there is a way round this problem. Manageable objects are defined in such a way that the agent associates certain actions with these objects.

In spite of the minimal command set, almost all operations between an SNMP client and an SNMP server can be executed. The names for the individual commands are as follows:

- Get Request;
- Get Next;
- Set Request;
- Get Response;
- Event/Trap.

Send functions

The following essential functions are executed when SNMP messages are sent:

- The computer wishing to send generates the necessary PDU command (for example, Get Request) as an ASN.1 object.
- This ASN.1 object is transferred, together with the Community Name, Source Transport Address and Destination Transport Address, to the service which produces the desired Authentication Scheme.
- From this information, the authentication service produces a further ASN.1 object.

- This object construct is then coded according to the ASN.1 Basic Encoding Rules and passed serially to the transport protocol for transmission to the Peer Transport Protocol.

Receive functions

The following functions are activated when SNMP messages are received:

- The incoming datagram is checked for the validity of the data transferred. If an error is found, the datagram will be destroyed and no further action will be taken.
- If the datagram is received correctly, the version number of the SNMP message is checked. If this does not correspond to the receiving SNMP version, the datagram will be destroyed, and no further action will be taken.
- If the SNMP version is correct, the community name and the data contained in the ASN.1 message object are transferred together with the source and destination addresses of the datagram to the authentication service.
- The authentication service either returns a new ASN.1 object or signals an authentication error. If there is an error, this will be registered, and a trap will be generated. The datagram will then be destroyed, and no further action will be taken.
- The ASN.1 object returned by the authentication service is also compared with the original PDU. If this comparison produces an error, the datagram will be destroyed and no further action will be taken. Otherwise, a defined SNMP community with all the associated profiles has been selected, and this will be processed by the PDU. A message created through this function is automatically returned to the Destination Transport Address of the message received.

4.2.1 SNMP commands

SNMP supports only five message types. In spite of this minimal command set, almost all operations between an SNMP client and an SNMP server can be executed. The names of the individual commands are shown below:

- Get Request;
- Get Next;
- Set Request;
- Get Response;
- Event/Trap.

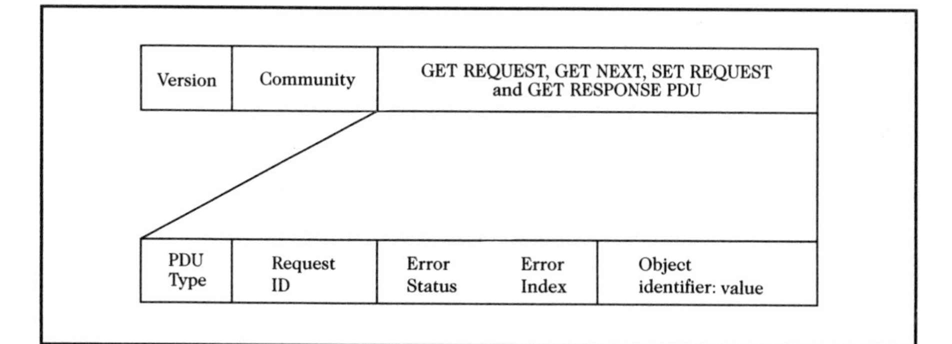

Figure 4.6 Get Request, Get Next, Set Request, Get Response PDU

Definition: Request/Response PDUs

```
PDUs ::= CHOICE {
            get-request
                GetRequest-PDU,

            get-next-request
                GetNextRequest-PDU,

            get-response
                GetResponse-PDU,

            set-request
                SetRequest-PDU,

            trap
                Trap-PDU

             }
```

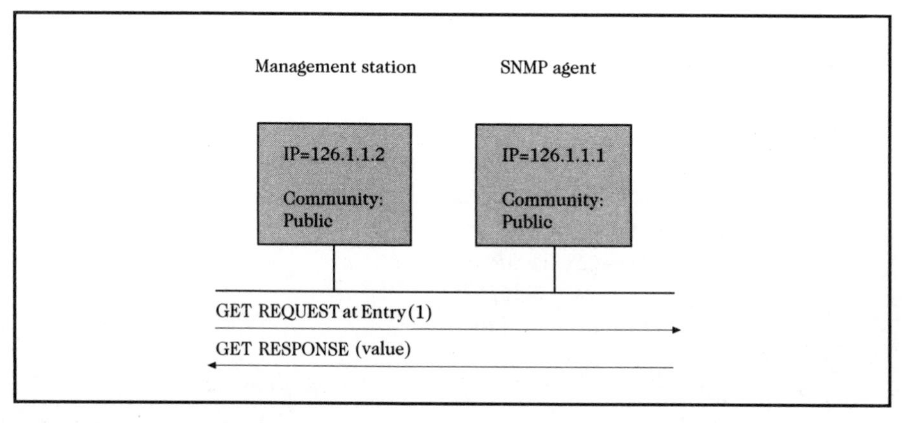

Figure 4.7 Example: Get Request

4.2.2 Get Request

The Get Request command enables a management system (client) to request a given variable in the MIB of an SNMP agent (server).

An object identifier is sent as an argument with this type of message. The client always receives a Get Response message in reply to a Get Request.

Example: SNMP GET REQUEST atEntry(1)

```
MAC:  ----- MAC Header -----
MAC:
MAC:  Destination = 080002001234
MAC:  Source      = 080002003456
MAC:  Ethertype  = 0800 (IP)
MAC:
IP:    ----- IP Header -----
IP:
IP:    Version = 4, header length = 20 bytes
IP:    Type of service = 00
IP:    Total length = 74 bytes
IP:    Identification = 12344
IP:    Flags = 000
IP:    Fragment offset = 0 bytes
IP:    Time to live = 35 seconds/hops
IP:    Protocol = 17 (UDP)
IP:    Source address = [126.1.1.1]
IP:    Destination address = [126.1.1.2]
IP:    No options
IP:
UDP:   ---- UDP Header -----
UDP:
UDP:   Source port = 5103 (SNMP)
UDP:   Destination port = 161
UDP:   Length = 54
UDP:   No checksum
UDP:
SNMP:  ----- Simple Network Management Protocol -----
SNMP:
SNMP:  Version = 0
SNMP:  Community = Public
SNMP:  Command = Get request
SNMP:  Request ID = 134567678
SNMP:  Error Status = 0 (No error)
SNMP:  Error index = 0
SNMP:  Object = {1.3.6.1.2.1.3.1.1}  (atEntry(1))
SNMP:  Value  = NULL
```

Definition: GetRequest PDU

```
GetRequest-PDU ::= [0]
                IMPLICIT SEQUENCE {
                    request-id
                        RequestID,

                    error-status          always 0
                        ErrorStatus,

                    error-index           always 0
                        ErrorIndex,

                    variable-bindings
                        VarBindList
                }
```

4.2.3 Set Request

The Set Request command enables a management system (client) to set certain specific variables in the MIB of an SNMP agent (server). An object identifier is sent as an argument with this type of message. If the Set Request command can be processed with the specified value from the agent, a Get Response packet is sent back and the operation is positively confirmed. If there is an error, a Get Response is created and sent back to the requester (management station) with the relevant error message.

```
MAC:  ----- MAC Header -----
MAC:
MAC:  Destination = 080002001234
MAC:  Source      = 080002003456
MAC:  Ethertype  = 0800 (IP)
MAC:
IP:   ----- IP Header -----
IP:
IP:   Version = 4, header length = 20 bytes
IP:   Type of service = 00
IP:   Total length = 74 bytes
IP:   Identification = 12344
IP:   Flags = 000
IP:   Fragment offset = 0 bytes
IP:   Time to live = 35 seconds/hops
IP:   Protocol = 17 (UDP)
IP:   Source address = [126.1.1.1]
IP:   Destination address = [126.1.1.2]
IP:    No options
IP:
```

```
UDP:  ----- UDP Header -----
UDP:
UDP:   Source port = 5103 (SNMP)
UDP:   Destination port = 161
UDP:   Length = 54
UDP:   No checksum
UDP:
SNMP:  ----- Simple Network Management Protocol -----
SNMP:
SNMP:  Version = 0
SNMP:  Community = Public
SNMP:  Command = Set request
SNMP:  Request ID = 144567678
SNMP:  Error Status = 0 (No error)
SNMP:  Error index = 0
SNMP:  Object = {1.3.6.1.2.1.1.1}  (sysContact)
SNMP:  Value  = Frank Patterson
```

Definition: Set Request PDU

```
SetRequest-PDU ::= [3]
                IMPLICIT SEQUENCE {
                    request-id
                        RequestID,

                    error-status          always 0
                        ErrorStatus,

                    error-index           always 0
                        ErrorIndex,

                    variable-bindings
                        VarBindList
                }
```

Structure of the Set Request PDU

The PDU code 3 has been assigned to the Set Request. After the PDU code, a Set Request message contains another four fields. The individual values are coded as follows:

- Request ID;
- Error Status;
- Error Index;
- Variable Bindings.

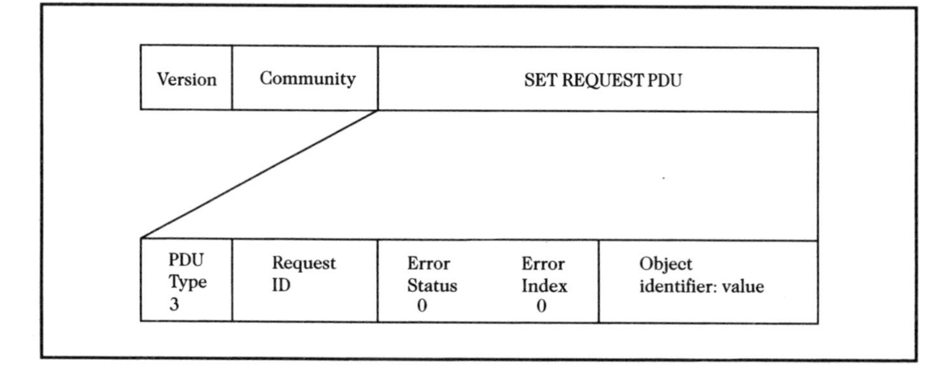

Figure 4.8 Set Request PDU

Request ID

Request IDs are generated only in order to check outstanding messages. On the basis of the Request IDs, the SNMP can match incoming responses to the relevant Requests sent. Since the SNMP is usually structured on the connection-free UDP service, messages may be lost or duplicated during transport through the network. Duplicates can easily be located because of the identification numbers.

Error Status

The Error Status field is always set to the value 0 in a Set Request.

Error Index

The Error Index field is always set to the value 0 in a Set Request.

Variable Bindings

The Variable Bindings field is defined by the object identifier requested. The relevant ASN.1 coded value is allocated to the value of the object variable in the Set Request command.

4.2.4 Get Next Request

The Get Next Request command enables a management system (client) to request a value for the next object in the MIB tree hierarchy. However, the argument transferred is not the value of the object identifier required; the last object identifier known is used. The Get Next operation is ideally suited for traversing tables such as AT tables or routing tables and for requesting consecutive objects quickly. This operation may also be advantageous if the manager does not know exactly which MIB the agent supports. In the case of unknown objects, it can be used simply to issue a Get Next Request to the directly preceding object. In response to a Get Next Request, the client always receives a message of the type Get Response. The values for the next object in the tree hierarchy are returned in this Get Response packet.

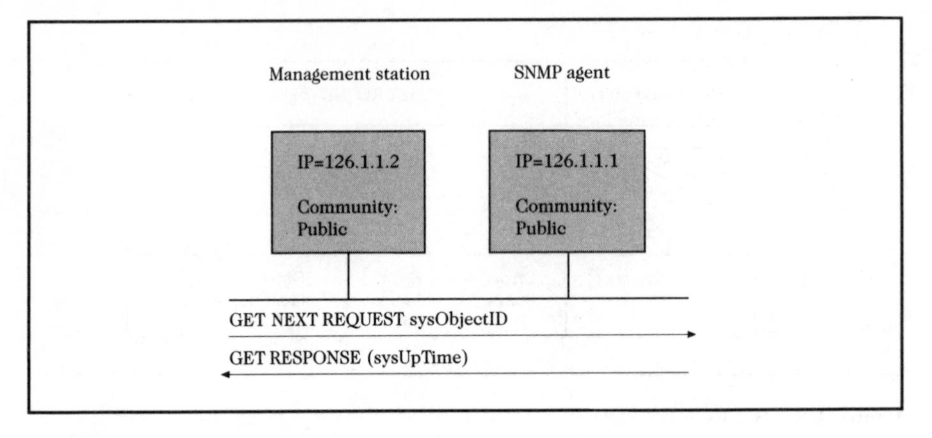

Figure 4.9 Example: Get Next Request

Example: SNMP Get NEXT REQUEST sysObjectID

```
MAC:  ----- MAC Header -----
MAC:
MAC:  Destination = 080002001234
MAC:  Source      = 080002003456
MAC:  Ethertype  = 0800 (IP)
MAC:
IP:   ----- IP Header -----
IP:
IP :   Version = 4, header length = 20 bytes
IP:    Type of service = 00
IP:    Total length = 74 bytes
IP:    Identification = 12344
IP:    Flags = 000
IP:    Fragment offset = 0 bytes
IP:    Time to live = 35 seconds/hops
IP:    Protocol = 17 (UDP)
IP:    Source address = [126.1.1.1]
IP:    Destination address = [126.1.1.2]
IP:    No options
IP:
UDP:   ----- UDP Header -----
UDP:
UDP:   Source port = 5103 (SNMP)
UDP:   Destination port = 161
UDP:   Length = 54
UDP:   No checksum
UDP:
SNMP:  ----- Simple Network Management Protocol -----
SNMP:
SNMP:  Version = 0
SNMP:  Community = Public
```

```
SNMP:   Command = GET NEXT Request
SNMP:   Request ID = 124567678
SNMP:   Error status = 0 (No error)
SNMP:   Error index = 0
SNMP:   Object = {1.3.6.1.2.1.1.2}  (sysObjectID)
SNMP:   Value  =
```

Definition: GET NEXT REQUEST PDU

```
GetNextRequest-PDU ::= [1]
                     IMPLICIT SEQUENCE {
                         request-id
                             RequestID,

                         error-status            always 0
                             ErrorStatus,

                         error-index             always 0
                             ErrorIndex,

                         variable-bindings
                             VarBindList
                     }
```

Structure of the Get Next Request PDU

The PDU code assigned to the Get Next Request is 1. After the PDU code, a Get Next Request message contains another four fields. The individual values are coded as follows:

- Request ID;
- Error Status;
- Error Index;
- Variable Bindings.

Request ID

Request IDs are generated only in order to check outstanding messages. On the basis of the Request IDs, the SNMP can match incoming responses to the relevant Requests sent. Since the SNMP is usually structured on the connection-free UDP service, messages may be lost or duplicated during transport through the network. Duplicates can easily be located because of the identification numbers.

Error Status

The Error Status field is always set to the value 0 in a Get Next Request.

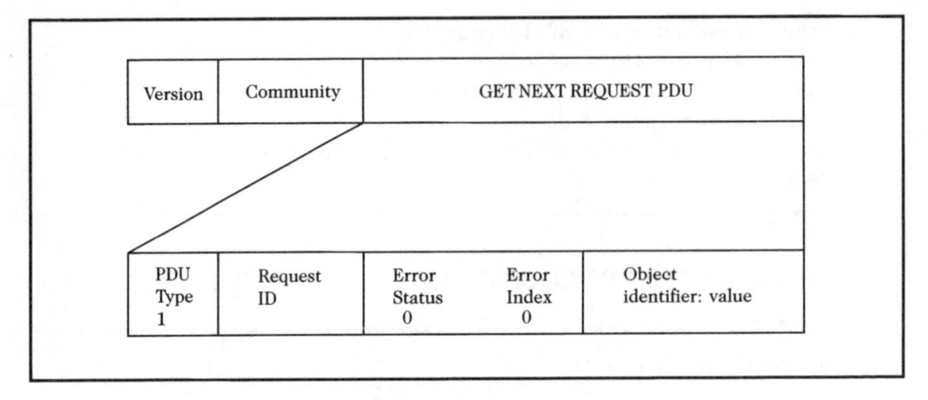

Figure 4.10 Get Next Request PDU

Error Index
The Error Index field is always set to the value 0 in a Get Next Request.

Variable Bindings
The Variable Bindings field contains the object immediately preceding the object required. The relevant ASN.1 coded value is allocated to the value of the object variable in the Set Request command.

4.2.5 Get Response

The Get Response command enables an agent (server) to respond to all Get Next Request, Set Request and Get Request queries from a management system (client). If the relevant command can be processed with the specified value from the agent, a Get Response packet is returned and the operation is positively confirmed. In a positive confirmation, the fields Error Status and Error Index are always coded with the value 0. If there is an error, a Get Response is created and returned to the requester (manager) with the relevant error messages. In an error message, the fields Error Status and Error Index are set to the relevant value. The values shown in Table 4.2 have been defined for the Error Status field.

Designation	Value
noError	0
tooBig	1
noSuchName	2
badValue	3
readOnly	4
genErr	5

Table 4.2

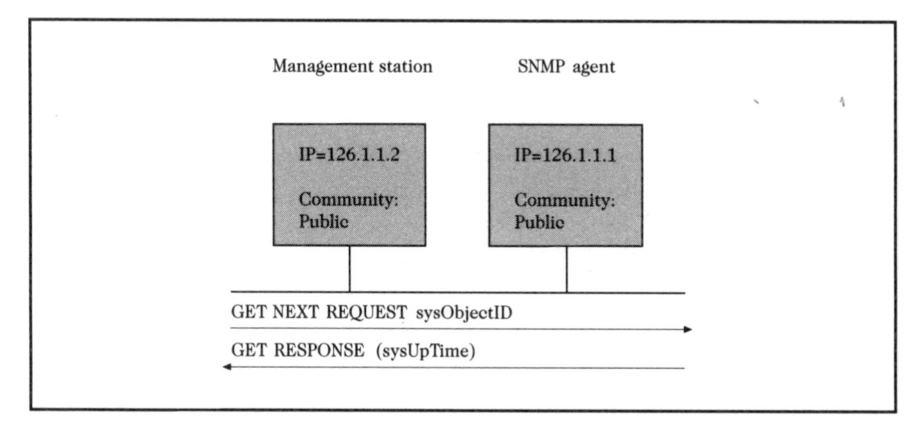

Figure 4.11 Example: Get Response

Example: SNMP Get Response sysUpTime

```
MAC:  ----- MAC Header -----
MAC:
MAC:  Destination = 080002001234
MAC:  Source      = 080002003456
MAC:  Ethertype   = 0800 (IP)
MAC:
IP:   ----- IP Header -----
IP:
IP:   Version = 4, header length = 20 bytes
IP:   Type of service = 00
IP:    Total length = 74 bytes
IP:    Identification = 12344
IP:    Flags = 000
IP:    Fragment offset = 0 bytes
IP:    Time to live = 35 seconds/hops
IP:    Protocol = 17 (UDP)
IP:    Source address = [126.1.1.1]
IP:    Destination address = [126.1.1.2]
IP:    No options
IP:
UDP:   ----- UDP Header ------
UDP:
UDP:   Source port = 5103 (SNMP)
UDP:   Destination port = 161
UDP:   Length = 54
UDP:   No checksum
UDP:
```

```
SNMP:  ----- Simple Network Management Protocol -----
SNMP:
SNMP:  Version = 0
SNMP:  Community = Public
SNMP:  Command = Get response
SNMP:  Request ID = 124567678
SNMP:  Error Status = 0 (No error)
SNMP:  Error index = 0
SNMP:  Object = {1.3.6.1.2.1.1.3}  (sysUpTime)
SNMP:  Value  = 1234567 hundredths of a second
```

Definition: Get Response PDU

```
GetResponse-PDU ::= [2]
                  IMPLICIT SEQUENCE {
                     request-id
                        RequestID,

                     error-status
                        ErrorStatus,

                     error-index
                        ErrorIndex,

                     variable-bindings
                        VarBindList
                  }
```

Structure of the Get Response PDU

The PDU code assigned to the Get Response is 2. After the PDU code, a Get Next Request message contains another four fields. The individual values are coded as follows:

- Request ID;
- Error Status;
- Error Index;
- Variable Bindings.

Request ID

In a Get Response message, Request IDs always relate to the response to the relevant request which has been activated. Duplicate messages can easily be located because of the identification numbers.

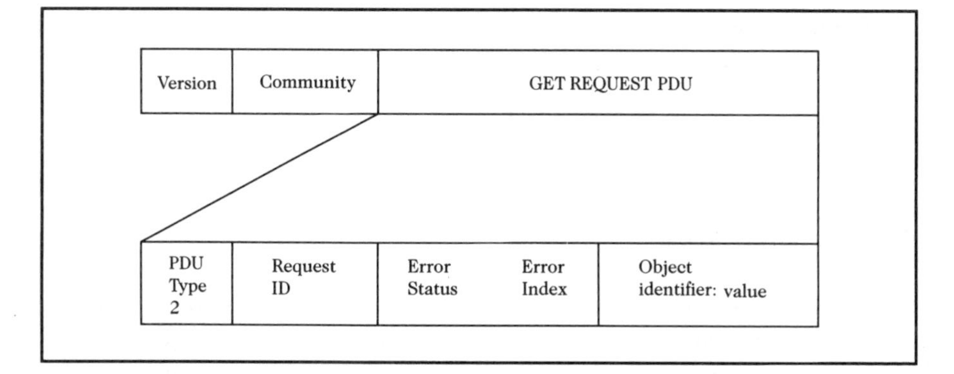

Figure 4.12 Get Response PDU

Error Status

The Error Status field in a Get Next Response always contains any of the following values:

NoError

If the Error Status is set to 0 during processing, this means that the request has been processed.

TooBig

The agent cannot accommodate the required data within a single SNMP message.

NoSuchName

When decoding the SNMP request, the agent has discovered an unknown variable name which it cannot process. This does not necessarily mean that the name is not present in the agent; it means that it cannot acknowledge it according to the predefined Community Profiles.

BadValue

When decoding, the agent has discovered incorrect syntax or an incorrect value which prevents it from altering the required variable.

ReadOnly

When decoding, the agent has discovered a variable which cannot be described in accordance with the Community Profile.

GenError

All other errors are marked by the agent as Generic Errors. More detailed coding is not provided in SNMPv1.

Error Index

If the Error Status field contains a value other than 0, this indicates that an error has been identified in the request just processed. The Error Index also contains additional information on the cause of the error.

Variable Bindings

The Variable Bindings field contains the definition of the object required. The relevant ASN.1 coded value is allocated to the value of the object variable in the Get Response command.

4.2.6 Event/Trap

SNMP is essentially based on a simple polling mechanism, according to which every network management station (client) has to implement all variable and status requests explicitly. In order to react to particular situations in a specific manner, the polling procedure has been expanded by integrating Events/Traps with the agents (servers). If an agent determines a particular situation, it sends a Trap message to the management station. This method enables the network management station to react immediately to the information sent. It also avoids the risk that the relevant change of status may not be recognized for some time by the polling. Sufficient resources are naturally required in order to create this trap. However, a trap must not contain too much information, otherwise the network management station may lose time in the selection of information. Traps should not occur too frequently because they would lead to a reduction in the available network bandwidth. This would in turn lead to agents generating new traps in order to notify the management station of the reduction in transmission bandwidth. For this reason, traps are only created if certain predefined thresholds are exceeded. This means that the agent is expected to check these threshold values continuously against the real circumstances. The agent therefore requires additional CPU resources. Since the agent processes only information relating to itself, it clearly cannot decide on the basis of global criteria.

The following traps have been established so far and specified in detail in RFC 1215 (under the title *Convention for Defining Traps*):

Designation	Value
coldStart	0
warmStart	1
linkDown	2
linkUp	3
authenticationFailure	4
egpNeighborLoss	5
enterpriseSpecific	6

Table 4.3 Generic traps

coldStart Trap

A Cold Start Trap signals to the network management station that the relevant agent is restarting.

```
coldStart TRAP-TYPE
   ENTERPRISE  snmp
   DESCRIPTION
   "A Cold Start Trap signals that the relevant agent has been
   re-initialized by changing the agent configuration or the
   protocol software."
   ::= 0
```

warmStart Trap

A Warm Start Trap specifies that the relevant agent has been re-initialized. The values for all variables remain unchanged.

```
warmStart TRAP-TYPE
   ENTERPRISE  snmp
   DESCRIPTION
   "A WarmStart Trap signals that the relevant agent has been
   re-initialized. The agent configuration and the protocol
   software have not been changed."
   ::= 1
```

linkDown Trap

The agent uses a Link Down Trap to signal that one of the connected interfaces has moved into the 'down' status and can no longer be reached.

```
linkDown TRAP-TYPE
   ENTERPRISE  snmp
   VARIABLES   { ifIndex }
   DESCRIPTION
   "A linkDown Trap signals that an error has been determined on
   one of the communication interfaces of the relevant agents."
   ::= 2
```

linkUp Trap

A Link Up Trap signals to the network management station that one of the connected interfaces has changed to the 'up' status and can be reached again.

```
linkUp TRAP-TYPE
   ENTERPRISE snmp
   VARIABLES   { ifIndex }
   DESCRIPTION
```

```
    "A linkUp Trap signals that a communication interface of the
    relevant agent has been reactivated."
    ::= 3
```

authenticationFailure Trap

An authentication failure trap informs the network management station that a false Community Name was contained in the SNMP transmitted.

```
authenticationFailure TRAP-TYPE
    ENTERPRISE  snmp
    DESCRIPTION
    "An authentication Failure Trap signals that an SNMP message
    received could not be correctly authenticated."
    ::= 4
```

egpNeighborLoss Trap

An EGP Neighbor Loss Trap signals to the network management station that an EGP neighbor, with which EGP Routing Protocol information is exchanged, can no longer be reached.

```
egpNeighborLoss TRAP-TYPE
    ENTERPRISE  snmp
    VARIABLES   { egpNeighAddr }
    DESCRIPTION
    "An egpNeighborLoss Trap signals that an EGP neighbor in an
    EGP Peer relationship has been coded as 'own'."
    ::= 5
```

enterpriseSpecific Trap

In addition to the predefined traps, users can define their own Events/Traps (enterpriseSpecific). In the following example, an enterprise specific trap is defined which is always sent when an error is detected on the communication link.

```
myEnterprise OBJECT IDENTIFIER ::= { enterprises 9999 }

myLinkDown TRAP-TYPE
    ENTERPRISE  myEnterprise
    VARIABLES   { ifIndex }
    DESCRIPTION
```

```
"A myLinkDown Trap signals that the SNMP application of the
sending agent has detected an error on one of the
communication links."
::= 2
```

Structure of Trap PDU

The PDU code 4 has been allocated to the Trap. According to the PDU coding, another six fields are contained in a Trap message. The individual values are coded as follows:

- Enterprise;
- Agent Address;
- Generic Trap;
- Specific Trap;
- Time Stamp;
- Variable Bindings.

Enterprise

The Enterprise field contains the value of the object identifier sysObjectID and therefore transfers an unambiguous identification of the agent that sent the trap.

Agent Address

The Agent Address field contains the IP address of the agent that sent the trap.

Generic Trap

The Generic Trap field contains an integer with which all fixed trap codes (coldStart, warmStart, linkDown, linkUp, authenticationFailure, egpNeighborLoss and enterpriseSpecific) are transferred.

Specific Trap

If the enterpriseSpecific code is set in the Generic Trap field, the integer in the Specific Trap field will transfer the relevant code of the enterprise specific trap.

Time Stamp

The time at which the trap was generated by the agent, registered in the variable sysUpTime (TimeTicks), is entered in the Time Stamp field.

Variable Bindings

The Variable Bindings field is used for allocating values to the relevant trap on the basis of variables that are of interest in terms of the relevant event.

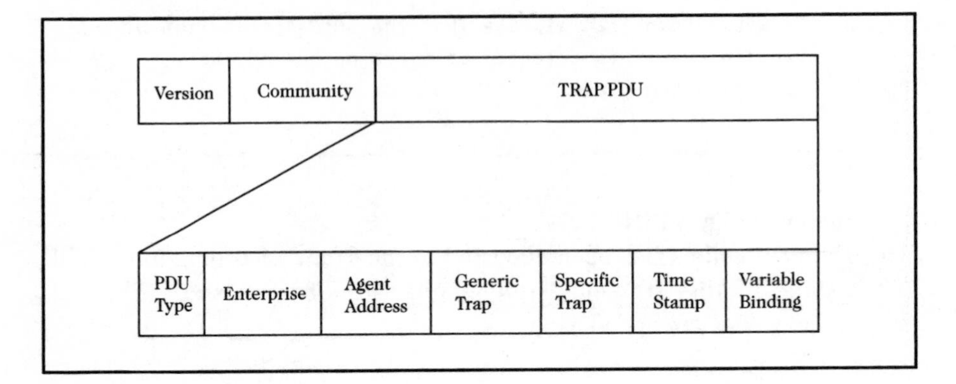

Figure 4.13 The Trap PDU

Definition: Trap/Event PDU

```
Trap-PDU ::= [4]
    IMPLICIT SEQUENCE {
       enterprise
          OBJECT IDENTIFIER,

       agent-addr
          NetworkAddress,

       generic-trap
          INTEGER {
             coldStart(0),
             warmStart(1),
             linkDown(2),
             linkUp(3),
             authenticationFailure(4),
             egpNeighborLoss(5),
             enterpriseSpecific(6)
          },

       specific-trap
          INTEGER,

       time-stamp
         TimeTicks,

       variable-bindings
          VarBindList
   }
```

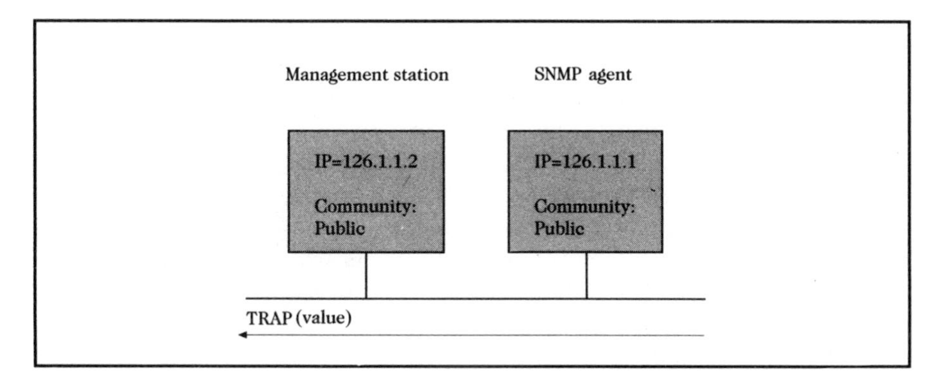

Figure 4.14 Example: TRAP

BASIC ASN.1 types	ID-value (hex)	(dec)
Integer	02	02
Octet string	04	04
Null	05	05
Object identifier	06	06
Sequence	30	48

Table 4.4 ASN.1 SNMP identification values

IPAddress	40	64
Counter	41	65
Gauge	42	66
TimeTicks	43	67
Opaque	44	68

Table 4.5 Basic SNMP application types

Get Request	A0	160
Get Next Request	A1	161
Get Response	A2	162
Set Request	A3	163
Trap	A4	164

Table 4.6 Constructed SNMP application specific types

4.3 The problem area of Private MIBs

As already described, the management tree branches into another four sub-branches below the Internet Node. These four branches are: Directory, Management, Experimental and Private. The private branch (Label=

private(4)) of the management tree has only one standardized node. This particular branch is referred to as Enterprises (Label= enterprises(1)). Using the Internet Assigned Numbers Authority, every manufacturer of management products has the option of having a manufacturer's code registered. Once a manufacturer has been issued with a registered code, he can define his own private objects without restriction and completely at his discretion. The Private MIB therefore provides the possibility of integrating resources such as manufacturer specific objects which extend beyond the fixed objects contained as standard within MIB II. Manufacturers have so far made extensive use of private MIBs.

One example of this type of private implementation is the Bridge/Router family of products developed by the Israeli firm Lannet/RND. In accordance with the SNMP standard, the Private MIB Identifier shown in Table 4.7 has been established for the company Lannet/RND.

private	Object Identifier::={internet 4}
enterprises	Object Identifier::={private 1}
Lannet/RND	Object Identifier::={enterprises 89}
RNDMng	Object Identifier::={rnd 1}

Table 4.7 The Lannet/RND Private MIB object list

```
OBJECT: rndSysId
   Syntax: INTEGER
            reb(1),
            ceb(2),
            cebib(3),
            xeb(4),
            xeb1(5),
            rebsx(6),
            rtb(7),
            ltb(8),
            lte(9),
            iprouter(10),
            ielb(11),
            leb(12)
   Definition: "Identification number of device."
   Access: read-only
   Status: mandatory

OBJECT: rndAction
   Syntax: INTEGER
            reset(1),
            deleteLanTab(7)
   Definition: "Variable, which enables the user to initiate
   one of the fixed actions in the network routing mechanism."
```

```
   Access: read-write
   Status: mandatory

OBJECT: rndFileName
   Syntax: OCTET STRING
   Definition: "Defines an internal filename which enables the
   transfer of IP routing tables."
   Access: read-write
   Status: mandatory

OBJECT: rndBridgeType
Syntax: INTEGER
         reb(1),
         ceb(2),
         cebib(3),
         xeb(4),
         xeb1(5),
         rebsx(6),
         rtb(7),
         ltb(8),
         tre(9),
         rte(10),
         xtb(11),
         ete(12),
         rete(13),
         ielb(30),
         leb(31)}
   Definition: "Identifies the bridge type."
   Access: read-only
   Status: mandatory

OBJECT: rndInactiveArpTimeOut
   Syntax: INTEGER
   Definition: "Defines the maximum time an entry remains in the
   ARP table. After expiry of this time, the entry is deleted
   from the table."
   Access: read-write
   Status: mandatory

OBJECT: rndErrorDesc
   Syntax: OCTET STRING
   Definition: "Textual representation of a trap which is to be
   sent to a network management station."
   Access: read-only
   Status: Status: mandatory

OBJECT: rndErrorSeverity
   Syntax: INTEGER
   Definition: "Classifies the enterprise-specific trap which is
   sent to a network management station."
   Access: read-only
   Status: mandatory
```

```
OBJECT: rndMaskTab
   SYNTAX: Sequence of rndMaskEntry
   Definition: "Contains a table including all the masks defined
   for the bridge."
   Access: read-write
   Status: mandatory

OBJECT: rndMaskType
   SYNTAX: INTEGER
            TX (1),
            RX (2),
            Compress (3),
            Priority (4)
   Definition: "Describes the type of filter mask. With the
   Lannet/RND bridge, only the transmission (TX) filter mask
   is used."
   Access: read-only
   Status: mandatory

OBJECT: rndIfPortNum
   SYNTAX: INTEGER
   Definition: "Defines the port number of the bridge for which
   the relevant filter mask has been defined."
   Access: read-write
   Status: mandatory

OBJECT: rndMaskNum
   SYNTAX: INTEGER
   Definition: "Defines the line number of the entry in the
   filter mask table."
   Access: read-write
   Status: mandatory

OBJECT: rndMaskDest
   SYNTAX: INTEGER
            unassigned_condition(1)
            all_messages(2)
            broadcast_messages(3)
            multicast_messages(4)
   Definition: "Defines the type of destination address for
   which the relevant filter was written."
   Access: read-write
   Status: mandatory

OBJECT: rndMaskPat1
   SYNTAX: OCTET STRING
   Definition: "Describes the mask field which may consist of a
   binary 16-bit or hexadecimal 4-character code."
   Access: read-write
   Status: mandatory

OBJECT: rndMaskActiveBit1
   SYNTAX: OCTET STRING
```

```
   Definition: "Defines the position at which the Don't care
   character (X) is located in the rndMaskPat1-field."
   Access: read-write
   Status: mandatory

OBJECT: rndMaskForm1
   SYNTAX: INTEGER
               mac(1)
               llc(2)
   Definition: "Defines the basis from which the offset value is
   calculated"
   Access: read-write
   Status: mandatory

OBJECT: rndMaskOffset1
   SYNTAX: INTEGER
   Definition: "Defines the size of the offset. The offset may
   be a value between 0 and 518."
   Access: read-write
   Status: mandatory

OBJECT: rndMaskCond1
   SYNTAX: INTEGER
               true(1)
               false(2)
   Definition: "Defines the logical operator of the bitmask.
   True - The condition corresponds to the position in the data
   packet which has been defined by the value rndMaskOffset 1.
   The data corresponds to the rndMaskPat1 value. False - The
   condition corresponds to the position in the data packet
   which has been defined by the value rndMaskOffset 1. The data
   does not correspond to the rndMaskPat1 value."
   Access: read-write
   Status: mandatory

OBJECT: rndMaskPat2
   SYNTAX: OCTET STRING
   Definition: "Describes the mask field which may consist of a
   binary 16-bit or hexadecimal 4-character code."
   Access: read-write
   Status: mandatory

OBJECT: rndMaskActiveBit2
   SYNTAX: OCTET STRING
   Definition: "Defines the point at which the Don't care
   character (X) in the rndMaskPat2 field is located."
   Access: read-write
   Status: mandatory

OBJECT: rndMaskForm2
   SYNTAX: INTEGER
               mac(2)
               llc(2)
```

```
   Definition: "Defines the base from which the offset value is
   calculated."
   Access: read-write
   Status: mandatory

OBJECT: rndMaskOffset2
   SYNTAX: INTEGER
   Definition: "Defines the size of the offset. The offset may
   be a value between 0 and 518."
   Access: read-write
   Status: mandatory

OBJECT: rndMaskCond2
   SYNTAX: INTEGER
               true(1)
               false(2)
   Definition: "Defines the logical operator of the bitmask.
   True - The condition corresponds to the position in the data
   packet which has been defined by the value rndMaskOffset 2.
   The data corresponds to the rndMaskPat2 value. False - The
   condition corresponds to the position in the data packet
   which has been defined by the value rndMaskOffset 2. The data
   does not correspond to the rndMaskPat2 value."
   Access: read-write
   Status: mandatory

OBJECT: rndMaskPat3
   SYNTAX: OCTET STRING
   Definition: "Describes the mask field which may consist of a
   binary 16-bit or hexadecimal 4-character code."
   Access: read-write
   Status: mandatory

OBJECT: rndMaskActiveBit3
   SYNTAX: OCTET STRING
   Definition: "Defines the point at which the Don't care
   character (X) in the rndMaskPat3 field is located."
   Access: read-write
   Status: mandatory

OBJECT: rndMaskForm3
   SYNTAX: INTEGER
               mac(1)
               llc(2)
   Definition: "Defines the base from which the offset value is
   calculated."
   Access: read-write
   Status: mandatory

OBJECT: rndMaskOffset3
   SYNTAX: INTEGER
   Definition: "Defines the size of the offset. The offset may
   be a value between 0 and 518."
```

```
   Access: read-write
   Status: mandatory

OBJECT: rndMaskCond3
   SYNTAX: INTEGER
               true(1)
               false(2)
   Definition: "Defines the logical operator of the bitmask.
   True - The condition corresponds to the position in the data
   packet which has been defined by the value rndMaskOffset 3.
   The data corresponds to the rndMaskPat3 value. False - The
   condition corresponds to the position in the data packet
   which has been defined by the value rndMaskOffset 3. The data
   does not correspond to the rndMaskPat3 value."
Access: read-write
   Status: mandatory

OBJECT: rndMaskOper
   SYNTAX: INTEGER
               block(1)
               forward(2)
               route(3)
               forward_route(4)
   Definition: "Defines the actions which the bridge must
   execute after the operator of the data packets agrees with a
   filter."
   Access: read-write
   Status: mandatory
```

As this example of a private implementation of MIB variables shows, this mechanism enables the implementation of every device in all its variety. However, the danger is that behind the colorful and varied range offered by manufacturers of network management products for every problem and every type of application, there lurks not only a universal panacea but also a uniquely idiosyncratic product. Among the manifold possibilities for combining products, there are many variants for the implementation of a manageable LAN. Once the basic decision has been made to install a managed data network in a company, the LAN just keeps on growing. Since these data networks do not generally evolve according to any definite plan, but tend to be extended as required, an unmanageable outcome is sooner or later bound to emerge. The logical arrangement of the overall system necessarily suffers under this type of uncontrolled organic growth. Personnel costs for purchasing, implementation and servicing of the system also grow at a considerable rate and can completely undermine the cost-benefit advantage, which is actually at the root of every LAN in the first place. It is as a result of this plethora of data, which must somehow be managed, that most users and network operators set foot into the Information MIB jungle. Cynics maintain that almost every conceivable variant is now represented in the many MIB standards. Since the standardization committees of the Internet community have been so preoccupied with the definition of these MIBs over recent years, nobody has remembered to inform the user of the useful things that can be done with these MIBs. Experience has shown that a large proportion of agents currently available have still not implemented SNMP and MIB II correctly. The implementation of countless private MIBs and functions has reduced the standard management system to a more or less proprietary system. Advertising for these products is based on slogans such as open system, SNMP compatible, SNMP standard, and so on. If one resists the appeal of this type of empty marketing and investigates the products using objective criteria, it becomes clear that many of the products are actually far from open. Supporting the SNMP protocol unfortunately says nothing about the quality of implementation. SNMP simply means that only one protocol has been integrated into one device with various functional modules – nothing more. It says nothing about which user service is available for communication with the protocol.

In the least favourable scenario, the user operates on the prompt and is able to send SNMP messages manually. There are still no standards governing how a component is graphically mapped or displayed. In practice, this can have serious consequences because two different products may well be based on the same standard but still not be fully compatible.

To minimize the problem of private MIBs and private functions and to protect their own network management implementations from interference by other management applications, a number of manufacturers have locked the Set Function on their machines. These vendors generally support access to their products only via the Telnet Protocol or via management stations developed by themselves. This means that the user must know very accurately which network management station provides complete support to which private MIBs, so that he/she can make full use of the range of functions offered by the products in use. It will no doubt be some time before manufacturers manage to achieve really compatible products in terms of networking, and before every machine can be managed from every station.

In selecting manageable network products, the following points should be borne in mind:

- Which version of the standard MIBs are supported by the device?
- How and to what extent are any private MIBs integrated?
- Can the network management system import additional manufacturer MIBs?
- Which auxiliary functions (for example, API, Application Builder) are available for integrating manufacturer MIBs into a management application?
- Are private MIBs from the relevant manufacturer supplied in ASN.1 format?

- How are updates carried out when the standard changes?
- Does a particular MIB compiler have to be installed on the relevant network management station?
- Is the Set Function supported for all variables?
- If the Set Function is not supported for all variables, the range of functions that cannot be implemented must be established.

4.4 Proxy SNMP

The basic model of SNMP determines how the SNMP agent is integrated with the Management Information Base (MIB) in the machine which is monitored and managed by the SNMP protocol. Before SNMP was developed, there were already several high-performance network management solutions. These management applications are generally based on proprietary specifications. The purpose of these systems was to increase the availability and reliability of the various components, for example workstations, servers, gateways, repeaters, printers and terminal servers. As a rule, such proprietary management systems specialized in the environment in which they were used. From the outset, multifunctionality was not desired, and this type of management technology was never widely distributed across the market. Because these devices and network management applications were already in use and available on the market, two approaches were used to ensure a transition to SNMP:

- Dispense with migration pathway;
- Expand the SNMP architecture model.

Dispense with migration pathway

Even on proprietary systems, network-relevant data is held in one or more databases (on servers); the network management systems (clients) have access to the data pools of these databases. For around ten years, manufacturers have been selling these supplementary features as network management functions as part of the overall solution. However, for historical and technical reasons, these devices do not always conform to the latest hardware and software technology. If the standardization groups of the Internet community, which were professionally engaged with this problem, had not been trying to integrate these systems into the new concept from the very start, the soft migration pathway would have been dispensed with. This would necessarily have led to manufacturers and users having no possibility of a gentle, gradual transition to a standardized system. In the worst

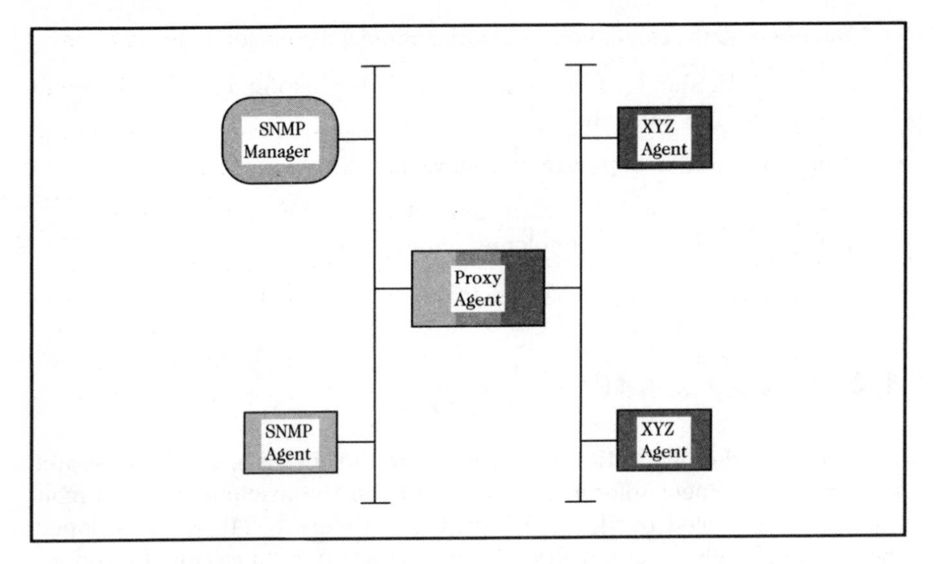

Figure 4.15 Proxy management

case scenario, network operators would have had to face the problem of several network management concepts being operated alongside each other for a certain period. This would have necessitated incisive measures both at a personnel level and in terms of costs.

Expand the SNMP architecture model

The development of network management began within the Internet community when, in 1987, a number of network gurus from the TCP/IP world recognized the signs of the times. The first practical step towards a network management concept was the development of the Simple Gateway Monitoring Protocol (SGMP). SGMP was accepted as a short-to-medium-term solution and was used on some Internet computers. At the same time however, the protocol was completely revised, giving birth to SNMP. As a 'proposed standard', the protocol developed by the Internet community then set out on the long march towards SNMP becoming a full standard. After the test period, it was able to attain the title of 'draft standard'. After further editing, commentary, implementations and all the accompanying tests, the protocol finally made it to the level of 'standard'. The Online Internet Draft Directorship has the right of precedence over publication of a proposed standard. Comments on this proposed standard may be issued by any Internet participant. The Internet drafts are generally working papers by the Internet Architecture Board (IAB) or by one of the project groups of the Internet Engineering Task Force (IETF). The Internet drafts are either presented to the publisher of the RFCs for publication or they are rejected within a few months. An RFC can only rise from the status of draft standard to a standard via the Internet Draft Publication and

Review Cycle. It has also become accepted that at least two fully independent and self-sufficient implementations of the protocol must be realized before a proposed standard can become a draft standard. On this long journey towards the status of a standard, more and more new requirements were integrated into the SNMP protocol.
One of the most demanding requirements on the protocol was to enable a certain degree of downward compatibility with already existing standards and also with proprietary solutions. To this end, the basic SNMP architecture model had to be submitted to further extensive expansion. This expansion is referred to as Proxy Management. According to this approach, a 'bilingual' agent enables direct conversion of the relevant management functions. This proxy gateway can be implemented in a separate agent or in the network management system itself. The proxy agent, in this case, acts on behalf of the network management system and converts all SNMP functions into proprietary management functions.

Advantages of proxy management

- All devices can be included in the overall concept.
- Favourable-cost migration to a new standard.
- Only one central station is needed.
- The users do not need to operate several management concepts or to understand the entire syntax.
- All proprietary functions can be integrated via private MIBs.

Disadvantages of proxy management

- Time limitation on support from manufacturer.
- Costly and time-consuming because special proxy implementations must be manufactured.
- Causes a flood of private MIBs.

Figure 4.15 shows the various communicative relationships between management stations, proxy agents and management agents.

4.5 Critique of SNMP Version 1

When the development of SNMP began in 1987, none of the people or companies involved in the processes of standardization and development could possibly have suspected the stormy events brewing in the field of data communications. SNMP was conceived as a practical approach to network management based on the Simple Gateway Monitoring Protocol (SGMP). The actual tasks of SGMP were simple monitoring functions which could be implemented on WAN IP Gateways (routers). The Internet team responsible for implementing SGMP next developed a successor with a wider range of functions. In its turn this development led to the now familiar SNMP. Since the Internet community has always based its research on the standards available internationally, it was obvious that the work of the ISO/OSI organization would be used as a basic framework for the development of the SNMP standard. SNMP is currently supported by almost every manufacturer. As a result, this protocol and its applications are spreading even more rapidly. Work on the SNMP standard was coordinated internationally by the Internet Engineering Task Force (IETF) and carried out by the various working groups. Among manufacturers, a few individuals and companies, sharing the SNMP source code market between them, have become established. Carnegie Mellon University (CMU), SNMP Research Inc., Peer Networks and Epilogue Technology Corporation are examples. Carnegie Mellon University has developed a Public Domain SNMP Code, which is available to all participants free of charge via the Internet. The CMU Code is – like all Public Domain software – not documented and may contain the usual programming errors. This code can only be brought to life through serious debugging and a great deal of 'trial and error'. In order to bring a viable product to the market, many companies are beginning to use commercially available products. Companies like SNMP Research Inc., Peer Networks and Epilogue Technology Corporation are therefore carving up the lion's share of the market between them.

General

SNMP developed slowly and has now penetrated areas for which it was never intended. During the development from the first simple protocol mechanisms of the Simple Gateway Monitoring Protocol (SGMP) to the current considerably extended claims and associated functions of SNMP network management, countless problem areas, which could never have been anticipated by the original SNMP specifications, have crystallized out. Supporting management functions in a range of complex devices (gateways, bridges, routers, terminal servers, and so on) now provide considerably more, highly detailed information and are based on the assumption that the network management protocol will offer the appropriate protocol mechanisms to process this information without difficulties. These new demands on protocol mechanisms can be categorized as follows:

- Simple structure;
- Heavy network loading;
- Rigid allocation of functions;

- Only for TCP/IP networks;
- Security of data;
- Limiting the range of functions;
- No certification.

Simple structure

Using the functions established in SNMP, only one management station (management implementation) can execute the commands Get Request, Get Next Request and Set Request. These commands are answered by the individual agents with Set Response packages. The trap is the only means available to the agent for sending messages to the manager. However, no confirmation is given by the manager in reply to the traps sent by the agent. The agent therefore always remains uncertain as to whether the trap has been received correctly. Using the Get Request command, the SNMP manager can request values for the variables supported by the agent. These variables must always be indicated exactly. The Get Next Request command, however, enables the immediate successor of any object in the agent to be read. This command primarily simplifies the reading of tables. However, it does mean that the variables in the agent must be sorted. This, of course, considerably increases the complexity of the implementation.

Heavy network loading

The Get Next function generally leads to an excessive burden on the network, because a Request and a Reply packet are sent via the network for every variable requested. This heavy network loading caused by the network management application reduces the bandwidth available for the actual network data. This has particularly serious consequences if there is a narrowband WAN connection between manager and agent.

Rigid allocation of functions

Because of the lack of manager-to-manager communication in the SNMPv1 standard, only flat network management structures can be implemented. A manager must always monitor the whole network or at least the whole community. If a network is subdivided into several communities and if several network management stations are also used, this leads to the formation of data and information islands which cannot communicate with each other. It is extremely difficult to preserve a clear overview of the complete network in this type of scenario. With SNMPv1, each manager has access to all data. Certain data areas cannot be masked according to predetermined criteria. As a result, a management station can only gain access either to all data or to none of the data.

Only for TCP/IP networks

In theory, SNMP can be used on any available protocol stack. In practice however, the internal structures (addresses, reserved ports, and so on) of SNMP have proved to be too inflexible to be integrated into a multiprotocol world without great difficulty. As a rule, the TCP/IP protocols have become established for SNMP applications and now dominate the world of network management. Only isolated implementations based on other protocols (usually IPX) have been developed.

Security of data

Data security in respect of SNMP was entirely neglected for a time or else was mentioned only in whispers. A number of definitions of security have been available since mid-1990, but these have been more or less ignored in current implementations of SNMP software. The Secure Working Group published an SNMP Security Variant in RFC 1352 under the title *SNMP Security Protocols* (July 1992). However, this document never rose above the status of a proposal. Secure SNMP establishes an independent authentication and coding mechanism. The major criticism of the Secure SNMP Proposal was that it did not guarantee downward compatibility with the existing SNMP protocols. The result of this was that all SNMP products installed had to be replaced or upgraded. This, of course, prevented wider distribution.

In terms of security, the following problems are associated with SNMP Version 1:

- Manipulation of packet contents;
- Correctness of sequence;
- Impersonation of a community;
- Unauthorized reading of information.

Manipulation of SNMP packages

In a network monitored and controlled by SNMP, it is always possible for an unauthorized user to capture the data packets and change the information (parameter values) for his or her own purposes. After this manipulation, the altered data packets are sent on to their actual target station.

The receiving device is unable to recognize this type of data manipulation. It therefore responds to the information contained in the packet as if it had been received directly from the management station.

Correctness of sequence

In general, all data between the management station and the connected agents are sent using the unsecured User Datagram Protocol service. Since the UDP does not guarantee sequential correctness of data, SNMP data can be delayed or may reach the recipient in an altered sequence, either passively, as a result of the dynamics of the LAN, or actively, through manipulation by a saboteur. Unauthorized users are therefore always in a position to alter data contents in their favour, and the recipient can to nothing to discover this form of manipulation.

Impersonation of a community

Simply by redefining the Community String, the owner of a network management station can gain access at any time to every agent connected to the network. This masquerade enables an unauthorized user to impersonate the identity of an authorized user, to read all information and implement all management operations. The agent has no means of distinguishing between the correct identity and the impersonator.

Unauthorized reading of information

Passive reading of data by unauthorized users using a data analyzer is a built-in problem with data networks. All the functions and devices normally used for network trouble shooting can also be misused at any time for illicit purposes. Any data (including passwords) can be read passively in the LAN and subsequently misused at some later date.

Limiting the range of functions

Because of the lack of security mechanisms in Version 1 of SNMP, a number of manufacturers have decided to suppress the Set Request functions in their SNMP agents for network management applications that they have not supplied themselves. However, a hacker can still read the data on the network, but cannot reconfigure the agent for his own purposes.

No certification

Another problem area connected with the SNMPv1 protocol is the lack of conformance testing. Any manufacturer can implement SNMP on his machines by relying on a Public Domain solution, a commercial solution or the talents of his own software engineers. A great many antiquated or difficult-to-implement SNMP solutions are currently available, which cannot, or can only partially, be brought up to the latest technical standards by means of an upgrade. From the user's viewpoint, certification and a conformance test for existing SNMP solutions would be highly desirable.

4.5.1 General critique of network management

Operating a data network and the many applications that can be used on it represents a productivity factor which should not be underestimated. In advanced data networks it is important to be able to request all data and information from any point in the system. Dependence on the availability of the data network and the connected terminal devices will naturally increase in proportion to the role played by data transfer in the internal processes of an organization. Any breakdown of these vital components will lead to considerable costs. The availability of a suitable network management system is indispensable for every data network. It is essential that a data network can be managed from one central position. This also contributes to shortening network downtime and preventing imminent breakdowns of the network or of components as far as possible, using appropriate means (preventive tools). The network management systems currently available in the LAN market have all implemented the standard SNMP as the basic protocol for network management and are open to subsequent expansion. The very mention of the topic 'network management' always seems to arouse the enthusiasm of technically minded people, who start to talk about SNMP, MIBs, RMON, configuration management and MIB browsers; the actual purpose of a network management system is often concealed behind all this 'techno-speak'. In this type of situation, the 'non-technical', who find it difficult to understand acronyms and abbreviations, are simply left shaking their heads incredulously. The economic benefits of this type of system ultimately remain a mystery to them.

Amongst the glittering array of products offered by manufacturers and distributors, there seems to be a uniquely 'perfect' product for every problem and every application. Engineers love to talk about technology and rapidly fall victim to subtle technical sales-talk. It is very easy to overlook the fact that the majority of products do not actually correspond to the state of the art in terms of technical maturity. This is especially true where the solution offered is restricted to the range of products from a single vendor. Advertising for these products often relies on slogans such as open system, SNMP compatible, SNMP standard, and so on. If one refuses to be taken in by marketing jargon and investigates these products according to objective criteria, it will soon become clear that many of the products are far from open. Unfortunately, supporting SNMP says nothing about the quality of implementation, and in most solutions, only a fraction of the internationally agreed standards have actually been integrated. To begin with, SNMP simply means that only one protocol with certain functional modules has been integrated into a machine – nothing more. It implies nothing about the user interface available for communication with the protocol. In the least favourable scenario, the user works on the prompt and can send SNMP messages manually. There are still no standards governing how a component is to be graphically mapped or displayed. In practice this can have serious consequences, because two different products may well be based upon the same standard, but still not be completely compatible. The excessive emphasis on technology is an extremely widespread phenomenon in the context of network problem solving. Technological problem solving tends to follow the kind of outline described below.

A problem and its symptoms are recognized. Because the network administrator is generally under enormous pressure of time, technical equipment takes the blame for the problem. This apportionment of blame often conceals a lack of knowledge or experience. A product or a solution that will solve this technical problem (as cheaply as possible) is sought. In this manner, treatment is found for the symptoms but not for the cause. After a certain time, the same problem recurs, albeit possibly in a slightly different form. Once again, a technical panacea is sought. If the problems really take the upper hand, the engineer can no longer avoid facing the actual cause of the dilemma. This means that many hours of expensive operating time are invested in the removal of symptoms before an investigation of the actual cause is even attempted. Since it used to be possible to achieve success through quick solutions, no time was spent on methodical investigation of causes. Now however, current problems can no longer be satisfactorily resolved before the next problems begin to emerge. Operational costs are rising and will soon no longer be economically viable. The troubleshooter now has to pay for this two- or threefold, investing a great deal of time and energy in looking for causes and actually solving the problems. They must step outside the operational role and develop realistic problem-solving strategies.

The approach to technical problem solving described above can be found in most companies. In such organizations, problem solving is carried out almost exclusively by the technical department. If computers and data networks are involved, the information technology department almost automatically assumes control of problem management. However, these technical departments focus primarily on the technical aspects (hardware conditions, compatibility, performance, technical peculiarities, support and possibly purchasing costs) of the products and technologies used. In order to gain more rapid control of technical problems, departments with a technical orientation become more vociferous in their demand for the introduction of a management system, because they hope this will enable them to gain better control over their technical products. This is known as the bottom-up approach.

Technical parameters and their consequences in a complete system are, of course, important factors in deciding on the introduction of a network management system. However, these criteria do not provide an adequate basis for coming to a decision on the type of system to install. The non-technical approach requires the preparation of a strategic catalogue in which all operating demands and aspects are taken into consideration. Technical aspects are only relevant when all the boundary conditions have been clarified. In this way, an organization can check, independently of the available technology, which demands are present and how they can best be met using the technology offered.

Technical resources are provided in an organization in order to support and simplify operating processes. However, this support is not provided by the infrastructure used, for example the cables, the network components, the protocols, the network operating system or the computer connected to the network. The applications and user-supported services are the actual criteria without which access to the common supply of data (accounting, stores, documents) would not be possible. Only the use of databases, E-mail services, and so on provides the user with information services via the network.

The top-down approach derives the requirements on a network system from the requirements of the applications. This is the only means of ensuring the efficient achievement of corporate goals and optimum, trouble-free support for employees. After the requirements of applications and services have been established, the demands on the network and on the quality and quantity of necessary network services can be derived. With the top-down approach, planning is continuous, and the overall plan includes solutions to potential, future problems. This way of thinking requires a more global strategy than the technical, bottom-up approach. The detailed analysis of requirements which precedes the global concept naturally increases the effort and expense which must be invested in the implementation of a network. However, a detailed analysis pays off in the long run, because although considerable problems may be encountered in achieving the strategic goals, these problems can ultimately be solved more quickly and with much less effort.

Network management is a fixed and essential component of a global networking concept. It must therefore be understood as a comprehensive, organizational and technical measure. The top-down approach requires collaboration between all corporate divisions. Corporate management must establish the requirements of subordinate organizational levels. The individual corporate levels must define the services needed for day-to-day operation. The IT department must plan the necessary resources in order to be able to implement requirements at network level and the associated network management. The analysis of all components of a global concept must not balk in the face of sacred cows, such as a favourite application program or computer system which is antiquated but still 'does the job'. The strategy of global thinking also implies cutting away the dead wood and replacing it with more effective mechanisms. With a strategic network concept, the basic services such as configuration management (documentation and alteration of the network configuration), error management (error recognition and removal), performance management (monitoring network loading), accounting management (calculation of network costs) and security management (management of users and monitoring access authorization) must be supplemented by additional features:

- Integration of applications;
- Possibility of constant growth;
- Flexible integration of new corporate concepts;
- Simulation as a basis for planning.

Integration of applications

A global network system covers all seven layers of the OSI reference model, from the physical level up to the applications level. However, the applications level defines only services that the network makes available to the actual applications. These applications, with which the user carries out his or her work, are used by the applications level of the network system. It is absolutely necessary to add this eighth level to the overall system and therefore also to the network management. The specific requirements of each application are administered through an applications management system and the resources and configurations required by the applications are provided dynamically. Unfortunately, the network management products currently on sale at this level offer virtually no possibility of integrating applications into a holistic system.

The possibility of constant growth

A global network concept and the resulting comprehensive network management concept creates the preconditions for supporting all services through the network. Since the requirements placed by communications philosophies are constantly being changed as a result of new services and strategies, for example multimedia, video networking, and so on, and since new goals are defined to preserve the competitiveness of an organization, the concept must contain the possibility of responding to constant growth and dynamic expansion.

Flexible integration of new corporate concepts

Rigid computer empires – and therefore also antiquated organizational hierarchies – are things of the past. Discussion of contemporary computer culture is dominated by terms such as downsizing or right-sizing. For reasons of cost, central IT services are subdivided into smaller units and replaced by decentralized client/server solutions with distributed applications. Narrowly circumscribed and functionally one-dimensional applications are replaced by open, network-compatible applications capable of integration. At the lower levels of the network, this necessitates the use of standards and multi-vendor interfaces and protocols. The resulting flexibility demands an unprecedented competence and responsibility from each independently organized corporate unit. Classic terminal networks have to be replaced by modular LANs and WANs. However, the new communications structure also sets new challenges for the individual specialist departments in terms of levels of training and motivation of employees.

Simulation as a basis for planning

Adapting a data network to constantly changing demands and implementing this adaptation without losing too much time requires a management function with which the corresponding parameters can be simulated. At a technical level, potential problems can only be identified in their early stages by monitoring all the important points of a plan. Procedural bottlenecks (network, applications and servicing) can be planned-in so that subsequent users of these services are not restricted or obstructed in their work. A complete simulation enables the network operator to resort to the appropriate measures at the right time, to minimize points of friction and the resulting expense. The more the demands on a network change, the more important it is to simulate the outcome at an early stage.

The introduction of a network management system into an organization requires a strategic approach. It must been understood as a management tool. For this reason, it must be dragged up from the depths of purely technical administration of bits, bytes and parameters. A management system is a management tool; it must therefore be derived from the strategic demands of the organization. It must support the operational boundary conditions and function as a linking tool for all software and hardware platforms used. It should also be capable of flexible expansion and adaptable to new organizational conditions. However, even the best network management system can only provide the maximum benefit if the goals and demands on the overall system are clearly defined.

4.6 Simple Management Protocol

As in most branches of industry, there is no shortage of brilliant individuals in the world of SNMP, who through their commitment become the human powerhouse behind their particular development. Often these people become renowned against their will and are associated with particular techniques and development stages. The SNMP protocol, especially Version 2, has become almost synonymous with the names Jeffrey Case (SNMP Research Inc.), Steve Waldbusser (Carnegie Mellon University, Pittsburgh), Marshall T. Rose (Dover Beach Consulting, Mountain View CA) and Keith McCloghrie (Hughes LAN Systems CA). In 1992, this 'Gang of Four' – as they have come to be known – gave a press conference in which they announced the availability of a new version of SNMP. In order to distance themselves completely from the world of SNMP, this specification was named Simple Management Protocol (SMP). SMP was taken up enthusiastically by the hungry specialist press. The SMP protocol was developed independently of normal IAB/IETF procedures. Its specifications are not even available as RFCs. In order to force the development of a new SNMP protocol, the authors decided to present the SMP specification to the IETF for certification, after the media storm over the SMP had settled down. Their new approach was based on practical experience with SNMPv1. It has considerably expanded the range of functions of network management.

4.7 The long route towards the SNMPv2 Standard

The Secure SNMP Proposal by Galvin, McGloghrie and Davin which was published in July 1992 as RFC 1352 can be considered a precursor to the SMP protocol. This working paper addresses a number of important problem areas connected with the SNMP protocol and defines, for the first time, independent authentication and coding mechanisms.

When the SNMP protocol was established and published in 1988, it was not possible to include security considerations for the following reasons:

- The individual standardization groups could not agree on a combined strategy.
- At the time there was little practical experience in this field.
- Users tended to remain silent about the topic and no pressure was put on the standardization groups.

RFC 1352 had provided an initial spark in terms of security. The document ensured that the discussion was opened on the offensive and pursued seriously by all the main groups in the Internet community.

The safety mechanism integrated in the SNMPv1 standard was based on a relatively simple mechanism. This mechanism has been described as 'trivial authentication'. In the SNMPv1 protocol, a Community String, which is contained in every SNMP packet, is compared with the configured SNMP Community String in the agent. A decision is made on the basis of the entries in the tables as to whether the message received is an authentic or a non-authentic message. To prevent misuse of the Community String, the SNMPv1 standard documents recommend that the Community String should be divulged only to devices (agent and management station) involved in the communication. The Community String was not coded, neither were any other mechanisms integrated to ensure its safety. In practice, all Community Strings were entered as ASCII text in every message. Any technician who knows anything about the internal attributes of the SNMP protocol can easily identify the packets and their contents. With this information, he can create his own management messages without great difficulty. This simply means that there is no effective data protection for the SNMPv1 protocol. The trivial authentication mechanism does not stop the protocol from being read illicitly. At best this mechanism means that protocol processing on the individual machines produces somewhat more overhead. As a result of this loophole in security, the SNMPv1 protocol was not used in many applications.

The Secure SNMP working group, the SMP group, tackled this security loophole and ultimately succeeded in publishing the relevant specification in the SNMPv2 protocol. RFC 1446 (*Security Protocols for version 2 of the*

Simple Network Management Protocol) and RFC 1447 (*Party MIB for version 2 of the Simple Network Management Protocol*) by Galvin and McCloghrie dealt extensively with the security functions of SNMP. These sub-standards enabled the manufacturers of SNMP products to integrate individually scaled security mechanisms.

In April 1993, work on the SNMPv2 standard was completed by the Internet Working Groups and passed on to the IETF for presentation and checking. These standards were published in the Requests for Comments 1441 to 1452. These several hundred page long documents form the basis for anyone interested in understanding the new SNMPv2 protocol and its various parameters. SNMPv2 is necessarily accompanied by a series of format and operational alterations. As a supplement to the old SNMP commands, the GetBulk Request was introduced. This considerably reduces the amount of data to be processed. The Remote Network Monitoring (RMON), which was developed in parallel with SNMPv2, benefits from the new functions. As a transitional solution until complete migration of all products to SNMPv2, all implementations will probably be implemented in 'bilingual' form. This will enable SNMPv2 agents to communicate directly with their management stations, but SNMPv1 stations will have to operate through a translator. In any case, SNMPv1 will eventually die out, making complete migration to SNMPv2 an inescapable necessity.

Without the precocious publication of the SMP specification by the Gang of Four, it would probably have taken even longer for the SNMPv2 standard to see the light of day. Public interest in the SMP specification placed such great pressure on the IAB and the Internet community that work on the new Internet management station was pushed ahead as quickly as possible.

5

Simple Network Management Protocol Version 2

After lengthy discussions and endless, arduous meetings of the Network Working Group, the specification for Simple Network Management Protocol Version 2 (SNMPv2) was published in April 1993. The complete SNMPv2 standard is set out in these Requests for Comments (RFC):

RFC 1441
Introduction to version 2 of the Internet Standard Network Management Framework

RFC 1442
Structure of Management Information for version 2 of the Simple Network Management Protocol (SNMPv2)

RFC 1443
Textual Conventions for version 2 of the Simple Network Management Protocol (SNMPv2)

RFC 1444
Conformance Statements for version 2 of the Simple Network Management Protocol (SNMPv2)

RFC 1445
Administrative Model for version 2 of the Simple Network Management Protocol (SNMPv2)

RFC 1446
Security Protocols for version 2 of the Simple Network Management Protocol (SNMPv2)

RFC 1447
Party MIB for version 2 of the Simple Network Management Protocol (SNMPv2)

RFC 1448
Protocol Operations for version 2 of the Simple Network Management Protocol (SNMPv2)

RFC 1449
Transport Mappings for version 2 of the Simple Network Management Protocol (SNMPv2)

RFC 1450
Management Information Base for version 2 of the Simple Network Management Protocol (SNMPv2)

RFC 1451
Manager-to-Manager Management Information Base

RFC 1452
Coexistence between version 1 and version 2 of the Internet-standard Network Management Framework

The SNMPv2 specifications established the basis of all requirements for an advanced management protocol. The considerably extended functional range of SNMPv2 compared with the original version of SNMP includes the following features:

Considerably extended communication model
The individual security and authentication mechanisms can be configured by the network administrator via parties. The various access rights, the perspectives on the Management Information Base, can be individually set by means of parties, and several network management stations can access one agent. A certain section of the MIB tree is configured for each of the parties (MIB View), so that each station can only read or write to the objects provided for it. The standard MIB had to be completely revised, to enable these functions in the protocol.

Extensions to the structure of management information

The administrative framework of SNMPv2 is based on the SNMP definition and was only slightly extended. The differences are primarily in the extended authentication and authorization functions.

Communication between manager stations

SNMPv2 also deals with another of the criticisms of SNMP. The rigid distinction between an agent (server process) and a network manager (agent process) has been broken down. From SNMPv2 onwards, a network manager can act both as an agent process and as a server process. This function enables manager-to-manager communication (implemented through a manager-to-manager MIB) within SNMPv2.

Security

In the SNMP protocol, a Community String, which is contained in every SNMP packet, is compared with the configured SNMP Community String in the agent. Any technician who knows the internal attributes of the SNMP can therefore easily identify the packets and their contents. With this information, he can simply create his own management messages. This represents a not inconsiderable security deficit in the SNMP standard. The Secure SNMP Working Group was set up to address this problem, and SNMPv2 has adopted a number of the solutions proposed. For example, the MD5 algorithm has been integrated for authentication. The MD5 algorithm forms a 16-byte individual fingerprint for each SNMPv2 packet by combining a type of checksum and a time stamp. This fingerprint enables the recipient to check the origin of a message received and to determine whether it has been transmitted without interference. There is also an encoding option. This prevents an outside observer of the network from understanding the message transmitted.

A further security aspect is the integration of time stamps for the complete life of an SNMP message. This is intended to prevent the repetition of a valid message at a later time. If this still fails to satisfy the security needs of some users, the optional coding of all data may be called upon. The coding mechanism provided is the DES (Data Encryption Standard) of the National Institute of Standards.

Transfer of bulk data in a PDU

The Get Bulk Request was introduced as a supplement to the old SNMP commands (Set Request, Get Request, Get Next Request and Response). A Get Bulk Request enables a complete MIB tree to be read with a single request. Since this considerably reduces the amount of data to be processed, the network transfer capacity for other data is preserved.

Extended error signalling

In the SNMP, the list of known errors was extended to 13 error codes. The information content of the traps can also be set with specific reference to the implementation.

The use of various transport services

True to the vision of a multiprotocol Internet, SNMPv2 was designed to be used with a range of different transport protocols. In addition to transport mapping on the basis of the User Datagram Protocol (UDP), which was already in use in the SNMP standard, the following access points have been determined for SNMPv2: SNMPv2 on OSI, SNMPv2 on DPP and SNMPv2 on Novell-IPX.

Downward compatibility

Until the complete migration of all products to SNMPv2, all of these codes have been implemented in two languages. This enables SNMPv2 agents to communicate directly with their management stations, while SNMPv1 stations must communicate via an SNMP language translator.

5.1 SNMPv2 SMI

As with SNMPv1, the Structure of Management Information (SMI) is also a fixed component of the new SNMPv2 specification. Compared with version 1, however, the SMI has changed in a number of respects.

Beneath the Internet subtree (1.3.6.1) of the management tree, important new branches have been added. The branching layout is now as follows:

directory	(internet 1)
mgmt	(internet 2)
experimental	(internet 3)
private	(internet 4)
security	(internet 5)
snmpV2	(internet 6)

The new SNMPv2 MIBs are integrated beneath the SNMPv2 branch with the prefix 1.3.6.1.6.

General SNMPv2 definitions:

```
SNMPv2-SMI DEFINITIONS ::= BEGIN

internet        OBJECT IDENTIFIER ::= { iso 3 6 1 }

directory       OBJECT IDENTIFIER ::= { internet 1 }
```

```
mgmt            OBJECT IDENTIFIER ::= { internet 2 }

experimental    OBJECT IDENTIFIER ::= { internet 3 }

private         OBJECT IDENTIFIER ::= { internet 4 }
enterprises     OBJECT IDENTIFIER ::= { private 1 }

security        OBJECT IDENTIFIER ::= { internet 5 }

snmpV2          OBJECT IDENTIFIER ::= { internet 6 }

-- Transport Domains
snmpDomains     OBJECT IDENTIFIER ::= { snmpV2 1 }

-- Transport Proxies
snmpProxys      OBJECT IDENTIFIER ::= { snmpV2 2 }

-- SNMPv2 Module
snmpModules     OBJECT IDENTIFIER ::= { snmpV2 3 }
```

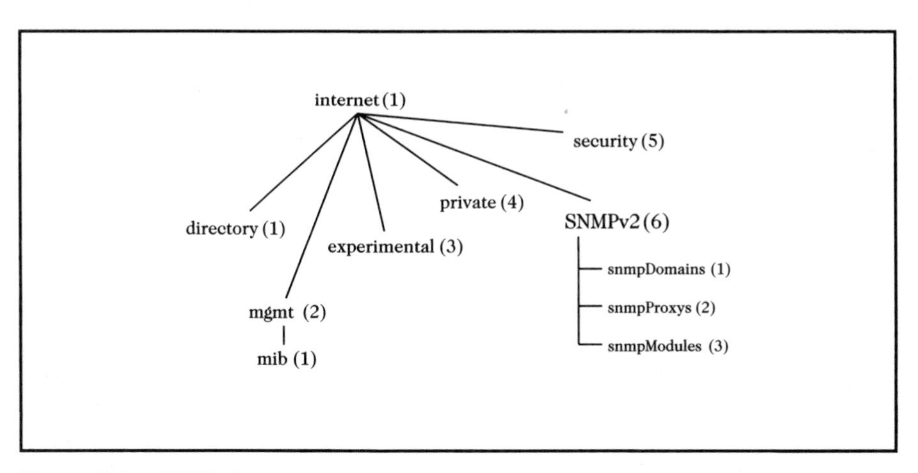

Figure 5.1 SNMPv2 management tree

The Structure of Management Information (SMI) in SNMPv2 consists of three parts:

- Module definitions;
- Object definitions;
- Trap definitions.

5.1.1 Module definition

The Module definition is used in the SMI to describe the information module. The ASN.1 Module Identity Macro describes the information module unambiguously.

Definition: Module Identity Macro

```
MODULE IDENTITY-MACRO ::=
BEGIN
    TYPE NOTATION ::=
                  "LAST-UPDATED" value(Update UTCTime)
                  "ORGANIZATION" Text
                  "CONTACT-INFO" Text
                  "DESCRIPTION" Text
                  RevisionPart

    VALUE NOTATION ::=
                  value(VALUE OBJECT IDENTIFIER)

    RevisionPart ::=
                  Revisions
                | empty
    Revisions ::=
                  Revision
                | Revisions Revision
    Revision ::=
                  "REVISION" value(Update UTCTime)
                  "DESCRIPTION" Text

    Text ::= """" string """"
END
```

In the Module Identity Macro, the relevant structure is established using the Type Notation. The Module Identity Macro must contain the following components:

- LAST-UPDATED;
- ORGANIZATION;
- CONTACT-INFO;
- DESCRIPTION.

LAST-UPDATED
Contains a local variable, whose value indicates the time (UTCTime) at which the module was last changed.

ORGANIZATION

Contains contact information relating to the organization responsible for the module.

Example

```
ORGANIZATION "Tristate Communications SNMPv2 Working Group."
```

CONTACT-INFO

Contains contact information relating to the editor responsible for the module.

Example

```
CONTACT-INFO
        "       David Griffiths

         Postal: Tristate Communications
                 Barton Park,
                 Marlborough, Wiltshire SN8 1TU
                 UK

            Tel: +44 672 516060
            Fax: +44 672 516125

         E-mail: davidg@cix.compulink.co.uk"
```

DESCRIPTION

Contains textual information relating to the relevant Module Identity Macro.

Example

```
DESCRIPTION
"The Tristate MIB module for all implementations of the Tristate
SNMP code <169>."
```

The optional Revision Part in the Module Identity Macro comprises two sections:

- REVISION;
- DESCRIPTION.

REVISION
Contains a local variable whose value indicates the time (UTCTime) at which the module was registered.

DESCRIPTION
This field describes the relevant revision in ASCII text.

Example

```
DESCRIPTION "First version of the MIB Module."
```

The Value Notation, which establishes the actual object identifier for the information module, is located at the end of the Module Identity Macro.

Example

```
::=  { SNMPModules 25 }
```

5.1.2 Object Identity Macro

Individual object identifiers in the SNMPv2 SMI are determined by means of an Object Identity Macro. The Object Identity Macro is composed of the following parts:

- STATUS;
- DESCRIPTION;
- REFERENCE.

Definition: Object Identity Macro

```
OBJECT-IDENTITY-MACRO ::=
BEGIN
    TYPE NOTATION ::=
                  "STATUS" Status
                  "DESCRIPTION" Text
                  ReferPart

    VALUE NOTATION ::=
                  value(VALUE OBJECT IDENTIFIER)

    Status ::=
```

```
                    "current"
                  | "obsolete"

    ReferPart ::=
                  "REFERENCE" Text
                | empty

    Text ::= """" string """"
END
```

STATUS
Defines the validity of the Object Identity Macro. The only values permitted are current and obsolete. The status field must be contained in every Object Identity Macro.

DESCRIPTION
Describes (in ASCII text) the meaning and purpose of the relevant Object Identity Macro. The Description field must be contained in every Object Identity Macro.

REFERENCE
The optional Reference field enables cross-references to other objects in other MIB modules to be entered.

Example

```
Tristate4760 OBJECT-IDENTITY
   STATUS  current
   DESCRIPTION
   "Used for the unique identification of the Tristate 4760
   Chipset."
   ::= { tristateChipSets 1 }
```

5.1.3 Object definitions

Manageable objects are unequivocally determined by the object definitions. The ASN.1 Object Type Macro is used for the exact description of manageable objects within the SMI.

Definition: Object Type Macro

```
OBJECT-TYPE MACRO ::=
BEGIN
    TYPE NOTATION ::=
```

```
                  "SYNTAX" type(Syntax)
                  UnitsPart
                  "MAX-ACCESS" Access
                  "STATUS" Status
                  "DESCRIPTION" Text
                  ReferPart
                  IndexPart
                  DefValPart

VALUE NOTATION ::=
                  value(VALUE ObjectName)

UnitsPart ::=
                  "UNITS" Text
                | empty

Access ::=
                  "not-accessible"
                | "read-only"
                | "read-write"
                | "read-create"

Status ::=
                  "current"
                | "deprecated"
                | "obsolete"

ReferPart ::=
                  "REFERENCE" Text
                | empty

IndexPart ::=
                  "INDEX"    "{" IndexTypes "}"
                | "AUGMENTS" "{" Entry      "}"
                | empty
IndexTypes ::=
                  IndexType
                | IndexTypes "," IndexType

IndexType ::=
                  "IMPLIED" Index
                | Index
Index ::=
                    -- use the SYNTAX value of the
                    -- corresponding OBJECT-TYPE invocation
                  value(Indexobject ObjectName)
Entry ::=
                    -- use the INDEX value of the
                    -- corresponding OBJECT-TYPE invocation
                  value(Entryobject ObjectName)
```

```
    DefValPart ::=
                   "DEFVAL" "{" value(Defval Syntax) "}"
                 | empty

    Text ::= """" string """"
END
```

Syntax

The syntax of the Object Type Macro determines the relevant ASN.1 syntax type for the object. The values determined for the syntax field include the basic types Integer, Object Identifier and Octet, which are familiar from SNMP version 1, with the addition of the Bit String type. The following additional, combined types are determined as Application Wide types: IpAddress, Counter32, TimeTicks, Opaque, NsapAddress, Counter64 and UInteger.

Example

```
TAddress ::= TEXTUAL-CONVENTION
   STATUS        current
   DESCRIPTION
   "Determines the Transport Service Address."
   SYNTAX        OCTET STRING
```

Integer32

For representing numbers in the SNM of SNMPv2, Integer32 can be used in addition to the Integer type. All numbers consisting of the digits 0, 1, 2, 3, 4, 5, 6, 7, 8 and 9 can be described using an Integer. The only exception is that the digit 0 can be used only in combination with other digits. It must not be used alone. The range of values for Integer32 extends from –2 147 483 648 to 2 147 483 647.

Example

```
snmpORIndex OBJECT TYPE
   SYNTAX     Integer32
   MAX-ACCESS not-accessible
   STATUS     current
   DESCRIPTION
   "This variable is used for unambiguous identification of an
   instance in the snmpORTable."
   ::= { snmpOREntry 1 }
```

Octet String

The Octet String type was defined in ASN.1 as the type for representing data contents (for example, texts).

Example

```
TAddress ::= TEXTUAL-CONVENTION
   STATUS      current
   DESCRIPTION
   "Determines the Transport Service Address."
   SYNTAX      OCTET STRING
```

Object Identifier

The object identifier is used in ASN.1 to describe abstract information objects. In the management MIB tree (object identifier tree) every node is labelled with an object identifier. Since the individual branches of the tree are represented by numbers, an object identifier is actually a sequence of integer numbers. An object identifier is always displayed in primitive form and contains one or more data octets.

Example

```
partyTDomain OBJECT TYPE
   SYNTAX      OBJECT IDENTIFIER
   MAX-ACCESS  read-create
   STATUS      current
   DESCRIPTION
   "Indicates the relevant Transport Service via which the
   Party receives all network management information."
   DEFVAL      { snmpUDPDomain }
   ::= { partyEntry 3 }
```

Bit String

The ASN.1 Bit String data type is used for the representation of values consisting of a sequence of binary characters.

IpAddress

The IpAddress type contains the 32-bit Internet address (IP) and is represented as a string of 4 octets.

Counter32

The Counter32 Type represents a non-negative counter which can only count upwards. Its range of values is defined from 0 to 429967295 (2^{32}–1). After wrap-around (overflow), the counter starts counting from 0 again.

Example

```
snmpStatsPackets OBJECT TYPE
   SYNTAX     Counter32
   MAX-ACCESS read-only
   STATUS     current
   DESCRIPTION
   "Contains the number of all data packets received from the
   SNMPv2 device via the Transport Service."
   REFERENCE
          "Derived from RFC1213-MIB.snmpInPkts."
   ::= { snmpStats 1 }
```

Gauge32

The Gauge32 type represents a non-negative counter which can be incremented as well decremented. Its range of values is defined from 0 to 4294967295 (2^{32}–1). The Gauge32 counter does not have a wrap-around and should never reach its maximum value.

TimeTicks

The TimeTicks type represents a non-negative counter (maximum value = 4294967296), which counts time in 1/100 second from the start or from the event.

Opaque

The Opaque type was introduced as a pseudo data type in order to circumvent any restrictions inherent in the definition of the SMI. An Opaque type enables the definition of any ASN.1 construction. The Opaque type is only supported to facilitate downward compatibility of SNMPv2.

NsapAddress

The NsapAddress type is used for the representation of an OSI address as an octet string of variable length. The first octet always contains a string, whose binary value (0–20) represents the number of octets in the NSAP address.

Counter64

The Counter64 type represents a non-negative counter which can only count upwards. Its range of values is defined from 0 to 18446744073709551615 (2^{64}–1). After a wrap-around (overflow), the counter starts to count from 0 again.

UInteger32

The UInterger32 Type is used for the unsigned representation of numbers. Its range of values is defined from 0 to 4294967295 (2^{32}–1).

Example

```
Clock ::= TEXTUAL-CONVENTION
   STATUS      current
   DESCRIPTION
   "The Authentication Clock of a Party is based on a non-
   negative integer and is incremented according to the rules
   of the Authentication Protocol."
   SYNTAX      UInteger32
```

Units

The code word Units enables the definition of units (for example, seconds) which are determined for the object variables.

Example

```
partyAuthLifetime OBJECT TYPE
   SYNTAX      INTEGER (0..2147483647)
   UNITS       "seconds"
   MAX-ACCESS  read-create
   STATUS      current
   DESCRIPTION
   "Defines an upper time limit (in seconds) up to which a
   message which has been sent from this Party may be
   delayed on its communication pathway."
   DEFVAL      { 300 }
   ::= { partyEntry 11 }
```

Max-Access

The code word Max-Access determines the access to the relevant object and may take the following values:

not-accessible

An object with this value in the Max-Access field cannot be read, written to or created.

read-only

An object with this value in the Max-Access field can only be read.

read-write

An object with this value in the Max-Access field can be read and written to (altered).

read-create

An object with this value in the Max-Access field can be read, written to (altered) and created.

Example

```
partyAuthPrivate OBJECT-TYPE
    SYNTAX       OCTET STRING
                   for v2md5AuthProtocol: (SIZE (16))
    MAX-ACCESS   read-create
    STATUS       current
    DESCRIPTION
    "Defines the coding mechanism of the Party."
    DEFVAL       { ''H }
    ::= { partyEntry 9 }
```

Status

The Status field for an object contains information on its meaning. With SNMPv2, the Status field may take various values:

current

Specifies that the currently valid version of the object is involved.

deprecate

This value enables certain sections of a MIB to be marked as obsolete (undesired). A variable marked 'deprecate' will be removed from circulation with 'obsolete' in a future version of the MIB.

obsolete

Determines that this object is no longer used.

Example

```
partyAuthPublic OBJECT-TYPE
    SYNTAX       OCTET STRING
                   for v2md5AuthProtocol: (SIZE (0..16))
    MAX-ACCESS   read-create
    STATUS       current
    DESCRIPTION
    "Defines a publicly readable value for this Party."
    DEFVAL       { ''H }
    ::= { partyEntry 10 }
```

Description

A textual description of the relevant managable object is stored in this field.

Example

```
partyAuthLifetime OBJECT TYPE
   SYNTAX       INTEGER (0..2147483647)
   UNITS        "seconds"
   MAX-ACCESS   read-create
   STATUS       current
   DESCRIPTION
   "Defines an upper time limit (in seconds) up to which a
   message, which has been sent from this Party, can be delayed
   on the communication pathway."
   DEFVAL       { 300 }
   ::= { partyEntry 11 }
```

Reference

With the optional Reference field, cross-references to other objects in other MIB modules can be determined.

Example

```
snmpV1BadCommunityUses OBJECT TYPE
   SYNTAX     Counter32
   MAX-ACCESS read-only
   STATUS     current
   DESCRIPTION
   "Number of SNMPv1 messages received, that define an operation
   which cannot be executed by the Community determined in the
   message."
   REFERENCE "Derived from RFC1213-MIB.snmpInBadCommunityUses."
   ::= { snmpV1 2 }
```

Index

The Index and the Argument code words are used for unambiguously specifying objects that belong to a table.

Example

```
partyEntry OBJECT TYPE
   SYNTAX       PartyEntry
   MAX-ACCESS   not-accessible
   STATUS       current
   DESCRIPTION
   "Locally stored information relating to an SNMPv2 Party."
   INDEX      { IMPLIED partyIdentity }
   ::= { partyTable 1 }
```

Defval

The defval value enables certain default values to be given to object variables. These values remain valid until they are actively overwritten by a network management station. Examples are listed in RFC 1442 (see Table 5.1).

ObjectSyntax	Defval
Integer32	1
Gauge32	1
TimeTicks	1
UInteger32	1
Counter32	0
Counter64	0
Integer	valid
Octet String	'ffffffffffff'H
Object Identifier	sysDescr
Bit String	{ primary,, secondary }
IpAddress	'c0210415'H – 192.33.4.21

Table 5.1 Defval values

5.1.4 Notifications

With SNMPv2, Notification Definitions are used to describe notifications. A notification may be a Trap or a Confirmed Event. An agent informs the manager about an unexpected event using a trap. A manager uses a confimed event to communicate an unexpected event to the other manager in a manager-to-manager communication. The Notification Type Macro unambiguously describes the structure and contents of traps and confirmed events.

Definition: Notification Type Macro

```
NOTIFICATION-TYPE MACRO ::=
BEGIN
    TYPE NOTATION ::=
                  ObjectsPart
                  "STATUS" Status
                  "DESCRIPTION" Text
                  ReferPart

    VALUE NOTATION ::=
                  value(VALUE OBJECT IDENTIFIER)

    ObjectsPart ::=
                  "OBJECTS" "{" Objects "}"
                | empty
```

```
        Objects ::=
                        Object
                      | Objects "," Object
        Object ::=
                        value(Name ObjectName)

        Status ::=
                        "current"
                      | "deprecate"
                      | "obsolete"

        ReferPart ::=
                      "REFERENCE" Text
                    | empty

        Text ::= """" string """"
    END
```

The code words of the Notification Type Macros are defined as follows:

Objects
Defines the objects which are components of this notification.

Status
The Status field in the Notification Type Macro defines the relevant status of the object and may contain the following values:

current
Specifies that the currently valid version of the object is involved.

depreciate
This value enables certain sections of a MIB to be marked as obsolete (undesired). A variable marked 'depreciate' will be withdrawn from circulation with 'obsolete' in a future version of the MIB.

obsolete
Specifies that this object is no longer used.

Description
A textual description of the relevant manageable object is stored in this field.

Reference
The optional Reference field enables cross-references to be made to other objects in other MIB modules.

Example of an SNMP Trap Definition

```
snmpTrapOID OBJECT TYPE
   SYNTAX     OBJECT IDENTIFIER
   MAX-ACCESS not-accessible
   STATUS     current
   DESCRIPTION
   "Specifies the identification number of the Trap sent."
   ::= { snmpTrap 1 }
```

5.1.5 Textual conventions

With the SNMP, the information to be managed is always drawn together into a Management Information Base (MIB). The corresponding objects are defined as a MIB Module and are based on a subset of the OSI ASN.1. A MIB Module must be designed in such a way that a programmer can introduce new types which are already present in the SMI in a similar form. The new types have different names and a similar syntax but the semantics are defined much more precisely. The semantics are referred to as textual conventions and they help to enable a reader to understand the modules more easily. The textual conventions for SNMPv2 were published in RFC 1443. This document describes a basic set of textual conventions which are available to all MIB Modules. All objects that use these textual conventions are coded as primitive types. Textual conventions are often based on special semantics. For this reason, an ASN.1 Textual Convention Macro has been defined in order to determine the syntax and semantics of these textual conventions precisely.

Definition of Textual Convention Macro

```
SNMPv2-TC DEFINITIONS ::= BEGIN

IMPORTS
    ObjectSyntax, Integer32, TimeTicks
        FROM SNMPv2-SMI;


-- Definition of Textual Conventions

TEXTUAL-CONVENTION MACRO ::=
BEGIN
    TYPE NOTATION ::=
                  DisplayPart
                  "STATUS" Status
                  "DESCRIPTION" Text
                  ReferPart
                  "SYNTAX" type(Syntax)

    VALUE NOTATION ::=
                  value(VALUE Syntax)

    DisplayPart ::=
                  "DISPLAY-HINT" Text
                | empty

    Status ::=
                  "current"
                | "deprecate"
                | "obsolete"
```

```
      ReferPart ::=
                    "REFERENCE" Text
                  | empty

        Uses the NVT ASCII-character set
      Text ::= """" string """"
  END
```

Further details of the individual code words of the Textual Convention Macro are given below:

Display-Hint
The code word Display-Hint determines how and in which form the individual integer or string values of each textual convention are to be interpreted or displayed. The following display hints have been established so far in the standard documents:

DisplayString
Specifies that the data in a string is displayed. The Display-Hint "255a" as a component of the DisplayString definitions indicates that all characters are to be displayed as ASCII characters.

Example

```
DisplayString ::= TEXTUAL-CONVENTION
   DISPLAY-HINT "255a"
   STATUS       current
   DESCRIPTION
   "Represents textual information using the NVT ASCII character
   set (Page 4, 10-11 RFC 854). No object with this Syntax may
   exceed the maximum length of 255 characters."
   SYNTAX       OCTET STRING (SIZE (0..255))
```

PhysAddress
The PhysAddress establishes the relevant interpretation and display for the physical address. The Display-Hint "1x:" indicates that the data is presented as hexadecimal numbers, whith each octet separated by a colon (08:00:02:12).

```
PhysAddress ::= TEXTUAL-CONVENTION
   DISPLAY-HINT "1x:"
   STATUS       current
   DESCRIPTION
   "Represents the physical address."
   SYNTAX       OCTET STRING
```

MacAddress

The MacAddress specifies that the six-octet 802 Mac Layer address is to be displayed according to the IEEE802.1a specifications in a canonical form. The Display-Hint "1x:" indicates that the data is presented as hexadecimal numbers, whith each octet separated by a colon (08:00:02:00:12:34).

```
MacAddress ::= TEXTUAL-CONVENTION
   DISPLAY-HINT "1x:"
   STATUS       current
   DESCRIPTION
   "Represents the 802 MAC Address in canonical form (according
   to IEEE 802.1a). The bit with the lowest value is always
   transferred first."
   SYNTAX       OCTET STRING (SIZE (6))
```

TruthValue

By establishing a TruthValue it is possible to specify a truth value according to Boolean rules.

```
TruthValue ::= TEXTUAL-CONVENTION
   STATUS       current
   DESCRIPTION
   "Represents a boolean value."
   SYNTAX       INTEGER { true(1), false(2) }
```

TestAndIncr

Management applications can be exactly synchronized by means of a TestAndIncr type. If an object with this syntax is to be modified, the new value must correspond exactly to the value of the relevant management instance. If there is an error, an Inconsistent Value error message will be displayed.

```
TestAndIncr ::= TEXTUAL-CONVENTION
   STATUS       current
   DESCRIPTION
   "If an object with this syntax is to be modified, the new
   value must correspond exactly to the value of the relevant
   management instance. If there is an error, an Inconsistent
   Value error message will be displayed. If the new value can
   be set, the counter will be incremented. After the counter
   has reached its maximum value (2147483647), it automatically
   restarts with the value 0."
   SYNTAX       INTEGER (0..2147483647)
```

AutonomousType

The autonomous type is used for referring to object identifiers in other parts of the management tree or defining special hardware or protocol types.

```
AutonomousType ::= TEXTUAL-CONVENTION
    STATUS       current
    DESCRIPTION
    "Represents an object identifier in other parts of the
    management tree or enables the definition of special
    hardware or protocol types."
    SYNTAX       OBJECT IDENTIFIER
```

InstancePointer

In SNMPv2, a table is formed from a number of conceptual rows (lines in the table). The InstancePointer type defines precisely the first object in the relevant row.

```
InstancePointer ::= TEXTUAL-CONVENTION
    STATUS       current
    DESCRIPTION
    "The InstancePointer type defines precisely the first object
    in the relevant row."
    SYNTAX       OBJECT IDENTIFIER
```

RowStatus

In order to define the status of the conceptual rows, each row must be provided with a defined field (RowStatus) for this purpose. The values in this field can be either read or changed by the network management station.

The following values have been established for the RowStatus field:

active

The relevant conceptual row can be used by the management system in question.

notInService

The relevant conceptual row is present on the agent, but cannot be used by the management system in question.

notReady

The relevant conceptual row is present on the agent, but certain information is missing, which prevents the management system from gaining access.

```
RowStatus ::= TEXTUAL-CONVENTION
   STATUS        current
   DESCRIPTION
   "The RowStatus textual convention is used for deleting or
   creating Conceptual Rows."
   SYNTAX        INTEGER {
                     active(1),
                     notInService(2),
                     notReady(3),
                     createAndGo(4),
                     createAndWait(5),
                     destroy(6)
                 }
```

createAndGo
Is sent from the management station in question, thereby initiating the creation of a new conceptual row. Access to this conceptual row can then be gained from the management station.

createAndWait
Is sent from the management station in question, thereby initiating the creation of a new conceptual row. Access to this conceptual row cannot be gained from the management station.

destroy
Enables the deletion of a conceptual row by the network management station.

TimeStamp
Enables the current time to be sent. The time of the TimeStamp is always measured in TimeTicks. It defines the time since the last rebooting operation.

```
TimeStamp ::= TEXTUAL-CONVENTION
   STATUS        current
   DESCRIPTION
   "Contains the value occupied by the Variable sysUpTime
   at the time of sending."
   SYNTAX        TimeTicks
```

TimeInterval
Measures the time interval between two events.

```
TimeInterval ::= TEXTUAL-CONVENTION
    STATUS        current
    DESCRIPTION
   "Defines a time interval and has the unit 0.01 seconds."
   SYNTAX        INTEGER (0..2147483647)
```

DateAndTime

DateAndTime enables the method of writing and displaying the dates to be set. The Display-Hint "2d-1d-1d,1d:1d:1d.1d,1a1d:1d" as a component of the DateAndTime definition indicates that all fields are to be interpreted according to the criteria shown in Table 5.2.

Octet	Meaning	Range of values
1-2	Year	0..65536
3	Month	1..12
4	Day	1..31
5	Hour	0..23
6	Minute	0..59
7	Second	0..59
8	1/10 Second	0..9
9	Direction of UTC	'+' / '–'
10	Hours from UTC	0..11
11	Minutes from UTC	0..59

Table 5.2

```
DateAndTime ::= TEXTUAL-CONVENTION
   DISPLAY-HINT "2d-1d-1d,1d:1d:1d.1d,1a1d:1d"
   STATUS       current
   DESCRIPTION
   "Sets the method of writing and displaying the date and the
   time."
   SYNTAX       OCTET STRING (SIZE (8 | 11))
```

Status

The Status field in the Textual Convention Macro defines the relevant status of the object. It may contain the following values:

current

Specifies that the currently valid version of the object is involved.

deprecate

This value enables certain sections of a MIB to be marked as obsolete (undesired). A variable marked 'depreciate' will be withdrawn from circulation with 'obsolete' in a future version of the MIB.

obsolete

Specifies that this object is no longer used.

Description

A textual description of the relevant manageable object is stored in this field.

Reference

The optional Reference field enables cross-references to be made to other MIB Modules.

Syntax

Defines the syntax associated with the relevant data type.

5.2 Introduction to the new protocol

Since there are many differences between the two SNMP standards in respect of functions and especially in terms of the definition of manageable objects, the authors of the SNMPv2 standard paid particular attention to ensuring a smooth transition between the two standards. Under the title *Coexistence between version 1 and version 2 of the Internet Standard Network Management Framework*, RFC 1452 establishes the individual stages of a migration strategy.

The following route is proposed as a migration strategy:

- If possible, all SNMPv1 agents should continue to be used in such a way that all investments made so far are saved. An abrupt transition which did not consider older versions was rejected for reasons of market acceptance.
- If possible, old SNMPv1 agents should gradually be converted to SNMPv2 via a software update.
- New agents should only be purchased on the basis of SNMPv2.
- At the same time, the network management station should be upgraded to SNMPv2.
- Since a number of SNMPv1 protocols will not be able to support the new version for some time, the network management station must be able to communicate bilingually until the migration of all products to SNMPv2 is complete. This transitional solution enables SNMPv2 agents to communicate directly with their management stations, while SNMPv1 stations must communicate via an SNMP language translator. Since the long-term aim is complete migration to SNMPv2, SNMPv1 will ultimately be superseded.

As shown in Figure 5.2, the management station in a bilingual solution is structured in such a manner that it can communicate with individual agents in the network via the appropriately supported protocol version. This bilingual solution does have the disadvantage that the software requirements for the management station are considerably augmented. However, the advantage is that the individual agents do not have to be implemented bilingually.

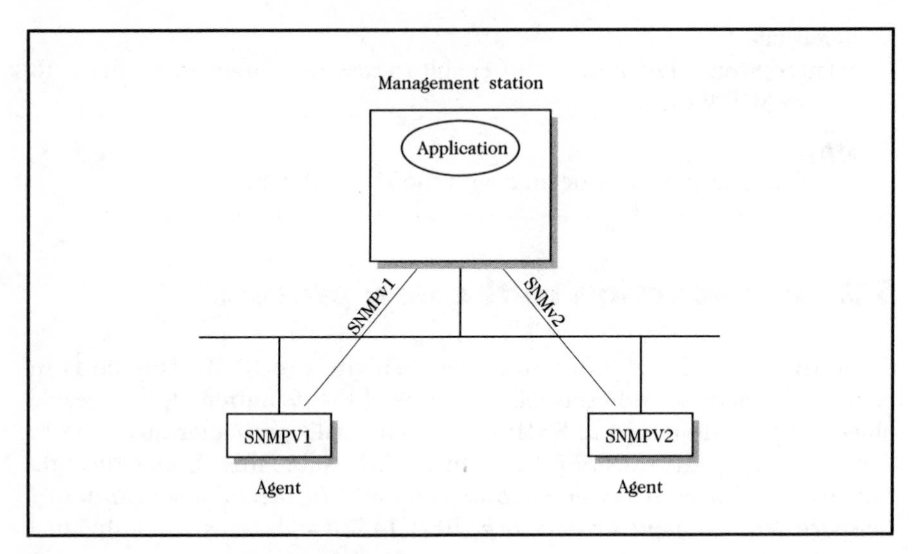

Figure 5.2 Bilingual SNMP implementation

In a transition from SNMPv1 to SNMPv2 the MIB definitions must also migrate to SNMPv2. The basic differences are as follows:

Syntax
The Syntax objects are shown in Table 5.3.

SNMPv2	SNMPv1
Bit String	–
Counter64	–
NsapAddress	–
UInteger	–
Integer32	Integer
Counter32	Counter
Gauge32	Gauge
Object Identifier	Object Identifier
Octet String	Octet String
TimeTicks	TimeTicks
IpAddress	NetworkAddress
Opaque	Opaque

Table 5.3 Syntax Objects

Units
The Units function was not available in SNMP version 1.

Max-Access
In SNMPv1, this function was simply designated as Access (see Table 5.4).

SNMPv2	SNMPv1
not-accessible	not-accessible
read-only	read-only
read-write	read-write
read-create	–

Table 5.4 Max-Access

Status
The Status field of an object contains information about its meaning (*see* Table 5.5).

SNMPv2	SNMPv1
current	mandatory
obsolete	optional
deprecate	obsolete
	deprecate

Table 5.5 Status field

Description
A textual description of the relevant manageable object is stored in this field. In SNMPv1, this field is described as the Definition field.

Reference
The Reference field, which could be implemented optionally under SNMPv1, enables cross-references to be made to other objects in other MIB modules.

Index
The optional value Index was introduced in SNMPv1 to enable unambiguous specification of objects belonging to a table.

Arguments
The Arguments function was not available in SNMPv1.

Defval
The Defval values were also available in SNMPv1. They enable default values to be given to the object variables.

5.2.1 SNMP on the various protocols

In the various publications from the Internet Architecture Board (IAB), reference is repeatedly made to the belief that, according to the latest technology, all IP and TCP/UDP implementations should run via network management functions (SNMPv1). This requirement presupposes the implementation of the Internet Management Information Base (MIB), as specified in the Request for Comments 1156 (RFC 1156) and one of the following management protocols: the Simple Network Management Protocol (RFC 1157) or the Common Management Information Services and Protocols over TCP/IP (RFC 1189). The SNMP protocol was conceived at the outset in such a way that it can be used on every reliable (error free) communication mechanism. In addition to the normal methods, that is, based on an IP/UDP Protocol Stack (preferred mapping), the SNMP protocol can also operate directly on the Ethernet Media Access Control (MAC) level (layer 2) or on the various layer 3/layer 4 protocols, for example, Novell's IPX Protocol, OSI, and so on.

The idea of multiprotocol support is continued with SNMPv2 and specified and implemented in more detail in RFC 1449 *Transport Mappings for version 2 of the Simple Network Management Protocol*.

SNMP/UDP

The SNMP protocol based on a User Datagram Protocol Stack is specified as the preferred mechanism with which all SNMP information is to be transferred between a network management station and the agents. In this case, all agents should be configured in such a way that they receive all PDUs from the management station via UDP port 161. All traps to the SNMP application of the network management station are passed on via UDP port 162. These values should be entered in the appropriate partyTable of the SNMPv2 party. Additionally, an SNMPv2 device must be able to receive data packets containing up to 484 octets.

SNMP/OSI

The OSI specifications provide the following two transport services on the transport level: the Connection-Oriented Transport Service (COTS) and the Connectionless Mode Transport Service (CLTS). The specifications of SNMP generally enable the support of both transport services, although the use of the Connectionless Mode Transport Service (CLTS) is the preferred method of transferring SNMP data via the network. All agents should be configured in such a way that they can receive all PDUs from the management station via the Transport Selector 'snmp-1' when using a Connectionless Mode Transport Service (CLTS). With CLTS, all traps are passed on to the SNMP application of the network management station via 'snmpt-1'. If the Connection Oriented Transport Service (COTS) is used, the Transport Selectors are named as follows: 'snmp-o' or 'snmpt-o'. These values should be entered in the relevant partyTable of the SNMPv2 party. An SNMPv2 device must be able to receive data packets containing up to 484 octets.

SNMP/DDP

The SNMPv2 protocol can also optionally be realized on the basis of the AppleTalk Datagram Delivery Protocol (DDP). The DDP protocol is one of the Network Layer protocols and is responsible for the socket-to-socket transport of datagrams. All SNMPv2 messages are sent with DDP protocol Type 8 packets. All agents should be configured in such a way that they can receive all PDUs from the management station via DDP socket 8. The agent process is unambiguously specified under the Name Binding Protocol (NBP). The code for the agent process has been set as the 10-character NBP type 'SNMP Agent'. All traps to the SNMP application of the network management station are passed on via DDP socket 9. The code defined for the network management process is the 17-character NBP type 'SNMP Trap Handler'. These values should be entered in the relevant partyTable of the SNMPv2 party. An SNMPv2 device must be able to receive data packets containing up to 484 octets.

SNMP/IPX

Because of the wide distribution of network management systems based on SNMP and the constantly growing popularity of Novell Netware products, a combination of both worlds was considered necessary. As an option, the SNMP protocol can be used on an IPX protocol stack. The Novell Internetwork Packet Exchange (IPX) protocol corresponds in terms of functions and services to the User Datagram Protocol. All SNMP data is sent in the IPX header with a packet type field = 4. The maximum packet length has been set at 546 bytes. An SNMP agent receives all commands via the following socket: 36879 (hexadecimal 900F). Traps are received by the network management station via IPX socket 36880 (hexadecimal 9010).

Proxy definitions for the support of SNMPv1

In order to ensure downward compatibility with Community-based SNMP management (version 1), the relevant authentication protocols must be established for these proxy relationships.

Transport Domain: rfc1157Domain

The Transport Domain (rfc1157Domain) establishes the mapping for the SNMP protocol in accordance with RFC 1157. If the Transport Domain (partyTDomain) was set as an rfc1157Domain, the following rules apply:

- The transport address of the party (partyTAddress) is always 6 octets long. The first 4 octets contain the IP address; the last 2 octets define the UDP port address.
- The authentication protocol of the party (partyAuthProtocol) is always set to the value rfc1157noAuth.

Authentication algorithm: rfc1157noAuth

The authentication protocol (partyAuthProtocol) of a party defines the mechanisms and the coding protocol used in order to ensure that the SNMPv1 or SNMPv2 PDU data from the party can be requested safely and unchanged. If the authentication protocol of a party is set to rfc1157noAuth, the values partyAuthPublic, partyAuthClock and partyAuthLifetime have no meaning. In this case, the private authentication code of the party (partySecretsAuthPrivate) for an RFC 1157 Community is used as a Community String.

Definitions

```
SNMPv2-TM DEFINITIONS ::= BEGIN

IMPORTS
    snmpDomains, snmpProxys
        FROM SNMPv2-SMI
    TEXTUAL-CONVENTION
        FROM SNMPv2-TC;

-- SNMPv2 over DP

snmpUDPDomain  OBJECT IDENTIFIER ::= { snmpDomains 1 }
The length of the SnmpUDP Address is 6:
--
-- Octets  meaning
--  1-4     IP-Address
--  5-6     UDP-Port
--
SnmpUDPAddress ::= TEXTUAL-CONVENTION
    DISPLAY-HINT "1d.1d.1d.1d/2d"
    STATUS       current
    DESCRIPTION
    "Represents the UDP Address."
    SYNTAX       OCTET STRING (SIZE (6))

-- SNMPv2 over OSI

snmpCLNSDomain OBJECT IDENTIFIER ::= { snmpDomains 2 }
snmpCONSDomain OBJECT IDENTIFIER ::= { snmpDomains 3 }
-- for an SnmpOSIAddress of length m:
--
-- Octets        Meaning
-- 1             Length of NSAP
-- 2..(n+1)      NSAP
--      (n+2)..m              TSEL
--
SnmpOSIAddress ::= TEXTUAL-CONVENTION
    DISPLAY-HINT "*1x:/1x:"
```

```
    STATUS       current
    DESCRIPTION
    "Represents the OSI Transport Address."
    SYNTAX       OCTET STRING (SIZE (1 | 4..85))

-- SNMPv2 over DDP

snmpDDPDomain  OBJECT IDENTIFIER ::= { snmpDomains 4 }
For an Snmp NBP Address of length m:
--
-- Octets                  Meaning
-- 1                       Length of object "n"
-- 2..(n+1)                Object
-- n+2                     Length of type "p"
-- (n+3)..(n+2+p)          Type
-- n+3+p                   Length of zone "q"
-- (n+4+p)..m              Zone
--
SnmpNBPAddress ::= TEXTUAL-CONVENTION
    STATUS       current
    DESCRIPTION
    "Represents an NBP Name."
    SYNTAX       OCTET STRING (SIZE (3..99))

-- SNMPv2 over IPX

snmpIPXDomain  OBJECT IDENTIFIER ::= { snmpDomains 5 }
--
-- Octets      Meaning
-- 1-4         Network number
-- 5-10        Physical Address
-- 11-12       Socket Number
--
SnmpIPXAddress ::= TEXTUAL-CONVENTION
    DISPLAY-HINT "4x.1x:1x:1x:1x:1x:1x.2d"
    STATUS       current
    DESCRIPTION
    "Represents the IPX Address."
    SYNTAX       OCTET STRING (SIZE (12))

For the Proxy-Function for Community-based SNMPv1 (RFC 1157)

rfc1157Proxy   OBJECT IDENTIFIER ::= { snmpProxys 1 }

uses SnmpUDPAddress
rfc1157Domain  OBJECT IDENTIFIER ::= { rfc1157Proxy 1 }

The Community based noAuth
rfc1157noAuth  OBJECT IDENTIFIER ::= { rfc1157Proxy 2 }

END
```

5.3 SNMPv2 commands

SNMPv2 is used for the exchange of messages between agents and management stations. The SNMP Protocol Data Unit (SNMP PDU) is packed in the message. The structure and form of the message are determined by the administrative framework which establishes the authentication and its rules. The SNMPv2 commands are set out in Request for Comments 1448 under the heading *Protocol operations for version 2 of the Simple Network Management Protocol (SNMPv2)*. An SNMPv2 device is described as an agent if this device carries out management functions (with the exception of Inform notifications) for SNMPv2 messages received or sends traps independently. An SNMPv2 device is described as a manager if it is capable of sending SNMPv2 protocol messages or implementing management operations in response to traps received or Inform notifications. In addition, an SNMPv2 device can act in the dual role as manager and agent. All SNMP messages are received via UDP Port 161. Only traps and Inform notifications use UDP Port 162. All implementations must be able to receive messages of at least 484 octets in length.

Definition: SNMPv2 PDUs

```
SNMPv2-PDU DEFINITIONS ::= BEGIN

     IMPORTS
         ObjectName, ObjectSyntax, Integer32
             FROM SNMPv2-SMI;

-- protocol data units

PDUs ::=
     CHOICE {
             get-request
                 GetRequest-PDU,

             get-next-request
                 GetNextRequest-PDU,

             get-bulk-request
                 GetBulkRequest-PDU,

             response
                 Response-PDU,
             set-request
                 SetRequest-PDU,

             inform-request
                 InformRequest-PDU,
             SNMPv2 Trap
                 SNMPv2 Trap-PDU
         }
```

```
-- PDUs

GetRequest-PDU ::=
    [0]
        IMPLICIT PDU

GetNextRequest-PDU ::=
    [1]
        IMPLICIT PDU

Response-PDU ::=
    [2]
        IMPLICIT PDU

SetRequest-PDU ::=
    [3]
        IMPLICIT PDU

 -- [4] is obsolete

GetBulkRequest-PDU ::=
    [5]
        IMPLICIT BulkPDU

InformRequest-PDU ::=
    [6]
        IMPLICIT PDU

SNMPv2 Trap-PDU ::=
    [7]
        IMPLICIT PDU

max-bindings

    INTEGER ::= 2147483647

PDU ::=
    SEQUENCE {
        request-id
            Integer32,

        error-status              -- sometimes ignored
            INTEGER {
                noError(0),
                tooBig(1),
                noSuchName(2),    -- for proxy compatibility
                badValue(3),      -- for proxy compatibility
                readOnly(4),      -- for proxy compatibility
                genErr(5),
                noAccess(6),
                wrongType(7),
                wrongLength(8),
                wrongEncoding(9),
```

```
                    wrongValue(10),
                    noCreation(11),
                    inconsistentValue(12),
                    resourceUnavailable(13),
                    commitFailed(14),
                    undoFailed(15),
                    authorizationError(16),
                    notWritable(17),
                    inconsistentName(18)
                }

            error-index          -- sometimes ignored
                INTEGER (0..max-bindings),

            variable-bindings    -- values are sometimes ignored
                VarBindList
        }

    BulkPDU ::=                  -- MUST be identical in
        SEQUENCE {               -- structure to PDU
            request-id
                Integer32,

            non-repeaters
                INTEGER (0..max-bindings),
            max-repetitions
                INTEGER (0..max-bindings),

            variable-bindings    -- values are ignored
                VarBindList
        }

    -- variable binding

    VarBind ::=
        SEQUENCE {
            name
                ObjectName,

            CHOICE {
                value
                    ObjectSyntax,

                unSpecified          -- in retrieval requests
                        NULL,

                                     -- exceptions in responses
                noSuchObject[0]
                        IMPLICIT NULL,

                noSuchInstance[1]
                        IMPLICIT NULL,
```

```
                endOfMibView[2]
                        IMPLICIT NULL
            }
        }

    -- variable-binding list

    VarBindList ::=
        SEQUENCE (SIZE (0..max-bindings)) OF
            VarBind

    END
```

Protocol specifications

Request IDs are used in version 2 as in SNMPv1. The Request IDs are only generated for monitoring outstanding messages. Request IDs enable SNMPv2 to match incoming answers to the Requests sent. Since the SNMP is normally based on the connectionless UDP service, messages may be lost or duplicated during transport via the network. Duplicates can be easily detected as a result of the ID numbers. The SNMPv2 commands are coded in Protocol Data Units (PDUs). SNMPv2 supports seven types of message. The SNMP messages are restricted to pure utilization data. This data orientation does not permit imperative commands to be issued to the network components managed. In spite of this minimal set of commands, practically all operations between an SNMP client and an SNMP server can be implemented. The individual commands are designated as follows:

- Get Request;
- Get Next;
- Get Bulk Request;
- Set Request;
- Response;
- Trap;
- Inform Request.

An SNMPv2 agent must be able to generate the following PDU types: Response PDUs and SNMPv2 Trap PDUs. In addition, all agent implementations must be able to receive or process the following PDU types: Get Request, Get Next Request, Get Bulk Request, SetRequest.
An SNMPv2 manager must be able to generate the following PDU types: Get Request, Get Nex tRequest, Get Bulk Request, Set Request, Inform Request and Response. In addition all SNMPv2 manager implementations must be able to receive or process the following PDU types: Response, SNMPv2 Trap and Inform Request.

5.4 SNMP Protocol Data Units

Compared with the five Protocol Data Units of SNMPv1, the commands and PDUs in version 2 have been expanded to include: Get Request, Get Next, Get Bulk, Set Request, Response, Trap and Inform Request.

5.4.1 Get Request PDU

Using the Get Request PDU, the management station can specifically request a known variable in the MIB of an SNMP agent. An object identifier is sent with this message type as an argument. In response to a Get Request, the client always receives a message of the type Response PDU. The PDU code 0 has been defined for Get Request. After the PDU code a Get Request message contains another four fields:

- Request ID;
- Error Status;
- Error Index;
- Variable Bindings.

Request ID
Request IDs are generated only for monitoring outstanding messages. Using Request IDs, SNMP can match incoming responses to the relevant Request sent.

Error Status
The Error Status field in a Get Request is always set to the value 0.

Error Index
The Error Index field in a Get Request is always set to the value 0.

Variable Bindings
The object identifier required is defined in the Variable Bindings field. The value of the object variables in the Get Request command is coded with the ASN.1 constant zero.

PDU Type 0	Request ID	Error Status 0	Error Index 0	Variable Bindings: Value

Figure 5.3 Get Request PDU

5.4.2 Get Next Request PDU

The Get Next Request command enables a management system to request the value of the next object in the MIB tree hierarchy. Instead of the value of the object identifier required, the last known object identifier is used as the argument. Get Next operations are ideally suited for traversing tables or quickly calling up consecutive objects. In the case of unknown objects, a Get Next Request for the directly preceding object can be issued. In response to a Get Next Request, the client always receives a message of the type Response. The values for the next object in the tree hierarchy are always sent back in this Response packet. The PDU code defined for the Get Next Request is 1. After the PDU code, a Get Next Request message contains another four fields:

- Request ID;
- Error Status;
- Error Index;
- Variable Bindings.

Request ID
Request IDs are generated only for monitoring outstanding messages. Using Request IDs, SNMP can match incoming responses to the relevant Request sent.

Error Status
The Error Status field in a Get Next Request is always set to 0.

Error Index
The Error Index field in a Get Next Request is always set to 0.

Variable Bindings
The object immediately preceding the object required is contained in the Variable Bindings field. The value of the object variables in the Get Next Request command is coded with the relevant ASN.1 value.

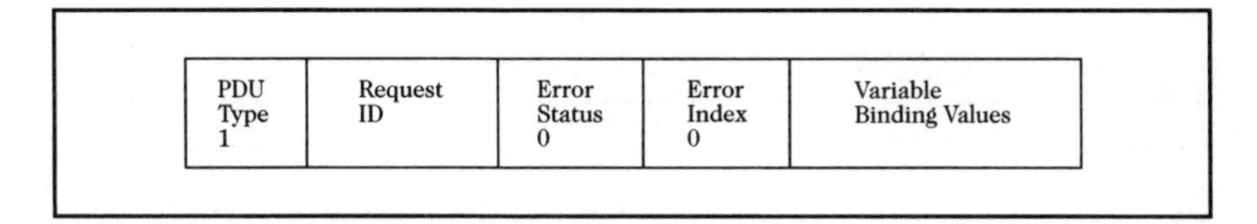

Figure 5.4 Get Next Request PDU

5.4.3 Set Request PDU

The Set Request command enables a management system to set specific variables on an agent. An object identifier is sent as an argument with this type of message. If the agent is able to process the Set Request command with the specified value, a Response packet will be sent back, thereby confirming the operation as positive. If there is an error, a Response is created and sent back to the requester (management station) with the relevant error messages. The PDU coding 3 has been defined for the Set Request command. After the PDU code, a Set Request message contains another four fields:

- Request ID;
- Error Status;
- Error Index;
- Variable Bindings.

Request ID
Request IDs are generated only for monitoring outstanding messages. Using Request IDs, SNMP can allocate incoming responses to the relevant Request sent.

Error Status
The Error Status field in a Set Request is always set to 0.

Error Index
The Error Index field in a Set Request is always set to 0.

Variable Bindings
The required object identifier is defined in Variable Bindings field. The value of the object variables in the Set Request command is coded with the relevant ASN.1 value.

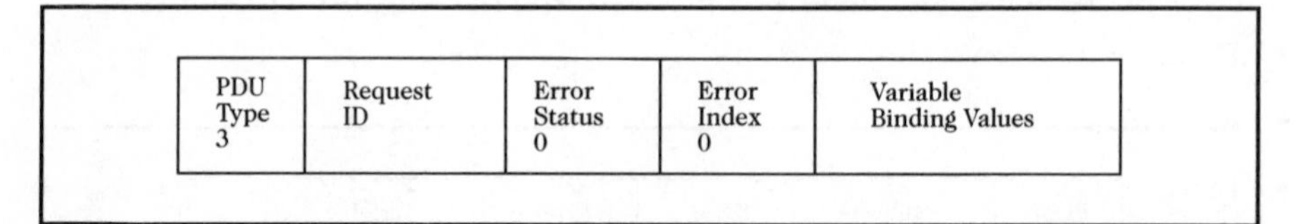

Figure 5.5 Set Request PDU

5.4.4 Response PDU

The Response command enables an agent to respond to all Get Next Request, Set Request, Get Bulk Request or Get Request queries from a management system. If the agent can process the Set Request command with the specified value, a Response packet will be sent back, thereby confirming the operation as positive. If the confirmation is positive, the Error Status and Error Index fields are always set to 0. If there is an error, a Response is created and sent back to the requester (management station) with the relevant error messages. In the case of an error message, the Error Status and Error Index fields are set to a predefined value. The values listed in Table 5.6 below have been established for the Error Status field:

Designation	Value
tooBig	1
noSuchName	2
badValue	3
readOnly	4
genErr	5
noAccess	6
wrongType	7
wrongLength	8
wrongEncoding	9
wrongValue	10
noCreation	11
inconsistentValue	12
resourceUnavailable	13
commitFailed	14
undoFailed	15
authorizationError	16
notWritable	17
inconsistentName	18

Table 5.6

The PDU coding 2 has been set for the Response command. After the PDU code, a Response message contains another four fields:

- Request ID;
- Error Status;
- Error Index;
- Variable Bindings.

Request ID

Request IDs in a Response message always relate to the response to the relevant query. Message duplicates can easily be detected by means of the ID numbers.

Error Status

The Error Status field in a Response always contains the following values:

TooBig

The agent cannot accommodate the required data in a single SNMP message.

NoSuchName

When decoding the SNMP Request, the agent has found an unknown variable name which it cannot process. This does not mean that the name is not present in the agent, but merely that it may not recognize the name according to the pre-set Community Profiles.

BadValue

During decoding, the agent has discovered an incorrect syntax or an incorrect value which prevents it from altering the required variable.

ReadOnly

During decoding, the agent has discovered a variable which cannot be written to, according to the Community Profile.

GenError

All other errors are marked by the agent as Generic Errors. Further coding is not provided in SNMPv2.

NoAccess

The variable is outside the predefined MIB View. This variable cannot be read or modified.

WrongType

The new, transferred value does not correspond to the correct ASN.1 data type.

WrongLength

The new, transferred value does not correspond to the correct length.

WrongEncoding

The new, transferred value was incorrectly coded.

WrongValue

The new, transferred value lies outside the value range for this object type.

NoCreation

The variable indicated does not exist, and the agent cannot create this object type.

InconsistentValue

The variable indicated is inconsistent with other variables of the agent.

ResourceUnavailable

The desired resource on the agent cannot be reserved.

CommitFailed

The transfer of a value in Variable Bindings could not be executed, and the changes were not carried out.

UndoFailed

The transfer of a value in Variable Bindings could not be executed, and the changes could not be reversed.

AuthorizationError

An error in authentication has been detected.

NotWritable

The variable indicated does not exist and cannot be created by the agent.

InconsistentName

The name indicated is not consistent with other names from the agent.

Error Index

If the Error Status field in a Response is set to a value other than 0, this indicates that an error has been detected in the Request just processed. The Error Index contains additional information which may be useful in identifying the cause of the error. Error Index definitions are shown in Table 5.7.

Name	Value
noSuchObject	0
noSuchInstance	1
endOfMibView	2

Table 5.7 Error Index definitions

noSuchObject

The required object is not supported by the agent or has not been implemented in the device.

noSuchInstance

An instance with this name is not supported by the agent or has not been implemented in the device.

endOfMibView

The end of the MIB for the relevant manager has been reached and no further values can be transferred.

Variable Bindings

The required object identifier is defined in the Variable Bindings field. The value of the object variables in the Response command is coded with the relevant ASN.1 value.

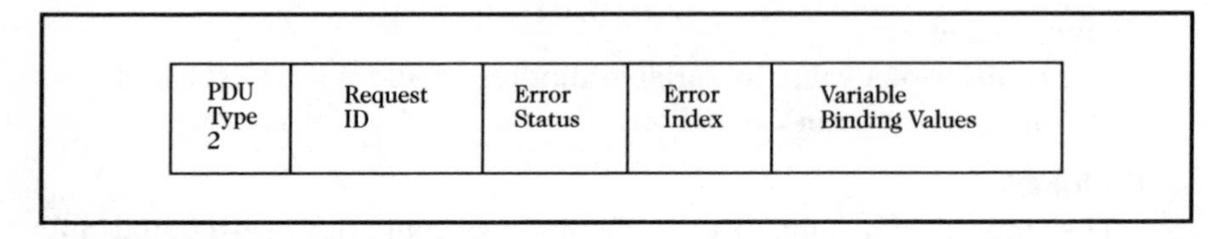

Figure 5.6 Response PDU

5.4.5 Get Bulk Request PDU

The protocol element Get Bulk Request was introduced with SNMPv2 and represents a generalization of the Get Next Request. The Get Bulk Request PDU enables large quantities of data, especially tables, to be read more efficiently. By contrast with the Get Next Request PDU, fewer packets are sent via the network. With Get Bulk Request, the repetition of basic operations is located in the agent. If the relevant command can be processed in the agent with the value specified, a Response packet will be returned, thereby confirming the operation positively. With a positive confirmation, the Error Status and Error Index fields are always set to 0. The PDU coding 5 has been set for the Get Bulk Request. After the PDU code, a Get Bulk Request message contains four fields:

- Request ID;
- Non-Repeaters;
- Max-Repetitions;
- Variable Bindings.

Request ID

Request IDs are generated only for monitoring outstanding messages. Using Request IDs, SNMP can match incoming responses to the relevant Request sent.

Non-Rrepeaters

The Non-Repeaters Parameter in a Get Bulk Request PDU indicates how many variables from the variable list are not subject to repetition.

Max-Repetitions

The repetition counter in a Get Bulk Request PDU defines how often the Get Next Operation should be carried out in an agent. The agent then packs the requested variable values in a single Response PDU. If the Response PDU reaches its maximum value, the remaining variable values will be rejected and must be requested by the management station again.

Variable Bindings

The required object identifier is defined in the Variable Bindings field. The value of the object variables in the Get Bulk Request command is coded with the relevant ASN.1 value.

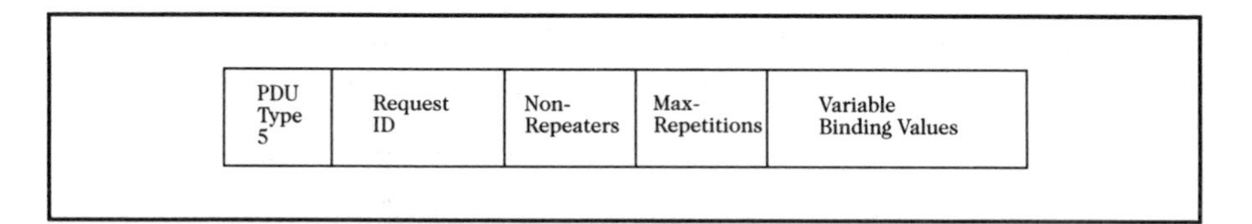

Figure 5.7 Get Bulk Request PDU

Definition: Get Bulk Request PDU

```
BulkPDU ::=                         -- MUST be identical in
    SEQUENCE {                      -- structure to PDU
        request-id
            Integer32,

        non-repeaters
            INTEGER (0..max-bindings),

        max-repetitions
            INTEGER (0..max-bindings),

        variable-bindings           -- values are ignored
            VarBindList
    }
```

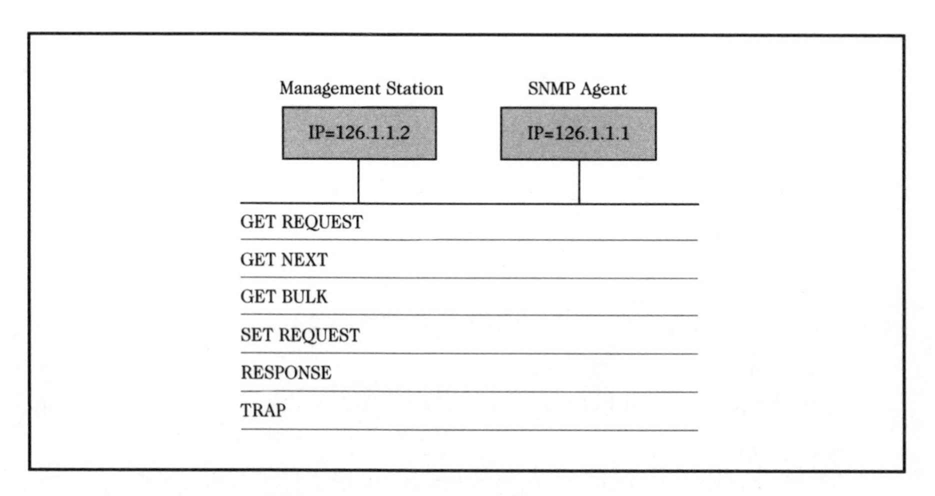

Figure 5.8 SNMPv2 client–server relationship

5.5 SNMPv2 traps

The SNMPv2 protocol is also structured on the basis of a simple polling mechanism. Every network management station (client), every variable request and status request must be executed via a command. In SNMPv2, the integration of traps and Inform Requests enables an agent to respond to particular situations. If an agent determines a special situation, it sends a trap-type message to the management station. With SNMPv1, the information content of traps was kept very low, and further information was left to the relevant implementations. The information content of traps in SNMPv2 is set out in Notation Type Macros. The Notation Type Macro has already been described in greater detail in Section 5.1.4. The coding set for the SNMPv2 Trap PDU is type 7.

An SNMPv2 Trap PDU is sent from an SNMPv2 device, which is acting as an agent, in order to communicate special circumstances in the network to one or more management stations, if the following conditions are met:

- The device (aclSubject) to which the trap is to be sent is entered in the aclTable.
- The value of aclPrivileges enables an SNMPv2 Trap PDU to be sent.
- The aclResources define the local SNMPv2 objects (resources) of the agent and refer to a MIB View in which the relevant object identifier is stored.

Only when all the conditions are met will an SNMPv2 trap be generated and sent to the manager defined under aclTarget. The format of the SNMPv2 Trap PDU is shown in Figure 5.9.

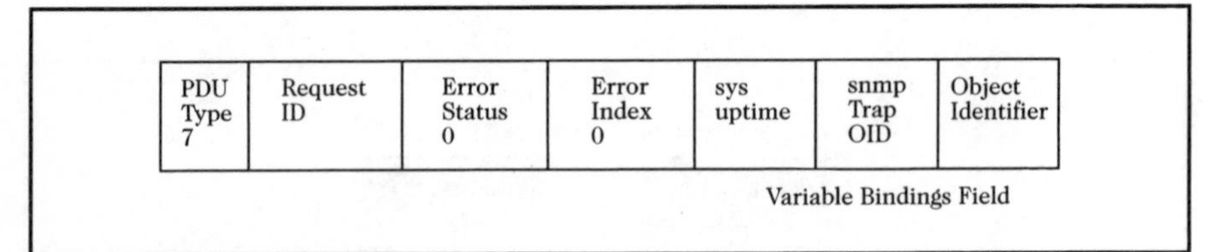

Figure 5.9 SNMPv2 Trap PDU

Request ID
Request IDs are generated only for monitoring outstanding messages.

Error Status
The Error Status field in a trap is always set to 0.

Error Index
The Error Index field in a trap is always set to 0.

Variable Bindings
The structure of the Variable Bindings field:

sysUpTime.0
The first variable in the Variable Bindings field is the value sysUpTime.0. The sysUpTime defines the time since the last reboot of the device.

snmpTrapOID
The second variable in the Variable Bindings field is the value snmpTrapOID.0. This value represents the fixed name of the relevant trap.

Object Identier
The third variable in the Variable Bindings field may be one or more object identifiers.

In RFC 1450, a number of traps are predefined for the SNMPv2 protocol:

Traps Group (RFC 1450)
All the objects predetermined for an agent which can be configured in order to transmit SNMPv2 Trap VDUs are subsumed in the Traps Group. The following object identifier has been issued for the SNMPv2 Traps Group.

```
snmpTrap        OBJECT IDENTIFIER ::= { snmpMIBObjects 4 }

snmpTrapOID OBJECT TYPE
   SYNTAX     OBJECT IDENTIFIER
   MAX-ACCESS not-accessible
   STATUS     current
   DESCRIPTION
   "Establishes the ID number of the Trap sent."
   ::= { snmpTrap 1 }

snmpTrapTable OBJECT TYPE
   SYNTAX     SEQUENCE OF SnmpTrapEntry
   MAX-ACCESS not-accessible
   STATUS     current
   DESCRIPTION
   "This table lists all Traps which have been sent to the
   SNMPv2 communication partners."
   ::= { snmpTrap 2 }

snmpTrapEntry OBJECT TYPE
   SYNTAX     SnmpTrapEntry
   MAX-ACCESS not-accessible
   STATUS     current
   DESCRIPTION
```

```
   "Defines the row entry for all Traps which have been sent to
   the SNMPv2 communication partners."
   AUGMENTS   { partyEntry }
::= { snmpTrapTable 1 }

SnmpTrapEntry ::= SEQUENCE {
   snmpTrapNumbers                    Counter32
}

snmpTrapNumbers OBJECT TYPE
   SYNTAX      Counter32
   MAX-ACCESS read-only
   STATUS      current
   DESCRIPTION
   "Counts all Traps which have been sent to SNMPv2
   communication partners since the last initialization."
   ::= { snmpTrapEntry 1 }

snmpTrapEnterprise OBJECT-TYPE
   SYNTAX      OBJECT IDENTIFIER
   MAX-ACCESS not-accessible
   STATUS      current
   DESCRIPTION
   "Contains the ID number of the relevant enterprise which was
   issued to the last Trap sent."
   ::= { snmpTrap 3 }

snmpV2EnableAuthenTraps OBJECT-TYPE
   SYNTAX      TruthValue
   MAX-ACCESS read-write
   STATUS      current
   DESCRIPTION
   "Marks whether an SNMPv2 agent has been configured in such a
   way that it can transmit Authentication Failure Traps."
   REFERENCE "Derived from RFC1213-MIB.snmpEnableAuthenTraps."
   ::= { snmpTrap 4 }
```

Well Known Traps

The following object identifier has been issued for the SNMPv2 Well Known Traps.

```
snmpTraps       OBJECT IDENTIFIER ::= { snmpMIBObjects 5 }
coldStart NOTIFICATION-TYPE
   STATUS   current
   DESCRIPTION
   "A coldStart Trap signals that an SNMPv2 agent has re-
   initialized because of a configuration change."
   ::= { snmpTraps 1 }
```

```
warmStart NOTIFICATION-TYPE
   STATUS  current
   DESCRIPTION
   "A warmStart Trap signals that an SNMPv2 agent has re-
   initialized and that no configuration change has been
   executed."
   ::= { snmpTraps 2 }

linkDown NOTIFICATION-TYPE
   OBJECTS { ifIndex }
   STATUS  current
   DESCRIPTION
   "A linkDown Trap signals that an SNMPv2 agent has detected an
   error on one of the connected links."
   ::= { snmpTraps 3 }

linkUp NOTIFICATION-TYPE
   OBJECTS { ifIndex }
   STATUS  current      DESCRIPTION
   "A linkUp Trap signals that the configured link of an SNMPv2
   agent has been activated."
   ::= { snmpTraps 4 }

authenticationFailure NOTIFICATION-TYPE
   STATUS  current
   DESCRIPTION
   "An authenticationFailure Trap signals that an SNMPv2 agent
   has detected an authentication error in a data packet
   received."
   ::= { snmpTraps 5 }

egpNeighborLoss NOTIFICATION-TYPE
   OBJECTS { egpNeighAddr }
   STATUS  current
   DESCRIPTION
   "An egpNeighborLoss Trap signals that an SNMPv2 agent has
   relinquished the communication process to an EGP neighbor."
   ::= { snmpTraps 6 }
```

5.5.1 The Inform Request PDU

By contrast with the SNMPv1 protocol, version 2 abandons the rigid subdivision into an agent (server process) and a network manager (agent process). The SNMPv2 protocol specifications introduce manager-to-manager communication, thereby enabling a network manager to behave as an agent process and also as a server process. Using the manager-to-manager communication model, it is possible to set up alarms on a manager/agent, with an upper and lower threshold for the value of an object variable. If the fixed threshold values are undershot or overshot, the superordinate management station will be informed of this event via an Inform Request. An Inform Request is always confirmed by the recipient with a Response Request. The structure of the Inform Request PDU corresponds to the Trap PDU. Type 6 has been defined as the code for the Inform Request PDU.

An Inform Request PDU is only sent to the recipient of the Inform Request PDU by an SNMPv2 device acting in the role of a manager/agent if the recipient has been entered in the snmpEventNotify table. Figure 5.10 shows the format of the Inform PDU.

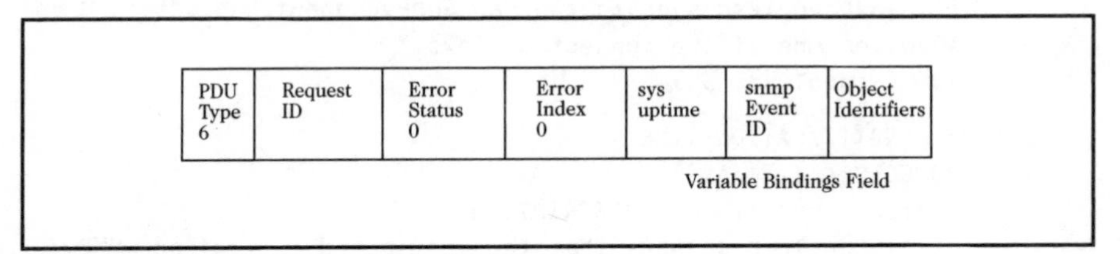

Figure 5.10 Inform Request PDU

Request ID
Request IDs are generated only for the purpose of monitoring outstanding messages.

Error Status
The Error Status field in a trap is always set to 0.

Error Index
The Error Index field in a trap is always set to 0.

Variable Bindings
The Variable Bindings field is structured as follows:

sysUpTime.0
The first variable in the Variable Bindings field is the value sysUpTime.0. The sysUpTime defines the time since the last reboot of the device.

snmpEventID
The second variable in the Variable Bindings field is the value snmpEventID.0. This value represents the fixed name of the relevant Inform Request.

Object Identifier
The third value in the Variable Bindings field may be one or more optional object identifiers.

A series of Inform Requests is defined in RFC 1450 for the SNMPv2 protocol:

Alarm Group

The Alarm Group enables the individual definition of alarm parameters. Threshold values can be set up and continuously compared with current values. If a threshold value is overshot, an event is created. The following object identifier has been issued for the Alarm Group within the Manager-to-Manager MIB:

```
snmpAlarm        OBJECT IDENTIFIER ::= { snmpM2MObjects 1 }

snmpAlarmNextIndex OBJECT TYPE
   SYNTAX      INTEGER (0..65535)
   MAX-ACCESS read-only
   STATUS      current
   DESCRIPTION
   "Contains the index number of the next non-fixed entry in the
   snmpAlarmTable. If the value is set to 0, the table contains
   no non-fixed values."
   ::= { snmpAlarm 1 }

snmpAlarmTable OBJECT-TYPE
   SYNTAX      SEQUENCE OF SnmpAlarmEntry
   MAX-ACCESS not-accessible
   STATUS      current
   DESCRIPTION
   "The table in which the SNMP alarms are listed."
   ::= { snmpAlarm 2 }

snmpAlarmEntry OBJECT-TYPE
   SYNTAX      SnmpAlarmEntry
   MAX-ACCESS not-accessible
   STATUS      current
   DESCRIPTION
   "In the SNMP alarm list, all parameters, which are monitored
   from time to time, can be defined by this field."
   INDEX       { contextIdentity, snmpAlarmIndex }
   ::= { snmpAlarmTable 1 }

SnmpAlarmEntry ::= SEQUENCE {
   snmpAlarmIndex                   INTEGER,
   snmpAlarmVariable                InstancePointer,
   snmpAlarmInterval                Integer32,
   snmpAlarmSampleType              INTEGER,
   snmpAlarmValue                   Integer32,
   snmpAlarmStartupAlarm            INTEGER,
   snmpAlarmRisingThreshold         Integer32,
   snmpAlarmFallingThreshold        Integer32,
   snmpAlarmRisingEventIndex        INTEGER,
   snmpAlarmFallingEventIndex       INTEGER,
   snmpAlarmUnavailableEventIndex   INTEGER,
   snmpAlarmStatus                  RowStatus
 }
```

```
snmpAlarmIndex OBJECT-TYPE
   SYNTAX     INTEGER (1..65535)
   MAX-ACCESS not-accessible
   STATUS     current
   DESCRIPTION
   "Using this index, an entry is individually identified in the
   SNMP alarm table for a static function."
   ::= { snmpAlarmEntry 1 }

snmpAlarmVariable OBJECT-TYPE
   SYNTAX     InstancePointer
   MAX-ACCESS read-create
   STATUS     current
   DESCRIPTION
   "Contains the Object Identifier of a variable with which
   statistics can be determined. Only variables which correspond
   to an ASN.1 INTEGER primitive Type (Integer32, Counter32,
   Gauge32, TimeTicks, Counter64 or UInteger32) are permitted."
   ::= { snmpAlarmEntry 2 }

snmpAlarmInterval OBJECT-TYPE
   SYNTAX     Integer32
   UNITS      "seconds"
   MAX-ACCESS read-create
   STATUS     current
   DESCRIPTION
   "Specifies the time during which data are collected and
   compared with the fixed lower and upper statistical limits."
   ::= { snmpAlarmEntry 3 }

snmpAlarmSampleType OBJECT-TYPE
   SYNTAX     INTEGER {
                  absoluteValue(1),
                  deltaValue(2)
              }
   MAX-ACCESS read-create
   STATUS     current
   DESCRIPTION
   "Defines the method according to which the statistics
   collected are compared with the fixed threshold values."
   DEFVAL { deltaValue }
   ::= { snmpAlarmEntry 4 }

snmpAlarmValue OBJECT-TYPE
   SYNTAX     Integer32
   MAX-ACCESS read-only
   STATUS     current
   DESCRIPTION
   "Contains the value of the last data collection period."
   ::= { snmpAlarmEntry 5 }
```

```
snmpAlarmStartupAlarm OBJECT-TYPE
   SYNTAX      INTEGER {
                   risingAlarm(1),
                   fallingAlarm(2),
                   risingOrFallingAlarm(3)
               }
   MAX-ACCESS read-create
   STATUS      current
   DESCRIPTION
   "Defines the type of the first alarm message and its setting
   value after the system was activated."
   DEFVAL { risingOrFallingAlarm }
   ::= { snmpAlarmEntry 6 }

snmpAlarmRisingThreshold OBJECT-TYPE
   SYNTAX      Integer32
   MAX-ACCESS read-create
   STATUS      current
   DESCRIPTION
   "Enables the definition of an upper threshold limit."
   ::= { snmpAlarmEntry 7 }

snmpAlarmFallingThreshold OBJECT-TYPE
   SYNTAX      Integer32
   MAX-ACCESS read-create
   STATUS      current
   DESCRIPTION
   "Enables the definition of a lower threshold limit."
   ::= { snmpAlarmEntry 8 }

snmpAlarmRisingEventIndex OBJECT-TYPE
   SYNTAX      INTEGER (0..65535)
   MAX-ACCESS read-create
   STATUS      current
   DESCRIPTION
   "Defines the index of the SNMP Event Entry which is used if
   an upper threshold limit is overshot."
   ::= { snmpAlarmEntry 9 }

snmpAlarmFallingEventIndex OBJECT-TYPE
   SYNTAX      INTEGER (0..65535)
   MAX-ACCESS read-create
   STATUS      current
   DESCRIPTION
   "Defines the index of the SNMP Event Entry which is used if a
   lower threshold limit is undershot."
   ::= { snmpAlarmEntry 10 }
```

```
snmpAlarmUnavailableEventIndex OBJECT-TYPE
   SYNTAX     INTEGER (0..65535)
   MAX-ACCESS read-create
   STATUS     current
   DESCRIPTION
   "Defines the index of the SNMP Event Entry which is used if
   no more variables are available."
   ::= { snmpAlarmEntry 11 }

snmpAlarmStatus OBJECT-TYPE
   SYNTAX     RowStatus
   MAX-ACCESS read-create
   STATUS     current
   DESCRIPTION
   "Sets the status of the relevent entry in the SNMP alarm
   table. This object cannot be activated if the following
   objects appear in the relevant row: snmpAlarmVariable,
   snmpAlarmInterval, snmpAlarmSampleType,
   snmpAlarmStartupAlarm, snmpAlarmRisingThreshold,
   snmpAlarmFallingThreshold, snmpAlarmRisingEventIndex,
   snmpAlarmFallingEventIndex and
   snmpAlarmUnavailableEventIndex."
   ::= { snmpAlarmEntry 12 }

snmpAlarmNotifications
              OBJECT IDENTIFIER ::= { snmpAlarm 3 }

snmpRisingAlarm NOTIFICATION-TYPE
   OBJECTS { snmpAlarmVariable, snmpAlarmSampleType,
             snmpAlarmValue, snmpAlarmRisingThreshold }
   STATUS  current
   DESCRIPTION
   "Defines the action which must be carried out after an upper
   threshold value has been overshot."
   ::= { snmpAlarmNotifications 1 }

snmpFallingAlarm NOTIFICATION-TYPE
   OBJECTS { snmpAlarmVariable, snmpAlarmSampleType,
             snmpAlarmValue, snmpAlarmFallingThreshold }
   STATUS  current
   DESCRIPTION
   "Defines the action which must be carried out after a lower
   threshold value has been undershot."
   ::= { snmpAlarmNotifications 2 }

snmpObjectUnavailableAlarm NOTIFICATION-TYPE
   OBJECTS { snmpAlarmVariable }
   STATUS  current
   DESCRIPTION
   "Defines the action which must be carried out after a
   monitored variable is no longer available."
   ::= { snmpAlarmNotifications 3 }
```

Event Group

In this group, it is possible to specify in an event table what the manager/agent must do if a given threshold value is overshot. The following object identifier has been issued for the Event Group in the Manager-to-Manager MIB:

```
snmpEvent       OBJECT IDENTIFIER ::= { snmpM2MObjects 2 }

snmpEventNextIndex OBJECT-TYPE
   SYNTAX     INTEGER (0..65535)
   MAX-ACCESS read-only
   STATUS     current
   DESCRIPTION
   "Contains the indexnumber of the next non-fixed entry in the
   snmpEvent Next Table. If the value is set to 0, the table
   does not contain any fixed values."
   ::= { snmpEvent 1 }

snmpEventTable OBJECT-TYPE
   SYNTAX     SEQUENCE OF SnmpEventEntry
   MAX-ACCESS not-accessible
   STATUS     current
   DESCRIPTION
   "Defines an Event List."
   ::= { snmpEvent 2 }

snmpEventEntry OBJECT-TYPE
   SYNTAX     SnmpEventEntry
   MAX-ACCESS not-accessible
   STATUS     current
   DESCRIPTION
   "Fixes the Event Parameters: the relevant action is initiated
   on the basis of these values."
   INDEX      { snmpEventIndex }
   ::= { snmpEventTable 1 }

SnmpEventEntry ::= SEQUENCE {
   snmpEventIndex          INTEGER,
   snmpEventID             OBJECT IDENTIFIER,
   snmpEventDescription    DisplayString,
   snmpEventEvents         Counter32,
   snmpEventLastTimeSent   TimeStamp,
   snmpEventStatus         RowStatus
}

snmpEventIndex OBJECT-TYPE
   SYNTAX     INTEGER (1..65535)
   MAX-ACCESS not-accessible
   STATUS     current
   DESCRIPTION
```

```
   "On the basis of this index, an entry is individually
   identified in the SNMP event table."
   ::= { snmpEventEntry 1 }

snmpEventID OBJECT-TYPE
   SYNTAX     OBJECT IDENTIFIER
   MAX-ACCESS read-create
   STATUS     current
   DESCRIPTION
   "Sets the Event ID for the relevant Event Type."
   ::= { snmpEventEntry 2 }

snmpEventDescription OBJECT-TYPE
   SYNTAX     DisplayString (SIZE (0..127))
   MAX-ACCESS read-create
   STATUS     current
   DESCRIPTION
   "Contains a comment describing the relevant entry in the SNMP
   Event Table."
   ::= { snmpEventEntry 3 }

snmpEventEvents OBJECT-TYPE
   SYNTAX     Counter32
   MAX-ACCESS read-only
   STATUS     current
   DESCRIPTION
   "Contains the number of events which have been created so far
   for this Event Type."
   ::= { snmpEventEntry 4 }

snmpEventLastTimeSent OBJECT-TYPE
   SYNTAX     TimeStamp
   MAX-ACCESS read-only
   STATUS     current
   DESCRIPTION
   "Contains the value sysUpTime, which was stored at the time
   the last Event was created for this Event Entry."
   DEFVAL { 0 }
   ::= { snmpEventEntry 5 }

snmpEventStatus OBJECT-TYPE
   SYNTAX     RowStatus
   MAX-ACCESS read-create
   STATUS     current
   DESCRIPTION
   "Sets the status of the relevant entry in the SNMP Event
   Table. This object cannot be activated if any of the
   following objects are contained in the relevant row:
   snmpEventID, snmpEventDescription,  snmpEventEvents and
   snmpEventLastTimeSent."
   ::= { snmpEventEntry 6 }
```

```
snmpEventNotifyMinInterval OBJECT-TYPE
   SYNTAX      Integer32
   UNITS       "seconds"
   MAX-ACCESS read-only
   STATUS      current
   DESCRIPTION
   "Defines the minimum time an SNMv2 device operated in a dual
   role will wait before an InformRequest PDU is re-
   transmitted."
   ::= { snmpEvent 3 }

snmpEventNotifyMaxRetransmissions OBJECT-TYPE
   SYNTAX      Integer32
   MAX-ACCESS read-only
   STATUS      current
   DESCRIPTION
   "Defines the maximum time an SNMv2 device operated in a dual
   role will wait before an InformRequest PDU is re-
   transmitted."
   ::= { snmpEvent 4 }

snmpEventNotifyTable OBJECT-TYPE
   SYNTAX      SEQUENCE OF SnmpEventNotifyEntry
   MAX-ACCESS not-accessible
   STATUS      current
   DESCRIPTION
   "This table contains all configurable Event Entries which
   this device can transmit".
   ::= { snmpEvent 5 }

snmpEventNotifyEntry OBJECT-TYPE
   SYNTAX      SnmpEventNotifyEntry
   MAX-ACCESS not-accessible
   STATUS      current
   DESCRIPTION
   "The type and recipient of the InformRequest PDU for an Event
   are established using this set of parameters."
   INDEX       { snmpEventIndex, contextIdentity }
   ::= { snmpEventNotifyTable 1 }

SnmpEventNotifyEntry ::= SEQUENCE {
   snmpEventNotifyIntervalRequested        Integer32,
   snmpEventNotifyRetransmissionsRequested Integer32,
   snmpEventNotifyLifetime                 Integer32,
   snmpEventNotifyStatus                   RowStatus
}

snmpEventNotifyIntervalRequested OBJECT-TYPE
   SYNTAX      Integer32
   UNITS       "seconds"
   MAX-ACCESS read-create
   STATUS      current
```

```
      DESCRIPTION
      "Defines the current interval at which an SNMv2 device
      operated in a dual role will transmit the InformRequest PDU
      for this Event Entry."
      DEFVAL { 30 }
      ::= { snmpEventNotifyEntry 1 }
   snmpEventNotifyRetransmissionsRequested OBJECT-TYPE
      SYNTAX     Integer32
      MAX-ACCESS read-create
      STATUS     current
      DESCRIPTION
      "Defines the retransmissions of the InformRequest PDU for
      this Event Entry."
      DEFVAL { 5 }
      ::= { snmpEventNotifyEntry 2 }
   snmpEventNotifyLifetime OBJECT-TYPE
      SYNTAX     Integer32
      UNITS      "seconds"
      MAX-ACCESS read-create
      STATUS     current
      DESCRIPTION
      "Sets the time (in seconds) after which the corresponding
      entry in the snmpEventNotifyStatus will be deleted."
      DEFVAL { 86400 }
      ::= { snmpEventNotifyEntry 3 }
   snmpEventNotifyStatus OBJECT-TYPE
      SYNTAX     RowStatus
      MAX-ACCESS read-create
      STATUS     current
      DESCRIPTION
      "Establishes the status of the relevant entry in the SNMP
      Event Notify Entry. This object cannot be activated if the
      following objects are contained in the relevant row:
      snmpEventNotifyIntervalRequested, snmpEventNotify-
      RetransmissionsRequested and snmpEventNotifyLifetime."
   ::= { snmpEventNotifyEntry 4 }
```

Name	Type number
GET REQUEST	0
GET NEXT	1
RESPONSE	2
SET REQUEST	3
not used	4
GET BULK	5
INFORM REQUEST	6
TRAP	7

Table 5.8 SNMPv2 PDUs

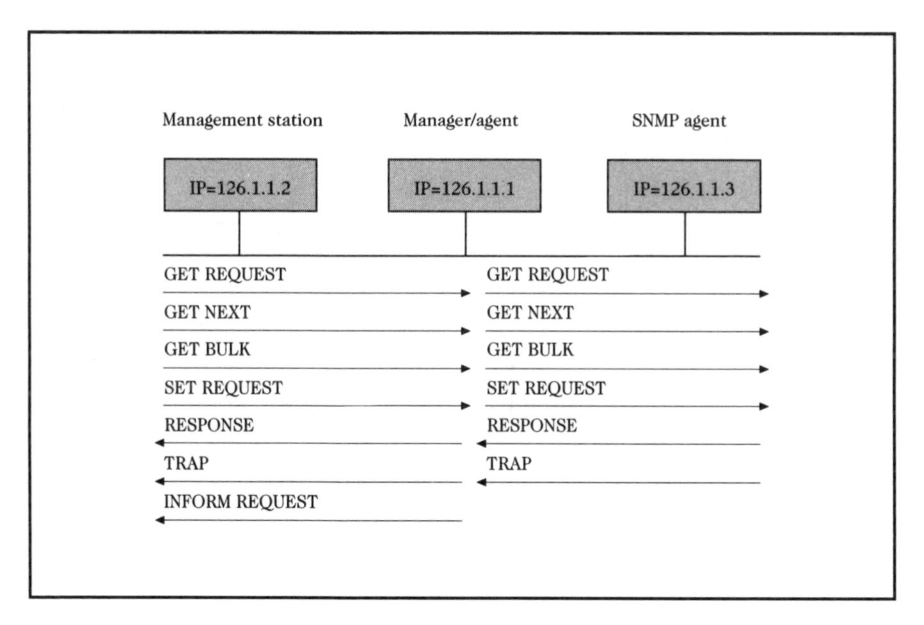

Figure 5.11 Communication relationships

5.6 Manager-to-manager management communication

The concept of a rigid dichotomy between management functions is broken down for the first time in the SNMPv2 protocol and replaced by a multi-level concept. While with SNMPv1, devices could only implement either manager functions or agent functions, a dual function is defined in version 2, enabling manager-to-manager communication. This means that a network manager can act as either an agent process or a server process.

In practice, this supplementary function enables the realization of a hierarchically graduated network management system which corresponds to the requirements of constantly expanding and ever more complex networks. A dual agent is referred to when a management station is capable of providing information to other management stations. This means that the services called up via an agent function are transferred to the next highest series of agents that consider this station to be their network management station.

In addition to the supplementary functions (that is, new PDUs) which are necessary for manager-to-manager communication, RFC 1451 also specifies the Manager-to-Manager Management Information Base. In this MIB, the concepts of Alarms, Events and Notifications are defined.

On the basis of definable alarm criteria, the following actions (events) are specified in the form of messages (notifications). The manager-to-manager MIB comprises three individual tables (the Alarm Table, the Event Table and the Notification Table) and the associated groups.

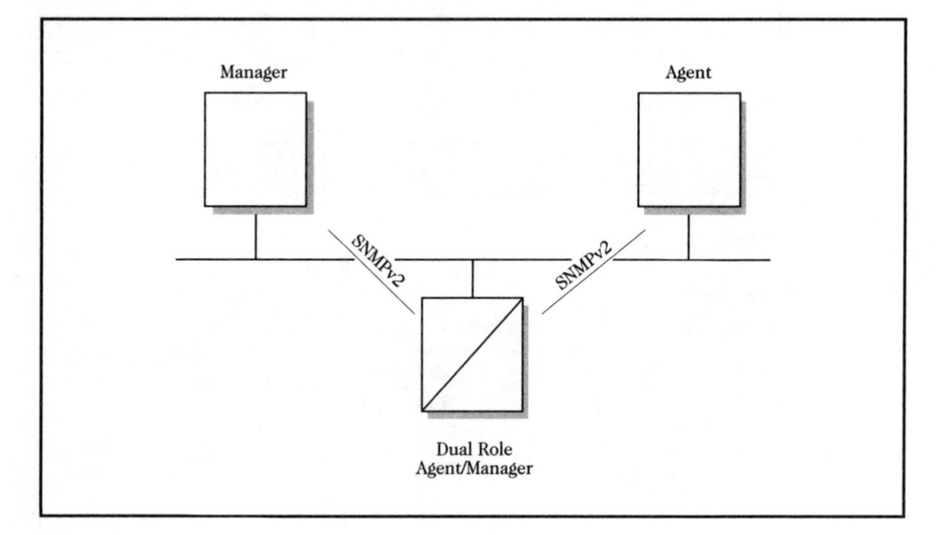

Figure 5.12 Hierarchical network management concept

Device	Receives	Transmits
Manager	INFORM Request RESPONSE SNMPv2 Trap	GET Request GET BULK Request GET NEXT Request SET Request INFORM Request RESPONSE
Agent	GET Request GET NEXT Request GET BULK Request SET Request	INFORM Request RESPONSE SNMPv2 Trap

Table 5.9 Agent/manager functions

Alarms

For every alarm, specific upper and lower thresholds can be defined for the value of an object variable. These threshold values are collected and monitored over a configurable period. Examples of this type of alarm may include the overshooting of error rates, loading limits or the failure of certain sections or segments.

Events

If the fixed threshold values are overshot or undershot, the alarm releases a configurable event.

Notifications

As a result of the event, this occurrence is communicated to the superordinate management station via an Information Request.

The configuration of alarms, events and notifications is carried out in the objects of the Manager-to-Manager MIB. Three individual tables are available for this purpose:

- The Alarm Table;
- The Event Table;
- The Notification Table.

Access to the individual tables is regulated in accordance with the Administrative Model of the SNMPv2 protocol on the basis of RFC 1445 (*Administrative Model for version 2 of the Simple Network Management Protocol*). This document specifies that information can only be sent to machines related to the Alarm Table and for which special provision has been made in the table. The entries in the Alarm Table enable the monitoring interval for the relevant MIB variable to be specified in the type of MIB View to which a specific context has been allocated. Interpretation of the alarm statistics is always based on a command received (Request). This Request is checked before an item of information is passed on, using the authentication procedure and/or the access and protection mechanisms agreed between the source party and the destination party. By convention, all SNMPv2 devices that have implemented an alarm table must support the following components for access control in the Initial MIB View:

```
viewSubtree   = { snmpAlarm }
viewStatus    = { excluded }
viewMask      = { ''H }
```

A management station can only access the MIB View with the allocated context (request context) through these access mechanisms and establish the individual alarm criteria.

Alarm Table

The Alarm Group enables alarm parameters to be defined individually. Threshold values which are constantly compared with the current values can thus be established. An event is created when a threshold value is exceeded.

```
snmpAlarmNextIndex OBJECT-TYPE
   SYNTAX     INTEGER (0..65535)
   MAX-ACCESS read-only
   STATUS     current
   DESCRIPTION
   "Contains the index number of the next, non-fixed entry in
   the snmpAlarm table. If the value is set to 0, the table
   contains no non-fixed values."
   ::= { snmpAlarm 1 }
```

```
snmpAlarmTable OBJECT-TYPE
   SYNTAX     SEQUENCE OF SnmpAlarmEntry
   MAX-ACCESS not-accessible
   STATUS     current
   DESCRIPTION
   "The table in which the SNMP-Alarms are listed."
   ::= { snmpAlarm 2 }

snmpAlarmEntry OBJECT-TYPE
   SYNTAX     SnmpAlarmEntry
   MAX-ACCESS not-accessible
   STATUS     current
   DESCRIPTION
   "In the SNMP Alarm List, all parameters, which are checked
   from time to time,  can be defined through this field."
   INDEX      { contextIdentity, snmpAlarmIndex }
   ::= { snmpAlarmTable 1 }

SnmpAlarmEntry ::= SEQUENCE {
   snmpAlarmIndex                    INTEGER,
   snmpAlarmVariable                 InstancePointer,
   snmpAlarmInterval                 Integer32,
   snmpAlarmSampleType               INTEGER,
   snmpAlarmValue                    Integer32,
   snmpAlarmStartupAlarm             INTEGER,
   snmpAlarmRisingThreshold          Integer32,
   snmpAlarmFallingThreshold         Integer32,
   snmpAlarmRisingEventIndex         INTEGER,
   snmpAlarmFallingEventIndex        INTEGER,
   snmpAlarmUnavailableEventIndex    INTEGER,
   snmpAlarmStatus                   RowStatus
}

snmpAlarmIndex OBJECT-TYPE
   SYNTAX     INTEGER (1..65535)
   MAX-ACCESS not-accessible
   STATUS     current
   DESCRIPTION
   "Using this index, each entry in the SNMP Alarm Table is
   individually identified for a static function."
   ::= { snmpAlarmEntry 1 }

snmpAlarmVariable OBJECT-TYPE
   SYNTAX     InstancePointer
   MAX-ACCESS read-create
   STATUS     current
   DESCRIPTION
   "Contains the object identifier for a variable used for
   collecting statistics. Only variables that correspond to an
   ASN.1 INTEGER primitive type (Integer32, Counter32, Gauge32,
   TimeTicks, Counter64 or UInteger32) are permitted."
   ::= { snmpAlarmEntry 2 )
```

```
snmpAlarmInterval OBJECT-TYPE
   SYNTAX     Integer32
   UNITS      "seconds"
   MAX-ACCESS read-create
   STATUS     current
   DESCRIPTION
   "Specifies the time in which data are collected and with
   which the fixed upper and lower limits of the statistics are
   compared."
   ::= { snmpAlarmEntry 3 }

snmpAlarmSampleType OBJECT-TYPE
   SYNTAX     INTEGER {
                  absoluteValue(1),
                  deltaValue(2)
              }
   MAX-ACCESS read-create
   STATUS     current
   DESCRIPTION
   "Defines the method by which the statistics collected are
   compared with the fixed threshold values."
   DEFVAL { deltaValue }
   ::= { snmpAlarmEntry 4 }

snmpAlarmValue OBJECT-TYPE
   SYNTAX     Integer32
   MAX-ACCESS read-only
   STATUS     current
   DESCRIPTION
   "Contains the value of the last period of data collection."
   ::= { snmpAlarmEntry 5 }

snmpAlarmStartupAlarm OBJECT-TYPE
   SYNTAX     INTEGER {
                  risingAlarm(1),
                  fallingAlarm(2),
                  risingOrFallingAlarm(3)
              }
   MAX-ACCESS read-create
   STATUS     current
   DESCRIPTION
   "Defines the type of the first alarm message and its set
   value after the system has been activated."
   DEFVAL { risingOrFallingAlarm }
   ::= { snmpAlarmEntry 6 }

snmpAlarmRisingThreshold OBJECT-TYPE
   SYNTAX     Integer32
   MAX-ACCESS read-create
   STATUS     current
   DESCRIPTION
   "Enables the definition of an upper threshold limit."
   ::= { snmpAlarmEntry 7 }
```

```
snmpAlarmFallingThreshold OBJECT-TYPE
   SYNTAX      Integer32
   MAX-ACCESS read-create
   STATUS      current
   DESCRIPTION
   "Enables the definition of a lower threshold limit."
   ::= { snmpAlarmEntry 8 }

snmpAlarmRisingEventIndex OBJECT-TYPE
   SYNTAX      INTEGER (0..65535)
   MAX-ACCESS read-create
   STATUS      current
   DESCRIPTION
   "Defines the index of the SNMP Event Entry used when an upper
   threshold limit is exceeded."
   ::= { snmpAlarmEntry 9 }

snmpAlarmFallingEventIndex OBJECT-TYPE
   SYNTAX      INTEGER (0..65535)
   MAX-ACCESS read-create
   STATUS      current
   DESCRIPTION
   "Defines the index of the SNMP Event Entry used when an upper
   threshold limit is exceeded."
   ::= { snmpAlarmEntry 10 }

snmpAlarmUnavailableEventIndex OBJECT-TYPE
   SYNTAX      INTEGER (0..65535)
   MAX-ACCESS read-create
   STATUS      current
   DESCRIPTION
   "Defines the index of the SNMP Event Entry used if a
   monitored variable is no longer available."
   ::= { snmpAlarmEntry 11 }

snmpAlarmStatus OBJECT-TYPE
   SYNTAX      RowStatus
   MAX-ACCESS read-create
   STATUS      current
   DESCRIPTION
   "Specifies the status of the relevant Entry in the SNMP alarm
   table. This object cannot be activated if the following
   objects are present in the relevant row: snmpAlarmVariable,
   snmpAlarmInterval, snmpAlarmSampleType,
   snmpAlarmStartupAlarm, snmpAlarmRisingThreshold,
   snmpAlarmFallingThreshold, snmpAlarmRisingEventIndex,
   snmpAlarmFallingEventIndex and
   snmpAlarmUnavailableEventIndex."
   ::= { snmpAlarmEntry 12 }

snmpAlarmNotifications
               OBJECT IDENTIFIER ::= { snmpAlarm 3 }
```

```
snmpRisingAlarm NOTIFICATION-TYPE
   OBJECTS { snmpAlarmVariable, snmpAlarmSampleType,
             snmpAlarmValue, snmpAlarmRisingThreshold }
   STATUS  current
   DESCRIPTION
   "Defines the action that must be carried out after an upper
   threshold limit has been exceeded."
   ::= { snmpAlarmNotifications 1 }

snmpFallingAlarm NOTIFICATION-TYPE
   OBJECTS { snmpAlarmVariable, snmpAlarmSampleType,
             snmpAlarmValue, snmpAlarmFallingThreshold }
   STATUS  current
   DESCRIPTION
   "Defines the action that must be carried out after a lower
   threshold limit has been exceeded."
   ::= { snmpAlarmNotifications 2 }

snmpObjectUnavailableAlarm NOTIFICATION-TYPE
   OBJECTS { snmpAlarmVariable }
   STATUS  current
   DESCRIPTION
   "Defines the action that must be carried out after a
   monitored variable is no longer available."
   ::= { snmpAlarmNotifications 3 }
```

Event Table

This table specifies what the agent/manager must do if a given threshold value is exceeded.

```
snmpEventNextIndex OBJECT-TYPE
   SYNTAX     INTEGER (0..65535)
   MAX-ACCESS read-only
   STATUS     current
   DESCRIPTION
   "Contains the index number of the next, non-fixed entry in
   the snmpEvent Next-Table. If the value is set to 0, the table
   contains no fixed values "
   ::= { snmpEvent 1 }

snmpEventTable OBJECT-TYPE
   SYNTAX     SEQUENCE OF SnmpEventEntry
   MAX-ACCESS not-accessible
   STATUS     current
   DESCRIPTION
   "Defines an Event List."
   ::= { snmpEvent 2 }
```

```
snmpEventEntry OBJECT-TYPE
   SYNTAX     SnmpEventEntry
   MAX-ACCESS not-accessible
   STATUS     current
   DESCRIPTION
   "Sets the event parameters: the relevant actions are
   initiated on the basis of these values."
   INDEX      { snmpEventIndex }
   ::= { snmpEventTable 1 }

SnmpEventEntry ::= SEQUENCE {
   snmpEventIndex          INTEGER,
   snmpEventID             OBJECT IDENTIFIER,
   snmpEventDescription    DisplayString,
   snmpEventEvents         Counter32,
   snmpEventLastTimeSent   TimeStamp,
   snmpEventStatus         RowStatus
}

snmpEventIndex OBJECT-TYPE
   SYNTAX     INTEGER (1..65535)
   MAX-ACCESS not-accessible
   STATUS     current
   DESCRIPTION
   "Using this index, each entry is individually identified in
   the SNMP Event Table."
   ::= { snmpEventEntry 1 }

snmpEventID OBJECT-TYPE
   SYNTAX     OBJECT IDENTIFIER
   MAX-ACCESS read-create
   STATUS     current
   DESCRIPTION
   "Specifies the associated Event ID for the relevant Event
   Type."
   ::= { snmpEventEntry 2 }

snmpEventDescription OBJECT-TYPE
   SYNTAX     DisplayString (SIZE (0..127))
   MAX-ACCESS read-create
   STATUS     current
   DESCRIPTION
   "Contains a comment which describes the relevant entry in the
   SNMP Event Table."
   ::= { snmpEventEntry 3 }

snmpEventEvents OBJECT-TYPE
   SYNTAX     Counter32
   MAX-ACCESS read-only
   STATUS     current
   DESCRIPTION
   "Contains the number of events so far created for this Event
   Type."
   ::= { snmpEventEntry 4 }
```

```
snmpEventLastTimeSent OBJECT-TYPE
   SYNTAX     TimeStamp
   MAX-ACCESS read-only
   STATUS     current
   DESCRIPTION
   "Contains the value sysUpTime which was stored the last time
   an event was created for this event entry."
   DEFVAL { 0 }
   ::= { snmpEventEntry 5 }

snmpEventStatus OBJECT-TYPE
   SYNTAX     RowStatus
   MAX-ACCESS read-create
   STATUS     current
   DESCRIPTION
   "Specifies the status of the relevant entry in the SNMP event
   table. This object cannot be activated if the following
   objects are present in the relevant row: snmpEventID,
   snmpEventDescription, snmpEventEvents and
   snmpEventLastTimeSent."
   ::= { snmpEventEntry 6 }

snmpEventNotifyMinInterval OBJECT-TYPE
   SYNTAX     Integer32
   UNITS      "seconds"
   MAX-ACCESS read-only
   STATUS     current
   DESCRIPTION
   "Defines the minimum time waited by an SNMv2 device operated
   in a dual role, before an Inform Request PDU is
   retransmitted."
   ::= { snmpEvent 3 }

snmpEventNotifyMaxRetransmissions OBJECT-TYPE
   SYNTAX     Integer32
   MAX-ACCESS read-only
   STATUS     current
   DESCRIPTION
   "Defines the maximum time waited by an SNMv2 device operated
   in a dual role, before an Inform Request PDU is
   retransmitted."
   ::= { snmpEvent 4 }

snmpEventNotifyTable OBJECT-TYPE
   SYNTAX     SEQUENCE OF SnmpEventNotifyEntry
   MAX-ACCESS not-accessible
   STATUS     current
   DESCRIPTION
"This table contains all configurable Event Entries that this
device is capable of transmitting."
   ::= { snmpEvent 5 }
```

```
snmpEventNotifyEntry OBJECT-TYPE
   SYNTAX     SnmpEventNotifyEntry
   MAX-ACCESS not-accessible
   STATUS     current
   DESCRIPTION
   "Using this set of parameters, the type and the recipient of
   the Inform Request PDU for a value are specified."
   INDEX      { snmpEventIndex, contextIdentity }
   ::= { snmpEventNotifyTable 1 }

SnmpEventNotifyEntry ::= SEQUENCE {
   snmpEventNotifyIntervalRequested        Integer32,
   snmpEventNotifyRetransmissionsRequested Integer32,
   snmpEventNotifyLifetime                 Integer32,
   snmpEventNotifyStatus                   RowStatus
}

snmpEventNotifyIntervalRequested OBJECT-TYPE
   SYNTAX     Integer32
   UNITS      "seconds"
   MAX-ACCESS read-create
   STATUS     current
   DESCRIPTION
   "Defines the current time interval in which an SNMv2 device
   operated in a dual role transmits the InformRequest PDU for
   this Event Entry."
   DEFVAL { 30 }
   ::= { snmpEventNotifyEntry 1 }

snmpEventNotifyRetransmissionsRequested OBJECT-TYPE
   SYNTAX     Integer32
   MAX-ACCESS read-create
   STATUS     current
   DESCRIPTION
   "Defines the InformRequest PDU retransmissions for this Event
   Entry."
   DEFVAL { 5 }
   ::= { snmpEventNotifyEntry 2 }

snmpEventNotifyLifetime OBJECT-TYPE
   SYNTAX     Integer32
   UNITS      "seconds"
   MAX-ACCESS read-create
   STATUS     current
   DESCRIPTION
   "Specifies the time (in seconds) after which the
   corresponding entry in the snmpEventNotifyStatus will be
   deleted."
   DEFVAL { 86400 }
   ::= { snmpEventNotifyEntry 3 }

snmpEventNotifyStatus OBJECT-TYPE
   SYNTAX     RowStatus
```

```
   MAX-ACCESS read-create
   STATUS     current
   DESCRIPTION
   "Specifies the relevant entry in the SNMP EventNotify Entry.
   This object cannot be activated if the following objects are
   present in the relevant row:
   snmpEventNotifyIntervalRequested,
   snmpEventNotifyRetransmissionsRequested and
   snmpEventNotifyLifetime."
   ::= { snmpEventNotifyEntry 4 }

snmpM2MConformance

              OBJECT IDENTIFIER ::= { snmpM2M 2 }
snmpM2MCompliances
              OBJECT IDENTIFIER ::= { snmpM2MConformance 1 }

snmpM2MGroups
              OBJECT IDENTIFIER ::= { snmpM2MConformance 2 }

snmpM2MCompliance MODULE-COMPLIANCE
   STATUS  current
   DESCRIPTION
   "Contains the Compliance Statement for all SNMPv2 Entities,
   which have implemented the manager-to-manager MIB."
   MODULE    this module
       MANDATORY-GROUPS { snmpAlarmGroup, snmpEventGroup }
   ::= { snmpM2MCompliances 1 }

snmpAlarmGroup OBJECT-GROUP
   OBJECTS { snmpAlarmNextIndex,
             snmpAlarmVariable, snmpAlarmInterval,
             snmpAlarmSampleType, snmpAlarmValue,
             snmpAlarmStartupAlarm, snmpAlarmRisingThreshold,
             snmpAlarmFallingThreshold,
             snmpAlarmRisingEventIndex,
             snmpAlarmFallingEventIndex,
             snmpAlarmUnavailableEventIndex,
             snmpAlarmStatus }
   STATUS  current
   DESCRIPTION
   "The SNMP Alarm Group contains  all the objects necessary for
   the configuration and description of alarm thresholds for an
   SNMPv2 manager in a dual role."
   ::= { snmpM2MGroups 1 }

snmpEventGroup OBJECT-GROUP
   OBJECTS { snmpEventNextIndex,
             snmpEventID, snmpEventDescription,
             snmpEventEvents, snmpEventLastTimeSent,
             snmpEventStatus, snmpEventNotifyMinInterval,
             snmpEventNotifyMaxRetransmissions,
             snmpEventNotifyIntervalRequested,
```

```
            snmpEventNotifyRetransmissionsRequested,
            snmpEventNotifyLifetime, snmpEventNotifyStatus }
    STATUS  current
    DESCRIPTION
    "This Group contains  all the objects necessary for the
    configuration and description of alarm thresholds for an
    SNMPv2 manager in a dual role."
    ::= { snmpM2MGroups 2 }
```

5.7 The Party MIB

The concept of manager-to-manager communication enables a hierarchically graduated network management concept. The multi-layer management functions of the SNMPv2 specifications presuppose that the various network resources will be able to be allocated individually to each manager. RFC 1445 (*Administrative Model for SNMPv2*) also describes the individual configuration models and possibilities for machines that can act as agent or as agent/manager. In the light of the security problems that became apparent through the practical operation of SNMPv1, the design of SNMP version 2 prevents SNMP packets from being captured by non-authorized stations and eliminates misuse of the information contained in the packets. Since communication between the SNMPv2 stations is still based on a more or less unsecured transport protocol, the design also provides guaranteed control of the data sequence. The whole function of the Community String has been discarded in favor of an authentication mechanism. The range of security problems, such as the unauthorized reading of data using a data analyzer, has been solved by introducing a graduated coding mechanism. Access rights and configurations in the SNMPv2 protocol are regulated via parties. The definitions of parties and of the individual objects have been published in RFC 1447 under the title *Party MIB for version 2 of the Simple Network Management Protocol*.

5.7.1 The SNMPv2 party

An SNMPv2 party describes a virtual environment in an SNMPv2 device, within which a communication partner can implement all forms of action. If an SNMPv2 device wishes to send an SNMPv2 message to a communication partner, it always acts according to restrictions (operations, commands, and so on) predetermined by the relevant party definition. The Party MIB enables the administrator to issue access rights to the individual SNMPv2 users, via freely definable MIB objects. For each party, the Party Table contains an indication of the name of the party, the coding process and its parameters (that is, public and secret codes), the authentication procedure and its parameters, and the transport address at which the party can be reached. This means that several network management stations can access one agent. A given region of the MIB tree is configured for each of the parties (MIB View), so that a station can only read or write to the objects allocated to it. The following groups are integrated within the Party MIB: SNMPv2 Party Database Group, SNMPv2 Contexts Database Group, SNMPv2 Access Privileges Database Group and the MIB View Database Group. Each party is therefore allocated the following values:

- An unambiguous party identity.
- A logical device, on which the party resides. The party is characterized by a Transport Protocol Domain and by its Transport Addresses.
- An authentication protocol and the associated parameters, which prevent the data in a protocol message from being falsified and ensure that data transmitters cannot be impersonated.
- A privacy protocol and the associated parameters, which ensure that the data is rendered unreadable by third parties, thereby preventing unauthorized reading.

Each SNMPv2 party is represented by the following ASN.1 sequence:

```
SnmpParty ::= SEQUENCE {
  partyIdentity
     OBJECT IDENTIFIER,
  partyTDomain
     OBJECT IDENTIFIER,
  partyTAddress
     OCTET STRING,
  partyMaxMessageSize
     INTEGER,
  partyAuthProtocol
     OBJECT IDENTIFIER,
  partyAuthClock
     INTEGER,
  partyAuthPrivate
     OCTET STRING,
  partyAuthPublic
     OCTET STRING,
  partyAuthLifetime
     INTEGER,
  partyPrivProtocol
     OBJECT IDENTIFIER,
  partyPrivPrivate
```

```
        OCTET STRING,
      partyPrivPublic
        OCTET STRING
   }
```

The following specifications have been established for all values of an SNMP party:

- The partyIdentity defines the identity of the party.
- The PartyTDomain designates the Transport Domain and represents the type of Transport Service through which a party receives the entire flow of data from the network. SNMPv2 Parties operating on the basis of the UDP protocol always use the Transport Domain: snmpUDPDomain.
- The partyTAddress defines the Transport Service Address, through which the party receives the complete flow of data from the network.
- The partyMaxMessageSize specifies the maximum length (in octets) of an SNMPv2 message, which the party is capable of receiving.
- The authentication protocol and its protocol mechanisms are determined by the partyAuthProtocol.
- The partyAuthClock, on the basis of which the current time of a party is transmitted, determines the authentication clock.
- The values of partyAuthPrivate specify the private coding mechanism of the authentication protocol.
- The partyAuthPublic component describes a public coding mechanism used by the authentication protocol.
- The partyAuthLifetime defines the upper time limit by which an SNMPv2 message may be delayed on its way between sender and receiver.
- The partyPrivProtocol component specifies the privacy protocol on the basis of which the protocol messages of a party are decoded.
- The values of the partyPrivPrivate component represent the secret coding key for the privacy protocol used.
- The partyPrivPublic component represents the public coding key for the privacy protocol used.

All parties which have been specified in an SNMPv2 device and in which the Authentication Protocol parameter is set to noAuth and the Privacy Protocol parameter is set to noPriv are defined as non-secure.

The actual SNMPv2 process implements all network management operations and generates or receives SNMPv2 protocol messages for the relevant party in accordance with the values specified in the party definitions. All SNMPv2 devices store all information on all parties known to them in a local database. All manageable object resources of the relevant device are administered in another local database. All access rights for the defined SNMPv2 parties are stored in a third database. With SNMPv2, an SNMPv2 management station undertakes the logical function of transmitting SNMPv2 protocol messages and reacts to traps received. The SNMPv2 agent implements the actions instructed by the management station or transmits unsolicited Trap messages.

The term View Subtree refers to a subset of all MIB object instances, which share a common ASN.1 object identifier. This subtree is identified on the basis of the longest object identifier prefix for all MIB objects in this subtree.

A MIB View represents a subset of all manageable variables available in the device, which are collated into any required quantity of View Subtrees. The entire MIB, one single object or any number of combinations of individual objects may be grouped in the MIB View.

5.7.2 Proxy communication

A Proxy Communication Relationship exists whenever a management request received by the local SNMPv2 device/functional module has to be passed on to another process (sub-agent) which is not logically located on the local device/functional module. An SNMPv2 functional module which implements management requests by means of proxy communication is described as a proxy agent. If communication between the remote sub-agent party and the proxy agent takes place via the SNMPv2 protocol, this proxy party relationship is described as an SNMPv2 native proxy relationship. If communication between the two parties is not via the SNMPv2 protocol, this is referred to as an SNMPv2 foreign proxy relationship.

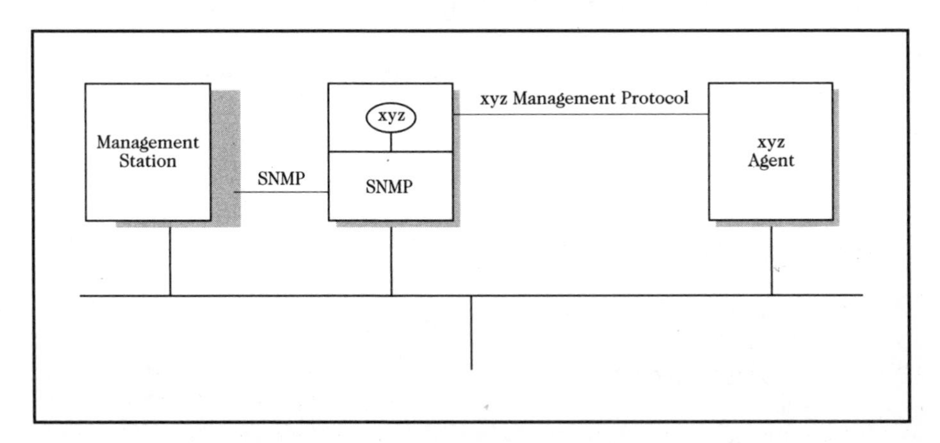

Figure 5.13 SNMPv2 proxy communication relationships

5.7.3 SNMPv2 context

In general terms, an SNMPv2 context defines a collection of manageable object resources to which an SNMPv2 device/functional module has access. The object resources determined by the SNMPv2 context may be implemented either locally or remotely. If an SNMPv2 context relates to the local object resources, this is described as the MIB View.

In this case, the SNMPv2 device/functional module gains access to the management information defined by the SNMPv2 context by means of a local access mechanism. If the SNMPv2 context relates to an object resource which is defined as a remote resource, this Context describes a proxy communication relationship, and the device acts as a proxy agent.

5.7.4 SNMPv2 management communication

Communication between management instances via SNMPv2 takes place only through given SNMPv2 parties. The SNMPv2 context specifies all management functions and their communication capabilities for the parties participating.

Management functions may appear as follows:

- The transmitting party sends a query for certain information to the relevant peer party. This is carried out via the Get Request, the Get Next Request, the Set Request or the Get Bulk Request command.
- The receiving party returns a response to the relevant peer party or automatically initiates a message. This is implemented via the Response Request, Inform Request or the SNMPv2 Trap commands.

A management communication relationship is determined by the following ASN.1 definition:

```
SnmpMgmtCom ::= [2] IMPLICIT SEQUENCE {
  dstParty
     OBJECT IDENTIFIER,
  srcParty
     OBJECT IDENTIFIER,
  context
     OBJECT IDENTIFIER,
  pdu
     PDUs
}
```

Communication between SNMPv2 parties takes place only when the following SnmpMgmtCom values are fulfilled:

- The value dstParty defines the destination SNMPv2 party to which the message is to be sent.
- The value srcParty defines the source SNMPv2 party from which the communication originates.
- The context component determines the specific SNMPv2 context and contains the management information necessary for the communication.
- The relevant PDU component corresponds to a valid format in accordance with RFC 1448.

5.7.5 Authentication of SNMPv2 management communication

SNMPv2 ensures that the transmitting party is reliably identified and that data cannot be falsified during transmission to the peer party. The authentication of the SNMPv2 management communication is ensured via the following ASN.1 construct:

```
SnmpAuthMsg ::= [1] IMPLICIT SEQUENCE {
  authInfo
     ANY,   defined by authentication protocol
  authData
     SnmpMgmtCom
}
```

The meaning of the ASN.1 SnmpAuthMsg construct values is as follows:

- The authentication information (authInfo) specifies values which guarantee the authenticity of the data in a message sent with the authentication protocol.
- The values of the authData component contain the data transmitted in the SNMPv2 management communication.

5.7.6 Private SNMPv2 management communication

Using a private SNMPv2 management communication, it is possible to code the data in the SNMPv2 message. The following ASN.1 construct specifies how and under which rules the SNMPv2 management information is coded:

```
SnmpPrivMsg ::= [1] IMPLICIT SEQUENCE {
  privDst
     OBJECT IDENTIFIER,
  privData
     [1] IMPLICIT OCTET STRING
}
```

The meaning of the ASN.1 SnmpPrivMsg construct is as follows:

- The privacy destination (privDst) specifies the SNMPv2 party with which communication is to be established.
- The privacy data (privData) component contains all the coded information for an authenticated SNMPv2 management communication.

5.7.7 SNMPv2 management communications classes

With the SNMPv2 protocol, individual PDUs are subdivided into management communication classes. Each management communication class is calculated on the basis of the constant 2 and the ASN.1 context-specific tag for the relevant SNMPv2 PDU type. A management communication class set is therefore described by an ASN.1 integer value, which represents the sum of all classes. The SNMPv2 management communication classes are shown in Table 5.10.

Get	1
GetNext	2
Response	4
Set	8
not used	16
GetBulk	32
Inform	64
SNMPv2 Trap	128

Table 5.10 Management communication classes

5.7.8 Access control policy

The SNMPv2 access control policy determines the operations which can be carried out by a source party in communication with a destination party on the basis of the specified SNMPv2 context. The Access control policy is defined in terms of four areas:

Target
Defines the SNMPv2 parties which a desired management operation is to implement on the basis of the Requests defined by the transmitting party.

Subject
Specifies the party of the sender, which is able to initiate a desired management operation.

Context
The SNMPv2 context defines the management information on which the desired management operation is to be implemented.

Privileges
Privileges determine which class of management communication can be implemented on a given SNMPv2 context.

Target	Subject	Context	Privileges
Gary	Lollo	local	35 (Get,, GetNext and GetBulk)
Lollo	Gary	local	132 (Response and SNMPv2 Trap)

Table 5.11 Example: Access authorization for an agent

The access control policy is determined via the following ASN.1 construct:

```
AclEntry ::= SEQUENCE {
  aclTarget
     OBJECT IDENTIFIER,
  aclSubject
     OBJECT IDENTIFIER,
  aclResources
     OBJECT IDENTIFIER,
  aclPrivileges
     INTEGER
}
```

The values of the ASN.1 aclEntry construct are mapped to the aclTable (acl = access control list). Their meanings are as follows:

- The term aclTarget defines the SNMPv2 party in terms of the Party Index for which access authorization has been defined.
- The term aclSubject specifies the SNMPv2 party in terms of the Party Index for which access authorization is available.
- The term aclResources defines the manageable object resources for which access authorization exists in terms of a fixed context (Context Index).
- The term aclPrivileges Component specifies the permitted management operations.

5.7.9 Protocol mechanisms

A more detailed description of the protocol procedures which must be enacted during the sending and receiving of SNMPv2 messages is given below:

Transmission processes

When transmitting management information, the transmitting device (functional module) or the transmitting party must follow the procedures below regardless of whether the message is a Command Request, an Inform Notification or a Trap:

1. On the basis of the SnmpMgmt construct, the transmitting source party (srcParty), the receiving destination party (dstParty), the manageable objects (context) and the desired management operations (operation) must be determined.
2. On the basis of the locally stored party information, a decision is made as to which authentication protocol is to be used between the transmitting and receiving parties.
3. On the basis of the SnmpAuthMsg construct, further information is then prepared as follows:

   authInfo

   Defines the relative value for the transmitting party in accordance with the authentication protocol. If the authInfo field produces the value noAuth, this field consists of an octet string of length 0.

   authData

   Contains the relevant data in accordance with the SnmpMgmtCom construct.
4. On the basis of the locally stored party information, a decision is made as to which data encoding protocol is to be used between the transmitting and receiving parties.
5. On the basis of the SnmpPrivMsg construct, further information is then prepared as follows:

   privDst

   Defines the receiving SNMPv2 party on the basis of an object identifier.

   privData

   The privData field contains the SNMPv2 authentication message (SnmpAuthMsg), which consists of octet strings and has possibly also been encoded. If no coding has been specified for the SNMPv2 party received (noPriv), the information will be transmitted uncoded.

6. The values of the SnmpPrivMsg construct are created as a serial data stream in accordance with the Transport Mapping Definitions (RFC 1449).
7. Finally, this information is transmitted to the Transport Address of the receiving party.

Reception processes

During the reception of management information, the receiving device (functional module) or receiving Party must carry out the following procedures:

1. The snmpStatsPacket counter is incremented. If an error is determined in the SNMPv2 message received, this message is rejected and the reception process is interrupted.
2. The local Party Information database is checked in terms of the privData field of the SnmpPrivMsg to determine whether it contains an entry relating to the receiving SNMPv2 party.
3. If no entry relating to the specified receiving party is found in the local Party Information database, the message is rejected and the snmpStatsUnknownDstParties counter is incremented.
4. On the basis of the privData component of the SnmpPrivMessage, an ASN.1 octet string is created by decoding the authentication protocol. The value of this string is compared with the corresponding value of the receiving party. For example, if no coding (noPriv) has been established for the receiving party and if the octet string corresponds to this value, the reception process can be continued.
5. If an error is determined during the creation of the octet string, the message received is rejected and the snmpStatsEncodingErrors counter ise incremented.
6. If the value of the dstParty does not correspond with the value in the privDst field, the message received is rejected and the snmp-StatsDstPartyMismatches counter is incremented.
7. The local party information database is then consulted to check whether there is an entry relating to the transmitting SNMPv2 party specified in the srcParty field.
8. If no entry is found in the local party information database relating to the transmitting party, the message received is rejected and the snmpStatsUnknownSrcParties counter is incremented.
9. The values for the SnmpAuthMsg construct received are then compared with the transmitting and receiving party definitions stored in the local Party Information database according to the rules of the

authentication protocol. For example, if the authInfo field produces the value noAuth, the SnmpAuthMessage is always evaluated as authentic.

10. If a problem is encountered when comparing the SnmpAuth message (for example, the comparison reveals that the message has been altered), the message received is rejected and an authorizationFailure trap is transmitted.
11. If no error is found, the values of the SnmpMgmtCom construct are created from the authData components of the SnmpAuth message.
12. Comparison of the context entries in the local Context Information database establishes whether the SNMPv2 context specifications contained in the SnmpMgmtCom construct are present.
13. If no entry is found in the local Context Information database, the SNMPv2 message is rejected and the snmpStatsUnknownContext counter is incremented.
14. The local database, in which all access authorizations are stored, is used to check whether the access rights of the transmitting SNMPv2 party agree with the rights of the receiving party.
15. On the basis of the SnmpMgmtCom value, the associated management communication class is then inspected. If the management communication class of the message received corresponds to the values 32, 8, 2 or 1 (Get Bulk, Set, Get Next or Get) and the SNMPv2 context does not enable the implementation of these operations, the message received is rejected and the snmpStatsUnknownContext counter is incremented.
16. If the management communication class of the message received corresponds to the values 128, 64 or 4 (SNMPv2 Trap, Inform or Response) and if the class does not correspond to the access privileges, the message received is rejected, and the snmpStatsBadOperations counter is incremented.
17. If no access authorisation has been specified for the communication class of the message received, the message is rejected and a Response message is created. This response message is addressed directly to the sending party, and the error index signals an Authorization Error.
18. If the SNMPv2 context corresponds to the local object resources, the relevant management operation is implemented by the receiving SNMPv2 device/process on the basis of the MIB View specified in the SNMPv2 context.
19. If the SNMPv2 context corresponds to the defined remote object resources, the relevant management operation is implemented on the basis of a proxy management relationship.

Transmitting a Response

When transmitting a Response to a Request, various procedures are performed:

1. On the basis of the SnmpMgmtCom construct received, the source party (srcParty) is sent to the destination party (dstParty). The source party (srcParty) of the transmitting SnmpMgmtCom construct is formed from the destination party (dstParty) of the message received. The context corresponds to the context of the message received, and the PDU variables consist of the values requested.
2. On the basis of the locally stored party information, a decision is made as to which authentication protocol is used between the sending and receiving parties.
3. On the basis of the SnmpAuthMsg construct, information is then prepared as follows:

   authInfo

   In accordance with the authentication protocol, this field defines the relevant value for the sending party. If the authInfo field contains the value noAuth, this field consists of an octet string of length 0.

   authData

   Contains the relevant data in accordance with the SnmpMgmtCom construct.
4. On the basis of the locally stored party information, a decision is made as to which data encoding protocol is used between the sending and receiving parties.
5. On the basis of the SnmpPrivMsg construct, information is then prepared as follows:

   privDst

   Defines the receiving SNMPv2 party on the basis of an object identifier.

   privData

   The privData field contains the SNMPv2 authentication message (SnmpAuthMsg), which consists of octet strings and may also be encrypted. If no coding has been specified for the receiving SNMPv2 party (noPriv) the information is transmitted uncoded.
6. The values of the SnmpPrivMsg construct are created as a serial data stream in accordance with the Transport Mapping Definitions (RFC 1449).
7. This information is then sent to the Transport Address and the Transport Domain of the receiving party specified in the Request message.

5.7.10 Configuration examples

Examples of various agent configurations are described below:

- Minimum agent configuration without security;
- Minimum agent configuration with security;
- MIB View configuration;
- Proxy configuration;
- Public key configuration.

Minimum agent configuration without security

The following example presents a minimum agent configuration which is provided for use in a non-secure environment and which communicates with one or more SNMPv2 management stations. Table 5.12 presents all the party information of the agent and the manager station. The agent party uses UDP port 161 above the IP address 192.1.1.1. The agent party has been allocated the name (Identity) Gary. The manager process (Identity: Lollo) is using UDP port 2001 on the computer with IP address 192.1.1.2 for communication. In a non-secure communication relationship, as an absolute minimum, only the Transport Addresses of the two SNMPv2 parties and their names (Identities) need to be specified.

Identity	**Gary (Agent)**	**Lollo (Manager)**
Domain	snmpUDPDomain	snmpUDPDomain
Address	192.1.1.1, 161	192.1.1.2, 2001
Auth Prot	noAuth	noAuth
Auth Priv Key	"	"
Auth Pub Key	"	"
Auth Clock	0	0
Auth Lifetime	0	0
Priv Prot	noPriv	noPriv
Priv Priv Key	"	"
Priv Pub Key	"	"

Table 5.12 Minimum agent party information

Table 5.13 represents the combined information for the local address policy.

Target	**Subject**	**Context**	**Privileges**
Gary	Lollo	local	35 (Get, GetNext and GetBulk)
Lollo	Gary	local	132 (Response and SNMPv2 Trap)

Table 5.13 Access information for a minimum agent configuration

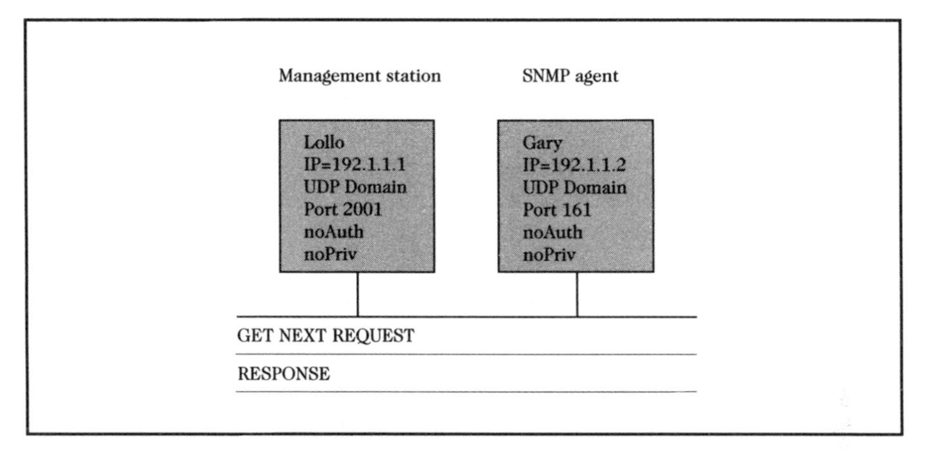

Figure 5.14 SNMPv2 client–server communication

Using a Get Next Request, the management party, Lollo, calls an SNMPv2 context (local) from the agent named Gary. The management station accordingly inspects the local Party Information Database and determines that the value noAuth has been defined for the authentication protocol of the party Lollo. It is also established that no privacy protocol (noPriv) has been defined for the party Gary. The Get Next Request message generated by the manager is therefore not protected or encrypted; it is sent directly to the Transport Address (IP address 192.1.1.1, UDP port 161).

When the Get Next Request is received from the agent, the receiving party (Gary) is identified and the Local Party Information Database is inspected for the party indicated. Because the value noPriv has been established for the privacy protocol of the party Gary, the message received need not be decoded. Since there is also no authentication protocol (noAuth) for the sending party Lollo specified in the Local Party Information Database, it is assumed that the incoming message is authentic. The message is then processed, provided the entries in the Local Access Policy Information Database permit the Get Next function between the party Lollo and the agent party Gary, in accordance with the SNMPv2 context 'local'. The Local Access Policy Information Database which permits this action is shown in Figure 5.14. At this stage, the Response message from the source party Gary is sent to the destination party Lollo. The agent station inspects the Local Party Information Database and establishes that the value noAuth has been defined for the authentication protocol of the party Gary. It is also established that no privacy protocol (noPriv) has been defined for the party Lollo. The Response message generated by the agent is accordingly not protected or encrypted; it is sent directly to the manager station.

Minimum agent configuration with security

The following example presents a minimum agent configuration which is provided for use in a secure environment and which communicates with an SNMPv2 management station. All the party information of the agent and the manager station is shown in Table 5.14. The agent party uses UDP port 161 above the IP Address 192.1.1.1. The agent party has been allocated the name (Identity) Brian. The manager process (Identity Virginia) uses UDP port 2001 on the computer with the IP Address 192.1.1.2 for communication. In a secure communication relationship, all protocol messages between the two communication partners are protected by means of authentication from falsification or impersonation of the sender. In our example, an additional encoding protocol is defined in order to be able to transmit the encryption key between source and destination using the SNMPv2 protocol.

Identity	Brian(Agent)	Virginia(Manager)
Domain	snmpUDPDomain	snmpUDPDomain
Address	192.1.1.1,161	192.1.1.2, 2001
Auth Prot	v2md5AuthProtocol	v2md5AuthProtocol
Auth Priv Key	'0123456789ABCDEF'	'GHIJKL0123456789'
Auth Pub Key	"	"
Auth Clock	0	0
Auth Lifetime	300	300
Priv Prot	desPrivProtocol	desPrivProtocol
Priv Priv Key	'MNOPQR0123456789'	'STUVWX0123456789'
Priv Pub Key	"	"

Table 5.14 Party information for a minimum agent configuration with security

Target	Subject	Context	Privileges
Brian	Virginia	local	35 (Get,GetNext and GetBulk)
Virginia	Brian	local	132 (Response and SNMPv2 Trap)

Table 5.15 Access information for a minimum agent configuration with security

As shown in Table 5.14, the management party (Virginia) communicates via UDP Port 2001 (IP Address 192.1.1.2) with the agent party (Brian) via UDP Port 161 (IP Address 192.1.1.1).

As a minimum configuration, a secure SNMPv2 agent must have a series of information available on both parties. The two parties (Brian and Virginia) authenticate all messages using an SNMPv2 authentication protocol (in this case it is the v2md5AuthProtocol) and the relevant private authentication codes (Brian = '0123456789ABCDEF' Virginia = 'GHIJKL0123456789').

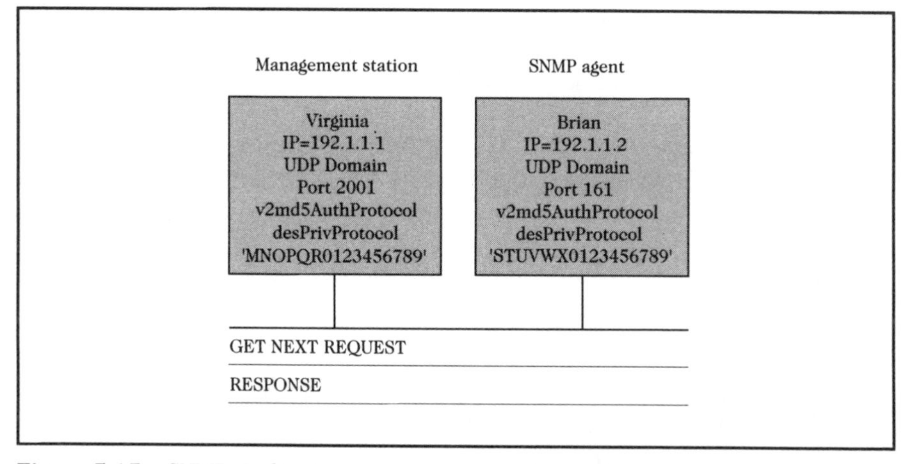

Figure 5.15 SNMPv2 client–server communication with security

All protocol messages to the party Virginia are coded using the agreed privacy protocols (desPrivProtocol) and the private encryption key 'STUVWX0123456789'. On receipt of this message, the data is decoded via the same encryption key or privacy protocol. In the reverse direction (Virginia → Brian), the privacy protocol (desPrivProtocol) and the private encryption key 'MNOPQR0123456789' are used.

MIB View configuration

By definition, a MIB View consists of any number of View Subtrees. In practice, a MIB View definition may comprise a very large number of View Subtrees. For this reason, the initiators of the SNMPv2 standard defined a number of conventions to simplify handling.

- The MIB View definitions are defined in the form of View Subtree families, which are either included in or excluded from a MIB View definition.
- A locally created table in every SNMPv2 entity contains all MIB Views for every SNMPv2 context and the resulting local object resources.
- Every entry in the MIB View Table represents a View Subtree Family.
- Every entry in the MIB View Table is provided with an object identifier value (Family Name) and a bit-string value (Family Mask). On the basis of the Family Mask, it is established which sub-identifiers of the relevant Family Name are of particular importance.

A MIB object instance belongs to a View Subtree Family under the following conditions:

- The object identifier name of a MIB object instance contains at least as many sub-identifiers as the Family Name in the table entry.

- Every sub-identifier in the name of a MIB object instance corresponds to the appropriate sub-identifier of the Family Name if the relevant bit in the Family Mask is not set to 0.

The accommodation of a MIB object instance in a MIB View for a specific SNMPv2 context depends on the relevant definition in the local MIB View Table:

- If a MIB object instance does not belong to a Subtree Family, this instance is not a component of the MIB VIew of the corresponding SNMPv2 context.
- If a MIB object instance belongs only to one Subtree Family of the MIB View Table entries, this instance may either be included in or excluded from a MIB View.
- If a MIB object instance belongs to more than one Subtree Family of the MIB View Table entries, this instance may either be included in or excluded from a MIB View.

Table 5.16 shows a minimum agent configuration with only one context entry. The SNMPv2 context (Frank) and the type (included) specify that all MIB object instances in the Subtree Family (internet) of the MIB View are permitted for the SNMPv2 context Frank. The Family Mask of length 0 indicates that the Subtree Family belongs to a single View Subtree.

Context	Type	Family Name	Family Mask
Frank	included	internet	“H

Table 5.16 MIB View definitions for a minimum agent configuration

Context	Type	Family Name	Family Mask
Frank	included	internet	“H
Frank	excluded	snmpParties	“H
Jeremy	included	System	“H
Jeremy	included	snmpParties	“H

Table 5.17 MIB Views for several context definitions

The MIB View definitions for an SNMPv2 entity shown in Table 5.17 contain several SNMPv2 context definitions with different MIB Views. The MIB View with the SNMPv2 context Frank contains all SNMPv2 objects with the exception of those needed for the administration of the SNMPv2 parties. The MIB View with the SNMPv2 context Jeremy, however, contains only MIB objects of the System Group and all objects needed for the administration of the SNMPv2 parties.

Context	Type	Family Name	Family Mask
Frank	included	System	“H
Frank	included	{ ifEntry 0 2 }	‘FFA0’H
Frank	excluded	{ ifSpeed 2 }	“H
Jeremy	included	icmp	“H
Jeremy	included	{ ifEntry 0 5 }	‘FFA0’H
Jeremy	included	{ ifInOctets 4 }	“H

Table 5.18 A more complex MIB View definition

As shown in Table 5.18, the agent also contains only two context definitions, but these have a considerably more complex structure. The MIB View of the SNMPv2 context Frank contains all object instances of the System Group and some information relating to a second network interface. In this context definition, access to the speed of transfer of the interface via the Family Mask value FFA0'H has been excluded. The value FFA0'H indicates that a MIB object belongs to the Subtree Family if the prefix of the object corresponds to the prefix of the ifEntry object, and the eleventh sub-identifier of the name is set to 2. The MIB View of the SNMPv2 context Jeremy contains all object instances of the ICMP Group, all information on the fifth network interface and all statistical data on the fourth interface (number of octets received).

Proxy configuration

Two advantages can be gained through the proxy functions of the SNMPv2 specification:

- Non-SNMP devices can be included in the overall concept via the foreign proxy functions.
- Native proxy functions can transfer the processing of management processes to the point of origin, enabling the agent to concentrate on collecting and passing on individual items of information.

Foreign proxy configuration

In the following example, a device which communicates only via a proprietary management protocol is to be supported by a management station. Consequently, an SNMPv2 proxy agent which converts all SNMPv2 management operations into the specific proprietary management functions is set up on the management station. Table 5.19 shows all the locally defined party information of the SNMPv2 parties in the SNMPv2 party agent.

Identity	Willy (Manager)	Huschu (Proxy agent)	Egbert (Proxy destination)
Domain	snmpUDP Domain	snmpUDP Domain	heinMgmtPrtcl
Address	192.1.1.1, 2002	192.1.1.2, 161	0x00704711
Auth Prot	v2md5Auth Protocol	v2md5Auth Protocol	noAuth
Auth Priv Key	'0123456789 ABCDEF'	'GHIJKL01234 56789'	''
Auth Pub Key	''	''	''
Auth Clock	0	0	0
Auth Lifetime	300	300	0
Priv Prot	noPriv	noPriv	noPriv
Priv Priv Key	''	''	''
Priv Pub Key	''	''	''

Table 5.19 Party information of a proxy agent

The proxy agent party (Huschu) uses UDP port 161 (IP Address 192.1.1.2). The manager (Willy) always communicates via UDP port 2002 (IP Address 192.1.1.1). Both parties (Willy and Huschu) authenticate all messages by means of an SNMPv2 authentication protocol (in this case it is the v2md5AuthProtocol) and the relevant private authentication codes (Willy = '0123456789ABCDEF', Huschu = 'GHIJKL0123456789'). Instead of the SNMPv2 protocol, the Party Egbert uses the proprietary management protocol (heinMgmtPrtcl) for communication.

Context	Proxy Destination	Proxy Source	Proxy Context
Flotowhaus	Egbert	n/a	n/a

Table 5.20 Proxy relationships for a proxy agent

Table 5.20 presents the defined proxy relationships of the SNMPv2 proxy agent according to the local context information. The SNMPv2 context Flotowhaus was specially created here for the communication relationship with the party Egbert. The Transport Domain of the proxy destination party determines the interpretation of the proxy source and the proxy context components. In the example, the use of the proprietary hein management protocol (heinMgmtPrtcl) determines that the proxy source and the context must be ignored.

In order to communicate with the proprietary device (party Egbert), an SNMPv2 Get Next Request is generated by the management station (Willy) as a component of the SnmpMgmtCom value, which in turn indicates the SNMPv2 context Flotowhaus. This is transferred to the party Huschu via

UDP port 161 (IP Address 192.1.1.2). This Request is authenticated using the private authentication code ‘0123456789ABCDEF’.

After the party Huschu has received the Request, the sender (Willy) is determined using the private authentication code ‘0123456789ABCDEF’. In the configuration, the party Willy has been enabled to send Get Next Requests to the party Huschu. The Request is accepted and processed according to the SNMPv2 context Flotowhaus and the relevant access control policy. The locally defined context information indicates that the SNMPv2 context Flotowhaus was defined for a proxy communication relationship. For this reason, the Request is converted into the specific operations of the hein management protocol (heinMgmtPrtcl) and passed on to the party Egbert with the address 0x00704711 in the heinMgmtPrtcl Domain.

After the proprietary protocol has sent a reply to the proxy agent Huschu, the agent (Huschu) constructs an SNMPv2 Response message according to the definitions of the context Flotowhaus. This is then passed on to the party Willy. This Response message is also saved using the authentication protocol (v2md5AuthProtocol) and encoded via the private coding key ‘GHIJKL0123456789’. The Response message is sent by the party Huschu to the SNMPv2 party Willy on the management station (IP Address 192.1.1.1, UDP port 2002).

After the party Willy has received the Response message, the sender of the message is checked, using the locally defined, private authentication key ‘GHIJKL0123456789’.

The party Huschu is permitted to send a Response message to the party Willy in accordance with the SNMPv2 context Flotowhaus. The Response is therefore accepted and the action is completed.

Table 5.21 shows the SNMPv2 party information set up in the management station.

Identity	Willy (Manager)	Huschu (Proxy agent)
Domain	snmpUDPDomain	snmpUDPDomain
Address	192.1.1.1 2002	192.1.1.2, 161
Auth Prot	v2md5AuthProtocol	v2md5AuthProtocol
Auth Priv Key	‘0123456789ABCDEF’	‘GHIJKL0123456789’
Auth Pub Key	‘’	‘’
Auth Clock	0	0
Auth Lifetime	300	300
Priv Prot	noPriv	noPriv
Priv Priv Key	‘’	‘’
Priv Pub Key	‘’	‘’

Table 5.21 Party information in the management station

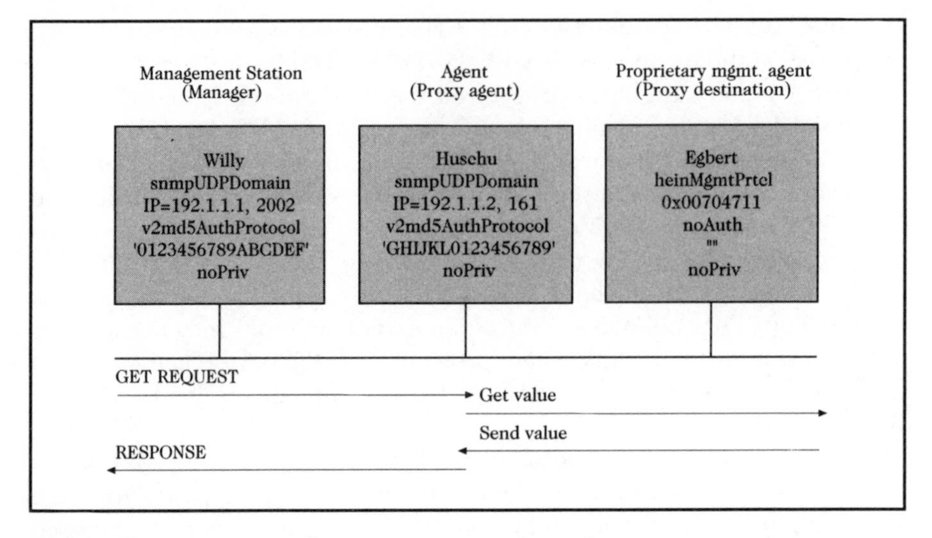

Figure 5.16 Foreign proxy communication relationship

Target	Subject	Context	Privileges
Huschu	Willy	Flotowhaus	35 (Get, GetNext & GetBulk)
Willy	Huschu	Flotowhaus	132 (Response & SNMPv2 Trap)

Table 5.22 Access information for a foreign proxy agent

Native proxy configuration

The following example describes the necessary configurations for a native proxy function. The introduction of native proxy management enables the processing of management processes to be transferred to sub-agents. In this case, the sub-agents act as pure proxy agents and communicate with the main agent via the SNMP protocol. The sub-agents may reside either in the same device as the main agent or may be located in other devices. Native proxy functions enable the implementation of modular SNMP agents which can produce the performance required, scaled according to needs and application. In terms of its function, the example of native proxy configuration is similar to foreign proxy configuration. However, in this case, the party Egbert receives all messages via the SNMP protocol. For this reason, an authentication mechanism is used for communication with the SNMPv2 proxy agent Huschu. Table 5.23 illustrates the party information of an SNMPv2 proxy agent.

Identity	Willy (Manager)	Huschu (Proxy agent)
Domain	snmpUDPDomain	snmpUDPDomain
Address	192.1.1.1,	2002 192.1.1.2,161

Auth Prot	v2md5AuthProtocol	v2md5AuthProtocol
Auth Priv Key	‘0123456789ABCDEF’	‘GHIJKL0123456789’
Auth Pub Key	‘’	‘’
Auth Clock	0	0
Auth Lifetime	300	300
Priv Prot	noPriv	noPriv
Priv Priv Key	‘’	‘’
Priv Pub Key	‘’	‘’

Identity	**Egbert (Proxy destination)**	**Zappa (Proxy source)**
Domain	snmpUDPDomain	snmpUDPDomain
Address	192.1.1.5, 161	192.1.1.2, 161
Auth Prot	v2md5AuthProtocol	v2md5AuthProtocol
Auth Priv Key	‘MNOPQR0123456789’	‘STUVWX0123456789’
Auth Pub Key	‘’	‘’
Auth Clock	0	0
Auth Lifetime	300	300
Priv Prot	noPriv	noPriv
Priv Priv Key	‘’	‘’
Priv Pub Key	‘’	‘’

Table 5.23 Party information of a proxy agent

Table 5.24 shows the proxy relationships stored in the context information of the SNMPv2 proxy agent.

Context	**Proxy destination**	**Proxy source**	**Proxy context**
Flotowhaus	Egbert	Zappa	Hexenhaus
Hexenhaus	Willy	Huschu	Flotowhaus

Table 5.24 Proxy relationships of the proxy agent

Table 5.25 shows the party information for all known SNMPv2 parties of the SNMPv2 management station.

Identity	**Willy (Manager)**	**Huschu (Proxy agent)**
Domain	snmpUDPDomain	snmpUDPDomain
Address	192.1.1.1, 2002	192.1.1.2, 161
Auth Prot	v2md5AuthProtocol	v2md5AuthProtocol
Auth Priv Key	‘0123456789ABCDEF’	‘GHIJKL0123456789’
Auth Pub Key	“	“
Auth Clock	0	0

Auth Lifetime	300	300
Priv Prot	noPriv	noPriv
Priv Priv Key	''	''
Priv Pub Key	''	''

Table 5.25 Party information for the management station

Table 5.26 shows all the locally defined access policy information.

Target	Subject	Context	Privileges
Huschu	Willy	Flotowhaus	35 (Get, GetNext and GetBulk)
Willy	Huschu	Flotowhaus	132 (Response and SNMPv2 Trap)
Egbert	Zappa	Hexenhaus	35 (Get, GetNext and GetBulk)
Zappa	Egbert	Hexenhaus	132 (Response and SNMPv2 Trap)

Table 5.26 Access information for native proxy functions

As shown in Table 5.23, the proxy agent party Huschu communicates via UDP port 161 (IP Address 192.1.1.2). The network management station (Willy) uses UDP port 2002 on IP Address 192.1.1.1. The proxy source party (Zappa) receives all messages via the Well Known UDP port 161 (IP Address 192.1.1.2), while the proxy destination party Egbert uses UDP port 161 on IP Address 192.1.1.5. All messages from the four parties are authenticated and use the authentication protocol v2md5AuthProtocol and the relevant private encryption code (Willy = '0123456789ABCDEF', Huschu = 'GHIJKL0123456789', Egbert = 'MNOPQR0123456789' and Zappa = 'STUVWX0123456789').

Table 5.24 presents all proxy relationships known to the proxy agent. The SNMPv2 context Flotowhaus is only used for communication if the SNMPv2 party Zappa is communicating with SNMPv2 party Egbert and the SNMPv2 context Hexenhaus has been specified.

For communication with the party Egbert, the management station Willy generates an SNMPv2 Get Next Request. This message contains the definition of the SnmpMgmtCom value which refers to the SNMPv2 context Flotowhaus. Before it is sent to the party Huschu (UDP port 161, IP Address 192.1.1.2), this message is encoded using the private encryption key '012345-6789ABCDEF'.

When the Get Next Request is received by the party Huschu, the sending party (Willy) is investigated using the locally stored, private encryption key '0123456789ABCDEF'. Since the party Willy is authorised to issue a Get Next Request to the party Huschu through the context Flotowhaus, the Get Next Request is accepted.

The locally stored context information indicates that the context Flotowhaus relates to a proxy communication. The Request is therefore transformed into a Get Next Request (with a reference to the context Hexenhaus) from the party Zappa to the party Egbert. The new message is encoded according to the private encryption key 'STUVWX0123456789' and transferred to the party Egbert (IP Address 192.1.1.5).

When the Get Next Request is received by the party Egbert, the sender party (Zappa) is investigated on the basis of the locally stored, private encryption key 'STUVWX0123456789'. Since the party Zappa is authorized to issue a Get Next Request to the party Egbert through the context Hexenhaus, the Get Next Request is accepted.

In reply, a Response message from the party Egbert is sent to the party Zappa with the SNMPv2 context Hexenhaus. The new message is encoded using the private encryption key 'MNOPQR0123456789' and transferred to the party Egbert (IP Address 192.1.1.2).

When the Response message is received by the party Zappa, the sender party (Egbert) is investigated on the basis of the locally stored, private encryption key 'MNOPQR0123456789'. Since the party Egbert is authorized to transfer a Response packet to the party Zappa through the context Hexenhaus, the message is accepted. From this information, the Response message is generated as a reaction to the initially received Get Next Request (with a reference to the context Flotowhaus). This Response message is encoded using the private key 'GHIJKL0123456789' and transferred to the party Willy (IP Address 192.1.1.1.).

When the Response message is received by the party Willy, the sender party (Huschu) is investigated on the basis of the locally stored, private encryption key 'GHIJKL0123456789'. Since the party Huschu is authorized to transfer a Response packet to the party Willy through the context Hexenhaus, the message is accepted. This brings the complete communication cycle between the management station and the proxy agent to a close (*see* Figure 5.17).

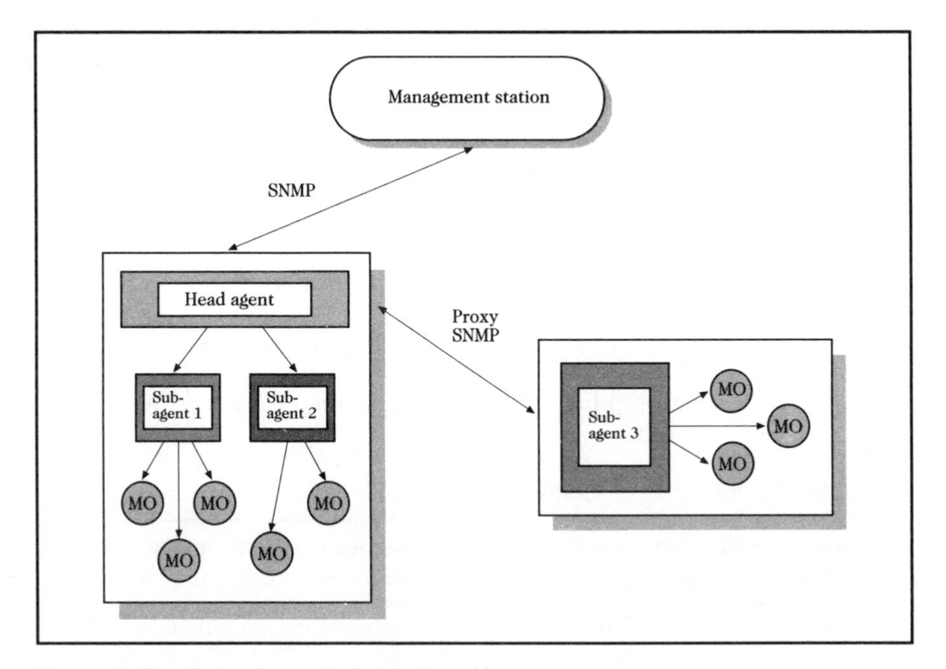

Figure 5.17 Native Proxy Relationships

Public key configuration

In this example, an imaginary security protocol is used, which ensures the encryption of the data so that the data can be protected from misuse on the way from the source to the destination. Table 5.27 presents a sample configuration for an SNMPv2 agent. This agent communicates only with an SNMPv2 management station.

Identity	Brian (Agent)	Virginia (Manager)
Domain	snmpUDPDomain	snmpUDPDomain
Address	192.1.1.1, 161	192.1.1.2, 2004
Auth Prot	mhAuthProtocol	mhAuthProtocol
Auth Priv Key	'0123456789ABCDEF'	''
Auth Pub Key	'0123456789abcdef'	'ghijkl0123456789'
Auth Clock	0	0
Auth Lifetime	300	300
Priv Prot	noPriv	noPriv
Priv Priv Key	''	''
Priv Pub Key	''	''

Table 5.27 Agent party information with a public key function

Table 5.28 presents the party information for the network management station.

Identity	Brian (Agent)	Virginia (Manager)
Domain	snmpUDPDomain	snmpUDPDomain
Address	192.1.1.1, 161	192.1.1.2, 2004
Auth Prot	mhAuthProtocol	mhAuthProtocol
Auth Priv Key	''	'GHIJKL0123456789'
Auth Pub Key	'0123456789abcdef'	'ghijkl0123456789'
Auth Clock	0	0
Auth Lifetime	300	300
Priv Prot	noPriv	noPriv
Priv Priv Key	''	''
Priv Pub Key	''	''

Table 5.28 Public key party information for the management station

Table 5.29 shows the local access policy of the agent and the network management station.

Target	Subject	Context	Privileges
Brian	Virginia	local	35 (Get, GetNext and GetBulk)
Virginia	Brian	local	132 (Response and SNMPv2 Trap)

Table 5.29 Access information for a minimum agent configuration with security

As shown in Table 5.27, the agent party (Brian) communicates via UDP port 161 (IP Address 192.1.1.1) with the network management station (Party = Virginia, UDP port = 2004, IP Address = 192.1.1.2). The messages transferred between the two parties are authenticated by means of the imaginary authentication protocol mhAuthProtocol and use the relevant private encryption codes (Brian = '0123456789ABCDEF', Virginia = 'GHIJKL0123456789'). Communication between the agent and the manager operates according to the same pattern as the example 'Minimum Agent Configuration with Security'.
The biggest difference is that none of the parties knows the relevant private encryption mechanism of the other parties. In order to decode the data correctly, a private encryption algorithm is transferred along with each message. Using this key and the known public authentication key, the content of the message can be deciphered.

5.7.11 Party MIB definitions

The Party MIB published in RFC 1447 enables the administrator to issue access rights individually to users via the freely definable MIB objects. A certain section of the MIB tree is configured for each of the parties (MIB View) so that a station can only read or write to the objects provided for it. The following groups are integrated in the Party MIB: the SNMPv2 Party Database Group, the SNMPv2 Contexts Database Group, the SNMPv2 Access Privileges Database Group and the MIB View Database Group.

```
TAddress ::= TEXTUAL-CONVENTION
   STATUS        current
   DESCRIPTION
   "Establishes a Transport Service Address."
   SYNTAX        OCTET STRING

Clock ::= TEXTUAL-CONVENTION
   STATUS        current
   DESCRIPTION
   "Establishes the Authentication Clock of the Party."
   SYNTAX        UInteger32

Context ::= TEXTUAL-CONVENTION
   STATUS        current
   DESCRIPTION
   "Establishes SNMPv2 context identifier."
   SYNTAX        OBJECT IDENTIFIER

StorageType ::= TEXTUAL-CONVENTION
   STATUS        current
   DESCRIPTION
   "Establishes how a row in a table is to be physically
   stored."
```

```
    SYNTAX        INTEGER {
                      other(1),
                      volatile(2),        eg.. in RAM
                      nonVolatile(3),     eg.. in NVRAM
                      permanent(4)        eg.. in ROM
                  }
```

The following object identifier has been issued for the SNMPv2 Party MIB:

```
partyAdmin      OBJECT IDENTIFIER ::= { partyMIB 1 }
```

Definition of the security protocol

```
partyProtocols      OBJECT IDENTIFIER ::= { partyAdmin 1 }

noAuth              OBJECT IDENTIFIER ::= { partyProtocols 1 }

noPriv              OBJECT IDENTIFIER ::= { partyProtocols 2 }

desPrivProtocol     OBJECT IDENTIFIER ::= { partyProtocols 3 }

v2md5AuthProtocol   OBJECT IDENTIFIER ::= { partyProtocols 4 }
```

Definition of temporal domains

```
temporalDomains     OBJECT IDENTIFIER ::= { partyAdmin 2 }

currentTime         OBJECT IDENTIFIER ::= { temporalDomains 1 }

restartTime         OBJECT IDENTIFIER ::= { temporalDomains 2 }

cacheTime           OBJECT IDENTIFIER ::= { temporalDomains 3 }
```

Definition of initial party and context identifiers

```
initialPartyId OBJECT IDENTIFIER ::= { partyAdmin 3 }

initialContextId    OBJECT IDENTIFIER ::= { partyAdmin 4 }

partyMIBObjects     OBJECT IDENTIFIER ::= { partyMIB 2 }
```

SNMPv2 Party Database Group

All locally stored MIB View values of an agent are collated in the Party Database Group. For each MIB View established, a series of corresponding values, such as Transport Service, Length of Message, Authentication Protocol, Authentication Clock, Time Delay Over Distance Travelled, Encryption Mechanism (for example, DES), the public variables and variables available only to certain parties are specified. For the SNMPv2 Party Database Group, the following object identifier has been specified within the Party MIB:

```
snmpParties     OBJECT IDENTIFIER ::= { partyMIBObjects 1 }
partyTable OBJECT-TYPE
   SYNTAX      SEQUENCE OF PartyEntry
   MAX-ACCESS  not-accessible
   STATUS      current
   DESCRIPTION
   "Contains all SNMPv2 Party Information."
   ::= { snmpParties 1 }

partyEntry OBJECT-TYPE
   SYNTAX      PartyEntry
   MAX-ACCESS  not-accessible
   STATUS      current
   DESCRIPTION
   "Locally stored information via an SNMPv2 Party."
   INDEX      { IMPLIED partyIdentity }
   ::= { partyTable 1 }

PartyEntry ::=
   SEQUENCE {
       partyIdentity         Party,
       partyIndex            INTEGER,
       partyTDomain          OBJECT IDENTIFIER,
       partyTAddress         TAddress,
       partyMaxMessageSize   INTEGER,
       partyLocal            TruthValue,
       partyAuthProtocol     OBJECT IDENTIFIER,
       partyAuthClock        Clock,
       partyAuthPrivate      OCTET STRING,
       partyAuthPublic       OCTET STRING,
       partyAuthLifetime     INTEGER,
       partyPrivProtocol     OBJECT IDENTIFIER,
       partyPrivPrivate      OCTET STRING,
       partyPrivPublic       OCTET STRING,
       partyCloneFrom        Party,
       partyStorageType      StorageType,
       partyStatus           RowStatus
   }

partyIdentity OBJECT-TYPE
   SYNTAX      Party
   MAX-ACCESS  not-accessible
   STATUS      current
```

```
   DESCRIPTION
   "Using the Identifier, the relevant SNMPv2 Party is
   unambiguously identified."
   ::= { partyEntry 1 }

partyIndex OBJECT-TYPE
   SYNTAX      INTEGER (1..65535)
   MAX-ACCESS  read-only
   STATUS      current
   DESCRIPTION
   "Defines an unambiguous value for every SNMPv2 Party."
   ::= { partyEntry 2 }

partyTDomain OBJECT-TYPE
   SYNTAX      OBJECT IDENTIFIER
   MAX-ACCESS  read-create
   STATUS      current
   DESCRIPTION
   "Indicates the relevant Transport Service, through which the
   Party receives all network management information."
   DEFVAL      { snmpUDPDomain }
   ::= { partyEntry 3 }

partyTAddress OBJECT-TYPE
   SYNTAX      TAddress
   MAX-ACCESS  read-create
   STATUS      current
   DESCRIPTION
   "Contains the Transport Service Address, through which the
   Party receives all network management information."
DEFVAL      { '000000000000'H }
   ::= { partyEntry 4 }

partyMaxMessageSize OBJECT-TYPE
   SYNTAX      INTEGER (484..65507)
   MAX-ACCESS  read-create
   STATUS      current
   DESCRIPTION
   "Defines the maximum permitted length (in octets) of an
   SNMPv2 message for this Party."
   DEFVAL      { 484 }
   ::= { partyEntry 5 }

partyLocal OBJECT-TYPE
   SYNTAX      TruthValue
   MAX-ACCESS  read-create
   STATUS      current
   DESCRIPTION
   "Determines whether the Party is located on this SNMPv2
   device. If the variable is set to the value = true(1), it
   will receive SNMPv2 messages for this Party via the address
   specified in partyTAddress. If the variable is set to the
```

```
   default value = false(2), it will receive no SNMPv2 messages
   for this Party via the address specified in partyTAddress."
   DEFVAL      { false }
   ::= { partyEntry 6 }

partyAuthProtocol OBJECT-TYPE
   SYNTAX      OBJECT IDENTIFIER
   MAX-ACCESS  read-create
   STATUS      current
   DESCRIPTION
   "Establishes the authentication protocol of the Party."
   DEFVAL      { v2md5AuthProtocol }
   ::= { partyEntry 7 }

partyAuthClock OBJECT-TYPE
   SYNTAX      Clock
   MAX-ACCESS  read-create
   STATUS      current
   DESCRIPTION
   "Contains the value of the Authentication Clock for the
   Party."
   DEFVAL      { 0 }
   ::= { partyEntry 8 }

partyAuthPrivate OBJECT-TYPE
   SYNTAX      OCTET STRING
                 for v2md5AuthProtocol: (SIZE (16))
   MAX-ACCESS  read-create
   STATUS      current
   DESCRIPTION
   "Defines the encryption mechanism for the Party."
   DEFVAL      { ''H }
   ::= { partyEntry 9 }

partyAuthPublic OBJECT-TYPE
   SYNTAX      OCTET STRING
                 for v2md5AuthProtocol: (SIZE (0..16))
   MAX-ACCESS  read-create
   STATUS      current
   DESCRIPTION
   "Defines a public, readable value for this Party."
   DEFVAL      { ''H }
   ::= { partyEntry 10 }

partyAuthLifetime OBJECT-TYPE
   SYNTAX      INTEGER (0..2147483647)
   UNITS       "seconds"
   MAX-ACCESS  read-create
   STATUS      current
   DESCRIPTION
"Defines an upper time limit (in seconds) by which a message
sent from this Party may be delayed on its communication
pathway."
```

```
   DEFVAL       { 300 }
   ::= { partyEntry 11 }

partyPrivProtocol OBJECT-TYPE
   SYNTAX       OBJECT IDENTIFIER
   MAX-ACCESS   read-create
   STATUS       current
   DESCRIPTION
   "Defines the private encryption protocol used."
   DEFVAL       { noPriv }
   ::= { partyEntry 12 }

partyPrivPrivate OBJECT-TYPE
   SYNTAX       OCTET STRING
                  for desPrivProtocol: (SIZE (16))
   MAX-ACCESS   read-create
   STATUS       current
   DESCRIPTION
   "Establishes the encryption key for the private encryption
   protocol."
   DEFVAL       { ''H }       an empty String
   ::= { partyEntry 13 }

partyPrivPublic OBJECT-TYPE
   SYNTAX       OCTET STRING
                  for desPrivProtocol: (SIZE (0..16))
   MAX-ACCESS   read-create
   STATUS       current
   DESCRIPTION
   "Defines a public readable value for this Party."
   DEFVAL       { ''H }       an empty String
   ::= { partyEntry 14 }

partyCloneFrom OBJECT-TYPE
   SYNTAX       Party
   MAX-ACCESS   read-create
   STATUS       current
   DESCRIPTION
   "Establishes the identity of the Party whose authentication
   and private parameters are to be cloned."
   ::= { partyEntry 15 }

partyStorageType OBJECT-TYPE
   SYNTAX       StorageType
   MAX-ACCESS   read-create
   STATUS       current
   DESCRIPTION
   "Defines the physical means of storing the table in the
   device."
   DEFVAL       { nonVolatile }
   ::= { partyEntry 16 }
```

```
partyStatus OBJECT-TYPE
   SYNTAX      RowStatus
   MAX-ACCESS  read-create
   STATUS      current
   DESCRIPTION
   "Determines the status of this row in the Party-Table."
   ::= { partyEntry 17 }
```

SNMPv2 Contexts Database Group

Information that is only of local importance can be specified in tables in the Contexts Database Group. This means that management functions can also be implemented by the SNMPv2 proxy. The following object identifier has been established for the SNMPv2 Contexts Database Group within the Party MIB:

```
snmpContexts   OBJECT IDENTIFIER ::= { partyMIBObjects 2 }

contextTable OBJECT-TYPE
   SYNTAX      SEQUENCE OF ContextEntry
   MAX-ACCESS  not-accessible
   STATUS      current
   DESCRIPTION
   "Contains the SNMPv2 context data."
   ::= { snmpContexts 1 }

contextEntry OBJECT-TYPE
   SYNTAX      ContextEntry
   MAX-ACCESS  not-accessible
   STATUS      current
   DESCRIPTION
   "Locally stored information on an SNMPv2 context."
   INDEX      { IMPLIED contextIdentity }
   ::= { contextTable 1 }

ContextEntry ::=
   SEQUENCE {
       contextIdentity         Context,
       contextIndex            INTEGER,
       contextLocal            TruthValue,
       contextViewIndex        INTEGER,
       contextLocalEntity      OCTET STRING,
       contextLocalTime        OBJECT IDENTIFIER,
       contextProxyDstParty    Party,
       contextProxySrcParty    Party,
       contextProxyContext     OBJECT IDENTIFIER,
       contextStorageType      StorageType,
       contextStatus           RowStatus
   }
```

```
contextIdentity OBJECT-TYPE
   SYNTAX       Context
   MAX-ACCESS   not-accessible
   STATUS       current
   DESCRIPTION
   "This context identifier is used to provide unambiguous
   identification of the relevant SNMPv2 context."
   ::= { contextEntry 1 }

contextIndex OBJECT-TYPE
   SYNTAX       INTEGER (1..65535)
   MAX-ACCESS   read-only
   STATUS       current
   DESCRIPTION
   "This context identifier is used to provide unambiguous
   identification of the relevant SNMPv2 context."
   ::= { contextEntry 2 }

contextLocal OBJECT-TYPE
   SYNTAX       TruthValue
   MAX-ACCESS   read-create
   STATUS       current
   DESCRIPTION
   "Establishes whether the relevant context in the SNMPv2
   device has been converted."
   DEFVAL       { true }
   ::= { contextEntry 3 }

contextViewIndex OBJECT-TYPE
   SYNTAX       INTEGER (0..65535)
   MAX-ACCESS   read-create
   STATUS       current
   DESCRIPTION
   "Defines whether the context represents a Proxy Management or
   a MIB View."
   ::= { contextEntry 4 }

contextLocalEntity OBJECT-TYPE
   SYNTAX       OCTET STRING
   MAX-ACCESS   read-create
   STATUS       current
   DESCRIPTION
   "Determines whether the MIB View represents the complete
   management information of the local device or only part of
   the information available in the device."
   DEFVAL       { ''H }       an empty String
   ::= { contextEntry 5 }

contextLocalTime OBJECT-TYPE
   SYNTAX       OBJECT IDENTIFIER
   MAX-ACCESS   read-create
   STATUS       current
   DESCRIPTION
```

```
    "If the value of a corresponding Instance with this Context-
    View is greater than 0, this identifies the current context
    of the management information in the MIB View."
    DEFVAL      { currentTime }
    ::= { contextEntry 6 }

contextProxyDstParty OBJECT-TYPE
    SYNTAX      Party
    MAX-ACCESS  read-create
    STATUS      current
    DESCRIPTION
    "If the value of a corresponding Instance with this Context-
    View-Index is equal to 0, this identifies a Proxy Management
    Destination."
    ::= { contextEntry 7 }

contextProxySrcParty OBJECT-TYPE
    SYNTAX      Party
    MAX-ACCESS  read-create
    STATUS      current
    DESCRIPTION
    "If the value of a corresponding Instance with this Context-
    View-Index is equal to 0, this identifies a Proxy Management
    Source."
    ::= { contextEntry 8 }

contextProxyContext OBJECT-TYPE
    SYNTAX      OBJECT IDENTIFIER
    MAX-ACCESS  read-create
    STATUS      current
    DESCRIPTION
    "If the value of a corresponding Instance with this Context-
    View-Index is equal to 0, this identifies a Proxy Management
    Resource."
    ::= { contextEntry 9 }

contextStorageType OBJECT-TYPE
    SYNTAX      StorageType
    MAX-ACCESS  read-create
    STATUS      current
    DESCRIPTION
    "Defines the physical means of storing the context table in
    the device."
    DEFVAL      { nonVolatile }
    ::= { contextEntry 10 }

contextStatus OBJECT-TYPE
    SYNTAX      RowStatus
    MAX-ACCESS  read-create
    STATUS      current
    DESCRIPTION
"Specifies the status of this row in the context table."
    ::= { contextEntry 11 }
```

SNMPv2 Access Privileges Database Group

All party access mechanisms for the relevant device are specified in this database in the form of a table. The following object identifier has been established for the SNMPv2 Access Privileges Group within the Party MIB:

```
snmpAccess     OBJECT IDENTIFIER ::= { partyMIBObjects 3 }

aclTable OBJECT-TYPE
   SYNTAX      SEQUENCE OF AclEntry
   MAX-ACCESS  not-accessible
   STATUS      current
   DESCRIPTION
   "Contains the Access Privileges Database."
   ::= { snmpAccess 1 }

aclEntry OBJECT-TYPE
   SYNTAX      AclEntry
   MAX-ACCESS  not-accessible
   STATUS      current
   DESCRIPTION
   "Defines the necessary Access Privileges for a defined SNMPv2
   context."
   INDEX      { aclTarget, aclSubject, aclResources }
   ::= { aclTable 1 }

AclEntry ::=
   SEQUENCE {
       aclTarget          INTEGER,
       aclSubject         INTEGER,
       aclResources       INTEGER,
       aclPrivileges      INTEGER,
       aclStorageType     StorageType,
       aclStatus          RowStatus
   }

aclTarget OBJECT-TYPE
   SYNTAX      INTEGER (1..65535)
   MAX-ACCESS  not-accessible
   STATUS      current
   DESCRIPTION
   "An SNMPv2 Party is identified by means of this value."
   ::= { aclEntry 1 }

aclSubject OBJECT-TYPE
   SYNTAX      INTEGER (1..65535)
   MAX-ACCESS  not-accessible
   STATUS      current
   DESCRIPTION
   "This value determines the SNMPv2 Party to which the relevant
   Access Privileges apply."
   ::= { aclEntry 2 }
```

```
aclResources OBJECT-TYPE
   SYNTAX       INTEGER (1..65535)
   MAX-ACCESS   not-accessible
   STATUS       current
   DESCRIPTION
   "The context of a specified Access Privilege is defined by
   means of this value."
   ::= { aclEntry 3 }

aclPrivileges OBJECT-TYPE
   SYNTAX       INTEGER (0..255)
   MAX-ACCESS   read-create
   STATUS       current
   DESCRIPTION
   "Specifies the implementation rights and the associated
   management operations for a Party in accordance with the
   relevant SNMPv2 context. The relevant privileges are formed
   as a sum of the following SNMPv2 PDU types:
   Get          :   1
   GetNext      :   2
   Response     :   4
   Set          :   8
   unused       :  16
   GetBulk      :  32
   Inform       :  64
   SNMPv2 Trap : 128"
   DEFVAL       { 35 }        Get, Get-Next & Get-Bulk
   ::= { aclEntry 4 }

aclStorageType OBJECT-TYPE
   SYNTAX       StorageType
   MAX-ACCESS   read-create
   STATUS       current
   DESCRIPTION
   "Defines the physical means of storing the Acl Table in the
   device."
   DEFVAL       { nonVolatile }
   ::= { aclEntry 5 }

aclStatus OBJECT-TYPE
   SYNTAX       RowStatus
   MAX-ACCESS   read-create
   STATUS       current
   DESCRIPTION
"Specifies the status of this row in the Acl Table."
   ::= { aclEntry 6 }
```

MIB View Database Group

All MIB Views for this device are specified in this database in the form of a table. The following object identifier has been established for the SNMPv2 View Database Group within the Party MIB:

```
snmpViews      OBJECT IDENTIFIER ::= { partyMIBObjects 4 }

viewTable OBJECT-TYPE
   SYNTAX      SEQUENCE OF ViewEntry
   MAX-ACCESS  not-accessible
   STATUS      current
   DESCRIPTION
   "Locally stored information on all MIB Views known to this
   SNMPv2 device."
   ::= { snmpViews 1 }

viewEntry OBJECT-TYPE
   SYNTAX      ViewEntry
   MAX-ACCESS  not-accessible
   STATUS      current
   DESCRIPTION
   "Contains all information on all specified View Subtrees,
   which are either included in or excluded from this MIB View."
   INDEX      { viewIndex, IMPLIED viewSubtree }
   ::= { viewTable 1 }

ViewEntry ::=
   SEQUENCE {
       viewIndex         INTEGER,
       viewSubtree       OBJECT IDENTIFIER,
       viewMask          OCTET STRING,
       viewType          INTEGER,
       viewStorageType   StorageType,
       viewStatus        RowStatus
   }

viewIndex OBJECT-TYPE
   SYNTAX      INTEGER (1..65535)
   MAX-ACCESS  not-accessible
   STATUS      current
   DESCRIPTION
   "Contains an unambiguous value for the identification of the
   MIB View."
   ::= { viewEntry 1 }

viewSubtree OBJECT-TYPE
   SYNTAX      OBJECT IDENTIFIER
   MAX-ACCESS  not-accessible
   STATUS      current
   DESCRIPTION
   "Defines the MIB Subtree."
   ::= { viewEntry 2 }
```

```
viewMask OBJECT-TYPE
   SYNTAX       OCTET STRING (SIZE (0..16))
   MAX-ACCESS   read-create
   STATUS       current
   DESCRIPTION
   "The relevant View Subtree Families are formed using this
   bit-mask."
   DEFVAL       { ''H }
   ::= { viewEntry 3 }

viewType OBJECT-TYPE
   SYNTAX       INTEGER  {
                    included(1),
                    excluded(2)
                }
   MAX-ACCESS   read-create
   STATUS       current
   DESCRIPTION
   "Determines whether a given View Subtree Family is a
   component of the SNMPv2 Context MIB View or whether this
   View Subtree has been excluded."
   DEFVAL       { included }
   ::= { viewEntry 4 }

viewStorageType OBJECT-TYPE
   SYNTAX       StorageType
   MAX-ACCESS   read-create
   STATUS       current
   DESCRIPTION
   "Defines the physical means of storing the View Table
   in the device."
   DEFVAL       { nonVolatile }
   ::= { viewEntry 5 }

viewStatus OBJECT-TYPE
   SYNTAX       RowStatus
   MAX-ACCESS   read-create
   STATUS       current
   DESCRIPTION
   "Establishes the status of this row in the View Table."
   ::= { viewEntry 6 }

partyMIBConformance
               OBJECT IDENTIFIER ::= { partyMIB 3 }

partyMIBCompliances
               OBJECT IDENTIFIER ::= { partyMIBConformance 1 }

partyMIBGroups
               OBJECT IDENTIFIER ::= { partyMIBConformance 2 }

unSecurableCompliance MODULE-COMPLIANCE
   STATUS  current
```

```
    DESCRIPTION
    "This Group may only be implemented by SNMPv2 devices which
    have implemented no authentication protocols and no private
    encryption mechanisms."
    MODULE     this module
        MANDATORY-GROUPS { partyMIBGroup }
    ::= { partyMIBCompliances 1 }

partyNoPrivacyCompliance MODULE-COMPLIANCE
    STATUS  current
    DESCRIPTION
    "This Group may only be implemented by SNMPv2 devices which
    have implemented an authentication protocol but which have
    not implemented a private encryption mechanism."
    MODULE     this module
        MANDATORY-GROUPS { partyMIBGroup }
    ::= { partyMIBCompliances 2 }

partyPrivacyCompliance MODULE-COMPLIANCE
    STATUS  current
    DESCRIPTION
    "This Group may only be implemented by SNMPv2 devices which
    have implemented an authentication protocol and a private
    encryption mechanism."
    MODULE     this module
        MANDATORY-GROUPS { partyMIBGroup }
    ::= { partyMIBCompliances 3 }

fullPrivacyCompliance MODULE-COMPLIANCE
    STATUS  current
    DESCRIPTION
    "This Group may only be implemented by SNMPv2 devices that
    have implemented an authentication protocol and a private
    encryption mechanism that can be used without restrictions."
    MODULE     this module
        MANDATORY-GROUPS { partyMIBGroup }
    ::= { partyMIBCompliances 4 }

partyMIBGroup OBJECT-GROUP
  OBJECTS { partyIndex, partyTDomain, partyTAddress,
           partyMaxMessageSize, partyLocal,
           partyAuthProtocol, partyAuthClock,
           partyAuthPrivate, partyAuthPublic,
           partyAuthLifetime, partyPrivProtocol,
           partyPrivPrivate, partyPrivPublic,
           partyStorageType, partyStatus,
           partyCloneFrom,
           contextIndex, contextLocal,
           contextViewIndex, contextLocalEntity,
           contextLocalTime, contextStorageType,
           contextStatus, aclTarget, aclSubject,
           aclPrivileges, aclStorageType, aclStatus,
           viewMask, viewType, viewStorageType, viewStatus }
```

```
STATUS  current
DESCRIPTION
 "SNMPv2 Parties can be defined and configured by means of
 this object."
::= { partyMIBGroups 1 }
```

5.8 Security functions

In the SNMP protocol, the whole dimension of security was neglected for a considerable time. This problem area was taken up in RFC 1446 (*Security Protocols for version 2 of the Simple Network Management Protocol*) and finally solved to the satisfaction of network critics. RFC 1446 was conceived by James M. Galvin and Keith McCloghrie and is based on the considerations raised in RFC 1352 (*SNMP Security Protocols*). Since this SNMP Security Variant never passed beyond the status of a proposal and was also not downwardly compatible with existing SNMP versions, it was not widely distributed.

Preliminary work on the SNMPv2 Security Standard was localized in the following areas:

- Changing the data
  The SNMPv2 protocol enables a management station to change the values of the manageable objects in an agent. However, there is a risk that a station on the transmission pathway between the sender and the recipient may intercept the data and change it without authorization. The SNMPv2 security concept created the possibility of coding the data information and the individual messages.

- Impersonation
  An essential component of the SNMPv2 architecture is the concept that access protection is guaranteed for the individual manageable resources. In practice, effective access protection is based on knowledge of the services and functions that a sender can provide or a recipient receive. Even impersonation by non-authorized users can no longer falsify authorized identities and implement management operations.

- Changing the sequence
  Like its predecessor, SNMPv2 is based on unsecured transport services. Since these transport services cannot guarantee sequential correctness of data, SNMP data may arrive at its destination either with a delay or after alterations have been made to its sequence. This may come about either passively as a result of the dynamics of the LAN or actively as a result of manipulation by a saboteur. SNMPv2 also addresses this area and uses an internal synchronization mechanism to ensure that no non-authorized users can intercept the data unnoticed and change the contents to their advantage.

Goals of the Standard

On the basis of the problem areas described in connection with network management, the following goals were defined for the Security Standard:

- For reasons of security, protocols should support the possibility of checking all SNMPv2 messages received for any modification carried out during the transport pathway.
- Protocols should support a mechanism for checking the sender of each SNMPv2 message.
- The protocol should insert the current time of sending in each SNMPv2 message and the recipient should check this time stamp.
- If required, the protocol should support an encryption mechanism for the data to be sent in an SNMPv2 message.
- Security mechanisms must be constructed in such a way that the basic specifications of the SNMP network management architecture retain their validity without change.

Security mechanisms

The security protocols of the SNMPv2 standard support differently graduated security mechanisms which can be configured explicitly according to security requirements and applications. The following mechanisms are available for use on the SNMPv2 protocol:

- To ensure integrity of data, an authentication algorithm is needed. This authentication algorithm is used to convert information in an SNMPv2 message into a key. The key can then be sent to the recipient together with the data as an electronic signature.
- To ensure that data is exchanged only between known senders and recipients, the electronic signature can be encrypted according to coding rules which are known only to the two communicating partners.
- To prevent the interception or repetition of SNMPv2 messages, each message can be given a time stamp. To this end, the two clocks must be synchronized between sender and recipient.
- To protect the data from unauthorized reading, data can be encoded according to an encryption algorithm before transmission.

In addition to the above measures, it should be possible to graduate all the security protocols and mechanisms of the SNMPv2 standard individually to meet specific requirements of each application. In practice, SNMPv2 devices can support all security classes from maximum security to no security.

Authentication mechanisms

With the SNMPv2 protocol, the MD5 algorithm is used to ensure integrity of data. The MD5 algorithm was published as C source code in RFC 1321, under the title *The MD5 Message Digest Algorithm*. The MD5 algorithm calculates a 128-bit checksum via the SNMPv2 message and is integrated into the PDU as a fixed component of the message. The use of the MD5 authentication mechanism as an authentication protocol is indicated by the ASN.1 object identifier value v2md5Auth protocol. Every SNMPv2 party that uses the authentication protocol v2md5Auth protocol also makes use of a private 16-octet (authDigest) authentication key.

Symmetric encryption algorithm

To ensure the confidentiality of data transmitted, the SNMPv2 protocol supports the Data Encryption Standard (DES). The DES encryption mechanism is operated in the Cipher Block Chaining Mode, according to which a given section of the message is encrypted and transmitted together with the message.

Every SNMPv2 party that uses the DES algorithm in a data encryption protocol indicates this through the ASN.1 object identifier of the Priv Protocol. Another private 16-octet authentication key is also used. The first 8 octets of the authentication key contain the DES key (56-bit algorithm plus 8-bit parity), while the second 8 octets contain the initialization vector.

Two US organizations have published standards for the Data Encryption Standard:

- The National Institute of Standards and Technology (NIST)
  - *Data Encryption Standard*, National Institute of Standards and Technology. Federal Information Processing Standard (FIPS) Publication 46-1, (January 1988).
  - *Guidelines for Implementing and Using the NBS Data Encryption Standard*, National Institute of Standards and Technology. Federal Information Processing Standard (FIPS) Publication 74, (April 1981).
  - *Validating the Correctness of Hardware Implementations of the NBS Data Encryption Standard*, National Institute of Standards and Technology. Special Publication 500-20.
  - *Maintenance Testing for the Data Encryption Standard*, National Institute of Standards and Technology. Special Publication 500-61, (August 1980).
- The American National Standards Institute (ANSI).
  - *Data Encryption Algorithm*, American National Standards Institute. ANSI X3.92-1981, (December 1980).

Security Classification

With the SNMPv2 protocol, the MD5 algorithm is defined as the mechanism for authentication of messages, and the Data Encryption Standard (DES) is defined as the mechanism for achieving privacy. Four classes of security for individual agents can be formed on the basis of the relevant parameters. These are shown in Table 5.30:

Security class	MD5	DES (only for security parameters)	DES (without restrictions)
unsecured	no	no	no
not configurable	yes	no	no
configurable	yes	yes	no
full privacy	yes	yes	yes

Table 5.30 Security classes

As can be seen from the list of security classes, only agents that have implemented the MD5 algorithm and the DES Data Encryption Standard can be fully managed via SNMPv2. If, for example, the DES standard is not supported in one agent, the configuration of security parameters cannot be fully implemented via the network.

The DES mechanism specified as the encryption mechanism in the SNMPv2 protocol is subject to US Government export restrictions, and software that contains the DES algorithm may not be sold freely, as a result. These restrictions may be numbered amongst the absurdities of free world trade, because as Public Domain software within the Internet, the DES algorithm is available to anyone interested. Non-American users or licensees, however, have to make do with SNMPv2 without this supplement. One day perhaps, such export restrictions, which have their origins in the Cold War, will be adapted to current realities, thereby enabling open trade of all products. In the long run, there is no way round the problem and complete implementation of the SNMP security functions, because the Internet community cannot afford to support two separate versions of SNMP.

SNMPv2 Party

As explained in Section 5.7, the SNMPv2 party describes a virtual environment within an SNMPv2 device. If a device is to send an SNMPv2 message to a communication partner, this device always acts according to restrictions (operations, commands, and so on) predetermined by the relevant party definitions. The Party MIB enables the administrator to issue access rights to the SNMPv2 users via freely definable MIB objects.

Each SNMPv2 party is represented by the following ASN.1 sequence:

```
SnmpParty ::= SEQUENCE {
  partyIdentity
    OBJECT IDENTIFIER,
  partyTDomain
    OBJECT IDENTIFIER,
  partyTAddress
    OCTET STRING,
  partyMaxMessageSize
    INTEGER,
  partyAuthProtocol
    OBJECT IDENTIFIER,
  partyAuthClock
    INTEGER,
  partyAuthPrivate
    OCTET STRING,
  partyAuthPublic
    OCTET STRING,
  partyAuthLifetime
    INTEGER,
  partyPrivProtocol
    OBJECT IDENTIFIER,
  partyPrivPrivate
    OCTET STRING,
  partyPrivPublic
    OCTET STRING
}
```

From the perspective of the authentication protocol, the following points in respect of the SNMP party definitions are of particular importance:

- The authentication protocol and its protocol mechanisms are determined by the values of the partyAuthProtocol. The following values have been specified in the Standard:

  noAuth
  No authentication protocol has been specified. Instead of the 128-bit checksum, an empty octet string is generated.

  v2md5Auth
  Using the MD5-algorithm, a 128-bit checksum is calculated for the complete SNMPv2 message and transmitted as a fixed component in the PDU.

- The current time of a party is communicated via the value party-AuthClock.

- The values for partyAuthPrivate specify the private encryption mechanism for the authentication protocol.

- The partyAuthPublic component describes a public encryption mechanism which is used by the authentication protocol.
- The partyAuthLifetime defines the upper time limit by which an SNMPv2 message may be delayed on its way between the sender and the recipient.

Parties that can send or receive SNMPv2 messages generated by means of an encryption protocol are defined in the party definitions using the following supplementary parameters:

- The partyPrivProtocol component specifies the decoding key for the privacy protocol on the basis of which the protocol message of a party can be decoded.
- The values for the partyPrivPrivate component represent the secret coding key for the privacy protocol used.
- The values for the partyPrivPublic component represent the public coding key for the privacy protocol used.

Authentication Protocol

The mechanisms for ensuring effective access protection of individual resources are described below. In the SNMPv2 protocol, this access protection is based on knowledge of the services and functions that a sender can achieve or that can be received by a recipient, and also on a mechanism for the unambiguous identification of data integrity. In turn, this integrity of data is based on a protocol mechanism which uses the MD5 algorithm. In this way, it is possible to guarantee that unauthorized users cannot impersonate an authorized identity or implement management operations. The only condition specified in the Standard for the use of the authentication protocol is that the parties involved only communicate with another party which is using the same authentication protocol. As explained, the management communication relationship of a party is specified by the following ASN.1 construct:

```
SnmpMgmtCom ::= [2] IMPLICIT SEQUENCE {
  dstParty
    OBJECT IDENTIFIER,
  srcParty
    OBJECT IDENTIFIER,
  context
    OBJECT IDENTIFIER,
  pdu
    PDUs
}
```

Communication between SNMPv2 parties only takes place if the values for the following SNMP management communication message (SnmpMgmt-Com) are fulfilled:

- The value dstParty defines the destination SNMPv2 party to which the message is to be sent.
- The value srcParty defines the source party from which the communication originates.
- The context component establishes the specific SNMPv2 context and contains the management information necessary for communication.
- The relevant PDU component corresponds to a valid format in accordance with RFC 1448.

The SNMPv2 security protocol also ensures that the sender party has been reliably identified and that the data have not been falsified during the transmission to the peer party. Authentication of the message is assured by means of the following ASN.1 construct:

```
SnmpAuthMsg ::= [1] IMPLICIT SEQUENCE {
  authInfo
    ANY, - defined by authentication Protocol
  authData
    SnmpMgmtCom
}
```

The meaning of the values for the ASN.1 SNMP authentication message (SnmpAuthMsg) construct is as follows:

- The authentication information (authInfo) specifies the values (noAuth and v2md5Auth) which guarantee the authenticity of the data in a message sent with the authentication protocol.
- The values of the authData component contain the data transmitted in the SNMPv2 management communication.

Exact details of the authentication mechanism are necessary in order to support an authentication protocol. These details are established via the following ASN.1 construct:

```
AuthInformation ::= >[2] IMPLICIT SEQUENCE {
  authDigest
    OCTET STRING,
  authDstTimestamp
    UInteger32,
   authSrcTimestamp
     UInteger32
}
```

The values of the ASN.1 AuthInformation constructs have the following meanings:

- The values of the authDigest (authentication digest) component in the MD5 authentication mechanism contain a private 16-octet authentication key.
- The value Authentication Source Timestamp (authSrcTimestamp) defines the time. The unit used for the Authentication Source Timestamp is always seconds.
- The value Authentication Destination Timestamp (authDstTimestamp) defines the time at which the message should be received by the receiving party (destination). The unit used for the Authentication Destination Timestamp is always seconds.

Sending an SNMPv2 message

If an authentication protocol is used for sending SNMPv2 messages, the sending device (functional module) or the sending party must follow the procedures below:

1. Using the SNMP management communication message (Snmp-MgmtCom) constructs, the sending source party (srcParty), the receiving destination party, (dstParty), the manageable object (context) and the required management operation (operation) are established.

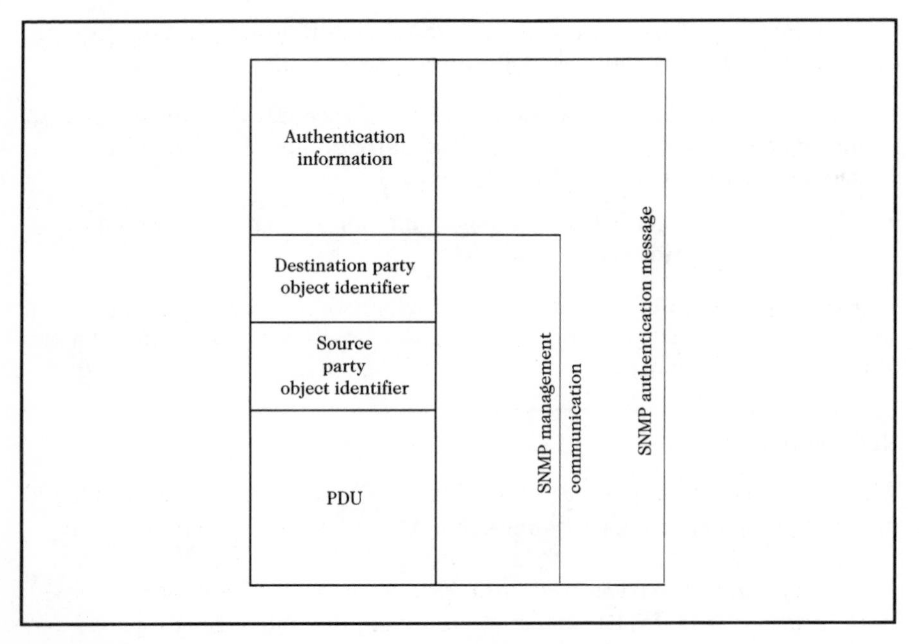

Figure 5.18 SNMPv2 Message with authentication header

2. Using the locally stored party information, a decision is made as to which authentication protocol is to be used between the sending and receiving parties.

3. Using the SNMP authentication message (SnmpAuthMsg) construct, the following information is prepared on the basis of the locally stored party information:

   authInfo

   Defines the relevant value of the sending party in accordance with the authentication protocol.
   If the authInfo field shows the value noAuth, the field will consist of an octet string of length 0.
   If the authInfo field shows the value v2md5, the MD5 algorithm is used to calculated a 128-bit checksum for the whole SNMPv2 message. This is then transmitted as a fixed component in the PDU.

4. The authentication data (authData) is inspected on the basis of the locally available information or counters:

   - The Authentication Source Timestamp (authSrcTimestamp) is set using the value of the authentication clock of the source party.
   - The Authentication Destination Timestamp (authDstTimestamp) is determined using the partyAuthClock of the receiving party. It contains the approximate time at which the message is to be received by the destination party.
   - The authDigest (authentication digest) is temporarily set to the private authentication key of the sending party.
   - A 128-bit checksum is then calculated for the SNMPv2 message and transmitted as a fixed component in the PDU.

5. The values of the SnmpPrivMsg construct are produced as a serial data stream in accordance with the Transport Mapping Definitions (RFC 1449).

6. Finally, this information is sent to the Transport Address and the Transport Domain of the receiving party.

Receiving a message

When receiving management information, the receiving device (functional module) or the receiving party must implement the following procedures:

1. The snmpStatsPacket counter is incremented. If an error is determined in the SNMPv2 message received, this message is rejected and the reception process is aborted.

2. Using the privData field of the SnmpPrivMsg, the local Party Information database is checked to see if it contains an entry for the receiving SNMPv2 party.
3. If the local Party Information Database does not contain an entry for the specified receiving party, the message is rejected and the snmpStatsUnknownDstParties counter is incremented.
4. Using the privData component of the SnmpPrivMessage, an ASN.1 octet string is produced by decoding the authentication protocol. This is then compared with the corresponding value for the receiving party. For example, if an authentication mechanism was specified for the receiving SNMPv2 party (v2MD5Auth) and if the octet string produced corresponds with this value, the reception process can be continued.
5. In an error is found when creating the octet string, the message is rejected and the snmpStatsEncodingErrors counter is incremented.
6. If the value of the dstParty does not correspond with the privDst field, the message received is rejected and the snmpStatsDstPartyMismatches counter is incremented.
7. The local Party Information Database is then consulted and checked to see if it contains an entry on the sending SNMPv2 party specified in the srcParty field.
8. If no entry for the sending party is found in the local Party Information Database, the message is rejected and the snmpStatsUnknownSrcParties counter is incremented.
9. The values of the SnmpAuthMsg construct received are then compared, according to the rules of the authentication protocol and other information, with the stored sender party and receiver party definitions in the local Party Information Database. For example, if the authInfo field produces the value noAuth, the SnmpAuthMessage is evaluated as non-authentic and the snmpStatsBadAuths counter is incremented. If the authInfo field produces the value v2md5Auth, the values authSrc Timestamp, authDstTimestamp and authDigest are filtered out from the SNMP authentication message (SnmpAuthMsg).
10. Using the locally stored sender party information, the authentication clock, the private authentication key and the lifetime of the SNMP message received are then inspected.
11. If, when calculating the authSrcTimestamp component plus the lifetime of the SNMP message, it is discovered that the total is less than the authentication clock, the message is rejected as non-authentic and the snmpStatsNotInLifetimes counter is incremented.

12. The value of the Authentication Digest (authDigest) component is then inspected and temporarily stored.

13. A new value for the SNMP authentication message (SnmpAuthMsg) is then calculated. The private authentication key and the other components are set to the values of the SNMP authentication message (SnmpAuthMsg). The value of the digest key is then calculated for the relevant section of the message.

14. If the value of the key inspected does not correspond with the temporarily stored key, the message is rejected as non-authentic and the snmpStatsWrongDigestValues counter is incremented.

15. If the value of the key inspected does correspond with the temporarily stored key, the message is accepted as authentic.

16. Using the locally stored party information, the privileges (commands) of the sending party are then checked. If this produces a positive result, the values of the authentication clocks for the sending party and the receiving party are both inspected.

17. Comparison of the context entries in the local Context Information Database is used to check whether the SNMPv2 context specifications contained in the SnmpMgmtCom construct are present.

18. If no entry is found in the local Context Information Database, the SNMPv2 message is rejected and the snmpStatsUnknownContexts counter is incremented.

19. Using the local database, in which all access privileges are stored, checks are carried out to determine whether the access rights of the sending SNMPv2 party correspond with those of the receiving party.

20. Using the SnmpMgmtCom value, the associated management communication class is investigated. If the management communication class of the message received corresponds to the values 32, 8, 2, or 1 (GetBulk, Set, GetNext or Get), and the SNMPv2 context does not permit the implementation of these operations, the message received is rejected and the snmpStatsUnknownContexts counter is incremented.

21. If the management communication class of the message received corresponds to the values 128, 64 or 4 (SNMPv2 Trap, Inform or Response), and the class does not correspond to the access privileges, the message received is rejected and the snmpStatsBadOperations counter is incremented.

22. If no access rights have been stipulated for the communication class of the message received, the message is rejected and a Response message is created. The Response message is addressed directly to the sending party and the error index signals an Authorization Error.

23. If no errors are found, the values for the SnmpMgmtCom construct are created from the authData component of the SnmpAuth message.
24. If the SNMPv2 context corresponds to the local object resources, the relevant management operation is carried out by the receiving SNMPv2 device/process using the MIB View specified in the SNMPv2 context.
25. If the SNMPv2 context corresponds to the remote object resources defined, the relevant management operation will be implemented on the basis of a proxy management relationship.

Symmetric Privacy Protocol

Using private SNMPv2 management communication, it is possible to encrypt the data in an SNMPv2 message. The following ASN.1 construct establishes how and under which rules the SNMPv2 management information is coded:

```
SnmpPrivMsg ::= [1] IMPLICIT SEQUENCE {
  privDst
    OBJECT IDENTIFIER,
  privDaten
    [1] IMPLICIT OCTET STRING
}
```

The values of the ASN.1 SNMP privacy message (SnmpPrivMsg) construct have the following meaning:

- The privacy destination (privDst) is used to specify the SNMPv2 party with which communication is to be taken up.
- The privacy data (privData) component contains all the encrypted information for an authenticated SNMPv2 management communication.

Generating an encrypted message

If an authentication protocol is used for the transfer of SNMPv2 messages, the following procedures must be implemented by the sending device (functional module) or the sending party:

1. On the basis of the SNMP management communication message (SnmpMgmtCom) Construct, the sending source Party (srcParty), the receiving destination party (dstParty), the manageable objects (context) and the desired management operation (operation) are specified.

2. Using the locally stored party information, a decision is made as to which authentication protocol is used between the sending and the receiving party.
3. Using the SNMP authentication message (SnmpAuthMsg) constructs, the authInfo information is then prepared on the basis of the locally stored party information. The relevant values for the sending party are defined in accordance with the authentication protocol. If the authInfo field produces the value noAuth, this field consists of a octet string of length 0. If the authInfo field contains the value v2md5Auth, the MD5 algorithm is used to produce a 128-bit checksum for the whole SNMPv2 message. This is transmitted as a fixed component in the PDU.
4. The authentication data (authData) is then inspected using the locally available information and counters:
   - The Authentication Source Timestamp (authSrcTimestamp) is set using the value from the authentication clock of the source party.
   - The Authentication Destination Timestamp (authDstTimestamp) is inspected using the partyAuthClock of the receiving party and contains the approximate time at which the message is to be received by the destination party.
   - The authDigest (authentication digest) is temporarily set to the private authentication key for the sending party.
   - Consequently, a 128-bit checksum is calculated for the SNMPv2 message and transferred as a fixed component in the PDU.
5. If the value for the SNMP authentication message (SnmpAuthMsg) cannot be formed in accordance with the rules of the digest authentication protocol, processing is aborted and the message is rejected.
6. If there are no errors, the locally stored information in the private privacy key, which defines the privacy of a message, is read for the receiving party.
7. The complete SNMP authentication message (SnmpAuthMsg) construct is produced as a serial data stream.
8. The octet sequence of the SNMP authentication message (SnmpAuth-Msg) is then encoded using the specified algorithm (for example, DES).
9. The value of the privData field is set to the value determined by the encryption process.
10. The values of the SnmpPrivMsg construct are produced as a serial data stream in accordance with the Transport Mapping Definition (RFC 1449).
11. This information is finally sent to the Transport Address and the Transport Domain of the receiving party.

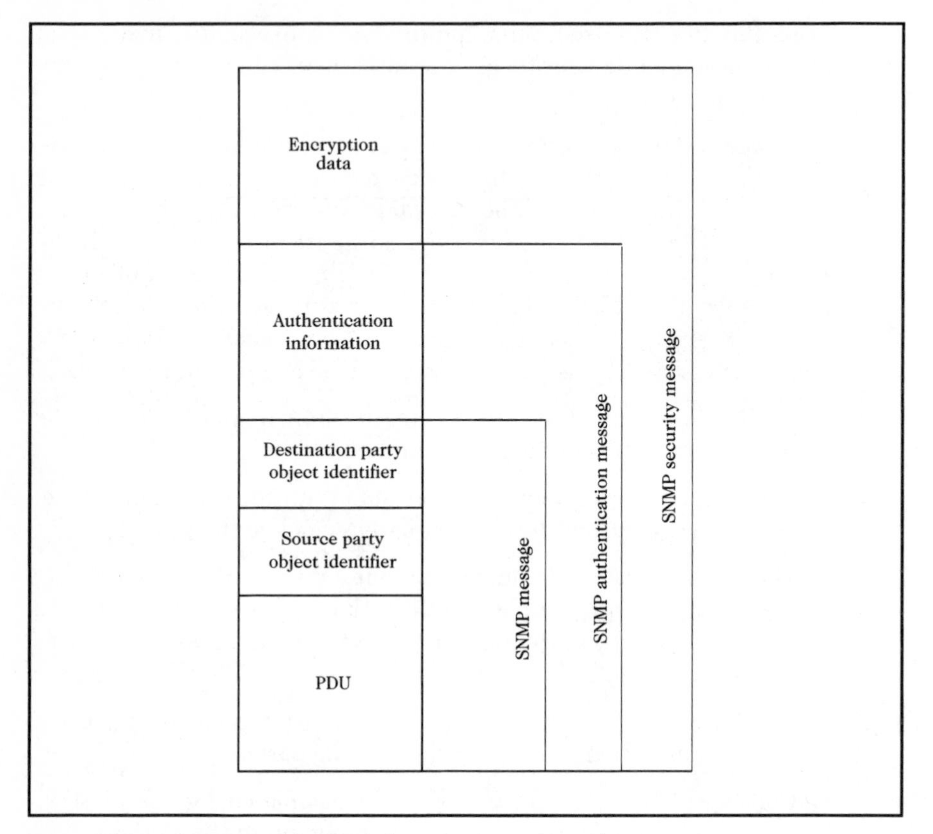

Figure 5.19 SNMPv2 Message with authentication and encryption

Receipt of an encrypted message

When receiving encrypted management information, the receiving device (functional module) or the receiving party must implement the following procedures:

1. The snmpStatsPackets counter is incremented. If an error is determined in the SNMPv2 message received, this message is rejected and the reception process is aborted.
2. Using the privData field of the SnmpPrivMsg, the local Party Information Database is checked to see whether it contains an entry relating to the receiving SNMPv2 party.
3. If no entry is found in the Party Information Database relating to the specified receiving party, the message is rejected and the snmpStats-UnknownDstParties counter is incremented.
4. Using the privData field of the SnmpPrivMsg, the local Party Information Database is checked and the privacy protocol used is

inspected. If a symmetrical privacy protocol such as DES is being used, the privacy key is read from the party Information.

5. This private privacy key is used to decode the PrivData field in the message.
6. Using the privData component of the SnmpPrivMessage, an ASN.1 octet string is produced by decoding the authentication protocol. This is compared with the corresponding value from the party received. For example, if an authentication mechanism was specified for the SNMPv2 party (v2md5Auth) and if the octet string corresponds to this value, the reception process can be continued.
7. If an error is determined when the octet string is created, the message received is rejected and the snmpStatsEncodingErrors counter is incremented.
8. If the value of the dstParty does not correspond to the value in the privDst field, the message received is rejected and the snmpStatsDstPartyMismatches counter is incremented.
9. The local Party Information Database is then consulted to check whether it contains an entry for the sending SNMPv2 party specified in the srcParty field.
10. If no entry relating to the sending party is found in the local Party Information Database, the message received is rejected and the snmpStatsUnknownSrcParties counter is incremented.
11. The values for the SnmpAuthMsg construct received are then compared, according to the rules of the authentication protocol, with the sending party and receiving party definitions stored in the local Party Information Database. For example, if the authInfo field produces a value noAuth, the SnmpAuthMessage is evaluated as non-authenticated and the snmpStatsBadAuths counter is incremented. If the authInfo field contains the value v2md5Auth, the values authSrcTimestamp, authDstTimestamp and authDigest are filtered out from the SNMP authentication message (SnmpAuthMsg).
12. Using the locally stored sending party information, the authentication clock, the private authentication key and the lifetime of the SNMP message are inspected.
13. If, when calculating the authSrcTimestamp component plus the lifetime of the SNMP message, it is determined that the total is less than that of the authentication clocks, the message is rejected as non-authorized and the snmpStatsNotInLifetimes counter is incremented.
14. The value of the authentication digest (authDigest) component is inspected and temporarily stored. A new value for the SNMP authentication message (SnmpAuthMsg) is then calculated. The private

authentication key and the other components are set to the values of the SNMP authentication message (SnmpAuthMsg) received. The value of the digest key is then calculated for the relevant section of the message.

15. If the value of the Key inspected does not correspond to the temporarily stored key, the message is rejected as non-authentic and the snmpStatsWrongDigestValues counter is incremented.
16. If the value of the key inspected does correspond to the temporarily stored key, the message is accepted as authentic.
17. Using the locally stored party information, the privileges (commands) of the sending party are then checked. If this produces a positive result, the values of the authentication clocks for the sending party and the receiving party are both inspected.
18. Comparison of the context entries in the local context information database is used to check whether the SNMPv2 context specifications contained in the SnmpMgmtCom construct are present.
19. If no entry is found in the local Context Information Database, the SNMPv2 message is rejected and the snmpStatsUnknownContexts counter is incremented.
20. Using the local database, in which all access privileges are stored, checks are carried out to determine whether the access rights of the sending SNMPv2 party correspond to those of the receiving party.
21. Using the SnmpMgmtCom value, the associated management communication class is investigated. If the management communication class of the message received corresponds to the values 32, 8, 2, or 1 (GetBulk, Set, GetNext or Get), and the SNMPv2 context does not permit the implementation of these operations, the message received is rejected and the snmpStatsUnknownContexts counter is incremented.
22. If the management communication class of the message received corresponds to the values 128, 64 or 4 (SNMPv2 Trap, Inform or Response), and the class does not correspond to the access privileges, the message received is rejected and the snmpStatsBadOperations counter is incremented.
23. If no access rights have been stipulated for the communication class of the message received, the message is rejected and a Response message is created. The Response message is addressed directly to the sending party and the error index signals an Authorization Error.
24. If no errors are found, the values for the SnmpMgmtCom construct are created from the authData component of the SnmpAuth message.

25. If the SNMPv2 context corresponds to the local object resources, the relevant management operation is carried out by the receiving SNMPv2 device/process using the MIB View specified in the SNMPv2 context.
26. If the SNMPv2 context corresponds to the remote object resources defined, the relevant management operation will be implemented on the basis of a proxy management relationship.

Clocks and secrets

The protocol procedures described presuppose the use of a clock mechanism and a method of ensuring that the values relevant to security can be safely transferred between parties. These mechanisms can be implemented only if three conditions are fulfilled:

- If the value of the authentication clock is increased, the private authentication key must also be altered.
- The private authentication key and the private privacy key may be known only by parties which are communicating with each other.
- In an SNMPv2 network, at least one SNMPv2 device must take on the functions of a network manager. The tasks of the management station include synchronizing the authentication clocks, and controlling and monitoring the values specified for data security. If several network management stations are operated in a hierarchical network management concept, these systems must come to a mutual agreement on the above functions.

Configuration

With an SNMPv2 device which has just been installed, the relevant parameters (Digest Authentication Protocol, Symmetric Privacy-Protocol) must be set manually on the device for at least one secure SNMPv2 party. Manual entry on the device ensures that the basic security parameters are known to the network administrator. Additional SNMPv2 parties can be configured via the manually entered basic setting of a secure SNMPv2 party relationship (on the network management station and the agent).

The basic settings for these parties should contain the following information on the network management station and the relevant agent:

- An SNMPv2 party in which the values noAuth and noPriv are specified for the parameters Authentication Protocol and Privacy Protocol respectively.
- An SNMPv2 party in which the authentication protocol is specified, but in which the value noPriv is defined for the privacy protocol.

- An SNMPv2 Party in which the authentication protocol and the privacy protocol are activated. A party relationship in which all relevant safety parameters are activated can be used for creating additional parties on the management station or the agent.

These initial parties must be created on the relevant management station and on the agent. The procedure is generally as follows:

1. The individual values for each Party Attribute must be specified by the network administrator. These values are derived as follows:
   - from the relevant MIB documents;
   - calculated by the network management station;
   - specified by the network administrator for the SNMPv2 network.
2. The individual parties are then configured in the management station, using the basic settings.
3. The basic settings for the relevant parties in the individual agents are then configured.
4. After the management station and the agents have been configured, the management station must synchronise the individual parties in the agents, using the authentication clocks.
5. When the clock synchronisation is complete, the network management station can alter the manually entered security values for the relevant peer parties and adapt them, via the network, to the current requirements for each party. However, this presupposes the use of an encryption mechanism (Symmetric Privacy Protocol) for the transfer of these values. If no encryption mechanism is used between the peer parties, the parameters can only be updated manually on each device involved.

Party clock

With the SNMPv2 protocol, the relevant management station is responsible for monitoring the authentication clock for each SNMPv2 party. In normal operation, the management station need only check the lifetime of an SNMPv2 message. However, the clock values may lie completely outside the possible range of values. To investigate this kind of anomaly, the SNMPv2 protocol proceeds as follows:

- If a considerable difference in the clock value is determined, and if the two mutually communicating SNMPv2 components both support a privacy protocol, the authentication clock and the private key for the relevant party will be changed simultaneously on both the management station and the agent. It must be ensured that the Request to alter values is also acknowledged as authentic by the receiving party. The authentication clock is therefore set before transmission to a value that will enable the recipient to accept the message.

- If an authentication clock reaches the maximum value, every SNMPv2 device must take special precautions to determine abnormal clock values. In order to avoid the need for integrating additional complicated mechanisms and to avoid complicating the implementation of the clock, the clock of a given party will stop when it reaches its maximum value. This maximum value is composed of the current clock time plus the lifetime of a message. If the clock is stopped in this way, the management station sends an Authentication Request to the relevant party. This Authentication Request sets the authentication clock and the private authentication key to new values.

Clock-Synchronization

In the case of SNMPv2, authentication clocks operating between two parties are always synchronized in such a way that the slower clock is adjusted to the faster. With SNMPv2, four different situations require alterations to the authentication clock:

1. The value of the management station authentication clock exceeds the value of the authentication clock for the corresponding (agent) party.
2. The value of the authentication clock for the manager party (mgrParty) in the management station exceeds the value of the agent authentication clock.
3. The value of the authentication clock for the agent party (agentParty) in the agent exceeds the value for the authentication clock in the management station.
4. The value of the authentication clock for the agent party exceeds the value of the authentication clock for the corresponding party (mgrParty) in the management station.

Error situations 1 to 3 are equalized and remedied by means of normal clock update procedures during communication between management station and agent through the protocol. Special error mechanisms are required only for situation 4:

1. The relevant management station saves the current value of the authentication clock for the relevant manager party (mgrParty).
2. The management station then attempts to ascertain the current value of the authentication clock for the relevant manager party (mgrParty) of the agent. Since the management station is not able to determine

whether the clocks are synchronised, this query is sent as an unauthorized Request. If the management station fails to receive a reply to the Request, the clock synchronisation procedure is aborted.

3. The Response from the agent is used to determine whether Error Status 4 is present. If this comparison is positive, the authentication clock of the manager party is adapted to the relevant clock of the agent.
4. It is then the task of the management station to compare the values of the authentication clock of the manager party (mgrParty) with the agent by means of an authentic Request. If there is no reply to the Request, the management station rejects the new values. The clock values saved in step 1 are reactivated and the synchronization procedure is aborted. If there is a reply from the Agent, the synchronization is complete.

During the synchronization of the clocks, management data must on no account be transferred between the two parties for reasons of data security.

Transfer of confidential information

Between two SNMPv2 parties, confidential information can be changed dynamically during operation. However, this presupposes that the SNMPv2 parties support a digest authentication protocol and a symmetric privacy protocol. For administrative purposes, for example if it is suspected that access has been gained to the information, the confidential information can be changed. With the SNMPv2 protocol, there is only one situation that automatically requires this information to be changed.

If the value of the authentication clock reaches its maximum, new values must be enforced between the two stations, in order to set the station to a new start value.

There are two reasons for modifying the confidential values for an SNMPv2 party (for example, private authentication key or private Privacy key) through the network management station:

- Establishing the confidential values when creating a new Party.
- Modification of confidential values on an existing Party.

Creating a new party

The following steps must be taken when transferring confidential information to a new party:

1. The relevant management stations generates the new confidential values for the new party.
2. if the source and destination parties support a digest authentication protocol and a private privacy protocol, the management station then produces an SNMPv2 Set Request message.

3. The new, confidential information is transferred via the Set Request message.
4. The receiving party processes the Request and generates a Response.
5. After the management station has received this Response message, the new values are stored in the local database for the relevant party and activated.

Modification of an existing party

The following steps must be taken when transferring confidential information to an existing Party:

1. The relevant management stations generates the new confidential values for the new party.
2. If the source and destination parties support a digest authentication protocol and a private privacy protocol, the management station then produces an SNMPv2 Set Request message.
3. The new, confidential information is transferred via the Set Request message.
4. The receiving party processes the Request and generates a Response.
5. After the management station has received this Response message, the new values are stored in the local database for the relevant party and activated.

If the management station fails to receive a Response to a Request, there are two possible causes:

- For various reasons, it may not have been possible for the recipient to receive the Request.
- For various reasons, it may not have been possible for the sender of a Request to receive the Response.

In order to intercept these two error situations, the relevant management station is required to check the newly transferred values in the receiving party. However, since the confidential information cannot be read directly, a strategy must be found which still enables the check to be made. The procedure is as follows:

- When a change is made to the private authentication key, the public authentication key is set to a readable value.
- When a change is made to the confidential privacy key, the public privacy key is set to a readable value.

These mechanisms enable the management station to react to missing Response messages and to check on the receiving party whether the value changes have been implemented.

If an SNMP party changes its own values, the recipient must first update the information in the local database before it can return a Response. The new values are therefore already contained in the Response. The relevant network management station only changes the values in the local database when this Response has been received and accepted as valid information.

The Response message received in this way is naturally registered by the network management station as non-authentic. Since this is a special status, the management station is able to process the non-authentic message or to check the information it contains in accordance with the above described scenario in respect of the public privacy key or the public authentication key.

The Practice

In practice, various mechanisms must be supported to ensure that the security functions can also be implemented on the individual SNMPv2 components.

RFC 1446 describes the following functions:

- A management station must refuse all SNMPv2 Response messages in which neither a Request ID nor the management information contained in a message received refer to an outstanding Request. This avoids the reception of message duplicates.
- A management station must never interpret an agent's failure to respond to an authentic SNMPv2 communication as a error in the agent. In practice, an authentication error trap may be lost because of a network error or may be suppressed because of an inconsistency in the authentication clock. Consequently, the management station must have integrated functions to intercept these error situations.

In the case of a system crash, communicative relationships between the manager party and the agent party must be carefully restored. All parameters (that is, Authentication Clock, Private Authentication Key, Private Privacy Key and Lifetime) for an SNMPv2 party must be stored in a local data store. This local data store should be realized as a non-volatile memory (NVRAM).

Since the authentication clock of an SNMPv2 party forms the basis of the security for the protocol mechanisms used, steps must be taken to ensure that the clock continues working even after a system-crash (or if the mains supply is interrupted). The simplest means of achieving this is to use a battery buffer for the clocks. After a system crash, the system administrator is responsible for checking the clocks involved and resetting the values is necessary.

If a crash occurs in an agent and the agent is not rebooted before the authentication clock reaches its maximum value, the clock is stopped during rebooting and restarted according to the above rules for party clocks.

Since all the parameters for a party cannot always be stored in a non-volatile RAM, these parameters need to be initialized when restarting after a crash, as follows:

- If the private authentication key does not contain an octet string of length 0, the authentication protocol defines the use of a digest authentication protocol.
- If the lifetime is not set, the relevant parameter is initialised with the value 0.
- If the privacy key does not contain an octet string of length 0, the privacy protocol defines the use of a symmetric privacy protocol.

If a management station has determined that an agent has been rebooted, all parameters for the parties supported which have not been stored in the NVRAM (Non-Volatile RAM) must be reset. If the lifetime of a Party is not stored in the NVRAM, the clock value is reset in accordance with the management station definition. In the first message, the authentication time stamp is formed from the sum of the current authentication clocks stored in the management station and the possible lifetime of the message.

SNMPv2 pre-conditions

In accordance with the Standard, an SNMPv2 implementation must fulfil the following pre-conditions:

1. The noAuth and noPriv protocol mechanisms must be implemented.
2. A digest authentication protocol must always be used in conjunction with the relevant algorithm.
3. At least one SNMPv2 party must be defined in the locally stored information. The values for the party must be set as follows:
   - The parameter partyAuth Protocol should be set to the value noAuth.
   - The parameter partyPriv Protocol should be set to the value noPriv.
   - This party must contain in its MIB View at least the authentication clocks of all other parties. Alternatively, the authentication clocks of all parties may be contained in separate configuration files.
4. Every locally configured SNMPv2 party must fulfil at least the following conditions:

- Precautions must be taken to ensure that the individual party parameters can never be set to an invalid value.
- The possibility of reading the private authentication key and the private encryption key must at all cost, be eliminated.
- The authentication clock of a party must be accessible using the specified security mechanisms in order to ensure synchronization of the sending and receiving parties.
- Alteration of the authentication clock of the party independently from the private authentication key must be prevented.
- Care must also be taken that the authentication clock of one party is increased to the maximum value, thereby setting the value to 0.
- It should not be possible to alter the maximum (transfer) lifetime of a message for a party, except via authorized commands through the network administrator.
- If the parameters of a party (the private authentication key or the private encryption key) are lost or destroyed, the values must be set in such a manner that the party values can be reset manually.

5. The new security values for a party must be selected in order to avoid invalid or easily guessed values (that is, all values set to 1).
6. It must also be ensured that if the sending party uses the digest authentication protocol in communicating with parties that do not support this mechanism, the message is always evaluated as non-authentic.

5.9 The SNMPv2 MIBs

Together with the SNMP Version 2 protocol specifications, a series of new SNMPv2 specific MIBs were created at the same time; the Manager-to-Manager MIB, the Management Information Base for SNMPv2 and the Party MIB for SNMPv2 were published.

5.9.1 SNMPv2 MIB Definition

RFC 1450 states that the SNMP Version 2 protocol incorporated its own Management Information Base (MIB). The following groups are integrated into the SNMPv2 MIB: the SNMPv2 Statistics Group, the SNMPv1 Statistics Group, the Object Resource Group, the Traps Group and the Set Group. The following definitions form the foundation for a single description of the object types prior to their compilation. The individual requirements can be seen in the complete text versions of the relevant RFCs.

Definitions

```
SNMPv2-MIB DEFINITIONS ::= BEGIN

IMPORTS
   MODULE-IDENTITY, OBJECT-TYPE, NOTIFICATION-TYPE,
   ObjectName, Integer32, Counter32, snmpModules
       FROM SNMPv2-SMI
   TruthValue, DisplayString, TestAndIncr, TimeStamp
       FROM SNMPv2-TC
   MODULE-COMPLIANCE, OBJECT-GROUP
       FROM SNMPv2-CONF
   system, ifIndex, egpNeighAddr
       FROM RFC1213-MIB
   partyEntry
       FROM SNMPv2-PARTY-MIB;

snmpMIB MODULE-IDENTITY
   LAST-UPDATED "9304010000Z"
   ORGANIZATION "IETF SNMPv2 Working Group"
   CONTACT-INFO
           "       Marshall T. Rose

            Postal: Dover Beach Consulting, Inc.
                    420 Whisman Court
                    Mountain View, CA  94043-2186
                    US
               Tel: +1 415 968 1052
               Fax: +1 415 968 2510

            E-mail: mrose@dbc.mtview.ca.us"
   DESCRIPTION
   "The MIB module for SNMPv2 entities."
   ::= { snmpModules 1 }
```

For the SNMPv2 MIB values the following object identifier has been defined:

```
snmpMIBObjects OBJECT IDENTIFIER ::= { snmpMIB 1 }
```

The SNMPv2 Statistic Group

With these objects SNMPv2 specific statistics can be grouped together. The SNMPv2 Statistics Group has the following object identifiers:

```
snmpStats       OBJECT IDENTIFIER ::= { snmpMIBObjects 1 }

snmpStatsPackets OBJECT-TYPE
   SYNTAX     Counter32
   MAX-ACCESS read-only
```

```
   STATUS     current
   DESCRIPTION
   "The total number of SNMP packets received by the device from
   the transport service."
   REFERENCE
           "Derived from RFC1213-MIB.snmpInPkts."
   ::= { snmpStats 1 }

snmpStats30Something OBJECT-TYPE
   SYNTAX     Counter32
   MAX-ACCESS read-only
   STATUS     current
   DESCRIPTION
   "The total number of packets (the initial octet is a value of
   30hex) received by the SNMPv2 device which does not suppport
   SNMPv1."
   REFERENCE "Derived from RFC1213-MIB.snmpInASNParseErrs."
   ::= { snmpStats 2 }

snmpStatsEncodingErrors OBJECT-TYPE
   SYNTAX     Counter32
   MAX-ACCESS read-only
   STATUS     current
   DESCRIPTION
   "The total number of packets received by the SNMPv2 device
   that were improperly encoded or had invalid syntax."
   REFERENCE "Derived from RFC1213-MIB.snmpInASNParseErrs."
   ::= { snmpStats 3 }

snmpStatsUnknownDstParties OBJECT-TYPE
   SYNTAX     Counter32
   MAX-ACCESS read-only
   STATUS     current
   DESCRIPTION
   "The total number of SnmpPrivMsgs delivered to the SNMPv2
   device for which the privDst field was not a known local
   party."
   ::= { snmpStats 4 }

snmpStatsDstPartyMismatches OBJECT-TYPE
   SYNTAX     Counter32
   MAX-ACCESS read-only
   STATUS     current
   DESCRIPTION
   "The total number of SnmpPrivMsgs delivered to the SNMPv2
   device containing a SnmpAuthMsg for which the
   authData.dstParty field did not match the privDst field in
   the SnmpPrivMsg."
   ::= { snmpStats 5 }

snmpStatsUnknownSrcParties OBJECT-TYPE
   SYNTAX     Counter32
   MAX-ACCESS read-only
```

```
   STATUS     current
   DESCRIPTION
   "The total number of SnmpAuthMsgs delivered to the SNMPv2
   device for which the authData.srcParty field was not a known
   remote party"
   ::= { snmpStats 6 }

snmpStatsBadAuths OBJECT-TYPE
   SYNTAX     Counter32
   MAX-ACCESS read-only
   STATUS     current
   DESCRIPTION
   "The total number of SnmpAuthMsgs delivered to the SNMPv2
   device which contained an authInfo field inconsistent with
   the authentication protocol associated with the source
   party."
   ::= { snmpStats 7 }

snmpStatsNotInLifetimes OBJECT-TYPE
   SYNTAX     Counter32
   MAX-ACCESS read-only
   STATUS     current
   DESCRIPTION
   "The total number of SnmpAuthMsgs delivered to the SNMPv2
   device deemed unauthentic due to their
   authInfo.authSrcTimestamp field being less than the source
   party's clock plus lifetime."
   ::= { snmpStats 8 }

snmpStatsWrongDigestValues OBJECT-TYPE
   SYNTAX     Counter32
   MAX-ACCESS read-only
   STATUS     current
   DESCRIPTION
   "The total number of SnmpAuthMsgs delivered to the SNMPv2
   device deemed unauthentic due to their authInfo.authDigest
   field being unequal to the expected digest value."
   ::= { snmpStats 9 }

snmpStatsUnknownContexts OBJECT-TYPE
   SYNTAX     Counter32
   MAX-ACCESS read-only
   STATUS     current
   DESCRIPTION
   "The total number of SnmpMgmtComs delivered to the SNMPv2
   device where the context field was not a known SNMPv2
   context."
   ::= { snmpStats 10 }

snmpStatsBadOperations OBJECT-TYPE
   SYNTAX     Counter32
   MAX-ACCESS read-only
   STATUS     current
```

```
    DESCRIPTION
    "The total number of messages delivered to the SNMPv2 device
    silently dropped because the PDU type referred to an
    operation not allowed in the aclTable."
    ::= { snmpStats 11 }

snmpStatsSilentDrops OBJECT-TYPE
    SYNTAX     Counter32
    MAX-ACCESS read-only
    STATUS     current
    DESCRIPTION
    "The total number of GetRequest-PDUs, GetNextRequest-PDUs,
    GetBulkRequest-PDUs, SetRequest-PDUs, and InformRequest-PDUs
    delivered to the SNMPv2 device silently dropped because the
    size of a reply containing an alternate Response-PDU with an
    empty variable bindings field was greater than either the
    maximum message size of the request's source party or a local
    constraint."
    ::= { snmpStats 12 }
```

The SNMPv1 Statistics Group

With these objects SNMPv1 specific statistics can be grouped together. The SNMPv1 StatisticsGroup has the following Object identifiers:

```
snmpV1         OBJECT IDENTIFIER ::= { snmpMIBObjects 2 }

snmpV1BadCommunityNames OBJECT-TYPE
    SYNTAX     Counter32
    MAX-ACCESS read-only
    STATUS     current
    DESCRIPTION
    "The total number of SNMPv1 Messages delivered to the SNMPv2
    device which used a community name not known to the SNMPv2
    device."
    REFERENCE "Derived from RFC1213-MIB.snmpInBadCommunityNames."
    ::= { snmpV1 1 }

snmpV1BadCommunityUses OBJECT-TYPE
    SYNTAX     Counter32
    MAX-ACCESS read-only
    STATUS     current
    DESCRIPTION
    "The total number of SNMPv1 Messages delivered to an SNMPv2
    device which contained an operation that was not allowed for
    the community named in the Message."
    REFERENCE "Derived from RFC1213-MIB.snmpInBadCommunityUses."
    ::= { snmpV1 2 }
```

The Object Resource Group

In the Object Resource Group all agent-embedded objects are gathered together, making dynamic configuration possible. For the SNMPv2 Object Resource Group the following object identifiers are relevant:

```
snmpOR          OBJECT IDENTIFIER ::= { snmpMIBObjects 3 }

snmpORLastChange OBJECT-TYPE
   SYNTAX     TimeStamp
   MAX-ACCESS read-only
   STATUS     current
   DESCRIPTION
   "The value of sysUpTime at the time of the most recent change
   in state or value of any instance of snmpORID."
   ::= { snmpOR 1 }

snmpORTable OBJECT-TYPE
   SYNTAX     SEQUENCE OF SnmpOREntry
   MAX-ACCESS not-accessible
   STATUS     current
   DESCRIPTION
   "The (conceptual) table which lists the dynamically
   configurable object resources in an SNMPv2 device acting
   in an agent role."
   ::= { snmpOR 2 }

snmpOREntry OBJECT-TYPE
   SYNTAX     SnmpOREntry
   MAX-ACCESS not-accessible
   STATUS     current
   DESCRIPTION
   "Defines an entry (conceptual row) in the snmpORTable."
   INDEX      { snmpORIndex }
   ::= { snmpORTable 1 }

SnmpOREntry ::= SEQUENCE {
   snmpORIndex                  Integer32,
   snmpORID                     OBJECT IDENTIFIER,
   snmpORDescr                  DisplayString
        }

snmpORIndex OBJECT-TYPE
   SYNTAX     Integer32
   MAX-ACCESS not-accessible
   STATUS     current
   DESCRIPTION
   "The auxiliary variable used to identify instances of the
   columnar objects in the snmpORTable."
   ::= { snmpOREntry 1 }

snmpORID OBJECT-TYPE
   SYNTAX     OBJECT IDENTIFIER.
```

```
   MAX-ACCESS read-only
   STATUS     current
   DESCRIPTION
   "An identification of one of the dynamically configurable
   object resources in an SNMPv2 device acting in an agent
   role."
   ::= { snmpOREntry 2 }

snmpORDescr OBJECT-TYPE
   SYNTAX     DisplayString
   MAX-ACCESS read-only
   STATUS     current
   DESCRIPTION
   "A textual description of one of the dynamically
   configurable object resources in an SNMPv2 device
   acting in an agent role."
   ::= { snmpOREntry 3 }
```

The Traps Group

In the Traps Group, all agent-embedded objects are gathered together once configured, generating SNMPv2 Trap PDUs. For the SNMPv2 Trap Group the following object identifiers are relevant:

```
snmpTrap       OBJECT IDENTIFIER ::= { snmpMIBObjects 4 }

snmpTrapOID OBJECT-TYPE
   SYNTAX     OBJECT IDENTIFIER
   MAX-ACCESS not-accessible
   STATUS     current
   DESCRIPTION
   "The reliable identification of the trap currently being
   sent."
   ::= { snmpTrap 1 }

snmpTrapTable OBJECT-TYPE
   SYNTAX     SEQUENCE OF SnmpTrapEntry
   MAX-ACCESS not-accessible
   STATUS     current
   DESCRIPTION
   "A table which keeps track of how many traps have been sent
   to each SNMPv2 device."
   ::= { snmpTrap 2 }

snmpTrapEntry OBJECT-TYPE
   SYNTAX     SnmpTrapEntry
   MAX-ACCESS not-accessible
   STATUS     current
   DESCRIPTION
   "Defines an entry which keeps track of how many traps have
   been sent to a particular SNMPv2 device."
```

```
    AUGMENTS   { partyEntry }
    ::= { snmpTrapTable 1 }

SnmpTrapEntry ::= SEQUENCE {
    snmpTrapNumbers
    Counter32
}

snmpTrapNumbers OBJECT-TYPE
    SYNTAX     Counter32
    MAX-ACCESS read-only
    STATUS     current
    DESCRIPTION
    "The number of traps sent to a particular SNMPv2 party since
    the last initialization of the SNMPv2 device, or the creation
    of the SNMPv2 party, whichever occurred first."
    ::= { snmpTrapEntry 1 }

snmpTrapEnterprise OBJECT-TYPE
    SYNTAX     OBJECT IDENTIFIER
    MAX-ACCESS not-accessible
    STATUS     current
    DESCRIPTION
    "The positive identification of the enterprise associated
    with the trap currently being sent."
    ::= { snmpTrap 3 }

snmpV2EnableAuthenTraps OBJECT-TYPE
    SYNTAX     TruthValue
    MAX-ACCESS read-write
    STATUS     current
    DESCRIPTION
    "Indicates whether the SNMPv2 device, when acting as an
    agent, is allowed to generate authenticationFailure traps."
    REFERENCE "Derived from RFC1213-MIB.snmpEnableAuthenTraps."
    ::= { snmpTrap 4 }
```

Well Known Traps

For the SNMPv2 Well Known Traps values the following object identifiers are used:

```
snmpTraps      OBJECT IDENTIFIER ::= { snmpMIBObjects 5 }

coldStart NOTIFICATION-TYPE
    STATUS  current
    DESCRIPTION
    "A coldStart trap signifies that the SNMPv2 device, acting as
    an agent, is reinitializing itself such that its
    configuration may be changed."
    ::= { snmpTraps 1 }
```

```
warmStart NOTIFICATION-TYPE
   STATUS  current
   DESCRIPTION
   "A warmStart trap signifies that the SNMPv2 device, acting as
   an agent, is reinitializing itself such that its
   configuration is unchanged."
   ::= { snmpTraps 2 }

linkDown NOTIFICATION-TYPE
   OBJECTS { ifIndex }
   STATUS  current
   DESCRIPTION
   "A linkDown trap signifies that the SNMPv2 device, acting as
   an agent, recognizes a failure in one of the communication
   links represented in its configuration."
   ::= { snmpTraps 3 }

linkUp NOTIFICATION-TYPE
   OBJECTS { ifIndex }
   STATUS  current
   DESCRIPTION
   "A linkUp trap signifies that the SNMPv2 device, acting as an
   agent, recognizes that one of the communication links
   represented in its configuration has come up."
   ::= { snmpTraps 4 }

authenticationFailure NOTIFICATION-TYPE
   STATUS  current
   DESCRIPTION
   "An authenticationFailure trap indicates that the SNMPv2
   device, acting as an agent, has received a protocol message
   that is not properly authenticated."
   ::= { snmpTraps 5 }

egpNeighborLoss NOTIFICATION-TYPE
   OBJECTS { egpNeighAddr }
   STATUS  current
   DESCRIPTION
   "An egpNeighborLoss trap signifies that an EGP neighbor has
   been marked down and the EGP peer relationship is no longer
   valid."
   ::= { snmpTraps 6 }
```

The Set Group

The Set Group is a collection of objects allowing several cooperating SNMPv2 devices, all acting as managers, to coordinate their use of the SNMPv2 set operation. For the SNMPv2 Set Group the following object identifiers are relevant:

```
snmpSet         OBJECT IDENTIFIER ::= { snmpMIBObjects 6 }

snmpSetSerialNo OBJECT-TYPE
   SYNTAX     TestAndIncr
   MAX-ACCESS read-write
   STATUS     current
   DESCRIPTION
   "An advisory lock used to allow several cooperating SNMPv2
   devices, all acting as managers, to coordinate their use of
   the SNMPv2 set operation."
   ::= { snmpSet 1 }

Conformance information:

snmpMIBConformance
              OBJECT IDENTIFIER ::= { snmpMIB 2 }

snmpMIBCompliances
              OBJECT IDENTIFIER ::= { snmpMIBConformance 1 }

snmpMIBGroups
              OBJECT IDENTIFIER ::= { snmpMIBConformance 2 }

Compliance Statements:

snmpMIBCompliance MODULE-COMPLIANCE
   STATUS  current
   DESCRIPTION
   "Defines the compliance statement for SNMPv2 devices
   implementing the SNMPv2 MIB."
   MODULE  RFC1213-MIB
       MANDATORY-GROUPS { system }
   MODULE    this module
       MANDATORY-GROUPS { snmpStatsGroup, snmpORGroup,
                          snmpTrapGroup, snmpSetGroup }
       GROUP   snmpV1Group
       DESCRIPTION
   "The snmpV1 Group is mandatory only for those SNMPv2 devices
   that also implement the SNMPv1 protocols."
   ::= { snmpMIBCompliances 1 }

Units of Conformance:

snmpStatsGroup OBJECT-GROUP
   OBJECTS { snmpStatsPackets, snmpStats30Something,
             snmpStatsEncodingErrors,
             snmpStatsUnknownDstParties,
             snmpStatsDstPartyMismatches,
             snmpStatsUnknownSrcParties, snmpStatsBadAuths,
             snmpStatsNotInLifetimes,
             snmpStatsWrongDigestValues,
             snmpStatsUnknownContexts,
```

```
                snmpStatsBadOperations,
                snmpStatsSilentDrops }
    STATUS  current
    DESCRIPTION
    "A collection of objects providing the basic instrumentation
    of the SNMPv2 device."
    ::= { snmpMIBGroups 1 }

snmpV1Group OBJECT-GROUP
    OBJECTS { snmpV1BadCommunityNames, snmpV1BadCommunityUses }
    STATUS  current
    DESCRIPTION
    "A collection of objects providing the basic instrumentation
    of a SNMPv2 device that also implements the SNMPv1 protocol."
    ::= { snmpMIBGroups 2 }

snmpORGroup OBJECT-GROUP
    OBJECTS { snmpORLastChange, snmpORID, snmpORDescr }
    STATUS  current
    DESCRIPTION
    "A collection of objects allowing an SNMPv2 device acting as
    an agent to describe its dynamically configurable object
    resources."
    ::= { snmpMIBGroups 3 }

snmpTrapGroup OBJECT-GROUP
    OBJECTS { snmpTrapNumbers, snmpV2EnableAuthenTraps }
    STATUS  current
    DESCRIPTION
    "A collection of objects which allow the SNMPv2 device, when
    acting as an agent, to be configured to generate SNMPv2 Trap
    PDUs."
    ::= { snmpMIBGroups 4 }

snmpSetGroup OBJECT-GROUP
    OBJECTS { snmpSetSerialNo }
    STATUS  current
    DESCRIPTION
    "A collection of objects which allow several cooperating
    SNMPv2 devices, all acting as a manager, to coordinate their
    use of the SNMPv2 set operation."
    ::= { snmpMIBGroups 5 }

END
```

5.9.2 Party MIB definitions

RFC 1447 makes it possible for the network administrator to grant access rights to parties or to a single user. It is possible that more management stations can be assisted by agents. For all of the parties, a certain partition of the MIB tree can be configured so that one station reads only one object or, rather, can only describe one object. In the Party MIB the following groups are integrated: the SNMPv2 Party Database Group, the SNMPv2 Contexts Database Group, the SNMPv2 Access Privileges Database Group and the MIB View Database Group. The following definitions form the foundation for a single description of the object types prior to their compilation. The individual requirements can be seen in the expanded text versions of the relevant RFCs.

Definitions

```
SNMPv2-PARTY-MIB DEFINITIONS ::= BEGIN

IMPORTS
   MODULE-IDENTITY, OBJECT-TYPE, snmpModules,
       UInteger32
       FROM SNMPv2-SMI
   TEXTUAL-CONVENTION, RowStatus, TruthValue
       FROM SNMPv2-TC
   MODULE-COMPLIANCE, OBJECT-GROUP
       FROM SNMPv2-CONF;
partyMIB MODULE-IDENTITY
   LAST-UPDATED "9304010000Z"
   ORGANIZATION "IETF SNMP Security Working Group"
   CONTACT-INFO
           "        Keith McCloghrie

           Postal: Hughes LAN Systems
                   1225 Charleston Road
                   Mountain View, CA  94043
                   US

              Tel: +1 415 966 7934
              Fax: +1 415 960 3738

           E-mail: kzm@hls.com"
   DESCRIPTION
"The MIB module which describes the SNMPv2 Parties."
   ::= { snmpModules 3 }
```

```
Party ::= TEXTUAL-CONVENTION
   STATUS       current
   DESCRIPTION
   "Indicates an SNMPv2 party identifier."
   SYNTAX       OBJECT IDENTIFIER

TAddress ::= TEXTUAL-CONVENTION
   STATUS       current
   DESCRIPTION
   "Indicates a Transport Service address."
   SYNTAX       OCTET STRING

Clock ::= TEXTUAL-CONVENTION
   STATUS       current
   DESCRIPTION
   "Indicates a party's authentication clock."
   SYNTAX       UInteger32

Context ::= TEXTUAL-CONVENTION
   STATUS       current
   DESCRIPTION
   "Indicates an SNMPv2 context identifier."
   SYNTAX       OBJECT IDENTIFIER

StorageType ::= TEXTUAL-CONVENTION
   STATUS       current
   DESCRIPTION
   "Describes what is in memory of a conceptual row."
   SYNTAX       INTEGER {
                    other(1),
                    volatile(2),    -- e.g. in RAM
                    nonVolatile(3), -- e.g. in NVRAM
                    permanent(4)    -- e.g. in ROM
                }
```

For the SNMPv2 Party MIB the following object identifiers apply:

```
partyAdmin     OBJECT IDENTIFIER ::= { partyMIB 1 }
```

The definition of the security-protocols

```
partyProtocols      OBJECT IDENTIFIER ::= { partyAdmin 1 }
noAuth              OBJECT IDENTIFIER ::= { partyProtocols 1 }
noPriv              OBJECT IDENTIFIER ::= { partyProtocols 2 }
desPrivProtocol     OBJECT IDENTIFIER ::= { partyProtocols 3 }
v2md5AuthProtocol   OBJECT IDENTIFIER ::= { partyProtocols 4 }
```

The definition of temporal domains

```
temporalDomains      OBJECT IDENTIFIER ::= { partyAdmin 2 }
currentTime          OBJECT IDENTIFIER ::= { temporalDomains 1 }
restartTime          OBJECT IDENTIFIER ::= { temporalDomains 2 }
cacheTime            OBJECT IDENTIFIER ::= { temporalDomains 3 }
```

The definition of initial party and context identifiers

```
initialPartyId       OBJECT IDENTIFIER ::= { partyAdmin 3 }
initialContextId     OBJECT IDENTIFIER ::= { partyAdmin 4 }
partyMIBObjects      OBJECT IDENTIFIER ::= { partyMIB 2 }
```

SNMPv2 Party Database Group

In the Party Database group all the MIB View values are stored locally with an agent. For every inbuilt MIB View value there are a series of corresponding values, for example the transport service, the message lengths, the interceding authentication protocol, the authentication clock, the time delay, the transport time, the coding mechanisms (for example, DES), the public and the private parties and the inbuilt variables. For the SNMPv2 Party Database Group the following object identifiers are relevant for the Party MIB:

```
snmpParties    OBJECT IDENTIFIER ::= { partyMIBObjects 1 }

partyTable OBJECT-TYPE
   SYNTAX      SEQUENCE OF PartyEntry
   MAX-ACCESS  not-accessible
   STATUS      current
   DESCRIPTION
   "The SNMPv2 Party database."
   ::= { snmpParties 1 }

partyEntry OBJECT-TYPE
   SYNTAX      PartyEntry
   MAX-ACCESS  not-accessible
   STATUS      current
   DESCRIPTION
   "Locally held information with respect to a specific SNMPv2
   party."
   INDEX      { IMPLIED partyIdentity }
   ::= { partyTable 1 }
```

```
PartyEntry ::=
   SEQUENCE {
       partyIdentity        Party,
       partyIndex           INTEGER,
       partyTDomain         OBJECT IDENTIFIER,
       partyTAddress        TAddress,
       partyMaxMessageSize  INTEGER,
       partyLocal           TruthValue,
       partyAuthProtocol    OBJECT IDENTIFIER,
       partyAuthClock       Clock,
       partyAuthPrivate     OCTET STRING,
       partyAuthPublic      OCTET STRING,
       partyAuthLifetime    INTEGER,
       partyPrivProtocol    OBJECT IDENTIFIER,
       partyPrivPrivate     OCTET STRING,
       partyPrivPublic      OCTET STRING,
       partyCloneFrom       Party,
       partyStorageType     StorageType,
       partyStatus          RowStatus
   }

partyIdentity OBJECT-TYPE
   SYNTAX      Party
   MAX-ACCESS  not-accessible
   STATUS      current
   DESCRIPTION
   "A party identifier which uniquely identifies a specific
   SNMPv2 party."
   ::= { partyEntry 1 }

partyIndex OBJECT-TYPE
   SYNTAX      INTEGER (1..65535)
   MAX-ACCESS  read-only
   STATUS      current
   DESCRIPTION
   "Defines a unique value for each SNMPv2 party. The value for
   each SNMPv2 party must remain constant at least from one
   reinitialization of the device's network management system to
   the next reinitialization."
   ::= { partyEntry 2 }

partyTDomain OBJECT-TYPE
   SYNTAX      OBJECT IDENTIFIER
   MAX-ACCESS  read-create
   STATUS      current
   DESCRIPTION
   "Indicates the type of transport service by which the party
   receives network management traffic."
   DEFVAL      { snmpUDPDomain }
   ::= { partyEntry 3 }
```

```
partyTAddress OBJECT-TYPE
   SYNTAX      TAddress
   MAX-ACCESS  read-create
   STATUS      current
   DESCRIPTION
   "The transport service address by which the party receives
   network management traffic, formatted  according to the
   corresponding value of partyTDomain."
   DEFVAL      { '000000000000'H }
   ::= { partyEntry 4 }

partyMaxMessageSize OBJECT-TYPE
   SYNTAX      INTEGER (484..65507)
   MAX-ACCESS  read-create
   STATUS      current
   DESCRIPTION
   "Defines the maximum length in octets of an SNMPv2 message
   that this party will accept."
   DEFVAL      { 484 }
   ::= { partyEntry 5 }

partyLocal OBJECT-TYPE
   SYNTAX      TruthValue
   MAX-ACCESS  read-create
   STATUS      current
   DESCRIPTION
   "An indication of whether this party executes at this SNMPv2
   device. If this object has a value of  true(1), then the
   SNMPv2 device listens for SNMPv2 messages on the
   partyTAddress associated with this party. If this object has
   the value false(2), then the SNMPv2 device will not listen
   for SNMPv2 messages on the partyTAddress associated with this
   party."
   DEFVAL      { false }
   ::= { partyEntry 6 }

partyAuthProtocol OBJECT-TYPE
   SYNTAX      OBJECT IDENTIFIER
   MAX-ACCESS  read-create
   STATUS      current
   DESCRIPTION
   "The authentication protocol by which all messages generated
   by the party are authenticated with respect to origin and
   integrity."
   DEFVAL      { v2md5AuthProtocol }
   ::= { partyEntry 7 }

partyAuthClock OBJECT-TYPE
   SYNTAX      Clock
   MAX-ACCESS  read-create
   STATUS      current
```

```
   DESCRIPTION
   "Contains the value of the authentication clock of the
   party."
   DEFVAL      { 0 }
   ::= { partyEntry 8 }

partyAuthPrivate OBJECT-TYPE
   SYNTAX      OCTET STRING
                 for v2md5AuthProtocol: (SIZE (16))
   MAX-ACCESS  read-create
   STATUS      current
   DESCRIPTION
   "Defines the encoding of the party's private authentication
   key which may be needed to support the authentication
   protocol."
   DEFVAL      { ''H }
   ::= { partyEntry 9 }

partyAuthPublic OBJECT-TYPE
   SYNTAX      OCTET STRING
                 for v2md5AuthProtocol: (SIZE (0..16))
   MAX-ACCESS  read-create
   STATUS      current
   DESCRIPTION
   "Defines a publicly readable value for the party."
   DEFVAL      { ''H }
   ::= { partyEntry 10 }

partyAuthLifetime OBJECT-TYPE
   SYNTAX      INTEGER (0..2147483647)
   UNITS       "seconds"
   MAX-ACCESS  read-create
   STATUS      current
   DESCRIPTION
   "Defines the lifetime (in units of seconds) representing an
   administrative upper limit on acceptable delivery delay for
   protocol messages generated by the party."
   DEFVAL      { 300 }
   ::= { partyEntry 11 }

partyPrivProtocol OBJECT-TYPE
   SYNTAX      OBJECT IDENTIFIER
   MAX-ACCESS  read-create
   STATUS      current
   DESCRIPTION
   "Defines the privacy protocol by which all protocol messages
   received by the party are protected from disclosure."
   DEFVAL      { noPriv }
   ::= { partyEntry 12 }

partyPrivPrivate OBJECT-TYPE
   SYNTAX      OCTET STRING
                 for desPrivProtocol: (SIZE (16))
```

```
    MAX-ACCESS  read-create
    STATUS      current
    DESCRIPTION
    "An encoding of the party's private encryption key which may
    be required to support the privacy  protocol."
    DEFVAL      { ''H }       the empty string
    ::= { partyEntry 13 }

partyPrivPublic OBJECT-TYPE
    SYNTAX      OCTET STRING
                  for desPrivProtocol: (SIZE (0..16))
    MAX-ACCESS  read-create
    STATUS      current
    DESCRIPTION
    "Defines a publicly readable value for the party."
    DEFVAL      { ''H }       the empty string
    ::= { partyEntry 14 }

partyCloneFrom OBJECT-TYPE
    SYNTAX      Party
    MAX-ACCESS  read-create
    STATUS      current
    DESCRIPTION
    "The identity of a party to clone authentication and privacy
    parameters from."
    ::= { partyEntry 15 }

partyStorageType OBJECT-TYPE
    SYNTAX      StorageType
    MAX-ACCESS  read-create
    STATUS      current
    DESCRIPTION
    "Defines the storage type for this conceptual row in the
    partyTable."
    DEFVAL      { nonVolatile }
    ::= { partyEntry 16 }

partyStatus OBJECT-TYPE
    SYNTAX      RowStatus
    MAX-ACCESS  read-create
    STATUS      current
    DESCRIPTION
    "Defines the status of this conceptual row in the
    partyTable."
::= { partyEntry 17 }
```

SNMPv2 Contexts Database Group

In the Contexts Database Group, the tables contain only locally stored information, through which SNMPv2 proxy management functionality is achieved. For the SNMPv2 Contexts Database Group the following object identifiers are incorporated within the Party MIB:

```
snmpContexts   OBJECT IDENTIFIER ::= { partyMIBObjects 2 }

contextTable OBJECT-TYPE
   SYNTAX      SEQUENCE OF ContextEntry
   MAX-ACCESS  not-accessible
   STATUS      current
   DESCRIPTION
   "Defines the SNMPv2 Context database."
   ::= { snmpContexts 1 }

contextEntry OBJECT-TYPE
   SYNTAX      ContextEntry
   MAX-ACCESS  not-accessible
   STATUS      current
   DESCRIPTION
   "Locally held information about a specific SNMPv2 context"
   INDEX      { IMPLIED contextIdentity }
   ::= { contextTable 1 }

ContextEntry ::=
   SEQUENCE {
       contextIdentity          Context,
       contextIndex             INTEGER,
       contextLocal             TruthValue,
       contextViewIndex         INTEGER,
       contextLocalEntity       OCTET STRING,
       contextLocalTime         OBJECT IDENTIFIER,
       contextProxyDstParty     Party,
       contextProxySrcParty     Party,
       contextProxyContext      OBJECT IDENTIFIER,
       contextStorageType       StorageType,
       contextStatus            RowStatus
   }

contextIdentity OBJECT-TYPE
   SYNTAX      Context
   MAX-ACCESS  not-accessible
   STATUS      current
   DESCRIPTION
   "Is a context identifier uniquely identifying a specific
   SNMPv2 context."
   ::= { contextEntry 1 }

contextIndex OBJECT-TYPE
   SYNTAX      INTEGER (1..65535)
   MAX-ACCESS  read-only
   STATUS      current
   DESCRIPTION
   "A unique value for each SNMPv2 context."
   ::= { contextEntry 2 }
```

```
contextLocal OBJECT-TYPE
   SYNTAX      TruthValue
   MAX-ACCESS  read-create
   STATUS      current
   DESCRIPTION
   "An indication of whether this context is realized by this
   SNMPv2 device."
   DEFVAL      { true }
   ::= { contextEntry 3 }
contextViewIndex OBJECT-TYPE
   SYNTAX      INTEGER (0..65535)
   MAX-ACCESS  read-create
   STATUS      current
   DESCRIPTION
   "If the value of an instance of this object equates to zero,
   this corresponding conceptual row in the contextTable refers
   to an SNMPv2 context identifying a proxy relationship."
   ::= { contextEntry 4 }

contextLocalEntity OBJECT-TYPE
   SYNTAX      OCTET STRING
   MAX-ACCESS  read-create
   STATUS      current
   DESCRIPTION
   "If the value of the corresponding instance of the
   contextViewIndex is greater than zero, then the value of an
   instance of this object identifies the local device whose
   management information is defined in the SNMPv2 context's MIB
   view."
   DEFVAL      { ''H }      the empty string
   ::= { contextEntry 5 }

contextLocalTime OBJECT-TYPE
   SYNTAX      OBJECT IDENTIFIER
   MAX-ACCESS  read-create
   STATUS      current
   DESCRIPTION
   "If the value of the contextViewIndex is greater than zero,
   then the value of an instance of this object identifies the
   temporal context of the management information in the MIB
   view."
   DEFVAL      { currentTime }
   ::= { contextEntry 6 }

contextProxyDstParty OBJECT-TYPE
   SYNTAX      Party
   MAX-ACCESS  read-create
   STATUS      current
   DESCRIPTION33
   "If the value of the contextViewIndex is equal to zero, then
   the value of an instance of this object identifies an SNMPv2
```

```
      party which equates to the proxy destination of a proxy
      relationship."
      ::= { contextEntry 7 }

   contextProxySrcParty OBJECT-TYPE
      SYNTAX      Party
      MAX-ACCESS  read-create
      STATUS      current
      DESCRIPTION
      "If the value of the contextViewIndex is equal to zero,
      then the value of an instance of this object identifies
      an SNMPv2 party which equates to the proxy source of a
      proxy relationship."
      ::= { contextEntry 8 }

   contextProxyContext OBJECT-TYPE
      SYNTAX      OBJECT IDENTIFIER
      MAX-ACCESS  read-create
      STATUS      current
      DESCRIPTION
      "If the value of the contextViewIndex is equal to zero,
      then the value of an instance of this object identifies
      the context of a proxy relationship."
      ::= { contextEntry 9 }

   contextStorageType OBJECT-TYPE
      SYNTAX      StorageType
      MAX-ACCESS  read-create
      STATUS      current
      DESCRIPTION
      "Defines the storage type for this conceptual row in the
      contextTable."
      DEFVAL      { nonVolatile }
      ::= { contextEntry 10 }

   contextStatus OBJECT-TYPE
      SYNTAX      RowStatus
      MAX-ACCESS  read-create
      STATUS      current
      DESCRIPTION
      "Is the status of this conceptual row in the contextTable."
   ::= { contextEntry 11 }
```

SNMPv2 Access Privileges Database Group

In this database, in the form of a table, all devices for the party access mechanism are stored. For the SNMPv2 Access Privileges Database Group the following object identifiers are defined within the Party MIB:

```
snmpAccess      OBJECT IDENTIFIER ::= { partyMIBObjects 3 }

aclTable OBJECT-TYPE
   SYNTAX       SEQUENCE OF AclEntry
   MAX-ACCESS   not-accessible
   STATUS       current
   DESCRIPTION
   "The access privileges database."
   ::= { snmpAccess 1 }

aclEntry OBJECT-TYPE
   SYNTAX       AclEntry
   MAX-ACCESS   not-accessible
   STATUS       current
   DESCRIPTION
   "Defines the access privileges for a particular SNMPv2 party
   when asking a particular target SNMPv2 party to access a
   particular SNMPv2 context."
   INDEX      { aclTarget, aclSubject, aclResources }
   ::= { aclTable 1 }

AclEntry ::=
   SEQUENCE {
       aclTarget         INTEGER,
       aclSubject        INTEGER,
       aclResources      INTEGER,
       aclPrivileges     INTEGER,
       aclStorageType    StorageType,
       aclStatus         RowStatus
   }

aclTarget OBJECT-TYPE
   SYNTAX       INTEGER (1..65535)
   MAX-ACCESS   not-accessible
   STATUS       current
   DESCRIPTION
   "Contains the value of an SNMPv2 party identifier."
   ::= { aclEntry 1 }

aclSubject OBJECT-TYPE
   SYNTAX       INTEGER (1..65535)
   MAX-ACCESS   not-accessible
   STATUS       current
   DESCRIPTION
   "Contains the value of an instance of this object which
   identifies an SNMPv2 party which is itself the subject
   of an access control policy."
   ::= { aclEntry 2 }

aclResources OBJECT-TYPE
   SYNTAX       INTEGER (1..65535)
   MAX-ACCESS   not-accessible
```

```
    STATUS      current
    DESCRIPTION
    "The value of an instance of this object identifies an
    SNMPv2 context in an access control  policy."
    ::= { aclEntry 3 }

aclPrivileges OBJECT-TYPE
    SYNTAX      INTEGER (0..255)
    MAX-ACCESS  read-create
    STATUS      current
    DESCRIPTION
    "The access privileges which determine what management
    operations a specific target party may perform with respect
    to a specific SNMPv2 context when requested by a specific
    party. These privileges are expressed as a sum of values,
    where each value specifies an SNMPv2 PDU type by which the
    subject party may request an allowable operation:
    Get         :   1
    GetNext     :   2
    Response    :   4
    Set         :   8
    unused      :  16
    GetBulk     :  32
    Inform      :  64
    SNMPv2 Trap : 128"
    DEFVAL      { 35 }        Get, Get-Next & Get-Bulk
    ::= { aclEntry 4 }

aclStorageType OBJECT-TYPE
    SYNTAX      StorageType
    MAX-ACCESS  read-create
    STATUS      current
    DESCRIPTION
    "Defines the storage type for this conceptual row in the
    aclTable."
    DEFVAL      { nonVolatile }
    ::= { aclEntry 5 }

aclStatus OBJECT-TYPE
    SYNTAX      RowStatus
    MAX-ACCESS  read-create
    STATUS      current
    DESCRIPTION
    "Defines the status of this conceptual row in the aclTable."
::= { aclEntry 6 }
```

MIB View Database Group

In this database, in the form of a table, all devices for the MIB Views are stored. For the SNMPv2 View Database Group the following object identifiers are defined within the PartyMIB:

```
snmpViews       OBJECT IDENTIFIER ::= { partyMIBObjects 4 }

viewTable OBJECT-TYPE
   SYNTAX       SEQUENCE OF ViewEntry
   MAX-ACCESS   not-accessible
   STATUS       current
   DESCRIPTION
   "Contains locally held information about the MIB views known
   to this SNMPv2 device."
   ::= { snmpViews 1 }

viewEntry OBJECT-TYPE
   SYNTAX       ViewEntry
   MAX-ACCESS   not-accessible
   STATUS       current
   DESCRIPTION
   "Contains information on a specific family of view subtrees
   included in or excluded from a designated SNMPv2 context's
   MIB view."
   INDEX       { viewIndex, IMPLIED viewSubtree }
   ::= { viewTable 1 }

ViewEntry ::=
   SEQUENCE {
       viewIndex          INTEGER,
       viewSubtree        OBJECT IDENTIFIER,
       viewMask           OCTET STRING,
       viewType           INTEGER,
       viewStorageType    StorageType,
       viewStatus         RowStatus
   }

viewIndex OBJECT-TYPE
   SYNTAX       INTEGER (1..65535)
   MAX-ACCESS   not-accessible
   STATUS       current
   DESCRIPTION
   "Contains a unique value for each MIB view."
   ::= { viewEntry 1 }

viewSubtree OBJECT-TYPE
   SYNTAX       OBJECT IDENTIFIER
   MAX-ACCESS   not-accessible
   STATUS       current
   DESCRIPTION
   "Defines the MIB subtree."
   ::= { viewEntry 2 }

viewMask OBJECT-TYPE
   SYNTAX       OCTET STRING (SIZE (0..16))
   MAX-ACCESS   read-create
   STATUS       current
```

```
   DESCRIPTION
   "The bit mask which, in combination with the corresponding
   representation of viewSubtree, defines a family of view
   subtrees."
   DEFVAL      { ''H }
   ::= { viewEntry 3 }

viewType OBJECT-TYPE
   SYNTAX      INTEGER  {
                   included(1),
                   excluded(2)
               }
   MAX-ACCESS  read-create
   STATUS      current
   DESCRIPTION
   "The status of an individual family of view subtrees within
   the specific SNMPv2 context's MIB view."
   DEFVAL      { included }
   ::= { viewEntry 4 }

viewStorageType OBJECT-TYPE
   SYNTAX      StorageType
   MAX-ACCESS  read-create
   STATUS      current
   DESCRIPTION
   "Defines the storage type for this conceptual row in the
   viewTable."
   DEFVAL      { nonVolatile }
   ::= { viewEntry 5 }

viewStatus OBJECT-TYPE
   SYNTAX      RowStatus
   MAX-ACCESS  read-create
   STATUS      current
   DESCRIPTION
   "Defines the status of this conceptual row in the viewTable."
   ::= { viewEntry 6 }

partyMIBConformance
              OBJECT IDENTIFIER ::= { partyMIB 3 }

partyMIBCompliances
              OBJECT IDENTIFIER ::= { partyMIBConformance 1 }

partyMIBGroups
              OBJECT IDENTIFIER ::= { partyMIBConformance 2 }

unSecurableCompliance MODULE-COMPLIANCE
   STATUS  current
   DESCRIPTION
   "Defines the compliance declaration for SNMPv2 devices
   that implement the Party MIB, but do not support any
   authentication or privacy protocols."
```

```
   MODULE    this module
       MANDATORY-GROUPS { partyMIBGroup }
   ::= { partyMIBCompliances 1 }

partyNoPrivacyCompliance MODULE-COMPLIANCE
   STATUS  current
   DESCRIPTION
   "This group defines the compliance declaration for SNMPv2
   devices that implement the Party MIB and support an
   authentication protocol, but do not support any privacy
   protocols."
   MODULE    this module
       MANDATORY-GROUPS { partyMIBGroup }
   ::= { partyMIBCompliances 2 }

partyPrivacyCompliance MODULE-COMPLIANCE
   STATUS  current
   DESCRIPTION
   "This group defines the compliance declaration for SNMPv2
   devices that implement the Party MIB, support an
   authentication protocol, and support a privacy protocol for
   the purpose of accessing security parameters only."
   MODULE    this module
       MANDATORY-GROUPS { partyMIBGroup }
   ::= { partyMIBCompliances 3 }

fullPrivacyCompliance MODULE-COMPLIANCE
   STATUS  current
   DESCRIPTION
   "This group defines the compliance declaration for SNMPv2
   devices that implement the Party MIB, support a privacy
   protocol, and support an authentication protocol without
   putting restrictions on its use."
   MODULE    this module
       MANDATORY-GROUPS { partyMIBGroup }
   ::= { partyMIBCompliances 4 }

partyMIBGroup OBJECT-GROUP
  OBJECTS { partyIndex, partyTDomain, partyTAddress,
          partyMaxMessageSize, partyLocal,
          partyAuthProtocol, partyAuthClock,
          partyAuthPrivate, partyAuthPublic,
          partyAuthLifetime, partyPrivProtocol,
          partyPrivPrivate, partyPrivPublic,
          partyStorageType, partyStatus,
          partyCloneFrom,
          contextIndex, contextLocal,
          contextViewIndex, contextLocalEntity,
          contextLocalTime, contextStorageType,
          contextStatus, aclTarget, aclSubject,
          aclPrivileges, aclStorageType, aclStatus,
          viewMask, viewType, viewStorageType, viewStatus }
```

```
  STATUS  current
  DESCRIPTION
   "This object group defines the set of objects permitting the
   description and configuration of SNMPv2 parties."
  ::= { partyMIBGroups 1 }

END
```

5.9.3 Manager-to-Manager MIB definitions

In RFC 1451 a managed object can be incorporated in the Manager-to-Manager MIB. Through this MIB a weakness was recognized in SNMP Version 1. The obvious division between an agent (server process) and a network management station (agent process) is now broken. A network management station can itself be both the agent process and the server process in SNMPv2. These functions enable a Manager-to-Manager communications connection. In this MIB the concepts of Alarms, Events and Notifications are integrated. With built-in Alarm criteria the following actions (Events) are added in the form of information (Notifications). Incorporated in the Manager-to-Manager MIB are three individual tables (the Alarm, Event and the Notification Tables). The following definitions form the foundation for a single description of the object types prior to their compilation. The individual requirements can be seen in the revised text versions of the relevant RFCs.

Definitions

```
SNMPv2-M2M-MIB DEFINITIONS ::= BEGIN
IMPORTS
   MODULE-IDENTITY, OBJECT-TYPE, NOTIFICATION-TYPE,
   Integer32, Counter32, snmpModules
       FROM SNMPv2-SMI
   DisplayString, InstancePointer, RowStatus, TimeStamp
       FROM SNMPv2-TC
   MODULE-COMPLIANCE, OBJECT-GROUP
       FROM SNMPv2-CONF
   contextIdentity
       FROM SNMPv2-PARTY-MIB;
snmpM2M MODULE-IDENTITY
   LAST-UPDATED "9304010000Z"
   ORGANIZATION "IETF SNMPv2 Working Group"
   CONTACT-INFO
          "          Steven Waldbusser
```

```
             Postal: Carnegie Mellon University
                     4910 Forbes Ave
                     Pittsburgh, PA  15213

                Tel: +1 412 268 6628
                Fax: +1 412 268 4987

             E-mail: waldbusser@cmu.edu"
   DESCRIPTION
"The Manager-to-Manager MIB module."
   ::= { snmpModules 2 }
```

For the Manager-to-Manager MIB values the following object identifiers apply:

```
snmpM2MObjects OBJECT IDENTIFIER ::= { snmpM2M 1 }
```

Alarm Group

The Alarm Group makes it possible to have individual definitions from Alarm parameters. Through this a threshold value can be included with the actual values remaining constant. This mechanism generates an event as a threshold is crossed (in the appropriate direction). For the Alarm Group the Manager-to-Manager MIB uses the following object identifiers:

```
snmpAlarm      OBJECT IDENTIFIER ::= { snmpM2MObjects 1 }

snmpAlarmNextIndex OBJECT-TYPE
   SYNTAX     INTEGER (0..65535)
   MAX-ACCESS read-only
   STATUS     current
   DESCRIPTION
   "Contains the index number of the next appropriate unassigned
   entry in the snmpAlarmTable. The value 0 indicates that no
   unassigned entries are available."
   ::= { snmpAlarm 1 }

snmpAlarmTable OBJECT-TYPE
   SYNTAX     SEQUENCE OF SnmpAlarmEntry
   MAX-ACCESS not-accessible
   STATUS     current
   DESCRIPTION
   "The Table listing the snmpAlarm entries."
   ::= { snmpAlarm 2 }
```

```
snmpAlarmEntry OBJECT-TYPE
   SYNTAX     SnmpAlarmEntry
   MAX-ACCESS not-accessible
   STATUS     current
   DESCRIPTION
   "Is a list of parameters which set up a frequent sampling
   interrogation to check for alarm conditions."
   INDEX      { contextIdentity, snmpAlarmIndex }
   ::= { snmpAlarmTable 1 }

SnmpAlarmEntry ::= SEQUENCE {
   snmpAlarmIndex                    INTEGER,
   snmpAlarmVariable                 InstancePointer,
   snmpAlarmInterval                 Integer32,
   snmpAlarmSampleType               INTEGER,
   snmpAlarmValue                    Integer32,
   snmpAlarmStartupAlarm             INTEGER,
   snmpAlarmRisingThreshold          Integer32,
   snmpAlarmFallingThreshold         Integer32,
   snmpAlarmRisingEventIndex         INTEGER,
   snmpAlarmFallingEventIndex        INTEGER,
   snmpAlarmUnavailableEventIndex    INTEGER,
   snmpAlarmStatus                   RowStatus
}

snmpAlarmIndex OBJECT-TYPE
   SYNTAX     INTEGER (1..65535)
   MAX-ACCESS not-accessible
   STATUS     current
   DESCRIPTION
   "An index that uniquely identifies an entry in the
   snmpAlarm table for an individual sampling context."
   ::= { snmpAlarmEntry 1 }

snmpAlarmVariable OBJECT-TYPE
   SYNTAX     InstancePointer
   MAX-ACCESS read-create
   STATUS     current
   DESCRIPTION
   "The object identifier of the specific variable to be
   sampled. Only variables that convert to an ASN.1 primitive
   type of INTEGER (Integer32, Counter32, Gauge32, TimeTicks,
   Counter64, or UInteger32) may be sampled."
   ::= { snmpAlarmEntry 2 }

snmpAlarmInterval OBJECT-TYPE
   SYNTAX     Integer32
   UNITS      "seconds"
   MAX-ACCESS read-create
   STATUS     current
   DESCRIPTION
```

```
   "Specifies the interval (in seconds) over which the data is
   sampled and compared with the ascending and descending
   thresholds."
   ::= { snmpAlarmEntry 3 }

snmpAlarmSampleType OBJECT-TYPE
   SYNTAX     INTEGER {
                 absoluteValue(1),
                 deltaValue(2)
              }
   MAX-ACCESS read-create
   STATUS     current
   DESCRIPTION
   "Defines the method of sampling the selected variable and
   calculating the value to be compared with the thresholds."
   DEFVAL { deltaValue }
   ::= { snmpAlarmEntry 4 }

snmpAlarmValue OBJECT-TYPE
   SYNTAX     Integer32
   MAX-ACCESS read-only
   STATUS     current
   DESCRIPTION
   "Contains the value of the statistic during the last
   sampling period."
   ::= { snmpAlarmEntry 5 }

snmpAlarmStartupAlarm OBJECT-TYPE
   SYNTAX     INTEGER {
                 risingAlarm(1),
                 fallingAlarm(2),
                 risingOrFallingAlarm(3)
              }
   MAX-ACCESS read-create
   STATUS     current
   DESCRIPTION
   "Describes the alarm that may be sent when this entry is
   first set to 'active'."
   DEFVAL { risingOrFallingAlarm }
   ::= { snmpAlarmEntry 6 }

snmpAlarmRisingThreshold OBJECT-TYPE
   SYNTAX     Integer32
   MAX-ACCESS read-create
   STATUS     current
   DESCRIPTION
   "Defines the alarm threshold for the rising sampled
   statistic."
   ::= { snmpAlarmEntry 7 }

snmpAlarmFallingThreshold OBJECT-TYPE
   SYNTAX     Integer32
```

```
   MAX-ACCESS read-create
   STATUS     current
   DESCRIPTION
   "Makes possible the definition of a falling alarm threshold."
   ::= { snmpAlarmEntry 8 }

snmpAlarmRisingEventIndex OBJECT-TYPE
   SYNTAX     INTEGER (0..65535)
   MAX-ACCESS read-create
   STATUS     current
   DESCRIPTION
   "Defines the index of the snmpEventEntry that is used when a
   rising threshold is crossed."
   ::= { snmpAlarmEntry 9 }

snmpAlarmFallingEventIndex OBJECT-TYPE
   SYNTAX     INTEGER (0..65535)
   MAX-ACCESS read-create
   STATUS     current
   DESCRIPTION
   "Defines the index of the snmpEventEntry that is used when a
   falling threshold is crossed."
   ::= { snmpAlarmEntry 10 }

snmpAlarmUnavailableEventIndex OBJECT-TYPE
   SYNTAX     INTEGER (0..65535)
   MAX-ACCESS read-create
   STATUS     current
   DESCRIPTION
   "Defines the index of the snmpEventEntry that is used when a
   variable becomes unavailable."
   ::= { snmpAlarmEntry 11 }

snmpAlarmStatus OBJECT-TYPE
   SYNTAX     RowStatus
   MAX-ACCESS read-create
   STATUS     current
   DESCRIPTION
   "The condition of this snmpAlarm entry. This may not be set
   to 'active' unless the following columnar objects exist in
   this row: snmpAlarmVariable, snmpAlarmInterval,
   snmpAlarmSampleType, snmpAlarmStartupAlarm,
   snmpAlarmRisingThreshold, snmpAlarmFallingThreshold,
   snmpAlarmRisingEventIndex, snmpAlarmFallingEventIndex,
   andsnmpAlarmUnavailableEventIndex."
   ::= { snmpAlarmEntry 12 }

snmpAlarmNotifications
          OBJECT IDENTIFIER ::= { snmpAlarm 3 }

snmpRisingAlarm NOTIFICATION-TYPE
   OBJECTS { snmpAlarmVariable, snmpAlarmSampleType,
          snmpAlarmValue, snmpAlarmRisingThreshold }
```

```
    STATUS  current
    DESCRIPTION
    "Is defined as an event which is generated when an alarm
    entry crosses its rising threshold."
    ::= { snmpAlarmNotifications 1 }

 snmpFallingAlarm NOTIFICATION-TYPE
    OBJECTS { snmpAlarmVariable, snmpAlarmSampleType,
              snmpAlarmValue, snmpAlarmFallingThreshold }
    STATUS  current
    DESCRIPTION
    "Is defined as an event which is generated when an alarm
    entry crosses its falling threshold."
    ::= { snmpAlarmNotifications 2 }

 snmpObjectUnavailableAlarm NOTIFICATION-TYPE
    OBJECTS { snmpAlarmVariable }
    STATUS  current
    DESCRIPTION
    "Is defined as an event which is generated when a variable
    which is monitored by an alarm entry becomes unavailable."
 ::= { snmpAlarmNotifications 3 }
```

Event Group

In this group an Event Table can be incorporated which the Agent/Manager has to follow when a definite threshold value is crossed. For the Event Group inside the Manager-to-Manager MIB the following object identifiers apply:

```
 snmpEvent      OBJECT IDENTIFIER ::= { snmpM2MObjects 2 }

 snmpEventNextIndex OBJECT-TYPE
    SYNTAX     INTEGER (0..65535)
    MAX-ACCESS read-only
    STATUS     current
    DESCRIPTION
    "Is the index number of the next suitable unassigned entry in
    the snmpEventTable."
    ::= { snmpEvent 1 }

 snmpEventTable OBJECT-TYPE
    SYNTAX     SEQUENCE OF SnmpEventEntry
    MAX-ACCESS not-accessible
    STATUS     current
    DESCRIPTION
    "Defines the Event list."
    ::= { snmpEvent 2 }

 snmpEventEntry OBJECT-TYPE
    SYNTAX     SnmpEventEntry
```

```
   MAX-ACCESS not-accessible
   STATUS     current
   DESCRIPTION
   "Is defined as a set of parameters that describe an event
   generated when certain conditions are met."
   INDEX      { snmpEventIndex }
   ::= { snmpEventTable 1 }

SnmpEventEntry ::= SEQUENCE {
   snmpEventIndex           INTEGER,
   snmpEventID              OBJECT IDENTIFIER,
   snmpEventDescription     DisplayString,
   snmpEventEvents          Counter32,
   snmpEventLastTimeSent    TimeStamp,
   snmpEventStatus          RowStatus
}

snmpEventIndex OBJECT-TYPE
   SYNTAX     INTEGER (1..65535)
   MAX-ACCESS not-accessible
   STATUS     current
   DESCRIPTION
   "Is an index that uniquely identifies an entry in the
   snmpEvent table."
   ::= { snmpEventEntry 1 }

snmpEventID OBJECT-TYPE
   SYNTAX     OBJECT IDENTIFIER
   MAX-ACCESS read-create
   STATUS     current
   DESCRIPTION
   "Is the unquestionable identification of the event type
   generated by this entry."
   ::= { snmpEventEntry 2 }

snmpEventDescription OBJECT-TYPE
   SYNTAX     DisplayString (SIZE (0..127))
   MAX-ACCESS read-create
   STATUS     current
   DESCRIPTION
   "Is a comment which describes this snmpEvent entry."
   ::= { snmpEventEntry 3 }

snmpEventEvents OBJECT-TYPE
   SYNTAX     Counter32
   MAX-ACCESS read-only
   STATUS     current
   DESCRIPTION
   "Comprises the number of events resulting from event
   generators associated with this snmpEvent entry."
   ::= { snmpEventEntry 4 }
```

```
snmpEventLastTimeSent OBJECT-TYPE
   SYNTAX     TimeStamp
   MAX-ACCESS read-only
   STATUS     current
   DESCRIPTION
   "Is the value of sysUpTime at the time this snmpEvent entry
   last generated an event."
   DEFVAL { 0 }
   ::= { snmpEventEntry 5 }

snmpEventStatus OBJECT-TYPE
   SYNTAX     RowStatus
   MAX-ACCESS read-create
   STATUS     current
   DESCRIPTION
   "Defines the status of this snmpEvent entry. This object
   cannot be set to 'active' unless the following columnar
   objects exist in this row: snmpEventID, snmpEventDescription,
   snmpEventEvents, and snmpEventLastTimeSent."
   ::= { snmpEventEntry 6 }

snmpEventNotifyMinInterval OBJECT-TYPE
   SYNTAX     Integer32
   UNITS      "seconds"
   MAX-ACCESS read-only
   STATUS     current
   DESCRIPTION
   "Defines the minimum interval that the SNMPv2 device acting
   in a dual role will wait before retransmitting an
   InformRequest PDU."
   ::= { snmpEvent 3 }

snmpEventNotifyMaxRetransmissions OBJECT-TYPE
   SYNTAX     Integer32
   MAX-ACCESS read-only
   STATUS     current
   DESCRIPTION
   "Defines the maximum interval that the SNMPv2 entity
   acting in a dual role will wait before retransmitting an
   InformRequest PDU."
   ::= { snmpEvent 4 }

snmpEventNotifyTable OBJECT-TYPE
   SYNTAX     SEQUENCE OF SnmpEventNotifyEntry
   MAX-ACCESS not-accessible
   STATUS     current
   DESCRIPTION
   "This table defines a list of protocol configuration entries
   for event notifications from this device."
   ::= { snmpEvent 5 }
```

```
snmpEventNotifyEntry OBJECT-TYPE
   SYNTAX     SnmpEventNotifyEntry
   MAX-ACCESS not-accessible
   STATUS     current
   DESCRIPTION
   "Is defined as a set of parameters that describe the type and
   destination of InformRequest PDUs sent for a particular
   event."
   INDEX      { snmpEventIndex, contextIdentity }
   ::= { snmpEventNotifyTable 1 }

SnmpEventNotifyEntry ::= SEQUENCE {
   snmpEventNotifyIntervalRequested        Integer32,
   snmpEventNotifyRetransmissionsRequested Integer32,
   snmpEventNotifyLifetime                 Integer32,
   snmpEventNotifyStatus                   RowStatus
}

snmpEventNotifyIntervalRequested OBJECT-TYPE
   SYNTAX     Integer32
   UNITS      "seconds"
   MAX-ACCESS read-create
   STATUS     current
   DESCRIPTION
   "Defined as the requested interval for retransmission of
   Inform Request PDUs generated on the behalf of this entry."
   DEFVAL { 30 }
   ::= { snmpEventNotifyEntry 1 }

snmpEventNotifyRetransmissionsRequested OBJECT-TYPE
   SYNTAX     Integer32
   MAX-ACCESS read-create
   STATUS     current
   DESCRIPTION
   "Defined as the requested number of retransmissions of an
   InformRequest PDU generated on behalf of this entry."
   DEFVAL { 5 }
   ::= { snmpEventNotifyEntry 2 }

snmpEventNotifyLifetime OBJECT-TYPE
   SYNTAX     Integer32
   UNITS      "seconds"
   MAX-ACCESS read-create
   STATUS     current
   DESCRIPTION
   "Is defined as the maximum number of seconds this entry
   shall live before the corresponding instance of
   snmpEventNotifyStatus is set to 'destroy'."
   DEFVAL { 86400 }
   ::= { snmpEventNotifyEntry 3 }
```

```
snmpEventNotifyStatus OBJECT-TYPE
   SYNTAX     RowStatus
   MAX-ACCESS read-create
   STATUS     current
   DESCRIPTION
   "Is the status of this snmpEventNotifyEntry. This object may
   not be set to 'active' unless the following columnar objects
   exist in this row: snmpEventNotifyIntervalRequested,
   snmpEventNotifyRetransmissionsRequested, and
   snmpEventNotifyLifetime."
   ::= { snmpEventNotifyEntry 4 }

snmpM2MConformance
              OBJECT IDENTIFIER ::= { snmpM2M 2 }

snmpM2MCompliances
              OBJECT IDENTIFIER ::= { snmpM2MConformance 1 }

snmpM2MGroups
              OBJECT IDENTIFIER ::= { snmpM2MConformance 2 }

snmpM2MCompliance MODULE-COMPLIANCE
   STATUS  current
   DESCRIPTION
   "Is the compliance statement for SNMPv2 devices that
   implement the Manager-to-Manager MIB."
   MODULE    this module
       MANDATORY-GROUPS { snmpAlarmGroup, snmpEventGroup }
   ::= { snmpM2MCompliances 1 }

snmpAlarmGroup OBJECT-GROUP
   OBJECTS { snmpAlarmNextIndex,
             snmpAlarmVariable, snmpAlarmInterval,
             snmpAlarmSampleType, snmpAlarmValue,
             snmpAlarmStartupAlarm, snmpAlarmRisingThreshold,
             snmpAlarmFallingThreshold,
             snmpAlarmRisingEventIndex,
             snmpAlarmFallingEventIndex,
             snmpAlarmUnavailableEventIndex,
             snmpAlarmStatus }
   STATUS  current
   DESCRIPTION
   "Is defined as a collection of objects permitting the
   description and configuration of threshold alarms from an
   SNMPv2 device acting in a dual role."
   ::= { snmpM2MGroups 1 }

snmpEventGroup OBJECT-GROUP
   OBJECTS { snmpEventNextIndex,
             snmpEventID, snmpEventDescription,
             snmpEventEvents, snmpEventLastTimeSent,
             snmpEventStatus, snmpEventNotifyMinInterval,
```

```
                snmpEventNotifyMaxRetransmissions,
                snmpEventNotifyIntervalRequested,
                snmpEventNotifyRetransmissionsRequested,
                snmpEventNotifyLifetime, snmpEventNotifyStatus }
    STATUS  current
    DESCRIPTION
    "Defined as a collection of objects permitting the
    description and configuration of events from an SNMPv2
    device which is acting in a dual role."
    ::= { snmpM2MGroups 2 }

END
```

5.10 Critique of SNMPv2

The development of the SNMP protocols began by using the Internet resources to administer and supervise, as a practical first step. The project began with the entry monitor functions of the Simple Gateway Monitoring Protocol (SGMP). The functionality of the SGMP protocols was considerably broadened through SNMPv1. Due to the functionality and simple methodology, the code was implemented and, with a worldwide protocol, a single market appeared which generally accepted that a Management Standard had been established. With the recognition of SNMPv2 and the position of the Management Information Base in today's market, MIB functionality will considerably increase. These developments naturally bring with them the risks that the protocols and the relevant sub-functions will become complex and therefore less cost-effective. The critics of the SNMP protocol rely on these issues for their arguments:

- Higher complexity;
- Higher overhead;
- Standard MIBs;
- Security of data;
- Low availability;
- No certification.

Higher complexity

As a result of the new ASN.1 macros and the new protocol functions, the SNMPv2 protocol is structured more clearly and simply in many respects.

This is particularly useful for the implementation and transfer of protocols. In practice, the new functions of SNMPv2 result from a comprehensive selection of new parameters which have to be taken into account when installing SNMPv2 devices. This version of the protocol contains the parameters required for every type of complexity. Cynics maintain that the first letter of the protocol name no longer stands for 'Simple', but now merely indicates 'Standard'. In many respects, SNMPv2 is based on the OSI structure. In the light of the convergence of different worlds, this is sensible. For the individual system administrator, SNMPv2 requires a certain amount of initial work in terms of new configuration parameters (that is, MIB Views, security parameters). Incorrectly entered parameter values may result in certain functions not being activated or failing to operate. Since the number of available SNMPv2 implementations is still relatively small, there is still a chance for manufacturers to develop protective mechanisms that will prevent the incorrect entry of parameters.

High Basic Loading

Integrating a network management system into the LAN does place a certain basic loading on the network. Encryption and authentication mechanisms also increase the overhead to be transferred. This is, however, compensated by the Get Bulk function. Furthermore, the network loading caused by the network management application reduces the available bandwidth for actual network data communication. This has particularly serious consequences if there is a narrow band WAN connection between manager and agent. The new SNMPv2 functions also have an impact on the CPU loading on the agent and/or management station. With the first SNMPv2 implementations in the Internet, it was discovered that the integration of the MD5 algorithm increases loading needed for processing the protocol by some 15–20%. Additional integration of the DES algorithm increases protocol processing by up to 100%. This means that under certain circumstances, the hardware on which the SNMPv2 protocols are implemented must be adapted to the new CPU-intensive functions.

Standard MIBs

The formal structures for data description introduced in the SNMPv2 are completely different from the structures of SNMPv1. This means that in the long term all MIBs will have to be converted to the new format. The full range of SNMPv2 features can only be implemented after this conversion has been made. Since the Internet community cannot afford to convert all Standard MIBs overnight, manufacturers and users will have to be prepared for a longer migration period.

Security of data

Particular emphasis is placed on data security in SNMPv2. The weaknesses of SNMPv1, namely changing packet contents, sequential accuracy and unauthorized reading of information, have been addressed, and the necessary protocol mechanisms have been integrated. These functions naturally increase the protocol overhead and give the CPU considerably more information to process. The clock mechanism, used for time synchronization between the two parties, also means that certain control mechanisms need to be implemented. With incorrect implementations, this can lead to a considerable protocol and CPU overhead.

Low availability

There is still a certain amount of confusion among manufacturers and users of SNMP products in respect of the new protocol specifications. SNMPv1 provided the first functional network management standard implemented by all manufacturers and SNMPv1 products are widely available. From the point of view of the user, an enormous wealth of knowledge concerning the use of SNMPv1 has built up. However, in the opinion of many SNMPv2 experts, the SNMPv2 protocol will bring about many improvements. It is for this reason that manufacturers feel compelled to implement the SNMPv2 protocol as quickly as possible. Users realize the advantages of the new standard but fear that the SNMP devices they have already installed will not transfer directly to the new protocol. The large manufacturers of management products such as HP, Sun, NetLabs, Network Managers Ltd and IBM are already working feverishly on transporting the new protocol. In terms of LAN terminals, the first implementations are already in existence. However, on a large scale, there is no discernible readiness to integrate the SNMPv2 protocols. The consequences and the cost which would accompany migration are still too extensive.

No certification

One problem area facing SNMPv2 is the lack of conformance and compatibility tests. So far, as in the case of SNMPv1, any manufacturer can implement the SNMP code in a device and claim that the device complies with and all the integrated protocols conform to the RFC Standard. Since there is no committee monitoring these statements, the customer is ultimately responsible for checking their truth. In the light of the complexity of material and the almost daily appearance of new extensions to individual sub-specifications (MIBs), the customer really has to trust these statements blindly. Only larger corporate groups can afford the luxury of employing highly paid experts to verify the implementation. As a result, some manufacturers of the SNMP code have decided to form a voluntary control association. They are now making the first tentative steps towards testing the source codes developed for conformance and compatibility before a larger committee. Unfortunately, none of the test results have yet been published, and the customer is forced to continue relying on rumours and suppositions as a source of information.

6

The Development of Private Network Management Solutions

The ability to support network management functions is clearly of great importance to any manufacturer of network products who is to operate successfully under current market conditions. Over recent years, SNMP has emerged as the ideal basis for network management. Accordingly, the following two strategies have been developed for integrating SNMP protocols in terms of the management station:

- Supporting a generic management platform;
- Developing a private management platform.

Generic management platforms

By complementary purchase of (or, to put it more succinctly, by supporting) one of the known generic management systems, a vendor of network components can rapidly offer a solution which is immediately available and has already been accepted by the market. The most widely distributed systems include HP Overview by Hewlett Packard, SunNet Manager from Sun Microsystems, Netview/6000 from IBM, the Lance+ system from Multinet, the NMC series from Network Managers Ltd. and the Overlord System from NetLabs Inc. The manufacturers named all offer a more or less convenient programming interface which can be integrated with private application modules. For the licensee, the choice of management system is ultimately a question of costs, existing sales and marketing goals. In terms of their functions and the applications they support, the systems exhibit very few differences. The main criterion for deciding for or against a given system is generally connected with the target markets and the available development resources (manpower). Most of these generic management platforms only support SNMP version 1. However, all manufacturers have now announced migration pathways towards SNMPv2 and have therefore begun to convert these specifications into real code. For this reason, it can be expected that all of these products will support version 2 of the SNMP protocol by the end of 1994.

Advantages of the generic management station

- Major market presence;
- Generally accepted market standards;
- Open programming interfaces;
- Migration to SNMPv2 announced or already in operation.

Disadvantages of the generic management station

- Relatively expensive;
- No optimized support for all hardware and software functions of the individual manufacturers.

Private management platform

As might be expected, the NIH syndrome (Not Invented Here) is also widely prevalent in the area of networking. Small companies, which occupy definite sections of the market or market niches, are particularly eager to distance themselves from general mainstream management applications by developing their own, private network management package. Some companies also believe that only their own implementation of certain special functions can fully support the hardware or software platforms they have developed. This type of development can be very expensive and there is no guarantee that the manufacturer will ever recoup the investment costs through sales of the system offered. In the near future, these management packages will also all be available on the basis of the SNMPv2 protocol.

In many cases, this relates primarily to the hardware supported. For example, the American firm Cabletron invested more than fifteen million dollars in the development of the UNIX-based Spectrum system. Even smaller companies, such as the German-based organization CompuShack, are trying their luck with a DOS/Windows-based SNMP system. This system is marketed under the product name CS-Care. In addition to the obligatory TCP/IP protocols, it also supports the Novell IPX protocols. A range of network management packages from different suppliers is also offered in the LAN hub market. This group includes products by Lannet, RAD, RND, Sumitomo, SynOptics, 3 Com Corporation, Ungermann Bass, Cabletron Systems and many more. These network management solutions rely mainly on supporting manufacturer-specific hardware functions and tend to neglect all-round, open, global approaches. Some of the systems are based on SNMP version 1. In the light of their availability and the discussion on SNMPv2 specifications, these manufacturers have been forced to show their colors. Either they convert their products in the medium term to the new system (which means high costs), or they freeze the system at the level of version 1. However, if a system is not being developed continuously on a large scale, it will eventually disappear from the market.

Advantages of the non-generic management station

- Generally more cost-favourable than generic systems;
- Optimized support of all hardware and software functions of the individual manufacturer;
- Alterations and extensions (customizations) can be realized relatively quickly;
- Support of special protocol and functions is possible.

Disadvantages of the non-generic management station

- Low market presence;
- Migration to SNMPv2 questionable;
- Long-term availability and further development questionable.

In the long term, it is expected by market experts that many of these suppliers will move from privately developed solutions to an open standard system after a certain period of transition. The market dominance of Sun Microsystems and Hewlett Packard is very oppressive, and these management applications will continue to set the pace of development in this specialist market segment. For reasons of cost, the often diverse and multifarious LAN market for management applications is likely to shift in the direction of more uniform solutions in the long term.

As regards agent software, the solution is unlikely to be as simple as in the field of management applications. The major manufacturers of management applications only market their own applications. However, the full realization of management functions also requires the implementation of a complete SNMP protocol stack in the agent.

Every company that has produced a LAN device has two options at its disposal for acquiring an SNMP code:

- Development of a private source code;
- Purchase the source code.

Private source code

The idea of having the code developed through in-house development facilities is often based on the Not-Invented-Here syndrome, as described above. In general, there are two reasons militating against the development of management software by the hardware manufacturer:

- Time;
- Cost.

The time factor is of inestimable importance in the development of such a complex product as the SNMP protocols. Sound development must evolve from an extensive analysis of the problems and associated boundary conditions. The time schedule needed to convert the predefined specifications into a final product is derived from this analysis. As a rule, a deadline by which the finished product should be available has also been indicated at the beginning of the project. Good software developers live with the dream of one day being able to write the perfect code, which all too often leads to the specified time limits being overshot. Specialists are seldom satisfied with a 90% solution; they try to perfect potential solutions without any regard for the time budget. This technically entirely justifiable and necessary attitude causes the collapse of the time schedule, which in its turn has negative commercial consequences because some or all of the new products offered by the firm cannot be supplied until the management software is complete. Ideally, however, the components already installed can be migrated cost effectively to the standard already sold.

The cost of private development often represents another problem area which corresponds closely to time planning. The cost of planning, development, error analysis and documentation for private developments can be unpredictably and immeasurably high. Every day by which a project is postponed because of problems or delay on the part of developers incurs enormous costs. The money lost in this way is then not available for marketing the products or for developing follow-on products.

Although the market for SNMP devices is constantly growing and promises high returns, hardware-oriented firms need to calculate precisely when and how they intend to participate in the field of management software development. The complementary purchase of ready-made software often presents more favourable options in the light of these considerations. There are currently a number of good, reasonably priced codes available, which have been developed by companies or institutes specializing in the SNMP field.

6.1 Public Domain SNMP software

In the eyes of the law, all the findings and developments from research carried out at American universities and colleges belong to the American people. These research findings are available to everyone and can be acquired in return for a contribution towards expenses. Public Domain software can be used freely and without restrictions. For example, TCP/IP protocols and the Berkley UNIX have been freely available as Public Domain software since 1983. Public Domain software is, by its nature, unsuitable for commercial purposes. One of the most well-known versions of SNMP is the SNMP Public Domain Version by Carnegie-Mellon University, Pittsburgh, PA, USA. SNMP Version 1 and SNMP Version 2 have both been published by this university. Both SNMP source codes are freely available via the Internet. One of the originators of the Carnegie-Mellon source codes is Steve Waldbusser, who was also jointly responsible for the development of the SNMP Version 2 specifications.

The significance of Public Domain codes can only be understood if one is familiar with the background. The majority of Public Domain codes were developed because no corresponding product was available on the commercial market. In certain cases however, a developer may develop an idea in which industry has no interest. To avoid leaving the code to fester in a drawer, the developer has the option of offering it to the public as Public Domain software. The classic example is the SLIP (Serial Line Interface Protocol) software by John Romkey, which was published as RFC 1055. This Public Domain code is now used by many manufacturers. In the world of communications, it counts as one of the standard mechanisms for data transfer over serial cables.

Steve Waldbusser's contribution to the development of SNMP Version 1 is closely associated with the distribution of the code as Public Domain software. It is primarily thanks to his commitment that SNMP source code is available free of charge via the Internet. The Carnegie-Mellon SNMP Version 1 was published without documentation, as is usual for Public Domain codes. The code was also not optimized for any specific application. This means that if a commercial organization wished to use an SNMP client/agent on the basis of a Public Domain source code, the company would initially have to become involved with the planning and design of the relevant code. After this, the source code would have to be transferred to the relevant CPU and operating system and optimized accordingly. After finishing the transfer and the successful completion of all tests, the software would have to be carefully documented before release and prior to the first customer installation.

Many companies and organizations are reluctant to use commercial SNMP source code products. This attitude is often justified in terms of lack of money or the relatively high consequential costs for binary licences required for the commercial codes. A number of companies still assume that the use of Public Domain software is always more cost-favorable than the complementary purchase of a commercial product. With such a complex product as the SNMP source codes, the principal cost factor is not usually the source code itself, but the associated consequential costs. The time factor also plays a significant role. Import of a source code generally requires detailed, professional and technical support in the following areas:

- Training and induction prior to importation;
- Assistance during the development phase;
- Ongoing support during operation.

Training and induction prior to importation

Even the best designed code cannot be understood unless the originator (ideally the developer) explains the important idiosyncrasies in the framework of a training session. This enables the functional modules to be better understood and speeds up the actual importing procedure.

Assistance during the development phase

During the porting of the code, questions that did not seem relevant during the induction period or were overlooked, may arise at any time. Problems caused either by a porting error or a software error may also occur.

If the advice of experts who know the code in detail can be called upon, it is much easier to surmount these difficulties and to complete the porting quickly.

Ongoing support during operation

During operation, even the best software requires ongoing extensions and new functions (*see* SNMPv1 and SNMPv2). These codes therefore require continuous supervision and maintenance. If the product was based on a Public Domain source code, it would be the responsibility of the manufacturer to implement these new functions. This, of course, involves an added work load which should actually be the responsibility of the commercial supplier.

Advantages of Public Domain software

- Low initial cost;
- Available for everyone;
- Not bound to licences.

Disadvantages of Public Domain software

- Not documented;
- No technical support;
- Difficult and costly to port;
- No repair of software errors;
- No guarantee of continued development.

6.2 Commercial vendors of SNMP

If one were to ask the technical specialists and market strategists about the possible market presence of SNMP, there would be unanimous agreement on a life span of two to three years for this experiment. With such meagre expectations and relatively unattractive future prospects, it is hardly surprising that very few suppliers have actually dared to develop an SNMP code. Apart from the Carnegie-Mellon Public Domain source code, only two commercial manufacturers offered SNMP sources on the market in late 1988. Both firms were, of course, from the USA. They were Epilogue Technology Corp. Inc. (based in Albuquerque) and SNMP Research Inc. from Knoxville. Both companies claim to have been the first to offer a commercial SNMP source code.

Epilogue Technology Corp.

Epilogue Technology was founded in 1986 by Karl Auerbach purely as an organizational consultancy and planning company. According to the founder, the field of network management was added almost by chance. To present the history of the SNMP code a little more graphically, we quote Karl Auerbach directly in an extract from his autobiography.

> 'When I was still working for the American software specialist Wollongong, I worked on the PC/IP source code, created under the guidance of John Romkey at the Massachusetts Institute of Technology (MIT), and I developed from it the first DOS-TCP/IP solution at that time. Altogether, this product was sold only twice (unit price US$ 1000). When John Romkey heard about it, he founded "FTP Software Inc." together with a few colleagues. For a number of years, I worked

as a freelance consultant, and it was during this time that "Epilogue Technology Corp." was also founded. Meantime, I was employed by a number of key firms on the development and implementation of the NetBIOS protocols based on a TCP/IP platform. This work came to light in the RFC 1001 and RFC 1002 specifications. Then I dived into the world of the X.400 E-Mail systems. At a meeting in Washington DC, I demonstrated the first X.400 products on an SNA protocol stack. Amongst others, Marshall T. Rose and Dan Lynch were participants at this meeting. I still remember some of the participant's questions. "Why are they using the SNA protocols instead of the TCP/IP protocols?" At that time, I answered out of true conviction, "SNA supports a wide range of management functions and enables one to manage and monitor the resources available. The TCP/IP protocols simply don't support these functions and services'.

'The first INTEROP demonstrations took place at around the same time. Only invited guests were permitted at the first meeting in Monterey, California. It was there that I finally met John Romkey in person. We had previously communicated with each other via E-Mail and had already developed a number of joint projects, but for various reasons, we had not yet met. During this INTEROP meeting, Dan Lynch formulated the requirements for future functions of the TCP/IP protocols. One definite component of his vision was the complete integration of management functions and specifications into the TCP/IP protocol stack. Epilogue Technology then began to work in the NETMAN Group, the first Internet Management Working Group. The first stage in the development of this project was for Marshall T. Rose, Amatzia Ben Artzi and myself to sit down together and plan the presentation level at which the OSI-CMOT protocol was to operate.'

'At around the same time, John Romkey decided to move to California to work with Epilogue. One day, John wrote a piece of router software. Since a certain amount of competitiveness had grown up between us, I took up the challenge and said that I would be able to convert this new SNMP specification into code in one weekend. Converting the specifications into code took a little longer than I had expected. In spite of my wealth of experience in the field of ASN.1 syntax and programming, it took me three full weeks to work out the basic framework for SNMP. I subsequently succeeded in implementing the first SNMP protocol on an intelligent Ethernet card (Contract for the American manufacturer TRW). In the same year (1988), at INTEROP, together with colleagues from the NETMAN Group, we produced the world's first SNMP ⇔ CMIP demonstration. As a consequence of this major event, we were commissioned by SynOptics to modify our code for their new Twisted Pair Ethernet Hub. This necessitated a complete rewrite of the code and the production of entirely new documentation. From this time, Epilogue Technology Corp has been one of the few manufacturers to offer the full SNMP source code as a commercial product.'

Epilogue Technology is now managed by Karen Auerbach. The following products are available in the field of SNMP protocols:

- Envoy
  SNMP source code based on Version 1 and Version 2.
- Emissary
  A special MIB compiler for the integration of manageable objects.
- Attaché
  UDP/IP source codes.
- Attaché Plus
  Complete TCP/IP source codes.
- Ambassador
  Remote Monitoring (RMON) source codes for the integration of RMON functions in an SNMP environment.

Epilogue Technology claims that the source codes were written completely independently from any given operating system or processor and are therefore not tied to any hardware-specific limits. Epilogue offers a technical introduction to the relevant products lasting at least two days, and guarantees that all updates and new developments in this field will be given to customers free of charge under maintenance contracts.

SNMP Research Inc.

The great competitor of Epilogue Technology was founded by Dr. Jeffrey Case under the company name SNMP Research Inc. The firm is based in Knoxville, Tenn, USA. As a result of his teaching at the University of Knoxville, Dr Case has made an essential contribution to the Internet world. He deserves particular recognition for the development of the SNMP specifications and made a key contribution to the following standards:

RFC 1028	Simple Gateway Monitoring Protocol
RFC 1067	Simple Network Management Protocol
RFC 1089	SNMP over Ethernet
RFC 1098	Simple Network Management Protocol
RFC 1157	Simple Network Management Protocol
RFC 1285	FDDI Management Information Base
RFC 1441 to RFC 1452	SNMP Version 2

The first commercial SNMP product by SNMP Research Inc. was supplied to IBM. All the products developed by SNMP Research (SNMP, UDP/IP, TCP/IP, RMON, and so on) are sold under the name 'Emanate' and are available either for version 1 or version 2. By contrast with Epilogue, SNMP Research has been working for years on the development of optimized codes for given platforms or operating systems, in addition to the generic SNMP protocol which can be transferred to all computers and operating systems. In many cases, this shortens the development time and can achieve dramatic cost reductions.

Over many years of hard work, both firms have been trying to demonstrate the advantages of SNMP. By 1992, SNMP Research and Epilogue were the only commercially oriented companies in the world offering SNMP source code.

Peer Networks Inc.

Peer Networks Inc. was founded in 1987 and set out to design a device called a 'Network Computer' which had the ability to run all seven layers of the OSI stack and network management. In 1990, Peer decided to drop its proprietary hardware platform and focus the company around its software expertise. The Peer multi-MIB SNMP agent was released in November 1991. According to the company, it was the first of its kind to employ the 'multi-MIB agent/sub-agent' architecture. The rationale according to Peer Networks is to make network management easy. All of their products are designed so that developers do not need to learn the SNMP protocol. This way they can continue to develop and create industry-leading products.

Their products are called S-2101 SNMP V1 Master Agent and Sub-agent Development Environment and S-2102 SNMP V1/V2/Bilingual Master Agent and Sub-agent Development Environment, which are applicable to SNMP versions 1 and 2. In addition to agents and development environments, Peer also have other network management products including a low-end SNMP management system called T-3001 Torpedo and a specialized sub-agent called Encapsulator S-2321 which allows the developer to have more than one V1 SNMP agent on a single platform.

If a developer buys the combined SNMP/SNMPv2 agent and development kit, a compile-time switch tells the C compiler to build the SNMP agent or the SNMPv2 agent. If the SNMPv2 agent is built, it can respond to SNMPv2 requests, and, if it receives an SNMP (v1) request, it will respond with an SNMP (v1) response.

The agent comes with the system and SNMP groups of MIB2 implemented. In addition, for SunOS, the TCP/IP groups of MIB2 are implemented. Peer's Torpedo network management station product includes most of the commonly used MIBs.

The PEER source code was designed to be portable from the beginning. As a result, it already runs on a wide variety of UNIX variants, as well as a number of commercial real-time operating systems. The code runs on a variety of chips, being independent of the hardware. Network byte ordering is handled automatically. Examples of the supported operating systems (either right out of the box, or through a compile-time switch) for their 'UNIX' distribution, are: SunOS, Solaris, SCO UNIX, AIX, Unixware, NCR System V, HPUX, Ultrix, Sequent, LynxOS, VRTX, pSOS, VxWorks, and others. Many of Peer's customers have ported the code themselves to other embedded operating systems, many of them 'homegrown'. Peer's agents were developed by them 'from scratch' and the code is not derived from any public-domain source.

The PEER development toolkit consists of the PEER MIB Compiler (it generates code as well as header files), cross-development scripts and makefiles, a very high-level API (that doesn't look like SNMP protocol, so the user doesn't have to be an expert in SNMP), and a set of run-time libraries. The run-time libraries perform a number of functions including BER encoding and decoding; SNMP COMMIT function for SETs; automatic range checking and enumerated-value checking. The user provides a set of concise MIB definitions, and 'annotates' the MIB with how the MIB variables are correlated to the C-language code that has access to the managed variables. These annotations are also processed by the Peer Networks MIB Compiler. When the SNMP GET, GET-NEXT and SET are received, the run-time libraries work with the MIB compiler output to automatically access the MIB variables as defined in the developer's code, or call-back functions provided by the implementor. Similarly, if the traps are defined with variables, or even indexed variables, in them, the run-time libraries gather up the variables and build the traps automatically, when the mgmt_trap API call is issued.

Peer also offer binary sub-agent development kits for the AIX environment, SCO UNIX, UnixWare, AT&T StarSENTRY Management Gateway and others. These are low cost and royalty free. The source code for Peer SNMP utilizes the Berkeley socket API to get access to transport services. Since Peer expect most of the operating systems to come with TCP/IP, they do not include a TCP/IP stack with the product (except for DOS).

Six months' telephone, fax, and email support is included. On-site support is optional, and Peer claim that it is not required in very many cases.

Public Domain or commercial code?

Some organizations and development departments decide against purchasing a commercial SNMP source code because of the licence fees which have to be paid in advance and the binary licence fees payable when the product is sold. Most fail to consider the reduction in development time and effort and therefore the lower costs. In America, the majority of vendors of network products have come to realize that only code developed by experts contains the functions and options needed to satisfy market demands.

The picture in Europe is completely different. Most organizations and companies refuse to make use of commercially produced SNMP codes. The following reason is sometimes given:

Cheaper and better code can be written privately

The available Public Domain code is fully adequate for the organization's needs.

In most cases, this means that the time needed (to write or to transfer the code and to produce the documentation) is completely underestimated and the availability of the product is considerably delayed. The real cost of development (in months or years of work) is often not clearly appreciated. This approach gives the competition the opportunity to bring an SNMP compatible product onto the market considerably more quickly. The organization in question is inevitably influenced by the Not-Invented-Here syndrome referred to previously.

It is interesting to note that by contrast with Europe, the majority of Israeli companies purchase commercially manufactured source codes in order to achieve rapid market presence with an SNMP compatible system.

6.3 The future

Over recent years, particularly since the mid-1980s, there have been radical changes in the world of communications. Nothing has seemed more constant than the constant change. In the not too distant past, corporate progress was dependent on telephone technology. In those days, telephones were supplied only by public, postal authorities and were installed and maintained only by them. Nowadays, the telephone market in most countries of the world is completely swamped. Neither the layman nor the specialist can claim to have a real overview of the vast and colorful range of products on offer. Changes in the world of networks have been equally rapid. In the mid-1980s, mainframe-oriented solutions were the norm. The availability of Ethernet and the Token Ring Standard have enabled the integration of many new products and functions. These new functions have led to radical changes in the world of computers. In the meantime, not only LANs and WANs, but also mobile phones, satellite communication and multimedia have become numbered amongst the challenges of the present.

Over the past decade, the communication standards of proprietary systems have moved towards generally agreed specifications. New developments are no longer created by individuals but by a large number of specialists from diverse organizations. The most widely known standardization bodies are the IEEE, the Internet community, the ITU and the ANSI. The only means of achieving cost-effective developments is through common standards which provide manufacturers with the guarantee that their products conform to the generally accepted market requirements.

In the network management market, especially in the area of the SNMP protocol, there is no doubt that SNMP Version 2 will come to dominate the future. The change-over will be initiated by users and organizations that already use the SNMPv1 code. These will necessarily be followed by other users who actively want to implement a freely available standard. The future of the SNMP protocol can best be described with a quotation from Karl Auerbach:

> 'I believe in the future of the SNMP protocol. The dynamic development of this specification has already withstood the test of time. It does not really matter whether future developments come to be known as Version 3 or Version 4. I have a feeling that we will continue to add to the functions and developments, while the SNMP protocols and functions themselves go on breaking new ground in the network world and adjoining areas. With the advent of global multimedia networks, I anticipate new technical needs which will not be covered by SNMPv2. As a result, there will have to be additions and new versions in the future.'

If we are to look into the future, we should be sure to have a clear picture of the present situation regarding SNMP. Thanks to the success of networks and the many systems operating within them, the SNMPv1 standard has been accepted. However, the updating intervals achieved by many firms and organizations have been slowed down because of the worldwide recession. It can therefore be assumed that products based on SNMPv1 will remain in operation for many years to come. The operators of network management systems should never lose sight of the need for downward compatibility.

Nothing is more expensive than having to replace network components. Even an upgrade to the latest state of technology is inevitably associated with considerable problems and costs.

However the market develops in the future, the functions of network management will remain. In the long term, the details and individual specifications will doubtless become more complex, but this is generally the result of pressure from users demanding the latest functions such as accounting, security and improved graphic interfaces. In the medium term also, SNMP management will be entering new territory (that is, Asynchronous Transfer Mode/ATM) with its more complex products. The SNMP protocol is still relatively young; it has only just reached market maturity. However, it also has a long voyage ahead of it and will doubtless have to penetrate many new and hitherto unsuspected realms.

Appendix I
Network Layers

Back in the 'Stone Age of communications', during the 1960s and 1970s, all protocols were developed according to manufacturer-specific (SNA, DNA) and organization-specific (DoD) models. In their diverse implementations, the individual models relied on network layers to which each of the services was allocated. In those days, data processing tended to be hierarchically structured and centralized. However, communication was only possible on a point-to-point basis from each terminal to the central computer.

In consequence of the revolution in data technology, the introduction of distributed systems and LAN systems, it became necessary to find new methods of communication and new explanatory models for the underlying technologies. The International Standardization Organization (ISO) began developing architecture directives in 1977. The aim was to enable communication between computer systems made by different manufacturers. In addition, this model was intended to enable the formation of 'primitive' processes such as the transfer of data or the control of input and output devices independently of the operating system of the computer or even independently of the applications used.

I.1 The Layer Model

The OSI Reference Model divides the functions and services of data transfer into seven layers. Each of the layers fulfils a certain task made available to the next highest layer as a service. The only exception, of course, is Layer 7. In turn, each layer relies on the services provided by the layer below (with the exception of Layer 1). Between two layers, communication takes place via precisely defined interfaces, known as Service Access Points (SAP). While the datastream flows vertically (that is, from Layer 7 to Layer 1 and vice versa), logical communication always takes place between the same layers of two or more computers in the network. Communication is regulated by means of a set of fixed protocols. If the data from an application (that is, Layer 7) is followed from one computer to another, it can be seen that in the source computer, on the way through the various layers, it is provided with a header and a trailer for each layer. In other words, it is 'packed'. The additional data is used for error recognition (checksum mechanism), and also provides important control information, that is, addresses or SAPs. Of course, this also creates additional data which has nothing to do with the original information from the sending layer. This additional data, however, has to be passed on to the next lowest levels or transferred to cable together with the actual information. The resulting additional overhead has a considerable influence on the throughput of data and on the performance of the network. This is not only because packing and transferring the data takes time, but also because the data has to be unpacked in the destination computer (from Layer 1 to Layer 7), in the reverse sequence to that of the source computer. If there are other network computers (known as gateways and routers) along the pathway between the source computer and the destination computer which also have to re-pack the data transferred, the true significance of the overhead of a protocol can be appreciated.

I.1.1 Layer 1

The lowest layer of the OSI reference model defines the transfer medium and the physical environment for data transfer, for which reason it is referred to as the Transfer Layer or Physical Layer. At this level, the actual physical transfer of data takes place in the form of a transparent bitstream. The access mechanisms are located in this layer alongside the topology and coding/modulation processes. Devices whose functions support only the essential transmission services, such as modems, transceivers, repeaters and media access units, operate on the Physical Layer. Repeaters link together two LAN segments at the lowest level. The signals received are simply amplified and regenerated as they pass through to the output. Repeaters are often used to adapt signals for other media (optical fiber, twisted pair, and so on).

I.1.2 Layer 2

Layer 2 is referred to as the Data Link Layer. At this level, the task is to ensure the error-free transfer of the physical bitstream. In this layer, the bits are subdivided into data packets. In addition to error recognition, it is also possible to carry out flow control here. In all LAN standards, the Data Link Layer is divided into two parts. The essential functions of the IEEE Standards 802.3 (CSMA/CD), 802.4 (Token Bus), 802.5 (Token Ring) and FDDI are located in Layer 2a, the Medium Access Control Layer (MAC). Layer 2b, the Logical Link Control Layer (LLC), is primarily determined by IEEE 802.2. LAN bridges, which are used for the logical, protocol-transparent connection of networks, operate in Layer 2. Bridges interpret the individual data packets received and effect a certain degree of routing on the basis of the information contained in the packets. Bridges can also block purely local data transfer from other networks. Another option is to configure filters, which are predetermined bit patterns for precisely predefined bit positions. If the bit pattern in a filter corresponds to the bit sequence in a packet, the bridge decides whether this packet is to be passed on or rejected.

I.1.3 Layer 3

The Network Layer basically provides the functions for routing. Using this layer, several networks can be linked to form an overall network. The functions of Layer 3 enable the construction of logically structured, hierarchical networks. The most well-known Layer 3 standard is the X.25 protocol used in packet-conveying networks. In the LAN field, the Internet Protocol (IP), the Xerox Network System Protocol (XNS), the Novell Network Protocol (IPX), the DECnet Protocol and a series of OSI protocols are used.

The devices used in Layer 3 are defined as gateways, network nodes or routers. Routers belong to a group of Transit Systems and only ever operate with a protocol located on Layer 3. By contrast with bridges, routers are always dependent in terms of their method of functioning and operating on the protocol implemented. An IP router cannot be used with non-IP protocols (XNS, IPX, DECnet and OSI). A router unpacks all data packets on Layer 3 and repacks them again on the other side of the network, together with the relevant network-specific protocol information. Routers are ideally suited for connecting different network topologies (for example, Ethernet to Token Ring (802.5), FDDI or X.25). By connecting networks and network structures, it may occur that a target network only enables the transfer of considerably smaller data packets than the sending network. When linking Ethernet (1514 bytes) to a X.25 (512 bytes), a router is needed to divide the large Ethernet packets into several smaller packets suitable for X.25. This process is known as fragmenting. The receiver then reconstitutes the 'original packet' from the many small data packets. One additional important task for routers is the actual process of routing through complex, extensive networks. To achieve this, routers send out control packets (Routing Information Packets) in order to learn the routes between networks. This enables redundant structures, for example, to be set up relatively easily.

I.1.4 Layer 4

The Transport Layer provides for transparent data transfer between terminal systems. Layer 4 Transport Protocols offer various classes and qualities of service, including error correction options and multiplex mechanisms. A further distinction is made between connection-oriented and connectionless protocols. While connection-oriented protocols (that is, TCP or ISO protocol 8072/73) guarantee safe transfer between the two terminal systems, datagram-oriented protocols (that is, UDP) do not check whether a packet is delivered correctly to the recipient. The advantage of this type of connectionless service is its improved performance. Layer 4 is considered the uppermost Network Layer or the lowest Application Layer. No devices operate on Layer 4 of the OSI Reference Model.

I.1.5 Higher layers

Layers 5–7 are described as the Application Layers. Layer 5 (Session Layer) deals with process communication, conversion and presentation of information exchanged between two (open) systems. The most well-known protocol on Layer 5 is the Remote Procedure Call (RPC) of the Network File System (NFS). Layer 6 (Presentation Layer) codes or decodes the data for the relevant system. The most well-known representative of Layer 6 protocols is ASN.1. Application-specific protocols are provided on Layer 7 (Applications Layer). Countless protocols appear at this level, including, for example, such diverse applications as file transfer (FTAM, FTP, TFTP), electronic mail (X.400, MHS, SMTP), name services and directory services (X.500, IEN 116, Domain Name Service) even a virtual terminal (VTS, TELNET, RLogin). Devices operating on these layers are described as gateways.

I.2 The Physical Network Layer

The lowest layer (Layer 1) of the OSI Reference Model is referred to as the Physical Layer. This bit-transfer layer determines the relevant transfer medium and the physical parameters for the data transfer. The transfer of data takes place in the form of a transparent, unstructured bitstream. The transfer media provide the basis for the network topology and the access procedures it supports. The various types of cable used in local networks on the physical layer can be subdivided into three categories: coaxial cable, twisted pair cable and optical-fiber cable.

Coaxial cable

In the basic band range, only two forms of coaxial cable are currently in use. They are known as Yellow cable and Cheapernet cable.

Yellow cable

Yellow cable, named according to the colour of its outer sheath, is used for the principal cabling within an Ethernet bus system. It meets the requirements of the IEEE 802.3 10 Base 5 Standard. The maximum bus length permitted is 500 m, which may be composed of several separate segments. The individual segments are linked together with connecting plugs. With lengths above 500 m, repeaters are used for signal regeneration. Yellow cable is fitted with connecting plugs of standard 'N' and must be provided with a terminal resistance (50 ohm) at both ends, to prevent signal reflections. The influence of perturbing radiation is minimized by the multi-layer, outer conductive shield.

Cheapernet cable

In structure, Cheapernet resembles coaxial cable of type RG 58 with an external diameter of 4.6 mm; however, it has better transmission qualities and complies with the requirements of the IEEE 802.3 10 Base 2 standard. Cheapernet cable can be used over shorter distances in office environments for low-cost Ethernet cabling. The maximum length of each segment is 185 m. This Ethernet coaxial cable is fitted with BNC plug connectors. The cable is connected to terminal devices with a BNC T-piece.

Twisted pair

Twisted pair cable consists of a copper cable twisted in pairs. Twisted pair cable can be used for the implementation of local data networks based on Ethernet, Token Ring and FDDI; and for ISDN, analog telephone connections and terminal communication. Typical twisted pair cabling set-ups are structured in a star shape, leading from local distribution centers to the connection sockets. With twisted pair cable, a distinction is made between shielded twisted pair (STP) and unshielded twisted pair (UTP).

Shielded twisted pair (STP)

Shielded twisted pair cable (STP) is based on twin pairs of copper wires with an impedance of 100 or 150 ohms. The twisted pairs in shielded twisted pair cables are individually shielded. This cable can be used for transfer systems operating up to data transfer rates of 100 Mbits/s. The cable is used in accordance with IEEE Standards 802.3 (10 Base-T), IEEE 802.5, in areas close to the work-place such as between floor distributors and the workstation, and ISDN (SO-Bus) up to a maximum length of 100 m.

Unshielded twisted pair cable (UTP)

Unshielded twisted pair cable (UTP) is based on twin paired copper wires with an impedance of 100 ohms. With unshielded twisted pair cable, only a joint external shield is used. These cables are suitable for local networks in areas close to the work-place such as between floor distributors and the workstation.

Optical fibers

Optical fibers are being used more and more frequently as a physical medium with Ethernet, Token Ring and FDDI systems. Many applications even provide for the use of optical fibers directly up to the data port. Because of the data security it offers, its immunity to interference and greater potential network size, this technology is certain to become even more firmly established. International standards in the field of local networks currently specify the following grades of optical fibers:

- 50/125 m;
- 62.5/125 m;
- 9/125 m.

I.2.1 Layer 2

In the OSI Reference Model, Layer 2 is described as the Security Layer or Data Link Layer. The tasks and functions of this layer include the error-free transfer of the bitstream from Layer 1 and the packaging of these data bits into packets or frames. In addition to error recognition, flow-control functions can also be implemented at this level. The Security Layer for LAN has been divided into two sub-layers: the MAC layer (Medium Access Control), to which parts of the IEEE standards 802.3, 802.4 and 802.5 (CSMA/CD, Token Bus, Token Ring) apply, and the LCC Layer (Logical Link Control), which is described in IEEE 802.2.

I.2.2 Ethernet

Towards the end of the 1970s, Digital Equipment Corp., Intel and Xerox (DIX) brought Ethernet (Version 1) onto the market. Ethernet Version 1 is sometimes also referred to as the DIX Standard. Ethernet is the most widely installed local data network in the world. It is characterized by ease of handling, a high degree of flexibility and versatility. In 1983, the basic version of Ethernet was replaced by a new, modified form, the IEEE 802.3 CSMA/CD (Carrier Sense Multiple Access/Collision Detection) standard.

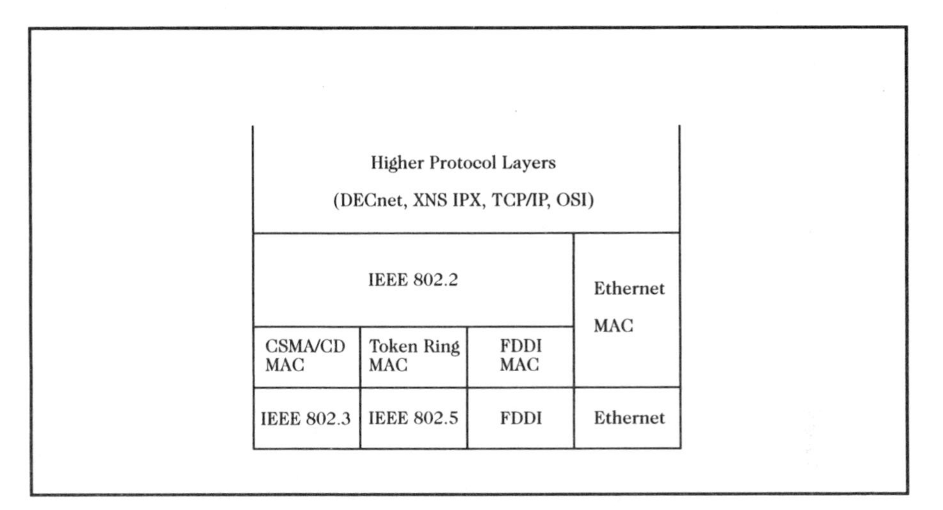

Figure I.1. The lower layers of the OSI Reference Model

This standard describes both the physical pre-conditions for a CSMA/CD LAN and the MAC Layer and its packet format. Ethernet version 2 is the adaptation of the DIX standard to the IEEE 802.3 specification.

In the original standard, Ethernet was conceived as a bus structure, based on coaxial cable, functioning as a transfer medium. For the user, these cables are easy to handle and trouble-free to install. As a result of frequent use in different environments, adaptations to other transfer media eventually became necessary. These adaptations were published as extensions to the standard. The IEEE 802.3 Standard currently includes the following sub-groups:

10 Base-5	Standard Ethernet (Yellow cable)
10 Base-2	Thin Ethernet (Cheapernet)
10 Base-T	Ethernet on twisted pair
10 Broad 36	Ethernet on broadband
10 Base-F	Ethernet on optical fiber

The Ethernet (CSMA/CD) mechanism is based on a non-deterministic method. All stations have equal rights and can gain simultaneous access to the network. In practice this means that every station checks whether data is being sent along the medium at a given moment or not (Listen Before Talking). If a station wishes to transmit, it waits for 9.6µs (the Interframe Gap) after the last transmission, before sending its data along the medium. Even during the transmission, the sender monitors the medium (Listen While Talking) in order to identify collisions. The simultaneous access of two stations to the same medium causes this type of collision. If this occurs, the two transmission signals are superimposed and can no longer be

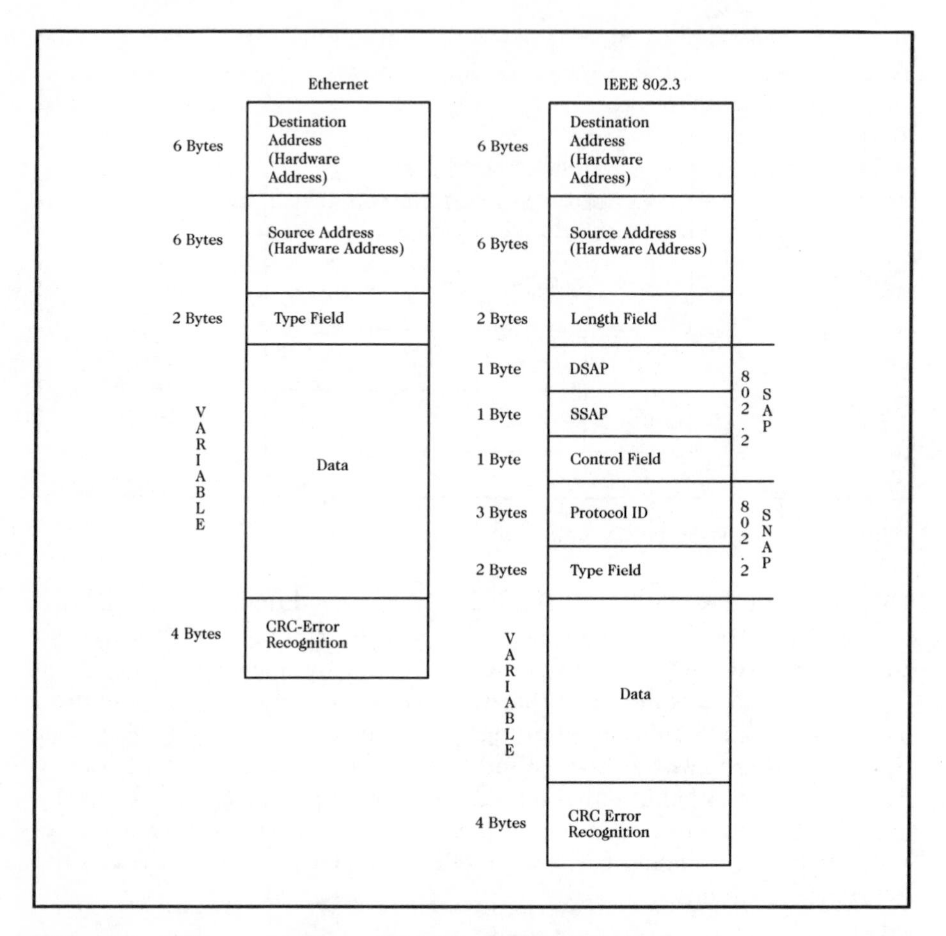

Figure I.2 Differences between Ethernet and IEEE 802.3

received (interpreted) unambiguously. If one of the sending stations identifies a collision, the transmission process is interrupted and a 32-bit signal, the JAM signal, is sent to all stations. The JAM signal ensures that all stations sending within the network are aware of the conflict. The senders involved in the collision wait a given time before resuming transmission. This waiting time is determined by a randomizer. After 16 unsuccessful attempts, the transmission is finally aborted, that is, it may possibly have to be restructured by the superordinate protocols.

Physical parameters

In terms of their physical parameters (cable length, number of segments permitted, and so on), the IEEE 802.3 and the Ethernet standards show only slight differences. At the physical level, manufacturers tend to focus on the somewhat more precise, higher- performance standard IEEE 802.3. On the MAC Layer (Layer 2a), the 'old-faithful', Ethernet version 2, is still used in 90% of implementations. The essential difference between the Ethernet Standard (Version 2) and the 802.3 Standard is in the packet structure. Both standards begin the data packet with a 6-byte (byte/octet) destination address and a 6-byte (byte/octet) source address. In accordance with ISO specifications, every workstation, every computer, every file server and any other device within a local network must have its own unique and unambiguous hardware address. A subdivision of the IEEE (Institute of Electrical and Electronic Engineers), which drew up the essential LAN standards, issues and registers addresses for manufacturers of network components. This procedure ensures that the addresses occur only once. A hardware address consists of a 6-byte, hexadecimal number. The source addresses are burned permanently into the controller (in the form of a chip). The two bits at the start of every address (also known as the High-Order Bits) have a very specific meaning. The first bit (Most Significant Bit), also known as the I/G bit, distinguishes between an individual address and an address for a group which can be addressed through broadcasts or multicasts. Depending on the application, network stations may support both types of address. The second bit, known as the U/L bit, distinguishes between universal addresses (issued by the IEEE) and local addresses (issued by the network operator). Locally issued addresses can only be used in isolated networks. Connection to worldwide transfer services, for example, is not permitted. The similarity between Ethernet and the IEEE 802.3Standard ends with the destination and source addresses.

In Ethernet, the next field is the type field, which identifies the next highest protocol.

Type-field value (hexadecimal)	Type-field value (decimal)	Protocol
0600	1536	Xerox IDP
0800	2048	IP
0806	2054	ARP
6001	24577	DECnet
6002	24578	DECnet
6003	24579	DECnet
6004	24580	DEC LAT
6005	24581	DECnet
6006	24582	DECnet
8035	32821	Reverse ARP
809B	32923	AppleTalk

Table I.1 Important Ethernet type numbers]

The data field which follows contains the information relating to the higher layers (IP, ARP or Decnet). The transfer of data is transparent, and the length of the data field is variable.

Under the IEEE 802.3 Standard, this field is interpreted as a length field which indicates the length of a data packet in bytes. In this context, the Standard defines a minimum (64 bytes) and maximum (1518 bytes) packet length. If a packet contains too little information to make up the minimum packet length, fill bytes are inserted. In this case, the length byte always indicates the end of the actual information. The length field in the IEEE packet is followed by fields for Layer 2b, in which the Logical Link Control (LLC, IEEE 802.2) is used. This requires at least three further fields (of 1 byte each) containing the DSAP (Destination Service Access Point) and SSAP (Source Service Access Point, for example, IP = 06) and a control field. If the 802.2 SNAP format is used (DSAP/SSAP = AA hex), this is followed by two further fields indicating the 802 network type (3 bytes) and containing the Ethernet type field (2 bytes). This feature enables the operation under 802.x of protocols for which no DSAP/SSAP is defined.

Ethernet bridges

In terms of their function, bridges operate on the MAC Layer (Media Access Control). Basically, they divide a data network into smaller, more manageable units. The local flow of data remains concentrated in these units, and only information destined for other units is transported from the bridge. The restrictions mentioned then relate only to these sub networks and not to the complete network. This means that there is no restriction on the size of network that can be set up. Filter mechanisms defined by the network operator enable further control over the network-wide flow of data, including the implementation of access control. In general, Ethernet uses only transparent bridges, with which the LANs can be linked. This means that the information can be passed on without any change in the data structure, if the bridge recognizes, on the basis of the address lists stored, that the receiver of the data packet is located in another subnetwork and no other filters have been set. The address lists are formed automatically by the bridge reading the source addresses for all data packets on the connected subnetworks (auto-learning bridges). Ethernet bridges also permit the realization of redundant network configurations in which there are several different transport routes between two stations, thereby still allowing the possibility of communication if an error occurs. The Spanning-Tree Method (IEEE 802.1) is used here, to guarantee that an unambiguous transmission route is selected in every case.

I.2.3 Token Ring

The most well-known form of local network in ring topology is the Token Ring. In ring topology, the terminal devices are connected together to form a physical ring. Each terminal has exactly one defined predecessor and one successor. All devices connected to the ring participate equally, and with the current access procedures, the complete flow of data is passed through each individual station. If a cable fails or even if a station fails, the entire system will crash. To counteract this serious disadvantage, a double ring is used so that not only cable faults but also the failure of a station can be survived. In fact, even with a single ring, there are mechanisms which enable a faulty station to be physically bypassed.

The Token Ring was developed in 1972 and brought onto the market early in the 1980s by IBM, under the aegis of IBM Cabling Systems (ICS). International standardization under IEEE 802.5 was not realized until the mid-1980s. The first generation of Token Ring components operate exclusively at a data transfer rate of 4 Mbit/s. Towards the end of the 1980s, an extension of the standard permitted an additional transmission speed of 16 Mbit/s. The only transmission medium standardized at present for the Token Ring is shielded twisted pair Cable (STP). The requirement for greater transmission ranges necessitates the use of optical fiber converters. Efforts are currently being made to unify the various requirements for optical fiber transmission (IEEE 802.5 draft J). The Token Ring topology consists of many stellar points connected together to form a ring. At these outer points, the terminals are linked to form a star shape. The stations in the Token Ring are thus connected in a physical and/or logical ring. Every station has an exactly defined (direct) predecessor and a successor. The Token Ring method is a deterministic approach according to which the maximum time for a station to transfer data to the network can be stated exactly. Transmission rights (the token) are passed from terminal to terminal so that each terminal is allocated a certain time in which it can send its data over the network. The token is received by all stations and – unless they have data to transmit – it is returned to the medium without change. If a station does have data to transfer, the (free) token is exchanged for a busy token. The data is immediately appended to this busy token and transferred to the cable. The data packet is then read, unchanged, by all stations and regenerated until it reaches the recipient. The target station, which is identified by its physical address, copies the packet into its memory, provides it with an acknowledgement flag and returns it unchanged to the cable. This bit pattern is passed on unchanged until it reaches the station that originally sent the data. This station checks whether the data were transferred correctly, removes the busy token from the network and places a new (free) token onto the network. Immediate transmission of new data is therefore not possible. Even in ideal conditions, a station wishing to send must wait for a complete circuit of the ring until it is once again able to transfer data to the network. Under the worst conditions, it may have to wait until all other stations have used the network. As a result of the (often) unnecessary circulation of the token around the Token Ring, a great deal of band width is lost. More advanced token techniques (for example, FDDI and 16Mbit/s Token Ring) use Early Token Release, according to which a new free token is generated immediately after sending a data packet. This means that more than one data packet can circulate around the ring at a given time.

Token Ring LANs were used initially only in pure IBM environments, but they are now beginning to penetrate all other computer environments.

Token Ring bridges

As in the case of Ethernet, Token Ring bridges also operate on the Media Access Control (MAC) Layer. At the same time as IBM presented the Token Ring in 1985, an alternative to the traditional transparent data transfer via bridges was also presented. In the Source Routing method, as this new approach was called, the information in the data packet is transferred together with information on the transport route. This shifts the decision on route selection to the terminal devices. The Ethernet and Token Ring methods both use the same address format in the header, consisting of the destination address, to which the packet is sent, and the source address, from which the message originated. With transparent bridges (Ethernet), no other address is used. However, with Source Routing, the address structure is extended to enable transmission via many bridges throughout the LAN.

Since the distinction between individual and group addresses (I/G bit) is not needed in the source address (a packet can be addressed to many stations that use the same group address, but it can never be sent from more than one given station in the network), this I/G bit is used in Source Routing as a Routing Information Indicator (RII). If the RII is set to the value 1, this indicates that additional routing information is contained in the header. The additional information may be up to 18 bytes long and describes the complete route from the source station to the destination station which is to receive the data packet. In order to fulfil this function, every LAN subnetwork must be allocated an unambiguous network number.

The routing information is basically a list of all subnetworks through which the packet must pass. In addition to the ring number, one other item of information is required in order fully to describe the route between source and destination. In practice more than one bridge may establish the connection between subnetworks. If parallel bridges are set up in this way, they must always be provided with an unambiguous identification (Bridge ID).

Source Routing

The term Source Routing accurately describes the technical implementation of the process. The sender, also known as the source, defines exactly the route which must be followed by a frame between its origin and its destination. This is achieved by inserting into the header of the data packet a Routing Information Field, which describes the complete route towards the destination. The first two bytes of the Routing Information Field are always control bytes. The first 3 bits (B) of these bytes contain information on the subsequent LLC header. The L bits define the length of the following routing information; the R bit indicates the direction in which this information must be processed. The F bits designate the maximum length of data packet that can be processed over the transmission pathway. The X bits are reserved for further user-specific information. The routing information Field may contain up to a maximum of 18 bytes of Routing Information (including the two control bytes). A Ring Number, which always consists of a 12-bit value, is combined with a 4-bit Bridge ID to form a 2-byte item of information. In practice this means that the available 18 bytes of routing information (minus two bytes for the control field) can contain a maximum of eight ring numbers. Each data packet can therefore pass through eight networks and a maximum of seven bridges on the pathway between sender and receiver. The maximum size for a configuration of Token Rings connected via Source Routing bridges is restricted to seven hops (transitions between subnetworks). In order to transfer the data packets correctly, a Source Routing bridge on every connected segment must receive every data packet. If the Routing Information Indicator in a packet received is 0, the bridge recognizes that the information in this data packet contains no routing information and is therefore destined for a station in the local subnetwork. Consequently, the bridge does not respond to this type of packet, that is, the data flow remains local and is not transferred to other subnetworks. However, if a data packet with a set RII bit is received, the bridge must evaluate the following routing information. The bridge checks whether the ring numbers appended correspond to its own ring number, that is, whether this information is presented in the Routing Information Field in the correct sequence. If all of this information agrees, the data packet is transferred to the other sub-network. No other frames can be transferred; all frames are filtered.

I.2.4 Fiber Distributed Data Interface

New computer architectures with a new generation of even faster CPUs require data networks with ever higher performance capabilities and even greater reliability. Manufacturers who consider the data network as a mere extension of the internal bus will quickly come up against the performance limits of Ethernet and Token Ring technologies. Especially in the field of CAD applications (graphics), innovative user profiles requiring very fast computer links are constantly being developed.

To meet the needs of manufacturers and users, it is clearly necessary for new communication techniques for data transfer to be developed. At an international level, new data networks are specified by standardization bodies such as the ISO and the Institute of Electrical and Electronic Engineering; specifications are standardized nationally by authorities such the American National Standards Institute (ANSI), the British Standards Institute (BSI) and the German Standards Institute (DIN). The most advanced network standard, the Fiber Distributed Data Interface (FDDI), originated in the USA.

The FDDI Standard defines only the two lowest layers (Physical Layer, Data Link Layer) of the OSI Reference Model. The basis for the FDDI Standard was drafted by the American National Standards Institute (ANSI). In defining the FDDI Standard, great importance was attached to conformity with the Open Systems Interconnect model (OSI) by the ISO. The Fiber Distributed Data Interface (FDDI) network system is based on a dual optical fiber ring with a data transfer speed of 100 Mbits per second. Computers (terminals) or, via bridges and routers, other networks (eg Token Ring or Ethernet) can be connected to an FDDI ring.

FDDI Standard

A Fiber Distributed Data Interface (FDDI) network is almost always used as a fast backbone (data highway). It is structured on the basis of a dual optical fiber ring. Up to 500 terminals (bridges, routers, gateways or hosts) can be connected to this backbone. Two FDDI stations may be a maximum of two kilometers distant from each other. Sometimes FDDI is also used as a Metropolitan Area Network (MAN) or City Network to cover requirements in towns, conurbations and large industrial complexes. The ring radius of an FDDI network may be up to 100 km. The smallest FDDI configuration comprises two FDDI stations connected by the Physical Layer (PHY). Connection to the physical medium is controlled by the access or removal algorithm of the Station Management (SMT) software.

The FDDI Standard is subdivided into four sub-standards: Physical Media Dependent (PMD), Physical Layer (PHY), Media Access Control (MAC) and Station Management (SMT).

Physical Media Dependent

The sub-standard ISO 9314-3 describes the lowest layer (1a) of an FDDI data network. This layer is described as Physical Media Dependent (PMD).

The PMD Layer determines the optical or electrical output, the jitter, the rise and fall times. Another component of the PMD Layer is the definition of the plug connection. In the early days of FDDI technology, only lengths of optical fiber were used to connect two individual FDDI computers. As a result, the PMD Standard defines only the support of gradient optical fibers of diameter 50/125 m or 62.5/125 m. The wavelength of the light used in FDDI is 1300 nm.

The PMD Standard would have become inflexible because of the one-sided specification of the optical fiber standard, and consequently new, extended PMD layers were established. These include the Single Mode Fiber Standard (SMF-PMD) supporting 9/125 m mono-mode fibers, the

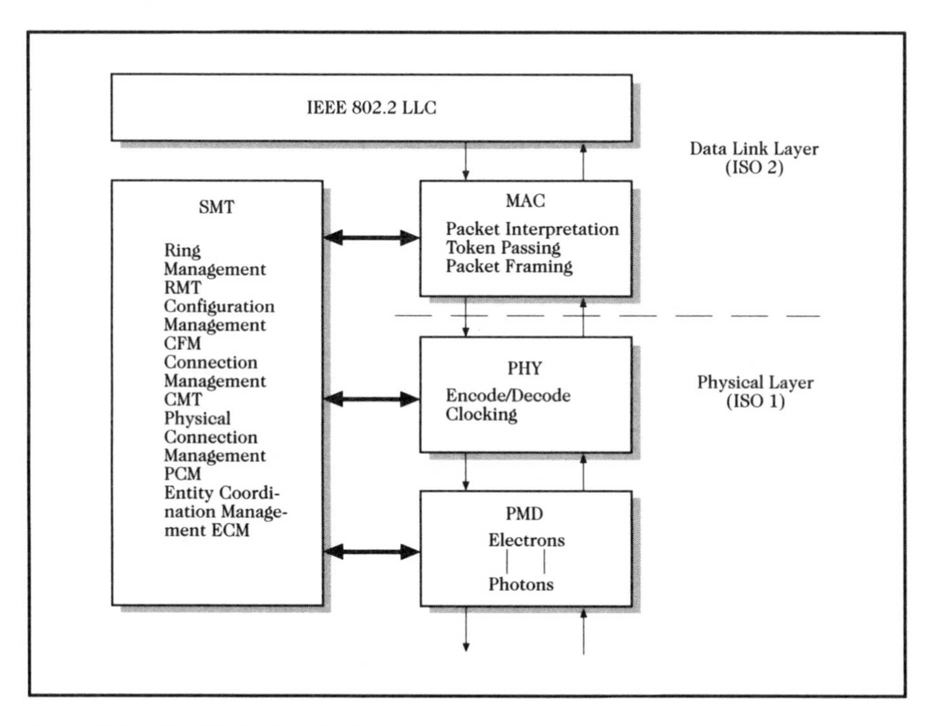

Figure I.3 The FDDI Standards

Low Cost Fiber Standard (LCF-PMD) for gradient fibers with a wavelength of 820 nm and the Twisted Pair Standard (TP-PMD) supporting shielded and unshielded twisted pair cables. As a result of these innovations, FDDI technology can be used on many physical media.

Physical Layer

The sub-standard ISO 9314-1 describes the upper layer of the Physical Layer (PHY) (Layer 1b) of an FDDI data network. The physical layer defines the complete FDDI transmission procedure and also determines the coding of the data. FDDI uses 4B/5B code, whereby four data bits are converted into a 5-bit value. Compared with the Ethernet Manchester Code, the 4B/5B code is considerably more efficient and enables transmission at 100 Mbits/s with an overall bandwidth of 125 MBaud. In addition to the functions of coding and FDDI timing, the PHY Layer continuously monitors the line status between neighboring FDDI stations.

Media Access Control

The sub-standard ISO 9314-2 describes the lowest layer (Layer 2a) of the Data Link Layer of an FDDI network. This layer is described as the Media Access Control (MAC) Layer. The MAC protocol defines the FDDI packet format, network access, FDDI address recognition, token

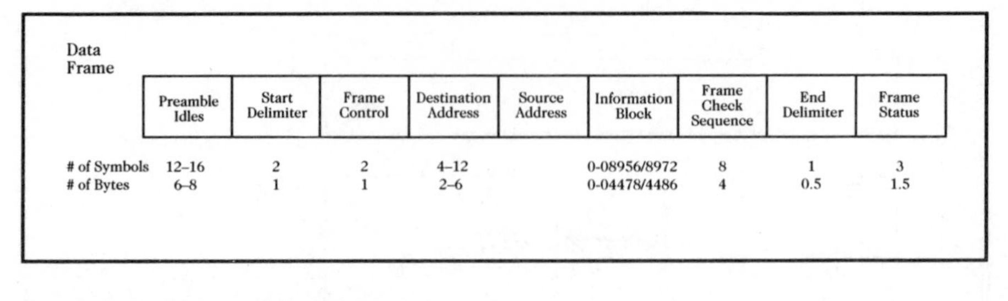

Figure I.4 The FDDI data format

administration and token timing. With stations which are integrated as active participants in the FDDI ring, the entire data stream of the ring passes through the MAC Layer and is transferred from the network input to the network output. If the MAC Layer itself wishes to transfer data, it has to wait until a token is received. The token is removed from the ring and the FDDI Controller sends the FDDI data packet to the ring. After this, another token is generated and the data are transferred from the network input to the network output.

Station Management

The Station Management defines the control of the FDDI protocol layers. The Station Management (SMT) recognizes errors, for example, loss of token, missing optical signal, optical signal too weak or CRC errors, which may occur in an FDDI network. This information is collected by the Station Management software, evaluated and, if required, any necessary response to these errors is initiated. If a (primary route) connection is interrupted between two FDDI computers, the Station Management software automatically switches the data pathway over to the secondary ring. If a token is lost, the Station Management deals with the reinitialization of the ring and the generation of a new token. Since the Station Management must be implemented in every FDDI Controller, each station individually registers error occurrences and responds dynamically to the current data loading on the ring. An additional function of the SMT is the ongoing collection of statistical data which can be passed to higher protocol layers to optimize the flow of data or for management purposes. All variables administered through the Station Management are determined in an SMT MIB (MIB = Management Information Base). Incorporation of a management agent enables the information collected from the FDDI SMT to be readily integrated into an SNMP system.

FDDI operation

An FDDI network is always structured as a dual ring topology. Under normal operating conditions (standard), all data is transferred via the primary ring.

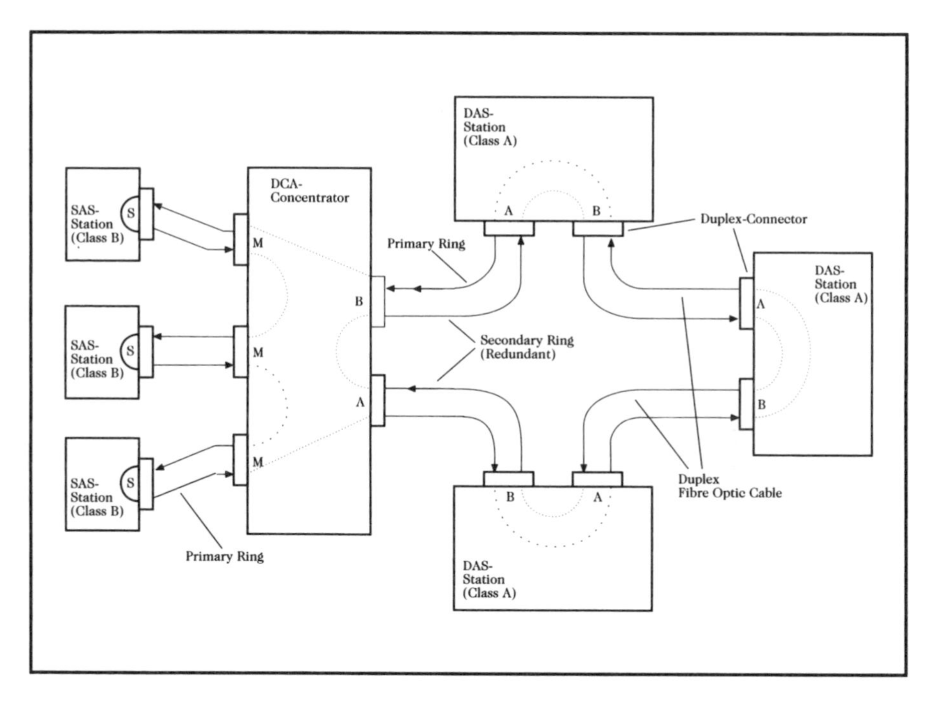

Figure I.5 FDDI ring under normal operating conditions

If an error occurs (line interruption), the FDDI stations nearest to the source of the error automatically switch to the secondary ring, thereby once again completing the FDDI ring.

After the line interruption (or error) has been remedied, the system immediately switches back to the primary ring. The connecting units (devices), that can be linked to an FDDI network are conventionally subdivided into two classes. Dual Attachment Stations (DAS) are amongst the devices included in Class A; Class B includes Single Attachment Stations (SAS).

Class A

All FDDI devices that can be connected directly to the FDDI ring belong to Class A. These devices are described as Dual Attachment Systems (DAS). The Physical Layer protocol (PHY) is implemented twice in DAS. All Class A devices have the option of rerouting the entire data flow from the primary ring to the secondary ring in cases of error. This means that the Station Management (SMT) protocol can unambiguously identify the section containing the error or the damaged station and cut it out of the ring. Even if a line is interrupted, the FDDI network remains fully operational. Concentrators are a special form of DAS which enable the connection of one or more Single Attachment Units (SAS) to the ring.

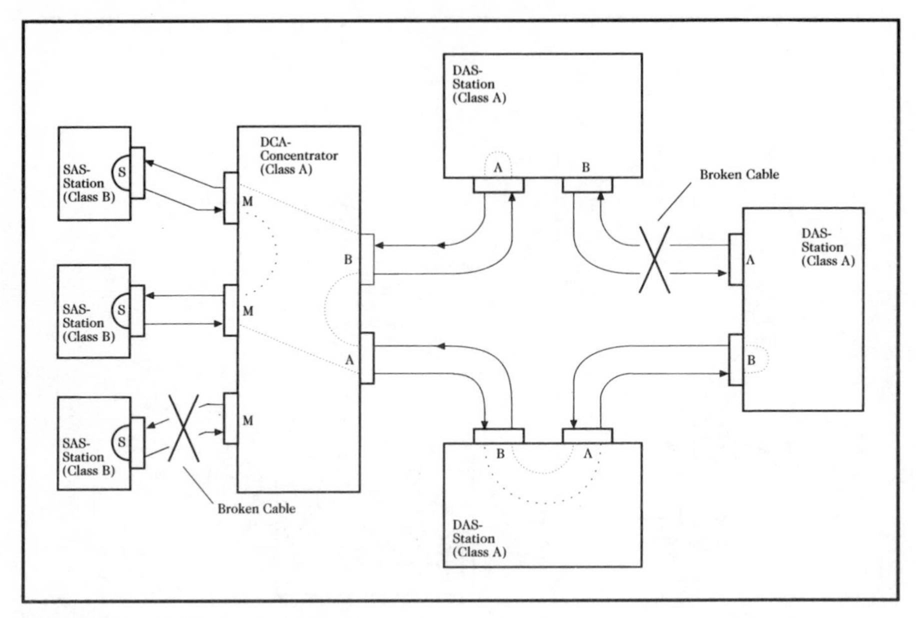

Figure I.6 FDDI ring in Error Status

Class B

All FDDI devices that cannot be connected directly to a dual FDDI ring belong to FDDI Class B. These devices are described as Single Attachment Stations (SAS). SAS are always connected to the FDDI network via concentrators. By contrast with the Dual Attachment Stations (DAS), only a physical connection (PHY) is implemented in the SAS. The SAS enables the cost-favorable connection of many simple terminal devices to the network.

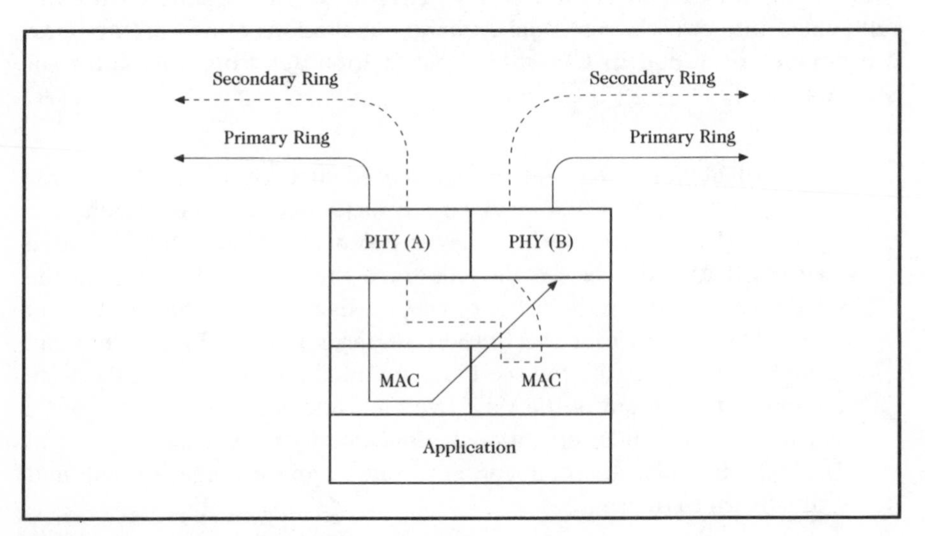

Figure I.7 Dual Attachment Station (DAS)

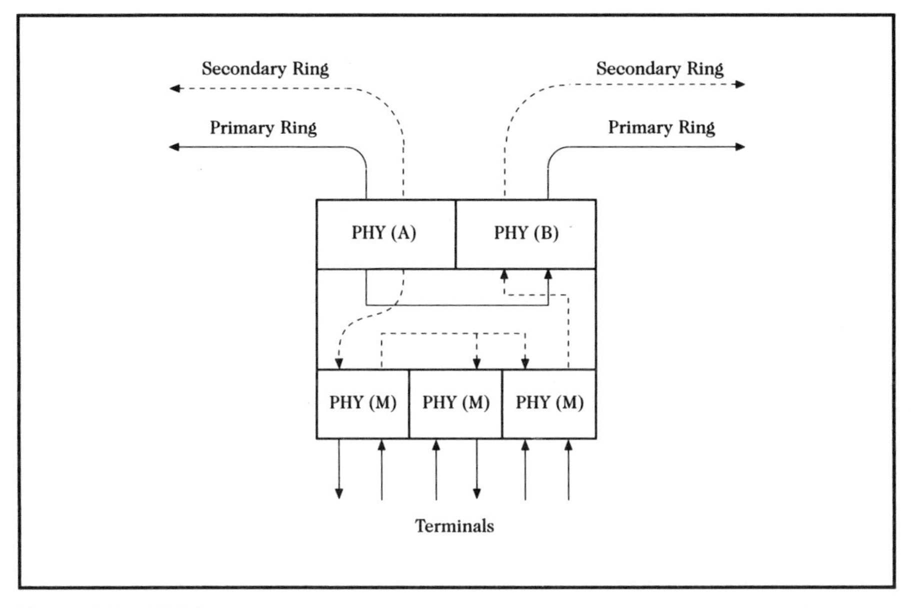

Figure I.8 FDDI concentrator

FDDI data networks are used primarily as fast data highways (backbones) between already existing slower data networks. The connection of the various data networks is usually implemented via routers or translation bridges. With both these methods, the Ethernet and Token Ring packets on the various layers are converted directly into FDDI packets. Direct coupling of FDDI computers to the network is generally via concentrators.

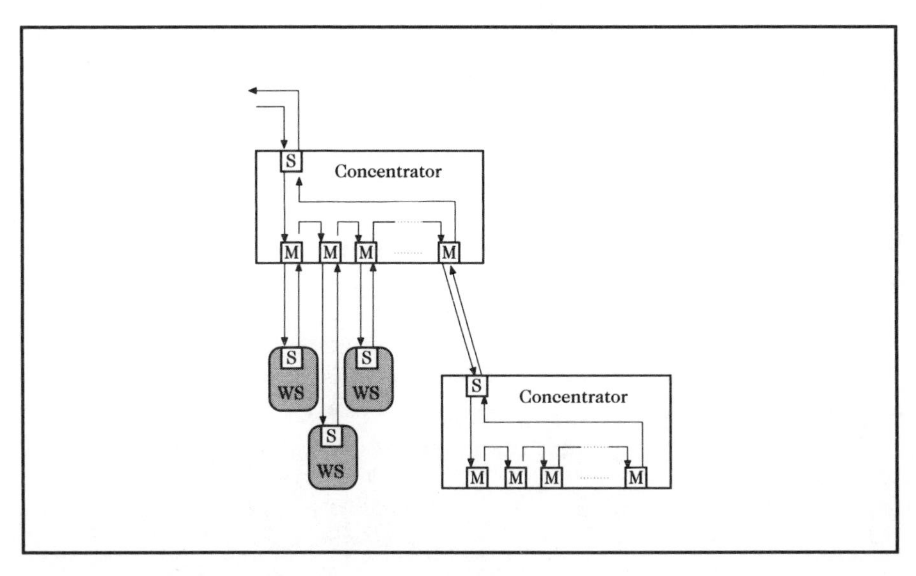

Figure I.9 Single Attachment Station (SAS)

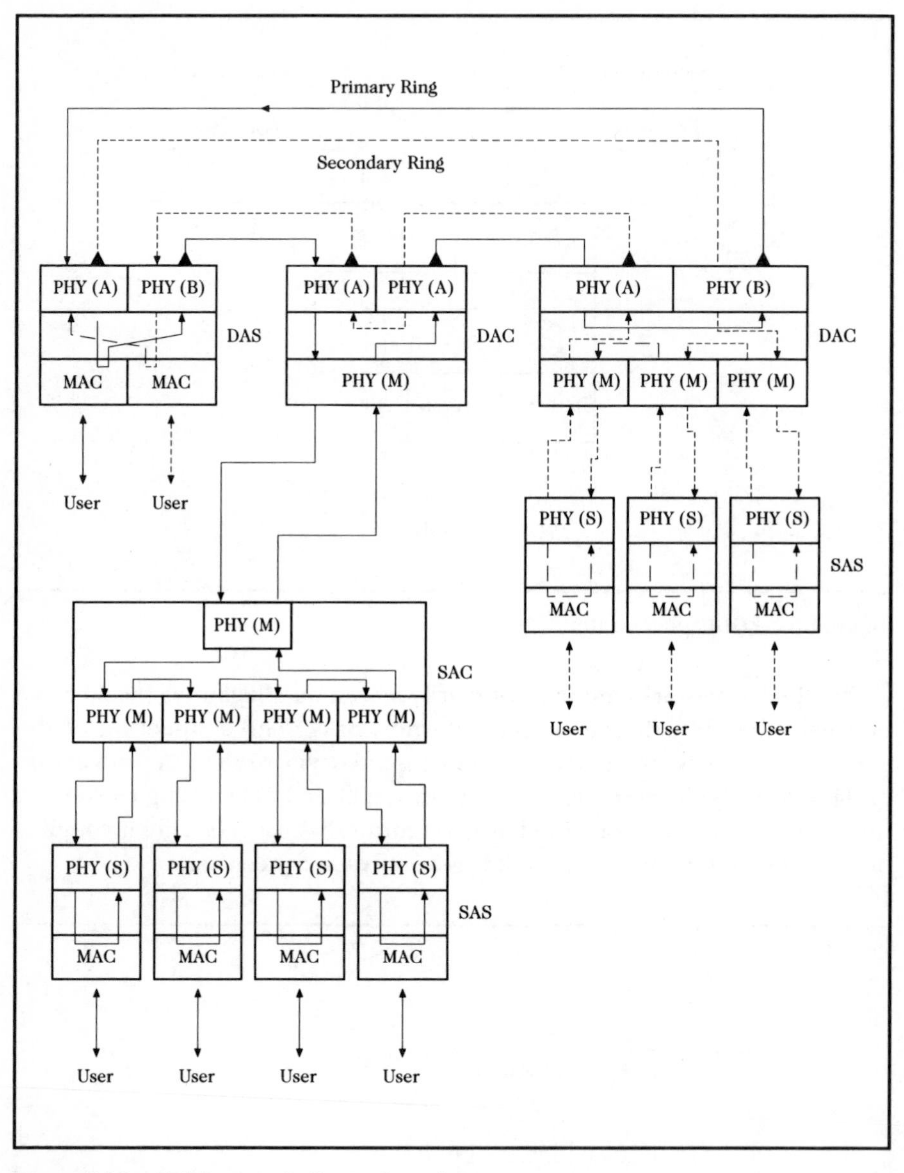

Figure I.10 FDDI network. Logical topology

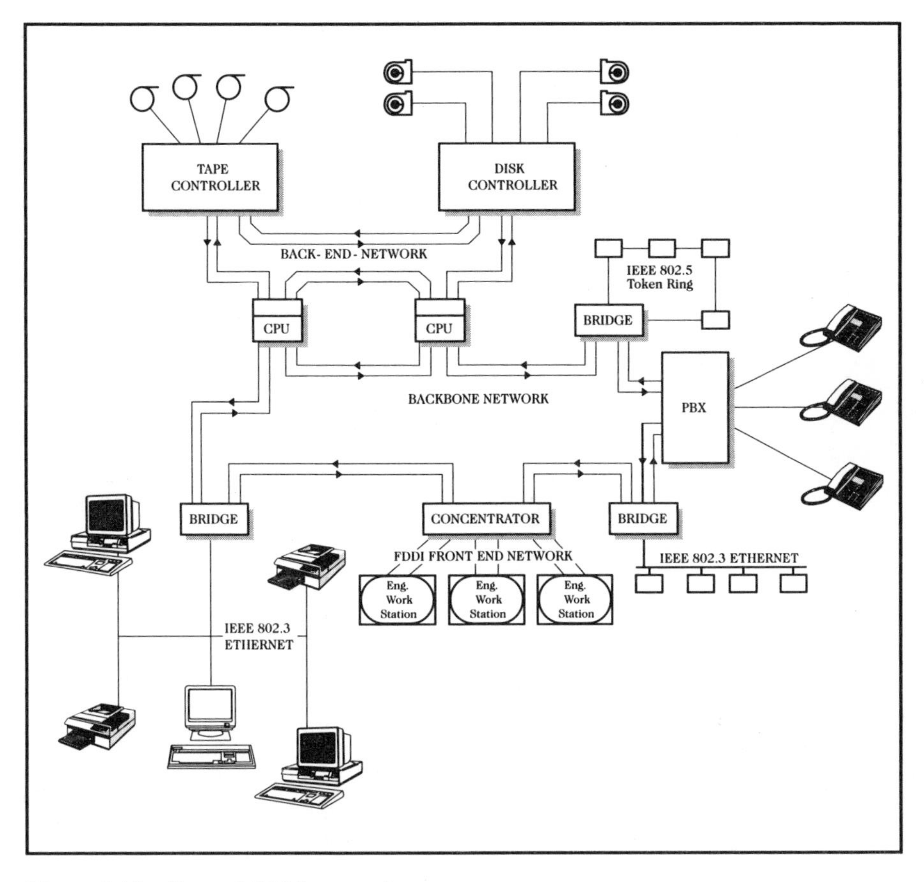

Figure I.11 Typical FDDI network

Appendix II

II.1 The higher protocols

In order to transmit data on the two lower layers, computers must agree on the transfer modalities. At its simplest, this may involve a raw data stream, in which the actual data is packed directly in a network-specific data packet and sent by means of Layer 2 mechanisms to the recipient. This strategy can be successfully implemented in certain applications; however, it is not advisable in a large-scale data network involving products from different vendors because it provides only very few error correction mechanisms. Communication between two computers is regulated via a private high-level language, the transfer protocol. For a long time, computer communication was dominated by a Babylonian chaos of languages because there were no conventions relating to these higher-level languages. The absence of standardization allowed manufacturers to develop diverse sets of protocols, resulting in several families of protocols.

Private protocols	Manufacturer protocols	General protocols
DECnet	Digital Equipment	OSI/ISO
LAT	Digital Equipment	TCP/IP
SNA/SDLC	IBM	XNS (up to Layer 4)
Netbios	IBM	X.25
XNS	Xerox	
IPX	Novell	
Xodiac	Data General	
XTP	Protocol Engine	
Vines	Banyan	
LANManager	Microsoft	

Table II.1 Important protocols

Over the years, a number of protocols which transcend the vendor-specific limitations have become established alongside the 'private' protocols. The XNS protocol specifications, developed by the American firm Rank Xerox, were published in the Xerox Integration Standard. This document defines all XNS protocols up to Layer 4. The release of these protocols enabled a certain compatibility to be achieved for the first time on Layers 3 and 4 between different manufacturers' products. For a long time, the XNS protocol dominated the LAN market as the only partially vendor independent protocol. In addition to the XNS protocol, a number of truly vendor-independent protocols have appeared over the past fifteen years. These have become internationally known under the names OSI and TCP/IP. The OSI protocols are determined by the ISO and define protocol sets based on the principles of Open System Interconnect (OSI). The OSI protocols are implemented in many products but because of the variety and power of their functions, they have not yet become established as 'communications protocols'. The protocols subsumed under the designation TCP/IP represent the actual market standard in the LAN field. TCP/IP protocols were initiated by the American Department of Defense/DoD). Their development was financed entirely through research grants. In terms of communication between computers made by different manufacturers, this standard is quite indispensable because TCP/IP is available for all types of computer and can be implemented at relatively low cost. The great variety of generally applicable and private protocols are transferred as data packets from the sender to the receiver via a packet-mediating data network. The various functions and tasks performed by a protocol enable classification in terms of 'Connectionless' and 'Connection oriented' protocols.

Connectionless protocols

Each data packet is transferred through the network to the receiver as a completely independent datagram. There is no procedure for establishment or termination of connections. The optimum route for each datagram within the network is investigated. In the process, datagrams may overtake each other and arrive at their destination in a modified sequence. A higher layer may take on the task of restoring the packets to the correct sequence and checking for errors (end-to-end check). A connectionless protocol cannot regenerate or retransmit any datagrams lost or rejected by the next lowest layer.

The great advantage of connectionless protocols is in their low overhead which is characterized by a high net data transfer rate.

Connection-oriented protocols

The following services are provided by connection-oriented protocols: secure establishment of connection, maintenance of the connection throughout the data transfer and secure termination of the connection. The data transferred over the connection is numbered continuously, checked for errors and monitored in terms of time. Faulty or lost data is retransmitted. As a result of the error handling mechanisms and the high protocol overhead, connection-oriented protocols are considerably slower than connectionless protocols. However, their advantage is in transferring large quantities of data or transmitting through transport media that are subject to high rates of error.

II.2 XNS protocols

The Xerox Network Standard protocols, better known as the XNS protocols, were developed in the late seventies and early eighties by the American manufacturer Xerox Corporation. The development of XNS protocols was carried out in the Xerox Laboratory in the Palo Alto Research Center, and they are also sometimes referred to as PARC protocols. In 1980, the XNS protocols were published in the Xerox System Integration Standard, up to Layer 4 of the OSI Reference Model. Almost all vendors built their first generation of LAN devices on the basis of these protocols.

Level 0 protocols

The Level 0 protocols of the XNS protocol define Layer 1 and Layer 2 (the various transmission mechanisms and the Media Access Control) of the OSI Reference Model. In XNS terminology, these protocols are described as Transmission Media Protocols. The most well-known Level 0 protocols are X.25, the IEEE 802.x networks (IEEE 802.3, CSMA/CD; IEEE 802.5, Token Ring), Ethernet, Netbios networks, Serial Lines, ARCNET Networks, Hyperchannel networks and FDDI networks.

Level 1 protocols

Level 1 protocols correspond to the functions of the ISO Layer 3 and are also referred to as the Transport Protocols of the first XNS level. With the XNS protocol, the Internetwork Datagram Protocol (IP) is located on this level. This is based on the services of ISO Layer 2 and is completely independent of the lower layers. The XNS protocol undertakes address and routing functions and enables datagrams to be sent.

Level 2 protocols

The XNS protocols located on the Transport Layer (Layer 4) are described as Level 2 protocols. Level 2 protocols are also known as 'Transport Protocols of the Second XNS Level'. There are five protocols on XNS Level 2: Echo Protocol, Error Protocol, Packet Exchange Protocol, Sequenced Packet Protocol and Routing Information Protocol. The Echo Protocol is used for testing a connection between communicating partners. The Error Protocol is used for sending error and status messages between communicating partners. Packet Exchange Protocol provides an unsecured transport mechanism; by contrast, Sequenced Packet Protocol supports a complete, secured, error-free transport service with full end-to-end control. Routing Information Protocol supports automatic route selection (routing) in LANs and WANs.

Level 3 protocols

The XNS protocols located on Layers 5 and 6 are known as Level 3 protocols. In XNS terminology, Level 3 protocols are referred to as Control Protocols. The XNS protocols above the Transport Layer have not been published by Xerox. Consequently, the manufacturers of XNS-based devices have had to implement their own vendor-specific Level 3 protocols.

Level 4 protocols

The XNS protocols implemented on Layer 7 are known as Level 4 protocols and are also referred to as Application Protocols. Since Xerox has not published the Level 4 protocols, there are a number of implementations of the XNS Application programs.

PX/SPX protocols

For its PC-LAN operating systems (Novell Netware), the American software and hardware manufacturer Novell Corporation Inc. uses a modified form of

7	Application	Level 4 Protocol (Application-Protocol)	Virtual Terminal
6	Presentation	Level 3 Protocol (Control-Protocol)	Courier Filling Printing Clearing House
5	Session		
4	Transport	Level 2 Protocol (Transport-Protocol)	Echo Error Sequenced Packet Packet Exchange Routing Information (RIP)
3	Network	Level 1 Protocol (Transport-Protocol)	Internet Datagram Protocol (P)
2	Logical Connection	Level 0 Protocol (Transmission Media-Protocol)	Ethernet Token Ring FDDI
1	Physical Connection		

Figure II.1 The OSI Reference Model and the corresponding XNS protocols

the XNS protocols. Novell Netware supports the following protocols: Medium Access Protocols, Internet Packet Exchange Protocol, Routing Information Protocol, Service Advertising Protocol and Netware Core Protocol. The Novell Netware Medium Access Protocols are located on the lowest two layers of the OSI Reference Model. These protocols support a number of network topologies (Ethernet, Token Ring, FDDI and ARCNET). The Internet Packet Exchange Protocol (IPX) in Novell Netware is used on Layer 3. The Internet Packet Exchange Protocol is a modification of the Internetwork Datagram Protocol developed by Xerox. The Novell Netware Routing Information Protocol (RIP) operates on Layer 4 of the OSI Reference Model. The Netware RIP protocol is used for finding the fastest and best connection between Netware routers. The Netware RIP protocol is a variant of the Xerox RIP protocol. The Service Advertising Protocol (SAP) enables the periodic announcement of Netware services via the network. The Netware Core Protocol provides services such as Connection Control and Service Request Encoding between clients and servers.

II.3 DECnet protocols

As a standard component of the Digital Networking Architecture (DNA), the DECnet protocols (DECnet Phase 1) were developed by the American manufacturer Digital Equipment Corporation (DEC) in 1976. DECnet Phase 1 enabled file transfer between two PDP-11 minicomputers. DECnet Phase 2 enabled communication with other computers (DEC-10, DEC-20, VAX). The functions were limited to pure point-to-point connections. DECnet Phase 3 was published in 1980 and introduced additional functions, such as routing and network management. A maximum of 255 computers could be supported by a network. Together with Intel and Xerox, DEC was one of the initiators of the Ethernet Standard. These companies are sometimes known as the DIX Group. In 1982, this distributed, combined communication medium was integrated for the first time in DECnet Phase 4 and used consistently for connection between DEC computers. Alongside LAN technology, the X.25 protocols used in the context of the Wide Area Network (WAN), a number of gateway functions (DECnet ⇔ SNA) and the support of large-scale distributed network structures were also integrated. DECnet Phase 4 is the most widely distributed variant of DECnet. Since 1989, a full TCP/IP protocol set has been available as an option for DEC computers. DECnet Phase 5 has been on the market since 1991 and may be interpreted as an expression of DEC's OSI strategy.

DECnet Phase 4

The DECnet Phase 4 of the DECnet Network Architecture (DNA) is based primarily on the Ethernet components manufactured by DEC. The connection between LANs is established via repeaters, bridges or routers. The DECnet nodes communicate with the LAN and WAN via separate physical controllers. As connecting mechanisms to the WAN, telephone lines (modems) and Packet Switched Public Data Networks (PSPDN) are supported via X.25. Three different Data Link Modules are integrated on the Data Link Layer (Layer 2), with different protocols in each case. The first module enables communication via point-to-point or multi-point connections on the basis of the Digital Data Communications Message Protocol (DDCMP). The DDCMP is a character-oriented protocol and can be used in asynchronous or synchronous mode. The second Data Link Layer module is used for communication with X.25 networks and supports the Link Access Procedure Balanced (LAPB) in accordance with ISO 7776. LAPB is a subset of the High-level Data Link Control (HDLC) protocol described in the standard ISO 7809. LAPB and HDLC are both synchronous communication procedures. As an additional Data Link Layer Module, communication via Ethernet is supported in DECnet Phase 4. By contrast with other communication protocols, DECnet Phase 4 is not capable of communicating with IEEE 802.3 devices. The Network Layer (DECnet Routing Protocol/DRP), Transport (DECnet End Communication

<table>
<tr><td>7</td><td>Application</td><td>Network Information and Control Exchange (NICE)
Command Terminal Protocol (CTERM)
Mail-11 Message Handling-Protocol
Data Access-Protocol (DAP)
Network Management</td></tr>
<tr><td rowspan="2">6

5</td><td>Presentation</td><td>Remote File Access Routines</td></tr>
<tr><td>Series</td><td>DNA Session Control</td></tr>
<tr><td>4</td><td>Transport</td><td>DECnet End Communication Layer (ECL)
Network Service Protocol (NSP)</td></tr>
<tr><td>3</td><td>Network</td><td>Routing-Module
DECnet Routing Protocol (DRP)</td></tr>
<tr><td>2</td><td>Logical Connection</td><td>DDCMP   LAPB   ETHERNET</td></tr>
<tr><td>1</td><td>Physical Connection</td><td>Line Controller for:
Ethernet
Point-to-Point Connections
Point-to-Multipoint
Telephone</td></tr>
</table>

Figure II.2 The OSI Reference Model and the DECnet Phase 4 Protocols

Layer/ECL, with Network Service Protocol/NSP) and Session Layer (Session Control Layer) are located above the Data Link Layer. These protocols do not correspond to any international standard and have not been published by DEC. The Application Layer in DECnet Phase 4 is known as Decnet Network Application and, like all the other protocols, it contains a range of applications. The most frequently used applications are the Data Access Protocol (DAP) and

<table>
<tr><td>7</td><td>Application</td><td>CTERM
NICE
MAIL
DAP
Network
Management</td><td>X.400
FTAM
CMIP</td></tr>
<tr><td>6</td><td>Presentation</td><td rowspan="2">DNA
Session
Control</td><td>OSI Presentation
(ASN.1)</td></tr>
<tr><td>5</td><td>Series</td><td>OSI Session
(X.25)</td></tr>
<tr><td rowspan="2">4</td><td rowspan="2">Transport</td><td colspan="2">Common Transport Interface</td></tr>
<tr><td>Network Services
Protocol (NSP)</td><td>OSI Transport
(X.24)</td></tr>
<tr><td>3</td><td>Network</td><td colspan="2">OSI CLNM OSI CONS

ISO 8473 CLNP
ISO 8348 CONS
ISO 9542 ES-IS Protocol
ISO 10584 IS-IS Protocol</td></tr>
<tr><td>2</td><td>Logical
Connection</td><td colspan="2">DDCMP LAPB ETHERNET LLC</td></tr>
<tr><td>1</td><td>Physical
Connection</td><td colspan="2">Telephone
Ethernet
Point-to-Point
Point-to-Multipoint
FDDI
Token Ring 802.5
CSMA/CD 802.3</td></tr>
</table>

Figure II.3 The OSI Reference Model and the DECnet Phase 5 protocols

the Command Terminal Protocol (CTERM). The DAP protocol enables access to data in a remote computer. CTERM is used for interactive communication between computers. One example is the Set Host command, which enables a remote terminal to log into a computer and to give the computer the impression that a local terminal is communicating with it.

This function is comparable with Telnet in the context of TCP/IP. The DAP and CTERM Services have been supplemented with a series of additional services, such as the Mail-11 Message Handling Protocol. The range of applications also includes Videotext, Remote Console, Diskless Bootservices and Bulletin Boards.

Two other protocols used in DECnet Phase 4 are the Local Area Transport protocol (LAT) and the Maintenance Operations Protocol (MOP). MOP and LAT are pure Data Link Layer protocols and communicate directly with the applications, bypassing Layers 3–5. The Local Area Transport Protocol is used for connecting terminals and printers via Terminal Server over Ethernet. The Maintenance Operations Protocol is responsible for booting Remote Diskless Clients via the network.

DECnet Phase 5

DECnet Phase 5 was announced in 1987, but was not actually released until 1991. Phase 5 is also referred to as DECnet/OSI, and as this name suggests, DEC is signalling its future strategic move towards OSI. In order to ensure that the many DEC users enjoy security of investment in terms of downward compatibility with older versions, DEC has included all DECnet Phase 4 and TCP/IP protocols in phase 5. In the long term, DEC users are to be provided with a complete OSI stack. DECnet Phase 5 does not only support Standard Ethernet; it also supports the IEEE 802.3 version, FDDI, IEEE 802.3 and the HDLC protocol on Layers 1 and 2. For the first time, modems (V.25 or Hayes compatible) can be fully integrated into a DEC concept. On the Data Link Layer, DEC supports full LLC and HDLC protocols. The DECnet/OSI protocol on the Network Layer corresponds to ISO standard 8473 (Connectionless Mode Network Service/CLNS) and ISO standard 8348 (Connection Mode Network Service/CONS). End-System-to-Intermediate-System (ES-IS) routing and IS-IS routing are fully supported. On the Transport Layer, DEC has implemented the OSI Transport Protocol (TP) in accordance with ISO 8073. Transport classes TP0, TP2 and TP4 are supported. In addition, the NSP protocol is supported in order to ensure communication between Phase 4 and Phase 5 devices. Above the Transport Layer, the protocol stack divides into two areas. DEC private protocols are used for communication between DEC machines. Pure OSI applications are provided for communicating with the 'rest of the world'. The OSI applications supported include the well-known File Transfer Access and Management (FTAM), X.400 Electronic Messaging and the Common Management Information Protocol (CMIP).

II.4 TCP/IP protocols

The protocols included under the heading 'Transmission Control Protocol/Internet Protocol' (TCP/IP) currently represent the *de facto* market standard in the LAN field, because TCP/IP is available for all major types of computer.

TCP/IP Standards

All developments relating to the TCP/IP protocols are coordinated by the Internet Engineering Task Force (IETF) and the ARPA Internet Advisory Board (IAB). After extensive tests on the ARPANET, the new protocol components are published by the IAB as technical innovations in the Internet Experiment Notes (IENs) or Request for Comments (RFCs).

These specifications (RFCs) used formerly to be adopted by the US Department of Defense (DoD) as a basis for the MIL standards for the Defense Data Network (DDN). The MIL standards describe the same functions as the RFCs, but they give more detail.

RFC 826	Address Resolution Protocol (ARP)
RFC 791	Internet Protocol (IP)
RFC 792	Transmission Control Messages Protocol (ICMP)
RFC 786	User Datagram Protocol (UDP)
RFC 793	Transmission Control Protocol (TCP)
RFC 854	Virtual Terminal Protocol (TELNET)
RFC 850	File Transfer Protocol (FTP)
RFC 821	Simple Mail Transfer Protocol (SMTP)

Table II.2 Request for Comments

MIL-STD 1777	IP
MIL-STD 1778	TCP
MIL-STD 1780	FTP
MIL-STD 1781	SMTP
MIL-STD 1782	TELNET

Table II.3 MIL Standards

Protocols

The architecture of TCP/IP is based on the DoD architectural model. This communications model originated in the mid-1970s and defines four levels of communication: Network Access Protocols, Internetwork Protocols, Transport Protocols and Application Protocols. TCP/IP protocols currently tend to be portrayed, with a greater or lesser degree of success, in terms of the OSI Reference Model.

Network Access Protocols

Network Access Protocols define Layer 1 and Layer 2 (the various transmission mechanisms and the Media Access Control) of the OSI Reference Model. The best known Network Access Protocols are the X.25 network, the IEEE 802.x networks (IEEE 802.3, CSMA/CD; IEEE 802.5, Token Ring), Ethernet, Netbios networks, Serial Lines, ARCNET networks, Hyperchannel networks and the FDDI networks.

Internetwork protocols (Layer 3)

The TCP/IP protocols are based on the services of ISO Layer 2 and are completely independent of the lower layers. The following protocols operate on the Internetwork Layer: the Address Resolution Protocol (ARP), the Reverse Address Resolution Protocol (RARP), the Internet Protocol (IP) and the Internet Control Message Protocol (ICMP). The following routing protocols are also located on the Network Layer: Exterior Gateway Protocol (EGP), Routing Information Protocol (RIP) and Open Shortest Path First Protocol (OSPF).

7	Application	Applications Protocol	TELNET FTP RLogin SMTP Socket Lib.
6	Presentation		
5	Series		
4	Transport	Transport Protocol	TCP UDP
3	Network	Internetwork Protocol	EGP,RIP IP ICMP ARP RARP
2	Logical Connection	Network Access Protocol	Ethernet Token Ring FDDI
1	Physical Connection		

Figure II.4 The OSI Reference Model and the TCP/IP protocols

Transport protocols (Layer 4)

Only two protocols are used to secure communication on the Transport Layer: the Transport Control Protocol (TCP) and the User Datagram Protocol (UDP).

Higher protocols

The Application Protocols correspond to OSI Layers 5–7. Of the wide range of protocols located on these layers, the following are used most frequently: File Transfer Protocol (FTP), virtual terminal access (TELNET), Remote User Login (Rlogin), electronic mail (SMTP), various name services (Domain Name, IEN 116), Boot Protocol (BootP), Simple Network Management Protocol (SNMP) and Network File System (NFS).

II.5 OSI protocols

Open Systems Interconnect (OSI) protocols are among the most recent protocols to enter the world of communications. After the acceptance of the OSI Reference Model as a standard in 1983, the international standardization bodies (ISO and CCITT) began 'filling in' the individual layers. Since the intention is to create unified protocols rather than manufacturer-specific applications and protocols, the publication of these protocols has been somewhat protracted. The first protocols to be agreed in 1984 were the Transport Protocols and the Session Protocol. These were followed in the same year by the first OSI application, X.400, which supports the exchange of E-Mail. New protocols and services offering even higher performance are constantly being developed, and some manufacturers (DEC, HP, Apple, Retix, The Wollongong Group, 3Com, IBM, and so on) are already beginning to integrate the ISO/OSI protocols either partially or fully.

Layer 1
On the Physical Layer, the ISO/OSI protocols support every conceivable mechanism, starting with the simple modem and extending up to the 2 GBit/s Cross Connect Switch.

Layer 2
In keeping with the concept of maximum variety on Layer 1, an equally diverse range of Data Link Layer Protocols must be supported on Layer 2. The most well known protocols are: High-level Data Link Control (HDLC) – ISO 7809, Logical Link Control (LLC) – ISO 8802-2, the CSMA/CD process – ISO 8802-3, Token Bus – ISO 8802-4, Token Ring – ISO 8802-5, FDDI – ISO 9314-1–ISO 9314-3, and LAN MAC Sublayer – ISO 10038.

Layer 3

The Network Layer provides routing functions which enable the construction of logically structured, hierarchical networks. The Network Layer in the ISO/OSI protocols is divided into two sections. Both Connectionless Services (ISO 8473) and Connection Mode Services (ISO 8348) are supported. Additional specifications which support the packet-mediating X.25 protocol (ISO 8878 and ISO 8208) are also included. The OSI Routing Protocols, the End System-to-Intermediate System (ES-IS) – ISO 9542 and the Intermediate System-to-Intermediate System (IS-IS) – ISO 10584 are to be found on this layer.

Layer 4

The Transport Layer ensures transparent connection between end systems. Layer 4 is also arranged in two sections supporting connection-oriented (ISO 8073) and connectionless (ISO 8602) services. The protocols of Layer 4 offer different classes and qualities of service.

Subdivision of the Transport Protocol into classes

Transport Class 0 (TP0) Simple Class

Class 0 provides the simplest type of transport connection. This class presupposes a reliable Network Service on Layer 3. In order to use TP0, the Connection Mode Network Service (CONS) must be implemented. The most well-known application using TP0 is the Telex Service.

Transport Class 1 (TP1) Basic Error Recovery Class

Class 1 was developed by the CCITT for the X.25 protocol. TP1 also presupposes the implementation of Connection Mode Network Service (CONS).

Transport Class 2 (TP2) Multiplexing Class

Class 2 is based on Class 0, but offers multiplex mechanisms and a flow control across the connection. TP2 also presupposes the implementation of Connection Mode Network Service (CONS).

Transport Class 3 (TP3) Error Recovery and Multiplexing Class

Class 3 provides a combination of Classes 1 and 2. The implementation of Connection Mode Network Service (CONS) is assumed.

Transport Class 4 (TP4) Error Detection and Recovery Class

Class 4 is the only transport class based on the Connectionless Mode Network Service (CLNM). It provides all services that ensure secure end-to-end control via a data network. TP4 is used primarily when operating on LANs.

Layer 5

The Session Layer is also divided into two sections consisting of Session protocols for connectionless services (ISO 8326) and connection-oriented services (ISO 8327). Layer 5 deals with process communication and the conversion and presentation of information exchanged between two systems.

Layer 6

The services of the Presentation Layer are defined in the standard ISO 8822. Layer 6 codes or decodes the data for the relevant system. The Presentation Layer protocol is specified in ISO 8823. ASN.1 is used as the coding and decoding language. The standards for ASN.1 are defined in ISO 8824 and 8825.

Layer 7

Application-specific protocols are prepared on the Application Layer. A vast number of protocols are located on this layer, the most important of which are File Transfer Access and Management Protocol (FTAM – ISO 8571), Electronic Mail (X.400, MHS – ISO 10021), Name and Directory Service (X.500 – ISO 9594), Virtual Terminal (VTS – ISO 9040, 9041), Common Management Information Protocol (CMIP – ISO 9596) and Common Management Information Service (CMIS – ISO 9595).

X.400

The X.400 standard describes a complete set of protocols for exchanging electronic messages and the services they contain. A model, known as the Message Handling System (MHS), has been established for Electronic Messaging. The basic core of the MHS is the Message Transfer System (MTS). MTS is used for transferring the various messages within the MHS system and consists essentially of several Message Transfer Agents (MTA). The MTAs route, store and transport the messages through the MTS. Other important components of the MHS are the User Agents (UA) and the optional Message Store (MS). Every message transported through the MTS comprises a document content (Message Section) and a Message Envelope. The task of the User Agent (UA) is to structure the content of the letter (Message Format and Content), to pack the message in an envelope, to send it, and unpack and correctly interpret the message after receipt. The Message Store (MS) represents an intermediate memory for messages delivered by the MTA, but not yet accepted by the recipient UA.

The X.400 specification was published in 1984 and considerably extended in 1988. The Message Store function was added in the 1988 standard and a number of protocols were defined more precisely. Supplementary functions were also added, that is, security and an interface with the X.500 Directory Services.

7	Application	X.400 (ISO 10021) FTAM (ISO 8571) CMIP (ISO 9596) CMIS (ISO 9595) X.500 (ISO 9594) VTS (ISO 9040,9041)
6	Presentation	OSI Presentation (ISO 8822/8823) Abstract Syntax Notation (ASN.1) (ISO 8824/8825)
5	Series	OSI Session ISO 8326 CLNP ISO 8327 CONS
4	Transport	OSI Transport ISO 8473 CLNP ISO 8327 CONS
3	Network	OSI CLNM OSI CONS ISO 8473 CLNP ISO 8348 CONS ISO 8878 and ISO 8208 –X.25 ISO 9542 ES-IS Protocol ISO 10584 IS-IS Protocol
2	Logical Connection	L A P B L L C CSMA/CD 802.3 Token Bus FDDI Token Ring 802.5
1	Physical Connecton	Telephone CSMA/CD 802.3 Point-to-Point Point-to-Multipoint FDDI Token Ring 802.5 ISDN

Figure II.5 The OSI Reference Model and the OSI protocols

File Transfer, Access and Management Protocol (FTAM)

The FTAM protocol enables the transfer of files to other computers and allows access to the contents and attributes of files. The Virtual Store (VS) is a component of the FTAM. The VS enables uniform presentation of disparate file systems. The FTAM application is responsible for converting this virtual file system into a real system.

Directory Services (X.500)

Directory Services (X.500) in ISO/OSI protocols undertake the uniform presentation of names, addresses and objects. The Directory Information Base, which contains the individual entries under a uniform heading, is a component of the X.500 service. The Directory Information Base has a tree-like structure starting from the root (/) and can therefore also be implemented on internationally distributed systems. This information is made available to the enquiring computer again, on request.

Virtual Terminal Service (VTS)

Since the very beginning of network technology, 'Remote Login' – that is, the possibility of operating on several computers from one point – has been one of the basic requirements placed on computer networks. With the ISO/OSI protocols, the Virtual Terminal Service (VTS) is used for these functions. The Telnet Service describes rules for communication between terminals and computer and simulates a fictional output/input unit. The Virtual Terminal Service makes the relevant terminal independent from the surrounding computer environment.

Common Management Information Protocol/Common Management Information Service (CMIP/CMIS)

The OSI management services CMIS and CMIP form the basis for all management functions of the ISO/OSI protocols. They enable the exchange of information and commands for network management between two applications sharing equal privileges on the same level. CMIP defines the protocol mechanisms. CMIS defines the service primitive and the information structure.

Appendix III

All Management RFCs at a Glance

RFC	Title
1516	Definitions of Managed Objects for IEEE 802.3 Repeater Devices. 1993 September (replaces 1368).
1515	Definitions of Managed Objects for IEEE 802.3 Medium Attachment Units (MAUs). 1993 September.
1514	Host Resources MIB. 1993 September.
1513	Token Ring Extensions to the Remote Network Monitoring MIB. 1993 September (replaces RFC 1271).
1512	FDDI Management Information Base. 1993 September (updates RFC 1285).
1503	Algorithms for Automating Administration in SNMPv2 Managers. 1993 August.

1493 Definitions of Managed Objects for Bridges. 1993 July (replaces RFC 1286).

1474 The Definitions of Managed Objects for the Bridge Network Control Protocol of the Point-to-Point Protocol. 1993 June.

1473 The Definitions of Managed Objects for the IP Network Control Protocol of the Point-to-Point Protocol. 1993 June.

1472 The Definitions of Managed Objects for the Security Protocols of the Point-to-Point Protocol. 1993 June.

1471 The Definitions of Managed Objects for the Link Control Protocol of the Point-to-Point Protocol. 1993 June.

1461 SNMP MIB extension for Multiprotocol Interconnect over X.25. 1993 May.

1452 Coexistence between version 1 and version 2 of the Internet-standard Network Management Framework. 1993 April.

1451 Manager-to-Manager Management Information Base. 1993 April.

1450 Management Information Base for version 2 of the Simple Network Management Protocol (SNMPv2). 1993 April.

1449 Transport Mappings for version 2 of the Simple Network Management Protocol (SNMPv2). 1993 April.

1448 Protocol Operations for version 2 of the Simple Network Management Protocol (SNMPv2). 1993 April.

1447 Party MIB for version 2 of the Simple Network Management Protocol (SNMPv2). 1993 April.

1446 Security Protocols for version 2 of the Simple Network Management Protocol (SNMPv2). 1993 April.

1445 Administrative Model for version 2 of the Simple Network Management Protocol (SNMPv2). 1993 April.

1444 Conformance Statements for version 2 of the Simple Network Management Protocol (SNMPv2). 1993 April.

1443 Textual Conventions for version 2 of the Simple Network Management Protocol (SNMPv2). 1993 April.

1442 Structure of Management Information for version 2 of the Simple Network Management Protocol (SNMPv2). 1993 April.

1441 Introduction to version 2 of the Internet-standard Network Management Framework. 1993 April.

1420 SNMP over IPX. 1993 March (replaces 1298).

1419 SNMP over AppleTalk. 1993 March.

1418 SNMP over OSI. 1993 March (replaces 1161, 1283).

1414 Identification MIB. 1993 February.

1407 Definitions of Managed Objects for the DS3/E3 Interface Type. 1993 January (replaces RFC 1233).

1406 Definitions of Managed Objects for the DS1 and E1 Interface Types. 1993 January (replaces RFC 1232).

1398 Definitions of Managed Objects for the Ethernet-like Interface Types. 1993 January (replaces RFC 1284).

1389 RIP Version 2 MIB Extension. 1993 January.

1382 SNMP MIB Extension for the X.25 Packet Layer. 1992 November.

1381 SNMP MIB Extension for X.25 LAPB. 1992 November.

1354 IP Forwarding Table MIB. 1992 July.

1353 Definitions of Managed Objects for Administration of SNMP Parties. 1992 July.

1352 SNMP Security Protocols. 1992 July.

1351 SNPM Administrative Model. 1992 July.

1321 The MD5 Message-Digest Algorithm. 1992 April.

1320 The MD4 Message-Digest Algorithm. 1992 April (replaces RFC 1186).

1319 The MD2 Message-Digest Algorithm. 1992 April.

1318 Definitions of Managed Objects for Parallel-printer-like Hardware Devices. 1992 April.

1317 Definitions of Managed Objects for RS-232-like Hardware Devices. 1992 April.

1316 Definitions of Managed Objects for Character Stream Devices. 1992 April.

1315 Management Information Base for Frame Relay DTEs. 1992 April.

1304 Definitions of Managed Objects for the SIP Interface Type. 1992 February.

1303 A Convention for Describing SNMP-based Agents. 1992 February.

1298 SNMP over IPX. 1992 February.

1289 DECnet Phase IV MIB Extensions. 1991 December.

1286 Definitions of Managed Objects for Bridges. 1991 December.

1285 FDDI Management Information Base. 1992 January.

1284 Definitions of Managed Objects for the Ethernet-like Interface Types. 1991 December.

1283 SNMP over OSI. 1991 December (replaces RFC 1161).

1271 Remote Network Monitoring Management Information Base. 1991 November.

1270 SNMP Communications Services. 1991 October.

1269 Definitions of Managed Objects for the Border Gateway Protocol (version 3). 1991 October.

1253 OSPF version 2: Management Information Base. 1991 August. (replaces RFC 1252).

1259 OSPF version 2: Management Information Base. 1991 August. (replaces RFC 1248; replaced by RFC 1253).

1248 OSPF version 2: Management Information Base. 1991 July. (replaced by RFC 1252).

1243 Appletalk Management Information Base. 1991 July.

1239 Reassignment of Experimental MIBs to Standard MIBs. 1991 June. (updates RFC 1229, RFC 1230, RFC 1231, RFC 1232, RFC 1233).

1238 CLNS MIB for use with Connectionless Network Protocol (ISO 8473) and End System to Intermediate System (ISO 9542). 1991 June (replaces RFC 1162).

1233 Definitions of Managed Objects for the DS3 Interface type. 1991 May.

1232 Definitions of Managed Objects for the DS1 Interface type. 1991 May.

1231 IEEE 802.5 Token Ring MIB. 1991 May.

1230 IEEE 802.4 Token Bus MIB. 1991 May.

1229 Extensions to the Generic-Interface MIB. 1991 May.

1228 SNMP-DPI: Simple Network Management Protocol Distributed Program Interface. 1991 May.

1227 SNMP MUX protocol and MIB. 1991 May.

1224 Techniques for Managing Asynchronously Generated Alerts. 1991 May.

1215 Convention for Defining Traps for Use with the SNMP. 1991 March.

1214 OSI Internet Management: Management Information Base. 1991 April.

1213 Management Information Base for Network Management of TCP/IP-based Internet: MIB II. 1991 March (replaces RFC 1158).

1212 Concise MIB Definitions. 1991 March.

1189 Common Management Information Services and Protocols for the Internet (CMOT and CMIP). 1990 October (replaces RFC 1095).

1187 Bulk Table Retrieval with the SNMP. 1990 October.

1186 MD4 Message Digest Algorithm. 1990 October.

1161 SNMP over OSI. 1990 June.

1158 Management Information Base for Network Management of TCP/IP-based Internet: MIB II. 1990 May (replaced by RFC 1213).

1157 Simple Network Management Protocol (SNMP). 1990 May (replaces RFC 1098).

1156 Management Information Base for Network Management of TCP/IP-based Internet. 1990 May (replaces RFC 1066).

1155 Structure and Identification of Management Information for TCP/IP-based Internet. 1990 May (replaces RFC 1065).

1098 Simple Network Management Protocol (SNMP). 1989 April (replaces RFC 1067; replaced by RFC 1157).

1095 Common Management Information Services and Protocol over TCP/IP (CMOT). 1989 April (replaced by RFC 1189).

1089 SNMP over Ethernet. 1989 February.

1067 Simple Network Management Protocol. 1988 August (replaced by RFC 1098).

1066 Management Information Base for Network Management of TCP/IP-based Internet. 1988 August (replaced by RFC 1156).

1065 Structure and Identification of Management Information for TCP/IP-based Internet. 1988 August (replaced by RFC 1155).

1028 Simple Gateway Monitoring Protocol. 1987 November.

1022 High-level Entity Management Protocol (HEMP). 1987 October.

1021 High-level Entity Management System (HEMS). 1987 October.

Appendix IV

IV.1 SNMP Codes

Management from all devices connected to the network is possible through SNMP RFC 1098 and the Common Management Information Protocol over TCP (CMOT). The functions and variables for the management of data networks are described in the *Structure and Identification of Management Information for TCP/IP based Internet (SMI) RFC-1065* and the Management Information Base for Network Management of TCP/IP-based Internet (MIB). The SMI establishes codes and parameters which enable a distinction to be made between private and general variables.

IV.1.1 SMI Network Management Directory Codes

Prefix: 1.3.6.1.1.

Decimal	Name	Description
all	reserved	reserved for future applications

IV.1.2 SMI Network Management Codes

Prefix: 1.3.6.1.2.

Decimal	Name	Description
0	reserved	–
1	MIB	–

IV.1.3 SMI Network Management Codes of the MIB II

Prefix: 1.3.6.1.2.1.x

Decimal	Name	Description
0	reserved	reserved
1	system	System
2	interfaces	Interfaces
3	at	Address Translation
4	ip	Internet Protocol
5	icmp	Internet Control Message
6	tcp	Transmission Control Protocol
7	udp	User Datagram Protocol
8	egp	Exterior Gateway Protocol
9	cmot	CMIP over TCP
10	transmission	Transmission
11	snmp	Simple Network Management
12	GenericIF	Generic Interface Extensions
13	Appletalk	Appletalk Networking
14	ospf	Open Shortest Path First
15	bgp	Border Gateway Protocol
16	rmon	Remote Network Monitoring
17	bridge	Bridge Objects
18	DecnetP4	Decnet Phase 4
19	Character	Character Streams
20	snmpParties	SNMP Parties
21	snmpSecrets	SNMP Secrets

IV.1.4 SMI Network Management Codes of the MIB II Transmission Group

Prefix: 1.3.6.1.2.1.10 (transmission)

Decimal	Name	Description
7	IEEE802.3	CSMACD-like Objects
8	IEEE802.4	Token Bus-like Objects
9	IEEE802.5	Token Ring-like Objects
15	FDDI	FDDI Objects
18	DS1	T1 Carrier Objects
30	DS3	DS3 Interface Objects
31	SIP	SMDS Interface Objects
32	FRAME RELAY	Frame Relay Objects
33	RS-232	RS-232 Objects
34	Parallel	Parallel Printer Objects

IV.1.5 SMI Network Management Experimental Codes

Prefix: 1.3.6.1.3.

Decimal	Name	Description
0	reserved	–
1	CLNS	ISO CLNS Objects
2	T1-Carrier	T1 Carrier Objects (obsolete)
3	IEEE802.3	Ethernet-like Objects (obsolete)
4	IEEE802.5	Token Ring-like Objects (obsolete)
5	DECNet-PHIV	DECnet Phase IV (obsolete)
6	Interface	Generic Interface Objects (obsolete)
7	IEEE802.4	Token Bus-like Objects (obsolete)
8	FDDI	FDDI Objects (obsolete)
9	LANMGR-1	LAN Manager V1 Objects
1	LANMGR-TRAPS	LAN Manager Trap Objects
11	Views	SNMP View Objects
12	SNMP-AUTH	SNMP Authentication Objects
13	BGP	Border Gateway Protocol (obsolete)
14	Bridge	Bridge MIB (obsolete)
15	DS3	DS3 Interface Type (obsolete)
16	SIP	SMDS Interface Protocol (obsolete)
17	Appletalk	Appletalk Networking (obsolete)
18	PPP	PPP Objects
19	Character MIB	Character MIB (obsolete)
20	RS-232 MIB	RS-232 MIB (obsolete)
21	Parallel MIB	Parallel MIB (obsolete)
22	atsign-proxy	Proxy via Community
23	OSPF	OSPF MIB (obsolete)
24	Alert-Man	Alert-Man
25	FDDI-Synoptics	FDDI-Synoptics

Decimal	Name	Description
26	Frame Relay	Frame Relay MIB (obsolete)
27	rmon	Remote Network Management MIB (obsolete)
28	IDPR	IDPR MIB
29	HUBMIB	IEEE 802.3 Hub MIB (obsolete)
30	IPFWDTBLMIB	IP Forwarding Table MIB (obsolete)
31	LATM MIB	
32	SONET MIB	
33	IDENT	
34	MIME-MHS	

IV.1.6 SMI Network Management Private Enterprise Codes

Prefix: 1.3.6.1.4.1.

Decimal value	Description
0	reserved
1	Proteon
2	IBM
3	CMU
4	UNIX
5	ACC
6	TWG
7	CAYMAN
8	NYSERNET
9	Cisco
10	NSC
11	HP
12	Epilogue
13	University of Tennessee
14	BBN
15	Xylogics, Inc.
16	Unisys
17	Canstar
18	Wellfleet
19	TRW
20	MIT
21	EON
22	Spartacus
23	Excelan

24	Spider Systems
25	NSFNET
26	Hughes LAN Systems
27	Intergraph
28	Interlan
29	Vitalink Communications
30	Ulana
31	NSWC
32	Santa Cruz Operation
33	Xyplex
34	Cray
35	Bell Northern Research
36	DEC
37	Touch
38	Network Research, Corp.
39	Baylor College of Medicine
40	NMFECC-LLNL
41	SRI
42	Sun Microsystems
43	3Com
44	CMC
45	SynOptics
46	Cheyenne Software
47	Prime Computer
48	MCNC/North Carolina Data Network
49	Chipcom
50	Optical Data Systems
51	gated
52	Cabletron Systems
53	Apollo Computers
54	DeskTalk Systems, Inc.
55	SSDS
56	Castle Rock Computing
57	MIPS Computer Systems
58	TGV, Inc.
59	Silicon Graphics, Inc.
60	University of British Columbia
61	Merit
62	FiberCom
63	Apple Computer, Inc.
64	Gandalf
65	Dartmouth
66	David Systems
67	Reuter
68	Cornell
69	TMAC

70	Locus Computing, Corp.
71	NASA
72	Retix
73	Boeing
74	AT&T
75	Ungermann-Bass
76	Digital Analysis, Corp.
77	LAN Manager
78	Netlabs
79	ICL
80	Auspex Systems
81	Lannet Company
82	Network Computing Devices
83	Raycom Systems
84	Pirelli Focom Ltd
85	Datability Software Systems
86	Network Application Technology
87	LINK (Local Informatics Network Karlsruhe)
88	NYU
89	RND
90	InterCon Systems Corporation
91	LearningTree Systems
92	Webster Computer Corporation
93	Frontier Technologies Corporation
94	Nokia Data Communications
95	Allen-Bradley Company
96	CERN
97	Sigma Network Systems, Inc.
98	Emerging Technologies, Inc.
99	SNMP Research
100	Ohio State University
101	Ultra Network Technologies
102	Microcom
103	Martin Marietta Astronautic Group
104	Micro Technology
105	Process Software Corporation
106	Data General Corporation
107	Bull Company
108	Emulex Corporation
109	Warwick University Computing Services
110	Network General Corporation
111	Oracle
112	Control Data Corporation
113	Hughes Aircraft Company
114	Synernetics, Inc.
115	Mitre

116	Hitachi, Ltd
117	Telebit
118	Salomon Technology Services
119	NEC Corporation
120	Fibermux
121	FTP Software Inc.
122	Sony
123	Newbridge Networks Corporation
124	Racal-Milgo Information Systems
125	CR SYSTEMS
126	DSET Corporation
127	Computone
128	Tektronix, Inc.
129	Interactive Systems Corporation
130	Banyan Systems Inc.
131	Sintrom Datanet Limited
132	Bell Canada
133	Crosscomm Corporation
134	Rice University
135	T3Plus Networking, Inc.
136	Concurrent Computer Corporation
137	Basser
138	Luxcom
139	Artel
140	Independence Technologies, Inc. (ITI)
141	Frontier Software Development
142	Digital Computer Limited
143	Eyring, Inc.
144	Case Communications
145	Penril DataComm, Inc.
146	American Airlines
147	Sequent Computer Systems
148	Bellcore
149	Konkord Communications
150	University of Washington
151	Develcon
152	Solarix Systems
153	Unifi Communications Corp.
154	Roadnet
155	Network Systems Corp.
156	ENE (European Network Engineering)
157	Dansk Data Elektronik A/S
158	Morning Star Technologies
159	Dupont EOP
160	Legato Systems, Inc.
161	Motorola SPS

162	European Space Agency (ESA)
163	BIM
164	Rad Data Communications Ltd
165	Intellicom
166	Shiva Corporation
167	Fujikura America
168	Xlnt Designs INC (XDI)
169	Tandem Computers
170	BICC
171	D-Link Systems, Inc.
172	AMP, Inc.
173	Netlink
174	C. Itoh Electronics
175	Sumitomo Electric Industries (SEI)
176	DHL Systems, Inc.
177	Network Equipment Technologies
178	APTEC Computer Systems
179	Schneider & Koch & Co.
180	Hill Air Force Base
181	ADC Kentrox
182	Japan Radio Co.
183	Versitron
184	Telecommunication Systems
185	Interphase
186	Toshiba Corporation
187	Clearpoint Research Corp.
188	Ascom Gfeller Ltd
189	Fujitsu America
190	NetCom Solutions, Inc.
191	NCR
192	Dr. Materna GmbH
193	Ericsson Business Communications
194	Metaphor Computer Systems
195	Patriot Partners
196	The Software Group Limited (TSG)
197	Kalpana, Inc.
198	University of Waterloo
199	CCL/ITRI
200	Coeur Postel
201	Mitsubish Cable Industries, Ltd
202	SMC
203	Crescendo Communication, Inc.
204	Goodall Software Engineering
205	Intecom
206	Victoria University of Wellington
207	Allied Telesis, Inc.

208	Dowty Network Systems A/S
209	Protools
210	Nippon Telegraph and Telephone Corp.
211	Fujitsu Limited
212	Network Peripherals Inc.
213	Netronix, Inc.
214	University of Wisconsin-Madison
215	NetWorth, Inc.
216	Tandberg Data A/S
217	Technically Elite Concepts, Inc.
218	Labtam Australia Pty. Ltd
219	Republic Telcom Systems, Inc.
220	ADI Systems, Inc.
221	Microwave Bypass Systems, Inc.
222	Pyramid Technology Corp.
223	Unisys Corp.
224	LANOPTICS LTD. Israel
225	NKK Corporation
226	MTrade UK Ltd
227	Acals
228	ASTEC, Inc.
229	Delmarva Power
230	Telematics International, Inc.
231	Siemens Nixdorf Information Sytems AG
232	Compaq
233	NetManage, Inc.
234	NCSU Computing Center
235	Empirical Tools and Technologies
236	Samsung Group
237	Takaoka Electric Mfg. Co., Ltd
238	Netrix Systems Corporation
239	WINDATA
240	RC International A/S
241	Netexp Research
242	Internode Systems Pty Ltd
243	netCS Informationstechnik GmbH
244	Lantronix
245	Avatar Consultants
246	Furukawa Electoric Co. Ltd
247	AEG Electrcom
248	Richard Hirschmann GmbH & Co.
249	G2R Inc.
250	University of Michigan
251	Netcomm, Ltd
252	Sable Technology Corporation
253	Xerox

254	Conware Computer Consulting GmbH
255	Compatible Systems Corp.
256	Scitec Communications Systems Ltd
257	Transarc Corporation
258	Matsushita Electric Industrial Co., Ltd
259	ACCTON Technology
260	Star-Tek, Inc.
261	Codenoll Tech. Corp.
262	Formation, Inc.
263	Seiko Instruments, Inc. (SII)
264	RCE (Reseaux de Communication d'Entreprise S.A.)
265	Xenocom, Inc.
266	AEG KABEL
267	Systech Computer Corporation
268	Visual
269	SDD (Scandinavian Airlines Data Denmark A/S)
270	Zenith Electronics Corporation
271	TELECOM FINLAND
272	BinTec Computersystems
273	EUnet Germany
274	PictureTel Corporation
275	Michigan State University
276	GTE Telecom Incorporated
277	Cascade Communications Corp.
278	Hitachi Cable, Ltd
279	Olivetti
280	Vitacom Corporation
281	INMOS
282	AIC Systems Laboratories Ltd
283	Cameo Communications, Inc.
284	Diab Data AB
285	Olicom A/S
286	Digital-Kienzle Computersystems
287	CSELT (Centro Studi E Laboratori Telecomunicazioni)
288	Electronic Data Systems
289	McData Corporation
290	Harris Computer Systems Division (HCSD)
291	Technology Dynamics, Inc.
292	DATAHOUSE Information Systems Ltd
293	DSIR Network Group
294	Texas Instruments
295	PlainTree Systems Inc.
296	Hedemann Software Development
297	Fuji Xerox Co., Ltd
298	Asante Technology
299	Stanford University

300	Digital Link
301	Raylan Corporation
302	Datacraft
303	Hughes
304	Farallon Computing, Inc.
305	GE Information Services
306	Gambit Computer Communications
307	Livingston Enterprises, Inc.
308	Star Technologies
309	Micronics Computers Inc.
310	Basis, Inc.
311	Microsoft
312	US West Advance Technologies
313	University College London
314	Eastman Kodak Company
315	Network Resources Corporation
316	Atlas Telecom
317	Bridgeway
318	American Power Conversion Corp.
319	DOE Atmospheric Radiation Measurement Project
320	VerSteeg CodeWorks
321	Verilink Corp.
322	Sybus Corportation
323	Tekelec
324	NASA Ames Research Center
325	Simon Fraser University
326	Fore Systems, Inc.
327	Centrum Communications, Inc.
328	NeXT Computer, Inc.
329	Netcore, Inc.
330	Northwest Digital Systems
331	Andrew Corporation
332	DigiBoard
333	Computer Network Technology Corp.
334	Lotus Development Corp.
335	MICOM Communication Corporation
336	ASCII Corporation
337	PUREDATA Research/USA
338	NTT DATA
339	Empros Systems International
340	Kendall Square Research (KSR)
341	Martin Marietta Energy Systems
342	Network Innovations
343	Intel Corporation
344	Proxar
345	Epson Research Center

346	Fibernet
347	Box Hill Systems Corporation
348	American Express Travel Related Services
349	Compu-Shack
350	Parallan Computer, Inc.
351	Stratacom
352	Open Networks Engineering, Inc.
353	ATM Forum
354	SSD Management, Inc.
355	Automated Network Management, Inc.
356	Magnalink Communications Corporation
357	TIL Systems, Ltd
358	Skyline Technology, Inc.
359	Nu-Mega Technologies, Inc.
360	Morgan Stanley & Co. Inc.
361	Integrated Business Network
362	L & N Technologies, Ltd
363	Cincinnati Bell Information Systems, Inc.
364	OSCOM International
365	MICROGNOSIS
366	Datapoint Corporation
367	RICOH Co. Ltd
368	Axis Communications AB
369	Pacer Software
370	Axon Networks Inc.
371	Brixton Systems, Inc.
372	GSI
373	Tatung Co., Ltd.
374	DIS Research LTD
375	Quotron Systems, Inc.
376	Dassault Electronique
377	Corollary, Inc.
378	SEEL, Ltd
379	Lexcel
380	W.J. Parducci & Associates, Inc.
381	OST
382	Megadata Pty Ltd
383	LLNL Livermore Computer Center
384	Dynatech Communications
385	Symplex Communications Corp.
386	Tribe Computer Works
387	Taligent, Inc.
388	Symbol Technology, Inc.
389	Lancert
390	Alantec
391	Ridgeback Solutions

392	Metrix, Inc.
393	Excutive Systems/XTree Company
394	NRL Communication Systems Branch
395	I.D.E. Corporation
396	Matsushita Electric Works, Ltd
397	MegaPAC
398	Pilkington Communication Systems
440	Amnet, Inc.
441	Chase Research
442	PEER Networks
443	Gateway Communications, Inc.
444	Peregrine Systems
445	Daewoo Telecom
446	Norwegian Telecom Research
447	WilTel
448	Ericsson-Camtec
449	Codex
450	Basis
451	AGE Logic
452	INDE Electronics
453	ISODE Consortium
454	J.I. Case
455	Trillium Digital Systems
456	Bacchus Inc.
457	MCC
458	Stratus Computer
459	Quotron
460	Beame & Whiteside
461	Cellular Technical Services

Appendix V

V.1 SNMP header formats

The SNMP Protocol is located on the Application Layer. It is therefore completely independent from the transport mechanisms at lower levels. With SNMP, every message is treated as a singular event and interpreted individually. The SNMP protocol normally uses the Connectionless Datagram Service UDP (User Datagram Protocol) for the transmission of information. However, this transport mechanism is not strictly prescribed. Other transport protocols, such as TCP, any OSI Layer (TP0–TP4) or even the MAC level directly, can be used.

V.1.1 SNMP over Ethernet

SNMP was originally designed for use on any reasonably reliable (error-free) transport mechanism. In view of the many components which in terms of their function have no higher transport protocols available (that is,

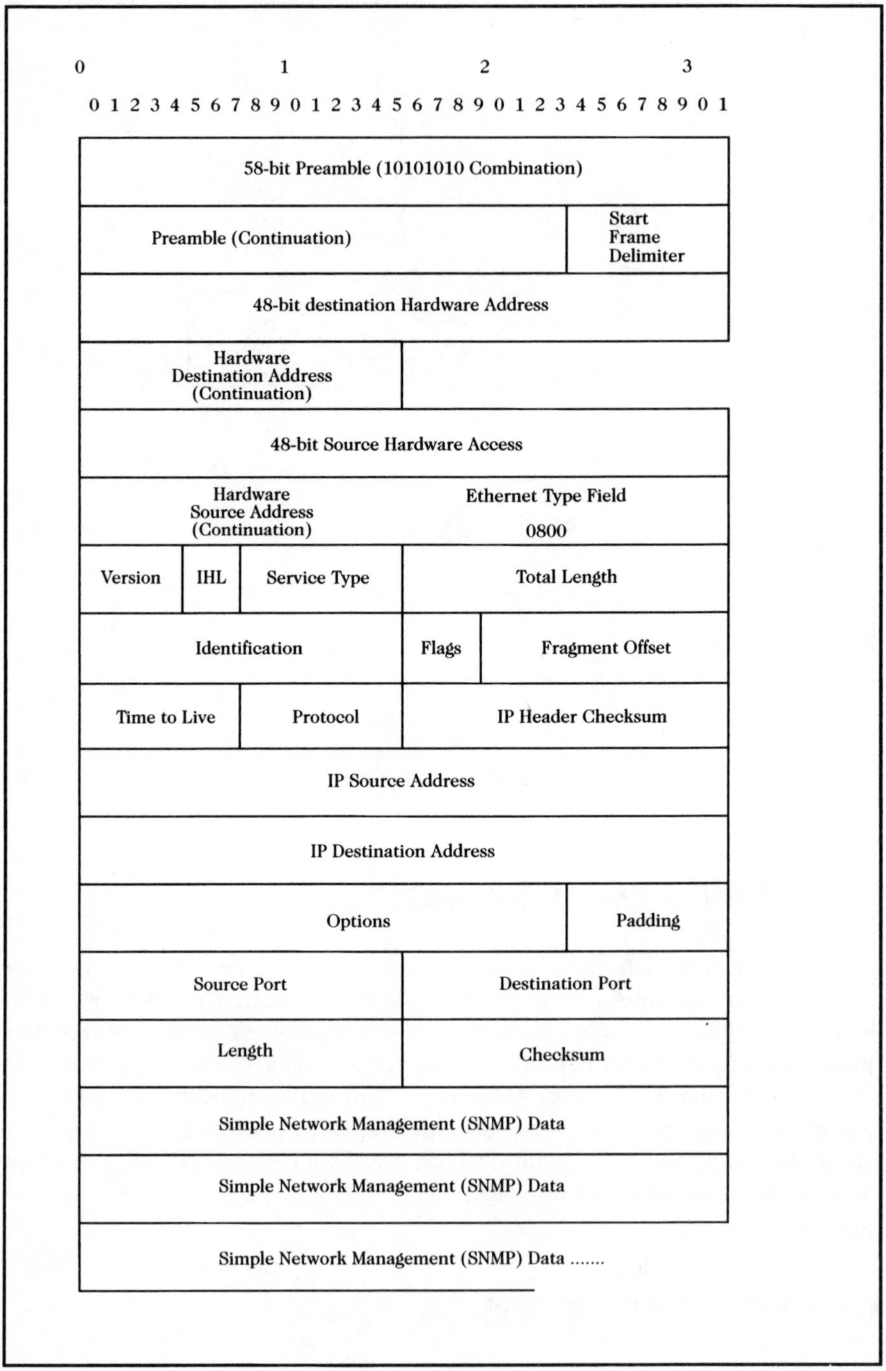

0 1 2 3

0 1 2 3 4 5 6 7 8 9 0 1 2 3 4 5 6 7 8 9 0 1 2 3 4 5 6 7 8 9 0 1

58-bit Preamble (10101010 Combination)

Preamble (Continuation) | Start Frame Delimiter

48-bit destination Hardware Address

Hardware Destination Address (Continuation)

48-bit Source Hardware Access

Hardware Source Address (Continuation) | Ethernet Type Field 0800

Version | IHL | Service Type | Total Length

Identification | Flags | Fragment Offset

Time to Live | Protocol | IP Header Checksum

IP Source Address

IP Destination Address

Options | Padding

Source Port | Destination Port

Length | Checksum

Simple Network Management (SNMP) Data

Simple Network Management (SNMP) Data

Simple Network Management (SNMP) Data ....

Figure V.1 IP/UDP/SNMP header

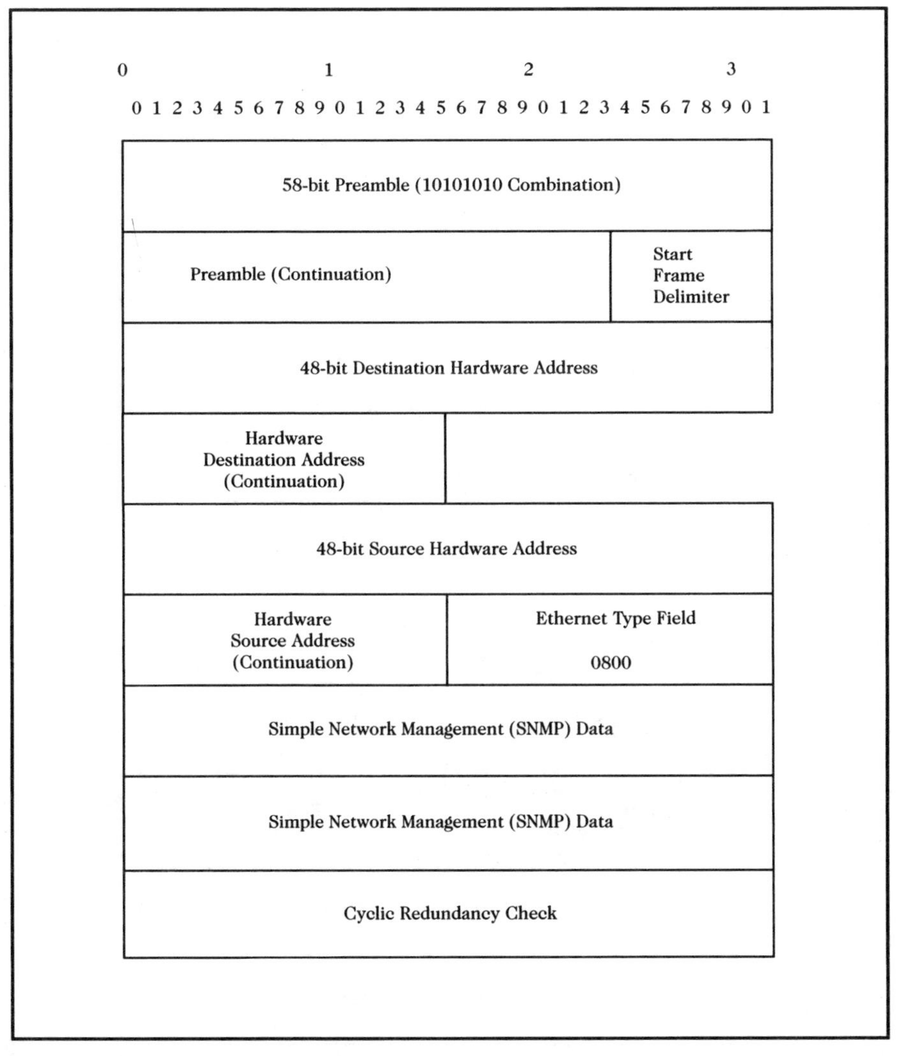

Figure V.2 Ethernet/SNMP header

repeaters, bridges, star couplers, fan-out units, and so on), it should be possible to integrate these devices into a global management concept. RFC 1089 (SNMP over Ethernet) describes how the management data in a Standard Ethernet/802.3 data packet can be packed.

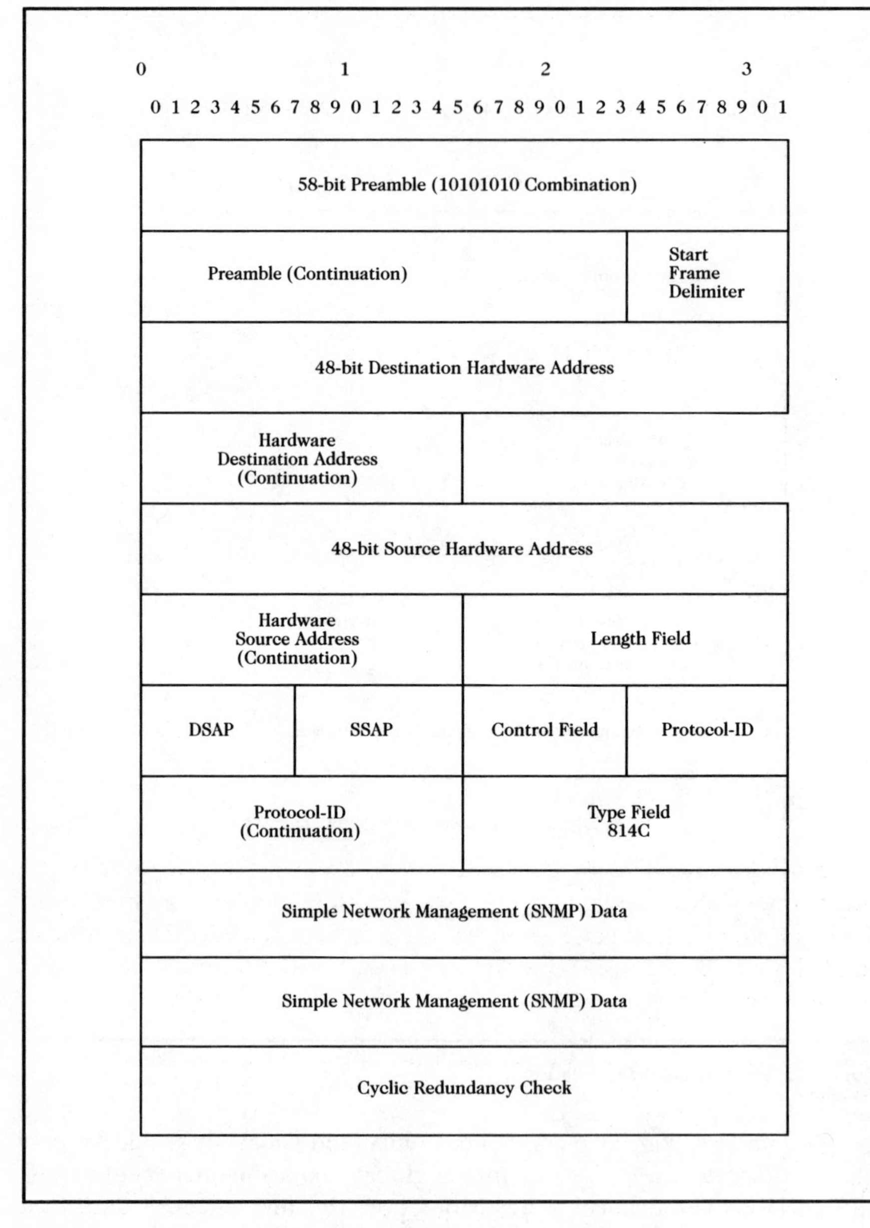

Figure V.3 IEEE 802.3/SNMP header

Appendix VI

VI.1 MIB II at a glance

The Management Information Base (MIB) was established at the same time as the Simple Network Management Protocol and the SMI. The first MIB (MIB I) contained a total of 114 entries which were subdivided into various regions. This MIB has been completely revised and published as MIB II (with a total of 117 objects). MIB II is subdivided into ten groups.

System	Information on the actual computer to be administered.
Interfaces	Network interfaces.
AT	IP Address Translation Tables and Information.
IP	Data on the Internet Protocol.
ICMP	Data on the Internet Control Messages Protocol.
TCP	Information on the Transmission Control Protocol.
UDP	Data on the User Datagram Protocol.
EGP	The Exterior Gateway Protocol.
Transmission	Contains media-specific information.
SNMP	Information on the SNM-Protocol.

Table VI.1 MIB II groups

VI.2 Groups and Object Identifier

sysDescr	Description of the hardware and operating system.
sysObjectID	Object Identifier, contains the identity of the agent (issued by manufacturer).
sysUpTime	Lifetime of the agent.
sysContact	Name of a contact person for the computer.
sysName	Name of the computer.
sysLocation	Physical location of the computer.
sysService	Number of services offered.

Table VI.2 The key MIB II Groups

VI.3 Interface Group

ifNumber	Number of system interfaces.
ifTable	List of interface entries.
ifEntry	Entry in the list with the following information:
ifIndex	Interface number.
ifDescr	Description of the interface.
ifType	Interface type (Ethernet, FDDI ...).
ifMtu	Size of MTU, maximum length of a packet to be transmitted.
ifSpeed	Data transfer rate.
ifPhysAddress	Interface address (medium-specific), for example, for Ethernet a.b.c.d.e.f.
ifAdminStatus	Desired status of the interface.
ifOperStatus	Actual status of the interface.
ifLastChange	Time of last status change.
ifInOctets	Total number of octets received.
ifInUcastPkts	Number of Unicast packets passed to the upper protocol layers
ifInNUcastPkts	Number of Multicast/Broadcast packets.
ifInDiscards	Number of packets discarded because of resource limitations.
ifInErrors	Number of errors in packets.
ifInUnknownProtos	Number of packets with unknown protocol.
ifOutOctets	Number of octets sent.
ifOutUcastPkts	Number of Unicast packets received from higher protocol layers.

ifOutUcastPkts	Number of Multicast/Broadcast packets.
ifOutDiscards	Number of packets discarded because of resource limitations.
ifOutErrors	Number of errors in packets.
ifOutQlen	Length of output queue.
ifSpecific	Medium-specific entry.

VI.4 Address Translation Group

atTable	Table of address translations between IP addresses and Layer 2 addresses.
atEntry	Entry in this table with the following information:
atIfIndex	Interface number.
atPhysAddress	Physical address of the mapping.
atNetAddress	IP address of the mapping

VI.5 IP Group

ipForwarding	Flag indicating whether IP packets are routed.
ipDefaultTTL	Default lifetime of an IP packet.
ipInReceives	Number of IP packets received (from the lower protocol layer.
ipInHdrErrors	Number of packets rejected because of format errors in the protocol header.
ipInAddrErrors	Number of packets rejected because of address errors.
ipForwDatagrams	Number of packets routed.
ipInUnknownProtos	Number of packets received with unknown protocols.
ipInDiscards	Number of packets rejected because of resource restrictions.
ipInDelivers	Number of packets received which are delivered to higher protocols.
ipOutRequests	Number of packets received from higher protocols.
ipOutNoRoutes	Number of packets rejected because of missing or unknown routes.
ipReasmTimeout	Timeout time for the reassembly of

	fragmented packets.
ipReasmReqds	Number of fragmented packets received.
ipReasmOKs	Number of successfully reassembled packets.
ipReasmFails	Number of unsuccessful attempts at reassembling packets.
ipFragOKs	Number of packets successfully fragmented.
ipFragFails	Number of unsuccessfully fragmented packets.
ipFragCreates	Number of unsuccessfully fragmented packets.
ipAddrTable	Table with address information.
ipAddrEntry	Entry in this table with the following information:
ipAdEntAddr	IP address of this entry.
ipAdEntIflIndex	Interface number.
ipAdEntNetMask	Subnetwork mask.
ipAdEntBcastAddr	Broadcast address.
ipAdEntReasmMaxSize	Maximum packet size that can be reassembled.
ipRoutingTable	Routing table.
ipRouteEntry	Entry in the routing table.
ipRouteDest	IP address of the target.
ipRouteIfIndex	Interface number through which routing is carried out.
ipRouteMetric1	Routing Metric #1.
ipRouteMetric2	Routing Metric #2.
ipRouteMetric3	Routing Metric #3.
ipRouteMetric4	Routing Metric #4.
ipRouteNextHop	IP address of the gateway through which routing is carried out
ipRouteType	Type of routing.
ipRouteProto	Routing protocol used.
ipRouteAge	Age of route; time elapsed since the last update through a routing protocol for this route was carried out
ipRouteMask	Subnetwork mask for this route.
ipNetToMediaTable	IP address translation table.
ipNetToMediaEntry	Entry in the above table with the following information:
ipNetToMediaIfIndex	Interface number.
ipNetToMediaPhysAddress	Physical address of the translation.
ipNetToMediaNetAddress	Logical (IP) address of the translation.
ipNetToMediaType	Process through which the above table is updated.

VI.6 ICMP Group

icmpInMsgs	Counts all ICMP packets received.
icmpInErrors	Counts all incorrectly received ICMP packets.
icmpInDestUnreachs	Counts all ICMP Destination Unreachable Messages.
icmpInTimeExcds	Counts all ICMP Time Exceeded Messages.
icmpInParmProbs	Counts all ICMP Parameter Problem Messages.
icmpInSrcQuenchs	Counts all ICMP Source Quench Messages.
icmpInRedirects	Counts all ICMP Redirect Messages.
icmpInEchos	Counts all ICMP Echo Request Messages.
icmpInEchoReps	Counts all ICMP Echo Reply Messages.
icmpInTimestamps	Counts all ICMP Timestamp Request Messages.
icmpInTimestampReps	Counts all ICMP Timestamp Reply Messages.
icmpInAddrMasks	Counts all ICMP Address Mask Request Messages.
icmpInAddrMaskReps	Counts all ICMP Address Mask Reply Messages.
icmpOutMsgs	Counts all ICMP messages sent.
icmpOutErrors	Counts all ICMP messages not sent.
icmpOutDestUnreachs	Number of ICMP Destination Unreachable Messages sent.
icmpOutTimeExcds	Number of ICMP Time Exceeded Messages sent.
icmpOutParmProbs	Number of ICMP Parameter Problem Messages sent.
icmpOutSrcQuenchs	Number of ICMP Source Quench Messages sent.
icmpOutRedirects	Number of ICMP Redirect Messages sent.
icmpOutEchos	Number of ICMP Echo Request Messages sent.
icmpOutEchoReps	Number of ICMP Echo Reply Messages sent.
icmpOutTimestamps	Number of ICMP Timestamp Request Messages sent.
icmpOutTimestampReps	Number of ICMP Timestamp Reply Messages sent.
icmpOutAddrMasks	Number of ICMP Address Mask Request Messages sent.
icmpOutAddrMaskReps	Number of ICMP Address Mask Reply Messages sent.

VI.7 TCP Group

tcpRtoAlgorithm	User retransmission algorithm.
tcpRtoMin	Minimum value for a retransmission timeout.
tcpRtoMax	Maximum value.
tcpMaxConn	Maximum number of simultaneous TCP connections.
tcpActiveOpens	Number of active connections set up (transition from CLOSED status to SYN-SENT status).
tcpPassiveOpens	Number of passive connections set up (transition from SYN-RCVD to LISTEN status).
tcpAttemptFails	Number of failed attempts at connection.
tcpEstabResets	Number of aborted connections.
tcpCurrEstab	Number of connections established at the moment.
tcpInSegs	Number of segments received.
tcpOutSegs	Number of segments sent.
tcpRetransSegs	Number of segments retransmitted.
tcpInErrs	Number of segments rejected because of format errors.
tcpOutRsts	Number of connection breaks initiated.
tcpConnTable	Table of current TCP connections.
tcpConnEntry	Entry in the above table with the following information:
tcpConnState	Status of the connection.
tcpConnLocalAddress	Local IP address.
tcpConnLocalPort	Local TCP port.
tcpConnRemAddress	IP address of the communication participant.
tcpConnRemPort	TCP port of communication participant.

VI.8 UDP Group

udpInDatagrams	Total number of datagrams delivered to the upper layers.
udpNoPorts	Number of datagrams destined for an unknown/ non-existent port.
updInErrors	Number of packets rejected because of format errors.
udpOutDatagrams	Total number of packets passed to lower

	protocol levels.
udpTable	Information on UDP terminals.
udpEntry	Entry in above table.
udpLocalAddress	Local IP address.
udpLocalPort	Local UDP port.

VI.9 EGP Group

egpInMsgs	Number of error-free EGP messages received.
egpInErrors	Number of incorrect EGP messages received.
egpOutMsgs	Number of EGP messages sent.
egpOutErrors	Number of EGP messages not sent.
egpNeighTable	EGP neighbor table.
egpNeighState	Status of the EGP system
egpNeighAddr	IP Address of the EGP neighbor.
Object type	
egpNeighAs	Autonomous System number of the EGP peer.
egpNeighInMsgs	Counts EGP messages from the EGP peer.
egpNeighInErrs	Counts incorrect EGP messages from the EGP peer.
egpNeighOutMsgs	Counts all EGP messages sent for the EGP peer.
egpNeighOutErrs	Counts all EGP messages not sent to the EGP peer.
egpNeighInErrMsgs	Counts all EGP error messages received.
egpNeighOutErrMsgs	Counts all EGP error messages sent.
egpNeighStateUps	Counts EGP State Transitions to the Up State EGP mode.
egpNeighStateDowns	Counts EGP State Transitions.
egpNeighIntervalHello	Time interval between EGP Hello commands.
egpNeighIntervalPoll	Time interval between EGP polls.
egpNeighMode	Polling Mode of the EGP.
egpNeighEventTrigger	Start and Stop of EGP neighbors.
egpAs	Autonomous System Number of the EGP device.

VI.10 Transmission Group

This group contains information on transmission medium-specific MIBs.

VI.11 SNMP Group

snmpInPkts	Number of all SNMP messages.
snmpOutPkts	Number of all SNMP messages sent.
snmpInBadVersions	Number of all SNMP messages with invalid SNMP Version.
snmpInBadCommunityNames	Number of all SNMP messages with incorrect Community Name field.
snmpInBadCommunityUses	Number of all SNMP messages with invalid Operation.
snmpInASNParseErrs	Number of all ASN.1 or BER errors.
snmpInTooBigs	Number of all PDUs received with the error status 'tooBig'.
snmpInNoSuchNames	Number of all PDUs received with error status 'noSuchName'.
snmpInBadValues	Number of all PDUs received with error status 'badValue'.
snmpInReadOnlys	Number of all PDUs received with error status 'readOnly'.
snmpInGenErrs	Number of all PDUs received with error status 'genErr'.
snmpInTotalReqVars	Number of all Get Request and Get Next Operations.
snmpInTotalSetVars	Number of all Set Request Operations.
snmpInGetRequests	Number of all Get Request Operation received.
snmpInGetNexts	Number of all Get Next Request Operations received.
snmpInSetRequests	Number of all Set Request Operations.
snmpInGetResponses	Number of all Get Response Operations received.
snmpInTraps	Number of all Traps received.
snmpOutTooBigs	Number of all PDUs sent with error status field 'tooBig'.
snmpOutNoSuchNames	Number of all PDUs sent with error status field 'noSuchName'.
snmpOutBadValues	Number of all PDUs sent with error status field 'badValue'.

snmpOutGenErrs	Number of all PDUs sent with error status field 'genErr'.
snmpOutGetRequests	Number of all Get Request PDUs sent.
snmpOutGetNexts	Number of all Get Next PDUs sent.
snmpOutSetRequests	Number of all Set Request PDUs sent.
snmpOutGetResponses	Number of all Response PDUs sent.
snmpOutTraps	Number of all Trap PDUs sent.
snmpEnableAuthenTraps	Enables Authentication Failure Traps to be sent.

Appendix VII

Addresses

Internet Activities Board (IAB)

Contact address:
Bob Braden
Executive Director of the IAB
USC/Information Sciences Institute
4676 Admiralty Way
Marina del Rey, CA 90292-6695
Tel. 001-213-822-1511
E-Mail: Braden@ISI.EDU

Internet Engineering Task Force (IETF)

Contact address:
Phil Gross
Chair of the IETF
Corporation for National Research Initiatives (NRI)
1895 Preston White Drive, Suite 100
Reston, VA 22091
Tel. 001-703-620-8990
E-Mail: PGross@NRI.RESTON.VA.US

Internet Research Task Force (IRTF)

Contact address:
David D. Clark
Chair of the IRTF
Massachusetts Institute of Technology
Laboratory for Computer Science
545 Main Street
Cambridge, MA 02139
Tel. 001-617-253-6003
E-Mail: ddc@LCS.MIT.EDU

Internet Assigned Numbers Authority

Contact address:
Joyce K. Reynolds
Internet Assigned Numbers Authority
USC/Information Sciences Institute
4676 Admiralty Way
Marina del Rey, CA 90292-6695
Tel. 001-213-822-1511
E-Mail: IANA@ISI.EDU

Request for Comments Editor

Contact address:
Jon Postel
RFC Editor
USC/Information Sciences Institute
4676 Admiralty Way
Marina del Rey, CA 90292-6695
Tel. 001-213-822-1511
E-Mail: Postel@ISI.EDU

The Network Information Center and Requests for Comments Distribution

Contact address:
SRI International
Room EJ291
333 Ravenswood Avenue
Menlo Park, CA 94025
Tel. 001-800-235-3155
001-415-859-3695
E-Mail: NIC@NIC.DDN.MIL

DDN Network Information Center

Contact address:
SRI International
Room EJ291

333 Ravenswood Avenue
Menlo Park, CA 94025
Tel. 001-800-235-3155
001-415-859-3695
E-Mail: NIC@NIC.DDN.MIL

NSF Network Service Center (NNSC)
Contact address:
NSF Network Service Center (NNSC)
BBN Laboratories, Inc.
10 Moulton St.
Cambridge, MA 02238
Tel. 001-617-873-3400
E-Mail: NNSC@NNSC.NSF.NET

NSF Network Information Service (NIS)
Contact address:
NSF Network Information Service
Merit Computer Network
University of Michigan
1075 Beal Avenue
Ann Arbor, MI 48109
Tel. 001-313-763-4897
E-Mail: INFO@NIS.NSF.NET

CSNET Coordination and Information Center (CIC)
Contact address:
CSNET Coordination and Information Center
BBN Systems and Technologies Corporation
10 Moulton Street
Cambridge, MA 02238
Tel. 001-617-873-2777
E-Mail: INFO@SH.CS.NET

Government Systems, Inc.
Contact address:
Attn: Network Information Center
14200 Park Meadow Drive
Suite 200
Chantilly, VA 22021
Tel. 001-800-365-3642
001-703-802-4535
Fax 001-703-802-8376
Network Address: 192.112.36.5 (NIC.DDN.MIL)
Root Domain Server: 192.112.36.4 (NS.NIC.DDN.MIL)

University of Dortmund
DENIC
Informatik IRB
44221 Dortmund
Germany
Fax 0231 7552386
E-Mail: hostmaster@deins.informatik.uni-dortmund.de

American National Standards Institute
(ANSI)
1430 Broadway
New York, NY 10018
USA

Electronic Industries Association
(EIA)
2001 Eye Street, NW
Washington, DC 20006
USA

European Computer Manufacturers Association
(ECMA)
114, rue de Rhone
1204 Geneva
Switzerland

Institute of Electrical and Electronics Engineers
(IEEE)
Secretary, IEEE Standards Board
345 East 47 Street
New York, NY 10017
USA

International Organization for Standardization
(ISO)
Central Secretary
1, rue de Varembe
1211 Geneva
Switzerland

The Simple Times
c/o Dover Beach Consulting Inc.
420 Whisman Court
Mountain View, CA 94043-2112
Tel. 001-415-968-1052
Fax 001-415-968-2510

Appendix VIII

Trademarks

Trademarks

Apple, AppleTalk, Finder, LocalTalk and Macintosh are registered trademarks of Apple Computer.

Transport Layer Interface, UNIX, UNIX System 5 are registered trademarks of AT&T.

DEC, DECmcc, DECnet, Ultrix VMS are registered trademarks of Digital Equipment Corporation.

Envoy, Attaché, Attaché Plus, Emissary, Diplomatic Pouch, Diplomatic Pouch Plus, Ambassador are registered trademarks of Epilogue Technology Inc.

IBM, PC/AT, PC/XT, SNA are registered trademarks of International Business Machines Inc.

INTEROP and ConneXions are registered trademarks of INTEROP Inc.

Appendix IX

References

Auffarth, Bernd:
Netzarbeit, TCP/IP. Grundlagen und Bedienung. In: iX Multiuser-Multitasking-Magazin. 1992.

Baker, Steven:
Just holding hands. Interoperability. In: LAN Magazine. 3. 1992. No 2.

Bernskötter, Georg:
HPs EASE Architektur. In: LANline. 1992. No. 10.

Bertsekas, Dimitri; Robert Gallager:
Data Networks. 2. Ed. New Jersey: Prentice-Hall. 1992.

Beyda, William:
Basic Datacommunications. A Comprehensive Overview. Hemel Hempstead: Simon & Schuster. 1991.

Bingham, Sanford:
What users want. Open Management, a guide for users. In: Communications Week International. 1992.

Black, Uyless:

Data Communications and Distributed Networks. 2. Ed. Hemel Hempstead: Simon & Schuster. 1991.

Network Management Standards. New York: McGraw-Hill. 1992.

TCP/IP and related Protocols. New York: McGraw-Hill. 1992.

OSI. A Model for Computer Communication Standards. Englewood Cliffs (New Jersey): Prentice-Hall. 1991.

Borchers, Detlef:

Über Grenzen hinweg. In: iX Multiuser-Multitasking-Magazin. March 1992.

Und der Sieger heißt: Netware contra LAN Manager. In: iX Multiuser-Multitasking-Magazin. September 1992.

Abgespeckt. Univel, das USL-Novell-UNIX. In: iX Multiuser-Multitasking-Magazin. February 1992.

Borowka, Petra; Mathias Hein:

Auswertung der Ausschreibung. Integrationslösung im Vergleich. In: PC Netze. 1993. No. 12.

Brant, Graham:

Asset Management. In: AIMS Conference Frankfurt. June 1992.

Bronold, Christoph:

Aufbau und Funktionsweise von MIBs. In: LANline. 1992. No. 10.

Carl-Mitchell, Smoot; John S. Quarterman:

Practical Internetworking with TCP/IP and UNIX. Wokingham: Addison-Wesley. 1993.

Carr, Jim:

Combatting Enterprise Entropy. In: LAN Magazine. March 1991.

Caruso, Richard:

Cooperating to achieve global communications. In: IEEE Communications Magazine. October 1992.

Case, Jeff; Keith McCloghrie; Marshal T. Rose (u.a.):

The Simple Management Protocol and Framework. In: Connections. The Interoperability Report. October 1992.

CCITT

CCITT X.208. Specification of Abstract Syntax Notation One (ASN.1). Genf. 1988.

CCITT X.209. Specification of Basic Encoding Rules for Abstract Notation One (ASN.1). Genf. 1988.

CERFnet

Captain Internet and CERFboy. Raiders of the lost ARP. San Diego: CERFnet. 1992.

Chappell, David:
The OSF Distributed Management Environment. In: Connections. The Interoperability Report. October 1992.

Cheifetz, Mike:
Networking 101. TCP/IP Why and how? In: WRQ Quarterly. 21. 1992. No. 3.

Chylla, Peter; Heinz-Gerd Hegering:
Ethernet-LANs. Planung, Realisierung und Netz-Management. Bergheim: DATACOM-Verl. 1992. (DATACOM-Fachbuchreihe).

Cohen, Alan M. A.:
Guide to Networking. Boyd & Fraser. 1993.

Corr, Frank; John Hunter:
Worldwide communications and information systems. In: IEEE Communications Magazine. October 1992.

Comer, Douglas:
Determining an Internet Address at Startup. In: Connections. The Interoperability. Report. 1989.
Internetworking with TCP/IP. Vol. 1. Englewood Cliffs (New Jersey): Prentice-Hall. 1990.

Comer, Douglas; David L. Stevens:
Internetworking with TCP/IP. Vol. 2. Englewood Cliffs (New Jersey): Prentice-Hall. 1992.

Compu-Shack
CS-Care Benutzerhandbuch. Neuwied: Compu-Shack Electronic. 1992. Rev.92/1.

Cox, Tracy; Deirdre Kostick; Kaj Tesink:
Sets are Fun. Introducing the SMDS Subscription MIB Module. In: The Simple Times. 1992. No. 5/6.

Crol, Ed:
The Whole Internet. Sebastopol (USA): O'Reilly. 1993. (User's Guide & Catalog).

Davis, J.; N. Dinn; M. Falconer:
Technologies for global communications. In: IEEE Communications Magazine. October 1992.

Davis, Rick:
Fast Packet Switching in Ethernet. In: LANline. 7. 1992.

DDN Protocol Handbooks I
Stanford: DDN Network Information Center. (ca. 1985).

DDN Protocol Handbooks II
Stanford: DDN Network Information Center. (ca. 1985).

DDN Protocol Handbooks III
Stanford: DDN Network Information Center. (ca. 1985).

5DDN RFC Update
Menlo Park (USA): DDN Network Information Center. 1993.

Dohmen, Andreas; Eric Wenig:
Bedarfsgerechte Netzwerkmanagement-Lösung für lokale Netze. In: Datacom. 1992. No. 10.

Ehrhardt, Johannes (Hrsg.):
Netzwerk-Dimensionen. Kulturelle Konfiguration und Management-Perspektiven. Bergheim: DATACOM-Verl. 1992. (DATACOM-Fachbuchreihe).

Emanuel, Michael:
Integrating Management Services. In: AIMS Conference Frankfurt. June 1992.

Epilogue Technology
The SNMP Porting Guide. Ventura: Epilogue Technology. (ca. 1991).
The Technical Guide. Ventura: Epilogue Technology. (ca. 1991).
The SNMP Programming Guide. Ventura: Epilogue Technology. (ca. 1991).
The MIB Compiler. Ventura: Epilogue Technology. (ca 1991).
Attache-Portable Transport Service. Ventura: Epilogue Technology. (ca. 1991).
Attache Plus-Portable Transport Service. Ventura: Epilogue Technology. (ca. 1991).
Emissary MIB Compiler. Ventura: Epilogue Technology. (ca. 1991).
Envoy–Portable SNMP source code. Ventura: Epilogue Technology. (ca. 1991).
Diplomatc Pouch. Ventura: Epilogue Technology. (ca. 1991).
Diplomatc Pouch Plus. Ventura: Epilogue Technology. (ca. 1991).
Technical Bibliography. Ventura: Epilogue Technology. (ca. 1991)

Estrada, Susan:
Connecting to the Internet. Sebastopol (USA): O'Reilly. 1993. (A Buyer's Guide).

Fedor, Richards, Schoffstall
Cutting Management Tasks down to Size with SNMP. In: LAN Technology. 1990.

Feit, Sidnie:
TCP/IP. Architecture, Protocols and Implementation. New York: McGraw-Hill. 1993

Finkel, Bettina:
SNI Transview-SNMP. In: LANline. 1992. No. 10.

Gilbert, William:
The five challenges of managing global networks. In: IEEE Communications Magazine. 1992. No. 10.

Gilster, Paul:
The Internet Navigator. New York: John Wiley. 1993.

Glaser, Gerhard:
(LAN-) Analysatoren und Netzwerkmanagement. Bergheim: DATACOM-Verl. 1990. (Datacom Netzwerkmanagement Special)
Kriterien zum Einsatz und Auswahl von LAN-Analysatoren. In: Datacom. June 1990.

Glaser, Gerhard; Mathias Hein:
Auswahlkriterien für Terminalserver. In: Datacom. January 1992.
Das TCP/IP-Kompendium. Bergheim: DATACOM-Verl. 1994. (DATACOM-Fachbuchreihe).

Glaser, Gerhard M.; Mathias Hein; Johannes Vogl:
TCP/IP-Protokolle. Projektplanung, Realisierung. 2., aktual. und erw. Aufl. Bergheim: DATACOM-Verl. 1994. (DATACOM-Fachbuchreihe).

Greenfield, David:
Putting Management into SNMP. In: Datacommunication. 1990. No. 9.

Grimshaw, Michael:
LAN Interconnections Technology. In: Telecommunications (North American Edition). February 1991.

Gronert, Elke:
MANs make their mark in Germany. In: Data Communications. May 1992.

Haupt, Wolfgang:
Moderne Anschlußtechnik. Der Weg zur universellen Lösung. In: LANline. 1992. No. 6.

Heilmeier, George:
"Global" begins at home. In: IEEE Communications Magazine. October 1992.

Hein, Mathias:
Protokoll Networking. In: Datacom. 1991. No. 3.
Neues TCP/IP-Routing-Protokoll. In: Datacom. 1992. No. 5.
Guide to TCP/IP Network Addressing. In: Datacom. 1992. No. 4.
Neue Netzwerkmanagement Arbeitsgruppe. In: Datacom. 1992. No. 9.
TCP/IP auf FDDI-Netzen. In: Datacom. 1992. No. 10.

Die Zukunft eines Veterans: Highspeed-Ethernet. In: PC-Netze. 1993. No. 10.
Kein Chaos im Netzwerk. In: PC-Netze. 1993. No. 7/8.
Die Sprache der LANs. In: PC-Netze. 1993. No. 7/8.
Netzwerke sicher im Griff. SNMP Version 2. In: PC-Netze. 1993. No. 6.
20 Jahre Ethernet. In: PC-Netze. 1993. No. 5.
Das Ende der IP-Adressen. In: PC-Netze. 1993. No. 4.
Stiefkind PC. In: PC-Netze. 1993. No. 3.
Nicht nur für IP-Welt. In: Gateway. 1993. No. 9.
Das Point to Point Protokoll. In: Datacom. 1993. No. 11.
SLIP, das Serial Line Interface Protocol. In: Datacom. 1993. No. 4.
Neue Adressen für die TCP/IP-Welt? In: Datacom. 1993. No. 12.
Stabile Verbindung. In: iX Multiuser-Multitasking-Magazin. 1994. No. 1.

Hemrick, Christine:
Building today's global computer Internetworks.
In: IEEE Communications Magazine. October 1992.

Henshall, John; Sandy Shaw:
OSI Explained. Hemel Hempstead: Simon & Schuster. 1991.

Hudgins-Bonafield, Christine:
Red Light, Green Light, Open Management, a guide for users.
In: Communications Week International. 1992.

Hunt, Craig:
TCP/IP Network Administration. Sebastopol (USA): O'Reilly. 1992.

Hunter, Philip:
Local Area Networking. Making the right choice. Wokingham: Addison-Wesley. 1993.

Information processing systems
Open Systems Interconnection. <192> Specification of Abstract Syntax Notation One (ASN.1)<169> International Organization for Standardization, International Standard 8824. December 1987.
Open Systems Interconnection. Specification of Basic Encoding Rules for Abstract Notation One (ASN.1). International Organization for Standardization, International Standard 8825. December 1987.

Janssen, Rainer; Wolfgang Schott:
SNMP – Konzepte, Verfahren, Plattformen (mit SNMPv2). Bergheim: DATACOM-Verl. 1993. (DATACOM-Fachbuchreihe).

des Jardins, Richard:
A protocol framework to achieve a single worldwide TCP/IP/OSI/CLNP Internet in the year 2000. In: Connections. The Interoperability Report. October 1992.

Jeanrond, Hans-Josef:
The future of Open Systems. In: AIMS Conference Frankfurt. June 1992.

Johnson, Till:
ATM. A dream comes true? In: Data Communications. March 1992.

Kehoe, Brendan:
Zen and the Art of the Internet. Englewood Cliffs (New Jersey): Prentice-Hall. 1992.

Kienle, Michael:
Aufsichtspersonal, Netzwerkmanagement/3. Wollongong Management Station, Release 3.0. In: iX Multiuser-Multitasking-Magazin. September 1992.

Kienle, Michael; Michael Kuschke:
Organisierte Komplexität, Netzwerkmanagement mit SNMP.
In: iX Multiuser-Multitasking-Magazin. February 1992.
Angewandtes Management, SNMP-Applikationen.
In: iX Multiuser-Multitasking-Magazin. February 1992.
Traumpaare, Netzwerkmanagement. Teil 4. Spider Systems Spider Manager, SpiderSentinel 2.0 und Chipcoms ONdemand NCS 1.0.
In: iX Multiuser-Multitasking-Magazin. February 1992.

Knippenberg, Gerd:
CS-Care, dem Fehler auf der Spur. In: Technik-News. 1992. No. 8.

Koren, Debby:
So many MIBs! In: International Journal of Network Management. 1992.

Kuo, Franklin F.:
Protocols and Techniques for Data Communication Networks. Hemel Hempstead: Simon & Schuster. 1990.

Kuschke, Michael:
Objektschau, Spectrum Version 1.1.1. In: iX Multiuser-Multitasking-Magazin. November 1992.

Kuschke, Michael; Michael Utermöhle:
Von Punkt-zu-Punkt, SLIP und PPP. Kommunikation über serielle Leitungen. In: iX Multiuser-Multitasking-Magazin. February 1992.

Kyas, Othmar:
ATM-Netzwerke. Aufbau-Funktion-Performance. Bergheim: DATACOM-Verl. 1993. (DATACOM-Fachbuchreihe).

Kyas, Othmar; Thomas Heim:
Fehlersuche in Lokalen Netzen. Bergheim: DATACOM-Verl. 1993. (DATACOM-Fachbuchreihe).

LaBarre, L.:
Structure and Identification of Management Information for the Internet. Internet Engineering Task Force working note. Network Information Center, SRI International, Menlo Park, California, April 1988.

LaQuey, Tracy; Jeanne Ryer:
The Internet Companion. A beginner's guide to global networking. Wokingham: Addison-Wesley. 1993.

Lebeck, Sue K.:
OSI and the seven layers. In: Connections. The Interoperability Report. 1989.

Leinwand, Allen; Karen Fang:
Network Management. (A practical perspective). Wokingham: Addison-Wesley. 1993.

Lynch, Daniel; Marshall T. Rose:
Internet System Handbook. Wokingham: Addison-Wesley. 1993.

Malamud, Carl:
Stacks. Interoperability in today's Computer Networks. Englewood Cliffs (New Jersey): Prentice-Hall. 1991.

Malamud, Carl:
Exploring the Internet. Englewood Cliffs (New Jersey): Prentice-Hall. 1992.

Marine, April; Susan Kirkpatrick; Vivian Neou (u.a.):
INTERNET. Getting Started. Englewood Cliffs (New Jersey): Prentice-Hall. 1993.

Markley; Richard:
Datacommunication and Interoperability. Hemel Hempstead: Simon & Schuster. 1991.

McCloghrie; Keith:
Security and Protocols. In: The Simple Times. July/August 1992.

McHale, John:
Netzwerkmanagement für 10 Base-T LANs. Fehler gar nicht erst entstehen lassen. In: LANline. 1991. No. 10.

Metz, Richard:
Vom Netz zum optimalen Netz. Was modernes Netzwerkmanagement heute leisten muß. In: LANline. 1991. No. 10.

Miller, Mark:
Troubleshooting Internetworks. Tools, Techniques and Protocols. Englewood Cliffs (New Jersey): Prentice-Hall. 1993.

Munro-Smith, Bryan:
Simulation within Network Management. In: AIMS Conference Frankfurt. June 1992.

Mutschler, Stefan:
Novell's Netware Management System (NMS). In: LANline. 1992. No. 10.

Palmer-Stevens, David:
Der Geheimagent. Cabletrons KI-basierendes Netz-Management. In: LANline. 1992. No. 10.

Partain, David L.:
An Implementation of SNMP Security. In: The Simple Times. July/August 1992.

Perlman, Radia:
Interconnections, Bridges and Routers. Wokingham: Addison-Wesley. 1992.

Rees, Simon:
The Telecommunications Management Network (TMN).
In: AIMS Conference Frankfurt. June 1992.

Reid, Peter:
Towards Integrated LAN Management. In: Telecommunications. December 1990.

Roberts, Erika:
Five percent improval over SNMP proposed.
In: Communications Networks. July 1992.

Romkey; John:
SLIP. Serial Line IP. In: Connections. The Interoperability Report. 1989.

Rose, Marshall T.:
Transition and Coexistance Strategies for TCP/IP to OSI.
In: IEEE Journal. Jamuar 1990.
Evolving the Internet-standard Network Management Framework.
In: The Simple Times. July/August 1992.
The Danger of Dreams: In: The Simple Times. September/October 1992.
The Little Black Book. Englewood Cliffs (New Jersey): Prentice-Hall. 1992.
The Open Book. Englewood Cliffs (New Jersey): Prentice-Hall. 1989.
The Simple Book. Englewood Cliffs (New Jersey): Prentice-Hall. 1994.

Rosenberg, Jerry:
Computers, Dataprocessing & Telecommunications. New York: John Wiley. 1988.

Saksena, Vikram; Tibor Schonfeld:
Customer Network Management of the InterSpan Frame Relay Service. In: The Simple Times. September/October 1992.

Schaad, Markus:
Network Management – a consultant's view.
In: AIMS Conference Frankfurt. June 1992.

Skorupa, Joe:
Managing the center of the universe. In: LAN Magazine. March 1991.

Sprung, Lance; Carol Tucker:
Netz-Management Glossar: Rund um SNMP. In: LANline. 1992. No. 10.

Stallings, William:
Handbook of Computer-Communications Standards. Vol 1. Indianapolis: Howard W.Sams.
Handbook of Computer-Communications Standards. Vol 2. Indianapolis: Howard W.Sams.
Handbook of Computer-Communications Standards. Vol 3. Indianapolis: Howard W.Sams.
Improving the LAN escape. Interoperability. In: LAN Magazine. 3. 1993. No. 2.
Networking Standards. A guide to OSI, ISDN, LAN and MAN Standards. Wokingham: Addison-Wesley. 1993.

Stewart, Ian:
The future of global private networks. In: Network Management Europe. March/April 1992.

Stewart, Robert L.:
Working Group Synopses. In: The Simple Times. 1992. No. 9/10.

Sluman, Chris:
Network and Systems Management in OSI. In: Telecommunications. 1990.

Stöttinger, Klaus:
Das OSI-Referenzmodell. Bergheim: DATACOM-Verl. 1989. (DATACOM-Fachbuchreihe).

Stephenson, Peter:
Solving the SNMP Manager Puzzle. In: LAN Magazine. March 1991.

Tannenbaum, Andre S.:
Computer Networks. Englewood Cliffs (New Jersey): Prentice-Hall. 1988.

Terplan, Kornel:
Ein Netz im Reich der Fantasie. In: Datacom. 1992. No. 10.

Tolly, Kevin:
Questioning Performance. In: Data Communications. April 1992.

Turner, Mary Johnston:
Putting the pieces together. Open Management, a guide for users. In: Communications Week International. 1992.

Waldbusser, Steven L.:
The Truth about SNMP Performance. In: The Simple Times. May/June 1992.
Today's MIB Compiler – Too much of a good thing? In: The Simple Times. 1992. No. 5/6.
Applications stand the benefit from SMP. In: The Simple Times. September/October 1992.

Walsh, Sheila:
Charting the European LAN connectivity frontier. In: Network Management Europe. March/April 1992.

Washburn, K.; J.T. Evans:
TCP/IP. Running a Successful Network. Wokingham: Addison-Wesley. 1993.

Welchering, Peter:
Vernetzte Probleme. In: iX Multiuser-Multitasking-Magazin. February 1992.

Wilder, Floyd:
A Guide to the TCP/IP Protocol Suite. Norwood: Artech. 1993.

Willetts, Keith:
The private/public life of network management. In: Network Management Europe. March/April 1992.

Wolfsgruber, Ulf:
SNMP – Simple Network Management Protocol. In: Technik-News. 6. 1992.

Appendix X
Glossary of Abbreviations

AARP	AppleTalk Address Resolution Protocol
ACSE	Association Control Service Element
dTable	Address Translation Table
ANSI	American National Standards Institute
ARP	Address Resolution Protocol
ASE	Application Service Element
ASIC	Application-specific IC
ASN.1	Abstract Syntax Notation One
AT	Advanced Technology
ATM	Asynchronous Transfer Mode
BER	Basic Encoding Rules
BGP	Border Gateway Protocol
BootP	Boot Protocol
BSI	British Standards Institute
CAD	Computer Aided Design
CCITT	Comité Consultatif International Télégraphique et Téléphonique
CHAP	Challenge Handshake Authentication Protocol

CIC	Co-ordination and Information Center CLNM
CLNP	Connectionless Network Protocol
CLNS	Connectionless Mode Network Service
CLTS	Connectionless Mode-Transport-Service
CMIP	Common Management Information Protocol
CMIP/CMIS	Common Management Information Protocol/Common Management Information Service
CMIS	Common Management Information Service
CMISE	Common Management Information Service Elements
CMOT	Common Management Information Protocol over Transmission Control Protocol
CONS	Connection-oriented Network Service
COTS	Connection-oriented Transport Service
CPU	Central Processing Unit
CRC	Cyclic Redundancy Check
CSMA	Carrier Sense Multiple Access
CSMA/CD	Carrier Sense Multiple Access/Collision Detection
CTERM	Command Terminal Protocol
DAP	Data Access Protocol
DAS	Dual Attachment Stations
DDCMP	Digital Data Communications Message Protocol
DDN	Defense Data Network
DDP	Datagram Delivery Protocol
DEC	Digital Equipment Corporation
DES	Data Encryption Standard
DIN	Deutsches Institut für Normung (German Standards Institute)
DIX	Digital Equipment Corp., Intel and Xerox
DLCMI	Data Link Connection Management Interface
DMI	Desktop Management Interface
DNA	Digital Networking Architecture
DoD	U.S. Department of Defense
DOS	Disk Operating System
DRP	DECnet Routing ProtocolDS
DSAP	Destination Service Access Point
DTE	Data Terminal Equipment
ECL	DECnet End Communication Layer
ECMA	European Computer Manufacturers Association
EGP	Exterior Gateway Protocol
EIA	Electronic Industries Association
ES-IP	End System-to-Intermediate System
ESF	Extended Superframe
FDDI	Fibre Distributed Data Interface
FTAM	File Transfer Access and Management
FTP	File Transfer Protocol
GDMI	Generic Definition of Management Information

GUI	Graphical User Interface
HDLC	High-level data link control
HEMP	High-level Entity Management Protocol
HEMS	High-level Entity Management System
IAB	Internet Architecture Board
ICMP	Internet Control Message Protocol
ICS	IBM Cabling Systems
IEEE	Institute of Electrical and Electronic Engineers
IENs	Internet Experiment Notes
IETF	Internet Engineering Task Force
IP	Internet Protocol
IPX	Novell Netware Protocol
IRTF	Internet Research Task Force
IS-IS	Intermediate System-to-Intermediate System
ISDN	Integrated Services Digital Network
ISO	International Standards Organization
KIP	Kinetics Internet Protocol
KSR	Keyboard Send Receive
LAN	Local Area Network
LAP	Link Access Procedure
LAPB	Link Access Procedure Balanced
LAT	Local Area Transport
LCF-PMD	Low Cost Fiber-Standard
LCP	Link Control Protocol
LLAP	LocalTalk Link Access Protocol
LLC	Logical Link Control
LPP	Lightweight Presentation Protocol
LQP	Link Quality Report
MAC	Media Access Control
MAN	Metropolitan Area Network
MAPDU	Management Application Protocol Data Unit
MAU	Medium Attachment Unit
MHS	Message Handling System
MIB	Management Information Base
MIBs	Management Information Bases
MIL	Military Standard
MOP	Maintenance Operations Protocol
MS	Message Store
MTA	Message Transfer Agents
MTS	Message Transfer System
MUX	Multiplexer
NBP	Name Binding Protocol
NCPs	Network Control Protocols
NFS	Network File System
NIC	Network Information Center
NIS	Network Information Service

NIST	National Institutes of Standards and Technology
NMC	Network Management Center
NNSC	NSF Network Service Center
NOC	Network Operations Center
NRI	National Research Initiatives
NS	Network Services
NSAP	Network Service Access Point
NSP	Network Service Protocol
NVT	Network Virtual Terminal
OS/2	Operating System 2
OSI	Open Systems Interconnect
OSPF	Open Shortest Path First Protocol
PABX	Private Automatic Branch Exchange
PAP	Password Authentication Protocol
PC	Personal Computer
PDUs	Protocol Data Units
PHY	Physical Layer
PMD	Physical Media Dependent
PPP	Point-to-Point Protocol
PSMs	Product Specific Modules
PSPDN	Packet Switched Public Data Networks
RAM	Random Access Memory
RARP	Reverse Address Resolution Protocol
RFCs	Request for Comments
RIP	Routing Information Protocol
RISC	Reduced Instruction Set Computer
RLogin	Remote User Login
RMON	Remote Monitoring
ROM	Read Only Memory
ROSE	Remote Operations Service Element
RPC	Remote Procedure Call
RTMP	Routing Table Maintenance Protocol
SAP	Service Access Points
SAS	Single Attachment Stations
SDLC	Synchronous Data Link Control
SMFA	Specific Management Functional Area
SGMP	Simple Gateway Monitoring Protocol
SLIP	Serial Line IP
SMF	Single Mode Fiber
SMI	Structure of Management Information
SMT	Station Management
SMTP	Simple Mail Transfer Protocol
SNA	System Network Architecture
SNMP	Simple Network Management Protocol
SPX	Sequenced Packet Exchange
SSAP	Source Service Access Point

STP	Shielded Twisted Pair
TCP	Transmission Control Protocol
TCP/IP	Transmission Control Protocol/Internet Protocol
TDR	Transfer Data Ready
TELNET	Virtual Terminal Protocol
TFTP	Triorial File Transfer Protocol
TP	Transport Protocol
TP	Twisted Pair
TP1	Transport Class 1
TP0	Transport Class 0
Trans	Transmission
UA	User Agents
UDP	User Datagram Protocol
UTP	Unshielded Twisted Pair
VF	Virtual File Store
VTS	Virtual Terminal Service
WAN	Wide Area Network
XNS	Xerox Network System protocol
ZIP	Zone Information Protocol

Index

T

U

V

W

X

Notes

Notes

Notes

Notes

Notes

Books from

International Thomson Computer Press

On The Internet

PIECING TOGETHER MOSAIC
Navigating the Internet and the World Wide Web

Steve Bowbrick, 3W Magazine

Mosaic is the most widely used browser for the Internet's World Wide Web and runs on UNIX, Macintosh and Microsoft Windows. Providing a multimedia interface to the Internet, Mosaic helps the user navigate the Internet and the World Wide Web, and explore the information superhighway. This title provides a user-friendly introduction to Mosaic. Fully illustrated throughout, this invaluable guide explains what Mosaic is and how it works, including: a quick start session for those people who already have a browser set up; details of how to obtain Mosaic from the Internet and configure it for your platform; Web navigation and search strategies; how to use Internet tools and services via Mosaic; an appendix listing useful World Wide Web sites; a glossary of terms; beyond Mosaic – how to set up a Web server and write HTML documents.

Spring 1995/300pp/1-850-32142-6/paper

SPINNING THE WEB
How to Provide Information on the Internet

Andrew Ford

An indispensable guide for all those who provide or intend to provide information on the World Wide Web, or want to make the most of their existing services, this book for the first time draws together all of the most up to date information and details of contemporary resources into one essential volume. Providing exclusive coverage of Web features, the book includes an overview of Web facilities, how to create hypertext documents, security issues, how to set up a server and the selection and evaluation of software. A variety of examples from current Web sources are included.

December 1994/250pp/1-850-32141-8/paper

INTERNET

Books from O Reilly & Associates

The Whole Internet User's Guide & Catalog

By Ed Krol
2nd Edition, April 1994
574pages, ISBN 1- 56592-063-5

The best book about the Internet just got better! This is the second edition of our comprehensive – and bestselling – introduction to the Internet, the international network that includes virtually every major computer site in the world. In addition to email, file transfer, remote login, and network news, this book pays special attention to some new tools for helping you find information. Useful to beginners and veterans alike, this book will help you explore what's possible on the Net. Also includes a pull-out quick-reference card.

"An ongoing classic."
– *Rochester Business Journal*

"The book against which all subsequent Internet guides are measured, Krol's work has emerged as an indispensable reference to beginners and seasoned travelers alike as they venture out on the data highway."
—*Microtimes*

"*The Whole Internet User's Guide Catalog* will probably become the Internet user's bible because it provides comprehensive, easy instructions for those who want to get the most from this valuable electronic tool."
—David J. Buerger, Editor, *Communications Week*

"Krol's work is comprehensive and lucid, an overview which presents network basics in clear and understandable language. I consider it essential."
—Paul Gilster, *Triad Business News*

!%@:: A Directory of Electronic Mail Addressing & Networks

By Donnalyn Frey & Rick Adams
4th Edition June 1994, 662 pages. ISBN 1-56592-046-5

This is the only up-to-date directory that charts the networks that make up the Internet, provides contact names and addresses, and describes the services each network provides. It includes all of the major Internet-based networks, as well as various commercial networks such as CompuServe, Delphi, and America Online that are "gatewayed" to the Internet for transfer of electronic mail and other services. If you are someone who wants to connect to the Internet, or someone who already is connected but wants concise, up-to-date information on many of the world's networks, check out this book.

"The book remains the bible of electronic messaging today. One could easily borrow the American Express slogan with the quip 'don't do messaging without it.' The book introduces you to electronic mail in all its many forms and flavors, tells you about the networks throughout the world... with an up-to-date summary of information on each, plus handy references such as all the world's subdomains. The husband-wife team authors are among the most knowledgeable people in the Internet world. This is one of those publications for which you just enter a lifetime subscription." – Book Review, *ISOC News*

The Mosaic Handbooks

Mosaic is an important application that is becoming instrumental in the growth of the Internet. These books, one for Microsoft Windows, one for the X Window System, and one for the Macintosh, introduce you to Mosaic and its use in navigating and finding information on the World Wide Web. They show you how to use Mosaic to replace some of the traditional Internet functions like FTP, Gopher, Archie, Veronica, and WAIS. For more advanced users, the books describe how to add external viewers to Mosaic (allowing it to display many additional file types) and how to customize the Mosaic interface, such as screen elements, colors, and fonts. The Microsoft and Macintosh versions come with a copy of Mosaic on a floppy disk; the X Window version comes with a CD-ROM.

The Mosaic Handbook for Microsoft Windows

By Dale Dougherty and Richard Koman
Ist Edition October 1994, 234 pages. ISBN 1-56592-094-5 (Floppy disk included)

The Mosaic Handbook for the X Window System

By Dale Dougherty, Richard Koman and Paula Ferguson
Ist Edition, October 1994, 220 pages, ISBN 1-56592-095-3 (CD-ROM included)

The Mosaic Handbook for the Macintosh

By Dale Dougherty & Richard Koman
Ist Edition October 1994 , 220 pages, ISBN 1-56592-096-1 (Floppy disk included)

Connecting to the Internet

By Susan Estrada
1st Edition, August 1993
188 pages, ISBN 1-56592-061-9

This book provides practical advice on how to get an Internet connection. It describes how to assess your needs to determine the kind of Internet service that is best for you and how to find a local access provider and evaluate the services they offer.

Knowing how to purchase the right kind of Internet access can help you save money and avoid a lot of frustration. This book is the fastest way for you to learn how to get on the Internet. Then you can begin exploring one of the world's most valuable resources.

"A much needed 'how to do it' for anyone interested in getting Internet connectivity and using it as part of their organization or enterprise. The sections are simple and straightforward. If you want to know how to connect your organization, get this book."
– Book Review, *ISOC News*

Learning the UNIX Operating System

By Grace Todino, John Strang & Jerry Peek
3rd Edition, August 1993
108 pages, ISBN I-56592-060-0

If you are new to UNIX, this concise introduction will tell you just what you need to get started and no more. Why wade through a 600-page book when you can begin working productively in a matter of minutes? It's an ideal primer for Mac and PC users of the Internet who need to know a little bit about UNIX on the systems they visit. This book is the most effective introduction to UNIX in print. The third edition has been updated and expanded to provide increased coverage of window systems and networking. It's a handy book for someone just starting with UNIX, as well as someone who encounters a UNIX system as a "visitor" via remote login over the Internet.

If you have someone on your site who has never worked on a UNIX system and who needs a quick how-to, Nutshell has the right booklet. *Learning the UNIX Operating System* can get a newcomer rolling in a single session. It covers logging in and out; files and directories; mail; pipes; filters; backgrounding; and a large number of other topics. It's clear, cheap, and can render a newcomer productive in a few hours." – *;login*

Smileys

By David W Sanderson
1st Edition March 1993, 93 pages, ISBN 1-56592-041-4

"For a quick grin at an odd moment, this is a nice pocket book to carry around :-) If you keep this book near your terminal, you could express many heretofore hidden feelings your email ;-) Then again, such things may be frowned upon at your company :-(No matter, this is a fun book to have around."
– Gregory M. Amov, *,News & Review*

TCP/IP Network Administration

By Craig Hunt
1st Edition August 1992, 502 pages ISBN 0-937175-82-X

TCP/IP Network Administration is a complete guide to setting up and running a TCP/IP network for administrators of networks of systems or lone home systems that access the Internet. It starts with the fundamentals: what the protocols do and how they work, how to request a network address and a name (the forms needed are included in an appendix), and how to set up your network. Beyond basic setup, the book discusses how to configure important network applications, including sendmail, the r* commands, and some simple setups for NIS and NFS. There are also chapters on troubleshooting and security. In addition, this book covers several important packages that are available from the Net (such as *gated).* Covers BSD and System V TCP/IP implementations.

Managing Internet Information Services

By Cricket Liu, Jerry Peek, Russ Jones, Bryan Buus & Adrian Nye
1st Edition Winter 1994/95 (est), 400 pages, ISBN 1-56592-062-7

This comprehensive guide describes how to set up information services to make them available over the Internet. Providing complete coverage of all popular services, it discusses why a company would want to offer Internet services and how to select which ones to provide. Most of the book describes how to set up email services and FTP, Gopher, and World Wide Web servers.

"Managing Internet Information Services has long been needed in the Internet community, as well as in many organizations with IP-based networks. Although many on the Internet are quite savvy when it comes to administering these types of tools, MIIS will allow a much larger community to join in and perhaps provide more diverse information. This book will be a welcome addition to my Internet shelf."
– Robert H'obbes' Zakon, MITRE Corporation

sendmail

By Bryan Costales, with Eric Allman & Neil Rickert
1st Edition November 1993, 830 pages, ISBN 1-56592-056-2

Although sendmail is used on almost every UNIX system, it's one of the last great uncharted territories – and most difficult utilities to learn – in UNIX system administration. This book provides a complete sendmail tutorial, plus extensive reference material. It covers the BSD, UIUC IDA, and VR versions of sendmail.

"The program and its rule description file, sendmail.cf, have long been regarded as the pit of coals that separated the mild Unix system administrators from the real fire walkers. Now, sendmail syntax, testing, hidden rules, and other mysteries are revealed. Costales, Allman, and Rickert are the indisputable authorities to do the text."
– Ben Smith, *Byte*

DNS and BIND

By Cricket Liu & Paul Albitz
Ist Edition October 1992, 418 pages ISBN 1-56592-010-4

DNS and BIND contains all you need to know about the Internet's Domain Name System (DNS) and the Berkeley Internet Name Domain (BIND), its UNIX implementation. The Domain Name System is the Internet's "phone book"; it's a database that tracks important information (in particular, names and addresses) for every computer on the Internet. If you're a system administrator, this book will show you how to set up and maintain the DNS software on your network.

"At 380 pages it blows away easily any vendor supplied information, and because it has an extensive troubleshooting section (using nslookup) it should never be far from your desk – especially when things on your network start to go awry :-)"
– Ian Hoyle, BHP Research, Melbourne Laboratories

MH & xmh: E-mail for Users & Programmers

By Jerry Peek
2nd Edition Septetnber 1992, 728 pages, ISBN 1-56592-027-9

Customizing your email environment can save time and make communicating more enjoyable. *MH & xmh: E-Mail for Users & Programmers* explains how to use, customize, and program with the MH electronic mail commands available on virtually any UNIX system. The handbook also covers *xmh,* an X Window System client that runs MH programs. The second edition added a chapter on mhook, sections explaining under-appreciated small commands and features, and more examples showing how to use MH to handle common situations.

Practical UNIX Security

By Simson Garfinkel & Gene Spafford
1st Edition June 1991, 512 pages, ISBN 0-937175-72-2

Practical UNIX Security tells system administrators how to make their UNIX system either - System V or BSD - as secure as it possibly can be without going to trusted system technology. The book describes UNIX concepts and how they enforce security, tells how to defend against and handle security breaches, and explains network security (including UUCP, NFS, Kerberos, and firewall machines) in detail. If you are a UNIX system administrator or user who deals with security, you need this book.

"Timely, accurate, written by recognized experts... covers every imaginable topic relating to Unix security. An excellent book and I recommend it as a valuable addition to any system administrator's or computer site manager's collection."
– Jon Wright, *Informatics (Australia)*

Where to purchase these books?

Please contact your local bookshop, in case of difficulties contact us at one of the addresses below -

ORDERS
International Thomson Publishing Services Ltd
Cheriton House, North Way, Andover, Hants SP10 5BE, UK
Telephone: 01264 332424/Giro Account No: 2096919/
Fax: 01264 364418
Email: UK orders - ITPUK@ITPS.CO.UK
Outside UK orders - ITPINT@ITPS.CO.UK

SALES AND MARKETING ENQUIRIES
International Thomson Publishing
Berkshire House, 168/173 High Holborn, London WCIV 7AA, UK
Tel: 0171-497 1422 Fax: 0171-497 1426
e-mail: Info@ITPUK.CO.UK

MAILING LIST
To receive further information on our Networks books, please send the following information to the London address -
Full name and address (including Postcode)
Telephone, Fax Numbers and e-mail address